Praise for *Latin America in the Modern World*

"*Latin America in the Modern World* provides readers with a careful, subtle interpretation of the peoples and cultures in the region now called Latin America. The dimensions of this historical account draw on the leading research of scholars across the region, the United States, and Europe. Yet despite the latest topics and methodologies, the authors provide a coherent narrative: individuals, events, and landscape combine into a comprehensive, articulate history shaped by men and women, random events, and natural phenomena.

—William H. Beezley, University of Arizona

"Latin America in the Modern World offers an insightful and enjoyably readable textbook that opens undergraduate students to the complexities of Latin American history. The text skillfully discusses the interplay between global, regional, and local events and ideas, and situates Latin American experiences within global social, economic, and political contexts. By using a thematic approach that explores questions of state formation, economic growth and crises, and how citizenship and national identity intersect with race, class, and gender, the text offers a welcome new introduction to the diversity of Latin American history."

—Catherine Nolan-Ferrell, University of Texas at San Antonio

"This is a superbly well-written and accessible survey of a complex and wide-ranging history. *Latin America in the Modern World* is deeply attentive to Latin America's global connections and sections on social upheaval, culture, and ideas make for a vibrant read. Few books can capture the intricacies of the large and dynamic region that is Latin America, and this work does. *Latin America in the Modern World* captures and captivates."

—Larisa Veloz, The University of Texas at El Paso

About the Cover

Diego Delso, "Indigenous people share maize while overlooking Quito from El Panecillo, Ecuador." (2015)

Over the past half century, Quito's population has more than doubled, and now approaches 3 million. Like most Latin American cities, it is characterized by great inequality and high levels of informality, or housing and employment created outside of official registries and codes. But like its neighboring countries in South America's Pacific Rim, Ecuador has prospered through growing trade with China and other Asian economies, and that growth creates new opportunities, as well as challenges. Ecuador's indigenous population has responded to these challenges and opportunities with heretofore unseen levels of political activism. That population is far from frozen in time: it helps to build the modern world that surrounds it. And yet aspects of traditional dress, culture and familial relations endure, giving Quito its unique and vital characteristics.

Latin America in the Modern World

Tradition and Modernity

Race and class in the Andean nations are vividly depicted in this 1952 photograph that contrasts an impoverished indigenous couple with a glamorous white fashion model. To sharpen the contrast, the three are strolling beside one of the quintessential examples of fine Inca stonework—the stone of 12 sides—fitted without a drop of mortar into the middle of this wall of Emperor Huayna Capac's palace.

Latin America in the Modern World

Virginia Garrard

Peter V. N. Henderson

Bryan McCann

New York   Oxford
OXFORD UNIVERSITY PRESS

With thanks to our families, mentors, colleagues and students who have supported us through all our academic endeavors

Oxford University Press is a department of the University of Oxford. It furthers the University's objective of excellence in research, scholarship, and education by publishing worldwide. Oxford is a registered trade mark of Oxford University Press in the UK and certain other countries.

Published in the United States of America by Oxford University Press
198 Madison Avenue, New York, NY 10016, United States of America.

For titles covered by Section 112 of the US Higher Education Opportunity Act, please visit www.oup.com/us/he for the latest information about pricing and alternate formats.

Library of Congress Cataloging-in-Publication Data

Names: Garrard, Virginia, 1957– author. | Henderson, Peter V. N.,
  1947– author. | McCann, Bryan, 1968– author.
Title: Latin America in the modern world / Virginia Garrard, Peter V. N.
  Henderson, Bryan McCann.
Description: New York, NY : Oxford University Press, 2017. | Includes
  bibliographical references and index.
Identifiers: LCCN 2017038752| ISBN 9780199340224 (pbk.) | ISBN 9780190874285
  (looseleaf) | ISBN 9780190859398 (ebook)
Subjects: LCSH: Latin America—Politics and government—1980– | Latin
  America—Social conditions—1982– | Latin America—Economic
  conditions—1982- | Latin America—History—21st century.
Classification: LCC F1414.3 .G375 2017 | DDC 980.03—dc23
LC record available at https://lccn.loc.gov/2017038752

9 8 7 6 5 4 3 2 1

Printed by LSC Communications Inc., USA

Contents

CHAPTER 3   First Attempts at State Formation: The Liberal-Conservative Debate, 1830–1875   98

CHAPTER 4   Exclusion and Inclusion: Everyday People, 1825–1880s   142

FEATURES:

CULTURE AND IDEAS
Photographs of Brazilian Slaves 163

CULTURE AND IDEAS
The Virgin of the Angels: A US Protestant Missionary (Mattie Crawford's) View, 1922 166

ECONOMICS AND COMMODITIES
Foreign Travelers in Andean Marketplaces 181

CHAPTER 6   Worlds Connecting: Latin America in an Imperial Age   238

FEATURES:

CHAPTER 7   Progress and Its Discontents, 1880–1920   286

PART THREE   The Call for Change: Twentieth-Century Transformations, 1930–1980   334

CHAPTER 8   The Great Depression and Authoritarian Populists, 1930–1950   338

CHAPTER 9   The Challenges of Modernity, 1930–1950   384

FEATURES:

CULTURE AND IDEAS
Latin American Baseball 565

SOCIAL UPHEAVAL
Mario Vargas Llosa
Contextualizes the Shining
Path 575

List of Maps

Note on Spellings

We have used modern Portuguese and Spanish spelling for relevant terms throughout. Terms in Portuguese have the *til* (˜) over nasalized vowels where relevant, as in Maranhão or *nações*. Portuguese terms including the "closed e" have the circumflex (ˆ) over the *e*, as in *inglês*. All Spanish terms have the accent over the stressed syllable if the syllable is not stressed as it would normally be, which is on the penultimate syllabus: for example, *comité*, *boliburguesía*, *petróleos*, and so forth. Spanish terms including the "enye" (ñ) have the tilde only over the n, as in *mañana*.

We also follow the correct convention of Spanish surnames (apellido), in which one uses both the patronymic (paternal) apellido first, and the matronymic (maternal) name second: for example, José Gonzales Morales would be known either as José Gonzales (using only the name he inherited from his father) or José González Morales (using both names), but not as José Morales (just his mother's name, which is not used alone). Women's names have historically changed with marriage, although this is custom is changing. As a single woman, she would, like a man, use both her paternal and maternal last names. Upon marrying, a woman drops her maternal last name to add her husband's paternal apellido—often with a "de" ("of") to indicate the husband's "possession" of her. Thus, if our example José's sister, María González Morales, marries Diego García, she would become María González de García, or, as more common today, María Gonzáles García.

Preface

The genesis of this book occurred when we collectively reflected that our students in the Modern Latin American History survey course would deepen their historical understanding if they approached learning about the region from a broader global context. Latin America is very much part of the Western tradition and the Atlantic World, but its unique geography, populations, climates, local worldviews, intellectual currents, religious expressions, cuisine, and many other factors have also rendered it distinct from the Old World in almost every possible aspect. As far back as the moment of independence in the early nineteenth century, Latin Americans shared the political theories of the Atlantic World and were affected by international events such as the US War for Independence, the French Revolution, and Emperor Napoleon's invasion of the Iberian Peninsula. Thereafter, North Atlantic political and economic theory as well as the Latin American elite's warm embrace of European ideas of modernization and technological advances in the nineteenth century strengthened that relationship. But these imported political ideas, economic models, and technologies from abroad did not always translate well into local contexts and conditions. The Brazilian Portuguese phrase, "*Só para Inglês ver,*" (for the English to see), meaning something that is aspirational or just for show, captures the ambivalence of Latin America's relationship with the Britain, Europe, and the United States during the nineteenth and much of the twentieth century.

As the world shrank in the twentieth and twenty-first centuries, Latin America deepened its connections with Eastern Europe, Africa, and Asia. To build this context, each chapter begins with a section titled "Global Connections." As we move toward the contemporary period and these connections intensify, we integrate more global material into the larger body of the chapter.

The authors wanted to emphasize the distinctive experiences of each of the Latin American countries rather than create a narrative that suggests that all Latin American nations have an interchangeable heritage, although, at the same time, we seek to clearly identify themes, topics, people, and intellectual currents that help to knit the history of modern Latin America into a coherent category of study. Likewise, we agreed that the book would not serve students well if it focused primarily on the history of the three largest countries (Mexico, Brazil, and Argentina) to the neglect of others like the Central American and Andean nations. As a consequence, we include case studies from almost all of the countries at some point in the narrative when their history effectively illuminates a theme or idea. In this fashion we hope students will come to appreciate the great diversity of history and culture within the Latin American region, while simultaneously understanding how it fits into the streams and currents of world history and events more broadly.

The text focuses on five general themes and illustrates how they evolve over four chronological periods: the early National Period (postindependence to roughly 1870; the age of progress and modernization (1870–1930); the age of greater inclusion, economic diversification, and greater egalitarianism (1930–1980); and the contemporary era with its legacies of revolution, repression, middle-class expansion, drug trafficking, and increased poverty for the poor. The five broad themes we feature over this journey are: state formation; the construction of national identity through popular culture and religion; economics and commodities; race, class, and gender; and finally, the environment.

Postindependence Latin America faced the complex question of state formation, the task of developing national governments out of whole cloth where none had previously existed, in an era when even the idea of what constituted a "republic" was new and contested. In the earliest years, the debate involved incessant wrangling and civil wars between those aspiring to implement North Atlantic liberal political theory, versus those who argued in favor of retaining much of the colonial historical tradition. In the twentieth century, a different set of conflicting ideologies dominated, all of which promised new and different solutions to long-standing issues such as the severe social and political inequalities that had plagued most Latin American countries since their inceptions. Some nations sought to broaden their choices and opted for new models of state formation such as communism (Cuba, for example), or populism (Venezuela, among others). Others (Mexico, Chile, Colombia, and more) held fast to their democratic governments, but often after paying a terrible price, such as the suspension of human rights and civil liberties, state-sponsored violence, and civil war.

Our second theme involves the creation of a distinctive national identity—the sense of a nation as a cohesive whole with distinctive traditions, culture, and sometimes language (Paraguay with Guarani, for example). In the early republican years, the Catholic Church controlled the hearts and minds of most Latin Americans and the Church's rituals and liturgical calendar made up much of popular culture. Over time, however, more secular traditions have largely replaced the influence of the Church in many areas, creating distinctive secular music, dance, literature, and film, in most countries. These popular culture traditions and growing religious diversity have become key elements in the construct of unique national personalities.

A third theme that appears in the pages to follow has to do with how global economics and commodity chains have linked Latin America to the world. In the nineteenth century, Latin America exported primary products (raw materials) that often provided a temporary economic boom because of the comparative advantage (i.e., little or no competition and hence higher prices) that these products commanded. New minerals (petroleum) and agricultural products that appealed to international taste buds (bananas and coffee) subsidized growth, modernization, and new technologies. Nations with multiple products for sale fared better than those limited to a single item (monoculture).

After 1930, many Latin American nations embarked on some form of industrialization to meet the demands of local consumers, while larger countries like Mexico and Brazil were able to manufacture and supply machinery, automobiles, and other large industrial products to their neighbors. But in other countries, local manufacturing remained small-scale, and the economies of those nations became locked in a closed circuit defined by the export of agricultural commodities and the importation of durable and consumer goods from large foreign producers. During the 1960s, policy makers described this cycle as economic dependence, and their analysis became known as "dependency theory." While this theory is no longer in vogue, the export-import circuit remains a reality in much of Latin America today, albeit with the United States' economic and political preeminence increasingly replaced by the economic power of China and other rising global trade networks.

Fourth, from a society once very exclusionary, where the vast majority of the population, whether indigenous or of African descent, suffered both legal and civil disabilities in the nineteenth century, Latin Americans since 1930 have slowly created more egalitarian societies, but the process remains, at best, incomplete. As too many examples demonstrate, people who are marginalized for their race, their gender, their ethnicity, or, in rare cases, their religion, tend to remain the poorest members of their societies. Women have overcome significant legal hurdles to gender equality in these years, but the social norms of patriarchy remain firmly ensconced.

Finally, in recent decades Latin Americans have come to grips with the environmental problems that they, along with the rest of the world, face. While in some instances environmental issues are the result of natural disasters (earthquakes, volcanoes, hurricanes) that are beyond human control, in other instances (such as air pollution and climate change–related catastrophes) environmental problems are man-made and have required political intervention to improve the situation.

Lessons not learned in the nineteenth century, such as the consequences of deple-tion of resources, still recur, while the environmentally catastrophic policies and development of the twentieth century—the massive consumption of fossil fuels, the destruction of ozone through carbon from industry and vehicles, widespread deforestation, the predation of the Amazon, the "lungs of the world"—have left a dire legacy for the people of Latin America and the world at large to deal with. Today, most major urban centers in Latin America are gridlocked in traffic and choking under polluted air and unsafe or impure water supplies insufficient to ser-vice their burgeoning populations.

But the environmental picture in Latin America is not universally grim. A few major cities, such as Curitiba, Brazil, are, through innovative urban planning, models of sustainable urban development; while Mexico City, once predicted to become the most populous metropolitan center in the world, has managed to im-plement effective programs to control population growth and improve air quality. Even tiny Costa Rica has moved into the vanguard as a world leader of model en-vironmental stewardship, by proving that protecting the environment is good for tourist dollars as well as helping save the planet.

The story of Latin America and its people is important not only as an intel-lectual end unto itself, but also because people of Latino descent represent the largest "minority" group in the United States today, and already constitute the majority of the population in some sections of the country. The US metropolises Miami, Los Angeles, Houston, and New York, and even the US capital of Wash-ington, DC, are "Latin American cities" in terms of demographics: one-in-ten residents of the Los Angeles-Long Beach area are Latino; Miami is home to the largest number of Cubans outside of Havana; and the three largest Texas cities—San Antonio, Houston, and Dallas—are either majority-minority Latino, or will be in the very near future. The "Latinization" of the United States adds enor-mously to the rich texture of US culture and is all the more reason that citizens need to understand the complexities of the cultures and historical experiences of the nations to the south. It is in the furtherance of this understanding that we have undertaken this work.

Acknowledgments

First, we thank the many scholars whose published works served as foundations for this text. We all appreciate the academic presses who remain true to their mission and continue to disseminate new knowledge. In addition, we express our appreciation to the numerous anonymous readers who commented on multiple early drafts of this textbook. Their careful reading, and thoughtful, useful, and sometimes very pointed suggestions significantly improved the final product.

At Oxford University Press, we thank Charles Cavaliere, who provided the inspired and imaginative leadership necessary to result in a student friendly textbook. We thank his assistants, Rowan Wixted who coordinated the permissions and prepared the final manuscript for transmission, and George Chakvetadze, who helped us with the design and construction of maps. At an earlier stage, Brian Wheel provided the impetus to move the project from conception to draft status. Development editor Meg Botteon made a number of important suggestions that sharpened the direction in which the project was moving. Thank you all for your patience and diligence.

We also owe debts of gratitude to several other individuals. Kim Morse and her class at Washburn University workshopped an early draft of the book. Michael Hironymous, the Rare Books Librarian at the Nettie Lee Benson Collection at the University of Texas, Austin produced many of the high-resolution images that grace this book; Robert Esparza from the Benson was very helpful in tracking down and making high-resolution images for us as well. Stella Villagran, the director of the Photographic Collection at the Columbus Memorial Library in Washington, DC, also provided us with access to many extraordinary images. Nicola Foote of Florida Gulf Coast University has increased the value of our work significantly by editing the documentary collection that accompanies this textbook. We want to thank the next generation of Latin Americanists, Oliver Horn and Eric Gettig of Georgetown University, and Rachel Fleming of the University of Texas, Austin, who ferreted out hard-to-locate images and documents and prepared the supplementary materials that enhance the value of this book for our undergraduate readers. And we thank the many hundreds of undergraduate students whom the three of us have taught in the Modern Latin American History survey; it was your questions, your insights, and your enthusiasm that convinced us that a book like this would be worth writing.

Lastly, Virginia Garrard and Bryan McCann thank our fearless leader, Peter Henderson, who has kept this project on track and generously tolerated two sometimes-distracted coauthors.

About the Authors

Virginia Garrard is director of the Teresa Lozano Long Institute of Latin American Studies and the Nettie Lee Benson Collection, and professor of History at the University of Texas, Austin. She received her PhD in history from Tulane University. Her most recent work, which she coedited with Stephen Dove and Paul Freston, *Cambridge History of Religions in Latin America*, was published in April 2016. In addition, she is author of *Terror in the Land of the Holy Spirit: Guatemala under General Efraín Ríos Montt, 1982–1983* (2010); *Terror en la tierra del Espiritu Santo* (2012); *Viviendo en la Nueva Jerusalem* (2009), and *Protestantism in Guatemala: Living in the New Jerusalem* (1998). She is coeditor, along with Mark Lawrence and Julio Moreno, of *Beyond the Eagle's Shadow: New Histories of Latin America's Cold War* (2013). She also edited *On Earth As It Is in Heaven: Religion and Society in Latin America* (2000) and coedited, with David Stoll, *Rethinking Protestantism in Latin America* (1993).

Peter V. N. Henderson is professor emeritus of history and the former dean of the College of Liberal Arts at Winona State University in Minnesota. He earned his PhD under the direction of Michael C. Meyer at the University of Nebraska–Lincoln. His book *In the Absence of Don Porfirio: Francisco León de la Barra and the Mexican Revolution* won the Thomas F. McGann Memorial Prize for the best monograph by a member of the Rocky Mountain Conference on Latin American Studies in 2001. Thereafter, he shifted his interest to the Andean region. Ecuador's *Academia Nacional de Historia* honored him with Corresponding membership because of his *Gabriel García Moreno y la formación de un Estado conservador en los Andes* (originally published in English as *Gabriel García Moreno and Conservative State Formation in the Andes* in 2008). Dr. Henderson's most recent work is a textbook titled *The Course of Andean History* (2013).

Bryan McCann is chair of the History Department at Georgetown University and president of BRASA, the Brazilian Studies Association. He is the author of several books on Brazilian history, including *Hard Times in the Marvelous City: From Dictatorship to Democracy in the Favelas of Rio de Janeiro* (2014), *Throes of Democracy: Brazil since 1989* (2009) and *Hello, Hello Brazil: Popular Music in the Making of Modern Brazil* (2004). Along with Brodwyn Fischer and Javier Auyero, he edited *Cities from Scratch: Poverty and Informality in Urban Latin America* (2014). Along with Gilmar Fraga and Daniela Vallandro de Carvalho, he is the author of the graphic history *The Black Lancers of Brazil* (forthcoming, 2019).

Prologue

The Land and the People

The story of modern Latin America began roughly twenty-five thousand years ago when the Americas' first inhabitants arrived from Asia. Centuries later, new arrivals from the Iberian Peninsula and Africa encountered these indigenous people, and created one of the most complex multicultural societies the world had ever experienced. In order to understand postindependence Latin America, we must take a brief journey through its earlier history.

☰ **Diego Delso.** "Indigenous people share maize while overlooking Quito from El Panecillo, Ecuador." (2015)

Topography and Basic Categories of People

Latin America's terrain is varied and challenging; its topography is vastly different from the flat arable land and navigable rivers facilitating commerce that greeted English and French settlers in North America. In an era in which the vast majority of the world's population sustained itself through agriculture, relatively small portions of Latin America's landscape lent themselves to dry farming (relying on rainfall alone to water crops). The best agricultural and pastoral lands, located in the **Southern Cone** nations of Argentina, Uruguay, and substantial portions of Brazil and Chile, were inhabited by people who survived by hunting, fishing, and gathering, rather than raising crops. Much of the remaining land, such as the valleys and slopes of the Andean region, the dry scrub forests of northern Guatemala, or the drought-prone areas north of Mexico City, required considerable ingenuity on the part of its inhabitants to raise adequate crops.

Acquiring adequate access to water resources also proved challenging to early Native Americans. Although South America possessed three large river systems (the Amazon; the Rio de la Plata in Argentina, Paraguay, and Uruguay; and the Orinoco in Venezuela), none of these systems experienced the benevolent annual floods that deposited rich alluvial soil along the floodplain and allowed for the emergence of complex civilizations as had occurred in Egypt and Mesopotamia. Nor did these rivers provide an internal trade network, unlike the pre-European upper Mississippi River, for example. Large portions of Latin America experienced either excessive or inadequate rainfall. As a result, in the Andean region, cultures had to construct sophisticated irrigation systems to capture and store the elusive flow of small rivers rushing from the mountains. Lakes, too, were relatively scarce and did not become settlement sites, with a few exceptions. Lake Texcoco in central Mexico fed many thousands of people because of the man-made floating gardens constructed in shallow eddies. Similarly, people living alongside Lake

Titicaca (located between Peru and Bolivia) not only fished the lake but also used its water to irrigate nearby cropland.

Historians have classified the peoples who lived in this challenging world into three categories: the nomadic, the semisedentary, and the densely populated complex civilizations. The nomadic peoples survived by hunting, fishing, and gathering local fruits, nuts, and edible vegetation. Typically, these groups lived in the most inhospitable areas, such as hot tropical places like present-day Panama, the western coast of Colombia, and the Amazon Basin as well as the drier and cooler locations on the pampas in the southernmost regions of South America. Even during the modern period, these nomadic people occupied vast portions of Latin America largely undisturbed by others in a true frontier zone. In contrast, semisedentary and sedentary peoples lived primarily by agriculture. One example of such a sedentary population was the Muisca of Colombia, who constructed wooden homes in small towns near present-day Bogotá, Colombia. They grew potatoes, beans, squash, and a rich variety of fruit, and traded their beautifully worked gold pieces for other desirable goods. The Tupí, who inhabited the Atlantic coast of what is now Brazil, were less sedentary but also relied on agriculture for sustenance. The Maya, who created advanced cities on the thin-soiled and dry Yucatán Peninsula, cultivated corn so successfully that their population eventually surpassed the land's ability to sustain them.

The Densely Populated Societies

Two densely populated civilizations flourished in Mexico and Central America (the Maya and the Aztec) and one in South America (the Inka). The Maya, the most disaggregated administratively, have been likened to the ancient Greeks in part because they configured themselves into city-states, or sovereign cities that also controlled the surrounding territory, mostly in present-day Guatemala and the Yucatán Peninsula of Mexico. Faced with a land characterized by thin soil, irregular rainfall, and deep forests, the Maya imaginatively developed a slash-and-burn form of agriculture that enabled them to manage these resources reasonably well. The Maya, whose Classic Period ran from approximately 250 to 900 AD, founded urban centers that included majestic steep-stepped pyramids and thriving markets and plazas. These urban centers were linked by networks of roads. The Maya's prowess with astronomy and mathematics, their precise calendar (which does not require adjustment through a leap year, unlike the Western calendar), and sophisticated writing system provided other reasons for the comparison to the Greeks. At the time of first contact with European explorers in the sixteenth century, however, many of the most important Maya cities had been abandoned or neglected. The Spaniards, disheartened by the local landscape and baffled by its inhabitants, nonetheless struggled to conquer the Yucatán Peninsula.

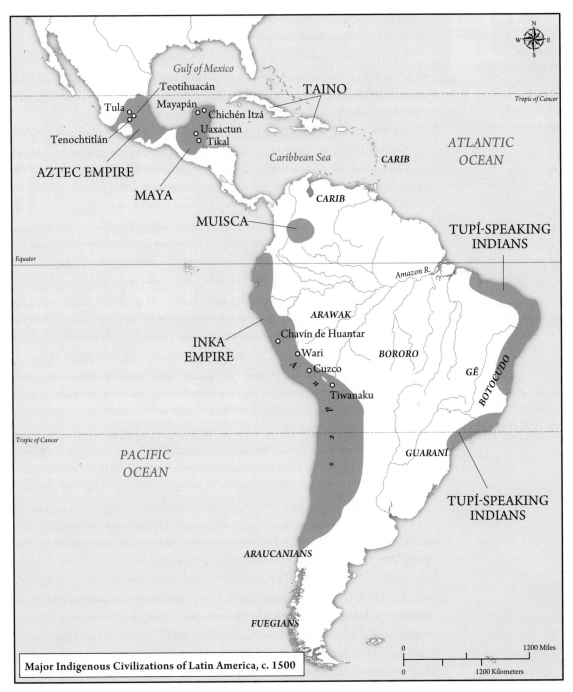

Major Indigenous Civilizations of Latin America, c. 1500

≡ **MAP. 0.1**

In the early 1400s the Mexica (more popularly called the Aztecs) began to consolidate their position among the city-states in the vicinity of Lake Texcoco in Mexico's great Central Valley. By 1519 the Aztec Empire controlled much of modern Mexico, stretching from the east coast as far south as Oaxaca and Guatemala. The streets of Tenochtitlán, the Aztec capital (now Mexico City), bustled with thousands of people, and its marketplace rivaled anything found in Europe.

Yet in these latter years of the Aztec Empire the great disparity in wealth between the privileged warrior-priest class and commoners, as well as the enmity between the Mexica and the people they had conquered, foretold potential problems. The subjugated population owed their overlords burdensome tribute, or taxes, and also had to adhere to the Aztec state religion, built around constant oblations of "holy liquid" (human blood) that demanded massive human sacrifice. Human sacrifice occurred elsewhere in pre-Hispanic America, but not on the massive scale of the Aztec rituals. When the Spanish arrived, they interpreted these rituals as evidence that Aztec culture was "demonic" in nature, justifying their subjugation and conversion to Christianity. Aztec influence endured long after Spanish conquest, in the magnificent pyramids they left behind, and in the survival of Nahuatl, the Mexica language. The Mexica had used Nahuatl as a tool to unify their vast empire. It remained the most common language spoken in central New Spain (Mexico) well after the arrival of the Spanish, and is still spoken today. The Mesoamerican diet of the Mexica also endures—corn tortillas, *ahuacatl* (avocados), *tomatl* (tomato), *chilli* (chile), *chocolatl* (chocolate), and *ahuacamolli* (guacamole) and continues to shape our perceptions of the region.

The third indigenous group, the Inka, constructed one of the largest empires in the world (it included modern Peru, Bolivia, Ecuador, and parts of Chile and Colombia) in the brief period between their emergence in 1438 and the arrival of the Spaniards in 1532. (As with the term Aztec, Inka is the popular term commonly used to designate the empire. Its own inhabitants referred to it as Tawantinsuyu, or the Land of Four Quarters, and used the term Inka only to refer to the supreme ruler.) The Inka civilization built on the achievements of numerous predecessors. Some writers have likened the Inka to the Romans because of their ability to design an imperial administrative structure that wove together peoples who spoke different languages and worshiped different gods. Although all subjects within the empire were required to worship Inti, the Inka Sun God, and theoretically speak Quechua, the Inka permitted conquered peoples to retain their own gods, worship their own ancestors, and maintain their traditional *huacas* (sacred places).

The 25,000-mile road system that radiated from the Inka capital of Cuzco (in modern Peru)—the word *"cuzco"* in the Inkan Quechua language means "navel," thus placing Cuzco as the center of the world—provided physical unity to the empire. The Inka labor draft (*mita*) that obligated men and women to provide service to the state (a practice later adopted by the Spaniards) made possible the construction of these roads and other examples of monumental architecture. With their *khipu* (rope writing system) the Inka could maintain records of taxes paid and foodstuff and treasure (woven cloth) stored in warehouses. The Spanish later concentrated their own administration in the Americas in the former lands of the Aztec and Inka, building on top of pre-existing structures of urban centers, extensive networks of communication and trade, and state systems of tribute and labor extraction.

The Iberians and the Africans

Even as the Aztec and Inka constructed their empires, the Iberian powers of Spain and Portugal consolidated their influence over their respective portions of the Iberian Peninsula and poised themselves for overseas expansion. The Iberian Peninsula was occupied largely by Moors (North African Muslims) from the year 711 until 1492. Although much of this period was peaceful—the smaller kingdoms that made up present-day Spain and Portugal enjoyed the benefits of Islamic learning in mathematics, poetry, and visual arts, for example, while the rest of Europe was plunged into the Dark Ages—by the time of Crusades, the Iberian Christian kingdoms were engaged in an all-out struggle to rid the peninsula of the Muslim North Africans.

This task—known as the **Reconquista**—was not fully complete until 1492, when the Spaniards expelled the last Moors from the southern city of Granada. That year, which witnessed the defeat of the Moors, the expulsion of Spain's significant Jewish population (in an ill-conceived attempt to unify the kingdom by ridding it of non-Christians), the production of the first Spanish-language dictionary (based on Castilian), and the first voyage of Columbus, marked the entry of Spain into the early modern world. Presciently, when the scholar and poet Antonio de Nebrija presented his newly compiled dictionary to Queen Isabella in 1492, he declared, "Majesty, the language is the instrument of the empire."

In the process of uniting their kingdoms, Spain and Portugal embraced certain values that would characterize their encounters with the Indians, as the explorer Christopher Columbus mistakenly named the native people of the Americas. (He believed he had arrived in Asia and had brought a Japanese dictionary along for the occasion). Because the kingdoms of Spain had spent seven hundred years attempting to reconquer their portion of Iberia from Muslim occupiers, Spaniards tended to have a distinctly militaristic outlook. Kings rewarded valor on the battlefield with grants of land and other wealth, encouraging their knights to fight for spoils to enrich themselves and enhance the status of their families.

In addition to glorifying military exploits and seeking personal wealth, the Christian kings and their feudal retainers engaged in this fight took on a crusading mentality as they battled the Muslim kingdom that occupied Spain. (The Portuguese, in contrast, had defined themselves as an empire of navigation well before they landed in the Americas. They did not emphasis proselytization in Brazil until the arrival of the first Jesuits in 1549, and even then never on the scale of the Franciscans in New Spain.) For the Spaniards, their militaristic spirit, crusading zeal, and hunger for gold and other forms of wealth would motivate them in their ambition to make a New World in the Americas. Columbus's errant but fortuitous effort to find an alternative trade route to "Asia" by sailing west could not have come at a better time for the growing Spanish Empire.

Finally, Africans represented a third significant presence in much of Latin America. The Spanish conquest depended, in part, on the skills of African fighters. Some of these black conquistadores arrived in the New World as slaves and then earned their freedom through their military prowess, becoming esteemed members of society. Over the course of the sixteenth century, the nature of the African presence in the Americas, and the nature of slavery itself, changed markedly. Sugar plantations in Brazil and the Caribbean relied on enslaved Africans in greater numbers, and subjected Africans and their descendants to more exhaustive forms of exploitation than ever seen before. Coastal Colombia, Mexico, and Venezuela as well as northern Peru also saw the rise of African slavery on plantations or **haciendas** (large, agricultural estates). These slave societies, in which slaves vastly outnumbered the free population, drew their wealth from the brutal exploitation of enslaved Africans.

Enslaved Africans often found a greater measure of autonomy, and longer life expectancy, in urban areas. Urban slaves worked as household servants or practiced trades such as metalworking and carpentry. Manumission, the freeing of slaves, was more common in urban areas: enslaved Africans in towns and cities often found opportunities to earn small amounts of money, saving it to purchase their own freedom. Urban slavery remained, nonetheless, a system of violent labor extraction, marked by the common practice of public corporal punishment.

The Conquest (Encounter) and Its Consequences

The Spanish conquest of the densely populated empires of the Aztecs and the Inka remains among the most dramatic episodes in world history. In the tales of these encounters, the best and the worst of human characteristics came to the fore, to be repeated in numerous lesser scenarios throughout the Americas. The aftermath of the Conquest resulted in a number of unintended consequences that are perhaps better described as an encounter that would have repercussions throughout the colonial period.

The Conquest of Mexico

By 1519, Spaniards had thoroughly explored the Caribbean Islands, which became the springboard to Mexico and Central America. In the Caribbean, the conquistadores first demonstrated their interest in colonizing the land and exploiting indigenous populations in the search for wealth. Their expansion onto the mainland, and the defeat and fragmentation of the Aztec Empire that ensued, was among the most consequential passages in human history. Historians have debated the details and implications of that Conquest for centuries. For the student of modern Latin America, it is fundamental to understand three aspects of that Conquest. First, it was improvised and contingent, rather than well planned and characterized by ineluctable domination. Second, it depended at all stages on the Spanish recruitment of indigenous allies. And finally, although the Aztec Empire disintegrated and the Spanish Empire expanded in its place, the indigenous inhabitants of the region influenced the Spanish and their descendants at least as much as the Spanish bent those indigenous inhabitants to their will.

On the first point, Hernando Cortés, the epitome of the conquistador, was not appointed to that role by the Spanish king, but seized leadership of a Spanish expedition from Cuba to the mainland in defiance of the Spanish governor of Cuba (who ostensibly held administrative authority for the expedition). Through a combination of flashes of tactical genius, outrageous good fortune, and the spread of Spanish-borne disease and dissent among indigenous populations, Cortés stumbled boldly forward toward conquest. This haphazard nature of expansion continued to play a role in Spanish administration in decades and centuries to come. The Spanish created a rich body of law, both ecclesiastical and secular, as well as enduring institutions to govern their colonial possessions. But the day-to-day application of those laws and operations of those institutions remained flexible, responding to local circumstances. (Indeed, when Spanish colonial dominion became less flexible in the late eighteenth century, it helped push the region toward independence.)

On the second point, nearly from the outset of his conquest, Cortés relied heavily on the abilities of an indigenous woman named Malintzin, his translator and lover, whom the Spanish called Doña Marina, but who Mexicans today remember as La Malinche. Malintzin helped translate between the Spanish and indigenous groups and also explained indigenous life and loyalties to Cortés. The Spanish also established a key alliance with Tlaxcala, an indigenous city-state that had long resisted Aztec rule. The Tlaxcalans saved the Spanish from destruction and then exacted favorable conditions as allies rather than subjects of Spanish dominion. This vital nature of indigenous assistance meant the Spanish could not usually function as oppressive overlords—they needed to work with indigenous power structures where possible. By far the greatest threat to indigenous survival came from the spread of European diseases like smallpox, not from Spanish military domination.

On the third point, the Spanish governed the Americas with a skeleton crew for two and a half centuries. Large regions of the interior—and entire populations of indigenous inhabitants—remained functionally autonomous from Spanish dominion well into the colonial period. Conquest and administration tended to be inversely proportional to the density and centralization of the indigenous population—decentralized and seminomadic indigenous populations effectively resisted or avoided Spanish rule. The **mestizo** population, of mixed Spanish and indigenous ancestry, outnumbered the Spanish population only a few decades into the colonial period, and continued to expand. In addition, cultural **mestizaje** (the blending of multiple indigenous, Spanish, and African influences) came to define cultural and religious practices in the region. Spanish America was always more American than Spanish, in the sense that it was defined by a process of demographic and cultural recombination determined within the Americas.

The Conquest of Peru and Elsewhere in South America

The conquest of the Aztecs established a pattern for the remainder of continental Spanish America. Few trained Spanish soldiers participated in these expeditions. The conquistadores' motivations, sometimes oversimplified as the "Three G's" (Gold, God, and Glory), remained consistent with the values associated with the long Reconquista in Spain. They sought wealth, whether in the form of gold and silver, or Indians in **encomienda**, a grant by the Spanish crown that gave individual conquistadores the right to exact labor and tribute from indigenous populations. Those holding such grants were known as *encomenderos*, the most influential group of Spanish colonists. Even minor conquistadores used the title of *hidalgo*, short for *hijo de algo*, or "son-of-something," an honorific that implied hereditary nobility in Spain itself but became increasingly commonplace in the Americas.

The Spaniards were also deeply committed to converting the natives to the Catholic faith, which for Spaniards was the hallmark of civilized culture and true humanity. In 1494, Spain and Portugal, prompted in part by the Spanish-born Pope Alexander VI, agreed to the Treaty of Tordesillas, which divided the New World in between these two empires. The treaty drew an imaginary line 100 leagues (about 320 miles) west of the Cape Verde Islands, giving lands and people found west of the line to Spain and those east of the line to Portugal. In theory, this gave the Spanish privileges over most of the Americas, leaving the land that would become Brazil for the Portuguese. This treaty offered further impetus for conversion, since possession of the new lands was contingent on the conversion of the people who lived in them. (It is worth mentioning that after the start of the Protestant Reformation in 1517, the newly Protestant countries such as England had no qualms about ignoring what had previously been considered a binding papal edict).

The story of the conquest of the Inka, the second most important conquest tale, recapitulates in many respects the improvised and contingent subjugation of the Aztec Empire. With even fewer men, Francisco Pizarro captured Atahualpa, the Sapa Inka (the sole Inka, or supreme ruler), and held him for ransom. Although a distant relative of Cortés, Pizarro was cut from coarser cloth, illiterate and an inveterate gambler willing to cheat his partners out of their share of the loot. As a result, Peru experienced both an Inka revolt that lasted until 1572 and a civil war between factions of the conquistadores. Pizarro's veterans later successfully subdued other portions of the Inka Empire (in modern Ecuador and Colombia), but met greater resistance from the Mapuche people of what is now Chile. There, the erstwhile conquistador, Pedro de Valdivia, after being captured in battle, had molten gold poured down his throat as a warning to other greedy Spaniards who might intrude into their territory.

Brazil and Other Conquest Experiences

The Portuguese navigator Pedro Alvares Cabral landed on the coast of what is now Brazil in 1500 and claimed the land in the name of his king, in accordance with the Treaty of Tordesillas. But Portugal was preoccupied with more immediately lucrative expansion in Asia, and placed little emphasis on colonization of this new dominion for nearly fifty years. During that period, the Portuguese did realize that the wood of a particular species of local tree could be exploited as a source of stable red dye—a precious commodity in European textiles of the period. The vivid red dye reminded the Portuguese of a burning coal, or *brasa*, prompting the naming of both the tree (brazilwood) and the new colony. Brazilwood became the first of the boom and bust commodities that would define Brazil's economy into the twentieth century. For several decades, Portuguese navigators scrambled to induce indigenous inhabitants to cut down as many trees as they could and drag them to the coast. Then, in the 1550s, a competing source of stable red dye called cochineal emerged—from a cactus-dwelling Mexican bug, no less. The price of brazilwood plummeted, and Brazil's economy was forced into sudden and painful reorientation. This pattern was to be repeated several times in the future.

As profits from brazilwood declined, Portuguese colonists in the New World turned to sugar. Portuguese planters on the Atlantic island of Madeira had already been exploiting African slaves in the cultivation of sugar on large estates for export to Europe for decades. Over the course of the sixteenth century, the Portuguese reproduced and greatly intensified this sugar complex—African slavery, large estates, and local mills producing for export—in Brazil.

The consequent rapid expansion of the African presence in Brazil would become the colony's most definitive demographic trend, one deeply shaping both its economy and its culture. As in Spanish America, the local indigenous population—mostly comprising branches of the Tupí population—suffered substantial demographic collapse as a result of the spread of European disease. In contrast to the core areas of Spanish America, the surviving indigenous population, characterized by semisedentary groups, largely avoided direct Portuguese administration for centuries. The Portuguese hugged the Atlantic Coast and sought to exercise brutal control over enslaved Africans, while indigenous inhabitants retreated to the interior.

The Consequences of the Conquest: The Columbian Exchange

The consequences of the Conquest weighed heavily on the people of the defeated empires. The noble families of the defeated indigenous empires found themselves subjected to the Spaniards, compelled to provide labor or tribute to the Spanish empire. Disease took the greatest toll. Indigenous people had no immunity to European pathogens, and experienced a demographic disaster of epic proportions. Diseases like smallpox, *peste* (typhoid fever), and what the Mexica called *matlazahuatl* (perhaps bronchial flu or typhus) devastated indigenous populations. Although statistics compiled in the sixteenth century are unreliable, by best estimate the Aztec empire once held 25 million people, while about 10 million inhabited the Inka realm. By 1625 no more than 675,000 Indians survived in Mexico and about 600,000 in the Andes. Some scholars estimate that by the start of the seventeenth century, the indigenous population of the Americas in their entirety may have declined by as much as 90 percent.

Contact had negative environmental effects, as well. The Spaniards especially exploited the landscape of the Americas by clearing primary growth forests. The importation of new invasive species such as pigs, sheep, and horses, though beneficial in terms of introducing new sources of protein and transportation to the New

World, also had negative consequences. They soon multiplied and overgrazed the terrain, damaging native flora and fauna. The cultivation of nonnative crops such as sugar (for trade and consumption) and wheat (for bread, a "food fit for Christian man," and also necessary for the Mass), transformed Latin America's relatively pristine lowlands and savannahs into domesticated agricultural landscapes.

On the positive front, the great **Columbian Exchange** (named for the explorer who "discovered" the Americas for Europe) reaped huge benefits for the world's population, especially in Europe. Latin America exported a variety of inexpensive crops to Europe that helped to prevent starvation. Maize, or corn, grew well in European soil. Potatoes, which produce dense food energy (calories) in small spaces, became a dietary staple of the poor in Ireland and northern Europe. Tomatoes, spicy peppers, and several varieties of beans also transplanted well. For the wealthier European consumer, Latin American food exports like sugar, tobacco, cacao (chocolate), and coffee became habit-forming necessities. For their part, Europeans brought such staples of the Spanish and Portuguese diets as wheat and grapes—which, in addition to food, provided the bread and wine needed for the Eucharist—and olives to the New World.

Colonial Administration and Economics

By the year 1750, Spanish officials could reflect back on the successes and failures of the colonial administrative and economic systems that had been created in the aftermath of the conquest. The system worked to some degree because the colonies still remained loyal to the monarchy after more than 200 years. But by 1750 clear fault lines had emerged. The colonial economy and tax system no longer provided sufficient revenue to the empire. The new dynasty of Bourbon kings would attempt to reform these institutions.

The Colonial Administration

The Hapsburg monarchs of the Spanish Empire (1519–1700) were the heirs to Ferdinand and Isabella. (The same royal family controlled the Holy Roman Empire, seated in Austria, but the Spanish and Austrian Hapsburgs diverged into two distinct branches after the mid-sixteenth century.) The Hapsburgs conceptualized the colonial administrative structure as a hierarchical pyramid, with the king and his Council of the Indies at the apex. Laws and decrees were transmitted from the apex to the most important of the administrators in the Americas, the viceroys (one situated in Peru, the other in Mexico). As their title suggests, the men acted like "vice-kings," cloaked with all the authority of the monarch. Within each viceroyalty were districts called *audiencias*, which in South America approximated the borders of the modern nations. In turn, each audiencia contained several subdivisions with different names such as *corregidor* or *alcalde mayor*. At each level, officials exercised executive, legislative, judicial, and even military powers, although obviously in diminishing degrees.

Reality on the ground proved quite different. Distance from Spain and the time it took for messages, orders, and appeals to crisscross the Atlantic ensured that decision-making was never swift. Colonials frequently appealed royal edicts and legislation that threatened important interests, often marking their communications with the wry but respectful phrase, "*Obedezco pero no cumplo*" (I obey but don't comply), thus offering tacit recognition on both sides of the ocean that Spain could not possibly speak to all possible New World realities across such a great distance.

Some proposed legislation proved so controversial that officials enforced it at their own risk. The New Laws of 1542, which prevented encomenderos (holders of encomiendas) from passing their privileges to exact labor and tribute on to the next generation, provides a good example. The viceroy of Mexico wisely exercised his discretionary power and did not enforce the New Laws, while the viceroy of Peru lost his office and his head to an army of angry encomenderos when he did attempt to enforce them. Even more commonly, members of the local elite discouraged royal officials from enforcing unpopular laws. Viceroys and other high-ranking royal officials were ostensibly banned from conducting business in their administrative districts, or allowing their children to marry members of the local elite, in attempts to hinder corruption. In practice, bureaucrats frequently engaged in both personal and economic relations with the people they were supposed to govern. As the Crown became more financially strapped during the seventeenth century, it sold lower-level offices to local elites, compounding their influence by 1750. Brazilian governors-general were vested with less power, and as many other officials reported directly to Lisbon, local interests often superseded the wishes of the monarchy.

The Church served as the moral guardian of the colonies and the partner of the king, using sermons to reinforce the colonists' loyalty to him. The friars who arrived in the sixteenth century performed three principal duties: converting the indigenous people to Christianity while administering the sacraments to both Spaniards and indigenous people, providing education for the Spaniards, and offering charity to unfortunate individuals, especially in cities. The spiritual conquest, however, achieved mixed results, as many indigenous people and Africans blended Catholic practices with their own beliefs, laying the foundation for Latin American popular religion.

One Spanish soldier who became a friar, Bartolomé de las Casas, vigorously denounced his fellow Spaniards for their brutal treatment of Indians and the failure of Spaniards to comply with their moral obligations. He petitioned the Spanish Crown for better treatment of indigenous people. Las Casas's diatribe against Spanish inhuman behavior during the early sixteenth century conquest of the Caribbean, *A Short Account of the Destruction of the Indies* (published in 1552), brought vivid attention to Spanish brutality. Because it was published during the height of hostilities between England and Spain during the wars of the Reformation, it was among the first books ever translated from Spanish into English—a translation that helped give rise to the "Black Legend," the perception among the English and other northern Europeans that the Spanish Empire was uniquely bloodthirsty and perverse. Las Casas's insistence on humane treatment for indigenous populations earned him both the title of Bishop of Chiapas and "Protector of the Indians."

In Brazil, the Jesuit Antônio Vieira bravely protested against exploitation of both Indians and enslaved Africans. To the north (as far as to what is now the US Southwest) and to the south (as far as the remote provinces of Paraguay and the Chaco), Iberian priests and friars built missions, worked toward conversion, and established what one scholar famously called the "Rim of Christendom." Over time, however, these efforts became routinized, incorporated into the messy business of colonial administration Many clergy enjoyed lives of luxury, funded by the profits derived from the enormous tracts of Church lands in rural areas and towns that, by law, remained inalienable. In the eyes of the Bourbon monarchs after 1750, the Church needed reforms as urgently as did the royal bureaucracy.

The Colonial Economy

The colonial economy depended on what turned out to be an ephemeral wealth, the silver of Peru and Mexico. Nevertheless, the shimmer of bullion (gold and silver) understandably captivated the Spanish monarchy, because the silver coins known as "pieces-of-eight" funded wars and bought consumer commodities. Brazil, at least until the eighteenth century, relied on the agricultural bonanza of sugar as its principal source of wealth. Both Iberian powers operated on the mercantile theory that the colonies existed to benefit the mother country. Thus tax revenue generated by mining (one-fifth of the value of the silver or gold mined) would be remitted to Spain to pay for defense, the costs of the colonial administrative system, and for expenses on the European continent, such as wars.

By 1750, the Spanish colonies operated at a loss. The costs of bureaucracy, especially salaries, consumed much of the tax revenue. Foreign enemies including pirates and smugglers beset the empire in an effort to seize ships laden with the silver from Potosí, Bolivia, and north central Mexico as well as gold and emeralds from Colombia. During the mid-eighteenth century, the Spanish government expended vast sums of money fortifying the key ports of Havana (Cuba), Cartagena, (Colombia), and Veracruz (Mexico) to protect the treasure fleets. For the first time, Spain created a militia and stationed a few regular army troops in the Americas. Clearly reforms had to occur if the colonial economies were to regain their status as profit centers.

Because Iberian cultural values disparaged manual labor, the elites and middle sectors of society required others to work the mines or plantations. Indians in *mita* (forced labor for a period of months) took turns at the mine in Potosí, the *"Cerro Rico"* (Rich Hill). The process was both dangerous and toxic. After digging the ore, workers carried it up rickety ladders to the surface. Next, they crushed it into a fine powder, which they mixed with water, chemicals, and mercury in a walled-in patio. Finally, they stirred the mixture with their feet until it "cooked" (a process that inflicted mercury poisoning on the workers themselves). Other workers then drained the patio, recovered the mercury, and gathered the remaining pure silver.

Obtaining gold, found in southwestern Colombia, the coast of Honduras, and the Caribbean, proved somewhat less hazardous. In all but Honduras, the mining of gold depended on the labor of African slaves, imported to replace indigenous labor after the demographic decline severely reduced the labor force. In Brazil, the heavy labor of sugar cultivation also depended entirely on enslaved Africans and their descendants, some two and a half million of them by 1800. Work on the plantation was harsh: planting and then cutting cane, feeding the stalks through the grinders of the mill to extract the juice, and then boiling the liquid to produce cane sugar—dangerous, exhausting labor.

Indigenous populations paid the bulk of the taxes, including a head tax (tribute extracted from every adult Indian) and a tithe (10% of their agricultural produce) that the Church and the government shared. Spaniards also found additional ways to extract money from Indians: Local officials could use the *repartimiento de bienes*, or division of goods, a system that obliged Indians to purchase merchandise from Spaniards at inflated prices. This practice introduced indigenous people to the market economy, and also allowed officials to recoup the price of the office they had purchased from the Crown.

Colonial Society

Postconquest society looked like a truncated pyramid with a few fortunate elite at its apex, a modest middle sector, and the vast majority (probably 90% or more) of the population holding up the elite and the middle class on their hard-working shoulders. The conquistadores initially constituted the elite sectors. But the decline of the encomienda caused by the demographic disaster of the sixteenth century soon propelled others into the elite class.

As time progressed, the European population itself divided into two sectors: **peninsulares** (Iberian-born Spaniards) and **criollos**, or "Spaniards" born in the New World. Although until the eighteenth century these two groups considered themselves as one, cultural drift (criollo Spaniards, for example, might have grown up with a Mexican or Peruvian accent, worldview, and preference) and genetic heritage (since some criollos were, in fact, biological mestizos or *castas* who had acquired the status of "Spaniards") began to take a toll. This would be one of the key factors in the growing fissure that would eventually split the New World from the Old.

The Elite, the Middle Sectors, and the Issue of Race

Soon after the Conquest, immigrants from Spain and Portugal poured into the New World to seek their fortunes, typically concentrating their activities in mining, trade, or plantation agriculture. These newer members of the elite, just like the conquistadores, preferred to live in cities and enjoy a more cosmopolitan lifestyle. Typically, they resided in the most fashionable neighborhoods adjacent to the central plaza. If their income was derived from ranching or agriculture, elites would also own sprawling haciendas in the countryside, though they seldom spent much time living there.

In the early years of the colonies, perceptions of race did not entirely define membership in the elite. In fact, the idea of "race" based on skin color— a social construction that varies from one society to another—originated much later in the eighteenth century, . In the early years, elite status was defined by the degree to which an individual possessed *calidad*, or "quality"—in practice, a set of attributes that included skin color, ancestry, occupation, wealth, language, and dietary preferences. Thus, in the early decades after the Conquest, members of the royal Mexica or the Sapa Inka's family enjoyed considerable social prestige. The descendants of the indigenous nobility struggled to maintain their position within the Spanish legal system, but gradually lost status. The descendants of the black conquistadores similarly found themselves losing ground in an increasingly stratified colonial society.

The middle sectors also generally lived in cities and towns. Spanish merchants were the wealthiest of all the individuals in the middle sector, especially the well-connected merchants in Lima or Mexico City who dominated international trade. Other middle sector professions included lawyers, estate managers, and members of the skilled artisan class such as silversmiths. Although small in number, members of the middle sectors, many of whom were literate, could be vocal in community affairs.

The majority of the colonial population lived in straitened circumstances. By the late sixteenth century, high-status indigenous men and women found themselves reclassified as "Indians" and subjected to a loss of their special privileges. For other Indians, the demographic facts speak for themselves. Although Spaniards did not understand the scientific reasons for the enormous number of deaths caused by epidemics, they were aware (especially the clergy) of the ill effects of hard treatment.

Spanish policy makers did employ ethnic labels to divide society into two groups: the *república de indios* and the *república de españoles*. Although Peru's viceroy Francisco de Toledo (1569–1581) professed altruistic motives for segregating the native population (theoretically, priests were the only Spaniards allowed in indigenous towns), the system of congregating indigenous people into towns also allowed for easier tax collection, facilitated drafts of men for mita service at the Potosí mine, and made for more efficient religious conversion. Many native communities retained their land throughout the colonial period and farmed it communally, although in times of prosperity Spanish *hacendados* (owners of large estates called haciendas) would encroach on indigenous property lines. Indigenous peoples continued to pay the bulk of the taxes, and harsh labor demands on bodies already weakened by disease wreaked havoc on their well-being.

Enslaved Africans also struggled to form families, retain cultural practices and carve out some degree of autonomy in the face of oppression. Africans in the New World combined Christianity and traditional beliefs and rituals, much as indigenous people did. Foods from Africa, like yams, became part of the Brazilian diet, and Bantu and Yoruba loan words became common in Brazil. Not surprisingly, Africans resisted slavery in a multitude of ways, whether slowing down their work, deliberately breaking machinery, or rising up against slave owners. And slaves frequently fled to remote areas where they formed communities called *quilombos*, some of which remained independent for decades, such as the famed quilombo of Palmares, in northeastern Brazil, which endured through most of the seventeenth century.

Changes in the Eighteenth Century

The last Hapsburg king died with no heir, leaving his French and Austrian relatives to engage in a thirteen-year war known as the War of the Spanish Succession (1700–1713) to determine which royal family would ascend to the Spanish throne. The victorious French royal family, the Bourbons, sought to reinvigorate the ties between Spain and its empire. Change came slowly, and although the Bourbons did strengthen the linkage between the Americas and the mother country, in the long run the unintended consequences of the reforms would contribute to the unraveling of the colonial world.

Piecemeal Reforms, 1713–1750

The **Bourbon reforms** essentially sought to increase tax revenues from the colonies, to shore up imperial defenses against Spain's European enemies who threatened the colonial periphery, and to increase the volume of trade between the mother country and the colonies. In the first portion of the eighteenth century, the monarchy was too engaged with attempts to reform Spain itself and its wars in Europe to accomplish much in the colonies.

Forces beyond the monarch's control contributed to policy changes. The European wars against Great Britain and its navy made the Spanish government reconsider the fleet system which semiannually conveyed treasure and goods between the colonies and Spain. Even in times of peace, fleets were regularly intercepted by privateers and pirates, often from Protestant countries such as England and Holland, who both welcomed the opportunity to steal the bounty of the galleons. The prices of goods collapsed when the fleet arrived, and spiked as supplies dwindled.

As a result, Spain gradually permitted individual ships to sail from Spain's legal ports to any location in the colonies, arguing that a single ship could better outmaneuver a British fleet. Beyond this, the Crown encouraged the development of new products in the peripheral areas. A monopoly company located in Venezuela marketed and sold cacao, making this once-neglected portion of the empire more valuable. Because the indigenous population had by now acquired immunity to European diseases, more labor was available for agriculture and mines. And increasing numbers of imported African slaves also augmented the labor supply.

Yet these gradual changes satisfied neither Spain nor the colonists. By the terms that ended the War of the Spanish Succession (1713), Spain yielded to the British a trade privilege known as the *asiento*, allowing the British to send a single ship per year to trade with the Spanish colonies. The British promptly abused the agreement, sending many ships. Few residents of Spanish America complained, for the asiento offered what they truly wanted: open trade with Great Britain for the cheapest and highest quality manufactured goods. Unregulated trade continued apace at the periphery, especially at Buenos Aires, in the remote Isthmus of Panama and the coves of Nicaragua, and along the coast of Peru and Chile. Mexico's far north also felt the lure of French and other European merchants.

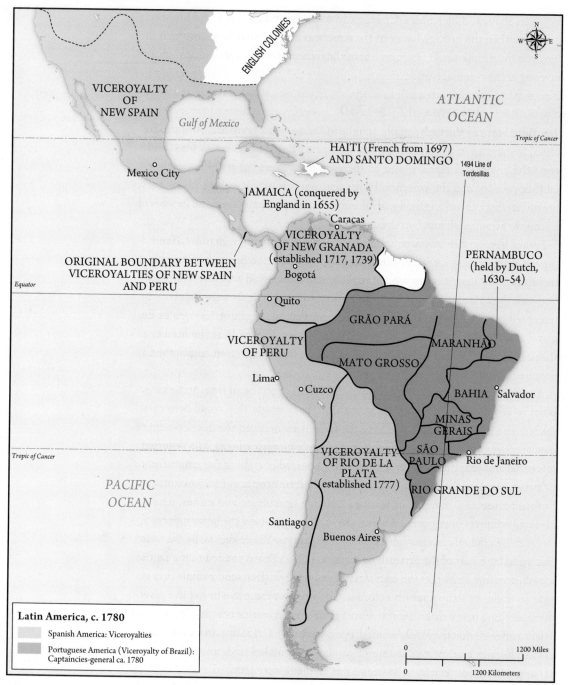

ENGLISH COLONIES

VICEROYALTY
OF
NEW SPAIN

Gulf of Mexico

*ATLANTIC
OCEAN*

Tropic of Cancer

HAITI (French from 1697)
AND SANTO DOMINGO

1494 Line of
Tordesillas

○ Mexico City

JAMAICA (conquered by
England in 1655)

Caracas ○

VICEROYALTY
OF NEW GRANADA
(established 1717, 1739)

PERNAMBUCO
(held by Dutch,
1630–54)

ORIGINAL BOUNDARY BETWEEN
VICEROYALTIES OF NEW SPAIN
AND PERU

Bogotá

Equator

○ Quito

GRÃO PARÁ

VICEROYALTY
OF PERU

MARANHÃO

MATO GROSSO

Lima ○

○ Cuzco

BAHIA

○ Salvador

MINAS
GERAIS

Tropic of Cancer

VICEROYALTY
OF RIO DE LA
PLATA
(established 1777)

SÃO
PAULO

○ Rio de Janeiro

*PACIFIC
OCEAN*

RIO GRANDE DO SUL

Santiago ○

Buenos Aires ○

Latin America, c. 1780

Spanish America: Viceroyalties

Portuguese America (Viceroyalty of Brazil):
Captaincies-general ca. 1780

0   1200 Miles

0   1200 Kilometers

≡ **MAP. 0.2**

The Later Reforms and the Enlightenment

The last two Bourbon kings insisted on more comprehensive reforms as the best means to restore Spain's greatness. Spain suffered the humiliating loss of its key port of Havana during the Seven Years' War (1756–1763), prompting King Charles III to turn his attention to colonial affairs. He intended to integrate the colonies more thoroughly with Spain and, in so doing, to squeeze more revenues from the Americas through higher taxes and a series of monopolies on popular pleasures (what we could today call "sin taxes" on such goods as tobacco, alcohol, and playing cards). The enhanced revenue would be used to defend colonial borders, strengthen fortifications, and introduce new bureaucrats to the Americas, improving the king's ability to exercise centralized control over the colonies.

Simultaneously, a reform-minded minister in Portugal, the Marquis de Pombal, undertook the rehabilitation of his country's largest possession, Brazil. Lionized because of the efficient manner in which he oversaw the reconstruction of Lisbon after a devastating earthquake destroyed the city in 1755, Pombal believed that Portugal should reap the benefits of its largest possession's prosperity. Earlier in the century, an enormous gold strike had shifted Brazil's focus from the sugar fields of the northeast further south. Even though the quantity of gold being mined had declined somewhat by the 1770s, the rich soils of the southeastern coast around Rio de Janeiro now grew crops like cotton, sugar, and eventually coffee. Like the Spanish Bourbon kings, Pombal believed that Portugal should seize the opportunities provided by Brazil's economic expansion.

Pombal moved Brazil's capital from Salvador to Rio de Janeiro in 1763, and made the colonial government more hierarchical, naming a viceroy who reported directly to the king. Pombal also took the radical step of expelling the Jesuits from all Portuguese dominions, enabling the imperial administration to seize the extensive Jesuit assets.

In Spain, King Charles III tightened the colonial reins even more than Pombal had in Brazil. The viceroyalty of Peru had proven unmanageably large and was challenged by especially difficult geography, which included not only the rugged Andes mountain range but also impenetrable tropical jungles, vast savannahs, and far-flung outposts and ports located across the continent from the viceregal capital of Lima. The Bourbons divided it into three: Peru, New Granada (Colombia, Ecuador, and Panama), and Río de La Plata (Argentina, Bolivia, and Paraguay). With a powerful viceroy in place in each capital, Charles believed he and his colonial minister would exert more forceful control over his subjects.

To reduce corruption, Charles created a new layer of bureaucrats (called intendants) to replace the lowest level of government officials. The size of an intendancy proved too large for a single man to govern effectively, so the Crown created a new category of low-ranking officials known as subdelegates—who often supplemented their meager salaries by accepting bribes. The intendants did collect taxes more efficiently, locating Indians who had escaped the tribute tax and rigorously collecting sales taxes from the rest of society. These "successes," however, provoked a series of violent rebellions in the Andean region during the 1780s. Like Pombal in Brazil, Charles III expelled the Jesuits from Spanish America, depriving the colonies of many of their teachers.

Spanish America's economy rebounded, at least until 1800. Charles instituted free trade within the empire in 1776, with a resulting increase in the volume of commerce and improved sales tax revenues. Royal monopolies on the sale of tobacco, alcohol, and playing cards filled the crown's coffers. Specialized monopolies, like the cacao monopoly in Venezuela, continued to earn great wealth for plantation owners. Mexico outdistanced Peru in the production of silver, and both surpassed the levels produced during the seventeenth century. Most interestingly, the neglected areas of Spanish South America, especially Venezuela, Argentina, and Cuba, now prospered. The vast grasslands around Buenos Aires allowed free-roaming cattle to proliferate, allowing for significant export of leather, tallow, and salted beef. Cuba surpassed Brazil in terms of sugar production. These economies were commercially linked to Europe and the United States, and as a result would suffer fewer economic reversals after independence than would the mining industry in Mexico and Peru.

Although the Bourbon reforms made Spanish kings more powerful, they did not please the local population, who yearned for the days when they enjoyed greater autonomy. Now *peninsulares* sat atop the social pyramid and cornered the most lucrative and prestigious positions in the bureaucracy and Church. Peninsulares tended to marry each other, reinforcing the clannishness of the elite. Criollos began to turn to liberal Enlightenment ideas, such as the idea that rational, innovative

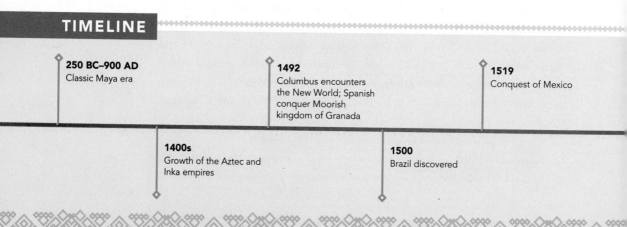

TIMELINE

250 BC–900 AD
Classic Maya era

1492
Columbus encounters the New World; Spanish conquer Moorish kingdom of Granada

1519
Conquest of Mexico

1400s
Growth of the Aztec and Inka empires

1500
Brazil discovered

strategies could improve economic efficiency, that individuals had inherent political rights, rather than privileges granted by the Crown, and that the best form of government was one chosen by citizens, rather than inherited by subjects.

At the same time, conditions for the lower tiers of society worsened after 1800. Emphasis on racial categories called **castas** increased. People of color were denied privileges and consigned to the lower realms of society. For the poor, the increasing level of taxation threatened their very survival, as did a series of famines in Mexico. Both in Spanish America and Brazil, protests against the reformed administration mounted at the dawn of the nineteenth century.

KEY TERMS

Bourbon reforms li	encomienda xlii	peninsulares xlix
castas lv	hacienda xl	Reconquista xxxix
Columbian Exchange xlv	mestizo xlii	Southern Cone xxxv
criollos xlix	mestizaje xlii	

Selected Readings

Burkholder, Mark, and Lyman Johnson. *Colonial Latin America*. New York: Oxford University Press, 2014.

Restall, Matthew, and Kris Lane. *Latin America in Colonial Times*. Cambridge: Cambridge University Press, 2013.

Twinam, Ann. *Purchasing Whiteness: Pardos, Mulattos, and the Quest for Social Mobility in the Spanish India*. Stanford, CA: Stanford University Press, 2015.

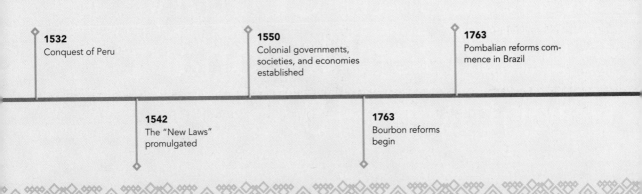

1532
Conquest of Peru

1550
Colonial governments, societies, and economies established

1763
Pombalian reforms commence in Brazil

1542
The "New Laws" promulgated

1763
Bourbon reforms begin

The Early Nineteenth-Century Search for National Identity to 1875

As the Prologue shows, the various regions of Latin America nurtured fascinating hybrids of culture, religion, language, and administration during the colonial period, making the region a fertile laboratory for innovation. In the early nineteenth century, inhabitants of mainland Spanish and Portuguese America faced a new challenge, as they struggled to construct viable nation-states. Inhabitants of the Spanish Caribbean, meanwhile, tried to make sense of their role in a declining Spanish Empire during a time of rapid change.

In Part One, we explore the challenges of the early decades of what historians call the "national period," from 1808 to the present, beginning with the formation of breakaway nations in the early 1800s. Just as the Bourbon reformers had introduced uncertainty into the colonial world, so too did the Enlightenment ideas of the eighteenth century provoke deep debates, about the ways in which the new nations ought to proceed. Would strong nation-states prevail against regional federations? Could Latin America gain a greater measure of prosperity than it had enjoyed in colonial times? Most divisively, would the Catholic Church continue to play a dominant role?

The colonial inheritance, which some historians describe as a long hangover, marked this passage to independence. Three hundred years of emphasis on exporting commodities like silver, sugar, tobacco, gold, diamonds, and emeralds had created economic patterns that were difficult to alter. In the nineteenth century, Latin Americans faced the difficulties of expanding domestic markets while weathering the shocks of volatile global commodity prices. In much of the region, agricultural production intensified and the meaning of land ownership changed along with it.

Even during the colonial period, large estates that participated directly in commodity booms were highly productive. The wheat grown on the haciendas of Mexico's Bajío region in the late sixteenth century perfectly complemented the silver extracted from mines in the same region, as new strategies of investment in these commodities facilitated innovation and expansion, generating exponential profits. The sugar plantations of northeastern Brazil in the seventeenth century generated a similar cluster of investment and expansion, in this case with direct ties to the Dutch joint-stock companies pioneering new strategies of global finance. Latin America's most productive large estates had long been engines of capitalist expansion and innovation.

Even in the core areas of Latin America, however, such as the hinterlands of Rio de Janeiro, titled nobility amassed lands merely as a function of their good relations with the Portuguese Crown. Over the course of the first half of the nineteenth century, the balance began to tip. Unproductive estates endured on the economic fringes, but in the areas of rapid growth (such as the coffee-growing areas of Brazil and Costa Rica, the cattle regions of the Rio de la Plata basin, and the sugar zones of Mexico, Puerto Rico, and Cuba), capitalist investment in agricultural production intensified. Land values soared as outputs increased.

This growth had environmental and social consequences. As more of Latin America's territory fell under cultivation, human intervention increased yields and decreased biodiversity. Rainforest, savannah, and rolling grasslands gave way to coffee, sugar, and grazing pastures. The subsistence agriculture that had survived the colonial period among indigenous communities, mestizo villages and Brazilian quilombos (communities of runaway slaves), faced new pressures. The resistance of small-scale cultivators to the encroachment of intensified production, rising land costs, and the displacement of traditional villages would shape many of the political conflicts of the nineteenth and even twentieth centuries.

The creation of new nation-states also raised questions of citizenship and rights. What forms would the new national governments take? After a few, failed attempts at monarchy, the new Spanish American nations adopted republican constitutions, usually modeled after that of the United States of America. These typically prescribed three branches of government, each vested with certain powers, with sovereignty resting in the people. As in the United States at independence, the vast majority of the population could not vote—these republics were not democracies and did not necessarily aspire to be. Indeed, most of nineteenth-century Latin America's republicans envisioned government of, by, and for men of property. (Brazil was a monarchal outlier: alone among the new nations of the Americas, Brazil made a transition from the Portuguese Empire to a new, independent Brazilian Empire, under the same royal dynastic family).

In both Brazil and the new Spanish American republics, the statesmen implementing new constitutions entered into fierce political conflict over political rights and procedures: who had the right to vote, which offices did they vote on, and what were the powers and limitations of government? Although women played important roles during the battle for independence, the strictures of patriarchal

culture denied them equal rights as citizens. Women nonetheless continued to exercise strong influence over both public and private life through their roles as property owners, entrepreneurs, tradeswomen and family members. During the early
nineteenth century, each nation stumbled toward its own solutions, in a process of
experimentation that shared common features throughout the region.

Beyond the question of who should have right to vote, Latin American nations
faced questions of how to redefine the hierarchies that had shaped colonial society.
The judicial structure of colonial Spanish America had separated indigenous communities from the mestizo world (the "Republic of the Indians" and the "Republic
of the Spanish"). In the early national period, most Spanish American nations did
away with this structure and sought to hold all citizens equal before the law—with
the catch that legal citizenship was limited to free, nonindigenous men. In practice,
adoption of new laws conferring equal, individual rights allowed the powerful to
exploit their fellow citizens in ways that eroded the autonomy of indigenous communities. One historian has described this as a passage "from two republics to
one, divided."

The new Spanish American nations succeeded in abolishing slavery in the early ✔
national period. Brazil and the sugar-producing islands of the Spanish Caribbean
clung to the pernicious institution much longer—and in both cases slavery and
the endurance of monarchy became deeply linked. The passage toward abolition
would be halting and arduous. Far from withering away, slavery intensified in the
first half of the nineteenth century, as exploitation contributed to rising agricultural production. The transatlantic slave trade itself continued to grow in volume
to Brazil and Cuba through the first half of the nineteenth century.

In most of Spanish America, the new republican governments that took power
in the 1820s failed to consolidate administrative control. Local strongmen, known
as *caudillos*, emerged to fill the power vacuum, maintaining the loyalty of their
followers by distributing benefits and upholding traditional privileges. These
caudillos sometimes rose to power at the national level but rarely held it for long.
Instead, conflict between those who sought to race toward their own vision of
modernity and those who sought to hold onto the hard-won stability of the past
continued. These conflicts never mapped easily onto social strata, as both humble
campesinos (agricultural workers) and powerful landowners often sought to hold
on to traditional structures, while both slaves and wealthy investors alike pressed
for change. For all these reasons, the conflicts and innovations that marked Latin
America in the first half of the nineteenth century would profoundly shape the later
growth of the region.

1

Latin America in the Age of Atlantic Revolution, 1789–1820s

Global Connections

Many historians consider the 1760s through the 1820s to be the "age of revolution," the dawning of the modern era across the globe, including Latin America. Three broad concepts underlay this transition to a more contemporary way of thinking. First, emerging ideas about the modern nation-state, republicanism, and popular sovereignty led to decolonization in the Western Hemisphere, dismembering centuries-old empires even as the British and French fired the opening salvos in their quest for new imperial ventures in Africa, the Middle East, and Asia. Second, the Industrial Revolution and the ideas associated with modern economics that began in western Europe abetted a long-standing growth in consumer-driven commerce all around the world. Finally, ideas about constitutionalism and the individual liberties that guaranteed equal rights for all citizens clashed with both religious beliefs and secular values held dear outside the Western world.

Western Europe's growing economic dominance adversely affected three of the world's longest-standing dynastic states: the Mughal Empire of India, the Ottoman Empire in the Middle East, and the Qing in China. Although these outdated dynastic empires quickly grasped the consequences of superior European firepower, they had more difficulty responding to the political and economic principles described above. In terms of economic consequences, for example, the Mughal Empire not only found itself displaced by the British East India Company, but also watched as English industrial textiles crowded Indian handmade cloth out of the marketplace in the Indian Ocean. The Ottomans in Turkey employed diplomacy and rivalries between the British, French, and Russians to hang on to their territory, but in the end could only feebly protest Egypt's growing autonomy (and the loss of Ottoman control over its valuable cotton crop) and Greece's outright independence. Although the Qing dynasty in China remained an economic powerhouse in 1800, the rot had set in and it found itself increasingly less able to compete with European pressure as British opium grown in South Asia reversed China's centuries-old favorable balance of trade. Decreasing tax revenues, as well as increasingly smaller plots for farmers because of rapid population increase, further stressed the empire.

During the age of revolution, however, political ideas proved far more important than the changing dynamics of the international marketplace. In many respects,

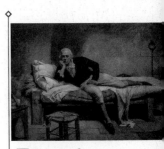

≡ **Francisco de Miranda Imprisoned in a Spanish Hulk.** Like most criollo patriot leaders, Francisco de Miranda, the so-called "Precursor" of the Spanish-American independence movements, had thoroughly read the writings of Enlightenment political thinkers. Even before Napoleon's invasion of Spain, Miranda had launched an attack on his native Venezuela. He returned to the fray as the head of Venezuela's First Republic in 1811 but was captured when it fell to royalist forces. Like many other independence leaders, Miranda became disillusioned with the cause. He spent the remainder of his life locked up in a Spanish prison ship.

GLOBAL CONNECTIONS
Latin America and the World in the Age of Revolution

NORTH
AMERICA

UNITED
STATES

MEXICO

ST. DOMINGUE/
HAITI

CENTRAL
AMERICA

PERU

BRAZIL

SOUTH
AMERICA

- Spanish Empire
- Portuguese Empire
- British, French, and Dutch colonial territories

Spain and Portugal had much in common with the aging dynastic empires elsewhere in the world. During the wars for independence, Spaniards and the Portuguese consistently resisted the idea that Latin Americans could become equal partners in the greater Iberian empires. Inhabitants of Latin America had good reasons to chafe under the rule of weakened empires that failed to defend their interests. Spanish Americans ultimately opted for the modern political idea of republican nation-states, some of the world's first such governments. (The Caribbean islands

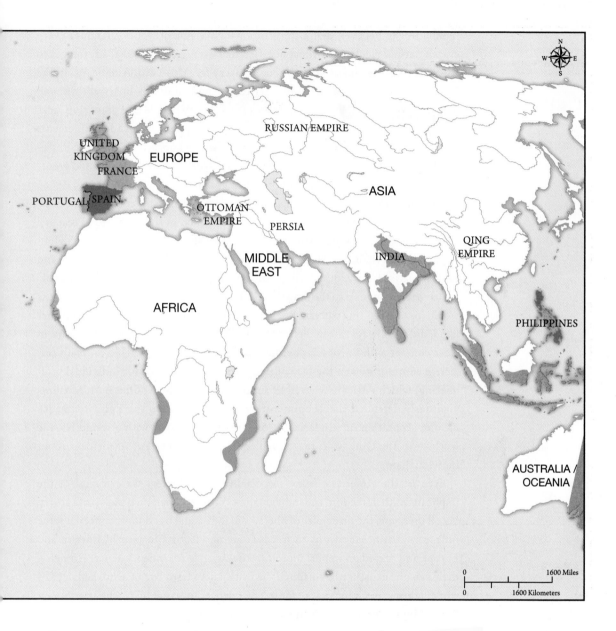

of Cuba and Puerto Rico, however, remained part of the Spanish Empire until the final years of the nineteenth century.) Through a curious process of royal migration and dynastic bifurcation explained in what follows, Brazil emerged into independence as a monarchy.

People in the Americas traded their status as subjects of a distant king not only to sever their ties with colonial overlords but also to gain the inalienable rights of citizenship. Most of those who championed the cause of independence and republicanism believed that a constitutional government would guarantee every citizen natural rights, individual liberties, and even grant personal advantages to specific groups, such as the abolition of slavery for Afro-Latin Americans. In the United States, France, and Latin America, the pursuit of life, liberty, and happiness (or property) offered opportunities for ordinary people and oppressed races to dream about self-betterment. Even so, these new opportunities and entitlements came at the price of a serious rupture with the status quo, and the effort to implement the Enlightenment's promises and values—or to resist them—would preoccupy Latin Americans for much of the nineteenth century.

For some areas of the world, Spanish America's turn to independence seemed only natural. To the north, the United States, which in the early 1820s reached only as far west as Louisiana—making it much smaller, and possibly less globally significant than, say, Mexico—was the first to establish its independence and build its nationhood around Enlightened principles, and it seemed only "rational" (to use a term popular to the day) that the other emerging nations in the Americas would follow the same pattern. But people in other parts of the globe, on the other hand, did not always line up behind the Enlightenment's ideas. West Africans, in close contact with Europeans because of the slave trade, struggled to retain collective communities in the face of the European preference for individual profiteering, which Africans viewed as simple greed. In the Middle East, Muslims vigorously defended their community of believers, seeing the Enlightenment's ideal of separation of religion and government as at odds with a sound Islamic worldview. The Qing in China proved equally resistant to European ideas about individualism.

Even in the Americas, some (especially certain elites) were fearful of the implications that freedom and individualism meant for their own status and power. Yet all the same, the principles of liberty and individual freedoms connected some influential Latin Americans to freedom-loving idealists in North America and Europe and played an important role in the struggle for independence. How else, then, can one explain what inspired the British poet Lord Byron, who died in 1824 while fighting in Greece's war for independence, to name his yacht after Simón Bolívar, internationally renowned as the "Liberator."

The Causes of Independence, 1789–1810

What would inspire reasonably content peoples inhabiting colonial empires to risk everything in a life-or-death struggle for independence? Although in 1810 only a few firebrands in Latin America favored outright independence, over time more individuals accepted the necessity for this radical change. Many factors contributed to Latin Americans' decision to sever their ties with Spain, Portugal, and France. This section of chapter 1 explores the general causes that contributed to that decision. Given the rich variety of historical experiences within Latin America, as well as the varied and complex societies and economies that had arisen there over three hundred years, different populations had different reasons for their growing malaise.

The External Causes of Independence

Four key factors contributed to the drive for independence. First, the ideas of the European **Enlightenment** carried serious implications for Latin Americans because they challenged colonial traditions. Although most eighteenth-century political theorists still believed that monarchy was the only acceptable form of government, for the first time they questioned whether royal power was God-given and absolute. A number of writers (like the English theorist John Locke or the French intellectual Jean-Jacques Rousseau) argued that a social compact, or contract, existed between monarch and subjects, requiring the monarch to govern with the consent of the people. Otherwise, in extreme instances (such as England's "Glorious Revolution" of 1688, which overthrew King James II, or even more violently, the French Revolution of 1789–1799, which destroyed the monarchy and much of the French aristocracy), those subjects could justifiably replace a king who, they believed, had violated the social contract with his subjects. More liberal authors like the French Charles-Louis de Secondat, the Baron de Montesquieu, posited an even more radical idea: that nations could adopt a republican form of government, responsive to the will of the majority, with three independent branches (executive, legislative, and judicial) that would protect citizens' individual liberties.

Enlightenment economists, like the Scotsman Adam Smith, advocated scrapping the antiquated system of mercantilism (theoretically a closed economic system wherein the profits generated benefited the colonizing power) for free trade. This idea played well with Latin American consumers and smaller-scale shopkeepers tired of paying upward of 60 percent taxes that only enriched Spain and Spanish merchants. This idea became even more tangible when Latin Americans experienced the benefits of freer trade during the intermittent global wars and the Bourbon Reforms of the late eighteenth century.

The late eighteenth-century Enlightenment also provided many Europeans with new knowledge about Spanish America, largely as the result of publications about the numerous scientific expeditions begun during the reign of Charles III (1759–1788). Curious to learn more about his realm, particularly its natural resources and economic prospects, Charles commissioned explorers like Italian-born Alessandro Malaspina to map the coastline of southern South America and the western coast of New Spain as far north at Nootka Sound in the Pacific Northwest. This Enlightenment quest for scientific knowledge culminated with the residence of the German geologist and botanist Alexander von Humboldt in the Americas between 1799 and 1804. During his stay, von Humboldt and his associate Aimé Bonpland traversed northern South America, observing rare pink dolphins and dangerous electric eels in the Orinoco River, climbing higher than any previous European (19,286 feet to within 1,000 feet of Ecuador's Mt. Chimborazo summit) collecting data on the effects of altitude on plant life, and discovering the rich fertilizer known as guano (chapter 3). While in New Spain, Humboldt accurately calculated the longitude of the Pacific port of Acapulco (the terminus of Spain's East Asia trade) and suggested scientific techniques to improve the productivity of the viceroyalty's silver mines. In all the metropolises that Humboldt visited, men and women gathered to share their thoughts with this renowned intellectual about matters political, economic, and scientific.

Political events elsewhere in the world also contributed to Latin American independence. The second external factor shaping independence in Latin America was the American Revolutionary War (1775–1783), which provided an example of a successful colonial rebellion. Latin Americans recognized that if the thirteen US colonies could force the world's most powerful nation to its knees, then Latin Americans should be able to expel the weaker colonial states of Spain and Portugal.

A third factor was the French Revolution, which (at least in its early stages) demonstrated the viability of Enlightenment political theory. That Revolution also directly contributed to the successful struggle for freedom in Haiti, where colonists, free blacks, and even slaves argued that they deserved the same personal liberties and rights of citizenship as European Frenchmen. By the same token, the French Revolution also provided an example where the peasantry and urban poor violently overthrew the nobility to gain these rights. But the French Revolution was also the source of a new technology of death, the guillotine, which "liberated" the heads from the bodies of some forty thousand French aristocrats between the years 1793–1794 to meet the demands of the revolutionary "*jacquerie*". Thus, the French Revolution also provided a shocking example of how, from an elite perspective, such movements could go very wrong by demanding that the rich and powerful sacrifice not only their privileges but also their lives.

Fourth, and finally, the French emperor Napoleon's invasion of the Iberian Peninsula in 1807 unleashed a series of events that triggered opportunities for change. Hoping to end British trade with Europe in defiance of his Continental

Blockade, Napoleon invaded Portugal, which caused the Portuguese royal family and its court to sail for Brazil escorted by a British fleet. For many years to follow, Rio de Janeiro would serve as the seat of the Portuguese empire, to the delight of many Brazilians. Meanwhile, Napoleon captured and imprisoned the recently deposed Spanish king and his slightly more likeable son, Ferdinand VII, initiating the Peninsular War (1807–1814) during which the Spanish people attempted to expel the French. Because the pope in 1493 had granted legal title to the Spanish Americas to the royal family rather than the kingdom of Spain, Napoleon's intervention and "unlawful" imposition of his brother, Joseph-Napoléon Bonaparte, on the Spanish throne raised a technical nicety. In the absence of a legitimate king, some Latin Americans would seize the opportunity to rule for themselves.

The Internal Grievances

Latin Americans' internal grievances, rather than the more distant external causes, proved to be the more telling factors leading to the demise of Spanish colonial rule. To begin with, the growing resentment of **criollos** (people of Spanish descent born in the New World) against the privileges, favored status, and snobbery of the **peninsulares** (Spaniards born in the Iberian Peninsula) gave rise to a generation of disgruntled patriots. They would be led by criollos whose first loyalty was to their place of birth in the Americas rather than to a distant Spanish monarch.

Centuries of distance between Spain and its colonies had produced profound differences between Spaniards from Spain and those born and raised in the New World. Some "Spanish" criollo families, in fact, had lived in the Americas for several generations. This concept of creole patriotism, expressed as resentment against peninsular Spaniards, had been muted for much of the colonial era. For example, under Spain's ineffectual seventeenth-century monarchs, criollos had purchased both high- and low-ranking offices in government and the church and had become wealthy owners of huge estates (haciendas), plantations, mines, and other businesses. Lax enforcement of mercantilist trade restrictions allowed for rampant smuggling of foreign-made goods, permitting the criollo elite to live luxuriously.

This period of salutary neglect (one that paralleled a similar process in the British colonies of North America) came to a halt with the accession of reform-minded King Charles III (1759–1788) to the Spanish throne. He and his prime minister, José de Gálvez, like most of their contemporaries in the Iberian royal administrations, looked down on the residents of their colonies in the Americas as inherently inferior, an inferiority they attributed to the maleficent influence of the tropics. Gálvez's lengthy visit to New Spain (Mexico) between 1765 and 1771 only reinforced his opinion. As a consequence, King Charles and Gálvez deemed criollos untrustworthy to hold administrative offices, and from that point forward almost exclusively appointed peninsulares to bureaucratic posts.

In 1804, King Charles's successor, Charles IV, further antagonized criollos by requiring the Catholic Church (Spanish America's principal banker) to demand full payment of the balance owed on outstanding long-term mortgages, which damaged many Mexican criollos economically (the decree apparently was less strictly enforced elsewhere). He also disallowed New World men to become priests, one of the most revered professions in Spanish society and a favored career option for second sons who could not inherit their family's property. Faced with this affront to their wealth and status, it is no wonder that creole patriotism expressed itself as a desire for some degree of Latin American autonomy (self-governance) within the imperial structure.

In addition, the poorer classes also felt pinched by Charles III's reforms. Because the indigenous population had finally recovered from the demographic disaster of the sixteenth century, burgeoning local populations, especially in Mexico, competed for land and access to water with expanding haciendas. Poverty increased for many indigenous people, who were now faced with the choice of either laboring for small wages on those haciendas or fleeing to the cities to scratch out a precarious living. While the availability of more workers revived the colonial economy, especially in the silver mining industry, it scarcely benefited those laborers. Finally, the reforms removed traditional indigenous leaders from their posts in villages and replaced them with outsiders.

Bourbon tax policy took its heaviest toll on the poorer classes. Charles III reconceptualized the New World "kingdoms" as mere colonies whose purpose was to provide more tax revenue, thereby allowing Spain to regain its proper place as a world power. As a result, King Charles and Gálvez rigorously collected taxes, especially the tribute levied mostly on indigenous people. In the Andean region, the more efficient bureaucrats enrolled tribute payers who had escaped the tax rolls previously, and, by so doing, simultaneously made them subject to the forced labor system used to draft workers for the mines. The king and Gálvez raised the sales tax rate from 2 to 6 percent. In addition, the reformers instituted government-owned monopolies on commodities such as tobacco and *aguardiente* (cheap grain alcohol), sin taxes on pleasurable vices that the poor enjoyed.

In regions with large slave populations, Latin Americans of African descent more openly resisted their mandatory servitude and sought emancipation. While the popular classes were unlikely to initiate independence movements, they certainly were restive forces that could be recruited to the broader project given the appropriate appeal. For criollos, the challenge would be how to win a greater degree of self-government without triggering a deeper revolution that would disturb their position atop the Latin American socioeconomic order.

The Haitian Revolution, 1789–1804

The uprising that ended slavery in the French colony of Saint-Domingue and brought independence to the country now called Haiti is the only fully successful slave revolt in history. Yet Haiti's war of independence was more than "just" a black rebellion. Not only did it seek to end French colonialism and the incredibly harsh conditions that Africans faced on sugar plantations but also it represented an effort to bring the promises of the French Revolution—*"liberté, égalité, fraternité"*—to full fruition in the New World. Finally, for colonial elites throughout the Americas, the Haitian Revolution was the nightmarish embodiment of their deep-rooted fears about race and power relations. Its promise for some and peril for others shaped subsequent revolutions in Spanish and Portuguese America.

Slavery in Saint-Domingue

Contrary to Haiti's reputation for poverty today, the French Caribbean colony of Saint-Domingue was among the most prosperous in the world at the end of the eighteenth century. The French had acquired the western half of the island of Hispaniola from Spain in 1697. By the early 1700s they had begun to extensively irrigate and convert agricultural production to sugarcane, an emergent commodity that helped to feed the sweet tooth of Europe's new emerging middle class. By 1740, French Saint-Domingue and the British colony of Jamaica produced much of the world's sugar (as well as coffee).

As in Brazil and the British colonies in the Caribbean, the French produced sugar on plantations, with labor provided by enslaved people from Africa. Saint-Domingue's tropical conditions, coupled with unusually harsh treatment of slaves by French masters, produced a slave milieu perhaps more brutal than any other in the Americas. France's **Code Noir** (Black Code), passed in 1685 (well before the heyday of Saint-Domingue's sugar production), attempted to regulate the treatment of black slaves by prohibiting beating, burning, and other forms of corporal punishment such as castration. Masters, however, paid little attention to the Code, and French authorities demonstrated little enthusiasm for enforcing it. In 1758, white French plantation owners created their own regulations to control society on their own terms.

This was a rigid caste system that divided society into three main categories: **blancs** (white, free, and mostly landowners); **gens de couleur libres**, or "free blacks" (often mixed-raced mulattos, frequently the children of white planters and enslaved mothers); and **noirs** (enslaved blacks). Because of this kinship and their relative "whiteness," in the racial thinking of the day, free blacks often held a favored position in society, including access to some education and, sometimes, the right to own land. The noirs, however, were entirely without social or political standing or, in fact, any right to personhood whatsoever.

With respect to those classified as noir, slave owners tended to think of New World–born slaves as more servile and trustworthy while regarding the majority African-born noirs with greater fear and distrust. These African-born noirs also retained strong personal and cultural memory of their homelands. Within the colony, people of African descent far outnumbered everyone else while slaves outnumbered whites in Saint-Domingue by a ratio of 10–1. The implicit tensions evident in this setting caused the eighteenth-century French writer, Honoré Gabriel Riqueti, Count of Mirabeau, to observe that Saint-Domingue's whites "slept at the foot of Vesuvius."

Yet when this volcano of rebellion erupted, it would be more than a revolt of enslaved people against their cruel masters. Haiti (as we hereafter refer to it) would become a test case for the values of the homeland, France, which by the 1780s would be deeply embroiled in the defining struggle of the eighteenth-century Enlightenment, the French Revolution (1789–1799). Although marked by the violent overthrow of the monarch and the landed class and by excessive social violence, the French Revolution at its foundation was about the implementation of radical new ideas forged by the Enlightenment, centered on the rights of mankind, equality, rationality, and natural law. These foundational ideas would also find voice in France's premier Caribbean colony.

While some of Haiti's white planters embraced the ideas of the Revolution and pressed for autonomy, most landed elites, whose counterparts were losing their heads to the guillotine back in France, did not. The specter of a race war seemed more threat than promise, even as the question of slavery itself fell under the scrutiny of Enlightenment thinking. Thus it would be not French planters, but the educated and francophone free blacks who, aware of the implications of France's revolutionary manifesto, the *Declaration of the Rights of Man and of the Citizen* (1789), would ultimately bring about both an end to slavery and to Haiti's colonial status.

Initially, the effort for equality in Haiti took a peaceful path. Two educated free blacks, Julian Raimond and Vincent Ogé, appealed unsuccessfully at different times to the French National Assembly for full civil equality with whites. Frustrated, Ogé initiated a small uprising in Haiti in early 1791. French authorities seized Ogé and, by way of example, sentenced him to death. He was "broken on the wheel," a public form of execution that involved breaking a victim's back across a wooden hoop

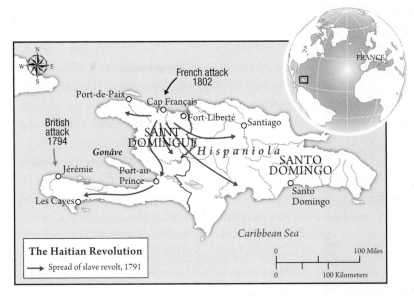

MAP. 1.1

and then beheading that person. This brutal execution was perceived by whites as a just punishment but by blacks as something closer to political assassination. The same month as Ogé's death, a meeting of enslaved African religious leaders, led by Dutty Boukman, a **Vodun** priest (Vodun is a Haitian belief system that combines elements of African spirit worship with Christianity) convened in the north of the island. There, they strategized a major slave insurrection, sacrificed a pig to seal the plan with sacramental power, and shared the pig's blood to symbolize the blood of whites that would soon flow across the island.

The Great Slave Rebellion

Boukman's slave insurrection broke out on August 21, 1791. Within ten days Boukman and the enraged slaves took over most of the Plaine du Nord, torturing and murdering their former masters, raping their wives and daughters, and pillaging and destroying the detested cane fields on which they had been forced to work. (In this respect, the rebellious slaves were not entirely unlike the subordinate peasants of France, who were humiliating and killing elites during the French Revolution's concurrent Reign of Terror). By year's end, former slaves controlled two-thirds of the island and most of the whites were either dead or doing everything in their power to flee Haiti. In a panic, in March 1794, the French Legislative Assembly voted to grant full civil rights to free men of color—but not to slaves.

≡ **Toussaint Louverture.** A self-educated free man of color, Toussaint Louverture had read some Enlightenment literature but had also applauded the reforms of the French Revolutionary government, especially the National Convention's abolition of slavery in 1794. Thereafter, he took up the banner of freedom in Haiti, leading not only the first independence movement in Latin America but also the first (and only) successful slave rebellion. A skillful strategist sometimes referred to as the Black Napoleon, he used his knowledge of the terrain and the environmental conditions to outmaneuver numerically larger British and French forces. Louverture finally surrendered to the French in 1802 and died in prison.

Into this maelstrom entered Toussaint Louverture, a free man of color who took up the torch of equality and provided the revolution with direction and order. Eventually nicknamed the "Black Napoleon" for his keen sense of strategy and political acumen, Louverture read widely and was inspired by the teachings of the Enlightenment. He adopted his surname (which means "the opening" in French) when he initially achieved notoriety fighting with Spanish forces located on the eastern half of Hispaniola. By 1794, Louverture, aided by several officers who would soon play prominent roles in the republic of Haiti's early history, including Jean-Jacques Dessalines and Henri Christophe, found themselves in trouble on every side in their battle for freedom as the British now invaded France's premier colony. Fortunately, an unseen ally would assist the Haitian rebels against their European enemies.

The Environment Assists the Haitian Revolutionaries

Despite their poorer weaponry and all too frequent desertions, the Haitians eventually prevailed against numerically superior and better armed British and French forces in large part because of the Haitians' knowledge of local environmental factors. Newcomers, who lacked immunity to yellow fever and malaria, had for centuries perished at much higher rates than those born on the island or in Africa because both of those populations had acquired antibodies that protected them against these mosquito-borne diseases. Deadly yellow fever flourished in Haitian ports where Europeans garrisoned their troops. Extended rainy seasons, such as the ones caused by the El Niño phenomenon from 1802 to 1804, worsened the situation for the invaders by providing a longer breeding season for the insects. Finally, as the invaders and the Haitian forces devoured the cattle that served as alternative hosts for the mosquitoes, the insects had no choice but to seek human substitutes.

Statistics bear out the effects of the environment on European troops. When the British invaded Haiti in 1793, they hoped that the seizure of France's most valuable overseas colony would weaken the French war effort. Instead, the British never enjoyed any success against Toussaint Louverture during their five-year campaign, largely because their troops were constantly ill. Britain sent 25,000 soldiers to fight in Haiti, 15,000 of whom perished (relatively few as a result of armed combat) before the survivors returned home.

In 1802 Napoleon decided to reconquer Haiti, imprison Louverture, and restore the plantation regime with 20,000 (soon increased to 65,000) experienced soldiers. By the time the army withdrew three years later, not only had Napoleon lost General Charles Leclerc, one of his most capable generals, but the bones of 55,000 troops remained buried in Haitian soil, four-fifths of whom perished as the result of disease. Medical science worsened the situation because bloodletting (the draining of blood from a sick person), the standard cure of this era, simply weakened them and hastened their demise. Taking advantage of the well-known inability of newcomers to adjust to the Haitian climate played a major role in Louverture's and other rebel commanders' strategic decision-making. Taking refuge in healthier mountainous zones during the rainy season, the rebels emerged to fight their weakened enemy in the dry season, when they faced their enemy on more favorable terms. Not surprisingly the French forces experienced low morale, making the restoration of Haiti to colonial status impossible. By 1804, Haiti had become the second independent republic in the Americas.

Violence and New Racial Hierarchies at the Dawn of the Republic

Independence did not bring peace and prosperity to Haiti. Twelve years of bloodshed had left the cane fields in ruins, the economy devastated, and the population decimated. As much as a third of the former slave population had died in the struggle, and only about 10,000 whites remained of the 30,000 who had lived in the colony in 1789. It was a moment for visionary leadership, but this was not in the cards. Haiti's first leader, Jean-Jacques Dessalines, named himself Emperor Jacques I of Haiti (1804–1806), and pledged to build his government around many of Toussaint Louverture's policies.

However, he also sought to follow through with the antiwhite practices that had started with the initial rebellion by severely limiting white citizenship in the new Haiti. He confiscated their land and, in 1804, ordered the extermination of many thousands of Haiti's remaining whites. In the end, Dessalines did not massacre all whites, but he did erase their identity in 1805, when he issued a new constitution that declared that all Haitians "henceforth will be known generically as black."

Emperor Jacques also discriminated against the elite mulattos (formerly the gens de couleur), and was killed trying to put down a revolt led by a mulatto leader named Alexandre Sabès Pétion. After Dessalines's death, Pétion and the black leader Henry Christophe divided Haiti between themselves. Competition between Pétion and Christophe, coming on the heels of Dessalines's slaughter of whites, set the precedence for a new racial hierarchy that would last for many years in Haiti, with the poor black majority deeply subservient to a small mulatto elite.

For the landholding classes in Spanish-, Portuguese-, and English-speaking America, the positive lessons of Haiti's struggle for independence and equality, embodied in the leadership of Toussaint Louverture, were almost completely overshadowed by the carnage that arose with the abolition of slavery. The massacre of white planters and their families—sometimes in ways that were as inventive as they were cruel—served as a cautionary parable to the landed elites. These people correctly understood that the plight of Saint-Domingue's whites—dead, or exiled forever to other colonies in the Caribbean rim (especially nearby Santo Domingo, Cuba, and slaveholding Louisiana), could easily be their own fate. Criollo elites outside of Haiti clearly grasped the potential for other types of ethnic uprisings (of blacks, indigenous, **castas**, and other subordinate people) that could upend the entire colonial socioeconomic hierarchy. In their perception, the violence of the Haitian Revolution seemed to confirm stereotypes of black "savagery." While many Spanish American creoles initially embraced the Enlightenment's promises of economic and political independence from Spain, the Haitian Revolution provided the strongest possible counterargument as to why revolution might be a very bad idea for them.

Independence in Mexico, 1810–1822

As was the case throughout the Spanish American world in 1808, Mexican criollos puzzled over the best way to respond to Napoleon's occupation of Spain and the imprisonment of Ferdinand VII. For disgruntled criollos, the absence of a legitimate monarch offered them the opportunity to exercise some form of autonomy (self-governance within the Spanish imperial structure) that would allow them to rule in the name of the absent king. To accomplish this, Mexicans elected representatives to the Cortes (Congress) meeting in Spain, which they hoped would devise a new imperial structure that would offer the Spanish American kingdoms home rule. Almost uniquely in Spanish America, the viceroy of New Spain in 1808 chose to side with the autonomy movement—although influential peninsulares

SOCIAL UPHEAVAL

The United States and the Haitian Revolution

When the Haitian Revolution broke out in 1793, Thomas Jefferson was a leading political figure in the United States of America, a relatively small, new nation that had emerged from its own war of colonial independence just ten years earlier. Jefferson was a great intellectual, and his own deep familiarity with the key writers of the Enlightenment allowed him to write the first true manifesto of Enlightened government, the United States' Declaration of Independence in 1776. It was Jefferson who authored the phrase, "We hold these truths to be self-evident, that all men are created equal, that they are endowed by their Creator with certain unalienable Rights, that among these are Life, Liberty and the pursuit of Happiness," that many consider to be the very credo of Enlightenment thought.

≡ **Haitian Blacks Killing Whites.**

But Thomas Jefferson was also a Virginian and a slave owner, and when the revolution in Saint-Domingue broke out, his sympathies for white planters and fear of a similar revolt coming to the United States trumped his Enlightenment principles. Echoing the fears of other white slaveholders in the United States, Jefferson proposed offering refuge to whites (and their slaves) who were fleeing Haiti. He also advocated providing limited aid to support those whites who remained behind, with the caveat that they should attempt to work out some plan that would eventually permit manumission and self-governance for former slaves in return for their willingness to support Saint-Domingue against foreign invasion, or some similar compromise arrangement. Jefferson was not yet president, however, and his influence was eclipsed with the election of John Adams to the presidency in 1796. A New Englander, Adams was staunchly antislavery. He had no qualms about throwing his support behind Toussaint Louverture and ending aid to Haiti's whites, especially during the British invasion of Haiti.

The election of Thomas Jefferson to the presidency following Adams in 1800, however, caused a reversal of this policy. Jefferson cut off US aid to Louverture and advanced a policy to isolate Haiti internationally after it gained independence in 1804. Dessalines's massacre of whites in Haiti reaffirmed Jefferson's conviction that the Haitian example was the American South's worst nightmare. As a result, the United States did not recognize Haiti diplomatically until Abraham Lincoln did so on July 12, 1862, just six months before he issued the Emancipation Proclamation freeing slaves in the Confederacy, when the sensibilities of white Southern landowners were no longer politically important.

- How do changing US policies toward Haitian independence illuminate the fragility of social revolution in the region?

and a few Spanish military officers quickly arrested him and restored the status quo ante. Events after 1810, however, soon moved beyond the quarrel between peninsulares and criollos as indigenous people and mixed-race mestizos joined the struggle for very different reasons, plunging Mexico into one of the bloodiest and most destructive of all the independence movements.

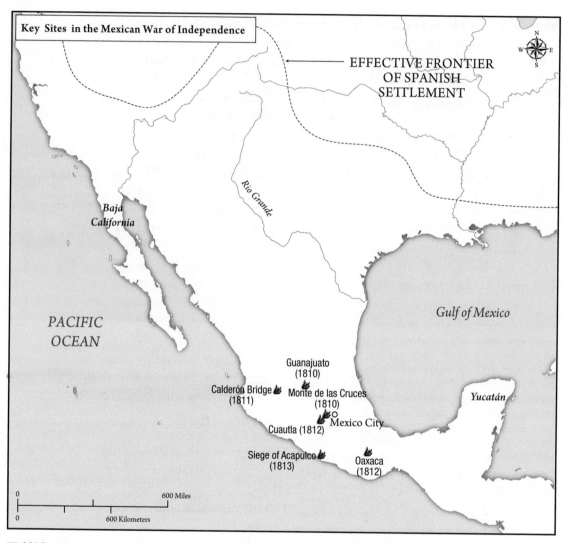

Key Sites in the Mexican War of Independence

EFFECTIVE FRONTIER OF SPANISH SETTLEMENT

Rio Grande

Baja California

PACIFIC OCEAN

Gulf of Mexico

Yucatán

Guanajuato (1810)

Calderón Bridge (1811)   Monte de las Cruces (1810)

Cuautla (1812)   Mexico City

Siege of Acapulco (1813)   Oaxaca (1812)

0   600 Miles
0   600 Kilometers

≡ **MAP. 1.2**

The Autonomy Movement versus the Hidalgo Rebellion

Most Mexicans in 1810 preferred a peaceful resolution to Spain's imperial crisis by reforming the imperial structure to grant Mexico more autonomy within a greater Spanish commonwealth. Unfortunately, this desirable solution proved politically impossible. Peninsular Spaniards held a majority of seats in the Cortes and could not be outvoted. Although Spain's Constitution of 1812 contained many liberal features, such as strong anti-clerical provisions, expanding the electorate and furthering democratic processes by mandating provincial and municipal elections, it too failed to restructure the empire into a commonwealth. Thus, while the autonomy movement was quite popular in the New World, it never gained traction in the Cortes. As a result, Mexicans and Spanish South Americans ultimately had to resort to force to achieve independence.

In a number of places in the interior of Mexico, but especially in the city of Querétaro, criollos used the subterfuge of meeting as a literary society to conspire to undo the coup of 1808 and substitute themselves for the hated *gachupines* (a derogatory slur for peninsulares). These conspirators generally favored autonomy, but circumstances eventually turned them more militant. The plotters differed as to the best method to advance their plan. Some wanted to recruit only criollo members of the militia into the conspiracy, while others believed they needed to create a broader multiclass alliance (including indigenous people, mestizos, and mulattos) to defeat the Spaniards.

Both strategies presented risks. On one hand, an exclusively criollo rebellion minimized any threat to the social order, but posed risks since only a minority of military officers seemed willing to commit to a plan to oust the peninsular leadership. On the other hand, a multiclass rebellion offered the unwelcome prospect of a popular revolt that could not be contained. Further, the political culture of the popular classes (which included those who were not from elite, landed families, those who worked with their hands or buying and selling in the marketplace, and those who struggled at the margins of society) differed from that of those few criollos leaning toward independence. Specifically, the former revered their distant monarch, who they believed would help them defend their community's interests against those who exploited them, be they peninsulares or criollos. In addition, most members of the popular classes were deeply religious and did not favor anticlerical Enlightenment thought. To create a multiclass alliance, the criollo leadership would have to avoid any discourse criticizing the Church or discussing a more extreme political objective, such as complete independence.

The individual who initiated the military phase of Mexico's independence movement, Father Miguel Hidalgo, is today honored as one of the nation's great heroes. An educated member of the criollo elite, well versed in the ideas of the French Enlightenment, Father Hidalgo once had a brilliant ecclesiastical career that ran into snags with higher authorities, perhaps because he allegedly mismanaged funds while serving as the *rector* (principal) of the College of San Nicolás Obispo. Demoted to the role of parish priest in Dolores, a small town in the heart of the Bajío region about twenty miles north of Querétaro, Father Hidalgo proved more interested in benefiting the material well-being of his parishioners than in observing his spiritual vows. Hidalgo befriended peninsulares, criollos, and

≡ **Father Hidalgo Initiating the Grito de Dolores.** Padre Miguel Hidalgo y Costilla, a priest, reformer, and former rector (principal) of a *colegio* (high school), initiated Mexico's struggle for independence on September 16, 1810 (today celebrated as Mexico's Independence Day), as depicted in this dramatic painting. A criollo with long-standing resentments against the peninsular establishment, Hidalgo temporarily forged together a multiclass alliance that threatened Spanish rule. But a series of incidents where indigenous people, the bulk of Hidalgo's army, indiscriminately slaughtered criollos as well as peninsulares turned the former against Hidalgo, who was captured and executed in 1811.

indigenous folk alike and enjoyed life to the fullest. (But not without paying a price for it; Hidalgo got into difficulties with the Inquisition because he questioned the virgin birth of Christ, denounced the pope as corrupt, and fathered five children by several different women).

Hidalgo joined the literary society in Querétaro, whose members shared their growing frustrations with peninsular rule and the ongoing imperial crisis in Spain. Other members included a few criollo militia officers, including the dashing and capable Captain Ignacio Allende. But as the conspirators attempted to recruit more criollos into their ranks, several of these contacts leaked details about the planned rebellion to Spanish authorities in Mexico City. Fearing arrest and the end of their prospects to unseat the peninsulares, the conspirators decided to risk everything and move forward. On the morning of September 16, 1810 (celebrated today as Mexico's Independence Day), horsemen rode to Dolores to warn Father Hidalgo that the authorities had orders to arrest every participant.

Ringing the bell of the parish church earlier in the morning than was customary signaled to the villagers that something was amiss. Father Hidalgo harangued his indigenous parishioners about the injustices of the Spanish colonial system. His people, who had suffered famine in 1808 and 1809, listened willingly. At the end of his speech Hidalgo offered his *Grito de Dolores* (Cry of Dolores), in which he probably said something to the effect of: "Long live Ferdinand VII; long live America; long live religion; death to peninsulares; and death to bad government," a slogan he hoped would resonate with criollos, mestizos, and indigenous people alike. References to Ferdinand VII and religion spoke to the interests of poor villagers; "long live America" and "death to peninsulares" appealed to criollos, while "death to bad government" found favor with everybody. To avoid offending those of his parishioners and criollos who aspired for autonomy, Hidalgo stopped short of declaring independence outright.

Grabbing shovels, hoes, slings, machetes, rocks, and anything else they could use as weapons (but almost no guns), the makeshift army composed mostly of indigenous people and mestizos swarmed onto the road and headed toward the mining city of Guanajuato. En route, they stopped in a small town whose parish church possessed a copy of the famous image of the Virgin of Guadalupe. The story of the appearance of a dark-skinned Virgin Mary to an indigenous shepherd in 1531, and his cloak's miraculous transformation into an image of Her, provided the most potent cultural symbol uniting Mexicans. When Father Hidalgo invoked the defense of religion in the Grito de Dolores, his foot soldiers immediately thought of the Virgin of Guadalupe. She became a source of unity for the movement, bringing together groups of disparate rebels who in many instances sought resolutions to very different local grievances.

Because of his inspired slogan and his regional popularity, Father Hidalgo, rather than Captain Allende, took command of the military operations. Hidalgo also had better rapport with those joining the rebel movement, who were overwhelmingly Indian. (Note: *indio*, or Indian, was the most common pejorative term for people of indigenous ancestry in Latin America in the early nineteenth century and remains the most common term today. In recent years, the term *pueblos indígenas*— *povos indígenas* in Portuguese—or indigenous peoples, has gained currency. To reflect both common usage and changing terminology, we generally use the term "indigenous people," but we do use the term "Indian" in direct quotations).

Placing Hidalgo in command, rather than the more experienced Allende, was ✓ probably a tactical mistake. Hidalgo allowed his followers to loot and pillage and ignored Allende's strategic advice. With tales of the bloody rampage circulating throughout the region, fearful peninsulares and criollos barricaded themselves in Guanajuato's sturdiest stone building, the municipal granary. For hours they held out, using shotguns to inflict casualties on the insurgents. When one of Hidalgo's men, a brave miner, sacrificed his life to burn down the wooden door to the granary, the enraged mob stormed the building and indiscriminately killed both peninsulares and criollos. Poor indigenous people had little reason to spare the lives of criollos who owned the haciendas, mines, and mills that paid low wages and made their lives miserable. For them this was a war against the propertied classes. But Hidalgo's failure to rein in his followers had important repercussions. Wavering criollos, who had sought political autonomy, were now confronted with a race war. They switched their sympathies to the Spanish cause, even enlisting in the royalist army.

Hidalgo, Allende, and the rebel insurgency now turned south. On the outskirts of Mexico City, they faced a well-disciplined and well-armed royalist force, which fought them to a draw but suffered so many casualties that the capital was left vulnerable. In retrospect, it is clear that Hidalgo erred when he decided to retreat northward. He occupied Guadalajara temporarily, executing scores of royalists. But his movement lost momentum, and in January 1811, was decisively defeated outside Guadalajara. By now Allende had openly quarreled with Hidalgo about his mismanagement of the insurgency. He argued that the Hidalgo's inability to restrain the largely indigenous army, his senseless brutality in executing so many Spaniards in Guadalajara, and his lack of knowledge of military strategy had caused the rebellion to fail. Not long thereafter, both shared the same fate: capture and execution. For the next decade what remained of their severed heads adorned two of the corners of Guanajuato's granary, serving as a grim warning to other rebels. Although a number of Hidalgo's contemporaries argued that he delayed independence by transforming the criollo conspiracy into a race war, today Mexicans pay homage to Hidalgo as the "Father of Mexican Independence."

Morelos's Insurgency

Following Hidalgo's capture and execution, the insurgency fragmented. Hidalgo's followers were of two minds. While the moderates sought to tamp down the excesses of the indigenous mobs and promote the idea of autonomy, the second and more radical faction demanded that the insurgents fight for independence and social change such as the abolition of slavery. While most criollos favored the autonomy movement, a few, mostly intellectuals living in Mexico City, advocated for the radicals and published pro-independence propaganda. Led by another priest, José María Morelos, the radicals' viewpoint soon dominated. Although inexperienced in warfare, Morelos quickly proved to be a more competent commander than Hidalgo because he combined a natural understanding of military tactics and guerrilla warfare with sound leadership principles. Morelos drew on prior experience and an extensive network of contacts in southern and western Mexico to form alliances with populations struggling to address local grievances. These local groups—predominantly mestizo, or of mixed African and Spanish ancestry—coalesced into small, mobile guerrilla units, operating nominally under Morelos's command. This decentralized structure frustrated the undermanned royalist army's attempts to snuff out the insurgency.

José María Morelos today is recognized as Mexico's second great independence era hero. Although he never quite gained the national stature accorded to Hidalgo, in many respects Morelos made a more durable contribution to independence because he clearly articulated the goals of the popular classes. Although his birth certificate proclaimed him to be a criollo, he had mestizo and possibly African ancestry, which may have contributed to his ability to appeal to the impoverished peoples in what is today the southern state of Guerrero. In addition, Morelos spent years working as a muleteer in that region, leading animals laden with goods to the port of Acapulco and, in the process, becoming well acquainted both with the terrain and local village leaders.

He and Father Hidalgo first met when Morelos gave up his job as a muleteer to study for the priesthood at the College of San Nicolás Obispo, where Hidalgo served as rector. Assigned thereafter to a small parish (a great disappointment), Morelos shared his mentor's casual approach to his priestly vows (although he only fathered four children). Hidalgo's Grito de Dolores struck a chord with Morelos, who quickly accepted a commission in the rebel army. Even during the Hidalgo movement, Morelos differentiated himself from his commander by disciplining his troops and prohibiting looting. In addition, he organized a congress of delegates from rebel-held territory to debate policy while he concentrated on the military campaign.

Despite the fact that the insurgency under Morelos's leadership lasted a full three years, his military campaign ultimately was doomed because his guerrilla forces never could capture any of the important cities of Mexico's central plateau. Instead, he occupied two peripheral municipalities, Oaxaca City and Acapulco, before surrounding Mexico City in 1813. In that year the capital's citizens faced incredible hardships because of the consequences of the misguided environmental policies of the Spanish conquerors. Unlike the Aztecs, who optimized the natural bounty of Lake Texcoco, the colonial regime viewed the lake that surrounded Mexico City as a flood threat and attempted to drain it, but never completely succeeded in doing so. To make matters worse, Spanish landowners cut down nearby forests to optimize grazing land, which only increased the flow of water into the city and, ironically, resulted in greater flooding.

In the early nineteenth century scientists had not yet uncovered the cause of water-borne diseases like typhus. In 1813, typhus and other deadly illnesses spread rapidly through the metropolis's population following unusually heavy summer rains. The resulting floods caused drainage canals, normally filled with human waste, garbage, and rotting animal carcasses, to overflow into the streets. Hundreds died and many more were sickened, including many members of the military defending the city, leaving it vulnerable. Like Hidalgo, however, arguably Morelos had strategic reasons for shying away from a confrontation with the well-armed Spanish army defending Mexico City. Despite these difficulties, the Spanish army rallied, broke the siege, and drove Morelos back to his former strongholds. His insurgency, like Hidalgo's, was always a rural movement dependent on local sympathizers and realistically had little chance of taking Mexico City. The insurgency would never succeed until the criollo-dominated urban centers joined the struggle.

Morelos's rebellion also proved more durable than that of Hidalgo because he clearly publicized the insurgents' objectives. By proclamation, Morelos abolished the caste system and the racial distinctions that had characterized the colonial period; instead, he declared that all Mexicans were "Americanos." Up to this time a person's race was noted in his or her birth registry in the parish church records. Morelos's decree forbade this practice. He furthered defined the revolution's goals by instructing his congress to write a constitution in 1814. That document, the *Constitution of Apatzingán*, declared Mexico's independence, established a republican form of government, abolished slavery, and retained the Roman Catholic Church's position as the only established church in the land.

External events, however, dulled the glamor of the constitution and Morelos's military victories in the rural areas. Napoleon's defeat in Europe meant the return of Ferdinand VII to the throne of Spain, and he soon restored absolutist rule. Ferdinand's return left those criollos who sought autonomy without a viable argument. Most chose to hope for the best from their new king. The combination of dwindling criollo support and the arrival of Spanish military reinforcements foretold the ultimate demise of Morelos's rebellion. His capture and execution in 1815 proved that the radical faction by itself could not achieve independence.

The Triumph of Criollo Patriotism

The six years following Morelos's execution are often described as a lull in the struggle for independence; some narratives even going so far as to claim that one of the most famous insurgents, Guadalupe Victoria, hid in a cave for much of the time. In reality, localized rebellions, now without the unifying leadership of a Morelos or Hidalgo, operated independently and caused considerable disorder in rural areas. One clan leader emphasized his group's autonomy from any central rebel leadership by claiming that "only the mountains were above him." These small bands of largely rural indigenous people and mulattos continued to seek some measure of social justice. The royalist armies could never extinguish these numerous rebellions.

By 1820, rural communities were not alone in their desire to sever ties with the Spanish state. Ferdinand VII had disappointed even his most loyal adherents by turning out to be despotic, vain, and incompetent. His rejection of constitutional monarchy and his return to absolutism proved very unpopular. Most Mexicans now supported some form of change. What they needed was a leader who could articulate the goals of criollo patriotism while also appealing to the ongoing insurgency. The task would require somebody who could put together a multiclass alliance.

Colonel Agustín de Iturbide fit the bill. A criollo best known as the royalist commander who had crushed José María Morelos's forces in a decisive 1813 battle, Iturbide enjoyed great prestige within the army's ranks. Cashiered from the service because of his excessive cruelty (he ordered many rebel executions) and alleged corruption, Iturbide was reinstated in 1820 and ordered to lead forces against the largest of the rebel bands, that of Vicente Guerrero. Instead, the two conducted secret negotiations over a period of weeks, ultimately agreeing on the Plan de Iguala, which called for independence, the creation of a constitutional monarchy under the terms of the liberal Spanish Constitution of 1812, and the maintenance of the Roman Catholic Church as the established church of Mexico.

Each of these goals met the spirit of criollo nationalism—the sense that Mexicans were distinct from Spaniards. For the popular-class rebels who inherited the mantles of Hidalgo and Morelos, the Plan de Iguala confirmed the idea that all Mexicans, be they creoles, mestizos, mulattos, Africans, or indigenous, were to be designated as "Americans" and citizens. Both parties agreed on the importance of the established Catholic Church, while the insurgents approved of many provisions of the liberal constitution. For criollos, the compromise left them atop the social structure and ended the threat of a social revolution like that of Haiti.

The incoming viceroy had sailed from Spain as the Cortes seemed about to approve greater autonomy in Mexico. He agreed to the terms of the Plan de Iguala, which held out the prospect of Ferdinand or one of his brothers serving as Mexico's king. After ten years of brutal fighting, during which approximately 10 percent of Mexico's population (about 600,000 people) perished and virtually all economic activity came to a standstill, Mexico had finally secured its independence.

The Liberation Movement in Spanish South America, 1808–1825

Not since the encounter/conquest of the Americas in the 1500s would events occurring in South America so captivate the attention of people around the globe. For individuals living on the right side of history in Spanish South America, the deeds associated with the wars for independence represented heroic, patriotic moments that would be celebrated for generations. In 1808, not surprisingly, most Spanish Americans preferred to take a safer stance in favor of seeking autonomy within the empire. For those committed to independence from the outset, their struggle began in the periphery of the empire in places like Argentina and Venezuela, far distant from the viceroy's standing army in Peru.

The Quest for Autonomy

As in Mexico, Napoleon's invasion of Spain in 1808 offered opportunities for South Americans to form **juntas** (governing committees) that paralleled those found in Spanish cities that were struggling against Napoleonic rule. The effort on the part of Iberians to expel the French took place region by region and was called the Peninsular War (1807–1814). Because the Peninsular War, by extension, had clear ramifications for Spanish and Portuguese holdings in the Americas, it inspired, or provided an excuse for, the creation of "loyal" juntas abroad, despite the fact that Napoleon obviously did not physically occupy any part of the New World.

The idea of self-governing juntas particularly appealed to Spanish Americans who sought a moderate, reformist middle ground between those committed to the traditional imperial system and the small minority in 1809 who wanted outright independence. The moderate middle ground proved attractive to many criollos because it allowed for assertions in favor of home rule (autonomy) while at the same time offering its prudent participants some degree of protection from charges of treason because they took these actions in the name of "beloved" King Ferdinand. While protesting their fealty to the deposed king, members of the South American juntas saw the opening as an opportunity to redress specific grievances.

The initial autonomy movements in the Andean region made little headway. A number of cities formed juntas in 1809 (Quito, La Paz, and Sucre being among the first). In each instance the criollo leadership carefully protested its loyalty to Ferdinand VII in an effort to convince royal authorities that they had not committed treason. Thus, the junta in Quito stated in its proclamation for autonomy: "Long Live Ferdinand VII; Long Live Religion; and Long Live the Fatherland" ("fatherland" was defined as the region of one's birth.) In each instance in the Andean world, the arrival of a royalist army from Lima crushed the junta and executed a number of its leaders to set an example. Thereafter, Andean elites responded tepidly to the events happening elsewhere in South America.

In 1810, representatives from Spanish and Spanish American juntas came together in the southern Spanish port city of Cádiz, one of the first locations to permanently expel the French, and home to one of the most vigorous and Enlightenment-inspired juntas on the peninsula. Not every Spanish American or Iberian junta sent a delegate to the Cortes (Court) in Cádiz, but those who did attend tended to represent some of the most liberal and progressive ideas from each of their regions.

The Cortes of Cádiz, while proclaiming all along its loyalty to the deposed king Ferdinand, worked to produce a new constitution to be implemented upon their king's return to the throne. The 1812 Constitution of the Cortes of Cádiz called for a series of unprecedented Enlightenment-inspired measures: universal voting rights (except for slaves, most free blacks, and women) free enterprise, freedom of the press, regional (and even, in some cases, national) autonomy; restrictions on the power of Catholic Church, and others. Most importantly, it created a constitutional monarchy, in which Ferdinand and all his successors would be subject to obeying the constitution. This demand fundamentally changed the king's status. Whereas previously the king was thought to rule by "divine right," his post was now dependent on his ability to serve his people.

When Ferdinand VII did return to power in 1814, he threw out the 1812 Constitution almost immediately and had all the monuments that had been built to commemorate it destroyed. After Ferdinand VII's restoration, the safe middle ground of autonomy turned to quicksand. Moderate Spanish Americans now had to choose between accepting Ferdinand's absolute rule or making a declaration for outright independence. Later, the 1812 Constitution became one model for the new national constitutions that would come into being in Latin American in the next decade. It would also, eventually, provide the basis for the constitutional monarchy that Spain would eventually adopt.

Meanwhile, proponents of outright independence in 1810 enjoyed a much greater likelihood of success in Spanish America's peripheral areas such as Argentina and Venezuela. Long ignored by Spain, these peripheral areas grew in importance during the eighteenth century largely because of Bourbon reforms that created the viceroyalty of the Rio de La Plata, opened Buenos Aires to direct trade from Spain, and created a profitable cacao (chocolate) industry in Venezuela. With a weaker Catholic tradition and greater access to Atlantic world Enlightenment ideas, these regions became the focal point of the Spanish American independence movement.

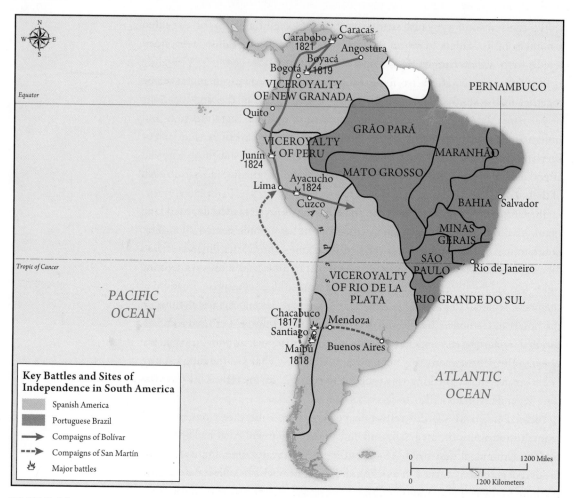

 MAP. 1.3

Independence in the Southern Cone

In Buenos Aires, the capital of the Spanish viceroyalty of the Río de la Plata, criollo merchants and their allies had responded both to local and hemispheric circumstances in pressing for greater autonomy and ultimately independence from the Spanish Empire. In 1806, the British invaded and occupied Buenos Aires. For the British, this was an opportunity to seize the advantage created by the Napoleonic wars in continental Europe and extend British influence in the Atlantic world. The British wanted to open the port of Buenos Aires to free trade, albeit on terms that favored the British over local interests. Not surprisingly, local residents resented their presence and organized to drive them out.

The Spanish viceroy himself was relatively ineffectual in this regard, fleeing to the interior. Instead, the expulsion of the British and defense against their return was led by a militia comprising residents of many social backgrounds, including slaves and free black volunteers, under the nominal command of Santiago Liniers, previously an officer in the Spanish navy. Soon afterward, Liniers was named the new viceroy. The successful fight against the British revealed that local mobilization counted for more than imperial administration in the turbulent world of the early nineteenth century.

Napoleon's occupation of much of Spain in 1808 confirmed that lesson. With Charles IV (Carlos) of Spain driven from the throne and his heir Ferdinand imprisoned, the Spanish American colonies could not rely on imperial forces to defend them. Viceroy Liniers attempted to restrict trade, but criollo merchants balked. Led by Manuel Belgrano and Mariano Moreno, they argued that Buenos Aires's prosperity depended on the free export of leather, dried beef, and silver and the free import of goods from across the Atlantic world.

When most of Spain finally fell to Napoleonic forces in 1810, the Spanish American colonies were functionally cut adrift. The criollo merchants of Buenos Aires, like their counterparts in many Spanish American cities, formed a governing junta. In May of 1810, they took the more radical step of driving the viceroy from the city, claiming that, given the disruption in Spanish administration, sovereignty lay with the people of Buenos Aires. At the same time, they remained nominally loyal to the imprisoned Ferdinand, a loyalty that remained untested as long as he was kept from the throne.

In the meantime, their greater challenge lay in asserting political control beyond Buenos Aires itself. Far-flung areas of the viceroyalty of Río de la Plata proved most resistant to the Buenos Aires junta. Events unfolded in differing ways in Paraguay, Upper Peru (later to become known as Bolivia), and the Banda Oriental (later to become known as Uruguay). In Paraguay, merchants and landowners in Asunción, led by José Gaspar Rodríguez de Francia, formed their own junta in 1811, declaring their autonomy not only from the Spanish Empire but also from the overweening merchants of Buenos Aires.

Upper Peru, home to the silver mines that had initially created the economic basis for the viceroyalty of Río de la Plata, proved an elusive prize for the Buenos Aires junta. Revolutionaries led by the Buenos Aires contingent sought control of the region, only to be driven back. The Spanish Empire had long maintained a well-armed presence in the mining regions, and called on those soldiers to resist the revolution. Once the Buenos Aires invaders were driven out, Upper Peru functionally reverted to the jurisdiction of the viceroyalty of Peru, and would await liberation from the north.

The Banda Oriental, directly across the Río de la Plata estuary from Buenos Aires, proved to be among the most turbulent regions in the Americas. The last Spanish governor of the territory resisted the authority of the Buenos Aires junta and claimed control, but was soon bedeviled by conflicts in the interior. Between 1810 and 1828, the viceroy, the Buenos Aires junta, the Portuguese Empire, the Brazilian Empire, and the British each attempted to subdue part or all of the Banda Oriental, to no avail. Instead, local heroes on horseback, leading small bands of men into conflict over ranchlands, dominated the countryside. The battles between them and the outsiders would continue to mark the first several decades of the history of independent Uruguay.

Ferdinand VII's restoration to the Spanish throne in 1814 reinvigorated Spain's attempts to bring the colonies into line. The Buenos Aires contingent refused to submit to renewed colonialism, and advocated autonomy for the former viceroyalty, which they now termed the United Provinces of the Río de la Plata. Liberal statesman Bernardino Rivadavia, by this point the foremost leader of the Buenos Aires junta, left for Europe in an attempt to secure tolerance from Spain and material support from England. Rivadavia still considered himself a loyalist, but wanted Ferdinand to name his nephew as a prince regent of the autonomous United Provinces.

In those heady days, any outcome seemed possible, from full-fledged republican independence to a return to colonial status, and Rivadavia sought to steer a middle course of autonomous monarchy with liberal reform. Other leaders within the Buenos Aires's leadership were more radical, favoring a clean break with Spain. And in the far reaches of the old viceroyalty, many local leaders rejected the free-trade policies of the Buenos Aires liberals, believing open ports benefited city merchants at the expense of rural producers. The so-called United Provinces, as a result, were divided by regional, economic, and ideological interests before they ever had a chance to cohere. In July 1816, at an assembly in Tucumán, in the northern reaches of the old viceroyalty, representatives of the United Provinces declared independence from Spain. The declaration did not resolve internal disputes, but did move the conflict decisively to the battleground.

The junta ruling the United Provinces appointed General José de San Martín, an Argentine who had spent most of his life in Spain, to accomplish this task. Unlike any other patriot leader, San Martín was a professionally trained officer who had fought against Napoleon during the Peninsular Wars. Along with other Argentines, he returned home in 1811 to offer his services to the United Provinces. Placed in command of the Army of the Andes that would invade Chile, San Martín stepped up the recruiting of slaves as soldiers. Offered freedom in exchange for military service and encouraged by the government's new legislation promising gradual abolition to other slaves, large numbers of slaves volunteered for the fight, constituting perhaps 40 percent of San Martín's army of five thousand men. Many owners agreed to free their slaves partially from patriotic motives but also because the government promised them compensation for their lost property. San Martín relied heavily on his black soldiers and referred to them as the fighting core of the Army of the Andes.

San Martín understood that the United Provinces would not be safe from Spanish resurgence unless the Spanish were driven from South America. In 1817, he made the daring decision to take his army across the spine of the Andes to Chile to wage a struggle for independence there, and then to move northward toward the heart of Spanish colonial power in Peru.

The Chileans, in the meantime, had already been through a parallel series of experiences, forming a governing junta in response to the ouster of Charles IV, and then suffering both internal division and royal reprisal following the restoration of Ferdinand VII. By the time San Martín crossed the Andes, the impassioned liberal Bernardo O'Higgins (son of a Spanish viceroy of Irish descent) had risen to the fore of advocates of Chilean independence. O'Higgins joined forces with San Martín, driving Spanish forces out of Chile by 1818. O'Higgins then consolidated power as a dictator in Chile until forced out of office in 1823, giving way to a fractious republic.

In the meantime, San Martín gathered his forces in Chile and prepared to sail north to Peru, gradually closing in on the royalist stronghold of Lima. But his

≡ **San Martín Crossing the Andes into Chile.** José de San Martín, an Argentine criollo who gained military experience serving as an officer in the Spanish army, returned home in 1811. Six years later he led the Army of the Andes, which contained a large contingent of Afro-Argentine soldiers and many Chileans under the leadership of Bernardo O'Higgins, into Chile. Crossing the very difficult terrain through the high passes of the mountain chain, San Martín's army descended north of Santiago, where they confronted Spanish forces. The battles of Chacabuco and Maipú secured Chile's independence as of April 1818.

outnumbered forces stalled. The remnants of the Army of the Andes, the Chilean volunteers would need to await reinforcements from the north.

The War in Northern South America, 1810–1816

The revolutions for independence in northern South America rivaled those of Mexico for violence, devastation, and duration, and raised many of the same bitter, divisive issues. As in the case of Mexico, independence occurred in three distinct phases—although in northern South America a single individual, Simón Bolívar, played a central role in all three. Frequently called the George Washington of South America, Bolívar and Washington shared many characteristics: a patrician background; an understanding of Enlightenment political theory; a growing discomfiture with slavery despite being slaveholders; and the ability to inspire men and women to the patriot cause. Perhaps most importantly, each faced the monumental task of having to convince political moderates (those favoring autonomy in this case) into siding with the cause of independence.

Unlike most cautious criollos, Bolívar favored independence even before the Napoleonic invasion of Spain. During his first attempt to liberate Venezuela in 1810, Bolívar teamed up with Francisco de Miranda, a disgraced Spanish military officer living in exile in London. Miranda had fought in the early stages of the French Revolution and had launched an unsuccessful invasion of Venezuela in 1806. Well known in European intellectual and social circles, Miranda had promoted the cause of Spanish American independence for many years. In July 1811, he and Bolívar collaborated to persuade Venezuela's newly elected assembly of thirty-one criollo aristocrats to reject autonomy and declare outright independence. Later, participants referred to this assembly as Venezuela's First Republic. But while the patriots held Caracas and its immediate environs, royalist forces dominated the countryside and other cities. Bolívar distinguished himself as the most competent of the criollo officers despite having no formal military training. Passionate, energetic, and bold, Bolívar overcame his lack of a military education by his inherent grasp of the fundamentals of strategy.

The First Republic collapsed in 1812 for a variety of reasons. First, criollo patriots feared a race war like the one in Haiti. Hence, although declaring an end to racial distinctions, the republic did nothing concrete to enlist either slaves or **pardos** (people with some African ancestry, who constituted about 50 percent of the Venezuelan population) to the patriot cause. Denied the vote or full rights of citizenship, the pardos felt no affinity for the criollo regime that wanted to maintain rigid social boundaries that excluded them. On the other hand, the royalists seemed more willing to contemplate the abolition of slavery (which, after all, struck hardest at criollo landowners), which encouraged pardos and African slaves to remain loyal to the king.

God and the forces of nature also opposed the First Republic, or so it seemed to many of the Catholic faithful. In March and again in April 1812, severe earthquakes shook Caracas. The roofs of many churches collapsed, trapping screaming victims beneath the rubble and taking a terrible toll. Ten thousand people in Caracas alone perished, as well as untold numbers in surrounding towns. The earthquake left royalist cities like Coro untouched. Because the initial quake

≡ **Two Different Portraits of Simón Bolívar.** Throughout the world Simón Bolívar is known as the Liberator of Spanish America. His charisma and military skills have earned him credit for freeing Venezuela, Colombia, Ecuador, Peru, and Bolivia. Because he died before photography was invented, artists have attempted to capture his likeness in portraits. By the end of the nineteenth century, the elite preferred to portray Bolívar as a light-skinned criollo (the figure on the right). But other artists depicted him more realistically with darker skin and curly hair, since, like many individuals in the Venezuelan elite, Bolívar likely had some African heritage.

happened on Holy Thursday, priests and the bishop of Caracas quickly pointed to the hand of God in the catastrophe, punishing the heathen patriots who had rejected king and Church. As the First Republic literally collapsed, Bolívar did his reputation a disservice by handing Miranda over to the Spanish authorities, who imprisoned him for the remainder of his life. Bolívar accepted a safe-conduct pass for himself and sailed to Cartegena in Colombia to serve the revolutionaries there.

Meanwhile, the patriots in New Granada (Colombia), having rid themselves of their viceroy, encountered very little military resistance in comparison to their Venezuelan compatriots. But instead of consolidating independence, the criollo elite quarreled amongst itself over political theory. Some patriots preferred a strong central government, located in the capital city of Bogotá, which would administer the entire nation, while others preferred a more federalist form of government that would grant provinces considerable autonomy. Thus began what Colombians came to call "*la patria boba*"—the foolish fatherland. This civil conflict between centralists and federalists lasted from 1810 to 1816, and foreshadowed many of the political disputes that would emerge in the postindependence era. In the meantime, it distracted Colombians from their greater purpose, winning the war against Spain.

For his part, Bolívar, whose primary goal was the liberation of Venezuela, mistakenly deduced the reasons for the failure of the First Republic. He concluded that the patriots had erred by being too soft on the enemy, failing to do their utmost to take royalist strongholds like Coro and execute royalists. Thus Bolívar now decided to treat captured Spaniards much more ruthlessly. After driving out the royalist forces occupying Colombia's Magdalena River basin, in May 1813 he requested permission from Colombia's congress to launch an overland strike against Caracas. Because the royalists had confiscated all property belonging to the patriots who had participated in the First Republic and treated patriot captives cruelly, sympathy in much of Venezuela swung to Bolívar's side. Three months later he entered the capital to a tumultuous welcome and established the Second Republic (1813–1815).

Bolívar's decision to take a tougher stand against the royalist foe was summarized in his *"War to the Death"* decree of June 1813. As the line between patriots and royalists hardened, both sides committed atrocities. Based on his experiences in the First Republic, Bolívar opted to grant no quarter to Spaniards found in possession of weapons. The decree meant no more prisoner exchanges and implemented the use of terror as a weapon, through indiscriminate execution of royalist prisoners. The Spaniards responded in kind, none more enthusiastically than Tomás Boves, a sadistic cattle dealer who commanded a cavalry force composed of cowboys (**llaneros**) from the plains south of Caracas. Armed with long lances tipped with steel, the llaneros feared nobody. Most llaneros were pardos (Boves was not) and they followed the royalist cause because they hoped to gain land and cattle at the end of the conflict.

By 1815, Boves's llaneros had proven too strong for Bolívar's army. Undisciplined though they were, the llaneros's cavalry charges swept the patriots from the field time and time again. In his wake Boves ordered the execution of all patriot prisoners, sometimes a thousand at a time. He took particular pleasure in the death of one of Bolivar's close friends, whom he ordered dismembered before frying his head in oil and displaying it publically. Civilian populations fled as the terror escalated. Boves himself was killed during the final battle of the Second Republic, while Bolívar again escaped. Venezuela and Colombia reverted to royalist control, and King Ferdinand VII dispatched 10,000 soldiers under the command of experienced Napoleonic war veteran Field Marshall Pablo Morillo to mop up the few remaining pockets of resistance.

Patriot Success in the North and the Andes, 1816–1825

Simón Bolívar faced a threefold challenge as he contemplated the future of the independence movement from his exile in the Caribbean in 1815. First, he realized he needed to broaden the patriots' base of support to create a multiclass alliance of Americanos as San Martín had done in Argentina and Iturbide would do in Mexico. Second, Bolívar had to create a unified command in order to quell the unruly subordinates who periodically questioned his leadership and prevented him from training a disciplined army. Finally, he needed to devise a strategy and tactics that relied on speed of movement and surprise attacks to defeat Morillo's numerically larger royalist forces. If he could achieve a series of consecutive victories, Bolívar would improve patriot morale.

Bolívar began to outline a broader appeal to his countrymen in his famous *Jamaica Letter* of September 6, 1815. In this document, he argued, much as José María Morelos had in Mexico, that Americans were substantially different from Spaniards. Regardless of race and class, Bolívar asserted, Americans had more in common with each other than they did with Spaniards. Further, all Americans deserved to enjoy the individual liberties and freedoms that Spanish tyranny denied them. Moreover, because Americans experienced discrimination under the imperial system, they were justified in rebelling. Not only were Spanish Americans denied their rightful positions in the bureaucracy but also Spain had organized the commercial system in a way that advantaged peninsulares and harmed colonials.

Soon Bolívar offered specific pledges designed to win over Americans of mixed races who to this moment had largely fought for the king. Obtaining supplies and some recruits from Haiti in 1816, Bolívar promised to end slavery in Venezuela. In addition, he publicly acknowledged the great social progress that some pardos had made during the conflict. To demonstrate his changing views about mixed-race Venezuelans, he confirmed the military ranks that pardo officers had awarded themselves. In addition, he reminded pardos that the Spanish Constitution of Cádiz of 1812 had broadened suffrage for many but had excluded slaves, most pardos, and women. Bolívar then went further than the language of the Constitution of Cádiz. Desperate for new recruits, he promised slaves their freedom if they joined his forces. As a result, the number of black soldiers in Bolívar's army increased markedly. Whether his promise to emancipate the slaves could be kept remained to be resolved later.

Landing on the coast of Venezuela with a relatively small number of soldiers, Bolívar faced the challenge posed by regional leaders who only nominally accepted him as the commander of the patriot army. These self-appointed officers, including some pardos, had kept the independence struggle viable while Bolívar remained in exile in Haiti and Jamaica. At first Bolívar proceeded gingerly, allowing his pardo generals to control their own regions of influence. Eventually he felt he needed to make an example of Manuel Piar, the most unruly of these pardo generals, who outright disobeyed Bolívar on several occasions. The Liberator had him captured and executed after a summary trial. Despite Bolívar's strong action against one of their own, the other pardo officers continued to accept his leadership as did the pardos and slaves among the rank and file.

Next, Bolívar spent well over a year organizing and training his recruits into a well-balanced army with infantry, cavalry, and artillery. To supplement his infantry and artillery, Bolívar relied on British volunteers, some two thousand strong, who soon numbered among Bolívar's most loyal and reliable forces. To upgrade the cavalry, he sought an alliance with the leader of the western llanos, José Antonio Páez, the most important of the llanero bosses. Riding virtually alone into Páez's camp, Bolívar proved his mettle by equaling the llaneros in games of horsemanship. Eventually, the llaneros gave him the admiring nickname *culo de hierro* ("iron ass") because of his ability to ride for hours at a stretch, a task necessary in the many long marches the army of liberation undertook.

Strategy also mattered. Instead of predictably attacking the royalist stronghold of Caracas, Bolívar decided to wade through the savannas of the llanos during the rainy season and ascend the steep slopes of the Andes with artillery in tow, surprising the less numerous royalists on the high plateau of central Colombia just outside of Bogotá. Using superior tactics and great bravado, the patriot army defeated the Spanish forces in August 1819. In consequence, Colombia became the first liberated country in northern South America.

Events in Spain now assisted the patriots. Field Marshall Morillo's forces during the past five years had been decimated by yellow fever and malaria as well as battle casualties, and desperately needed reinforcements. But in 1820, the Spanish colonel Rafael Riego led a successful rebellion against King Ferdinand, forcing him to restore the Constitution of 1812. Skeptics pointed to a possible second motive for the Riego revolt. He and other rebels, part of the expeditionary forces bound for Mexico and Venezuela, worried that many of the troop transports were unseaworthy. In addition, many of these reluctant volunteers had heard stories about the poor provisions, low pay, and extreme violence of the conflicts in the New World and preferred to stay home in their own safe beds. The Riego revolt assured the patriots that Field Marshall Morillo would receive no reinforcements for his troops, and he soon retired. Morale declined within the royalist army. Thus, the patriots' prospects looked remarkably brighter in 1820 than at any previous point in the independence period.

≡ **Simón Bolívar and His Generals Planning the Attack on Colombia.** Knowing that the royalist general Pablo Morillo anticipated that Bolívar and the patriots would attempt to liberate Caracas first in 1817, Bolívar decided on a surprise attack on Bogotá instead. In this painting, he and his generals plan the details of their march through the savannahs of the Orinoco River and up the slopes of the Andes. The march took quite a toll, as even the experienced British Legion that had fought against Napoleon lost many lives because of the difficult terrain and lack of provisions. But the surprise worked, as the patriots defeated the royalists at the bridge of Boyacá in 1819 and liberated Colombia.

By now patriots recognized Bolívar as the master of the long march who could inspire officers and soldiers alike to great heroic feats. Another quick strike brought the patriot forces into the heart of Venezuela, where they faced a demoralized royalist army. Bolívar used Páez and his llaneros to maximum advantage, resulting in a great victory and a triumphant return to Caracas in June 1821. Next, he determined to extend the battle to less familiar territory, the Andean region of Ecuador. Dispatching his favorite general, Antonio José de Sucre, to Guayaquil with orders to consolidate independence there and then march to Quito, Bolívar's army moved south from Bogotá. He encountered unexpected resistance in southern Colombia, where indigenous peoples remained loyal to the Crown because of the legal protections that Spanish law afforded communal land holdings. The two patriot generals had planned to meet in Quito, but the fierce resistance of royalists in southern Colombia delayed Bolívar and gave Sucre the honor of liberating

Ecuador, defeating the royalists on the slopes of the mountain overlooking Ecuador's capital in May, 1822.

Bolívar and General San Martín had reached the same strategic conclusion: that Spanish American independence could not be assured if any Spanish forces remained in South America. Thus, the two men met in Guayaquil in July 1822 to discuss how to eliminate the single remaining royalist army in Peru. Because Bolívar had more soldiers and more enthusiasm for the difficult task, San Martín

Bolívar and San Martín Meet at the Guayaquil Conference. The only meeting between Spanish South America's two great liberators took place at Guayaquil, Ecuador, in July 1822. The purpose of the meeting was to strategize about completing the independence movement by liberating Peru and Bolivia, the royalists' remaining strongholds. The two generals met alone, and as a result historians have speculated about the precise nature of the conversations that took place over the next two days. At the conclusion of the meeting, San Martín retired from the struggle, leaving Bolívar with the task of liberating the region most loyal to Spain.

yielded the field and retired to Europe. The patriots' task would not be easy because a sizable number of Peru's criollo elite still favored the king's cause. Equating the liberal language of the patriots with the prospects of another race war like the ones Peruvians had experienced in the 1780s in which nearly 100,000 people were killed, most criollos felt safer under the king's protection.

When Bolívar arrived in Peru with his army in 1823, he immediately felt the resentment of Peruvians who preferred to work out their own solution to the independence crisis. Although many Peruvians did not love King Ferdinand's arbitrary rule, they disliked their Colombian, Argentine, Chilean, and Ecuadorian liberators even more. As a result, Bolívar left Lima and the quarreling Peruvians to their own devices and concentrated his efforts against the royalist army in the *sierra* (highlands).

For the most part, foreign forces liberated Peru and Bolivia. Bolívar, Sucre, and their international army fought the Spaniards in August 1824, in what some have called the Battle of the Centaurs because it was fought entirely on horseback. Unfortunately for the Spaniards, they had decided to lessen the strain on their backs and the burden on their horses by cutting three feet off the shafts of their lances. As a result, the patriots' traditional longer lances gave them a huge advantage as they impaled hundreds of royalists. Four months later, Sucre delivered the final blow to royalist hopes at Ayacucho. By now, the royalists had no realistic prospects for victory, and all but the diehards surrendered and departed for Europe. Bolívar, celebrated in triumph in Lima and La Paz, thoroughly enjoyed the fame and glory he had earned. Truly deserving of the title Liberator, the deeper question for him and other patriot leaders and soldiers was: what had the wars for independence accomplished, and what would happen to the newly independent nations?

"The Loyal Caribbean," 1800–1860s

The Caribbean was the oldest outpost of the Spanish empire, the first land "discovered" by Christopher Columbus. Columbus himself had established the first Spanish settlement on the island of Hispaniola (1493), and had either visited or sighted and claimed Cuba, Puerto Rico, Montserrat, St. Kitts, Grenada, St. Vincent, and Trinidad. But despite some early excitement over alluvial gold in the Caribbean, the Spaniards soon deemed the islands a disappointment, their remaining small indigenous populations after twenty years of contact too sick and disinclined to work for the Spaniard's behalf, and their relative riches paled next to the glorious gold, silver, large labor pools, and other treasures that Spain would soon encounter in New Spain and Peru. As a result, Spanish settlement in the Caribbean was

SOCIAL UPHEAVAL

Manuela Sáenz de Thorne

Women took advantage of the opportunities proffered by the tumultuous events of the wars of independence to take on new roles previously denied to them. None did this more notoriously than Manuela Sáenz de Thorne, Simón Bolívar's celebrated companion and lover. In an age when elite women like Sáenz were expected to marry and live quietly in privacy, she defied this convention. Even during the early years of her unhappy marriage to the British businessman James Thorne, she helped to manage his affairs when his work required him to travel. By 1821, she and other elite women in Lima had become partisans of the cause of independence. In this role, they spread propaganda and recruited officers, including Sáenz's brother, to serve in José de San Martín's army of liberation.

Sáenz and her husband left Peru for Ecuador the following April; he to conduct business in the thriving port of Guayaquil, and she to visit her family in Quito. She arrived at her destination soon after Sucre's patriot forces defeated the royalist army in Ecuador. Bolívar galloped into Quito shortly thereafter to a hero's welcome and met the beautiful and vivacious Manuelita (as she was known to her friends) at a party given by one of Ecuador's elite families. The couple spent the early part of the evening dancing, and the rest of the night in bed. (This was common practice for Bolívar).

Yet the couple's relationship endured, not just because of Manuela's physical attractiveness, but also because of her lively intelligence and loyalty to Bolívar. She became his archivist and confidante, following him during his campaign in Peru, occasionally dressing in uniform, and serving as a trusted member of his staff. After the wars ended, the couple lived together in Bogotá during Bolívar's presidency, where she famously saved him from assassination in 1828. (Sáenz stalled would-be assassins outside Bolívar's bedroom by telling them she had no idea where he was, while Bolívar escaped via the window).

Today Manuela Sáenz de Thorne is the best known of all the women associated with the wars of independence and is a hero in her native Ecuador. Often called the Lady Liberator, she exemplified the new roles that women carved out for themselves during this decade and a half. Many other women contributed to the patriot cause as well: recruiting volunteers, providing and smuggling food and supplies, raising money, spying, nursing wounded soldiers, and even taking up arms. Sáenz's relationship with Bolívar allowed her to participate more visibly in the public sphere—in the government and politics of the day. But Manuela's outspokenness and her flouting of traditional behavior by living openly with Bolívar wore thin after his death. As the process of nation building began in the mid-1820s, traditional social conventions were revived and women lost many of the freedoms that they had enjoyed during the independence era. Sáenz's fate resembled that of most such women: she now could only assert her diminished political influence behind the scenes through male family and friends.

- How did Sáenz's life challenge gender expectations in early nineteenth-century Spanish America? How did it fulfill those expectations?

desultory for many years, even after the introduction of sugar cane—the product that would eventually determine the course of Caribbean history—in the early 1500s.

Sugar and Slavery in the Caribbean

Unfortunately for Spain, the Caribbean's charms were not lost on new players from European countries such as England, the Netherlands, and Denmark. These

Protestant nations and sworn enemies of Spain each coveted Spain's vulnerable possessions for their own. Despite the ultimate ownership of the various islands, a single commodity, cane sugar, converted the Caribbean from a backwater to a colonial jewel, a sentiment that Cuba's nickname, "the pearl of the Antilles," conveyed. Although Christopher Columbus had been the one to introduce sugarcane to the islands, and Spanish settlers had exported the first sugar to Spain very early (even before the conquest of Mexico), it was not until the mid-1600s that the cultivation of sugar as a commercial commodity began to transform the Caribbean. An emerging collective European sweet tooth and developing consumer markets impelled Spanish settlers and their European rivals to step up cultivation of a product that they had grown on a modest scale since the earliest days of the colony.

Large-scale plantation production, worked not by local settlers or Indians but by slave labor imported from Africa by Spanish and Portuguese slave traders, now became the norm. Thus commenced a brutal slave trade of horrific proportions. Over the 350-year span of the transatlantic slave trade, the Caribbean absorbed more than 50 percent of all Africans that arrived in the New World, with the Spanish Caribbean importing around 580,000 enslaved Africans in the last half of the eighteenth century alone. It is little wonder that Cuba and Puerto Rico, along with the rest of the sugar Caribbean, developed a "plantocracy," a society built around a social pyramid with white sugar planters at the top, a moderate sized group of white settlers and free blacks and mixed race people in the middle, and a huge enslaved population of blacks at the bottom.

Retaining the Colonial Order

Following the Haitian slave revolt, Cuba and Puerto Rico's white planters became acutely aware of the danger of slave revolts, even though the planter and white settler population on both islands (nearly 60 percent in the case of Cuba and 51 percent for Puerto Rico) was significantly larger than Haiti's miniscule blanc population had been. Santo Domingo, home to a tiny population that shared the island of Hispaniola with Haiti, was most fearful of all, especially after Haiti overran the Spanish colony and occupied it between 1822 and 1844. After overthrowing the Haitian occupation in 1844, Santo Domingo proclaimed itself the Dominican Republic. But the new nation was so unstable, so underpopulated, and so fearful of reconquest by Haiti that in 1861 its president, Pedro Santana, requested that Spain reacquire it as a province, with Santana as its governor. Spain reluctantly did so, but quickly found Santo Domingo to be both ungovernable and unprofitable, and abandoned the island in 1865. The little nation then reverted to its status as the Dominican Republic.

At the same time, Cuba was prospering gloriously, basking in what some have called Cuba's "Golden Age." As the other islands of the Caribbean made the difficult transition from plantation to free labor economies, Cuba's sugar industry, built around a unique system of slave labor and small producers who sent their cane to centralized mills called *ingenios.* The system was unique, and produced high-quality sugar that sold at top price in the world's markets.

So why should Cuba desire independence from Spain? Simply put, the planter colonial elite (at least) emphatically did not. As the historian Franklin Knight has pointed out, "The colonial status was an important factor . . . [Spanish] Caribbean slave societies always required the military, psychological and economic support of the metropolis." Moreover, the dependency ran in both directions. By the middle of the nineteenth century, income from Cuban sugar accounted for almost 25 percent of Spain's national income, and any pressure that Spanish merchants might have felt to abolish slavery was entirely offset by their desire not to antagonize prosperous Cuban planters. In turn, Cuban and Puerto Rican criollos as well were dependent on Spain, which provided all manufactured goods, facilitated the international trade of their product, helped to keep restless slaves in line, and offered protection against outside attack. Thus, at the "revolutionary moment" when the rest of Spanish America sought to sever its ties with Spain, the Spanish Caribbean found every reason to tighten them.

Brazil's Path to Independent Empire, 1807–1822

Brazil did not so much win independence as stumble into it, in a strange mix of happenstance and compromise. Between 1808 and 1822, Brazilian land- and slave-owning elites reacted to the collapse of Portuguese sovereignty in ways that would bolster their own power. The final result was the creation of a Brazilian Empire, independent but dynastically linked to the Portuguese Empire. This new constitutional monarchy allowed for limited representative government but at the same time greatly expanded the ranks of the titled nobility and in most regards catered to its needs.

The Portuguese Court in Brazil

Already in the late eighteenth century, Brazilian merchants and freethinkers had begun to chafe at the strictures of the Portuguese Empire, and had initiated a series of conspiracies and uprisings aimed toward independence. Best known among these uprisings was the *Inconfidência Mineira,* or Minas Gerais Conspiracy, hatched in the region of that name by a collection of officers, writers, and tradesmen inspired by Enlightenment thought and the American Revolution. The

Inconfidência Mineira was later celebrated as one of the roots of independence, ✓ but it was stifled easily in the short term, with no threat to the Portuguese Empire.

The most radical of the late colonial rebellions was the 1798 multiracial *Tailors' Rebellion* in the northeastern Brazilian port city of Salvador da Bahia. As the name suggests, petty tradesmen, as well as disaffected soldiers, led the rebellion. They demanded free trade, the declaration of a republic, and the abolition of slavery— the only Brazilian movement to advocate this trifecta of liberal reforms. But the Tailors, like previous initiatives, were easily crushed. Independence, when it came, would emerge in more cautious and conservative guise, responding to pressure from without while continuing to suppress dissent within.

In 1807, Napoleon's forces invaded Portugal. In an ingenious maneuver, Dom João, prince regent of Portugal, abandoned Lisbon and fled to the New World. After stopping in Salvador da Bahia, he reestablished court life in Rio de Janeiro early in 1808. Rio de Janeiro became, in effect, the provisional capital of the global Portuguese Empire, while Napoleonic forces occupied much of mainland Portugal. Seeking protection from further Napoleonic aggression, Dom João allied with the British, granting them favorable trade status, and linking nineteenth-century Brazilian development firmly to British mercantile interests.

The presence of the royal court transformed Rio de Janeiro. Dom João founded the Royal Library and the Royal Press, institutions that would survive subsequent political transitions with little change through the remainder of the nineteenth century. And he permitted, for the first time, the foundation and circulation of newspapers. Overnight, Rio de Janeiro became more cosmopolitan. At the same time, the power of the prince, wielded through personal favors granted in face-to-face encounters with supplicants ranging from powerful landowners to humble merchants, instilled a tendency toward political patronage that would also endure.

Meanwhile, back in mainland Portugal, the combined forces of local residents and British troops expelled the Napoleonic army by 1814. Portuguese landowners grew restless in Dom João's absence and pressed for his return, while their Brazilian cousins sought greater leverage. Late in 1815, Dom João officially granted Brazil the status of "co-kingdom," recognizing it as an equal partner rather than a colony within the united Portuguese Empire. In 1818, Dom João's official coronation as King João VI, which took place in Rio de Janeiro, further stoked Brazilian pretensions to metropolitan status.

Independence

For elites on the Portuguese mainland, these measures threatened the loss of colonial tax revenue. In 1820, they formed a parliament, called for the immediate return of the king, and began drafting a constitution—one that would reassert Portuguese authority over Brazil, returning that land to colonial status. Brazilian representatives in this parliament were quickly marginalized, pushing them toward advocacy of full independence.

In 1821, threatened by turbulence in both Lisbon and Rio de Janeiro, João VI returned to Portugal. His 23-year-old son, Pedro, remained in Rio de Janeiro. Pedro was more favorable toward liberal reform than his father. Pedro's dynastic inheritance was Portuguese, but his sympathies lay with the Brazilian modernizers. Early in 1822, he declared his intent to remain in Brazil. On September 7 of that year, joined by his liberal allies, he formally declared Brazilian independence, and prepared for a constitutional assembly granting limited representative government.

But this did not mean a decisive break with Portugal. Instead, it opened a series of negotiations, carried out in the midst of extensive civil conflict within Portugal.

≡ **The Coronation of Pedro I.** Alone among the Latin American states, Brazil achieved independence relatively peacefully and with many of its colonial institutions, including the monarchy, intact. Pedro I and the House of Braganza provided the continuity that enabled Brazil to remain comparatively stable and prosperous during the nineteenth century. The formal coronation of Pedro I instilled the institution of the monarchy as well as a traditional court system. For years Brazil remained an exception to the turmoil that characterized much of Spanish America and Haiti.

CULTURE AND IDEAS

José Bonifácio de Andrada e Silva

The life of José Bonifácio de Andrada e Silva exemplifies many of the challenges and contradictions of the independence period in Brazil. Andrada e Silva was the most influential statesman of the era, in some ways more powerful than Pedro I. Without his vision and statecraft, Brazil might easily have broken into several smaller units in the early 1820s. But he was reviled by many, and Pedro I alternately relied on and resented him. He helped usher a united Brazilian Empire into independence, but his most contentious proposed reforms were put off for generations.

Andrada e Silva was born in Santos, São Paulo, in 1763, to Portuguese nobility. Like other bright boys of his social station, he quickly surpassed the meager offerings for formal education available in Brazil, and was sent to study at the great Portuguese university at Coimbra. He soon realized that Coimbra was a hidebound institution and departed for northern Europe, studying both the latest methods of mining and engineering and acquainting himself with Enlightenment political theory. By the time he returned to Brazil in 1819, he had been gone for over thirty years. Rio de Janeiro had become the seat of empire and was transforming rapidly, but Andrada e Silva was quick to perceive that slavery remained both the basis of the economy and the greatest obstacle to development. Like his contemporary Simón Bolívar, he advocated emancipation primarily on economic grounds, abhorring slavery more as an inefficient mode of production than as a moral offense.

Andrada e Silva's experience and insight made him a key interlocutor for Dom Pedro, as the vacillating prince regent demurred on whether to return to Lisbon or to remain in Rio de Janeiro. Andrada e Silva became a steady, forceful advocate for the integrity and autonomy of Brazil, if not necessarily its

independence. When São Paulo sent six delegates to the Lisbon parliament of 1821, Andrada e Silva dispatched them with a series of "Notes and Reminders." This became a foundational document for Brazilian independence, insisting, among other things, on the necessity of self-government of a united Brazil. Andrada e Silva's notes also advocated public education, the creation of a university, the development of the interior, the prohibition of the transatlantic slave trade, and the gradual emancipation of slaves. In all these regards, his suggestions not only horrified the Portuguese parliament but also moved against the short-term interests of Brazilian elites. As a result, Andrada's suggestions went unheeded until the late nineteenth century.

On the issue of autonomy and unity, however, Andrada e Silva's guidance proved decisive. Over the course of the next year, he persuaded Dom Pedro to remain in Brazil and to reject new colonial laws passed by the Portuguese parliament. His ability to isolate both radicals and reactionaries in the far-flung Brazilian territories and to bring them (at least temporarily) into line enabled Brazil to enter independence without civil war.

After declaring independence, Dom Pedro (now Pedro I of Brazil) soon rejected Andrada e Silva's counsel and exiled him late in 1823. Nonetheless, eight years later as Pedro I prepared to enter into exile himself, leaving behind his young son as prince regent, he called on his former adviser whom he could trust to tutor the boy. Andrada e Silva was as influential in shaping the ideas of the future Emperor Pedro II as he was in ushering Brazil into independence.

- What does Andrada e Silva's career tell us about the limits and possibilities of enlightened statecraft in early nineteenth-century Brazil?

Only in 1825 did Portugal—pressed by British merchants powerful in both Lisbon and Rio de Janeiro—officially recognize Brazilian independence.

Thus, Brazil emerged as an independent empire with no dynastic transition. Pedro (now Pedro I, Emperor of Brazil) carried out liberal economic reforms, granting free trade. And he continued his father's creation of modern local institutions, laying the groundwork for a stable administration. But he dared not contemplate one particular liberal reform: the abolition of slavery. To do so would strike too deeply at the social and economic power of his closest supporters.

Conclusion

The age of independence brought primarily political change to the former colonies of Spain, Portugal, and France. Enlightenment political theory rejected the colonial system's formal values of hierarchy and privilege in favor of a concept of citizenship that endowed all (except slaves and women, meaning mainly free men) with individual liberties. Popular sovereignty, the idea that the people (however defined) could direct their own destiny, replaced submission to the whims of a distant sovereign. Criollos seized on these principles after Napoleon invaded the Iberian Peninsula to either assert claims for autonomy in the Spanish world or to work with the exiled Portuguese monarch to better their circumstances within imperial structures. With the restoration of Ferdinand VII in 1814, those Spanish Americans favoring the prudent middle ground had to make the difficult choice between the royalist or patriot side.

Independence ultimately offered a broad spectrum of results, ranging from Haiti (which became a republic of former slaves) to Brazil (which installed a branch of the Portuguese dynasty in the newly independent nation). As a general rule, the successful campaigns for independence in Spanish America after 1818 required the criollo leadership to put aside memories of racial conflicts and to structure a multiclass alliance, calling on all Americans to rally together against the common

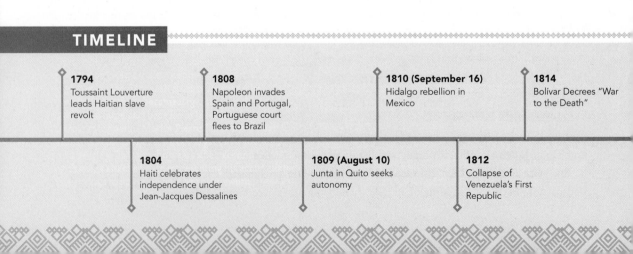

TIMELINE

1794
Toussaint Louverture leads Haitian slave revolt

1804
Haiti celebrates independence under Jean-Jacques Dessalines

1808
Napoleon invades Spain and Portugal, Portuguese court flees to Brazil

1809 (August 10)
Junta in Quito seeks autonomy

1810 (September 16)
Hidalgo rebellion in Mexico

1812
Collapse of Venezuela's First Republic

1814
Bolívar Decrees "War to the Death"

enemy. Ferdinand VII ultimately lost because he refused to compromise with the autonomist faction when he had the opportunity, and alienated many with his draconian policies.

The deeper implications of independence resonated for generations. Patriotic holidays associated with independence provided some of the first building blocks of national identity. The wars saw the reemphasis of fealty to one's *patria*, or region of birth, as evidenced both in the rise of regional military leaders and the election of regional delegates to the Cortes. Independence created a cult of charismatic heroes, like Bolívar, who presumed they deserved a place on the political stage. Promises for a more egalitarian society were soon betrayed, as slaves remained in bondage, Indians continued to pay discriminatory taxes, mixed-race populations lost the right to vote, and women returned to more modest roles. True, some

KEY TERMS

blancs 15	Enlightenment 11	noirs 16
castas 20	gens de couleur libres 15	pardos 36
Code Noir 15	juntas 30	peninsulares 13
criollos 13	llaneros 38	Vodun 17

1815
Ferdinand VII returns to Spanish throne, nadir of independence movements

1819–1822
Bolívar liberates northern South America

1822
Pedro I declares Brazil independent

1823–1826
Bolívar campaigns in Peru and Bolivia

1816
Argentina and Paraguay independent

1821
Independence of Mexico

1823
Formation of Central American Union

1861–1865
Spain regains the Dominican Republic

fortunate pardo and mestizo military officers obtained land and won the hands of gentrified women, thereby gaining entrée into society. At the same time the decade of violence cost thousands of lives, ruined the economy in much of Latin America, and left the criollo elite quarreling about the best way to structure their new nations.

Selected Readings

Blanchard, Peter. *Under the Flags of Freedom: Slave Soldiers and the Wars of Independence in Spanish South America.* Pittsburgh, PA: University of Pittsburgh Press, 2008.

Brading, David A. *The First America: The Spanish Monarchy, Creole Patriots, and the Liberal State, 1492–1867.* New York: Cambridge University Press.

Chasteen, John C. *Americanos: Latin America's Struggle for Independence.* New York: Oxford University Press, 2008.

Dubois, Laurent. *Haiti: The Aftershock of History.* New York: Picador Books, 2012.

Hamnett, Brian R. *Roots of Insurgency: Mexican Regions, 1750–1824.* New York: Cambridge University Press, 2002.

Henderson, Timothy J. *The Mexican Wars for Independence.* New York: Hill and Wang, 2009.

Hochschild, Adam. *Bury the Chains: The British Struggle to Abolish Slavery.* New York: Houghton Mifflin Harcourt, 2006.

James, C. L. R. *The Black Jacobins: Toussaint Louverture and the San Domingo Revolution.* New York: Vintage Books, 1963.

Lynch, John. *Simón Bolívar: A Life.* New Haven, CT: Yale University Press, 2006.

McNeil, J. R. *Mosquito Empires: Ecology and War in the Greater Caribbean, 1620–1914.* Cambridge: Cambridge University Press, 2010.

Murray, Pamela. *For Glory and Bolívar: The Remarkable Life of Manuela Sáenz.* Austin: University of Texas Press, 2008.

Paquette, Gabriel. *Imperial Portugal in the Age of Atlantic Revolutions: The Luso-Brazilian World, c. 1770–1850.* Cambridge: Cambridge University Press, 2013.

Prou, Marc E. "Haiti's Condemnation: History and Culture at the Crossroads." *Latin American Research Review* 40, no. 3 (2005): 191–201.

Rodríguez O, Jaime. *The Independence of Spanish America.* Cambridge: Cambridge University Press, 1998.

Rodríguez O., Jaime. *"We Are Now the True Spaniards": Sovereignty, Revolution, Independence and the Emergence of the Federal Republic of Mexico.* Stanford, CA: Stanford University Press, 2012.

Zahler, Reuben. *Ambitious Rebels: Remaking Honor, Law, and Liberalism in Venezuela, 1780–1850.* Tucson: University of Arizona Press, 2013.

2

Latin America: Regionalism and Localism

Global Connections

In most of today's Latin America, the concept of regionalism (the preference for identifying with a smaller, autonomous geographical entity rather than the nation-state) has melted away as steadily as the glaciers atop the Andean mountains. Yet regionalism proved a major obstacle to the formation of viable nations in the years immediately following the achievement of independence. Regionalism resulted not only from peoples' state of mind, but also from geographical obstacles that divided nations physically. Between 1825 and the early twentieth century, regionalism not only dominated the political and economic history of Latin American but also was a global phenomenon.

Until 1871, the modern nations of Germany and Italy did not exist; instead, a host of warring regional principalities and city-states, and "sovereign villages" that zealously guarded their privileges and frontiers, held sway. Regional differences prevailed even in already established nation-states, like France and Spain. The 1844 novel *The Three Musketeers* by Alexandre Dumas delighted Parisian readers with its caricature of the hero D'Artagnan's provincial accent and country ways, while admiring his swashbuckling swordsmanship, just as Latin Americans loved their literary works produced by local authors and paintings that depicted regional scenes from everyday life and popular customs. In East Asia, China's long-standing Qing dynasty experienced increased regionalism following the Opium War (1839–1842), particularly during the Taiping Rebellion (1850–1864), when overwhelmed Confucian bureaucrats had to rely on foreign mercenaries to maintain the imperial order. In the Middle East, both the Ottoman and the Persian empires weakened in the face of regional forces, with provinces of the former, like Egypt, asserting autonomy.

Meanwhile, the United States, one of the few nation-states expanding in geographical size during this era, struggled to maintain its union because of significant regional conflicts between the Northeast, the West, and the South. Varying accents, foods, and customs differentiated the three regions. By midcentury, while northeastern factory-owners accumulated fortunes and immigrants toiled in textile and shoe-making mills, western farmers harnessed horse to plow to till the soil of the Great Plains, contending with the hardships of life in sod houses and conflicts with displaced Native Americans. In the south, "King Cotton" dominated, which led to the most divisive issue among the regions: the question of human bondage. Planters and politicians in the southern states insisted on their right to maintain

≡ **John Gast's Painting** *Spirit of the Frontier.* John Gast's painting provides deep insights into the notion of Manifest Destiny that swept the United States in the 1840s. Portraying the story of pioneers expanding the frontier westward, Gast's classically clothed figure embodies the ideals of republicanism. Other elements depict the advance of technology, such as the telegraph wire she holds in her hand, the railroad, and the steel plow. The east, from whence she comes, is bathed in light while the west, still inhabited by indigenous people and buffalo, is shrouded in darkness.

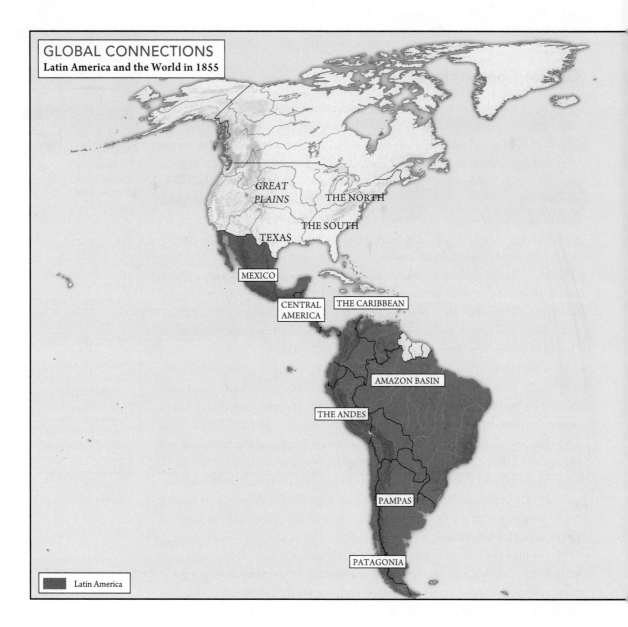

GLOBAL CONNECTIONS
Latin America and the World in 1855

GREAT PLAINS

THE NORTH

THE SOUTH

TEXAS

MEXICO

CENTRAL AMERICA

THE CARIBBEAN

AMAZON BASIN

THE ANDES

PAMPAS

PATAGONIA

Latin America

slavery and pressed for expansion of slavery into western territories. (They also occasionally pressed for annexation of slaveholding areas of Latin America, such as Cuba). Abolitionists in the northern states demanded an end to slavery, and recognized that expansion of slavery to western territories could lock the United States into the system indefinitely. These regional differences led to the Civil War (1861–1865), the bloodiest confrontation in US history or in the Americas as a whole. Even in the aftermath of the war, white Southerners continued to view

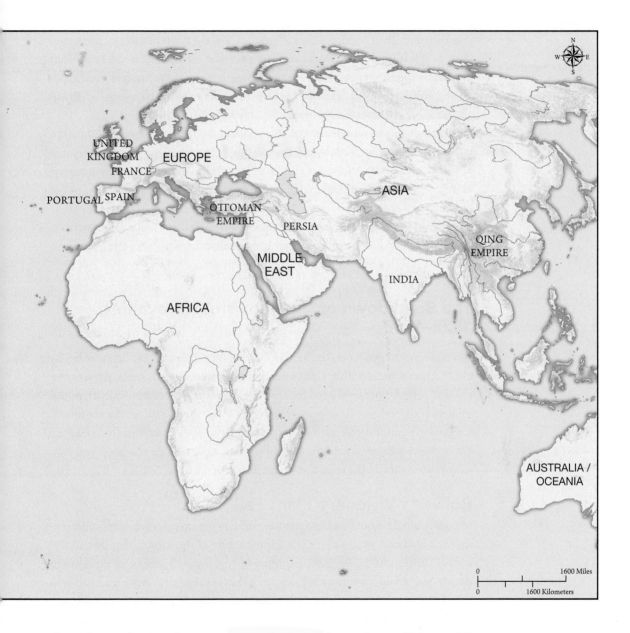

themselves as sharing a distinctive regional culture whose values and lifeways differed sharply from those of the "Yankees."

Like the rest of the world, Latin Americans contended with the forces of regionalism despite the hopes and dreams of a number of the independence leaders. Visionaries like Simón Bolívar aspired to create grander geographical entities, hoping to emulate the United States by maintaining the physical boundaries of the old viceroyalties. But geographical obstacles, like the mountain ranges that ✔

dominated much of Mexico, Central America, and the Andean nations, prevented most people from experiencing a world beyond their own birthplace. Yet it was not geography alone that determined regional sentiments. Over time, historical experiences created regional customs, diets, and traditions even in countries like Brazil and Argentina, where fewer geographical impediments existed.

Regionalism was reinforced in Latin America between 1825 and 1870 by the emergence of popular leaders called **caudillos**, who generally relied on a regional power base. Caudillos created coalitions of loyal followers and fought for influence and the interests of their regional home district, much as the principal families of local elites had squabbled among themselves during the colonial period. The combination of geographical obstacles, regional historical and cultural differences, and the emergence of caudillo leadership made Bolívar's dream for Pan-American unity an unlikely prospect in the early nineteenth century.

The Breakdown of the Spanish Viceroyalties, 1825–1830

Having won independence, the heroic liberators now faced the challenge of building functional states within clearly defined geographical boundaries. Even in the colonial period, borders shifted for a variety of reasons. More importantly, as the soldiers of the independence era noted during their marches across the continent, tremendous cultural distinctions existed between the newly liberated peoples. Given these realities, would the idea of supra-states based on the borders of the viceroyalties survive the postindependence era?

Bolívar's Visionary Plans Fail

Not surprisingly, a bold and imaginative military commander like Simón Bolívar also had bold and imaginative ideas for the future of the nations that he had liberated. During the 1820s, Bolívar proposed two Spanish-American *supra-states* (states that would have included several of the modern Latin American nations) that would reassume the territorial boundaries of former viceregal units, in part for defensive reasons. Bolívar worried that Spain, in concert with Europe's conservative Quadruple Alliance, would attempt the reconquest of the former colonies even after the last royalist army was expelled in 1825. (The Quadruple Alliance of England, Austria, Prussia, and Russia sought to preserve the post-Napoleon status quo and prevent renewed French aggression).

With that fear in mind, he urged each newly independent nation to appoint representatives to the Congress of Panama in 1826 to discuss a common foreign policy and defensive strategy. Only four republics sent delegates to this first Pan-American meeting (Gran Colombia, Peru, Mexico, and the United Provinces of Central America), and they failed to agree on anything meaningful. Bolívar's fears were nonetheless never realized, because the threat of the powerful British fleet accomplished what the Congress of Panama could not: defend the security of the Americas. The failure of the Congress of Panama, however, suggested that Bolívar's larger visions would not carry the day.

Bolívar's longest lasting supra-state, Gran Colombia, survived from 1821 to 1830. An attempt to maintain intact the boundaries of the Viceroyalty of New Granada (Colombia, Venezuela, Panama, and Ecuador), Gran Colombia faced insurmountable barriers in part because of the contentious personalities and ambitions of the leaders of this cobbled-together republic. During the war years (1819–1826), Bolívar left the administration of Gran Colombia to his vice president, the lawyer Francisco de Paula Santander. But Santander, the "Man of Laws'" openly favored Colombians and demonstrated his disdain for Venezuelans, especially the rough horsemen of the plains, the *llaneros*, reputedly because they mocked his poor horsemanship. Many contemporaries viewed Santander as cold and ruthless, which further distanced him from the mixed-race llaneros. The llaneros and their general, José Antonio Páez, returned Santander's antipathy.

While Bolívar fought in Peru, stress fractures quickly appeared in his Gran Colombian edifice as both Páez and Santander furthered their own regional interests. Bolívar himself recognized the cultural differences between the three component parts of Gran Colombia and succinctly quipped, "Venezuela is a barracks, Colombia a university, and Ecuador a monastery." Santander the lawyer and Páez the soldier personified the distinction between Colombia and Venezuela. As Bolívar dallied in Lima in 1826, enjoying the adulation of the crowds and the endless parties thrown in his honor, his two principal lieutenants nearly came to blows. Bolívar rushed home, and with honeyed words of praise for Páez, temporarily patched up the quarrel. But Bolívar's embrace of Páez alienated Santander, who became increasingly critical of the Liberator and his "dictatorial" ways.

Meanwhile, Bolivar pressed an even more unrealistic scheme on his unwilling wartime compatriots—The Federation of the Andes. His new idea would have joined Peru and Bolivia to Gran Colombia while allowing the former considerable autonomy. Although the Liberator had spoken the language of liberalism early in his career, by the mid-1820s his endless conflicts with uncooperative congresses had made him more cynical and conservative. Evidence of the Liberator's disillusionment appears in Bolivia's Constitution of 1826, which

☰ MAP. 2.1

called for a president for life to be succeeded by a vice president, also chosen for life—hardly a promising premise for democracy. The Bolivians dutifully named Bolívar's favorite general, the Venezuelan Antonio José de Sucre, to the presidency, and adopted the constitution. As soon as Bolívar left Lima, Peru rejected the proposal. Simultaneously, Santander dismissed the Federation of the Andes as absurd, and vowed that Gran Colombia would not participate in the experiment; this was certainly a blow to Bolívar's ego. Any lingering hopes for the success of the Federation ended when the Bolivians drove Sucre into exile two years later.

Reluctantly accepting the failure of the Federation, Bolívar struggled to keep Gran Colombia alive during the final three years of his life. In 1828–1829, General Sucre and General Juan José Flores defeated a Peruvian invasion in the far south, keeping Guayaquil and southern Ecuador as part of Gran Colombia for the moment. Attempting to halt further disorder, Bolívar assumed dictatorial powers and cultivated conservative institutions like the army and the Church. Santander condemned this drift away from the liberal principles of the independence movement, and may have even been the inspiration behind an unsuccessful plot to assassinate Bolívar in September 1828. Gran Colombia's economic policies further reduced its likelihood of success. Free trade not only cost the country needed tax revenues but also crippled domestic cloth manufacturers in Ecuador and Colombia. Corruption abounded. Bolívar refused to reduce the size of the army, placing an impossible burden on the treasury. Finally, the government squandered the loan it had received in 1822 and 1824 from Great Britain, defaulted on repayment, and ruined its credit rating.

Like a Shakespearean metaphor, the diseased state of Gran Colombia mirrored Simón Bolívar's failing personal health, as years of hard campaigning and tuberculosis took their toll. With Bolívar's health and prestige continuing to decline, Páez and his Venezuelan followers decided to break away from Gran Colombia in 1830. Shortly thereafter, Juan José Flores followed suit in Ecuador, thereby completing the destruction of Bolívar's most viable attempt to retain the boundaries of a viceroyalty. Disillusioned because of the failure of his grand enterprises, Bolívar famously lamented, "We have plowed the sea." Bolívar found his final refuge on a Spaniard's estate, where he died on December 17, 1830, in Santa Marta, Colombia.

Plans for Supra-States after Bolívar's Death

The idea of resurrecting a supra-state died hardest among those officers whom Simón Bolívar had cultivated. Because the charismatic Bolívar spoke passionately about his vision for a greater state, a number of these men absorbed his enthusiasm.

Between Bolívar's death and the 1860s, several of his aides-de-camp authored plans to reconstitute states whose borders resembled those of the Spanish South American viceroyalties. The Peru-Bolivia Confederation, the brainchild of Andrés Santa Cruz, one of Bolívar's principal generals during the key battles for independence in Peru during the 1820s, was the most successful of these ventures. Born in the city of La Paz, Bolivia, an urban area historically connected with southern Peru, Santa Cruz, like many people during the postindependence era, believed himself to be a citizen of both nations. Elected president of Bolivia in 1828, Santa Cruz proved a capable administrator, keeping the new country stable and holding the military in check.

Peru did not fare so well. With the exception of the presidency of Agustín Gamarra (1829–1833), Peru disintegrated into chaos, partly because of the traditional rivalry between the coastal region and the highlands and partly because of the ambitions of a host of generals. Given the anarchy reigning in Peru, Santa Cruz's offer to create his Peru-Bolivian Confederation in 1836 met with considerable popular acclaim. Well aware of the issue of geography, Santa Cruz proposed three semiautonomous entities (North Peru, South Peru, and Bolivia), which would be largely self-governing. Real authority rested in the "Supreme Protector" (Santa Cruz himself), who was elected to this office for a ten-year term and enjoyed the power to appoint officials, conduct foreign policy, regulate commerce, and command the army. Never popular in the north, where the population viewed the entire project as the conquest of Peru by a Bolivian, the Confederation also met with considerable opposition from Peru's southern neighbor, Chile, which interpreted the creation of the Confederation as a commercial and military threat.

As a result, the Chileans launched a preemptive strike, deploying their navy to blockade Peruvian ports and bringing the commerce of the north coast to a halt. Santa Cruz attempted to negotiate with the Chileans but they refused his terms. Santa Cruz's Peruvian rivals, and especially his nemesis Gamarra, joined the Chileans. The Chilean military captured Lima, marched into the highlands, and defeated Santa Cruz at the battle of Yungay in 1839, ending the Confederation. Gamarra also believed in a supra-state but on terms more favorable to Peru. But when he attempted to invade Bolivia in 1841 to achieve this end, he was shot and killed by one of his own troops.

In 1863 another of the Liberator's former aides-de camp, Tomás Cipriano de Mosquera, made one final attempt to create a supra-state, this time proposing the resurrection of Gran Colombia. After leading his party to victory in New Granada's civil war (in what is now Colombia), the bombastic and ambitious Mosquera announced his plan for union. Venezuela had sufficient military strength to simply ignore Mosquera, but the smaller Ecuador was more vulnerable. Its president persuaded retired independence hero and former president Juan José Flores to organize a volunteer army to fight the Colombians. Flores's untrained volunteers did not fare well against Mosquera's battle-hardened veterans. Mosquera seemed poised to take Quito and extinguish the Ecuadorian state as the first step toward reconstituting Gran Colombia. Just when all seemed lost for Ecuador, Flores appealed to his friendship with Mosquera as comrades of Bolívar. Simultaneously, Colombia's legislature forced Mosquera to halt the invasion. Ultimately, Mosquera saved face and signed a peace treaty with Ecuador, declaring he was satisfied with an *abrazo* (hug) from his old friend, and agreed to forego the plan to reunite Gran Colombia. After this debacle, the forces of regionalism and a growing sense of nationalism prevented any further attempts to create larger states in Spanish South America.

≡ **A Human Burden Carrier in Ecuador.** In the early nineteenth century, transportation in the northern Andean countries was very difficult because no roads existed in many areas. As a result, indigenous people were pressed into service as porters. Not only did they carry luggage, but in Colombia and Ecuador they also carried people, presumably members of the elite or foreign visitors, up steep slopes. To manage this task, porters strapped a chair-like wooden frame on their backs, as in this picture of an indigenous man carrying someone up one of the Guacamayo Mountains.

CULTURE AND IDEAS

Women Travelers in the Andean Nations

Physical geography hampered nation building, perhaps nowhere more noticeably than in the Andean nations of Colombia, Ecuador, Peru, and Bolivia. There, nearly every foreign traveler commented on the rugged topography and the absence of modern systems of transportation, both of which profoundly contributed to regionalism and economic stagnation. Each of the Andean countries contained three distinctive regional zones: a hot coastal plain; ranges of craggy, snowcapped volcanic peaks with valleys in between; and an Amazonian tropical forest.

Each region presented its own geographical challenges. Colombia's verdant shores proved inhospitable because of incessant rains that promoted fevers, while Peru and Bolivia shared the equally inhospitable coastal Atacama Desert, one of the driest places on earth. Each nation had sparsely settled but vast Amazonian reaches. Most foreigners, like the majority of Andeans, preferred the milder climates of the agriculturally productive valleys between the mountain chains, but commented on the hardships associated with the journey to these higher elevations.

Elite women, who were constrained by many rules and social norms that limited many aspects of their lives and personal mobility, did travel in Latin America during these times, but they needed to conform to the norms of approved behavior in order to be accepted socially. For example, Flora Tristan, the illegitimate daughter of an elite Peruvian, left France in 1833 to claim her inheritance from her uncle. Seeking him in the city of Arequipa, she joined a party of upper-class Peruvians and rode a mule inland, nearly dying of thirst in the desert. When the travelers finally reached the mountains, her sure-footed mule frightened her out of her wits as it jumped crevasses, clambered up rocks, and meandered along dangerous precipices. Yet Tristan admitted that although the journey nearly cost her life, the spectacular scenery made the trip worthwhile. Her status (her uncle had briefly been president of Peru) and her well-to-do companions protected her from physical harm and served as suitable chaperones, even though in the end her quest for her inheritance came to naught.

Ida Pfieffer, a middle-class teacher from Germany who crossed the Pacific during an around-the-world tour, had a very different experience. She made the mistake of arriving in Ecuador without a suitable male companion (Latin American society assumed that single women traveling alone were immoral) and as a result found herself constantly cheated (one unscrupulous merchant charged her the exorbitant price of eight dollars for a worn saddle that turned out to be unusable). She was physically miserable: frequently wet, cold, and suffering from altitude sickness. She complained that rooms in roadside inns were tiny and flea-ridden, and that the hosts seldom had more than a bowl of soup to offer their hungry visitors. In her own words, "I was more comfortable among the cannibals of Sumatra than among the so-called Christian rabble" of Ecuador. To compound her misery, on the return trip to the coast she fell out of the boat on the Guayas River and none of the crew lifted a finger to save her. Finally, another passenger pulled her aboard just as she was about to drown.

- How did gender, class, and geography shape women's travel in the nineteenth-century Andes?

The Breakdown of New Spain, 1821–1835

At the time of independence, the Viceroyalty of New Spain consisted of modern Mexico, the southwestern portion of the United States, and today's Central American nations except for Panama. Each section was further divided into autonomous jurisdictions. Overseeing this vast territory had challenged even the most capable viceroy. Despite the theoretically unified nature of the Kingdom of New Spain, the

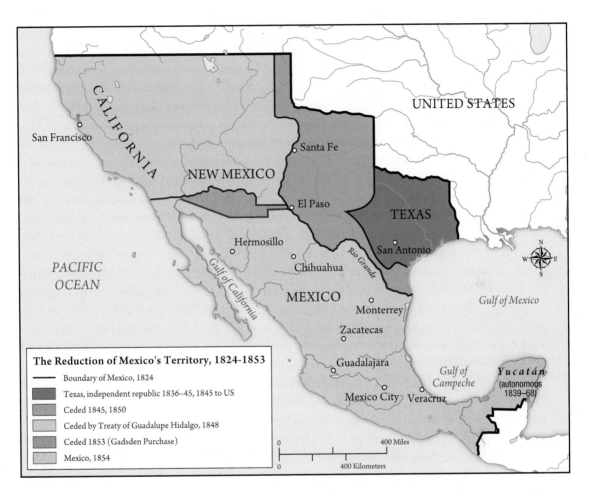

The Reduction of Mexico's Territory, 1824-1853

—— Boundary of Mexico, 1824

▨ Texas, independent republic 1836–45, 1845 to US

▨ Ceded 1845, 1850

▨ Ceded by Treaty of Guadalupe Hidalgo, 1848

▨ Ceded 1853 (Gadsden Purchase)

▨ Mexico, 1854

≡ **MAP. 2.2**

wars for independence revealed profound regional rifts with the colony and would present a major challenge for Mexico.

Iturbide's Empire

Agustín de Iturbide was committed to a unified Mexican empire, but was less emphatic than Bolívar about retaining control over distant provinces. In a postscript to the Plan de Iguala, declared, "Long Live Northern America, independent from all the nations of the globe. Long live the union that makes our happiness." With this commitment to unity, even before his coronation Iturbide attempted to coax the Central American provinces to remain within Mexico.

Like many of his contemporaries, Iturbide believed that only monarchy could provide the symbolic unity necessary to control this vast geographical area. The *Plan de Iguala* had called for a Bourbon prince to assume the throne of Mexico, but when Spain refused to acknowledge Mexico's independence in 1821, this solution became impossible. Therefore, Iturbide's friends proclaimed him emperor in May 1822. However, many monarchists doubted the wisdom of elevating a criollo who lacked European royal bloodlines to the throne.

Iturbide temporarily succeeded in maintaining his empire intact. The province of Yucatán grudgingly accepted but remained a strong proponent of regional autonomy, soon to be followed by Chiapas. Its delegates to the Constituent Congress consistently raised objections to Iturbide's attempts to strengthen the national government. Similarly, Guatemala's representatives shared these concerns, but took solace in the understanding that Spain's Constitution of 1812, which protected regional liberties, remained the law of the land. The remaining four Central American provinces (Honduras, Nicaragua, El Salvador, and Costa Rica, as well as Chiapas), ultimately opted to join the empire, although Iturbide had to send an army to persuade El Salvador. The northern provinces of Mexico followed a similar pattern. New Mexico and Texas reluctantly accepted the inevitable, while only the threat of force brought the Californians into the fold.

Emperor Agustín I did not fare well in office. Military expenses mounted, especially as ambitious junior officers clamored for promotions and Iturbide refused to reduce the size of the army. Pomp and ceremony drained the treasury, while Iturbide and Congress quarreled over policy. By the end of Iturbide's reign, the more geographically remote regions were only nominally under the control of Mexico City. As in South America, regional interests overpowered Iturbide's efforts to create a unified state.

By February 1823, a coalition of independence-era military officers and provincial elites decided to end the empire. In addition to seeking payment of the army's salaries, the rebels advocated greater regional autonomy. The once powerful and unified army had become politicized, prone to following their district commanders rather than civilian authority. In the far south, only Chiapas maintained its ties to Mexico, while the remainder of Central America went its own way. As one leader in Chiapas allegedly retorted, quoting an old Sephardic proverb, "It is better to be the tail of a lion than the head of a rat." The far north remained Mexican territory, at least for the moment.

Iturbide's end proved tragic. Attempting to return to Mexico from a short exile in England he was captured and executed in 1824. Even after his demise, however, the idea of monarchy enjoyed many supporters in Mexico. Perhaps with a legitimate European prince instead of a native imposter, some conservatives reasoned, respect for monarchy could be revived.

Mexican National Politics from Iturbide to the Texas Rebellion

Following Iturbide's ouster, the victors called for a congress that ultimately produced Mexico's first constitution, the Constitution of 1824. Delegates hotly debated the shape that the government would take. Would it be centralist, with a powerful executive and the locus of power in Mexico City as had been the case during the colonial period and the recent empire? Or would it be federalist like the United States, with most powers reserved to the legislature and the individual states? After much deliberation, the delegates chose the latter alternative because it seemed to better protect individual liberties and guard against despotism as well as to allow tax revenues to remain in local hands. Federalism neatly dovetailed with the regionalist sentiment prevalent in Mexico's outlying states.

Second-tier military figures from the wars of independence led both federalists and centralists into the electoral frays of the next few presidential elections. As in early US history, the Constitution permitted the possibility that the president and vice president could come from different parties. In Mexico, this led to a series of military coups by vice presidents. After losing the election of 1828, for example, the independence hero and unsuccessful candidate Vicente Guerrero seized the presidency. During his short time in office, Guerrero abolished slavery, which would have important consequences on the coming fracas with immigrants to Texas from the US south.

Being financially strapped exacerbated the difficulties of the national government. Expenditures always exceeded revenue streams, in large measure because the Church owned about one-fifth of all Mexican property and by law was exempt from taxation. To balance the budget, the government borrowed, initially seeking a loan from Great Britain, whose banks and private citizens eagerly sought to speculate in emerging markets like Mexico. But Mexico's dreams to resuscitate mining and modernize infrastructure failed in the Global Panic of 1825.

The ongoing political and economic crises convinced Mexicans in 1832 to elect as president the one individual who had had successfully navigated the country's troubled political waters with resolution and charisma. Antonio López de Santa Anna, by now a general and a wealthy *hacendado* from the coastal state of Veracruz, had been a royalist officer who had signed onto Iturbide's Plan de Iguala for independence. In 1829, he defeated an attempted Spanish reconquest of Mexico. Commanding both popular respect and the support of the army, Santa Anna easily won the election of 1832, the first of eleven times that he would hold the presidential office. Although he soon became bored with the day-to-day administrative duties of his office and returned to his hacienda, Santa Anna remained at the ready to retake the presidency and defend Mexico against danger, such as the one that would engulf the country with the breakaway of Texas in 1835.

Independence Comes to the Isthmus of Central America

During the colonial period, the Kingdom of Guatemala was an administrative unit under New Spain, serving as an administrative, judicial, and political entity that included Chiapas (now a state of Mexico), Guatemala, Belize, El Salvador, Honduras, Nicaragua, and Costa Rica. While the capital of the Kingdom of Guatemala was located in present-day Guatemala City, provincial capitals in each district enjoyed considerable autonomy and municipal authority.

During the initial stage of the independence movement, seven Central American representatives served prominently at the Cortes of Cadiz (1810–1814), and voiced opinions favoring greater Spanish-American autonomy. The more radical among the prosperous Central American elites preferred independence instead of autonomy. In 1811, unsuccessful independence movements broke out in El Salvador, and revived stirrings for independence erupted again after the restoration of Ferdinand VII in 1814. In 1821, a congress of Central American elite criollos declared their independence from Spain effective September 15 of that year, a date that Central Americans today celebrate as their independence day. Shortly thereafter, Central America joined the Mexican Empire.

When Mexico became a republic in 1823, Central America (Guatemala, Honduras, El Salvador, Nicaragua, and Costa Rica) broke away. On July 1, 1823, the Central American elites declared independence from Spain, Mexico and all foreign powers and established a new federated republic called the **United Provinces of Central America** (*Provincias Unidas del Centro de América*, or UPCA). The region now known as Belize theoretically remained an internal province within Guatemala, though informally controlled by Great Britain, which called the territory British Honduras. The Central American leadership proposed a federated republic with its capital in Guatemala, the wealthiest and most populous of the states. Significant power lay in the provincial capitals, where local elites remained in control over day-to-day life.

Mexico Loses More Territory: The Effects of Manifest Destiny, 1835–1853

Mexico's geographical disintegration continued in the years between 1835 and 1853, not as a result of provinces peacefully leaving the union, but as the result of external aggression. Weakened by regional divisions and internal political disputes, Mexico fell victim to the expansionist dreams of its northern neighbor, the United States. The results would be catastrophic for the country and would poison the relationship between the neighboring nations for at least a century.

The Idea of Manifest Destiny

During the mid-nineteenth century, most US politicians and citizens believed that the nation enjoyed a special destiny. They deemed their country unique and especially blessed, as the refuge of so many from Europe's social and political ills, a land of rich natural resources, and the birthplace of a democratic government based on Enlightenment principles. This perception of "American exceptionalism" continues to influence American popular thought. The concept of Manifest Destiny grew out of this understanding of American exceptionalism, in ways specific to the nineteenth century. Manifest Destiny was the understanding that God had granted a covenant to the United States to spread across the North American continent "from sea to shining sea." This involved appropriating new lands from Texas to California from Mexico, and fully absorbing the diverse populations who already lived there into the Protestant, Anglo-Saxon culture, values, religion, and political system of the United States. Although the self-serving aspects of Manifest Destiny were obvious even at the time, Americans perceived that Providence had blessed their land and given them a mission to spread American ideals throughout the land.

Manifest Destiny was a concept, not an explicit policy or mandate. The actual term did not come into popular use until 1845, when the American journalist John L. O'Sullivan coined the phrase. He wrote, "[It is] our manifest destiny to overspread the continent allotted by Providence for the free development of our yearly multiplying millions [of people.]" The heyday of Manifest Destiny took place between the Andrew Jackson administration and the start of the US Civil War (1828–1861) and corresponded directly to the greatest period of territorial expansion in US history.

The concept of Manifest Destiny had clear and threatening implications for people living outside of what was the United States at the time (which effectively ran no farther west than Louisiana and Missouri), including Native Americans who populated the entire western region and who would eventually be almost completely displaced or eliminated by white settlers. But the implications of Manifest Destiny were especially dire for Mexico, whose territory from Texas to California constituted their northern *Provincias Internas* (Interior Provinces).

Because the Interior Provinces were sparsely populated and remote from the metropolitan center of Mexico City, this large area, bordering its territorially aggressive northern neighbor, was vulnerable from the moment of Mexico's independence in 1821. Some of Spain's last colonial edicts in Mexico in 1822 had permitted Anglo-American immigrants to purchase land in Texas, on the condition that they take learn Spanish, become Catholics and take Mexican citizenship. The goal was to make these new Mexican citizens a buffer against US encroachment. This policy badly misfired when these Anglo-American settlers led a breakaway movement for Texas independence: a rebellion prompted largely by their desire to retain slavery despite Mexico's passage of abolition. The Texas Revolution succeeded, following a final confrontation at San Jacinto (Texas) on April 21, 1836, when the Texan forces captured the Mexican commander, General Antonio López de Santa Anna, and made the province's independence a condition for his release.

Texas remained an independent republic for nearly a decade. Throughout this period, the Lone Star Republic entertained the prospect of annexation to

PLUCKED:

OR,

THE MEXICAN EAGLE BEFORE THE WAR!   THE MEXICAN EAGLE AFTER THE WAR!

≡ **Plucked: The Mexican Eagle before and after the War.** This cartoon, published in Cornelius Mathew's humor magazine *Yankee Doodle*, in 1847, graphically demonstrates the results of Manifest Destiny on Mexico. Mathews, the leader of the "Young America" movement, advocated for the creation of a national literature, less beholden to English models. The song "Yankee Doodle" became the most popular anthem of the volunteer soldiers as they invaded Mexico. During the US-Mexican War, Mexico was stripped of almost half of her national territory, including everything north of the Rio Grande and all of what is now the western United States. The cartoon exhibits no remorse about the forcible seizures of our peaceful neighbor's real estate, but instead mocks the Mexican eagle, picturing it as a chicken about to be roasted for Sunday dinner. Given the prevalence of Manifest Destiny and Mathew's nationalistic beliefs, the cartoon depicts the popularity of the United States' first international war.

the United States, a prospect made more difficult by a dispute about where the Republic of Texas's borders actually lay. Several of the borders were contested, but the most problematic was the southern boundary, which Texas claimed was the Rio Grande, but which Mexico argued was the Rio Nueces, farther north.

The Mexican War

The conflict between the United States and Mexico between 1846 and 1848 had its roots in the long anticipated annexation of Texas in 1845 and the ongoing westward thrust of American settlers. It is usually called the Mexican War, the Mexican-American War, or, in Mexico, "the American War." The two nations understood the war in very different terms. For Mexico, it was fought to preserve national sovereignty. By contrast, a number of different factors impelled the United States to war, including the sense of Manifest Destiny; this assumed a divine right to "liberate" the lands held by Mexico for democracy, Protestant religion, and "Anglo-Saxon" values. Last but not least, the expansionist US presidents of the mid-nineteenth century correctly assessed that Mexico's internal political instability made its northern territories ripe for the taking.

In 1845, James K. Polk became president of the United States. An expansionist, Polk aspired to settle the Texas issue and, as well, press for the spread of US settlement across "Indian territory" and "the Great American Desert" onward to California, thus laying the groundwork for US territorial claims all the way to the Pacific Ocean. Texas had declared its independence, and its borders remained under dispute. But Mexico had incontrovertible sovereignty over the lands from New Mexico to California. Shortly after taking office, however, Polk attempted to secure Mexican agreement to setting the boundary of Texas at the Rio Grande and to arrange for the sale of Mexico's province of northern California (Alta California) to the United States. Mexico had no inclination to sell. Polk failed to realize that even his carefully orchestrated policy of graduated pressure on Mexico to cede or sell land to the United States would not work. Although Mexico's internal politics were chaotic, no Mexican politician would willingly agree to the alienation of any territory to the aggressive neighbor to the north. Polk nonetheless pressed the issue with formal annexation of Texas, which joined the United States as the twenty-eighth state in December of 1845, its southern border still under dispute.

In January of 1846, Polk directed General Zachary Taylor's army at Corpus Christi to advance to the Rio Grande. The Mexican government viewed the incursion as an act of war. On April 25 the Mexican troops at Matamoros crossed the river and ambushed an American patrol. Polk seized on the incident to secure a declaration of war on May 13 on the basis of the shedding of "American blood upon American soil." Mexicans pointedly did not agree that this was American soil: they insisted it was still part of Mexico.

Santa Anna, who had fled to exile after the Texas debacle, returned to Mexico in mid-August 1846 to help Mexico fend off the United States. The general, who once called liberty "folly" and boasted, "[in] a hundred years to come, [the people of Mexico] will not be fit for it," initially claimed that he did not wish to return to Mexico as its president. He quickly reneged on that promise, however, in part

"A LITTLE MORE GRAPE CAPT BRAGG"

GENERAL TAYLOR AT THE BATTLE OF BUENA VISTA FEBY 23? 1847.

A Little More Grape, Captain Bragg. This Currier and Ives print depicts a critical moment in the battle of Buena Vista in February 1847. General Zachary Taylor ("Old Rough and Ready") was the beloved military hero of the Mexican War, well known for his taciturn nature. According to contemporary accounts, at a critical moment in the battle, General Taylor uttered the sparse words in the caption, which thwarted an advance by General Santa Anna's soldiers. Although technically the battle was a draw at the end of the day, Santa Anna elected to retreat southward, allowing Taylor to claim the first major victory of the war. The slogan "A Little More Grape, Captain Bragg" became part of General Taylor's successful presidential campaign in 1848.

hoping to vindicate himself for the loss of Texas ten years earlier. Again, Santa Anna would lead his nation to perdition.

Combat lasted a year and a half until the fall of 1847. American forces occupied New Mexico and California, then invaded parts of northeastern Mexico and northwest Mexico. Meanwhile, the Pacific Squadron blockaded California ports, and took control of several garrisons on the Pacific coast further south in Baja California. A second US army under General Winfield Scott captured Mexico City. As Scott's troops approached in September 1847, six teenage cadets at the national military academy located in Chapultepec Castle heroically and tragically did their best to defend the capital. According to patriotic legend, the cadets, later known as the *Niños Heroes* (child heroes) of Chapultepec, all died. According to legend, they threw themselves off the Castle's parapets rather than surrender, one wrapping his body in a Mexican flag. The Castle, as well as the rest of the capital city, fell to the Americans. But the Niños Heroes remain symbols of patriotism, and bravery in Mexico to the present day.

Despite their valor, the war ended in a victory for the United States. On February 6, 1848, the US and Mexico signed the Treaty of Guadalupe Hidalgo with the former acquiring California, Arizona, New Mexico, and the Rio Grande boundary for Texas, as well as portions of Utah, Nevada, and Colorado. This territory became known in the US as the "Mexican Cession." In 1853, as Americans came to covet more Mexican territory south of the Gila River for a railroad route, the United States negotiated a new treaty providing for the Gadsden Purchase, adding a small strip of land across New Mexico and Arizona, establishing what remains the boundary between the United States and Mexico. At the time, the acquisition of these territories seemed to many Americans to be the embodiment of Manifest Destiny and evidence of the superiority of US nationalism and purpose. Mexico, for its part, lost more than half its national territory, and Mexicans emerged with their sense of national honor and pride badly damaged.

Anecdotal evidence suggests that two words that would become crucial to understanding the US presence in Latin America emerged from the Mexican War. The first is the pejorative term "**gringo**," which purportedly came from Mexicans' hearing the American troops' singing a popular song based on a poem by Robert Burns, "Green grow the rushes, oh." The second word, is "*jingo,*" or "*jingoism,*" a word that means "belligerent nationalism." (The word "jingo" was a popular English slang word similar to "gosh" that came to mean someone with finger-snapping audacity. A famous song written in 1878 by G. W. Hunt further popularized the word's modern meaning: "We don't want to fight, but, by jingo if we do, / We've got the ships, we've got the men, we've got the money too.")

SOCIAL UPHEAVAL

The San Patricios

The Saint Patrick Battalion, or the **San Patricios**, was a mainly Irish-American battalion that fought for Mexico during the Mexican War. During the 1840s tens of thousands of Irish emigrated to the United States to escape starvation during the Great Potato Famine. They received a lukewarm welcome at best in the United States. Often stereotyped as wily drunkards, they encountered deeply rooted social, economic, and political prejudice in their new homeland. Because the military offered employment and prospects for social mobility, many Irish joined the US Army to fight in the Mexican War.

Even in the army, however, Irish-American soldiers experienced discrimination, and soon some discovered that they seemed to have more in common with Mexico (like Ireland, a poor and Catholic nation) than with the United States. In mid-1846, John Riley, an Irish-American who had left the US Army just prior to the start of the Mexican War, organized the St. Patrick Battalion, or *San Patricios*, named in honor of Ireland's patron saint. The battalion was made up mainly of Irish defectors from the US Army, determined to fight for Mexico. The San Patricios fiercely engaged American troops at the battles of Monterrey, Buena Vista, and Cerro Gordo, all of which Mexico lost.

The battle of Churubusco, in August 1847, was the San Patricios' final and most memorable fight. When Mexican troops tried to surrender, the San Patricios repeatedly tore down the white flag; they refused to lay down their arms until their ammunition ran out. Most of the San Patricios died at Churubusco, but the US Army took eighty-five of them prisoner. In September 1849, the American forces under General Winfield Scott court-martialed thirty of the San Patricios for desertion and sentenced them to death by hanging. Because their leader, John Riley, had resigned from the army before the war commenced, he could not be charged as a deserter. Nevertheless, because he had taken up arms against his country, he received two brands of a "D" on his face—the second because the first brand had been put on upside down "by mistake." While US history remembers the San Patricios, if at all, as traitors, Mexican history regards them as them heroic and patriotic martyrs to their (second) adopted country.

- Would you consider the San Patrícios heroes, traitors, or adventurers?

The Brazilian Counterexample: Unity despite Regionalism, 1822–1845

The great triumph of the Brazilian Empire was its ability to avoid the splintering that characterized the former Spanish viceroyalties. The empire's fatal flaw was the expansion of African slavery throughout its length and breadth. As in most cases, triumph and flaw were inextricably linked, for it was the awful machinery of slavery that bound the empire together and precluded separatist movements from gaining momentum. Only after the long overdue abolition of slavery in 1888—an abolition that made the empire obsolete—did Brazil inaugurate a republic. By that time, the territorial extent and integrity of the nation had been secured.

The Contours of Empire

Brazilians living during the 1820s and 1830s had grave doubts that the empire would hold together. Brazil's cautious path to independence had forestalled convulsions but also precluded satisfying resolutions. In 1822, Dom Pedro I, emperor of independent Brazil, was also the presumptive heir to the throne of Portugal, where his father reigned. In northern Brazil, Portuguese loyalists advocated the full restoration of Brazil to the Portuguese Empire, whereas other Brazilians feared that outcome. In Rio de Janeiro, meanwhile, liberal constitutionalists pressed the new emperor for representative government.

These statesmen were united in their desire for a constitution but divided about its governing principles. The most radical among them, known as the *exaltados* (exalted ones), went so far as to contemplate republicanism and the end of monarchy; but the moderates, who sought to preserve monarchy while influencing the administration through the legislature, generally prevailed. And in moments of crisis, the moderates tended to lose out to the conservatives, who defended the power of the monarch. What radicals, moderates, and conservatives had in common was that they were men of property and slave owners. Many of them were the beneficiaries of royal titles and perquisites. As a result, even professed liberals failed to question the existence of slavery before the 1850s, with a few exceptions. For the duration of the empire, limits on slave-owner power were as likely to come from the monarch himself as from liberal statesmen.

Dom Pedro I abhorred the idea of a constitution but could not resist the momentum of the 1820s, when the choice was either constitutional monarchy or republican rule. In 1824, Pedro I duly issued a constitution, a concession which itself indicated that power continued to emanate from the monarch rather than arise from the people. The document created a Senate of lifetime members chosen by the emperor from a list of three possibilities selected by the electoral assembly, and a rotating, indirectly elected Chamber of Deputies. The constitution granted the emperor Moderating Power, described as "the key to all Political organization." The Moderating Power gave the emperor the authority to enact or annul all legislative decisions at his discretion. He further held the power to name cabinet ministers, along with presidents of the various Brazilian provinces (the equivalent of governors). In theory, the constitution allowed the emperor to tame the passions of the popular will and avoid the turbulence of representative government. Under the willful Pedro I, this was a recipe for conflict. Under his careful, deliberate son, however, it provided the basis for stable governance.

The real check on the emperor's power came not from the constitution but from the weakness of the state. The imperial bureaucracy was minimal, and funds for the army and navy depended on the goodwill of provincial elites. In practice, both Pedro and his successor were beholden to these elites. For Pedro I, this meant a short and tempestuous reign. His son, Pedro II, learned the lesson and acted cautiously.

The Cisplatine War (1825–1828), fought against Argentina over the territory that would eventually become Uruguay, threatened the unity of Brazil and stretched resources thin. The death of the emperor's father, Dom João VI of Portugal, in 1826 further complicated Pedro's position. Many Brazilians feared he would use his father's death as a pretext to reunite Brazil and Portugal. For the next five years, Pedro I struggled to put these fears to rest. Hounded by liberal opponents and increasingly unpopular in the capital of Rio de Janeiro, he finally abdicated the Brazilian throne in 1831, returning to Portugal in an attempt to guarantee his daughter's succession to the Portuguese throne.

He left behind his five-year-old son as heir to the Brazilian Empire, imposing the condition that a three-person regency govern the nation until Pedro II came of age. There followed the most turbulent period in the Brazilian Empire, as competing factions sought to exert their political will. Partly in response to this upheaval, in 1835, a series of provincial revolts rocked the empire, threatening its fragmentation.

The Regency Revolts

The most radical and bloodiest of the provincial conflicts was the *Cabanagem*, which erupted in the Amazonian port city of Belém do Pará. The Amazon, then known as Great Pará, had been a separate Portuguese viceroyalty during much of the colonial period and had not yet settled equably into the Brazilian Empire. The Cabanagem, so named for its origins in the *cabanas* (shacks) of its humble participants, began with local opposition to the provincial president, an outsider appointed by the regency. In January 1835, liberal rebels assassinated the provincial president and claimed political control. The rebels began fighting among themselves, with a radical wing advocating complete separation from Brazil and a moderate wing advocating compromise. The radicals killed many of the moderates, leading to a civil war within the province.

Imperial forces reestablished control in the provincial capital of Belém by mid-1836. By then, however, rebellion had spread throughout the Amazonian river network, where increasing competition for river and forest resources had created conflicts between indigenous groups, mixed-race communities practicing subsistence fishing and gathering, and landowning elites. Members of the mixed-race subsistence communities seized the opportunity presented by the revolt to attack local elites, triggering violent retribution. Indigenous groups sought to defend their own interests in a chaotic series of conflicts. It took imperial forces another five years to impose order. By the early 1840s, thousands were dead, the mixed-race subsistence communities were devastated, and local indigenous groups had been driven further upriver. The suppression of the Cabanagem was a war of internal colonialism, as imperial forces crushed a popular, local rebellion in order to assert national control.

The January 1835 *Malê Revolt* in the northeastern port of Salvador da Bahia was short-lived but even more horrifying to the imperial government, as it struck close to the bone of slave-owning power. "**Malê**" was the Bahian term for Muslim, and African Muslim slaves planned and initiated the Malê Revolt. It was more an African revolt than a slave rebellion, as non-Muslim freed slaves of African birth joined the Muslim slaves, but Brazilian-born slaves did not. Such distinctions revealed the fault lines of slavery in Bahia, where African-born slaves and freedmen, exploiting the relative flexibility offered by urban slavery, maintained their own cultural and social networks in defiance of slave-owner proscriptions. Ironically, the Muslim slaves could read and write Arabic, while many of their Brazilian slave owners were illiterate in any language. Literacy was a luxury in nineteenth-century Bahia, whereas slave owning was nearly universal among the free population.

The revolt was more a dramatic assertion of autonomy than an attempt at mass liberation: rebels ran through the streets of the city, skirmishing with soldiers and attempting in vain to free a Muslim leader from the imperial jail. Local forces crushed the revolt within a day, but it left lingering fears in the minds of slave owners. Several other rebellions in the north and northeast in the mid-1830s heightened those fears.

A lengthy upheaval on the southern frontier, meanwhile, revealed the limits of separatist sentiment in Brazil. The *Farroupilha*, or Ragamuffin Revolt—a name that initially referred to the antimonarchical sentiments of the revolt's leaders, and was later associated with the ragged clothing worn by the rebel soldiers—was the longest and the most threatening of the provincial revolts, posing the prospect of the breakaway of Brazil's southernmost province, São Pedro do Rio Grande do Sul. In September 1835, local ranchers toppled the president of the province and demanded the end of import taxes on the salt they needed to manufacture dried beef. Rebuffed, they escalated to full-scale revolution, declaring independence from the Brazilian Empire in 1836. Their rhetoric was eloquent and inflamed, lent heat by the contributions of Italian revolutionary collaborators like Giuseppe Garibaldi. But the Ragamuffin leaders were far from radical revolutionaries. They were slave owners and ranchers, and they wanted independence without social upheaval.

The regency revolts left all factions in the capital exhausted and eager for compromise. In 1841, fifteen-year-old Pedro II was crowned and consecrated Emperor of Brazil. His coronation formally ended the regency, enabling him to suppress lingering provincial rumblings. It took five more years to hem the last Ragamuffins into an indefensible corner, forcing their final surrender, but the rebellion's separatist momentum had effectively been checked much earlier. The defeat of the Ragamuffins consolidated the rise of the conservatives, paving the way for the foundation of a Conservative Party that would shape Brazilian politics for the remainder of the empire. The Brazilian Empire now entered a period of stability and internal development.

ECONOMICS AND COMMODITIES

Domingos José de Almeida: Race and Rebellion in Nineteenth-Century Brazil

The life of Domingos José de Almeida exemplifies the complexities of race, mercantile growth, and commodity trading in early nineteenth-century Latin America. Almeida was born in 1797 in a remote diamond mining town in Minas Gerais, Brazil, the son of a poor Portuguese immigrant and a Brazilian woman of humble birth, who was herself likely the daughter or granddaughter of African slaves. As a young man, Almeida resided in the viceregal capital of Rio de Janeiro, finding employment as a shipping clerk. In 1822, at the time of Brazil's independence, he moved to Pelotas in southernmost Brazil to take advantage of the opportunities offered by the expanding cattle economy of the southern plains. Pelotas was an emerging center for the *saladeros* (salting plants like the one portrayed above), where beef was dried and salted before shipment to the capital. Most of that *charque* (beef jerky), was used for slave rations on the coffee plantations near Rio de Janeiro.

≡ **The Paysandu Saladero**

Almeida leveraged his skill as a literate clerk into a leading role in the local trade, marrying into a prominent Pelotas saladero family. By the mid-1830s he owned *saladeros* and dozens of slaves, and served as a representative in the provincial assembly. A modernizer, he invested in the region's first steam-powered cargo barge, a breakthrough in the dried-beef trade. Like many of the southern cattle barons, he resented the Brazilian Empire's taxes on salt imports, and its reluctance to tax imports of Uruguayan and Argentine dried beef. When the cattle barons rose in arms in the 1835 Ragamuffin Revolt, Almeida joined them.

He became a leader in the revolt, and in 1836 coauthored a manifesto proclaiming the separation of the "*Riograndense Republic*" from the Brazilian Empire. He subsequently served as the minister of the interior in the rebel province, administering the precarious Ragamuffin finances. The revolt complicated Almeida's trajectory as a slave owner. The Ragamuffins promised liberation for any slave who fought against the empire, but Almeida sold many of his own slaves into continued bondage to raise funds for the revolt. He used those funds to buy a printing press for the Ragamuffin newspaper, *O Povo (The People)*, which then became the foremost platform for republican sentiment in Brazil. All the while, Almeida looked out for his private interests, moving some of his slaves across the border to Uruguay in order to avoid their induction as soldiers in the rebel troops. The revolt's failure only temporarily interrupted Almeida's operations.

Almeida's life reminds us that Brazilians of African ancestry could rise to positions of political prominence but that doing so usually meant reproducing the barbarity of slavery. Republican rebels used the rhetoric of slave liberation but were not abolitionists. And in the first half of the nineteenth century, economic modernization and a vigorous political press went hand-in-hand with the expansion of slavery.

- What does Almeida's career suggest about the interaction of slavery, race, and regionalist rebellion?

The regency revolts showed that Brazil had much in common with its Spanish-American neighbors: Here, too, pronounced regionalism threatened to break apart the new nation. The empire's survival depended on its ability to appease and contain movements for regional autonomy, based always on the shared commitment of powerful Brazilians to maintaining slavery.

The Viceroyalty of La Plata Continues to Fragment, 1820s–1850s

South of Brazil, the mostly dismembered Viceroyalty of La Plata found itself in the same predicament as the other Spanish-American territorial units as it struggled to preserve its unity. Even after Bolivia and Paraguay split off during the wars of independence, the inhabitants of the La Plata basin attempted to find some commonality that would justify the unity of the remaining United Provinces of the La Plata (including what would become Uruguay). Here, geography appeared more favorable and ethnic differences more surmountable than in other parts of Spanish America. But even the more circumscribed United Provinces of La Plata, already popularly known as Argentina, were troubled by pressures that led to further fragmentation.

Argentina's Unitarians and the Federalists

Today's Argentina and Uruguay occupy a landscape of stunning beauty and diversity. From the Andean spine running south from Tucumán to Patagonia, from the high desert of the Gran Chaco in the north to the rolling **pampas** grasslands of the central provinces to the bustling port of Buenos Aires, the United Province's diverse populations and customs threatened unity. Indigenous groups such as the Charrúa in the northeast, the Wichí in the northwest, and the Ranquelche in the central provinces continued to control territory and trading routes, despite Argentine claims to dominion. The founders of the new nation did not even pretend to control territory south of the Río Salado, a mere 105 miles from Buenos Aires, labeling the lands beyond that stream as "Indigenous Dominions." This recognition of indigenous control in no way indicated respect for those people, as the expansion of the Argentine frontier at the catastrophic expense of indigenous life and autonomy would be one of the defining themes of the nineteenth-century nation. In these regards Argentina was typical of attitudes throughout the Americas, and although ethnic diversity presented challenges, it did not immediately threaten the existence of the nation.

Economic and regional tensions proved more divisive. A liberal, republican elite in Buenos Aires, who had long acquaintance with English merchants, clergy, and diplomats who lived and worked in Argentina, adopted British customs and rhetoric, while rough horsemen of the interior disdained cosmopolitanism and looked to charismatic local leaders. These tensions played out against the backdrop of one of the more striking environmental transitions in the history of the Americas. When the Spanish brought horses and cattle to the sparsely settled pampas in the colonial period, they set in motion a quadruped colonization that far exceeded human density and control. By the mid-eighteenth century, vast herds of wild horses and cattle roamed the grasslands. The fortuitous meeting of European ruminants and

American terrain created a natural resource of epic proportions. Human conflicts over the how this natural resource would be controlled and channeled determined much of Argentine history over the next century and half.

Independence accelerated the rise of the cattle economy and the distribution and settlement of frontier land. The end of Spanish dominion eliminated any restrictions on international investment in Buenos Aires, leaving the field clear for British investors and local merchants to increase the shipment of dried beef, hides, and tallow to ports throughout the Atlantic world. Sudden economic acceleration generated new pressures, contributing to military conflict and further territorial fragmentation by the end of the decade.

First to take advantage of the favorable economic context of the early 1820s were Buenos Aires's statesmen, who looked to British economic, social, and political philosophy for inspiration. They firmly believed that Argentina's best hopes lay in drafting a constitution that would make individual citizens equal before the law and encourage untrammeled merchant capital to develop the vast reaches of the interior. Foremost among these statesmen was Bernardino Rivadavia, a politician who had passed much of the wars for independence in Britain, rallying political and financial support for the United Provinces.

In Britain, Rivadavia had been strongly influenced by the philosopher Jeremy Bentham, whose ideas about everything from constitutional law to prison reform grew from a firm belief in the perfectibility of policy. In Bentham's view, and consequently in Rivadavia's, rational law could shape men and direct their actions. The new Argentina seemed to present the perfect test case for this belief: As Rivadavia drafted the first laws for the new nation, he sought to assure Bentham they were "entirely based on the unimpeachable and indisputable truths contained in your work." Following Bentham, Rivadavia advocated a central government for the entire nation. Adopting this principle of unitary government as their standard, Rivadavia and his allies became known as the Unitarians.

To local authorities in the provinces, accustomed to rallying men on horseback through a vigorous but carefully calibrated combination of coercion, persuasion and negotiation, the Unitarians were offensive. The provincial leaders believed that law emerged from customs and was best kept local. Their belief in a loose federation of locally-governed provinces made them Federalists, although their politics were more practical than ideological. They resented the political authority and rational planning of the Unitarians in the capital and wanted to determine their own course.

As long as the economic boom lasted, the Unitarians held the upper hand. Rivadavia seized the moment to distribute millions of acres of land through *emphyteusis*, the temporary leasing of public land. Rental rates were intentionally low, with the goal of making land productive and facilitating exports rather than raising direct revenue for the government. Merchant families of Buenos Aires, unable to compete with more efficient British commercial firms newly established in the capital, snapped up these emphyteusis leases, diversifying their operations.

The Unitarian heyday did not last. London experienced an economic crisis in the Panic of 1825–1826, partly precipitated by the failure of speculative investments elsewhere in Latin America. British investors went bankrupt while others withdrew their capital from Argentina. To exacerbate matters, the United Provinces found themselves embroiled in an international war. The region known as the **Banda Oriental**, or Eastern Shore, across the Río de la Plata estuary from Buenos Aires, had been a zone of Portuguese and Spanish conflict for centuries. In 1820, first the Portuguese king and then his successor Pedro I annexed the Banda Oriental and renamed it *Cisplatina*, to the dissatisfaction of local Spanish-speaking leaders, who saw no benefit in paying fealty to a Brazilian emperor. In 1825, these local leaders allied with compatriots across the estuary and rebelled against Brazilian control.

The ensuing **Cisplatine War** (1825–1828) tested the newly independent nations of Brazil and Argentina. The Brazilian Empire, the larger and wealthier power, was preoccupied by regional conflicts in the north and could not direct the weight of its resources to its southern frontier. In the United Provinces, the war initially played into Rivadavia's hands, justifying his desire for a strong national executive rather than a confederation of provincial governors. As a result, early in 1826, Rivadavia was elected the first president of Argentina. But the cost of the war threw his plans into disarray, pushing his constitutional government toward authoritarian control. In 1827, abandoned by his own party and hounded by the opposition, Rivadavia relinquished the presidency.

The British stepped in to mediate a truce in the Cisplatine War. Under its terms, the Banda Oriental became the independent nation of Uruguay, a buffer zone between the regional powers of Argentina and Brazil. For Uruguay, independence was neither the beginning nor the end of conflict, as the small nation would be torn by civil war for the next three decades. In Argentina, Rivadavia's renunciation led to a period of instability and bloody conflict between Unitarians and Federalists. Only the rise to national power of the strongest Federalist, Juan Manuel de Rosas, in 1830, would bring stability that prevented further splintering of Argentina.

Buenos Aires versus the Provinces; Rosas versus Sarmiento

Born into the provincial criollo landowning elite, Juan Manuel de Rosas played no significant part in the struggle for independence but seized the opportunities it created. In the vanguard of the expanding cattle economy, he amassed estates and served as the agent for similar acquisitions by kinsmen and allies. Much of this land was carved from the "indigenous dominions" south of the Río Salado, and Rosas's success in negotiating with key indigenous leaders and pushing back those who refused to negotiate earned him a reputation as a capable leader. His successful management of vast estates, in turn, became the basis for his administrative strategy. As both commander and landowner, Rosas emphasized hierarchy, loyalty, and the fulfillment of obligations, backed by unstinting use of force.

In the turbulent aftermath of Rivadavia's resignation from his presidency, Rosas parlayed his growing reputation into a post as the militia commander of the province of Buenos Aires. This strengthened his power without changing its nature; the provincial militia, like the crew of gaucho cowboys on Rosas's estates, functioned more as a voluntary cavalry than as a regular army. Its members followed Rosas because he never failed to provide for them.

Late in 1829, Rosas marched on the capital and seized political control. In his own view, his actions were necessary and inevitable: "Society was in a state of utter dissolution.... The inevitable time had arrived when it was necessary to exercise personal influence on the masses to re-establish order, security and laws." The Buenos Aires House of Representatives capitulated, electing Rosas governor of the province and granting him "extraordinary powers." Aside from a brief interregnum from 1832 to 1835, when he ruled through a figurehead leader, Rosas remained governor until 1852. He eliminated the office of president as a symbol of his rejection of the Unitarian national project, but no one doubted he was the most powerful individual in the country.

≡ **A Gaucho in Argentina.** Gauchos (cowboys) worked on the great haciendas south and west of Buenos Aires for much of the nineteenth century. For the Argentine writer and president (1868–1874) Domingo Faustino Sarmiento, the **gauchos** represented the barbarism of the provinces, a violent people who need to be civilized by the European elites of Buenos Aires. Ironically, gauchos became Argentina's national symbol in large part because of José Hernández's heroic epic poem, "Martín Fierro." This somewhat romanticized image captures the gaucho's costume and bearing. This gaucho wears a belt around his waist with coins attached to it, representing his accumulated life savings to use when he is too old to work.

As governor of Buenos Aires, Rosas not only functioned as dictator of the province but also determined Argentina's international relations and exercised a chokehold on its vital overseas commerce. He used these powers to reward his followers and punish enemies. He ended the practice of emphyteusis, instead selling public lands at a bargain to allies. This led to a land rush on the southern frontier in areas cleared by the violent eviction of indigenous groups. Vast estates ruled by staunch Rosistas soon dominated the interior. The free range once roamed by wild cattle and autonomous herdsmen began to disappear.

Rosas insisted on expressions of loyalty, such as the display of his portrait in all public buildings and churches. He sponsored the public festivities of his followers, including the Afro-Argentine dockworkers of Buenos Aires, and received in turn their pledges of service. Young women from Rosista families wore red ribbons in their hair; young men wore red kerchiefs, the color of the blood running in the Buenos Aires stockyards. The enemy Unitarians wore sky blue, suggesting their high-minded political theories. While these early manifestations of propaganda were minimal in comparison to the image-making of twentieth-century dictators, they were immediately indicative of adherence in 1830s Argentina.

Those who refused to adhere suffered the consequences. Rosas deployed a band of enforcers and secret police known as the *mazorca* to enforce his rule. The term initially referred to a corn cob, and was applied to Rosas's enforcers to indicate that they were as close and inseparable as kernels of corn on the cob. Like many tyrants, Rosas loved the law but held himself above it. He forcefully rejected the prospect of any binding national constitution but deftly used individual laws to bolster his own power and persecute rivals.

He was, consequently, the scourge of the committed Unitarians, who continued to espouse individual equality before the law. But Rosas effectively marginalized the principled opposition by enriching the export sector. The Buenos Aires elite and their British peers may not have liked his manners, but they benefited from his economic strategy, which proscribed international commerce through any port other than Buenos Aires. Under Rosas, the capital and its connection to overseas trade grew indispensable to the national economy.

When decisive opposition to Rosas finally emerged, it came not from the Unitarians in the capital but from rivals in the interior, who overthrew him in 1852. A new generation of Unitarians opened the Paraná and Uruguay rivers to international commerce, and restored the office of the presidency. Rosas fled into exile, but he had already left his profound mark on the nation. The cattle economy would remain Argentina's lifeblood for most of the next century.

Rosas's Unitarian opponents were not silent during his long rule. The intellectual and writer Domingo Faustino Sarmiento went into exile in Chile, and authored the most stinging refutation of all that Rosas represented. In 1845 Sarmiento published his masterpiece, *Civilization and Barbarism: The Life of Juan Facundo Quiroga*, translated into English under the title *Life in the Argentine Republic in the Days of the Tyrants*. The book contrasted the enlightened, cultured city of Buenos Aires to with the benighted countryside, plagued by barbaric ignorance and ruffians like

Facundo, its title character. Facundo was not a fictional character, but a real caudillo, one whose ruthless tactics Sarmiento had witnessed in action. But Sarmiento described him as an archetype, manifestation of a political illness plaguing the nation. And he made similarities between Facundo and Rosas transparently clear. Sarmiento's book offered one of the clearest descriptions and denunciations of caudillo rule in nineteenth century Latin America, and remains among the best-known works of Latin American literature.

Regionalism and the Demise of the UPCA, 1830s–1840s

The forces of regionalism also plagued the United Provinces of Central America (UPCA) following its declaration of independence from Mexico. As in the Andean countries, the physical geography and the absence of effective systems of transportation and communication contributed to the tendency of the UPCA to disaggregate. In addition, Central Americans found cultural ways to distinguish themselves from one another. As Sarmiento wrote in the mid-nineteenth century, "The South American republics have all, more or less, passed through the propensity to decompose into small fractions, attracted by an anarchical and rash aspiration to a ruinous, dark independence. [But] Central America has made a sovereign state of every village."

Growing Tensions in the UPCA

In the years following the independence of the Central American states, two key factors led to the growing drive for regional autonomy that ultimately resulted in the UPCA's dissolution. First, regional elites had differing visions of what served their best interests; and second, provincial capitals competed among themselves for supremacy. Central America nevertheless asserted its independence with several advantages over Mexico and South America. It achieved independence bloodlessly, because none of the battles for independence were fought in its territory; its relative isolation meant that it could avoid much outside influence or interference during its early years; and its small but powerful governing elites were bound by common linkages of family, power, and influence. Yet within only a few years, Central America succumbed to the same centrifugal forces that broke apart the former viceroyalties of South America and Mexico.

From the beginning, the UPCA shared a common problem with the disparate regions of Mexico and South America. Like those regions, the UPCA struggled with redefining a common locus of sovereignty in a way that could hold together

The United Provinces of Central America

Gulf of Mexico

YUCATÁN
(1842)

MEXICO

BELIZE
(1834)
LOS ALTOS
(1838)
IZABAL
(1840)

SOCONUSCO
(1824)
GUATEMALA
(1823)
HONDURAS
(1823)

EL SALVADOR
(1823)
NICARAGUA
(1823)

Caribbean Sea

*PACIFIC
OCEAN*

COSTA RICA
(1823)

PANAMA

0   300 Miles

0   300 Kilometers

≡ **MAP. 2.3**

distant communities. Citizens of the republic had no sense of being part of a national "imagined community," and shared little beyond a common language, religion, and colonial heritage (and not even that in parts of Guatemala, where the dominant Maya population maintained an entirely separate tradition of languages and culture). Instead, they thought of their community in terms of the "*patria chica*," or small country. Ordinary people's allegiances formed around family, community, and regional loyalties rather than around an amorphous "nation," about which they had little or no understanding or social investment.

Furthering this idea of regionalism and localism, the Spanish colonial system had considered urban municipalities as sovereign units and administrative centers. These municipalities also constituted religious, social, and economic units that had real cultural meaning and resonance for the people who lived within them. Yet language, religion, and heritage alone *could* have been enough to create a national consolidation among the provinces had there been the social and political will to do so on the part of regional elites. But there was not. Costa Rica provides an excellent example of this phenomenon.

During the colonial period, Costa Rica had rested at the periphery of the periphery: It was the most remote province in continental New Spain. The journey by oxcart from Costa Rica to the regional capital of Guatemala, then to the viceregal capital in Mexico City, and beyond that to Spain could take many months. In an era when no news, goods, people, or services could travel faster than a person on horseback, this isolation sealed colonial Costa Rica's fate. Although Columbus was so inspired by its physical beauty that he had christened it with its charming name (literally, "Rich Coast"), Costa Rica did not, from a Spanish perspective, live up to its moniker. The territory was short on the sorts of fungible natural resources (such as gold, silver, or dye stuffs) that lured Spaniards to other regions; and the indigenous population was small and sufficiently dispersed that they did not readily conform to Spanish labor systems. Finally, the hot, disease-ridden tropical climate (at least in the lowlands) further discouraged Spanish immigration.

These factors, combined with its location at the virtual "ends of the earth," made Costa Rica attractive to a different sort of Spanish immigrant than more popular destinations in Latin America. Although, as in other parts of the Americas, there were some large estates and elite landholders in control of servile labor in Costa Rica during its colonial period, most settlers to the region were neither elite nor wealthy. Instead, Spanish immigrants to Costa Rica tended to be content to live in small, homogeneous communities and till the soil, generally without benefit of forced labor. Spanish settlements were clustered in Costa Rica's narrow but lush *meseta central*, its central valley.

By 1824, the year of the separation of the UPCA from Mexico, the total population of Costa Rica was only around 50,000 people, scattered about twenty-one small towns and villages. This reality helped to create Costa Rica's "myth of the yeoman farmer": the genesis of a sense of Costa Rican exceptionalism, based in egalitarian community cooperation, political moderation, democratic values, and, to some extent, a certain pride in its "whiteness," due to its small indigenous and African-descendent population. The people, history, and customs of Costa Rica, in short, were different from those of the other Central Americans, providing little basis for a sense of patriotism or allegiance to the UPCA.

The Collapse of the Union

Because of such provincial diversity, the founders of the UPCA established a form of government in which the regional governors and regional elites wielded more influence in their provinces than did the national government. The national government's weakness, its mishandling of a cholera outbreak, and internal policy disputes led in March 1837 to a series of rebellions breaking out in Guatemala's western highlands. These forces eventually coalesced under the leadership of a **ladino** (the Central American word for mestizo) a non-elite military leader named Rafael Carrera. Carrera, by uniting the disparate groups of rural ladinos

THE ENVIRONMENT

The 1837 Cholera Epidemic

In late 1836 or early 1837, an epidemic of *cholera morbus* spread from southern Mexico via Belize into the highlands of Guatemala, the most densely populated and most indigenous area of the province. Cholera is a highly contagious bacterial gastrointestinal ailment usually transmitted by eating food or drinking water contaminated by the feces of an infected person. In the era before potable water, modern latrines, or antibiotics, untreated cholera could kill a formerly healthy human being within a matter of hours; an epidemic could kill large numbers of people in a very short time. Death from cholera is ghastly; the patient experiences fatal dehydration after severe diarrhea and vomiting.

Because the epidemic struck Mexico before it came to Guatemala, the chief-of-state Mariano Gálvez had prepared for the crisis by implementing a series of public health measures designed to reflect the most modern epidemiological theories of the day. He ordered the creation of **cordons sanitaires** (sanitary barriers) to quarantine infected areas, and mandated that the bodies of victims not be buried in churches or under the floors of homes (as was the Mayan custom), but that they be cremated or interred in new public cemeteries, a measure that violated both Maya and Catholic beliefs. Because the disease vectors of cholera were not well understood at the time, the government, equating indigenous lifestyles with the spread of the disease, also forbade the consumption of "Indian" foods and drinks such as chocolate and homemade alcohol. Ironically, this decree left only water, the actual source of cholera infection, for people to drink.

Although Gálvez's efforts were well intentioned, they did little to staunch the flow of the disease. They did much to alienate the local population, however, who saw the modern public health measures as heretical and hostile to their way of life. When government officials tried to add medicine to drinking water systems, people believed the state was trying to poison them. When the epidemic continued to spread unabated, many came to see cholera as divine retribution for Gálvez's hostility against the Catholic Church. In later years, Liberal historians accused Catholic priests of encouraging this belief in order to undermine Gálvez. The cholera epidemic hit Maya populations particularly hard, exacerbating the displacement they had already suffered under Liberal rule. The epidemic struck most harshly in the Maya highlands, rather than in the *ladino* (nonindigenous) towns, giving the epidemic a logic of its own, one that helped to define and represent new racial identities in the new nation.

- How does a natural disaster like an epidemic produce a logic of its own that affects social and political conditions?

and indigenous people opposed to the government into a formidable but informal "army," would ultimately topple the Liberal president Mariano Gálvez's government and bring Conservative rule to Guatemala in 1838. By the middle of the same year, anti-Liberal revolts had broken out from Guatemala to Costa Rica.

Carrera's revolt, known as the "war of la Montaña," met with quick success. Early in 1838, his forces took Guatemala City, and by March of that year, the province withdrew from the UPCA. By 1840, all of the provinces had seceded from the union as Central America fragmented into five small states: Guatemala, El Salvador, Honduras, Nicaragua, and Costa Rica. The failure of union was complete. In the words of a Guatemalan statesman, Juan José de Aycinena, "Our pueblos did not present the aspect of a kingdom ruled by a unitary government, but of many factions dislocated with no unity of center."

Physical Geography and Popular Culture in Mexico, 1820s–1850s

Throughout Latin America, the vibrant variety of popular cultures, in large measure the consequence of physical geography within a given country, reflects the historical significance of regionalism. In Mexico, for example, dynamic and diverse regional cultures emerged even before the colonial period. Not surprisingly, under both Aztec and Maya rule, and during the Spanish colonial administration, these geographical circumstances encouraged a kaleidoscope of cultures to emerge. Isolation allowed regions to create unique forms of music, dance, art, and cuisine.

The state of Jalisco in western Mexico gave birth to mariachi music, for example, which bears an indigenous name but evolved during the nineteenth century to include European stringed instruments and later added the trumpets for which mariachis are so well known today. Mariachi band members wear the regionally popular **charro** (cowboy) outfits with wide-brimmed sombreros also associated with Jalisco. Jalisco also was the source of the famed Mexican hat dance, a courtship dance condemned by the Church in colonial times as morally offensive. In this expression of popular culture, men wear their charro outfits while their partners dress in a white blouse and an embroidered skirt. The dance becomes increasingly flirtatious as the rhythm of the music intensifies. Farther north, in the former Mexican province of Texas, these same musical elements during this period fused with the instruments and styles of German and Czech immigrants to the region, specifically the use of the accordion, which brings characteristic brio to both Tejano and northern Mexican ranchero music.

The popular culture of Veracruz has very different origins. Because this coastal state housed

≡ **La Coca Performing the Jarabe, the Mexican Hat Dance.** Mexican popular culture, whether food, music, dance, or plastic arts, varies tremendously from region to region, which prompted one early historian to title his book *Many Mexicos*. This photograph depicts a woman preparing to do the famous romantic courtship "Hat Dance" typical of the state of Jalisco. In the more circumspect nineteenth century, the hat initially separated the dancing couple, thereby maintaining the proprieties. (The Church still saw fit to forbid the dance as too salacious). As the dance became more lively and the couple's movements more flirtatious, the woman picked up the hat to demonstrate her interest in the man. At the end, the woman held the hat in front of the couple's faces, behind which they were presumably kissing. During the course of the nineteenth century the dance became so popular that Mexican's ultimately recognized it as their national dance.

the port through which thousands of African slaves entered Mexico, Veracruz was home to a diverse population. African influences played a vital role in local cuisine. The popular seafood dish, red snapper *a la veracruzano*, flavored the fish with a delicious tomato sauce, made piquant with spices and flavors familiar to African palates. The state's traditional music, which features a harp, violins, and guitar, sounds quite different from that of Jalisco. Veracruz's unique dance, the Dance of the Flyers (*voladores*), had indigenous origins, probably as a tribute to the god of rain. Five participants climb a 100-foot pole, and while one of them plays a flute and a drum, the other four slowly twirl on ropes tied to their feet as they descend headfirst to the ground. During the nineteenth century, foreign travelers commonly remarked on the remarkable diversity of regional popular cultures in Mexico.

Regionalism and Caudillos, 1820s–1870s

The presence of military figures, often the former heroes of independence, would further complicate the process of creating viable nation-states in the early republican period. Most of these informal military leaders operated on the regional level, but the more skilled eventually became players on the national stage. For the elite politicians, these men were wild cards who could provide either great benefits, such as law and order, or cause chaos.

Characteristics of a Caudillo

Caudillos (strongmen-politicians), political leaders unique to Spain's former colonies, exacerbated Latin America's tendency toward regionalism in the early nineteenth century. First elevated to prominence as leaders of impromptu military forces during the wars of independence, caudillos relied on their patria chica as a regional base, one that provided them with recruits and supplies in good times and a place of refuge in bad ones.

Caudillo armies made important contributions to the patriots during the wars of independence because they were less costly to maintain than formally enlisted soldiers. Caudillo armies subsisted on livestock and foodstuffs they commandeered during campaigns. But caudillo armies proved less reliable than regulars, as they sometimes refused to leave their familiar surroundings to wage war elsewhere. Although caudillo armies cost less initially, once in power they often proved very expensive. With the caudillo's success came expectations on the part of his followers that he would use his powers of patronage to reward them with jobs and opportunities for corruption.

The age of caudillos, which lasted roughly until the 1870s, was an era of self-proclaimed heroes who often favored their own self-interest above the good of the nation. More interested in personal relationships than in ideology, caudillos proved to be uncertain allies for any regime. Frequently changing sides even in the middle of a civil war, caudillos valued loyalty more than abstract theoretical platforms. To woo followers, successful caudillos relied on *personalismo* (charisma). Gregarious, cruel, and ruthless in turn, the larger-than-life personalities of the caudillos astonished foreign visitors more accustomed to staid politicians in their own countries.

Generally, the elite found caudillos useful. In an age of continuous civil war, caudillos promised temporary stability. Because caudillos often identified with elite interests, they defended property rights and prevented social or racial uprisings, while at the same time using their charisma to maintain their personal relationship with their followers. Because caudillos rarely paid attention to constitutional term limits, they tended to believe in **continuismo**—their right to remain in office indefinitely. Such a belief made presidential succession difficult to predict, leading to further instability. Caudillos were usually either driven out of office or killed by rivals.

There were some exceptions to this broad-brush description of caudillos. A few caudillos, sometimes described as folk caudillos, fought for policies favoring their constituents rather than the elite. Some countries experienced variants on the caudillo theme, or avoided them altogether. Chile, for example, had little experience with caudillos. Liberated very quickly, Chile had a single leader of independence, Bernardo O'Higgins, who might have qualified as a caudillo, but he so botched his term of office that his countrymen exiled him and plunged the country into a brief ideological civil war before achieving stability under a constitutional government. In short, caudillismo, like so many other aspects of life in Latin America, cannot be reduced to a simplistic formula. A closer look at three caudillos and their careers will provide a better understanding of both the general characteristics of caudillos and demonstrate the varieties of the caudillo experience.

José Antonio Páez

Unlike Simón Bolívar, who was born of privilege, José Antonio Páez came from a humble immigrant background. Accused as a teenager of killing a man, he fled from his small village near the coast for the interior of Venezuela, where he worked as a herder under the supervision of an enslaved overseer. He honed his skills as a cowboy on the llanos, or plains of the interior. Before the wars for independence broke out, he got married and ran a few head of cattle on the open range. Much of the llanos remained unfenced, and cowboys retained significant autonomy. When economic times got bad, Páez occasionally engaged in banditry, typical for his time and

≡ **José Antonio Páez in Arturo Michelena's Painting.** *About Face* Páez was one of Venezuela's quintessential early nineteenth-century caudillos. Raised on the llanos, Páez won recognition as one of Simón Bolívar's most important collaborators during the wars for independence, known for his skills on horseback and with a lance. This painting portrays one of Páez's best-known heroic episodes, where he single-handedly turned his retreating troops around by the sheer force of his personality, and led them to victory against the royalist forces. Military prowess proved a vehicle that allowed such men to achieve political power in the postindependence era.

place. In short, Páez acquired sufficient life experiences in his formative years to be able to take advantage of the opportunities for personal advancement offered during Venezuela's war for independence and to establish his patria chica in the llanos.

Páez rose to prominence during the latter stages of the wars, aligning his cowboy followers with Bolívar's troops in 1817. Páez allegedly could outride, out-rope, and outswim any other llanero. In battle, he had more skill with the lance, the typical weapon of the llaneros, than any of his compatriots. Coupled with his physical gifts, his abilities as a natural leader enabled him to take command of the mixed-race cowboys on the western llanos and turn them into an effective cavalry unit. In short, he exuded *personalismo*. Páez's troops played a key role at the battle of Carabobo, which liberated Venezuela. Because of his leadership in this decisive victory, Bolívar named Páez as the commander-in-chief of the Venezuelan forces when the

Liberator left his homeland to free Ecuador, Peru, and Bolivia. Over the next few years, Páez drove the remaining royalists out of Venezuela, acting virtually autonomously from the government of Gran Colombia.

Bolívar divided Gran Colombia into three departments in 1821, assigning one to each of the principal caudillos. By 1827, Páez had outmaneuvered his rivals and had become the national caudillo, in part because he cleverly created a multiclass alliance with the *hacendados*, merchants, and politicians of the center-north, the location of Venezuela's cacao and coffee plantations. With the power to redistribute land seized from royalist sympathizers, Páez deeded most of this land to his friends who were high-ranking military officers, while keeping a substantial share for himself. In addition to cattle haciendas, Páez owned cacao plantations and coffee **fincas** (farms).

Like almost all caudillos, Páez solidified his relations with the elite by reducing export taxes. This made Venezuelan cacao and coffee competitive on the world market. To be worthy of his new status, he overcame his illiteracy, learning to use a fork and knife in order to host state dinners. Yet he retained his common touch. Páez loved cockfights, typically a pastime of rural peoples, where he could socialize with his former soldiers. Páez's average followers gained few tangible rewards but they remained loyal to him.

As president (1831–1835, 1839–1843), Páez offered the country stability. Even when out of office, Páez dominated his puppet presidents (1835–1839, 1843–1847) and continued to serve as an enforcer for law and order. He also provided some worthwhile benefits for the nation: founding primary schools, creating the National Library, abolishing the slave trade, and declaring religious tolerance. To save money, he reduced the size of the army in 1843 to five hundred men, because by then he rarely had to use force against his rivals. Overconfident, he refused a third term in 1847 and agreed to allow the second most important caudillo in the country to become president. This maneuver backfired and Páez soon found himself exiled. For most of the remainder of his life, he lived comfortably in New York City, dying there in 1873.

José Gaspar Rodríguez de Francia

The republic of Paraguay is a landlocked nation inhabited by the indigenous Guaraní and initially settled by Jesuit and Franciscan missionaries who congregated indigenous inhabitants into semiautonomous colonies called "*reducciones*." Its independence came about as the result of the May 1810 revolution of Buenos Aires, when Argentina separated from Spain. Conservative criollo leaders in the Paraguayan capital, Asunción, declared that they would remain loyal to Spain, though they hoped to retain good relations with the free port of Buenos Aires, Paraguay's lifeline to the outside world. When Buenos Aires responded by sending five thousand troops to control the province, Liberal criollos took over the capital and declared Paraguay's independence in May 1811. After two years of semi-chaotic Liberal rule, José Gaspar Rodríguez de Francia seized control of the government. Francia, who had no confidence in democracy, named himself "Supreme Dictator of the Country" in 1814. Two years later he assumed a new title: "Supreme Perpetual Dictator" for life (*El Supremo*, for short), an apt title he retained until his death in 1840.

Francia was a unique caudillo, and his iron-fisted control of Paraguay established a long tradition of dictatorship for the new country. Francia was an intellectual, the product of an elite family. He first studied for the priesthood, earning advanced degrees in theology and philosophy, but eventually became a lawyer. Francia became selectively enamored with the new political and social theories of the Enlightenment and the French Revolution, especially the French philosopher Rousseau's idea of a social contract, which suggested that humans cede their natural rights to a leader or government in return for their mutual preservation, but this "contract" between governed and government is valid only so long as the authority rules for the larger interests of the governed.

Francia's rule was despotic but populist, as he dismantled the vestiges of the Spanish-imposed caste system in Paraguay. After unearthing an 1820 plot to assassinate him, Francia arrested and executed nearly two hundred Paraguayans. He came from Paraguay's elite but did not trust his peers. To weaken them, he abolished municipal governments in the larger towns, promoted state-operated cattle ranches and state commerce, and took over such traditional functions of the Roman Catholic Church as collecting tithes, leasing out Church-owned lands, and paying clergy's salaries. He also established a brutal secret apparatus called the *pyragües* (hairy feet, in Guaraní) to enforce loyalty to him throughout the country.

Paraguayan Woman Making ñandutí. Regionalism also expressed itself in the production of unique handicrafts. Here a Paraguayan woman is engaged in producing fine embroidered lace, known locally as ñandutí, which means "spiderweb" in Paraguay's indigenous language Guarani. The lacework is designed on a spoke-like structure, often with floral patterns. Paraguay's enforced isolation during the dictatorship of the caudillo José Gaspar Rodríguez de Francia contributed to its ability to retain a number of its cultural attributes such as ñandutí and the language of Guarani.

Francia is perhaps best remembered for his concerns for security. Internally, he suppressed banditry, became a protector of indigenous people and their still widely spoken language (even by the nonindigenous), and paid careful attention to government expenditures to make sure the new nation would not lose its financial independence. Most famously, he sealed the borders of Paraguay against Argentina in 1819 and again in 1823 and 1840, imprisoning foreigners who strayed across the frontier, and redirecting Paraguay's trade when Argentina's caudillos attempted to bully Paraguay into reassuming its subservience to Buenos Aires.

Francia's long twenty-four years of rule were dictatorial and often ruthless. But his government was also stable and efficient, and, overall, ordinary people (if not elites) benefited from El Supremo's paternalistic, populist rule. By the time of his death in 1840, Paraguay was firmly independent and prosperous, thanks to years of isolation and dictatorship. As the Scottish essayist Thomas Carlyle wrote of Paraguay shortly after El Supremo's death, "Liberty of private judgment, unless it kept its mouth shut, was at an end in Paraguay . . . [but] Dr. Francia, we may conclude, at least, was not a common man, but an uncommon one."

Antonio Abad Huachaca

Far more obscure than either Páez or Francia, Peru's Antonio Abad Huachaca exemplifies a local caudillo, or *cabecilla*, who also qualifies as a folk caudillo because he represented the interests of the poor indigenous people of his patria chica rather than the elite. An illiterate indigenous man, Huachaca earned his living as a muleteer who transported coca from small haciendas and farms to the city of Ayacucho. (Although coca is today the base commodity from which cocaine is

TIMELINE

1814–1840
Francia declares Paraguay's autonomy and isolates it from Argentina

1819–1830
Rise and fall of Simón Bolívar's Gran Colombian state

1821–1831
Pedro I rules Brazil as an empire

1822–1823
Iturbide's empire in Mexico and Central America fails

1823
Central America leaves Mexico and forms the United Provinces of Central America

1826–1829
Rivadavia and the Unitarios dominate Argentina

1829
The Cisplatine War creates the nation of Uruguay

1830–1845
Caudillo José Ar Páez rejects Gra Colombia and d nates Venezuela

produced, Andean people have used coca for many generations to alleviate hunger pangs and fatigue.)

During his travels, Huachaca befriended many people of various classes in the Huanta district of the highlands. He joined the royalist army, and before the battle of Ayacucho (1824), its commander, the viceroy, informally awarded him the title of "general." As a result of this honor, Huachaca commanded respect. Huachaca was one of the leaders of a multiclass revolt that lasted from 1825 to 1828, vainly seeking to restore Spain's rule in Peru. He fought in part because he and the people of Huanta resented the huge fine the patriot government imposed upon them for siding with King Ferdinand. After the revolt failed, Huachaca disappeared into the high sierra.

He reemerged in the 1830s, again defending the interests of the popular classes. Asked by a Liberal president for assistance to fend off a military coup, Huachaca's forces helped the former retain control over southern Peru. As a reward, the caudillo demanded that the government eliminate some taxes that indigenous people paid and permit him to retain others collected locally for use by the municipality. The caudillo protected his followers from greedy landlords by forcing those landlords to pay their workers a decent wage. Given the chaotic state of Peruvian politics in the 1830s, the president could only agree, essentially allowing Huanta to become an autonomous district in the sierra under Huachaca's control. During the troubled times of the Peru-Bolivian Confederation, Huachaca and his indigenous volunteers took up arms in defense of Santa Cruz's government in exchange for the continuation of the district's special privileges. Huachaca asked only that he be named the justice of the peace of his home town. Although the Confederation ultimately lost and any further trace of Huachaca disappeared from the historical record, his career demonstrates that at certain moments a folk caudillo and the popular classes could assert their own interests to win benefits for themselves.

1831–1841
Pedro I abdicates, Regency rules in Brazil

1835–1852
Juan Manuel Rosas returns as governor of Buenos Aires province

1836–1854
Mexico loses its northern territories

1835
Cabanagem, Malê, and Ragamuffin regional revolts in Brazil

1836–1839
The Confederation of the Andes fails

1838
The United Provinces of Central America dissolve their union

Conclusion

In the maelstrom that followed the advent of independence, the new nations of Latin America were pulled by both centripetal and centrifugal forces. The centripetal forces included the lure of the unity of the old viceroyalties and the intoxicating dream of the Liberator, Simón Bolívar, who unceasingly advocated for supra-states in the Americas. The centrifugal forces were those of regionalism, shaped by long histories of local cultural, and ethnic differences. Regionalism fostered loyalty to the patria chica, rather than the new nation. The centrifugal prevailed in the decades following independence, not only because the majority of the elite thought in terms of their parochial interests but also because caudillos had the military might to tip the scales in favor of regional solutions.

Without the phenomenon of regionalism, the modern-day countries of Paraguay, isolated by its dictator, Francia), and Uruguay (created as a result of the Cisplatine War and British intervention) would not exist. Neither would the original five Central American nations (Guatemala, Honduras, Nicaragua, El Salvador, and Costa Rica), whose elite leadership decided that each province had such individual identities that each deserved independence from the United Provinces of Central America. Even in Brazil, the one colonial entity that remained united, regionalism remained an important phenomenon. Yet regionalism does not entirely account for Latin America's general pattern of instability in the early republican era. The dominant elites and voices from the popular classes also engaged in heated debates about politics, society, the economy, and the nature of the state. Participants in these debates eventually cohered into two warring camps, the Liberals and Conservatives. Their conflict, and its variations throughout the hemisphere, are the subject of chapter 3.

KEY TERMS

Banda Oriental   81

caudillos   58

charro   88

Cisplatine War   81

continuismo   90

cordons sanitaires   87

fincas   92

gauchos   82

gringo   73

ladino   86

Malê   77

Manifest Destiny   69

pampas   79

San Patricios   74

United Provinces of Central America (UPCA)   68

Selected Readings

Adelman, Jeremy. *Republic of Capital: Buenos Aires and the Legal Transformation of the Atlantic World*. Palo Alto, CA: Stanford University Press, 2002.

Anna, Timothy. *Forging Mexico:1821–1835*. Lincoln: University of Nebraska Press, 1998.

Brown, Matthew, and Gabriel Paquette, eds. *Connections after Colonialism: Europe and Latin America in the 1820s*. Tuscaloosa: University of Alabama Press, 2013.

Dym, Jordana. *From Sovereign Village to National States: City, State and Federation in Central America, 1759–1839*. Albuquerque: University of New Mexico Press, 2006.

Grandin, Greg. *The Blood of Guatemala: A History of Race and Nation*. Durham, NC: Duke University Press, 2000.

Guardino, Peter. *Peasants, Politics, and the Formation of Mexico's National State: Guerrero, 1800–1857*. Stanford, CA: Stanford University Press, 1996.

Harris, Mark. *Rebellion on the Amazon: The Cabanagem, Race and Popular Culture in the North of Brazil, 1798–1840*. Cambridge: Cambridge University Press, 2010.

Lynch, John. *Argentine Caudillo: Juan Manuel de Rosas*. New York: Rowman and Littlefield, 2001.

Méndez, Cecilia. *The Plebian Republic: The Huanta Rebellion and the Making of the Peruvian State, 1820–1850*. Durham, NC: Duke University Press, 2005.

Needell, Jeffrey. *The Party of Order: The Conservatives, the State, and Slavery in the Brazilian Monarchy, 1831–1871*. Palo Alto, CA: Stanford University Press, 2006.

Sobrevilla Perea, Natalia. *The Caudillo of the Andes: Andrés de Santa Cruz*. Cambridge: Cambridge University Press, 2011.

Williams, John Hoyt. *The Rise and Fall of the Paraguayan Republic, 1800–1870*. Austin: University of Texas Press, 1979.

Woodward, Ralph Lee, Jr. *Central America: A Nation Divided*. Oxford: Oxford University Press, 1999.

3

First Attempts at State Formation: The Liberal-Conservative Debate, 1830–1875

Global Connections

As Latin America took its first tentative steps toward state formation in the half century after independence, other portions of the globe also experienced conflicts between liberal and conservative ideologies. Politicians and thinkers in western Europe and throughout the Americas experimented with the legacies of Enlightenment and the French Revolution, and explored new ideas of liberal reform at the same time. By the mid-nineteenth century, however, debates about constitutional governance, economic theory, and secularizing the state intensified worldwide. Conservatives initially rejected liberal proposals in their entirety. Rivalries between Conservatives and Liberals divided Latin American throughout the first decades following independence. This made the new nations vulnerable to foreign intervention, instability, and territorial loss.

In the mid-1820s, Latin America and other parts of the world became enmeshed in the first great global economic meltdown, the Panic of 1825. British bankers made speculative investments in the emerging Latin American markets, lured by the prospects of repairing and reopening mines in countries like Mexico, Peru, and Colombia as well as the likely profits to be made from investing in modern infrastructure. In the most notorious case, Gregor MacGregor, a Scot who had fought briefly for Simón Bolívar, peddled bonds in the London stock market for a nonexistent Central American province he had named Poyais (part of Honduras). Because he promised to pay bondholders a high rate of interest, nobody fact-checked Poyais's existence, to the regret of those fleeced. When the London Stock Exchange crashed in 1825, many of the newly independent Latin American nations were saddled with enormous debts that took generations to repay.

In the same decades, the Napoleonic Wars had intensified nationalism, the emotional and intellectual bond uniting a territory with a common language, customs, and historical experiences. The new ideas of nationalism and liberalism threatened dynastic empires that contained multiple ethnic groups, whether in eastern Europe (the Austro-Hungarian Empire), the Middle East (the Ottoman Empire), or East Asia (the Qing Empire of China). Attempting to preserve the Ottoman Empire, the so-called Tanzimat reforms allowed greater civil liberties to non-Turks, diminishing legal distinctions between Muslims and non-Muslims within the empire. The Qing Empire attempted to resist European influence, but following the Opium Wars had to cede Hong Kong to the British and open other ports like Shanghai to global trade.

Constitutionalism, initially rooted in western European nations such as the Netherlands, Belgium, and Switzerland, eventually influenced dynastic empires

≡ **President Ismael Montes and the Archbishop of La Paz Dedicating Bolivia's Railroad.** The debate about the relationship between the Catholic Church and the State (the national government) became the most divisive political issue of the nineteenth century. In this photograph from early twentieth-century Bolivia, the president, members of the elite, and the archbishop all joined together to demonstrate their consensus that railroad construction would benefit the nation and lead to greater prosperity. Although Liberals usually led the onslaught against the Catholic Church, in this instance the Liberal president Ismael Montes soft-pedaled any ideological differences in order to create a sense of national unity that outweighed anticlericalism.

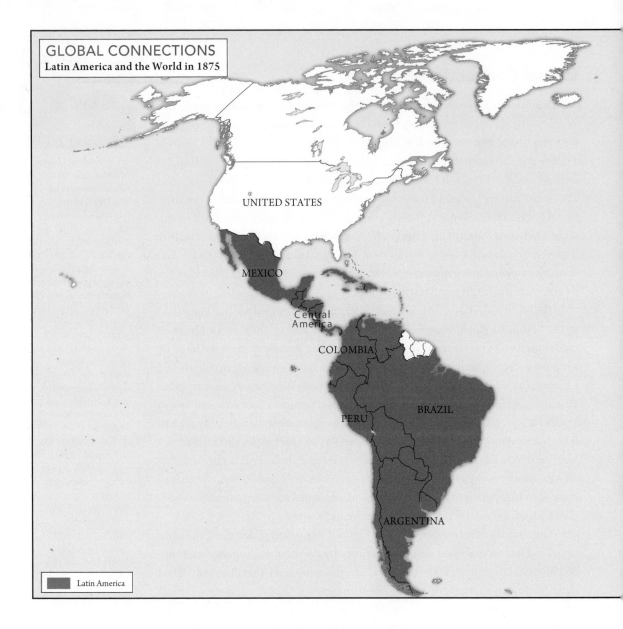

GLOBAL CONNECTIONS
Latin America and the World in 1875

UNITED STATES

MEXICO

Central
America

COLOMBIA

PERU

BRAZIL

ARGENTINA

Latin America

like Russia and others around the globe. These empires conceded limited political institutions and individual liberties to at least some of its citizens. Of all the
nonwestern nations, Japan adopted constitutionalism most wholeheartedly. Its
Constitution of 1887 formalized imperial rule, but required that the emperor
govern with the consent of an assembly of notables. This constitution granted

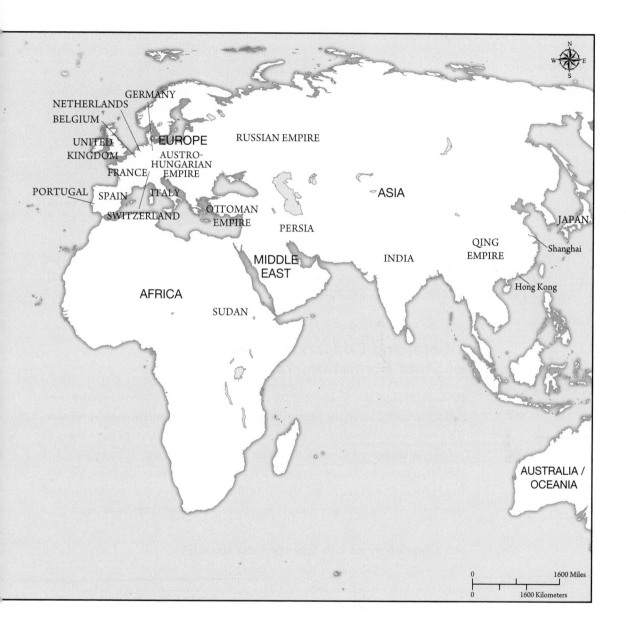

Western-style individual liberties such as the freedom of speech, assembly, and religion (although Shintoism was made the official state religion).

Many states across the globe, but especially in western Europe and the Americas, became increasingly secular during the course of the nineteenth century. Unified Germany provides an excellent example. The Iron Chancellor, Otto von Bismarck (chancellor, 1873–1890), launched the *kulturkampf*, or clash of cultures, between his secular political party and the Catholic Church. Following the lead of the United States, von Bismarck argued that Germany should not have an established church nor should the Catholic Church influence politics. But secularism was not universal. Only a small portion of the Islamic world became more secular; religion continued to play a vital role in Middle Eastern states.

Liberals and Conservatives across Latin America confronted similar issues, debating the the proper form and structure of government, the degree of civil liberties that individual citizens ought to enjoy, the economic policies likely to bring prosperity to the country, and (most divisively) the role of the Catholic Church. Although the two factions shared similar elite backgrounds and often even family ties, they ossified into ideologically opposed parties that would drive much of Latin America's political history until the 1870s. Each nation responded somewhat differently to these basic questions. Their trajectories were roughly parallel, with many idiosyncrasies and detours in each case.

Liberal and Conservative Visions of State Formation, 1830–1875

In the years around independence, elites in Latin American grouped into two competing political ideologies, liberalism and conservatism. The distinction between the two was not immediately evident, as both parties drew from the same group of people—rich, powerful, and influential property owners, who at first glance had more in common with one another than they did with the ordinary people who lived in their emerging nations. Similarity of origin, however, did not diminish and may well have intensified hostility of engagement between these two camps.

An Overview of the Competing Visions

Members of the **Liberal** parties were modernists who wished to see their young countries catapult quickly forward. (It is important to note that it was not until later that these two sets of political ideologies actually solidified into formal "parties." At first they were simply ideological alliances and tendencies). Liberals looked to European ideas for models and inspiration, and sought to emulate what they saw as the success of modern nations like France and England. They favored free trade, immigration, foreign investment, and the assimilation of the "folk" (indigenous, Afro-descendants, poor mestizos, castas) into a modern labor force. Because of their embrace of foreign models for development, Liberals often disdained the colonial Spanish inheritance. Their scorn was nowhere more evident than in their attitude toward the Catholic Church, which they believed represented the worst of the Spanish legacy. Liberals also resented the fact that popular classes often expressed greater loyalty to the Church than to the new nation.

Members of the **Conservative** parties, by contrast, sought to protect tradition and inherited order. Even after independence, many favored retaining some kind of monarchy. Failing that, they were willing to put their trust in strong, often unelected, leaders who would establish a centralized state with authority resting in the chief executive at the national capital. They expected such leaders to rely on armed forces loyal to the leader himself, rather than to the abstract nation. Conservatives wished to see, at most, a gradual transition in old colonial economic and political patterns. They viewed the great landed estates as the key to social and economic order. They viewed the Catholic Church as Spain's greatest legacy and as the institution most able to assure stability. Conservatives were generally suspicious of foreigners (especially Protestant foreigners, such as the English), and their motives for investment and political interests in the New World. They were skeptical, as well, of democracy, and clung to an ideal of a two-tiered society in which the elite made all political decisions.

In theory, Liberals favored the idea of citizen participation in government, and occasionally even full-fledged democracy. In order to permit citizens to exercise individual liberties, Liberals often embraced the new governing philosophy of federalism, devolving administrative power to subnational governments, such as states or provinces. Questions of the proper form of government, along with debates over the extent of individual liberties, mark the first and second controversies that divided Liberals and Conservatives. Because Liberals consistently believed that federalism allowed for the freest exercise of individual liberties, while Conservatives argued that centralized states should restrict citizens' liberties in order to preserve order, these two issues are treated simultaneously in the following examples of Colombia, Chile, and Ecuador.

Colombia's Liberal Experiment with Extreme Federalism

Colombia's Liberal experiment between 1861 and 1886 offers the most extreme example of the governing philosophy of federalism. Following a three-year civil war, Colombia's Liberal Party drafted the Constitution of 1863 (also known as the Rionegro Constitution) to clarify their governing principles. Like Liberals elsewhere in Latin America, the Colombian Liberals believed that sovereignty resided in the people and that the people best expressed their will through the electoral process. Colombia's well-educated Liberal Party leaders based their Constitution of 1863 on European Enlightenment doctrines propounded by liberal thinkers such as Montesquieu, Voltaire, and Adam Smith.

The Rionegro Constitution hobbled the authority of the national government for the express purpose of maximizing individual citizens' civil liberties. Presidents served short two-year terms and could not be immediately reelected. Aside from directing foreign policy, organizing the defense of the nation in the event of external aggression, and minting coins, the federal government had little authority. Only Congress could authorize sending troops to intervene in a civil war, and the Supreme Court could not strike down a state statute it deemed unconstitutional. Individuals enjoyed unlimited free speech, freedom to assemble, and freedom of religion. The constitution prohibited the death penalty and limited jail terms for any crime, however heinous, to ten years. Individuals who rebelled against their state's government, for example, were exiled, rather than imprisoned. In short, under this constitution, not only did citizens enjoy unrestricted liberties, but the nine states of Colombia were essentially sovereign and semiautonomous. The Constitution of 1863 created a system of extreme states-rights as the surest guarantee for individual liberties.

Democratic Aspects of the Rionegro Constitution

The Rionegro Constitution also encouraged each state legislature to broaden its electorate. With few exceptions, almost all nineteenth-century Latin American constitutions had restricted suffrage to male property owners (sometimes further restricted to literate male property owners) in order to guarantee elite domination of the political system. As a result, less than 5 percent of the male population elsewhere in Latin America typically was eligible to vote. Colombia's Liberals rejected this model, opening the polls to all males. Hence this government was democratic as well as republican. Newly enfranchised individuals took their responsibilities as voters seriously, as participation rates in elections during the 1860s exceeded 50 percent of eligible voters. As a result of broader-based political participation, Afro-Colombians and indigenous people won seats on municipal councils and sometimes even higher offices. The Constitution mandated frequent elections, as governors, judges, deputies, national office holders, and municipal council members all served two-year terms. The constant practice with exercising the franchise deepened the democratic process among the popular classes.

By the 1870s, however, moderate Liberals expressed doubts about the wisdom of both extreme federalism and broadly based democracy. After all, like their Conservative counterparts, most Liberal politicians hailed from the elite, and were as assiduous in their zeal to protect private property as the Conservatives. Under federalism, Colombia's economy had stagnated in the absence of a highly profitable export commodity. Permitting states to collect their own tariffs had starved the national government of revenues, hampering trade even within the nation.

Richer states invested in development projects like railroads while poorer states lagged behind. The weak national government and a dearth of serious penalties for criminal activity invited an atmosphere of lawlessness. Civil wars broke out frequently, and the poor often settled on vacant land that elites viewed as sacrosanct private property.

Like elites elsewhere, Colombia's Liberals ultimately concluded that the lower classes were ignorant and superstitious. With education, Liberals believed they might be redeemable, but the weak federalist state lacked the resources to invest in public schools. In the meantime, they were willing to relegate indigenous and Afro-Colombians to the kind of disenfranchised cheap labor force that investors found attractive. Towards the end of the nineteenth century, moderate Liberals allied with Conservatives and formed the Regeneration movement, which in 1886 replaced the Rionegro Constitution with a more centralized state.

This backlash against both federalist devolution and broad-based democracy was typical across the region. By 1875, Liberals across most of Latin America had accepted the hard lesson that only a more centralized form of government could provide the necessary unity and stability to permit a nation to modernize along the lines of western Europe and the United States.

Chile, Diego Portales, and Conservative Centralism

Chile provided the most likely proving ground for the Conservative experiment in postindependence Latin America. Its population was small (no more than 600,000), and the great majority of it was concentrated in a fertile valley folded between the Andes and the Pacific. The valley's geography facilitated the Conservative project: Spanish and mestizo society was concentrated here, while the native Mapuche indigenous population was shut out, pushed to less hospitable lands farther south and east. Through most of the nineteenth-century, Chilean elites viewed the Mapuche as an external threat. Decades would pass before the Mapuche would be included in Chilean nation-building, even on unequal terms.

At the same time, central Chile was not isolated. The port of Valparaíso, already a key node of maritime commerce, grew rapidly in importance in the decades after independence. As Peru's and Bolivia's economies faltered in the aftermath of independence, Chilean silver and copper mining prospered. Chilean agricultural production also grew in response to overseas demand, particularly from California. British merchants and engineers became a common presence in Valparaíso, in the capital of Santiago, and in the mining towns.

Given this context, those who occupied vital commercial positions stood to prosper greatly and had a strong interest in protecting stability. Diego Portales became the foremost such citizen. He rose to prominence as a businessman in the early 1820s, as a partner in a firm that held the state monopoly on the valuable commodities of tobacco and tea. But when he lost his monopoly contracts in a period of political turbulence later that decade, he faced commercial disaster, prompting him to take a stronger political role. He became the key member of a cohort that assumed power in 1830. Portales himself opted for cabinet ministries rather than the presidency, but used these positions to exercise the real power behind the administration.

Portales and his allies acted to strengthen the institutions that guaranteed commercial and social stability. They drafted the authoritarian Constitution of 1833, one that would structure Chilean politics through the nineteenth century. That document created a unitary state with a strong president who had the prerogative to serve a ten-year term. In practice, the president also held powers enabling him to control elections to make sure his friends won offices in the provinces. Portales also created a new national guard to police internal order. He reinforced the link between church and state, returning expropriated lands to the Catholic Church in return for its collaboration in upholding social order. He purged political opponents from government employment and executed those accused of conspiracy, and kept Chile's press on a short leash. Chile became the first stable, constitutional state to emerge in Spanish South America.

Portales was heavy-handed, but the institutions created under the Constitution of 1833 were neither arbitrary nor easily swayed by personal connections. The key players in Chile's state—large landowners, merchants, foreign businessmen, clergy, and the military—all approved of his policies. Above all else, his interest in commercial stability and export-oriented production (copper, silver, and wheat) allowed Chile to become the foremost economic power in Spanish South America in the early nineteenth century. Portales himself died in 1837, assassinated by a political rival. The political structure he helped create, however, endured for decades longer.

Extreme Centralism: Ecuador's Constitution of 1869

Ecuador's tangled political history began after its separation from Gran Colombia in 1830. From that moment until 1860, Liberals and Conservatives were at each other's throats, as a series of elite politicians and military figures shuttled in and out of the presidential palace. This age of chaos culminated in a destructive civil war during which the four regions of the country fought each other while Peru's caudillo, Ramón Castilla, opportunistically attempted to seize the port of Guayaquil and two adjacent provinces. In September 1860, the civilian Gabriel García Moreno rallied his conservative followers from the highlands, emerged victorious, and preserved the nation intact.

Like many other members of the elite in nineteenth-century Latin America, García Moreno dedicated his life to public service and politics. His vision for unifying the nation included road construction projects to create physical unity and a project bolstering the Catholic faith to promote cultural unity. His dynamic personality enabled him to serve two terms as president and dominate Ecuadorian politics from 1860 until 1875, when he was assassinated by a disgruntled army officer, in a conspiracy with others among García Moreno's liberal opponents. While briefly acting as Ecuador's diplomatic envoy to Chile, García Moreno became enamored of Diego Portales's centralist Constitution of 1833. At the beginning of his second presidential term (1869–1875), García Moreno and his fellow Conservatives drafted a new constitution heavily influenced by the Chilean document.

Overall, the Constitution of 1869 expressed conservative nationalist principles intended to create order and stability under a strong president who held office for six years, with the possibility for reelection. The legislature scarcely met (only a few weeks every other year), and when it was not in session the president could rule by decree. Although the constitution permitted personal liberties like free speech, freedom of the press, and freedom of assembly, the president could suspend those liberties at any time to preserve order.

While on paper the constitution created a unitary state, the rugged topography of the Andes impeded this ideal. García Moreno created Ecuador's first functional bureaucracy in order to overcome this challenge. His reputation for toughness, even cruelty, and his willingness to punish political opponents allowed him to insist that all governors, *jefes políticos* (essentially the heads of counties), municipal officials, bishops, and road and school inspectors regularly send him extensive reports. He had the work ethic to read and analyze this information, the firmness to make decisions based on this data, and the reputation for ruthlessness to make certain his orders were followed.

For García Moreno and other modern Conservative nation-builders, the centralized state was not an end unto itself, but rather a means toward helping Ecuador to progress materially. But the momentum of centralization led to authoritarian

≡ **Gabriel García Moreno.** Gabriel García Moreno served two terms as Ecuador's president, and even when out of office, he and his fellow Conservatives dominated politics. His portrait shows him to be a stern individual (his Liberal opponents would say ruthless) who used strong methods (exiling many Liberals) to centralize the government and bring order to one of South America's most unstable nations. García Moreno pursued stability as a means of modernizing Ecuador by increasing spending on Church-run primary education (even for girls) and building the first viable highway linking Quito to Guayaquil.

excesses and the suppression of individual rights. Extreme centralism failed in Ecuador, as it did elsewhere in Latin America, because it so curtailed individual liberties. In 1895, the Liberals, led by Ecuador's national hero, Eloy Alfaro, overthrew the Conservatives and implanted a regime led by coastal planters, bankers, and a largely Afro-Ecuadorian army. This long-running contest between Liberals and Conservatives was typical of the region.

The Benefits (and Costs) of Moderation, 1830s–1880s

While Liberal-Conservative debates tore apart most Latin American nations, two South American countries (Brazil and Chile) and one Central American nation (Costa Rica) made reasonable progress in resolving these differences, achieving a measure of stability during the early national period. Consequently, each was in a position to begin to modernize and follow in the footsteps of western Europe and the United States and turn their attention to achieving a greater degree of material progress. At the same time, moderation could have significant costs: In Brazil, Liberals and Conservatives compromised primarily in order to preserve the pernicious institution of slavery. The social costs of compromise in Chile and Costa Rica were not as high, but still considerable.

Moderate Leadership Emerges in Costa Rica

During the most contentious years of the United Provinces of Central America (UPCA) in the 1830s, Costa Rica's leadership feared that the larger and more populous regions (especially Guatemala) would overwhelm their interests. But the province's small size and isolation made it relatively immune from the struggle and violence of the UPCA. In fact, Costa Rica soon took the opportunity to go its own way. In 1834, Braulio Carrillo held office as Costa Rica's official head of state (*jefe de estado*) a post intended to function like a governorship, but which Carrillo, a Conservative, considered to be more like a presidency. He withdrew Costa Rica from the UPCA, establishing it as an independent nation, with the town of San José as its capital.

Carrillo ruled the country as a dictator. He served two terms of office, the first from 1835 to 1837, and a second beginning in 1838. In 1841, Carrillo named himself president for life, although he actually served only one more year in office. Despite his authoritarian tendencies, however, Braulio Carrillo set Costa Rica's state-formation project in motion. Carrillo was a Conservative and a caudillo, but in typical Costa Rican fashion, a moderate version of both. He clamped down on crime and vice in the interest of public safety, and also ushered in new forms of economic development, especially the cultivation of coffee. Carrillo also attempted to open communication between San José and the unassimilated Caribbean coastal region, so isolated that it had at one time served as a home base for British pirates. Not entirely successful in his policy initiatives, Carrillo's moderate approach did allow for an eventual transition to liberalism as the century progressed.

Carrillo's successor, Juan Rafael Mora Porras, built on Carrillo's economic policy and expanded the development of agrarian capitalism through coffee, which grew abundantly in the temperate volcanic soils of Costa Rica's mountains. Mora cultivated markets for coffee in Europe and oversaw the transformation of Costa Rica's campesinos from subsistence farmers to small-scale agrarian producers. By 1850, coffee had become the nation's most lucrative national export. Mora was expelled from power in 1860, after which a Liberal government assumed leadership of the nation, emphasizing a project of national modernization. The Liberals focused on further investment, the acquisition of additional foreign markets, and the emergence of a new "middling" class. This new class would form the backbone of moderate Costa Rican politics through the remainder of the century.

The moderate register of Costa Rica's nineteenth-century history provides a counterpoint to the violent conflicts that played out between Liberals and Conservatives during the same period elsewhere in most of Latin America. Costa Rica's caudillos adhered to their Conservative political ideology, but not at the price of innovation. Importantly, Costa Rica's forays into commercial coffee cultivation under Carrillo and Mora set the stage for the full-scale introduction of the commodity that would transform nearly all of Central America in the decades to come.

Moderation Prevails in Chile

The authoritarian principles of the 1833 Constitution notwithstanding, stability in Chile only prevailed because that nation's Conservative leaders adopted moderate policies. Manuel Bulnes, Chile's president from 1841 to 1851, was a decorated military officer and married to the daughter of an important Liberal politician. He had the leverage and the connections to bring moderate Liberals into his government. He also regularly consulted Congress, which the Constitution did not require. Chile's free press and stable state encouraged exiles like Argentina's Domingo F. Sarmiento to seek asylum there. Although a staunch Liberal in Argentina, Sarmiento befriended a number of Chilean Conservatives and endorsed Bulnes's Conservative successor in print.

A brief but bitter civil war over the 1851 election ended when Bulnes and the unsuccessful Liberal candidate (who also happened to be his cousin) signed a peace agreement over lunch. By then, a new generation of Chilean political leadership was emerging. The younger generation of both parties, endorsed the expansion of personal liberties without threatening the Constitution's emphasis on order. Bulnes's civilian successor also restricted some of the privileges of the Catholic Church. Moderate Conservatives, now calling themselves the Nationalists, nominated José Joaquín Pérez for the presidency in 1861. Pérez won the election handily by appealing to Liberal voters. The last of Chile's ten-year presidents, Pérez approved in 1865 a law that reinterpreted Article 5 of the Constitution of 1833 to mean that Chile would permit religious toleration (the exact opposite meaning of its literal wording). With this gesture, Chile reinforced its reputation for moderation, and opened the south to settlement by foreign immigrants, most notably German Protestants. At the same time, the Chilean military conducted a series of skirmishes against the Araucanians (now properly called the Mapuche), defeated them, and pushed them to even more remote locations. The Mapuche had resisted colonization for hundreds of years, but could not defend themselves against contemporary artillery or the repeating rifle. Their retreat before the forces of Chilean modernization was typical of the social costs of nation-state consolidation in nineteenth-century Latin America.

Brazil under Pedro II: A Third Example of Moderation

With the final suppression of the Ragamuffin Revolt in 1845, the Brazilian Empire entered its most stable period. Regional dissent was contained, no longer threatening territorial dissolution. The Liberal and Conservative parties competed for positions in the Senate, and in the Imperial Cabinet of Ministries. But leaders in both parties had a tacit agreement to contain dissent to the drawing room. The binding glue of this political agreement was a shared investment in the institution of slavery.

Brazil's monarchy succeeded in part because of the esteem in which Brazilians held Pedro II. Known as the "Citizen Emperor," Pedro mingled with ordinary Brazilian citizens and opened the palace two days a week to hear his subjects' concerns. His intellectual curiosity and fascination with science (he befriended the biologist and chemist Louis Pasteur and telephone-inventor Alexander Graham Bell) were renowned. The stability of Pedro II's long rule brought gradual modernization, as the country saw the laying of hundreds of miles of rails and telegraph lines, and the installation of the first telephone in South America.

Regularly scheduled elections ensured smooth transitions in Brazil's Senate and its Chamber of Deputies. Pedro II alternately favored Liberals and Conservatives in the Cabinet, depending on circumstances. He installed a Liberal cabinet when he wanted to make incremental progress in reining in the slave trade, then called on the Conservatives when he needed to raise resources for war. His middle-of-the-road government guaranteed free speech and other personal liberties to Brazilian citizens, but limited citizenship to free men.

CULTURE AND IDEAS

Pedro II and the Sciences

≡ **Portrait of Emperor Pedro II**

Brazil's Pedro II was a bundle of contradictions: he was one of history's longest-ruling monarchs but showed little regard for the trappings of royal life. He had a profound distaste for military affairs but prosecuted a war of total annihilation against neighboring Paraguay. Elegant and reserved in public, he was gluttonous and a severe patriarch in private. He had a fondness for liberal ideas but ruled an empire dependent on slavery. He professed esteem for the study of arts and sciences but did little to support education in Brazil.

Pedro II himself was a man of letters, corresponding with distinguished authors and jurists such as the American essayist and philosopher Ralph Waldo Emerson and Supreme Court justice Oliver Wendell Holmes. He was a dedicated amateur scientist, installing his own chemistry and physics laboratory in the royal palace. Photography and the telephone, two of the nineteenth-century's greatest technological advances, attracted his particular interest. He was among the first photographers in Latin America, experimenting in the 1840s both with daguerreotypes (unique images photographically impressed on copper plates) and calotypes (reproducible images impressed on paper sensitized with a silver iodide solution), the two competing processes of the medium's early history.

In 1876, Pedro II joined US President Ulysses S. Grant in inaugurating the Philadelphia Centennial Exposition, the world's largest science and industry fair to that point. In Philadelphia, Pedro II met the inventor of the telephone, Alexander Graham Bell, and was the first to buy stock in Bell's new company. Pedro II was an early adopter of the telephone, installing one in his summer palace outside of Rio de Janeiro.

These pursuits were more than flights of fancy: Pedro II was keenly interested in scientific advance and dreamed of bringing such innovation to Brazil. And yet in practice Pedro II did little to foster science and industry outside the palace and the royal academies of science and the arts. Brazil lagged behind its Spanish American neighbors in support for both higher education and primary schools. Pedro II's scientific interests were typical of the contradictions of liberal ideals of progress and modernization in nineteenth-century Brazil. In a nation whose economy still rested on the exploitative foundations of slavery, science and technological innovation remained the pursuit of the few and the privileged.

- What kind of obstacles might Pedro II have faced in attempting to bring scientific progress to nineteenth-century Brazil? Why didn't Pedro II support creation of public schools, like Argentina's Liberals in the same period?

Pedro II exercised executive power carefully in order to avoid measures that might awaken renewed regional or social rebellion. His own political vision was more closely aligned with the Liberals as he sought to strengthen banks and facilitate the first cautious steps of industrial growth. But he needed the support of the Conservative Party in order to collect imperial revenues, and catered to its needs where necessary. This balancing act resulted in political initiatives that fulfilled some Liberal objectives without threatening Conservative interests.

The Brazilian Land Law of 1850, for example, was designed to encourage increased agricultural production by breaking up unproductive colonial estates and selling off imperial lands, facets it held in common with liberal land laws passed elsewhere in the mid-nineteenth century Americas. But the Brazilian law prohibited small farmers from staking claims based on their active production on rural land, and instead delivered large tracts to the rural elite, reinforcing the power of well-connected planters and ranchers. Rather than undermining the power of slave owners, the Land Law encouraged the expansion of intense slave exploitation to areas where slaveholding had previously been sparse, such as the fertile western lands of the province of São Paulo. The Land Law was typical of the compromises of Pedro II's long reign. It helped create the foundations for a more modern and productive economy, but at the same time preserved social hierarchy, expanded exploitation of slave labor and limited the opportunities of the landless poor.

The moderate political course set by Brazil, Chile, and Costa Rica became the norm for most of Latin America by the 1870s. By then, most nations had rejected both Colombia's model of extreme federalism and Ecuador's model of extreme centralism in favor of moderate centralism characterized by a strong chief executive and moderate restrictions on civil liberties. This form of government generated stability that contrasted markedly with the turbulent transitions of the early republican era.

Economics and the Environment, 1830s–1880s

Liberals and Conservatives also differed over exploitation of natural resources. Liberals tended to reject colonial trade restrictions and advocated free trade, especially with Great Britain. Conservatives tended to prefer protectionism (taxes on imports) to defend local industries, such as textiles, against European manufactured imports. New primary products, like coffee and guano, emerged as the region's most valuable exports, and Latin Americans embraced the idea of economic "comparative advantage," exchanging their higher-priced raw materials for inexpensive western European manufactured goods. The British and other European powers, for their part, concentrated on securing favorable agreements with trading partners in Latin America.

Coffee

Historian Eric Hobsbawm once declared that coffee, as a commercial agricultural commodity, signaled two "firsts" in nineteenth-century Latin American history. It was both a product of the new free trade ideology of the era and also the first "drug food" not controlled by colonial or imperial ideologies. The cultivation and development of the bean that produced what one American consumer called the "nerve food" to confront the "pressures of the machinery of civilized life" was in some respects the perfect staple for the industrializing nineteenth century. As the ideal commodity for the emerging Latin American states, coffee demanded international trade networks and markets, and the labor systems to sustain them. In some countries this entailed experiments with new forms of wage labor and smallholding. In others it entailed an intensification of slave labor.

In the case of places like Brazil, Colombia, and Venezuela, coffee cultivation offered an incentive for coffee "pioneers" to expand the frontier and plant the crop. New coffee growers then demanded roads, trains, and modern ports to move their product to market. Coffee would radically transform both landscape and society in every country in which it grew, and in the cases of Medellín, Colombia, and São Paulo, Brazil, its profits would lay the foundation for industrialization. All of these elements supported and advanced the Liberal state-formation project.

Coffee as a commodity long predated the nineteenth century. The product had deep roots in Africa, where Arab and Turkish traders had purchased and trafficked in the bean since the 1400s. In the Middle East, coffeehouses became spaces for male sociability. During the colonial period, Spaniards had planted coffee in the temperate, volcanic highlands of Central America, as did the Portuguese in Brazil, but difficulties in transporting and marketing the product had discouraged its cultivation. Only in the 1830s, when innovations from the United States and Europe in processing and marketing the bean suddenly made coffee profitable did the coffee industry in the Americas take off. Coffee production increased exponentially over the course of the nineteenth century. Latin America produced 90,000 metric tons of coffee for world trade in 1820, 450,000 metric tons in 1870, and 1,600,000 metric tons in 1920. No wonder economic historians sometimes call the 1800s Latin America's "coffee century."

No single location in Latin America can claim to have originated modern coffee cultivation, but Costa Rica may have the best case. In the late 1820s, the regional government opened up unused lands in the nation's Meseta Central to cultivation,

≡ **Coffee Bag Manufacturing in São Paulo.** Although generally Latin American nations did not create industrial facilities until after the Depression of 1930, Brazil and Mexico were exceptions to the general rule. By the mid-nineteenth century, Brazilian industrialists had opened plants that provided ancillary products for the export trade. In this instance, coffee needed to be shipped in burlap sacks, and so this factory in Sao Paulo met that demand. The equipment to produce the bags was manufactured in Great Britain, and in many instances foreigners were the skilled mechanics, the management, and even the owners of these plants.

and in 1832 sold Costa Rica's first coffee abroad. Costa Rican peasants moved readily into these areas, which proved ideal for the cultivation of very high quality varieties of the smooth-tasting *Arabica* bean. The nation's experience was atypical of that of other locations, such as Brazil and Colombia, where coffee was (re)introduced around the same time. Because Costa Rica was small and its population relatively homogeneous, its coffee industry developed a unique labor system. Costa Ricans tended to grow coffee on small estates, often along with subsistence farming, relying on one another for labor during the intensive period of harvest and planting. Costa Rican farmhands were wage laborers. When its coffee market exploded in the 1830s, the people as a whole prospered. Costa Rica became a model for economic innovation in the region.

Brazilian coffee production and export also accelerated rapidly in the 1830s. As in Costa Rica, Brazilian coffee pioneers advanced the lines of a vast frontier, first into the Paraíba Valley of Rio de Janeiro and later onto the plateau of western São Paulo. Coffee planters devastated the South Atlantic forest region, hacking down irreplaceable species of trees to expand plantations and burning huge quantities of wood in coffee and sugar mills.

So too, did a "coffee frontier" emerge in Colombia, where, like Brazil, patterns of internal migration saw settlers move into the then-remote western portions of the province of Antioquia and later into Santander in the north. The same pattern pushed Venezuelan settlers away from the coast and toward foothills of the Andes. Unlike Costa Rica, however, planters in Brazil, Colombia, and Venezuela experienced what the Colombians called a "falta de brazos," a shortage of cheap available labor, the solutions to which would help redefine social and power relations in each of these regions for years to come.

In Brazil, land and labor relations followed patterns established by the earlier sugar industry, meaning that Brazilian coffee growers (**fazendeiros**) ended up accumulating enormous estates holding hundreds of thousands of coffee trees and slaves. Coffee planters relied predominantly on slave labor until the 1880s. During the first half of the nineteenth century, Brazil imported an astonishing 1.5 million African slaves. By the 1830s, coffee had become Brazil's most important product, surpassing cotton and sugar. By the 1840s, coffee constituted 40 percent of Brazil's exports and made Brazil the number one coffee-producing nation in the world. Large-scale coffee planters grew fabulously wealthy and politically influential, slowing Brazil's halting progress toward the abolition of slavery. Planters only began to recruit free immigrant labor in large numbers in the 1870s, and even then most continued to cling to a combination of slave and free labor until Brazil's abolition of slavery in 1888.

Colombia also moved toward a hacienda system of great estates, often owned by rich Bogotá merchants who relied on administrators and tenants (*colonos*) to pick, process, and export the coffee. Some small producers continued to participate in the coffee industry alongside the large estates. As in Brazil, coffee made Colombian hacendados rich, and coffee dramatically increased their country's gross national income and its networks with markets abroad. But coffee's benefits did not extend to the colonos who picked and handled the crop, as the Costa Rican example proved difficult to replicate.

El Salvador and Guatemala offered different examples of coffee's effect on landscape, labor, and national development. Unlike their South American counterparts, neither El Salvador nor Guatemala had available frontier land; both were fairly densely populated countries, with the indigenous populations engaged in subsistence farming. In both cases, the development of the lucrative coffee industry encouraged local elites, aided by Liberal legislation, to displace these populations so that the lands could be put into coffee production for the *finqueros'* private gain, worked by the very people whom the coffee *fincas* had just displaced.

In Guatemala, where the indigenous Maya constituted the great majority of the rural population, this was not easily accomplished. Coffee elites nonetheless found ways to confiscate common lands. Maya people largely remained in their villages, feeding themselves through subsistence farming, but they were obliged both by necessity and by law to work on the coffee fincas as well. In El Salvador, emergent coffee elites could not afford such niceties. Instead, in hand with the Liberal government, they brutally displaced the natives and **peones** (workers) and indentured them as permanent colonos, bound to serve on the coffee fincas in perpetuity.

The symbiotic relationship between coffee elites and Liberal governments, though well illustrated by the cases of El Salvador and Guatemala, was common. Virtually everywhere that coffee became "king," the state responded to the needs and whims of the planters, forming what some historians have called an "oligarchic pact." Liberal reforms freed up resources for the development of agricultural export economies, while disciplining labor forces and subjecting them to planter control.

Guano and Resource Depletion

Peru's guano industry, which flourished between 1845 and 1875, should have exemplified the success of liberal economic theory. Guano is the accumulated droppings of birds or bats, which nest in colonies in the same locations for thousands of years. Because the material provides a potent and concentrated source of certain minerals, it makes excellent fertilizer for crops. Peru marketed this unique, much-in-demand commodity, one that consistently commanded high prices on the international market. Despite all of these favorable circumstances, Peru squandered this valuable resource and so mismanaged the guano industry that it provided a keen lesson in poor environmental planning. In thirty years, Peru nearly depleted the valuable resource that the Inka had taken great pains to preserve for centuries.

Guano provided the best answer to the economist Thomas Malthus's dire prediction for humanity's future. In his 1798 "An Essay on the Principles of Population," Malthus demonstrated that prosperous economic times in the eighteenth century had encouraged population growth. He argued that the rising population would outstrip the food supply, resulting in starvation and misery. In addition, the problem of food shortages would be compounded by centuries of land overuse that had left British and continental European soils depleted of minerals. The fertilizer revolution of the 1840s proved Malthus wrong.

Peru's Chincha Islands contained the world's largest supply of high-quality guano fertilizer for several reasons. Because the nearby Humboldt current's rich supply of fish attracted huge flocks of seabirds that nested on the three rocky islands, enormous quantities of guano, hundreds of feet thick, had been produced over the centuries. These rocky islands experienced no rainfall, meaning the nutrients contained in guano (nitrogen, phosphates, and potassium) never leached out. In terms of quality and quantity, Peruvian guano had no effective competition in the international market.

The British company of Anthony Gibbs and Sons determined to exploit guano's commercial possibilities. Since Peru, rather than private individuals, owned the Chincha Islands, the government controlled the supply but granted consignment rights (roughly between one-fifth and one-third of the profits) to Anthony Gibbs and Sons for promoting, transporting, and selling the product. The Gibbs family's newfound wealth surely made up for the teasing of their friends, who mocked them for having made their fortune "selling turds of foreign birds." Peru retained a substantial share of the profits—much higher, for example, than the Spanish Crown had earned from the mining of silver and gold during the colonial period. Between 1845 and 1875, Peru exported over ten million tons of guano to Great Britain.

Peru also maximized its profits by keeping labor costs low. Although initially the government hoped that highland indigenous people would perform the work, they proved unwilling. To replace them, the government encouraged the importation of Chinese migrant laborers and paid them abysmally low wages. Workers endured horrific conditions. They used dynamite to blast the hardened mounds of guano before separating the loose guano from rock, shoveling it into wheelbarrows, and dumping the guano into chutes leading to the holds of ships. In addition to the heat and noxious smells, the work filled the air with toxic fecal dust.

In short, liberal economic theory worked in the short term, as Peru took advantage of its favorable position in the international marketplace to earn significant profits from its niche export. Yet by 1875, the country had little to show for all this revenue. Peru did not employ the wrong economic theory, nor did foreigners cheat them. Rather, Peru mismanaged its guano earnings. Ramón Castilla, Peru's president (1845–1851, 1855–1862) for much of the Age of Guano, chose to spend the money in three ways. First, he paid off Peru's foreign debt and made the treasury solvent for the first time since independence. This positive step, however, had negative consequences. As Peru's credit rating improved, foreign banks offered new loans, which the government accepted without regard as to how it could repay the money. Second, Castilla paid off the internal debt, much of which was based on inflated claims for property damage occurring during Peru's many civil wars and for bogus compensation to slave owners for their emancipated slaves.

≡ **Workers Digging Guano in Peru.** Between 1850 and 1875, Peru based its export economy almost exclusively on the extraction of guano (bird dung). When indigenous people refused to perform this unhealthy, filthy labor, Peru lured workers from China as substitutes with false promises of fair wages. Guano brought considerable prosperity to Peru, much of which funded railroad construction. Although the peak of the guano era ended in 1875, when overproduction depleted the precious resource, a few workers have continued to scratch out a livelihood extracting guano despite the health hazards associated with the work.

Third, Castilla briefly flirted with the conservative economic doctrine of protectionism to promote Peru's fledgling industries, such as textile manufacturing. Not only was Peru's internal market too small to make such ventures profitable, but political pressure and common sense forced Peru in the direction of free trade, which allowed the elite and business classes to import better quality and cheaper goods from Great Britain and France. Castilla's successor had even grander illusions for the guano revenue. He hoped to build a series of railroad lines connecting coastal ports to highland cities. This dream bankrupted the Peruvian state by 1875, leaving Peru as the second most indebted nation in the world after the Ottoman Empire.

In addition to providing a lesson about the pitfalls of excessive borrowing, Peru's guano bonanza proved instructive about the environmental consequences of resource depletion. Because of guano's extreme profitability, the government rushed to market as much of the product as quickly as possible. The pace of guano mining outstripped the birds' ability to replace the commodity. Unrestricted mining practices further contributed to depleting the resource. Although the birds tolerated mining operations next to their nests, greedy miners went further: pushing birds off nests, destroying eggs, all in their rush to get at the guano deposits beneath. By 1875, the guano fields were essentially played out.

By the 1870s, most Latin American nations had turned away from the conservative doctrine of protectionism in favor of a modified version of the liberal ideology of free trade (some export and import taxes were imposed to raise revenue). By pursuing the export of valuable commodities like coffee and guano, Latin Americans believed that they would seize the comparative market advantage of high prices for luxury goods, and use this wealth to become modern, prosperous states. But only in rare cases were nation-states able to harness the revenues from export commodities in ways that led to sustainable growth.

The Church-State Issue, 1830s–1880s

The role of the Catholic Church proved the most contentious of the issues dividing Liberals and Conservatives. Liberals saw the Catholic Church as a hindrance to modernity, especially in countries where the Church was particularly strong as a social and political force. Early Liberal reforms included transferring public record-keeping on births and deaths from the Church to public registries and suppressing special clerical privileges. By the 1850s, Liberal anticlerical measures became more radical, as new statutes expropriated Church-owned properties. Conservatives, as strong defenders of the institutional role of the Catholic Church, resisted these measures.

Liberals, Conservatives, and the Church

By the time of independence, there were many diverse expressions of the Catholic faith across Latin America. These ranged from European orthodoxy to Enlightenment-influenced "freethinkers," and also encompassed indigenous syncretic religion and the fusions of African and Christian beliefs found in Brazil and the Caribbean. In one way or another, almost all of these diverse religious expressions fell under the umbrella of "Catholicism." Most Latin Americans, even those who were not personally devout, still demonstrated a strong sense of religious belonging through active participation in Church ceremonies and rituals.

The same could not be said for their feelings toward the new nations they inhabited. For these new political units, ordinary people initially tended to express little affinity or loyalty. One of the first Liberal state-formation projects was to try to shift the allegiance of ordinary people away from the Church and to the new states. This was not an easy task, as the secular leaders of the new nations as well as nearly all the new citizens identified themselves as Catholics. Unlike the United States, where people saw the separation of church and state as providing protection for minority religions, in Latin America the separation of church and state demanded the suppression of the single religion that commanded the loyalties and affections of nearly everyone.

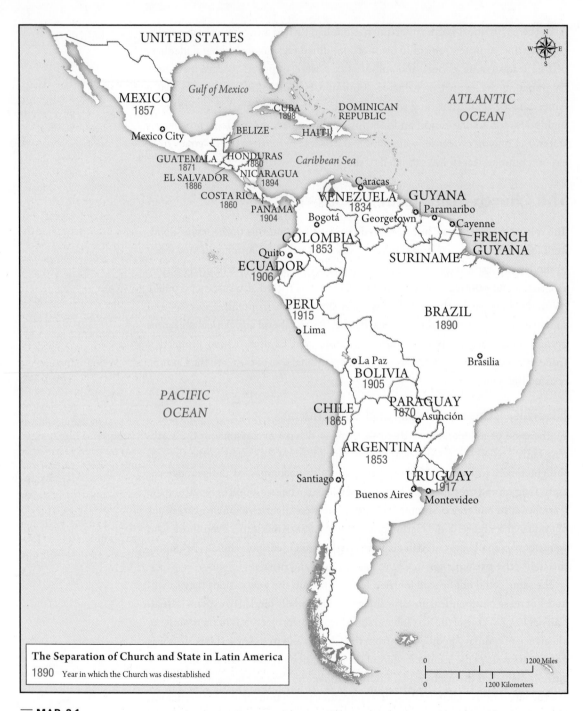

The Separation of Church and State in Latin America

1890   Year in which the Church was disestablished

≡ **MAP. 3.1**

SOCIAL UPHEAVAL

Mandeponay, a Chiriguano Leader in Bolivia

While Liberals and Conservatives vied for the spoils of national power in Latin America in the nineteenth century, indigenous leaders sought to defend their communities from threats such as the expropriation of traditional communal lands, forced labor on export-oriented estates, and suppression of indigenous religion. The life of Mandeponay, leader of the Macharetí Chiriguano Indians in Southeastern Bolivia, exemplifies the possibilities and limitations of indigenous responses to religious and economic transformation.

The Chiriguano had remained among Latin America's most independent indigenous groups throughout the colonial period and into the nineteenth century, resisting repeated attempts at colonization and religious conversion. But by the mid-nineteenth century, mestizo cattle ranchers encroached on Chiriguano traditional lands and pressured Bolivia's Liberal regime to support their efforts. In 1855, Mandeponay's father had led an attack a Franciscan mission in an attempt to drive out the friars. But by the end of the 1860s, Mandeponay realized he needed to call on those same Franciscans in order to defend his community. He welcomed the establishment of a new mission. The Franciscans, in turn, helped protect the Chiriguano from displacement and economic exploitation.

But Mandeponay did not submit to their authority. He resisted baptism himself, as did most of the adults in his community. Mandeponay had numerous wives, as did most Chiriguano men. The Franciscans called on the Bolivian government to punish Mandeponay, but the indigenous leader successfully played the state against the friars. He traded valuable information about frontier politics to civic authorities in return for their indulgence of Chiriguano marital arrangements. When the missionaries attempted to ostracize Mandeponay, most of the local Chiriguano simply abandoned the mission. For more than twenty years, Mandeponay managed to use the Franciscans for protection while resisting proselytization. In the words of historian Erick Langer, Mandeponay "combined the skills of a caudillo and of a traditional chieftain."

This sheltered autonomy could only endure so long. In 1892, Apiaguaiqui, another Chiriguano leader, rose in violent rebellion against both the Franciscans and the white settlers. Mandeponay counseled in vain against war and carefully guarded his neutrality during the rebellion. When the Bolivian army suppressed the rebellion, Mandeponay managed to secure his authority and his community's autonomy temporarily. But Franciscan education was gradually changing Chiriguano lifeways. And even the Franciscan missions could not keep out the incursions of a modernizing economy. By the end of the century, Mandeponay turned to serving as a middleman in an international labor migration that sent many Chiriguano to work in Argentina.

Over the course of Mandeponay's lifetime, the Chiriguano were reduced from an autonomous indigenous group roaming the vast hinterland of the Andean foothills to a dependent population, subject to the discipline of Franciscan education and the strains of low-wage labor. Mandeponay's nimble negotiations among the Franciscans and civic authorities delayed this outcome, but could not prevent the inevitable.

- Did Mandeponay do the right thing in striking a compromise in return for some protection of Chiriguano community? Or should he have risen in vain rebellion like Apiaguaiqui?

Liberal governments across Latin America in the nineteenth century undertook an extensive program of anticlericalism. The severity of the anticlerical reforms varied from one country to another, but they generally included the following: seizure of Church-held lands; legalization of alternative religions (mainly Protestantism); secularization of birth, death and marriage registries; and secularization of education. In some cases, Liberal governments placed serious limitations on clerical activity, including the expulsion of archbishops.

Whenever Conservatives took power, they tended to champion Church privilege and pledged to return it to its former status of power and authority. Conservatives reinstated relations with the Vatican, elevated clergy to positions of religious and political authority, and attempted to restore Catholicism as a unifying and edifying force in public and private life. (They were not, however, nearly as eager to return expropriated property to the Church, as much of it had been sold already to the elite supporters of both parties.) In return for their support, the Church offered Conservatives a preexisting system of symbols and images on which the state could hang the trappings of secular nationhood. Such was the case, for example, with the Virgin of Guadalupe in Mexico, who was co-opted from strictly Catholic significance into the symbol of Mexican nationalism. The Virgin of Caridad de Cobre in Cuba, the Sacred Heart of Jesus in Ecuador, and the Black Christ of Esquipulas in Guatemala performed similar functions and became the focus of national identities in the nineteenth century.

The Mexican Reforma

After the demise of Iturbide's empire, Mexicans in 1824 turned to federalism as the form of government that best reflected its regional traditions. Like the Colombian federalist government of the 1860s and 1870s, the constitutional structure promoted autonomy, popular sovereignty, and municipal self-governance. By the 1830s, Mexican federalists turned their reformist attentions to trimming the influence of the Church. In the 1830s they abolished the mandatory tithe that required all citizens to pay one-tenth of their income to the church and modified the schedule of fee payments for sacraments (baptism, marriage, burial) that weighed most heavily on the poor.

Conservative retrenchment in the 1830s–1840s beat back these Liberal reforms and temporarily reinforced Church power. But the Conservatives proved unable to live up to their promises of economic growth and social harmony, creating an opening for Liberal renewal.

The new generation of Liberals that rose to prominence in the 1850s demanded more extensive anticlerical reforms. Reduction of Church power became the hallmark of the Liberal Constitution of 1857. The debate culminated with the three-year long War of the Reform (1858–1861). Although the war resulted in considerable property damage, relatively few people participated in the fighting (some estimates are as low as 25,000 individuals).

Led by Benito Juárez, Mexico's third great nineteenth-century hero (after Padres Hidalgo and Morelos of the independence era), the Liberals had articulated a program designed to secularize the nation and eliminate the privileges of corporate (nonindividual) entities. Juárez, an Indian born into poverty in a small village in the mountains of Oaxaca, earned his law degree and used it as a ticket into politics and public service. He became governor of his home state and won the admiration of his fellow Mexicans through his stalwart defense of the nation and the Liberal cause, initially against the final dictatorship of Santa Anna. Despite being Mexico's first indigenous president, Juárez viewed himself first and foremost as a Liberal, not an Indian, and firmly defended Liberal policies even when they adversely affected the indigenous population.

Mexico's Liberal reformers had a twofold agenda with regard to the Church and passed a series of statutes known as the Reform Laws to weaken the Church. First, Liberals wanted to make the institution subject to the authority of the state and to eliminate all special privileges for clergymen, making them citizens of Mexico like everybody else. Benito Juárez himself wrote the *Ley Juárez* (Juárez Law) which ended corporate **fueros** (privileges). No longer did clergymen (or military officers for that matter) have access to special courts where their transgressions would be judged by peers. Instead, when a clergyman or military officer committed a criminal or civil offense, they were tried in the same legal system as all other Mexicans. An even more important statute weakened the Church by disestablishing it, or, in other words, allowing religious toleration. This allowed the State to dominate the Church in all matters except those of the faith itself.

These measures struck at the Church's institutional power. A third important law, the **Lerdo Law** (named after the Liberal politician Miguel Lerdo de Tejada), hit the Church in its pocketbook. This statute confiscated all corporately held property. For the Church, this meant the forfeiture of its rural estates and urban properties on which the Church had collected rents for centuries. (The Church owned approximately one-fifth of Mexico's territory). Only the land on which church edifices stood was exempt. Under the terms of the law, the property was to be sold at auction with the proceeds going to the Church.

Liberals hoped that the indigenous tenants would purchase the plots they had rented and become small-scale

Benito Juárez. The personification of nineteenth-century Mexican liberalism, Benito Juárez led the struggle to defeat the Conservatives in both the War of the Reform and during the French intervention. A full-blooded Zapotec Indian from the sierra of Oaxaca, Juárez as president did not represent indigenous people, but rather embraced the liberal ideas of his colleagues, including the division of indigenously owned communal properties (*ejidos*) into individual parcels. Faced with the realities of racism during his lifetime, Juárez often lightened his complexion with rice powder on formal occasions.

capitalist farmers, thus better integrating them into the nation. The fact that tenants rarely had the ready cash or access to sufficient credit to bid at the auction meant that in many instances, Liberal elites (landowners, merchants, and professional people) gobbled up the property. The inclusion of indigenous communally held property, the **ejidos**, in the Lerdo Law had even more drastic consequences (as chapter 4 relates). Elsewhere in Latin America, similar broad statutes also allowed Liberals to "recover" corporate properties for private use and to move the original owners into the wage economy. Throughout the region, these measures provoked considerable backlash: the clergy enjoyed vast popularity, particularly among indigenous peoples, in many Latin American nations. Liberals believed anticlerical policies designed to secularize the state had the force of history on their side, but Conservatives pushed back.

García Moreno and the Catholic Nation in Ecuador

Gabriel García Moreno's vision of the relationship between the Catholic Church and the state of Ecuador diametrically opposed that of Benito Juárez and the Liberals in Mexico. Many Latin American conservatives in the early republican years believed that the traditional, colonial-era partnership between Church and State ought to be retained in its entirety. By midcentury, modernizing conservative nationalists like García Moreno sought a different relationship: to transform the Church into a highly respected, but subordinate, servant of the state. García Moreno believed that secularizing the Ecuadoran state would deprive the country of its core identity; recall that in a poetic moment, Simón Bolívar had metaphorically compared Ecuador to a monastery.

Visitors to Ecuador commented on the extreme religiosity of highland Ecuadorians. The ringing of church bells at the moment of the Elevation of the Host in the Cathedral and other churches in Quito brought traffic and commerce to a halt. Even today, the lengthy Good Friday procession there, just as in García Moreno's time, features scores of devout men bearing heavy wooden crosses through the downtown streets. In short, he saw Ecuadorians' devotion to the Catholic faith as an essential instrument advancing nation building.

While the Mexican Liberals sought to weaken the Church and subordinate it to the State, García Moreno moved in the opposite direction. He established a Concordat, or formal treaty with the Vatican, formalizing the union of church and state in Ecuador. Under the agreement, Catholicism remained Ecuador's official religion, and the Catholic Church retained its real estate and its ability to collect tithes. At the same time, the agreement granted the Ecuadorian government the power to appoint clergy to key offices and to expel corrupt priests and monks.

CULTURE AND IDEAS

The Sacred Heart of Jesus

The devotional cult of the Sacred Heart of Jesus came to stand for the conservative opposition to secular liberalism in nineteenth century Latin America. Seventeenth-century sources related that a French nun repeatedly saw visions of Jesus, bathed in blood from his crucifixion wounds. Reports of these visions spread. Popular religion soon associated the Sacred Heart with miracles such as the relief of a plague epidemic in Marseilles, France. The nun's artistic rendition of the Sacred Heart, a heart surrounded by a crown of thorns, became a popular devotional adornment in times of crisis.

The French Revolution brought the cult of the Sacred Heart to greater prominence when the soon-to-be guillotined King Louis XVI allegedly promised to consecrate France to the Sacred Heart if God would deliver him and France from the bloody Revolution. Conservative peasants and nobility from the Vendée region wearing the insignia of the Sacred Heart rebelled against the Revolution in the name of King Louis's martyrdom and the Catholic faith, making the Sacred Heart the symbol of opposition to liberalism. After the disastrous Franco-Prussian War in 1871 and the repression of the Paris Commune, the Sacred Heart reached the zenith of its popularity.

The Sacred Heart performed the same function for Latin American conservatives as it did for French conservatives, symbolizing the rejection of secular liberalism. Although García Moreno was the first to consecrate his country to the Sacred Heart, others followed suit over the next three decades. Peru's longest serving president, Augusto Leguía (1908–1912, 1919–1930), dedicated his country to the Sacred Heart as a tactic to reach out to conservative Catholic faithful while embracing the idea of Catholic labor unions. Although no entire Latin American nation today is dedicated to the cult, Sacred Heart parishes exist in many countries, especially in Colombia, Peru, and Ecuador.

- How did the religious image of the Sacred Heart become a political symbol in Spanish America in the nineteenth century? Can you think of other examples where this happened?

García Moreno also expanded the public school system for both boys and girls by hiring Christian Brothers' friars and Sisters of the Sacred Heart to teach in primary schools, and Jesuits to staff secondary schools and the universities. All of these measures served his greater vision of creating what he called the Catholic nation, in which the Roman Catholic faith served as the basis of national unity. Incorporating adults into the Catholic nation proved a greater challenge, as new laws against public drunkenness and extramarital sex failed to alter popular practices. Indigenous couples practiced trial marriages, for example, and were loath to give up the practice. Attempts to outlaw cockfights, bullfights, and even Carnival proved similarly unsuccessful.

García Moreno's evocation of the Catholic nation was more effective at the symbolic level than the legal level. In 1873, he became the first Latin American president to dedicate his country to the cult of the Sacred Heart of Jesus. For his conservative friends, this gesture demonstrated Ecuador's devotion to the faith and the idea of the Catholic nation, while for his liberal critics, it demonstrated García Moreno's fanaticism. When García Moreno was assassinated two years later, it only deepened the convictions of Conservatives that the Catholic nation remained Ecuador's best hope. Liberals were forced to wait in the wings until near the close of the nineteenth century. Throughout portions of Latin America, the Church-State issue remained a bone of contention into the early twentieth century.

Gender, Families, and Liberal Lawmaking, 1830s–1880s

Liberalism transformed Latin American politics. Its influence on gender relations was more subtle. Because women were not citizens, they were not equal under the law. Liberal prescriptions affected them profoundly, but mostly in indirect ways.

The Family Structure

To preserve social order, Spanish laws and customs decreed a paternalistic familial system wherein husbands ruled and wives and children played subordinate roles. So strong was this tradition that the conquistadores imposed it on the generally more egalitarian gender relationships of indigenous families. Male domination allowed the patriarch and his male relatives to preserve the family's all-important honor.

While men could gain honor through heroic deeds of valor, women could at best maintain their honor. To do so, women had to remain chaste until marriage and thereafter remain faithful to their husbands. As a practical matter, the code of honor required that women be secluded under the protection of a male family member at all times, or else remain safely behind convent walls. In an example of the unfulfillable ideals of probity of the day, one popular saying held that a "lady" left her house only three times in her life: for her baptism, for her marriage, and for her funeral. While this depiction was greatly exaggerated, even for sheltered elite women, it indicates the emphasis on restricting women to the private sphere. Only elite women could live these rigidly prescribed lives. Poorer women, also subject to patriarchy but forced to contribute to their family's livelihood, shared bustling streets, job sites, and marketplaces with male strangers.

Spanish legal codes gave husbands control over almost all property. In addition to his own holdings, a husband gained access to his bride's dowry, a wedding gift from the bride's parents viewed as a down payment on her future inheritance. In addition, the husband managed the couple's commonly held property (all the revenue that both parties earned during the course of the marriage). The bride retained ownership only of her jewels and clothing. Only upon the death of the husband, or in the rare instance of the dissolution of the marriage, did the spouse regain her dowry and take possession of one-half of the property earned during the course of the marriage.

Although married women could neither manage their dowry nor sign binding contracts, single women of age and widows enjoyed greater legal rights. Since Spanish law required that decedents' estates be divided in equal shares among all legitimate children, elite single women had every expectation of receiving an inheritance upon their father's death. Spanish law also granted widows the freedom to contract and to own property. Many widows became successful managers of extensive real-estate holdings. Although constrained in some senses, unmarried and widowed elite women continued to enjoy relative autonomy in the early nineteenth century.

Liberalism and Elite Women

The language of liberalism employed in many constitutions (individual freedoms, the right to private property and the free-

≡ **Mexican Lady at Home.** Elite women, like the one in this image, were expected to live secluded lives in their homes in order to protect their honor. The notion of honor hung over from the colonial period, and essentially referred to a woman preserving her sexual purity (virginity before marriage and chastity thereafter). Being secluded allowed a male relative to protect her honor. Elite women played an important role in child rearing, teaching all her children Christian values and additional practical homemaking skills to her daughters.

dom to contract) would seem to imply that independence opened up greater opportunities for Latin American women. But where liberal constitutions directly changed the status of indigenous people and freed slaves, for example, they offered only indirect changes to women. Elite women and the and the daughters of merchants and professional men received increased educational opportunities, but such schooling was intended only to further traditional patriarchal social goals, now redefined as "republican" motherhood. In early independent Mexico, for example, the number of girls' primary schools in urban areas increased, providing instruction not only in reading, writing, and arithmetic but also in national history, religion, and practical subjects like cooking and sewing. The overall intent of providing education for girls in Latin America, however, was not to prepare women for work outside the home, but to make them better mothers and enable them to tutor their children in desirable civic values.

Family law for married women changed little before 1870. Two reasons may explain the reluctance of male legislators to reform the system. First, because families lay at the heart of Latin American society, radical changes in family law would have threatened the core values of the culture. Equally important, the status quo offered married women more protection than the other possible alternative, the system of **coverture** then employed in the contemporary United States, Great Britain, and other common law jurisdictions. Coverture held that a wife's legal rights were entirely subsumed under those of her husband, who therefore outright owned all of her property, whether dowry, inheritance, earned income, or real estate. In the Spanish American republics, in contrast, widows recovered their dowries and inherited half of the community property acquired during the marriage.

Liberals interested in reducing the Catholic Church's secular power used the debate about the nature of marriage and divorce as a wedge issue to further their agenda. While Conservatives viewed marriage as a holy sacrament, Liberals insisted marriage was simply a civil union, thereby removing one of the Church's most important influences over families. Social pressures mounted for other changes in family law as well. As the custom of giving dowries disappeared, Liberal reformers sought other guarantees to provide for a widowed or divorced wife's financial future, such as legally ensuring her a statutory share of her former husband's estate. Women lobbied for equal opportunities to raise a couple's children in the event of divorce, arguing that single motherhood was an appropriate role for women. Across Latin America, legislators also questioned the humanity of laws that permitted a husband to kill his wife and her lover when caught in bed together. Although custom still frowned on upper- and middle-class women earning their own living outside the home, a few talented elite and middle-class women gained fame as literary figures, penning novels and popular journals. Nevertheless, the legal status of women in Latin America changed little until after 1870.

Foreign Influence, 1840s–1880s

Both Liberal or Conservative factions looked to foreign alliances, depending on the circumstances. In an era where North Atlantic nations felt no ethical qualms about interfering in the domestic affairs of weaker governments, or even invading and annexing portions of their territory, the Latin American states had to fend off as best they could the advances of the western European countries and the United States. In these years Great Britain, France, and the United States successfully carved out zones of influence, sometimes seizing territory but more often simply dominating trade and commerce.

The Era of Filibusters: Narciso López in Cuba

The effort to acquire land and influence in Latin America during the age of Manifest Destiny took several shapes. In some instances, individual citizens or groups of citizens, often but not always from the United States, took advantage of national disorder and internal conflicts in Central America and the Caribbean to probe the possibilities. Such political adventurers were called filibusters. Some filibusters focused their attention on Cuba, which seemed to hold special promise as a potential US slave state. Its close proximity to the United States and its status as a plantation society based on slave labor were especially appealing to American Southern expansionists. They were not the least troubled by Cuba's Spanish heritage and language, since the same was true of all the western territory acquired by the United States as a result of the Mexican War.

Yet Cuba's most notorious filibuster would not be an American, but a Venezuelan, an anti-Spanish radical named Narcisco López. López's main initial goal was to help Cuba win its independence from Spain. As an advocate of slavery himself, however, López also believed that the support of US Southerners was essential to this process. He was not averse to the thought that Cuba might eventually become part of the United States, just as Texas had.

In 1845, López traveled first to New York and then to New Orleans, where he gained the support of American backers, including the journalist John L. O'Sullivan (who coined the term "Manifest Destiny"), for a military expedition to Cuba. He also courted assistance from key Southerners, including Robert E. Lee and Jefferson Davis, who would later lead the Confederacy. Both men approved of López's project but declined to offer financial backing. After several initial setbacks, López invaded Cuba with a small army of men in August 1851. Spanish forces captured the rebels and executed most of them, including López himself. López's defeat notwithstanding, some American Southerners continued to advocate for annexation of Cuba as a slave state.

William Walker and Nicaragua

Just a few years after López's execution, another expansionist scheme unfolded in the Central American nation of Nicaragua. Nicaragua's geography made it the most likely location for a transoceanic canal from the Caribbean to the Pacific coast. The California gold rush of 1849 intensified interest in Nicaragua as the location for a potential canal. The US railroad magnate Cornelius Vanderbilt established the Accessory Transport Company in the early 1850s, conveying passengers by steamship, small boat, and even stagecoach across Nicaragua and onward to the California goldfields. But the country itself was unstable; near constant rivalry between Liberals and Conservatives since the years of independence had left Nicaragua fragmented and vulnerable. Even the capital city changed depending on whichever party was in power. The 1852 compromise that made Managua the nation's permanent capital city was not enough to reassure either foreign investors or imperialists of the country's political stability.

In 1854, members of the Nicaraguan Liberal party invited William Walker, an American journalist, lawyer, one-time medical student, and filibuster to help them defeat their Conservative opponents. They came to lament this invitation. Walker called on allies from United States slaveholding states to bring an army of fellow adventurers to Nicaragua. Walker's forces took over the republic of Nicaragua in 1856.

Rather than sharing power with the Liberals, Walker declared himself President of Nicaragua. President Franklin Pierce of the United States recognized the legitimacy of his government. Nicaragua had abolished slavery in 1824, but Walker reinstated it, with an eye to possible statehood down the road. He also declared English to be the official national language, and implemented a series of policies designed to encourage large-scale immigration from the United States to Nicaragua in return for free land.

Walker's shocking mendacity forced a rare show of Central American unity against the filibuster. In 1856, Costa Rica's Juan Rafael Mora Porras formed a combined Central American army and led an assault to unseat Walker, an offensive known as the National War. The Central American army defeated Walker and his troops, who were badly weakened by cholera, at the town of Rivas on the Nicaragua–Costa Rica border, in April of 1856. Walker surrendered, and after his release returned to the United States.

In late 1857, Walker returned to Central America via Honduras to try to repeat his previous success. Instead, British military forces captured him and handed him over to the Honduran authorities, who executed Walker by firing squad in 1860. His posthumously published memoir, *The War in Nicaragua*, made him a hero among US Southerners. Although Walker is largely forgotten in US history, Central Americans view Walker as a symbol and archetype of US imperialism. They also remember resistance against Walker as a singular display of Central American unity during the era of Manifest Destiny.

The British and the Miskito Coast

The Atlantic Coast of Central America, much like the Caribbean, served as a contested zone for imperial power, first between Spain and Britain and later between Britain and the United States. Present-day Belize was the northernmost and most unpopulated district of Guatemala. Privateers founded Belize in the 1660s, and their descendants turned to dyewood and logging before ultimately taking up sugar cultivation, for which they introduced African slave labor. In 1783 the British officially

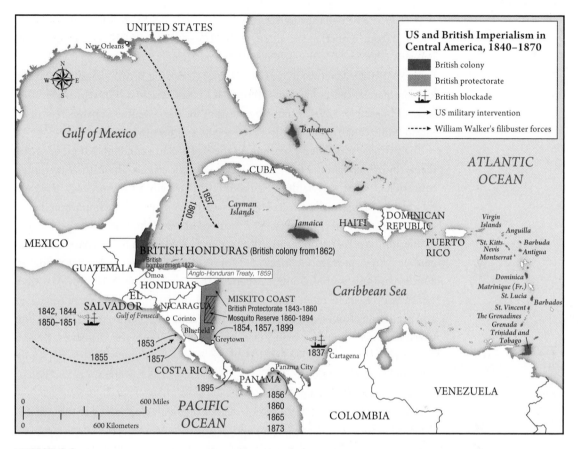

US and British Imperialism in Central America, 1840–1870

- British colony
- British protectorate
- British blockade
- US military intervention
- William Walker's filibuster forces

≡ **MAP. 3.2**

recognized Spain's sovereignty over Belize in exchange for the right to extract dye-woods, but continued to occupy the region as if it belonged to them, christening it British Honduras and treating it as a colony. British Honduras became the center of British interests in Central America. In 1859, Guatemala agreed to surrender its claim to its province in return for Great Britain's construction of a road from Guatemala City to the Atlantic Coast. The British never kept their end of the bargain.

Further south, the even more remote Miskito Coast was the region that pirates, mainly from Britain, used as a base for their illicit activities during the eighteenth century. It extended south through the heartlands of Honduras and Nicaragua to the Matina Valley of Costa Rica. The area took its name not from the insects that infest the coast's mangrove-lined shores, but from the Miskito indigenous population, who lived there along with the Rama and Sumu indigenous groups and Afro-descendent populations, many of them descendants of runaway slaves.

In 1839, the British captured the town of San Juan del Norte, a key regional trade entrepôt (transit port) at the mouth of the Rio San Juan, which marked the border between what would become Costa Rica and Nicaragua. Renaming it Greytown (after the British governor of Jamaica Charles Grey), the British developed it into a key commercial center for their interests in Central America. Greytown's location seemed to offer the most promising location for the potential construction of an interoceanic canal, dramatically increasing its strategic value.

The British established garrisons on the Bay Islands and founded other settlements, most importantly the port of Bluefields, Nicaragua. The British attempted to introduce export agriculture without much success. In the process, however, they brought in Afro-descendent laborers who ended up making important demographic and cultural contributions to the population of the Miskito Coast.

The admixture of people and cultures that took place on the Miskito Coast, including British, indigenous, black, and a sprinkling of other immigrants, produced a society unique within Central America. The people of the Miskito Coast were typically Protestant, often English (or Creole) speaking, with different foodways and livelihoods from the mestizos of the highlands and capital cities. The Miskito Coast in many ways remained a land unto itself. In 1816, the British crowned a "monarch," King George Frederick II, of the "Mosquito Kingdom," through whom they could rule the region and make it, effectively, a British protectorate, a relationship that was formalized in 1843.

Despite such efforts, Great Britain's relationship with Central America's Atlantic Coast was more commercial than political, thanks to the efforts of British consuls such as Frederick Chatfield, who grasped that Britain could exploit the region effectively without taking outright sovereign control over it. By the middle decades of the nineteenth century, however, it became clear that a new foreign power loomed on the horizon to compete with Britain for the Miskito Coast: the United States. In 1846, the United States signed the Bidlack Treaty with New Granada (Colombia), guaranteeing the US right of transit across Panama. A year later, a US company began work on the Panama railway, prompting the British to expand their own presence.

Anglo-American rivalry on the coast prompted both powers to meddle in the domestic affairs of Central American nations. The British threw their support behind Conservatives while the Americans supported the Liberals, complicating the political divides throughout the region. In 1850, the United States and Great Britain signed the Clayton-Bulwer Treaty, which provided for joint control over any route across the isthmus, and the furor slowly began to subside. The British tested US resolve by declaring the Honduran Bay Islands to be a British colony, but protests from both the United States and Honduras impelled Britain to withdraw the claim in 1859. The following year, Britain agreed to withdraw from the Miskito

Coast altogether, tacitly ceding imperial control to the Americans. The British presence receded from Central America's Atlantic Coast, with the exception of British Honduras, which remained a British colony until it won independence as the nation of Belize in 1981. British occupation and its consequences, however, left behind a legacy of language, religion, and ethnic blending that continue to contribute to the region's distinctive identity.

The British in the Southern Cone

British influence in the **Southern Cone** of South America took a different shape, one primarily of mercantile presence and political persuasion rather than militarized occupation or extensive settlement. Through much of the nineteenth century, British investors supplied capital, British engineers supplied expertise, and British merchants offered commercial contacts for endeavors in Argentina, Chile, Uruguay, Paraguay, and Brazil. While the British presence was most noticeable in the major port cities, its influence stretched as far as the railways that began to spread throughout the region in the mid-nineteenth century, and as deep as the mines they served. As long as relations between British investors and local elites remained harmonious, no serious objections to this influence arose. When those harmonious relationships broke down, the British acted to protect their interests. Argentina provides a clear example.

As early as 1825, an Anglo-Argentine Treaty of Friendship, Commerce and Navigation required the two nations to treat each other equitably. This facilitated British access to Argentine markets while enabling the Argentine government to draw on British capital at low interest rates. Even during the Rosas period, with its emphasis on self-sufficiency and internal development, connections between Argentine ranchers and British investors continued to grow. After Rosas's fall, British diplomats sought to protect these interests by persuading Governor Justo José de Urquiza to allow British ships free navigation of the Paraná River. This set the stage for a new phase of the British-Argentine relationship in the 1870s and beyond, one that would be characterized by a strengthening of commercial and cultural ties.

France, Latin Americans, and the Empire in Mexico

In the main, Latin Americans perceived France in a more positive light than they did the United States or European powers like Spain and even Great Britain. French intellectuals stressed the commonality of the culture of "Latin" peoples, those who spoke Romance languages and adhered to the Roman Catholic faith. Latin Americans embraced France because of its cultural heritage, perceived by nineteenth-century Latin American elites to represent the pinnacle of refinement. Most importantly, Latin Americans wanted to differentiate themselves from the imperialistic Anglo-Saxons of the United States, and their support for filibusters like William Walker.

Both Liberal and Conservative members of Latin America's political elite, like Ecuador's Gabriel García Moreno, spent their time in exile in Paris. Because France epitomized civilization, fashion, and modernity, young, elite Latin Americans traveled there to study, to pursue commercial interests, and to enjoy the good life. For literary figures like Nicaragua's poet Rubén Darío and other intellectuals, Paris allowed them to enjoy the stimulating atmosphere of salons and other less formal gatherings of artists, writers, and other intellectuals.

The high regard in which Latin Americans held France diminished temporarily in the 1860s because of the imperialistic ambitions of its emperor, Napoleon III. In emulation of his uncle, Napoleon the Great, Napoleon III drew up his own "Grand Design," which intended to make France the principal Latin power in the Americas and erect a Latin buffer zone against further US territorial ambitions. After a brief flirtation with the idea of extending a protectorate over García Moreno's Ecuador, Napoleon III turned his attention to Mexico.

Mexican monarchists had convinced him that their countrymen would welcome a return to monarchy. Without sharing the details of his broader ambitions, Napoleon III convinced Spain and Great Britain to mount a joint expedition to Mexico to collect long-standing debts. Once the other two countries became aware of France's true intentions, they withdrew. Meanwhile, the Mexican monarchists (including Juan Almonte, the son of independence hero José María Morelos), scoured Europe to find a suitable candidate for the throne. Ultimately, they joined Napoleon III in persuading the naïve Prince Maximilian of Austria and his ambitious wife Carlotta to rise to the bait—although neither Maximilian nor Carlotta realized in time that after forty years of republicanism, most Mexicans had little taste for monarchy.

Meanwhile, the vaunted French army suffered a serious setback. Outside the city of Puebla on May 5, 1862, the Liberal army routed the overconfident French, giving rise to one of Mexico's most important patriotic holidays, the Cinco de Mayo. A year later, the now-reinforced French army took Puebla and marched on Mexico City. Maximilian and Carlotta landed in Veracruz, where Mexicans greeted them with stony silence. The French army drove Benito Juárez and the Liberals to the northwestern border of Mexico, but were scattered too thinly to control the country effectively. When the US Civil War ended in 1865 and the US government announced it would not tolerate further violations of the Monroe Doctrine, Napoleon III began withdrawing his troops.

Maximilian's own foolhardy policies hastened his demise. Rather than throwing himself into the arms of the Conservative party that had brought him to power, Maximilian indulged his Liberal proclivities and approved all of the anticlerical legislation of the Reforma. This left Maximilian with no party to defend him.

≡ **Edouard Manet's Painting *The Execution of Maximilian*.** The French Impressionist painter Edouard Manet produced several versions of one of his most famous paintings, *The Execution of Emperor Maximilian*. The emperor's execution shocked and horrified European governments and the public at large, who characterized the act as regicide and denounced the "savage Indian" Benito Juárez. But for patriotic Mexicans, Juárez remained the quintessential symbol of nationalism for the defense of Mexico against the French intervention, saving the republic from foreign domination.

His second miscalculation was to declare Liberal soldiers captured under arms to be bandits and subject to immediate execution. This also backfired: Juárez's principled stand against the foreign invader encouraged localized popular uprisings against the empire. The Liberals captured Maximilian only months after the French army withdrew. On the morning of June 19, 1867, Emperor Maximilian I was executed by a firing squad. His last words were, "I forgive everyone, and I ask everyone to forgive me. May my blood which is about to be shed, be for the good of the country. Viva Mexico, viva la independencia!" Carlotta, meanwhile, fled to Europe to seek papal assistance, only to succumb to madness. This royal misadventure ended the possibility of resurrecting European monarchies in mainland Spanish America.

The War of the Triple Alliance, 1864–1870

While the Liberal-Conservative divide conformed to general patterns through-out the region, contests between these two factions within each nation rarely spilled over borders to become international wars. The most notable exception was among Latin America's most horrific conflicts. **The War of the Triple Alliance** (1864–1870), known in Brazil as the Paraguayan War, brought Brazil, Argentina, and Uruguay into battle against landlocked Paraguay. The war was an unmitigated disaster for both the losers and the ostensible winners, and produced the worst loss of life in in the region since the Conquest.

The Conduct of the War

Uruguay, which joined Brazil and Argentina in the Triple Alliance, had the small-est role in the war, but one decisive at its beginning. The local Conservative party, known as the Blanco, or white party, governed Uruguay in the early 1860s. The Blancos struck an alliance with Paraguayan dictator Francisco Solano López, granting passage to Paraguayan vessels on the Uruguayan river network. At the same time, the Blancos provoked Brazil by expropriating Uruguayan borderlands owned by Brazilian ranchers. The Brazilian ranchers demanded that Pedro II defend their interests. In a rare and unfortunate instance of Brazilian-Argentine cooperation, in 1864 Pedro II joined forces with Bartolomé Mitre's Liberal govern-ment in Argentina to force regime change in Uruguay.

Francisco Solano López attempted to restore the Blancos to power in Uruguay by striking out against Brazil. In November of 1864, his forces seized a Brazilian steamboat and sent Paraguayan troops into Brazilian territory. Early in 1865 Solano López's troops crossed Argentine territory on their way to Uruguay. Pedro II and Mitre treated these incursions as acts of war. In May of 1865, Brazil, Argentina, and the newly installed Liberal government in Uruguay sealed the Triple Alliance and attacked Paraguay. Paraguay was at a decisive strategic disadvantage. It was smaller and poorer than its rivals, and could easily be cut off from the Atlantic shipping that might have allowed it to acquire crucial munitions. In the long run, Paraguay stood no chance. In one telling moment, when the Brazilians finally rousted Paraguayan forces after a months-long siege of the fort at Uruguaiana, the Brazilian commander took one look at the hungry, bedraggled Paraguayan troops, many of them boys in tattered uniforms, and remarked, "The enemy was not worthy of being beaten."

Yet it took over five years for the struggle to play out, greatly protracted by the difficulties Brazil and Argentina faced in mustering and supplying troops, training them to fight in distant and unfamiliar terrain, and above all the Triple Alliance's insistence on the capture or death of Solano López himself. This last condition, ap-parently designed to prevent Solano López from returning to power in the pattern

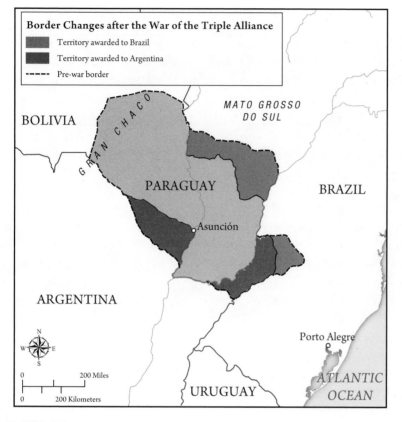

Border Changes after the War of the Triple Alliance
  ▨ Territory awarded to Brazil
  ▨ Territory awarded to Argentina
  ----- Pre-war border

BOLIVIA

GRAN CHACO

MATO GROSSO DO SUL

PARAGUAY

BRAZIL

Asunción

ARGENTINA

N
W · E
S

0   200 Miles
0   200 Kilometers

Porto Alegre

URUGUAY

ATLANTIC OCEAN

≡ **MAP. 3.3**

of many caudillos, turned the war into a personal vendetta. By the time Brazilian troops finally killed their quarry, the nation of Paraguay was devastated. Historians continue to argue over what percentage of the Paraguayan nation died in the war, but there is no doubt that it was one of the most cataclysmic defeats in history. The War of the Triple Alliance showed that Liberalism could turn into imperialism. Pedro II and Argentina's Liberal leaders objected to Solano López as both a threat to their trade network and an affront to their sensibilities. Their war against him was catastrophically destructive.

Results of the Conflict

Paraguay, the vanquished nation, lost about a third of its national territory and much of its population. The latter stages of the conflict were fought entirely on Paraguayan territory, and threw every aspect of national development into disarray. The loss of men in the war was so great that the Paraguayan Catholic Church allowed a "dispensation" for polygamy to help repopulate the country, a process that took

several generations. The war set Paraguayan development back several decades in other ways as well. The protected local development that had characterized Paraguay in the 1830s–1840s turned into impoverished isolation following the war.

While Brazil, the ostensible winner, did not suffer anywhere near comparable material losses, it did suffer deleterious political effects. In turning the energy of the Brazilian Empire toward a protracted struggle on a distant frontier, the war reinforced an emphasis on the maintenance of social order, delaying progress toward abolition. It also exacerbated abusive conditions within the Brazilian armed forces. The war did

TIMELINE

1830–1838
Diego Portales creates foundations for Conservative era in Chile

1841–1889
Pedro II is emperor of Brazil, contends with slavery and development of coffee

1843
British take Miskito Coast

1840–1875
The Guano Age in Peru

1842–1860
Carrillo and Mora lay foundations of Costa Rican state

1851–1857
US filibusters in Cuba and Nicaragua

≡ **Scenes from the War of the Triple Alliance.** The War of the Triple Alliance was the first extensively photographed war in Latin America. Photography remained a time-consuming, expensive practice: Images were made on wet collodion plates of either fragile glass or heavy metal, then transferred to delicate albuminate paper. The few images that survive reveal the course of the war in vivid detail. Page 138 shows Paraguayan prisoners of war. They are mostly indigenous, wearing a combination of indigenous and Western dress. They are barefoot and bedraggled; some are clearly injured. This photograph was taken in 1866, when most Paraguayan soldiers were grown men. As the war ground on, the Paraguayan Army turned to drafting adolescents. The prisoners appear to be guarded by Brazilian soldiers who are themselves young, of African ancestry, and barefoot—an indication that they were likely former slaves who enlisted in return for manumission. Page 139 shows the ruins of the Humaitá Fortress, key to the Paraguayan defenses. Brazilian and Argentine forces laid siege to the fortress between November and July 1868, gradually reducing the complex—including the old Jesuit church at its heart—to rubble through bombardment. The grinding reduction of Humaitá was emblematic of the larger course and consequences of the war.

1857–1860
The War of the
Reforma in Mexico

1863–1886
Extreme federalism pre-
vails in Colombia

1864–1870
War of the Triple Alliance;
Paraguay loses

1861–1875
Gabriel Garcia Moreno
and the Catholic nation in
Ecuador

1863–1867
Napoleon III and the
Mexican Empire

force the Brazilian army to professionalize, creating greater national cohesion among the officer corps. But treatment of common soldiers was often characterized by abuse and neglect. In Argentina, the war consolidated the power of the Liberals and reinforced their interest in extending their territorial dominance, fueling a campaign of eradication of indigenous groups from much of the Argentine interior.

Conclusion

Early republican nation builders eventually reached a meeting of the minds on most of the issues they faced. By 1870, they had developed a greater sense of national identity, sometimes as a response to foreign aggression. Liberals eventually agreed that extreme federalism had failed, and that a moderately centralist state better promoted stability. Conservatives also agreed to accept moderation. Both Liberals and Conservatives concurred that citizens, meaning men of property, should enjoy a reasonable amount of civil liberties. Conservatives came to accept the liberal emphasis on reducing tariffs and encouraging trade.

The question of the role of the Catholic Church, however, continued to leave the two parties at complete loggerheads. No other issue acted as a surer litmus test of a politician's convictions and no issue led to a greater number of contentious civil wars in early republican history than did the controversy about the relationship between Church and State. By the 1870s and 1880s, however, the Liberals had generally prevailed. As the institutional Church lost more and more authority and property, a more secular society emerged.

KEY TERMS

Conservative 103	fueros 123	Southern Cone 133
coverture 128	Lerdo Law 123	War of the Triple Alliance 136
ejidos 124	Liberal 102	
fazendeiros 115	peones 116	

Selected Readings

Adelman, Jeremy. *Republic of Capital: Buenos Aires and the Legal Transformation of the Atlantic World*. Palo Alto, CA: Stanford University Press, 2002.

Collier, Simon. *Chile: The Making of a Republic, 1830–1865: Politics and Ideas*. New York: Cambridge University Press, 2003.

Cushman, Gregory. *Guano and the Opening of the Pacific World: A Global Ecological History*. New York: Cambridge University Press, 2013.

Dando-Collins, Stephen. *Tycoon's War: How Cornelius Vanderbilt Invaded a Country to Overthrow America's Most Famous Military Adventurer*. Cambridge, MA: Da Capo Press, 2008.

Gootenberg, Paul. *Imagining Development: Economic Ideas in Peru's "Fictitious Prosperity of Guano,"1840–1880*, Berkeley: University of California Press, 1993.

Hamnett, Brian. *Juárez*. London: Longman, 1994.

Henderson, Peter V. N. *Gabriel García Moreno and Conservative State Formation in the Andes*. Austin: University of Texas Press, 2008.

Kraay, Hendrik, and Thomas Whigham, eds. *I Die with My Country: Perspectives on the Paraguayan War, 1864–1870*. Lincoln: University of Nebraska Press, 2005.

Langer, Erick. "Mandeponay: Chiriguano Indian Chief on a Franciscan Mission." In *The Human Tradition in Latin American History: The Nineteenth Century*, edited by Judith Ewell and William H. Beezley, 280–295. Wilmington: Scholarly Resources, 1989.

May, Robert E. *Southern Dreams of a Caribbean Empire*. Athens: University of Georgia Press, 1989.

May, Robert E. *Manifest Destiny's Underworld: Filibustering in Antebellum America*. Chapel Hill: University of North Carolina Press, 2002.

Needell, Jeffrey. *The Party of Order: The Conservatives, the State and Slavery in the Brazilian Empire, 1831–1871*. Palo Alto, CA: Stanford University Press, 2006.

Roseberry, William, et al. *Coffee, Society, and Power in Latin America*. Baltimore: Johns Hopkins University Press, 1995.

Sinkin, Richard N. *The Mexican Reform, 1855–1876: A Study in Liberal Nation Building*. Austin: University of Texas Press, 1979.

Wheelan, Joseph J. *Invading Mexico: America's Continental Dream and the Mexican War, 1846–1848*. New York: Carroll and Graf, 2007.

Wood, James A. *The Society of Equality: Popular Republicanism and Democracy in Santiago de Chile, 1818–1851*. Albuquerque: University of New Mexico Press, 2011.

4

Exclusion and Inclusion: Everyday People, 1825–1880s

Global Connections

Over the course of the nineteenth century, the rise of new patterns of global trade and forms of state management created new expressions of inclusion and exclusion. Traditional peasant communities tended to be the losers in this new world order. As these peasant communities were highly diverse, they did not simultaneously dissolve before an advancing tide of commercial agriculture. Instead, many adapted or retreated while still holding onto traditional lifeways. Even at the end of the nineteenth century, much of the world's population consisted of people living in rural, subsistence communities. But in regions closer to major port cities, to valuable resources, or to spreading rail lines, traditional peasantries faced new threats in the mid-nineteenth century. As rural populations grew, subsistence farmers were confined to smaller plots. Community resources were spread thin. External pressures and increasing demand for fertile land left communities vulnerable.

In this context, natural disaster levied a heavy toll. The Irish potato blight of 1847–1848, caused by a type of fungus, struck the Irish rural poor in a period of rising population, growing land pressure, and increasing British colonial demands. The potato, originally an Andean crop, demonstrated one of the problems of the Columbian exchange. It had become almost the sole source of nutrition for many poor Irish families by the eighteenth century. But while Andean villagers relied on hundreds of varieties of potato growing in microclimates, the Irish farmed only a few varieties in a climate where potato blight spread easily, destroying the crop. Although Britain could have helped sustain Ireland by importing food aid to its colony, it did little to ameliorate Ireland's suffering. Hundreds of thousands died in the ensuing famine, while tens of thousands more emigrated, the majority of them to the United States.

The Indian subcontinent experienced dramatic transitions in agriculture and commodity export over the course of the nineteenth century, first through the influence of the British East India Company, later under the rule of the British Raj, as the period of British rule in India from 1858–1947 is known. Under this system, the British consolidated the many princely states of the South Asian continent—which varied dramatically from one another in language, custom, and religion—into a single colonial entity under British tutelage. At first, the British strongly encouraged subsistence farmers to switch to cultivation of crops like cotton and opium for export, through favorable loans and persuasion. As the nineteenth century wore on, the export of opium grown in India to China became a vital part

≡ **Aymara Carnival in Bolivia.** Carnival, the three days before Ash Wednesday and the beginning of Lent, is widely celebrated in almost all Latin American nations. This photograph depicts the celebration mounted by the Aymara Indians, the majority indigenous population of Bolivia, have congregated in La Paz for the annual parade. Celebrants dressed in spectacular costumes, wore masks, danced, and consumed massive amounts of alcohol. Because the popular classes often became "unruly" and "disrespectful" during Carnival festivities, elite government in the nineteenth century attempted to ban them, usually to no avail.

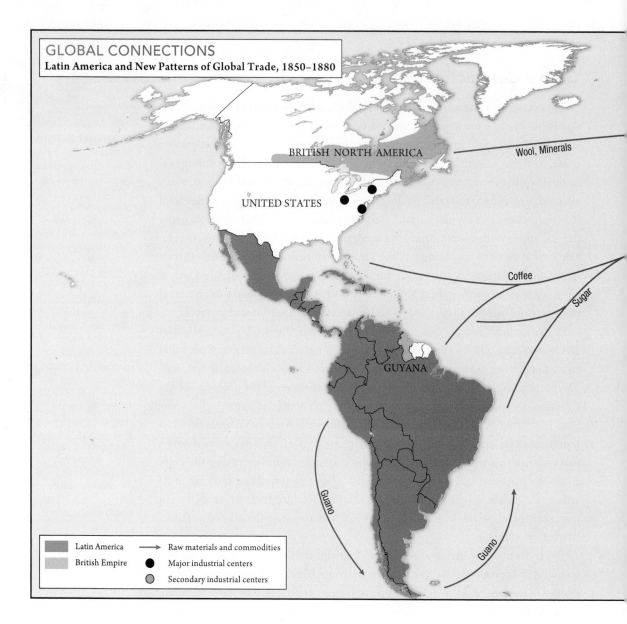

GLOBAL CONNECTIONS
Latin America and New Patterns of Global Trade, 1850–1880

of British trade, and the British gave local farmers no option, requiring them to cultivate opium. Subsistence agriculture waned as export commodity agriculture supervised by a trading empire grew.

Latin American peasants may not have been vulnerable to the potato blight or to demands for opium cultivation, but they suffered similar pressures, as traditional forms of communal landholding eroded in the face of Liberal law and commercial

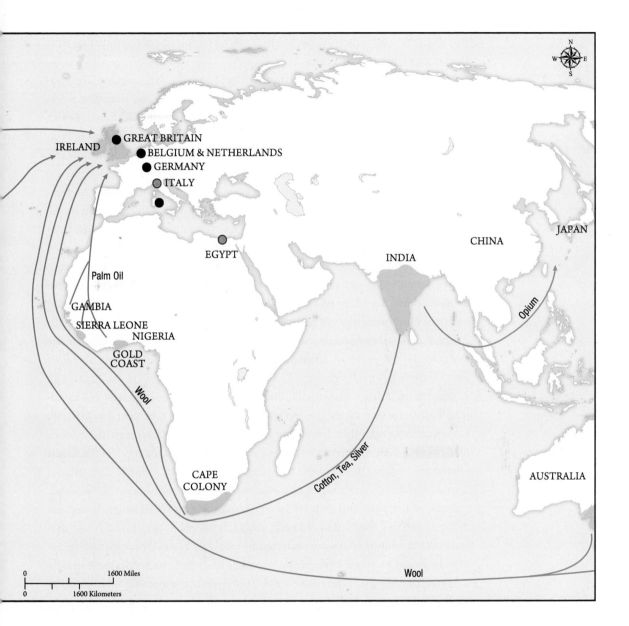

agriculture. Not all peasants suffered, as new trade demands could temporarily enrich humble rural producers. But global trade tended toward booms and busts, enriching speculators while shifting risk onto small-scale producers. The price of food became an issue of rising concern for both the rural poor and urban working class, leading to worldwide protest movements. As villagers in Mexico fought to protect communal maize fields, urban dwellers in Great Britain protested the

British Corn Laws, which imposed high tariffs on imported grain, protecting local landowners while raising prices.

Social struggles created their own forms of inclusion. The British Anti-Slavery Societies of the 1820s–1830s mobilized tens of thousands of citizens, from dockworkers in Liverpool to carriage drivers in London, to press for **abolition**, first in British imperial dominions, and then globally. The movement, linked to new forms of Protestant social mobilization, offered a new expression of solidarity both within and across working communities. Although it took longer to emerge in Latin America, the abolitionist movement created similar groups of like-minded campaigners, including freeborn, former slaves, and even slaves themselves. The abolition of the Atlantic slave trade reoriented the West African economy, which had in itself been closely linked to the transatlantic slave trade. Now Africa supplied products such as palm oil from Nigeria, used to lubricate machinery and make high-quality soap.

Around the globe, centralizing states created new military institutions to enforce domestic order. These armed agents enforced new laws against previously accepted practices. Many countries criminalized vagrancy and large public gatherings. South Africa, Australia, New Zealand, and the US South, enshrined racial segregation in law and enforced it at gunpoint. Latin America's social codes were rarely explicitly racial, but they could be equally exclusive. In Rio de Janeiro, for example, it was illegal to go barefoot in the lush downtown parks created by the imperial government, and also illegal for slaves to wear shoes. The implications were obvious. (Like most laws in Brazil, these were inconsistently enforced; but arbitrary enforcement was part of the strategy of exclusion.) New military institutions also displaced lingering relics of the feudal aristocracy. In Japan, for example, the emperor abolished the samurai, the medieval warrior class, in 1873 and created a national army, which many former samurai joined.

Some of the poor and dispossessed rejected the new social order, living and dying as outlaws. Particularly in rural areas facing new forms of land concentration, tales of bandits who were protected by local folk against incompetent agents of order became a staple of nineteenth-century life. While such tales were usually exaggerated, they spoke to a collective will to celebrate those who lived beyond the walls and fences of order.

Indian Subjects Become Indigenous Citizens, 1820s–1889

In Latin America, the role of indigenous people changed markedly during the early nineteenth century. The colonial era had theoretically segregated Indians (the *república de indios*) from Spaniards (the *república de españoles*), for mixed motives.

For humanitarian reasons, the Crown and the Church wanted to protect indigenous people from further exploitation and to convert them to the Catholic faith. On the other hand, separating natives from Spaniards simplified tax collection and the organization of labor drafts. After independence, however, the Liberal project decreed that indigenous people were no longer subjects of Spain but legal citizens of the new republics. Liberals wanted to eliminate distinct indigenous status, in part because this made it easier to acquire and sell lands formerly held in common by indigenous villages.

The End of "Indian" Tribute

The tribute was a form of taxation historically levied on people living in conquered provinces (for example, Roman Judaea in antiquity). For the Spanish colonial administration, the payment of tribute symbolized native people's postconquest subjugated status. Yet tribute also offered indigenous people certain protections. In addition to the all-important understanding that they could continue to hold land communally, the colonial pact also provided native peoples with special courts and exempted them from other taxes like the oppressive sales tax. In return, the native people implicitly promised to be loyal subjects of the Crown and faithful adherents of the Catholic religion. Republican constitutions eliminated indigenous tribute, but in the process eliminated access to special courts, and exposed indigenous populations to the sales tax.

In Mexico in 1821, Agustín de Iturbide and guerrilla insurgents like Vicente Guerrero agreed in the Plan de Iguala to consider everybody living in Mexico (except Spaniards) as *Americanos*. The practical consequence of eliminating distinctions based on the colonial caste system (race) was to eliminate tribute. To replace lost tribute revenue, Emperor Iturbide created the personal contribution head tax, levied on every citizen regardless of race. In South America, the Liberators shared Iturbide's dim view of the discriminatory tribute tax. Because they hoped to recruit indigenous soldiers for the wars, both Simón Bolívar and José de San Martín promised to end tribute. This promise held little appeal for indigenous populations, who understood that eliminating tribute also eliminated their right to hold lands in common. Although the Liberals governing Gran Colombia decreed the end of tribute during the wars, President Bolívar reinstated the tax in 1828 to raise revenue, changing its name from "tribute" to the "personal contribution" in order to maintain the positive image of Liberal republicanism.

In Ecuador, Peru, and Bolivia, the tribute remained the government's principal source of revenue for most of the nineteenth century. In Peru, with mining and

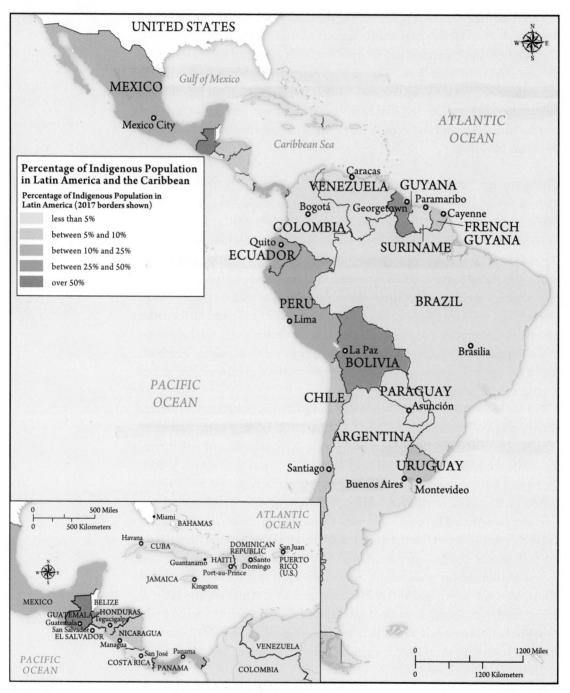

Percentage of Indigenous Population in Latin America and the Caribbean

Percentage of Indigenous Population in Latin America (2017 borders shown)

- less than 5%
- between 5% and 10%
- between 10% and 25%
- between 25% and 50%
- over 50%

≡ **MAP. 4.1**

commerce in the doldrums, tribute provided 40 percent of government revenues prior to the guano era. As in Mexico, indigent Peruvian governments sought to broaden the tax to increase revenues, and so enacted the *contribución de castas* (personal contribution) in 1826 to include people of all races, including the mestizos of the highlands and the freed Afro-Peruvians residing on the coast. The latter tax proved impossible to collect, in part because of the poverty of the *castas* and in part because they received no tangible benefit from the tax, unlike indigenous people, whose right to hold property communally depended on payment of the tribute.

A similar attempt to impose a broader tribute in Ecuador in 1843 was abandoned after it led to riots. Both Liberals and Conservatives felt they had no choice but to endorse this racist reminder of the colonial period. Only when revenues from export taxes rose in these three countries could tribute be abolished (Ecuador in 1854, Peru in 1854, and Bolivia in 1866). Even then, provincial highland departments in Peru and Bolivia continued to collect tribute well beyond the time of its official abolition.

Communal Land Issues in Central America: El Salvador and Guatemala

At the beginning of the national period, much of the land in El Salvador and Guatemala was not privately owned, but held in common. The Spaniards had introduced the idea of private property in the sixteenth century, and wealthy families acquired private landed estates by sale and inheritance. But at the time of independence, the indigenous populations and the Catholic Church were the region's main landholders. The Catholic Church, which had lost much of its property during the late colonial period, lost still more in the early 1800s, when early Liberal governments expropriated most of its properties, leaving common lands as the most widely practiced form of land use. Indigenous communities all held common lands, while non-elite ladino (nonindigenous) municipalities also laid claim to what were known as *tierras del común*, or commons. All this would change with the introduction of coffee in the middle part of the nineteenth century.

The majority of the indigenous population in El Salvador and Guatemala lived in the temperate mountainous zones, where they tilled the volcanic soil much as their ancestors had for generations. To their misfortune, however, this land was also suitable for the planting of coffee. Conservative leaders initially promoted coffee growing throughout Central America, but the cultivation of the product did not initially disrupt landholding patterns. Conservative policies under Guatemala's Rafael Carrera, in fact, had expressly protected indigenous communal land holdings by law until Carrera's death in 1865. When the Liberals returned to power after Carrera's death, however, they sought to expand commercial productivity and to assimilate the indigenous into the general population as laborers.

The transition from communal to private lands was most ruthless and abrupt in El Salvador. In 1879, a government survey revealed that more than one-quarter of the nation's land, almost all of it ideal for coffee cultivation, belonged to indigenous communities. In fact, some indigenous people had begun to cultivate coffee themselves. Ladino growers had also begun the process of claiming title to *tierras baldías* (public lands, though in fact indigenous common lands) to create coffee haciendas. Even so, for the Liberal government of Rafael Zaldívar, for whom "progress" was a watchword, the process of converting common to private lands could not move fast enough. That same year, he issued the first in a series of laws that led to the virtual abolition of communal lands.

The first of these laws allowed for any individual to lay claim to private ownership of communal lands if they agreed to plant at least one-quarter of it with coffee. Next, in 1881 and 1882, the government abolished indigenous and then municipal ejidos outright. Although the former occupants of these lands were theoretically allowed to purchase title to their own lands, few could afford to do so. Instead, large-scale commercial coffee *finqueros* (estate owners) absorbed indigenous common lands into their estates, and the people who had once lived and worked the lands became their landless tenants. In 1897, the government passed a statute which gave the state the right to expropriate common lands and turn them over to the coffee finqueros, thus forcing the indigenous and ladino campesinos to work as **colonos** (sharecroppers) on the large estates.

The Maya population constituted a much larger proportion of Guatemala's population than did the indigenous population in El Salvador. Mayan common lands also offered great promise for the widespread cultivation of coffee, and Guatemala's Liberals took steps to expropriate and privatize these lands. But the sheer size of the Maya population complicated this scenario. Liberal leaders recognized the value of leaving enough communal lands intact for Mayan farmers to feed themselves, not so much out of a respect for custom, but because the *finca* system could operate more cheaply that way.

During the 1870s, under the regime of Liberal leader Justo Rufino Barrios, legislation permitted the privatization of common lands for coffee cultivation. In 1877, the government passed new laws by which individuals could gain title to any indigenous common lands that they had previously leased or illegally used. As in El Salvador, the government labeled many indigenous lands as "tierras baldías" (public lands) and sold them to private owners. Between the 1860s and 1880s, the Guatemalan government actively encouraged the immigration of Germans—preferred for their reputed industriousness—into the Alta and Baja Verapaz regions. The Germans introduced new cultivation methods to enhance the quality of Guatemalan coffee overall and to market the product abroad. By 1900, Germans alone owned around one hundred large estates in the departments of Alta and Baja Verapaz. But in the process, the native Q'eqchi' and Poqomchi' Maya lost their vast communal holdings and found themselves able to subsist only by going to work for the fincas.

Unlike El Salvador, however, Guatemala never outlawed the ejidos outright, especially those located at higher altitudes where coffee would not grow. But the size of indigenous common lands was greatly reduced, forcing the Maya to work on the coffee fincas on a seasonal basis as wage labor.

Land Conflicts in Bolivia

The conflicts between large estates (haciendas) and *ayllus* (communities that held their land in common) in the Andes were similar to those that occurred in Central America and also dated from the sixteenth century. The liberal ideals expressed in Spain's Constitution of 1812 and reiterated by Simón Bolívar sought to reform Andean landholding and tribute-paying patterns based on the colonial pact. As part of their ideological attack on corporate (group) privilege, Liberals sought to end communal landholding practices by subdividing community-held land into individually owned private properties. Fortunately for Bolivia's indigenous Aymara communities, the postindependence Bolivian state was both too weak and too poor to consider Bolívar's reform seriously and thus left colonial landholding institutions intact.

As was the case in Peru and Mexico, the devastating effects of the wars for independence ruined Bolivia's mines. Lacking access to foreign capital and new technology, the mines were largely shut down. Agricultural production replaced silver exports as Bolivia's most significant economic activity until the late 1860s. Both hacendados and ayllus produced foodstuffs (such as potatoes, quinoa, corn, and wheat) to sell to the urban and small town populations. The most successful hacendados and ayllus took advantage of the time-honored Andean ecological-niche strategy of verticality, which recognized that different crops flourished in different ecological zones to provide a variety of foodstuffs to markets. Villagers raised llama and alpaca for wool at very high altitudes, grew potatoes and quinoa at fairly high altitudes (8,000 to 12,000 feet), and cultivated corn and wheat in the warmer temperatures and longer growing season of lands below 8,000 feet.

Slow market growth meant the competition between ayllus and haciendas for land, labor, and access to water diminished. As a consequence, the reduced economic activity during the early nineteenth century had positive consequences for the environment and indigenous people both in Bolivia and other Andean nations.

Producing fewer goods for export minimized resource depletion and allowed for more sustainable growth. Both ayllus and haciendas could leave sufficient land fallow in order to prevent soil exhaustion.

Members of indigenous ayllus nonetheless remained the poorest members of Bolivian society. Working as a peon on a hacienda meant more security: the hacendados paid the peon's tribute, offered rations in times of distress, and gave his family a small parcel of land to farm. On the other hand, hacienda workers labored long hours for somebody else, and on many occasions performed humiliating, unpaid service called *pongueaje,* a demeaning term for a person who guarded the hacendado's door and slept on the floor. In contrast, while ayllu members received their allotment of communal property according to their family's needs and

≡ **Indigenous Bolivian Woman Weaving.** Indigenous people in the Andean nations during the early nineteenth century continued to live much as they had in the colonial period. The woman with her back to the photographer is weaving clothing for her family and with the intent to sell any surplus at a local market. The animal pens indicate that this relatively prosperous family kept llamas or possibly alpacas for their wool, as the weaver has skeins of yarn to her left. Meanwhile, her two daughters are learning how to ply this ancient craft.

maintained a close cultural identity connected to their traditional lands, they had to earn enough cash in their spare time to be able to pay tribute.

Bolivia's economic depression ended in the early 1860s when technological advances (such as more efficient pumps to drain mines) triggered new investments in the silver mining industry. The country also earned other revenues by leasing portions of its distant Pacific coast, rich in nitrates used as agricultural fertilizers, to Chilean miners. (This arrangement came back to haunt Bolivia in the War of the Pacific of 1879–1883, when Chile, Bolivia, and Peru fought to control this territory and its resources. Chapter 6 discusses the War of the Pacific in detail.) Bolivia's infamous caudillo Mariano Melgarejo, who gained the presidency by shooting his opponent in the head at a political rally, surrounded himself with friends representing the silver mining interests. These advisors convinced Melgarejo to adopt free trade, which reduced taxes on exported silver and also urged him to eliminate indigenous tribute and break up communally held ayllu lands.

Melgarejo's 1866 statute privatizing indigenous land ownership caused an uproar. Potential investors protested when the corrupt regime only permitted the dictator's friends to bid on the newly privatized lands, while indigenous communities complained because the conversion from communal to individual private landholding forced them off traditional lands. Even after a coup terminated Melgarejo's presidency in 1870, the Liberal elite pressed the new caudillo to end indigenous communal landholding practices. Thus, an 1874 statute expropriated the "excess" land of the ayllus (defined as land not currently under cultivation, or land lying fallow) and further permitted ayllu members who owned individual plots to sell their farms to outsiders. For several years this law remained dormant because the mining sector's high profits lured investment capital away from real estate. Eventually, however, those profiting from the mining boom decided to diversify by speculating in land, especially around the city of La Paz.

In the aftermath of Bolivia's participation in the disastrous War of the Pacific, Bolivia's elite sought stability in the creation of the same kinds of Liberal and Conservative parties common elsewhere in the region. The Conservatives won the first election in 1880 and unleashed an assault on ayllu properties. Between 1880 and 1900, roughly 30 percent of ayllu land in the rich **altiplano** (high plains) near La Paz had been sold to hacendados despite the indigenous attempts to contest these sales in court. No wonder that many Aymara, led by Pablo Zárate Willka, joined the Liberals when they rebelled and unseated the Conservative government in 1899. But the Liberals disappointed the Aymara. Not only did the Liberals accelerate ayllu land grab, but they also continued to assess the provincial tribute, now called the *contribución territorial*, well into the twentieth century.

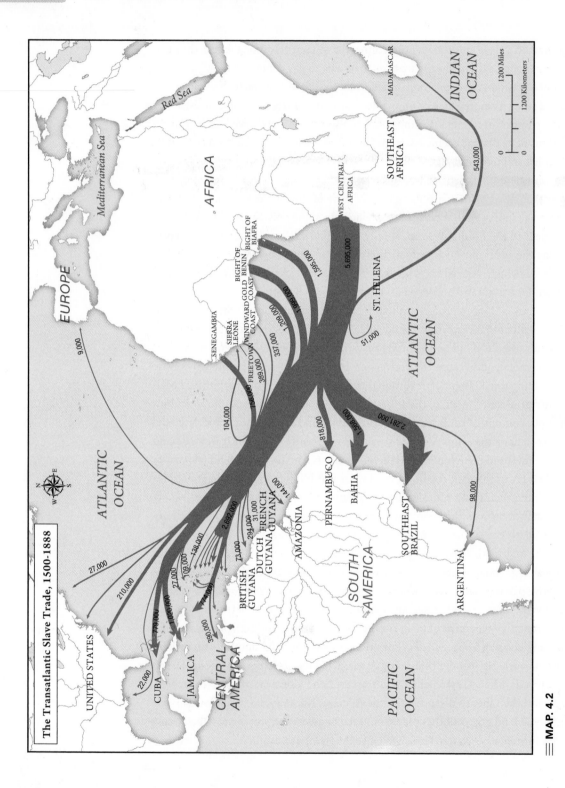

The Transatlantic Slave Trade, 1500-1888

MAP. 4.2

The End of the Transatlantic Slave Trade and the Long Path to the Abolition of Slavery in Latin America, 1820s–1880s

The end of the transatlantic slave trade and the abolition of slavery throughout the Americas was a slow process of social reform. Abolitionists in each nation fought to pass domestic laws and change practices, gradually beating back the evil institution. These national struggles were linked through the spread of abolitionist ideas. Legislators, publishers, slave owners, and slaves themselves were acutely aware of their counterparts elsewhere in the Americas, and where they stood on the great questions of slavery. Nowhere was this consciousness more acute than in Brazil and in Cuba, where the slow progress toward abolition was both a source of shame to many and cold comfort to those slave owners who clung to the institution.

Throughout the Americas, wherever African slavery existed, so-called **maroon societies**—colonies of runaway slaves—emerged. The name came from the Spanish *cimarrón*, for untamed (itself probably a derivation from a similar Taíno indigenous word). Most maroon societies were small and short-lived (with a few notable exceptions). In the nineteenth century, they existed at the margins of free societies, characterized by trading and raiding—exchange of crops and resources with local farmers, accompanied by occasional pilfering of guns and other goods. The maroon societies rarely challenged the slaveholding order directly—their endurance depended on flexibility rather than confrontation. But as a symbol of liberation they held enduring power. And in many cases these communities persisted through the twentieth century, rare examples of black landholding and autonomy.

Sugar in the Americas

For nearly five centuries, sugar and slavery expanded together in the Atlantic world. In the 1400s, the Portuguese named the island of Madeira (wood), off the west coast of Africa, for its hardwood timber, useful in ship building. By the end of that century they had deforested much of the island and were using the land to cultivate sugar. Madeira had no indigenous population, so the Portuguese forcibly imported slaves purchased on the African coast for labor on the new sugar plantations. The slaves felled the remaining timber, chopped the sugar cane, built the mills and turned the grindstones, a backbreaking labor regime exacerbated by sugar cane's rapid growth. Twice or even thrice-yearly harvests offered no season of diminished exploitation for slaves on sugar plantations.

By the early 1500s, the Portuguese had transplanted both sugar and the use of slaves for its cultivation to Brazil. They were soon frustrated in their attempts to enslave enough Indians to work the land, and again turned to Africa for slave labor. Ultimately almost five million enslaved Africans would be transported to Brazil. By the early seventeenth century, sugar and slavery were so intimately linked that subsequent colonial powers scarcely contemplated alternatives. In Saint-Domingue and Martinique, Jamaica and Puerto Rico, Barbados and the Bahamas, Curaçao and Surinam, the French, Spanish, British, and Dutch followed the Portuguese lead. Competition among these colonial powers exacerbated demands for more fertile land and more slave labor.

The insatiable desire of European and North American consumers for sugar seemed limitless. As increased cultivation lowered the price, cane sugar went from a luxury item to an everyday staple. Like coffee, tea, and tobacco, it became one of the addictive stimulants whose consumption seemed a necessary part of life in the industrializing world.

As Europeans consumed sugar, sugar consumed slaves and the land. Average life expectancy for slaves on sugar plantations varied over time and throughout the region, but was always dramatically shorter than that of free persons in the same society. And as sugar denuded and degraded one island after another, it stoked the desire of planters to claim and monopolize land. Sugar cultivation went hand in hand with concentration of land and power in the hands of a few. Those who attempted to slow this concentration and the destruction that went along with it generally lost out to planter interests.

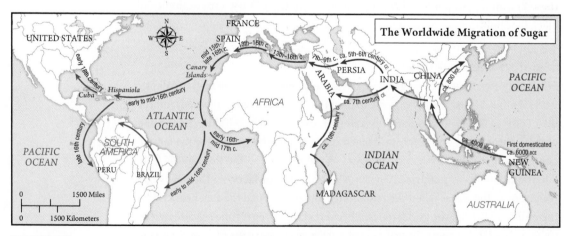

≡ **MAP. 4.3**

Nowhere was this pattern stronger than in Cuba and in northeastern Brazil. In Cuba, sugar marched eastward across the island from Havana to Santiago. As that march picked up pace over the course of the nineteenth century, plantations got larger. The growth of a few **centrales** (large, industrialized sugar mills) increased capacity for sugar export, stoking the deforestation of eastern Cuba and the increased exploitation of slave labor. In Brazil, as well, the landscape of sugar meant captivity and exploitation for labor.

From the 1820s on, abolitionist pressure from the British threatened the sugar and slavery complex. The resistance of slaves themselves, along with the pressure exerted by domestic abolitionists, intensified as well and forced reform. In Brazil, where coffee had already supplanted sugar as the most lucrative crop, that trajectory unfolded differently than it did in Cuba, where sugar remained king. In both places, the links between sugar, environmental destruction, and labor exploitation persisted beyond abolition.

Environmental Factors Intensify Cuba's Sugar Production

Early in the nineteenth century, Cuba enjoyed a balanced export agricultural economy, shipping tobacco, sugar, and (especially) coffee to Spain and other international markets. Coffee farms flourished in western Cuba, where planters produced between fifty million and eighty million pounds annually. Because coffee production needed smaller capital investments, it appealed to the modest planters whose farms dotted the Cuban landscape. Coffee had other advantages. Because the beans ripened slowly and were harvested only when ready, labor exploitation was less exhaustive on the coffee plantations than on the sugar plantations. In addition, coffee plants provided shade where slaves could grow crops to sustain their families. As a result, life expectancy of slaves on coffee plantations exceeded that of slaves on sugar plantations. But environmental circumstances, specifically the devastating hurricanes of 1844 and 1846, radically transformed the nature of Cuban agriculture.

These hurricanes, among the strongest ever to strike tropical storm-prone western Cuba, laid ruin to large portions of the island just as the harvest season began. The storm surge flooded low-lying coastal regions as well as the streets and suburbs of Havana, where hundreds of people drowned. Waves as high as thirty feet washed over coastal communities, spreading brackish water over the fields for miles into the interior, rendering them infertile. It took years of fresh rainfall before nature leached the salt from the soil and made the land productive again. Winds of over 140 miles per hour whipped up the storm surge and tore millions of coffee plants up by the roots, laying waste to farm after farm. Poorly built slave quarters collapsed, killing many people. Flood waters drove thousands from their homes.

The hurricanes of 1844 and 1846 contributed to Cuba's shift from balanced agriculture to a sugar monoculture. The expansion of sugar production first began between 1794 and 1804, when numerous Haitian planters, fleeing the Revolution, sought refuge in Cuba. There, they reinvested in sugar operations. In the wake of the hurricanes, planters in western Cuba largely abandoned coffee; it took years for a tree to mature, and many feared that another natural disaster would ruin their investment. With abundant vacant land, wealthy planters purchased huge tracts and felled much of the forested area to create and expand sugar plantations. The world market rewarded their investment.

With Haitian competition eliminated and European and US consumers hungering for sweets, world demand for sugar increased in the remaining decades of the 1800s. In the 1820s, sugar had represented only about 26 percent of Cuba's agricultural exports, by 1860 that had increased to 61percent. The new sugar monoculture increased the brutality of the slave labor regime and simultaneously accelerated ecological degradation.

Slave Trade and Abolition in Cuba

Of the million slaves brought from Africa to Cuba over the course of the Atlantic slave trade, 85 percent arrived during the nineteenth century. Between 1830 and 1850, a time that the African slave trade was on a steep decline elsewhere in the world, an estimated 10,000 new slaves arrived in Cuba each year. The Spanish Empire did not eliminate the transatlantic slave trade to Cuba until 1867, well after most of the Americas had ended the practice. Sugar planters and mill owners invested in modern technology in the same decades, transforming sugar cultivation from a a low-tech colonial plantation system to a modern complex based on steam, railroads, and extensive **ingenios** (sugar cane mills). Technological modernization, however, only intensified demand for slave labor.

The sugar boom also delayed Cuban independence. In contrast with criollos in other parts of Spanish America, Cuban elites did not push for independence from Spain. Instead, they clung to their colonial relationship in the belief that the mother country could protect them from the kind of massive slave uprising that had destroyed Haiti's French planters. Planters well remembered a series of rebellions that had roiled the island in 1812, incidents in which slaves and members of the free black population collaborated, communicating through underground networks spreading across the island. They relied on the Crown to protect them from the possibility of more extensive rebellion.

Nonetheless, slavery's days were numbered. The abolitionist movement had gained unstoppable momentum over the course of the nineteenth century. Britain outlawed its slave trade in 1807 and slavery outright in 1833 in all its colonies, and used its influence as the most powerful nation in the world to push the other European nations to do the same. The United States outlawed the trans-Atlantic slave trade in 1808, although the trafficking of humans within the country remained legal. By midcentury, only three places in the New World (the United States, Brazil, and the Spanish Caribbean colonies) remained slaveholding territories. Of the Caribbean Spanish colonies, Cuba was the most prosperous and most committed to retaining its slaves.

But by midcentury, loyalist sentiments toward Spain began to unravel, as Spanish administration of Cuba became more lackadaisical. As fears rose that Spain might capitulate to Britain's pressure to end the slave trade, Cuban planters began for the first time to consider the possibility of independence from Spain. As in earlier decades, the issues of independence and slavery were intertwined, but by this time the equation was reversed. In the minds of some prominent Cuban planters, independence from Spain (or possibly annexation to the United States as part of the slaveholding South) seemed to offer the best possibility for maintaining slavery and avoiding slave rebellion.

Enslaved people themselves, meanwhile, sought every opportunity for greater autonomy, whether through subtle resistance, community building or outright rebellion. Enslaved people in Cuba developed institutions like the *cabildos de naciones*, religious and benevolent mutual-aid societies. They were also places of sociability that fostered community, dignity, and empowerment for people whose cruel circumstances otherwise deprived them of basic opportunities. Slaves and some free people of color used the cabildos not only as places where they could try to retain their culture and identity, but also as venues in which they could form networks contesting slavery and colonial order. While some Cuban planters began to see independence from Spain as a means of retaining slavery, slaves saw emancipation and independence from Spain as linked struggles.

Spain's imperious treatment of Cuba further provoked a desire for independence. In the early 1860s, Spain reacted to a series of workers' protests and strikes in Havana with severity, including the silencing of free speech, imprisonment, and the imposition of new taxes and tariffs on the island. These measures infuriated not only Cubans in the capital but also the sugar barons in the remote eastern part of the island. Colonial ties frayed to the breaking point. In 1868, when a group of eastern conspirators declared the "Grito de Yara," a declaration of independence for Cuba from Spain, many Cubans, from sugar planters to urban bourgeoisie and free people of color, cautiously supported the movement.

Thus began the **Ten Years' War** (1868–1878), an inconclusive war for independence that ravaged Cuba for a decade. One of the key intellectual authors of the war was a planter from Oriente province named Carlos Manuel de Céspedes, who was among those who issued the Grito de Yara. Céspedes freed his own slaves at the same time, inviting them to take up arms with him against Spain. However, Céspedes's linking the cause of independence for Cuba with abolition of slavery cost him the support of most of Cuba's affluent planters, especially those living on the richer western part of the island.

Instead, the fight for Cuba's freedom would largely fall to lower-class rebel forces, led for most of the war by a Dominican-born former Spanish cavalry officer named Antonio Maceo. Maceo, a mulatto, introduced the battle tactic of the "machete charge," wherein troops used their ubiquitous field tool against Spanish swords to deadly effect. Maceo's rebel army was largely made up of guerrilla soldiers called **Mambises** (a term of disputed origin that came to refer to all those who volunteered for the fight against Spain—most of them free blacks and escaped slaves). Although poorly armed and trained, these volunteers slowly beat back the better-equipped Spanish forces.

While the rebels were able to take over significant amounts of territory in eastern Cuba, they were less successful in the west, where the specter of the machete-wielding Mambises cooled the ardor that many white planters had momentarily felt toward independence. Yet Spain's drastic reaction to the independence uprising completely offset any Cuban goodwill they might otherwise have regained. In early 1868, Spain launched a war of extermination against the rebels, killing off their leadership, committing widespread extrajudicial executions, and placing women and other noncombatants into deadly concentration camps. Never again could Cubans consider themselves to be full Spanish citizens.

The war ended in a stalemate in 1878, with the Pact of Zanjón between Cuba and Spain. The pact offered a compromise: Cuba remained a Spanish colony and slavery was abolished. The terms to end slavery, however, still disingenuously forced slaves to "work off" their purchase price to their former masters over a certain period of years. Maceo refused to sign the pact. Spain eventually relented and lifted restrictions on emancipation, finally abolishing slavery in 1886. But the clouds of war remained on the horizon, as another war for Cuban independence, soon to be led by the veterans of the Ten Years' War, lay in the near future.

Abolition in Brazil, the End of Empire/Creation of the Old Republic

As in Cuba, Brazil's path toward abolition was bound up with the history of international war. The War of the Triple Alliance (1864–1870) had two major consequences for slavery in Brazil. The first was that the Brazilian Empire pressed thousands of slaves into military service, or accepted them as substitutes for slave owners seeking to exempt themselves from military obligation, which amounted to the same thing. These slaves were nominally freed to become soldiers, but faced reenslavement if they deserted. Those who survived the war and the constant threat of disease at the front only tasted real freedom after the war's end, when they were released from military service and their emancipation was confirmed. While armed service became a path to freedom for some slaves, officers also used it as justification for harsh treatment of their men. Brazil's armed forces became notorious for miserable conditions and use of corporal punishment, characteristics that would outlast the abolition of slavery itself.

The second consequence was the installation of a Conservative cabinet that diverted gathering pressure for emancipation by passing the 1871 Law of the Free Womb, which declared that children born to enslaved mothers would henceforth be considered free. The law also stipulated, however, that these children would remain in the custody of the slave owner until age twenty-one, an arrangement that continued to subject them to forced labor. Together with the prior suppression of the slave trade, this law guaranteed the eventual disappearance of slavery in Brazil. But it did so in the most gradual way imaginable, protecting the interests of slave owners. If no further steps toward abolition had been taken, the Law of the Free Womb would have allowed slavery to exist until the mid twentieth century. Brazilian abolitionists like Joaquim Nabuco expressed frustration with the law's modest achievements. It was not a progressive law, but rather a rear-guard defense fought by slave owners.

Between 1871 and 1881 the political power of those slave owners began to erode for different reasons. As coffee planters from São Paulo made a transition to immigrant wage labor, they became less invested in slavery, depriving the institution of its most powerful advocates. Abolitionism spread from a marginal position to the mainstream of Brazilian political debate, and was embraced by the free press. Abolitionists emerged within both the Liberal and Conservative parties. Most importantly, slaves themselves seized the opportunity to intensify their resistance not just against individual enslavement, but against the institution.

Brazilian slaves had always struggled for greater autonomy, through rebellion, escape and everyday strategies of resistance. As the slave order broke down in the 1880s, however, slaves finally had the opportunity to act collectively and more openly. Small communities of runaway slaves on the outskirts of Rio de Janeiro made a transition from covert survival to open occupation, defying authorities to try to rein them in. Slave owners urged the emperor to repress these communities, but imperial forces were leery of inciting widespread rebellion. For urban slaves, it became clear that the house of slavery was tottering.

In the countryside, meanwhile, imperial soldiers—some of them freed slaves themselves—ignored calls from planters to capture and imprison runaway slaves. This left slave owners themselves to carry out repressive measures. By the mid-1880s, they no longer had the will or the manpower to do so. On the coffee planta-tions of western São Paulo, collective slave flight became common. By 1886 there were cases of dozens of slaves walking away together, an expression of hard won autonomy and mobility.

Finally, on May 13, 1888, the empire issued a short declaration outlawing slav-ery and overturning any prior contrary legislation. Princess Isabel signed the law while her father, Emperor Pedro II, was away in Europe—with his blessing, but in a way that separated him from the act. The law offered no compensation to slave owners. It also provided for no assistance for freed slaves. In the aftermath of the Golden Law, as it became known, many former slaves drifted to the growing cities of Rio de Janeiro and São Paulo to look for work.

Abolition was the last significant political act of the Brazilian Empire. For de-cades, Pedro II had conciliated between Liberals and Conservatives, wielding power in a way that preserved a social order built on slavery. With slavery gone, the aged emperor lost the ability to reconcile competing political groups. A cohort of military officers and political renegades began organizing a movement to over-throw the empire and inaugurate a republic, with a president chosen by men of property rather than a hereditary monarch. They stitched together an alliance pushing for the creation of a republic, in which the armed forces would assume something like the moderating role previously played by the emperor. When the military cohort deposed the emperor on November 15, 1889, Pedro II realized resistance was pointless. With much of the officer corps supporting the coup, he could not call on the armed forces, and whatever popular sympathy he continued to enjoy could not prevent his ouster. Instead, he chose to depart quietly for exile. The transition happened without bloodshed and with little immediate significance for most citizens.

CULTURE AND IDEAS

Photographs of Brazilian Slaves

Photographs constitute one of the most valuable sources of documentary evidence of the everyday nature of slave life in nineteenth-century Brazil. An extraordinary quantity of photographs of Brazilian slaves survives, more extensive than that of any other slave society—a consequence both of Brazil's slow progress toward abolition and the popularity of photography in its growing cities. Why did photographers make these images? In some cases they were made for foreign travelers, as keepsakes of exotic Brazil. In others they were made for the Emperor Pedro II, supplying him with a vast photographic record of life in the empire. And in still more instances, they fulfilled the ambitions of individual photographers to document social types, a common preoccupation among photographers of the time.

The photo below shows slaves on a coffee plantation in 1882. Several are adolescents. The men and boys wear trousers of durable canvas, the women wear ragged cotton dresses: Slave owners invested the minimum possible in feeding and clothing their labor force. They either carry shallow sieves designed to separate coffee berries from twigs and leaves, or deep baskets designed to carry heavy loads of picked

≡ **Brazilian Slaves and Senhora**

berries. Behind them to the right of the image is a mature coffee bush, source of the commodity whose production largely governed their lives—or at least those facets that could be controlled by the slave owner. The photo conveys the relative isolation of the rural world, where the slave owner's word was law.

The photo above shows the contrasting urban world. These slaves were dressed in relatively luxurious attire, displaying the slave owner's wealth in the streets of the city, as does the ornate sedan chair, the fine cloth of the slave owner's dress, and her dangling earrings. The slaves are nonetheless barefoot: slaves were prohibited from wearing shoes, precisely to make their status clear in an urban world populated by many free people of color. (This prohibition was often flouted, but it did mean that anyone seen barefoot in the street was almost certainly a slave.) The slaves look downward, as they were expected to do in the presence of slave owners. The slave owner herself, in contrast, gazes directly at the lens, a woman confident of her stature in the ruthlessly hierarchical world of nineteenth-century Brazil.

- Why might consumers have been interested in acquiring photographs of slaves? Were slaves necessarily passive subjects of the photographer, or could they shape their own image in some way?

≡ **Brazilian Slaves Mustering for Work in the Fields**

The Rise of Popular Religion, 1830s–1890s

Across Latin America, the Roman Catholic Church rather than the new national governments claimed most peoples' hearts and minds in the decades following independence. Even those who were not overly religious tended to think of themselves as Catholic. Latin Americans followed the cycles of the Catholic liturgical calendar, named their children after patron saints, and were baptized and buried through the Church. Catholicism in Latin America, however, was far from monolithic. During the early nineteenth century, the traditional Church would be challenged in multiple and novel ways.

The Emergence of Popular Catholicism

The elite discourse between the emerging Liberal state and the Catholic Church had a profound impact on local populations, although not necessarily in the ways which Liberal policy makers anticipated. This was particularly true in areas of Latin America where the indigenous population was large and the colonial influence of the Church had been strong, such as in the Maya areas of southern Mexico and the highlands of Guatemala. Many Maya considered the church an ally against the kinds of Liberal innovations that brought ladino lowlanders onto traditional indigenous lands and pushed Indians into wage peonage on agricultural estates. This is not to say that indigenous people necessarily found champions in the local clergy, whom they often considered to be greedy, or in the orthodox doctrines of Catholicism, with which they were often unfamiliar. But in many instances, native populations recognized that the Church shared a common enmity toward Liberal reformers who represented a way of life hostile to their shared interests.

When Liberals regained control of most areas of Latin America in the second half of the nineteenth century, their agendas of "order and progress" had powerful anti-Catholic implications. These measures undermined the stature of the institution of the Roman Catholic Church, without necessarily diminishing popular religiosity. Liberal restrictions on clergy meant that the number of priests declined precipitously, leaving many pulpits empty and depriving congregations of sacraments like baptism. The Church's decline was particularly evident in predominantly indigenous areas, and in the frontier regions of the emerging states.

While the Church as an institution began to recede, however, Catholicism as a lived religion continued to thrive. In the wake of the institutional Church's decline, a type of popular Catholicism practiced by an enthusiastic local laity quickly emerged. This popular faith supplemented and in some cases replaced orthodox Catholicism in indigenous regions and on the frontier, where it developed and thrived without Church sanction or clergy. The manifestations of popular religion in these areas were not merely reactions to the reduced presence of the Church, but instead represented local adaptations of vital elements of the faith, with or without the blessing of the official Catholic Church.

This **folk Catholicism,** as some have called it, grafted elements of local spirituality, legend, and shamanism onto orthodox Catholic dogma, creating a fusion of indigenous and Catholic beliefs. In some cases, traditional beliefs, which years of Christian contact had never fully snuffed out, gained new public exposure. Some of these, such as Maya fire ceremonies in Guatemala or rituals devoted to the Andean goddess Pachamama in Bolivia, fell far outside the norms of Catholic dogma. Others, which elevated the devotions to popular images of Christ, the

≡ **Religious Procession in Huárez, Peru.** In the indigenous communities in the Andes, Catholic religious holidays scarcely resembled orthodox Christianity. In fact, one foreign traveler noted that he wished he were rich, because he would like to pay the pope's fare to the Andes to watch such ceremonies. Here, the villagers are processing the patron saint of the community of Huárez. The statues have indigenous features, and other symbols of pre-Christian Andean traditions accompany the celebrants. The men are doffing their hats out of respect for the saints and/or their ancient deities associated with the saints.

CULTURE AND IDEAS

The Virgin of the Angels: A US Protestant Missionary (Mattie Crawford's) View, 1922

In the early 1920s, the American missionary Mattie Crawford left the evangelical hotbed of Los Angeles for Central America. She traveled on mule back through Mexico, Guatemala, and Nicaragua attempting to spread her understanding of the Gospel. Even though Crawford did her work in the 1920s, the people she encountered lived much the same as they did in the nineteenth century. Crawford herself saw the world through a Victorian worldview: she interpreted popular religion as superstition. Her description nonetheless offers a glimpse of the power of passionate faith.

"The people worship many different kinds of idols. Sometimes they walk hundreds of miles to do penance to some stick of wood or piece of stone which has been set up by the priests.

We met one young man who told us he had crawled three hundred miles carrying a golden dish, valued at ten thousand dollars. This idol to which he crawled is in Costa Rica and is called 'The Virgin of the Angels.' The people have been made to believe that this little image of black stone three and a half inches high can perform all sorts of miracles such as opening blind eyes, healing the deaf, and driving away evil spirits. The temple in which this idol is kept was built at a cost of one million dollars. Once a year this 'Virgin of the Angels' is carried to visit all the other santos (saints-idols) that she may bless them and give them more power for the ensuing year. This immense temple is literally lined with gold and silver dishes and cooking utensils brought there by the rich inhabitants of the country with the hope that the image would bless and heal them. Just outside the temple are stacks of corn, bananas, coffee, sticks and stones, which the poor people have brought that they too might have their sins taken away and their diseases healed.

They are begging for the Gospel. Their call comes to you and me, 'Come over and help us!' and God asks, 'Who will go for us?' Isaiah 6:8. Who will leave home and loved ones and go out not knowing whither they go? They will have to eat native foods that are unclean and unwholesome and may cause fevers and various sicknesses. They may have to sleep in old dirty native huts where mosquitos, scorpions, bats, and vermin will attack them. Nevertheless, God is calling now, as He called in Isaiah's day, 'WHO WILL GO FOR US?' Jesus is Coming Soon! The message must go forth regardless of the cost."

- How does this account of popular religion reveal the biases of its author? Can we read past these biases to gain greater understanding of the rituals and their social context?

Virgin Mary, and the saints, and sacred geography (such as holy mountains and caves), fused local belief with Christianity in innovative ways that were as resonant with local religious sensibilities as they were alien to orthodox Catholicism.

In a very real sense, the anticlerical pressures of the nineteenth century forced Latin American Catholicism to transform itself from a colonial institution to a force for social innovation and local agency, a uniquely "Latin American" Catholicism that some historians have paradoxically referred to as "Catholicism without priests." The formal, institutional Church did not disappear in the face of the Liberal reforms of the late nineteenth century. But it was the vitality of its believers rather than the strength of its institutions that kept the faith vibrant, a phenomenon that would continue well into the twentieth century (see chapter 7).

Political, Social, and Economic Responses of the Popular Classes, 1840s–1880s

Urban and rural workers also found ways to participate in the Liberal-Conservative debates that divided Latin America politically through much of the nineteenth century. They voiced their opinions in the streets, in broadsheets, occasional riots, and at the ballot box, in those rare instances where they were permitted to vote. With the export economy in the doldrums and the elite dominating politics, the popular classes took advantage of the occasional openings in the political system to protest their poverty.

Popular Liberalism and Conservativism in Mexico

During early federalist administrations in the 1820s, members of the popular classes took advantage of the decentralized administrations to participate in local civic associations and municipal government. The federalists' agenda of keeping taxes low and using those financial resources for local projects (such as building schools and bridges) appealed to many poorer Mexicans. Plans to broaden suffrage to indigenous men and former slaves, following the abolition of slavery in Mexico in 1829, also appealed to the poor .

This experiment with federalism encouraged popular elements within the states to voice their opinions about the important issues of the day. Some scholars have described these forces as "popular federalists": their interests did not always align perfectly with those of elites in the Federalist Party, but they occasionally pulled in the same direction. Looking across Latin America, we can describe these common folk who pushed for reform as "popular liberals," for their strategic support of some liberal reforms. In southern Mexico in 1853, popular liberals initiated the Revolution of Ayutla, a rebellion that ultimately placed Benito Juárez and his fellow Liberals in office. (After a brief pause, the conflict reignited as the War of the Reform, see chapter 3). The popular liberals demanded a restoration of universal suffrage (meaning all men—women remained excluded) and the expanded roles of municipalities. In addition, popular liberals pleaded for an end to military conscription. Conscription struck hard at poor families who depended on both the husband and wife to share in the labor necessary to enable the family to feed itself. Indigenous villagers belonging to the Liberal coalition hoped, too, that Liberals would help them regain possession of disputed lands.

Popular liberalism was more egalitarian than Conservative models, advocating a voice for every citizen in local affairs, a vote, and the full expression of individual liberties. Popular liberals opposed high taxes, and argued that tax revenues should be invested in local infrastructure. Elites in both the Liberal and Conservative parties viewed the popular liberals with caution, and sometimes with outright disdain, blaming them for disorder. By the 1870s, the demands of popular liberals in Mexico had largely been suppressed. But the impulse behind popular liberalism, pressing for greater popular participation in the political life of the republic, would remain strong not only within Mexico, but throughout the region.

Conservatives could also rely on popular support throughout Latin America, particularly over the issue of Church-State relations. Mexico provides two good examples. There, residents of some remote rural areas sided with national Conservatives to protect the Church against Liberal efforts at secularization, especially in the 1850s. In western Mexico, for example, the former bandit Manuel Lozada led a popular conservative uprising against the Laws of the Reform and in defense of indigenous community boundaries and property rights.

Lozada formed a multiclass alliance with merchants, foreign businessmen, and local authorities to defend popular Catholicism. Rallied by the slogan, "Long Live Religion," he and has fellow popular conservatives fought against the Liberal state until he was captured and executed in 1873. A similar situation emerged in the Mixteca Baja province of Oaxaca state, which had experienced a re-Christianization after independence with an influx of new clergy, the expansion of the parochial school system, and a widespread agreement on the importance of Christian morality. Community members saw the Laws of the Reform as an attack on the faith and their way of life. They particularly objected to the Ley Lerdo (Lerdo Law), which threatened to confiscate the land belonging to their *cofradías*, or religious brotherhoods. Although Liberals snuffed out the revolt in 1860, popular conservativism remained a vibrant force in the region.

Popular Liberals and Popular Conservatives in Colombia

The Liberal-Conservative debate in Colombia also included people from the popular classes, who can be similarly divided into popular Liberals and popular Conservatives. In most instances, members of the poorer sectors of society fought alongside an elite leader because that individual promised rewards, such as future employment, or because they owed the leader loyalty as an employee, ranch hand, laborer, or friend. In a few instances, most noticeably when liberals opened the franchise to universal suffrage and encouraged widespread political participation, the popular classes played a larger role than usual. When Colombia's Liberal Party instituted Latin America's boldest constitutional experiment with democracy between 1849 and 1886 (chapter 3), the popular classes took this opportunity to bargain with the Liberal leadership for concrete benefits.

Simón Bolívar nicknamed Colombia "the university" for the interest of the local population in higher learning and French publications, in particular. Given this reputation, it is not surprising that ideas associated with the French Revolution of 1848 flourished here. Intellectuals devoured Parisian newspapers detailing the events of February 1848 and the fall of the French monarchy. The swelling tide of liberalism in Europe rejuvenated Colombia's Liberal Party during the hotly contested election of 1849. Intimidated by a mob led by artisans (handicraft workers such as shoemakers, tailors, tinkers, masons, and carpenters), Congress chose Liberal General José Hilario López as Colombia's next president.

Over the next four years President López enacted numerous liberal reforms, such as expulsion of the Jesuit monastic order, universal suffrage for men, and reduction of the army to four hundred soldiers and three generals, largely replacing it with a citizens' militia. To improve the nation's economy, López agreed to a measure of free trade (tariff reduction), which infuriated his former friends the artisans, but which was consistent with liberal economic theory. Most importantly, in 1852 the Liberals abolished slavery. Abolition strengthened the Liberal's political hand in southern Colombia, where approximately 27,000 Afro-Colombians still suffered under the yoke of bondage, and along the Caribbean and Pacific coasts, also home to large numbers of Afro-Colombians.

With the broadening of suffrage, Afro-Colombians leapt into the political fray. In addition to voting, they joined the numerous Liberal Party "Democratic Societies" that emerged during the decade of the 1850s. These new political clubs were open to all social groups, including those who wore *ruanas* (ponchos) and went barefoot, as one Liberal politician bragged. In these societies, the newly emancipated listened to newspapers being read and attended classes where they learned about democracy.

Afro-Colombians also participated in the new democratic experiment by volunteering to serve in the popular militias. David Peña personified popular liberalism. Well educated and a sterling orator, Peña fought for Liberal causes from 1851 until his death in 1878. Afro-Colombians had shed blood fighting for the Liberals, and insisted on access to land redistributed from expropriated haciendas in return. Peña led the campaign. Liberal elites, however, balked at legislation infringing on private property rights, a principle they cherished. As a consequence, Afro-Colombians resorted to extralegal measures, such as squatting on land belonging to haciendas and ejidos, stealing wood and food from estates, and refusing to pay rent on properties they had leased. As a legislator, Peña penned a statute permitting these actions. When Afro-Colombians sacked the city of Cali in 1877 demanding land titles, however, the Liberal and Conservative elite united in opposition to their demands.

Colombia's Conservative Party enjoyed substantial popular support, as well, but among a different constituency: the indigenous communities. Because of Conservatives' interest in preserving corporate privileges (the rights of groups), the Conservatives defended the rights of indigenous communities to *resguardos*, or communal landholdings. Indigenous communities asserted that they, as citizens possessing the same constitutional liberties as other Colombians, could choose communal landholding forms instead of being forced to accept individual proprietorships. Popular conservatives also formed political clubs. In Bogotá, the conservative "Popular Society" spoke out against the Liberal Party's anticlerical reforms and protested the expulsion of the Jesuit order, an issue that also appealed to indigenous communities.

Women from the popular classes enjoyed fewer opportunities for political participation, as both the Constitution of 1853 and that of 1863 denied them the vote. (Indeed, no country in the world permitted women to vote in the 1800s, with the exception of New Zealand, in 1893). Nevertheless, women from all social classes participated in the political process and made their voices heard. Afro-Colombian women approved of the Liberals' free trade and antimonopoly stance because many of them were small-scale producers of distilled sugar cane alcohol, up to this time a monopoly dominated by elite landowners. Ending that monopoly legalized the women's businesses. Female popular liberals also ran taverns where the Democratic Society clubs met, and joined men in political rallies and in tearing down fences that hacendados erected to keep the poor from using their lands. Because of the passions associated with the Church-State debate, Conservatives probably recruited more women to their cause than did Liberals. Elite women hosted other women at political gatherings, and supported Conservative petition drives against the "Reds," or Liberals, in defense of the Catholic Church.

As mentioned in chapter 3, Conservatives and moderate Liberals alike became fearful about the political activities of the popular classes and the obvious lack of law and order during the 1860s and 1870s. Moderate Liberals believed that the popular classes lacked the education and discipline to respect the inviolability of private property, and had failed to understand that citizenship incurred obligations as well as granting rights. Conservatives and moderate Liberals alike recognized that the proliferation of guns in the hands of the popular classes contributed to the lack of order. These elite concerns and hesitation undermined Colombia's experiment in broad-based democracy. From 1886 to 1930, Conservatives and the elite again dominated politics.

The Popular Classes and the Economy

Throughout Latin America, the popular classes also weighed in on the economic debate between supporters of protectionism and the advocates of free trade.

Although popular-class artisans were few in number, they played a disproportionate role in discussions about economic policy. Organized during the colonial period into guilds (medieval entities that created a monopoly over production and marketing of a particular product), artisans in the early national period rallied to the side of Conservative politicians and caudillos who advocated continuing high import taxes. Such taxes protected local craftsmen by artificially raising the prices of mass-produced goods from Europe.

In the late 1840s, the Liberals pushed for modified free trade, which lowered prices for consumers while still providing revenue for the treasury. Colombia's Law of June 14, 1847, reduced the tariff by 30 percent, ruining many artisans. Taking advantage of the opening political system, tradesmen formed an Artisan Society, which played a major role in the presidential election of 1851. But Colombia's artisans were unsuccessful in the advocacy for restoring high import tariffs, and never regained the relatively privileged status they enjoyed in earlier periods.

In Lima, Peruvian artisans offered political support and campaign contributions to Conservatives and caudillos who legislated tariffs as high as 85 percent on foreign-made shoes and clothing. But the rising Liberal tide in the late 1840s ended artisans' hopes. The Liberals reduced tariffs and then abolished guilds entirely in 1862—one of several Liberal reforms designed to destroy corporate protections and foster free trade and individualism. Artisans remained politically active; some even joined the Liberal party, usually because they preferred the Liberals' more open views on society and politics even as their identity as artisans was subsumed into the working class. Working-class people in Bolivia came down on both sides of the economic issue. Wheat growers in northern Bolivia preferred tariff protection against cheaper Chilean grain, while miners and traders in the south allied with free trade regimes that allowed them to ship goods beyond Bolivia's borders without burdensome taxes.

Social Banditry in Mexico and Brazil

The notion of social banditry has intrigued historians, some of whom believe that a few outlaws were righteous men of the people fighting for social justice. The idea of the social bandit, however, is largely a romantic exaggeration. In Mexico, bandits joined national rebellions, like the War of the Reforma (1857–1861), but did so because they were self-interested and saw participating in the war as a means of gaining access to opportunities otherwise denied to them. In times of peace, bandits robbed for a variety of reasons, including boredom and adventure as well as the simple lust for loot.

During the colonial period, banditry certainly existed, but the breakdown of law and order during the wars for independence allowed bandits to cloak their activities in the guise of patriotism and expand their activities. As the Mexican state further weakened during the early republic, theft and robbery grew more widespread. This lawlessness appalled foreign visitors. On more than one occasion, travelers journeying along the only road from Veracruz to Mexico City reported that their stagecoach was held up multiple times with each successive gang stealing something. By the time they arrived in Mexico City, the now-naked travelers had to sprint for their hotels dressed in nothing but newspapers! (As with Mattie Crawford's description of popular religious rituals, these tales tell us as much about the perception of foreign visitors as about local practices. But they do indicate the expectation of banditry in rural Mexico.)

Mexican banditry reached its heyday during the decade of the War of the Reforma and the ensuing French intervention in Mexico (1857–1867), when the government was largely unable to provide any sort of law and order. The most notorious bandit gang, the Plateados, consisted of the former soldiers of one of the most important Liberal generals. When these mustered-out soldiers received no reward for their services in the War of the Reforma, they kept their weapons and took up banditry in the state of Morelos, just southeast of Mexico City. Hacendados and merchants moving goods along the roads had no choice but to pay protection money to the bandit gangs, supplying them with horses, guns, and other goods. The widespread lawlessness convinced Benito Juárez and the Liberal government in 1861 of the necessity for creating a rural police force called the **rurales**.

As had occurred in many other countries historically, Juárez recruited amnestied bandits and former soldiers and hired them as his policemen. After all , who knew the lay of the land and the practices of banditry better than former bandits themselves? The government paid members of the rurales fairly well (certainly more than what they could earn as soldiers or farmers) and with more certainty and less danger than what bandits earned by robbing stagecoaches. Resplendent in *charro* (cowboy) outfits with grey jackets, braided suede pants adorned with silver buttons, leather boots, and a wide sombrero, the rurales cut a jaunty figure. But as long as the Mexican state remained weak, the rurales were an untrustworthy force. When the temptation to loot became too great, rurales sometimes reverted to banditry. Only under the stabilizing influence of Porfirio Díaz's dictatorship after 1876 would the rurales become an effective mechanism of social control.

In Brazil, rural banditry arose in the context of the economic decline of northeastern Brazil in the nineteenth century. As the focus of agricultural production shifted to the southeast, the population of the arid interior of the northeast dropped. Landowners clung to large but unproductive estates, while tenant farmers struggled to survive. The Guarda Nacional, responsible for internal security, was barely existent in this region. Instead, feuding landowners relied on their own private guards, rough and ready locals who knew the territory well. In times of increased economic stress, such as the periodic droughts that lacerated the *sertão* (hinterland), these private guards sometimes quit their landowning patrons.

When they struck out on their own, raiding farms for supplies and holding up mule-trains, they became known as *cangaceiros*, or backwoods bandits. Like their Mexican counterparts, the Brazilian cangaceiros balanced intimidation with rewards in order to move freely among local populations. Their leather clothing, distinctive hats with a broad, raised brim, and feats of derring-do made them iconic figures. Agents from outside the *sertão* (the Brazilian outback) sent to capture them usually failed. The transition from empire to republic in 1889 only stoked the phenomenon of rural banditry, as the new state levied taxes that outstripped its own capacity of enforcement. Not until the 1930s would a combination of political centralization, improved communication, and vigorous pursuit enable more enduring repression of cangaceiros.

Poor Women in Latin America, 1820s–1880s

During the early republican era, the lives and concerns of women who lived in poverty differed from those of the elite and middle-class women described in chapter 3. Although poor women also used the legal system to defend their persons and assert property claims, their struggle against poverty took priority. Nineteenth-century legal codes figured men as heads of the household, complicating the political and economic activity of women in the popular classes. Female-headed households were common in practice, but the women who led them always faced greater legal challenges than men in the same situation. Urban women had more opportunities than did rural women, but still faced great obstacles as they strove to feed their families and keep a roof over their heads.

Patriarchy and Poor Rural Women

Many poor indigenous women, especially in Mexico, Guatemala, and the Andean nations, lived with their families on communally held lands. Under these circumstances, culture and tradition tempered the harsh rules of patriarchy. Women living in the great pre-Hispanic indigenous civilizations had enjoyed more independence and equality than Spanish women, and these cultural norms persisted into the nineteenth century and beyond. Young indigenous Andean couples frequently cohabited with one another in a trial marriage to test their compatibility before finally tying the knot, for example. Women in these trial marriages could reject their potential spouse without shame and select an alternative mate. While custom permitted the husband to "discipline" his spouse (a euphemism for beating), the same custom allowed the wife to flee or take a protective lover. Although the law preferred male property ownership, under various circumstances women obtained a share of the community's land. Finally, women from indigenous communities enjoyed the freedom to engage in the community's social, economic, and cultural events, whether selling *chicha* (corn beer), plying their wares in marketplaces, sharing chores with female friends, or dancing in festivals.

The bonds of patriarchy more tightly constricted the lives of indigenous women residing on haciendas. There, marriage offered both indigenous men and women a more secure life because only married couples were entitled to the use of

≡ **Tortilla Maker in Mexico.** This woman is in the midst of making her family's basic food, the tortilla. The finished tortilla is designed to hold beans, chili peppers, and perhaps a little meat inside. She has already soaked corn kernels in water enriched with calcium and now she is grinding the corn with the stone *mano* (hand grinder) on the *matate* to make corn meal. She will pat out the corn meal into tortillas and then place them on the *comal* (grill) to cook for a few moments. Even before the Spaniards brought cattle, sheep, and chickens to the New World, the basic tortilla stuffed with beans, squash, tomatoes, chili peppers, and other vegetables provided Meso-American indigenous people with a nutritious, balanced diet.

subsistence plots of land belonging to the hacienda. Being a tenant farmer provided the family with economic security as well as access to credit, a much less vulnerable status than that of daily wage laborers, who could be turned out of the hacienda gate at a moment's notice. Hacendados insisted on the requirement of marriage because wedded couples provided the social stability demanded by the patriarchal estate system.

Indigenous wives on haciendas experienced significant exploitation. They were expected to work beside their husbands in the fields during the planting and harvest seasons for little or no wages. In addition, these wives toiled in the estate owner's home: cooking, cleaning, doing laundry, and performing other tasks. Sexual exploitation by the hacendado or administrator was not uncommon. Most importantly, indigenous women had no legal status. In estate account books, women's wages were added to those of their husband with no notation, so that no legal mark of their existence remained. Paternalism weighed heavily on these rural women well into the twentieth century.

Patriarchy and Poor Urban Women

Poor women in urban areas like Mexico City labored to survive. Prohibited by law from joining the guilds that allowed male tradesmen to earn a decent living, women spun wool or cotton and fashioned clothing without guild protection. Other women waited tables in restaurants, sold food in the streets, or acted as midwives. In Brazilian cities, women in street markets sold sugar cane juice, fruit, coffee, honey, salt, sugar and other small-scale household necessities. By far the largest number of women, especially single women, worked in elite and middle-class homes as domestic servants. Even these poorly paying jobs enticed women to migrate from rural areas to cities.

A significant percentage of poor families had single, never-married women as their head of household. Women typically left the workforce for some time in order to give birth and raise families. But whereas even young children shared the burden of agricultural labor in rural settings, in urban settings children imposed greater costs on the family. Infant mortality rates were also often higher in poor urban quarters than in traditional rural settings. As a result, urban women tended to have smaller families than their rural counterparts.

Women constituted the majority of the population in most Latin American cities, in part because of the high mortality rate men experienced during the independence and other wars, and in part because so many unmarried women fled rural areas seeking better opportunities in the cities. Urban women worked in the streets or in factories in the company of unrelated men, challenging gender norms that equated female honor with confinement to a private sphere. Urban women also defied expectations in cases where they used the law to divorce husbands when faced with physical abuse or a failure to provide. Neighbors, friends, and family would often testify on behalf of the abused spouse because the thin walls of boarding houses where the poor huddled together allowed them to overhear violent quarrels. As a result, poor urban women tended to have greater autonomy and opportunity than their rural counterparts.

Haciendas and Urban Life: The Role of Elites, 1830s–1880s

The elite, played a disproportionate role in Latin American politics and society between independence and the Great Depression of 1929, and in some instances, beyond. Rich in land but cash-poor during the early republican years, the elite constituted approximately 1 to 3 percent of any given nation's population. Elite families that owned haciendas or plantations formed alliances with other elite families through marriage and other relationships, guarding against upheaval in turbulent political environments. At the same time, rival family networks usually joined opposing political parties.

Elites and Comparative Ranching in the Rio de la Plata Basin

The grasslands of the Río de la Plata basin, covering parts of southern Brazil, nearly all of Uruguay, and a large portion of Argentina, had long been recognized as uniquely suitable for raising cattle. The ports of Buenos Aires, Montevideo, and (to a lesser degree) Rio Grande, Brazil, stood ready to export beef to markets throughout the Atlantic world. Until the early 1850s, however, the productivity of these lands was limited by wars between caudillo factions. Producers in Brazil, Uruguay, and Argentina exported beef, but primarily in the form of salted jerky to a regional market. Much of this beef jerky was purchased by slave owners in Brazil and Cuba, where minimal rations of beef jerky were the principal source of protein in the slave diet.

The end of the Ragamuffin Revolt in southern Brazil in 1845 and the fall of Rosas in Argentina in 1852 (chapter 2) set the stage for a period of increased productivity and export. (Caudillo wars in Uruguay continued for another decade, but Uruguay did not lag far behind Argentina in beef exports.) Improved productivity coincided with rising demand for beef in industrializing western Europe, primarily in Great Britain, where per capita beef consumption doubled in the second half of the nineteenth-century. The challenge for Argentine, Uruguayan, and Brazilian producers lay in how to bring their beef to hungry markets. Their contrasting answers reveal much about the expectations and ambitions of rural elites in these locations.

Producers initially sought to expand the market for salted beef, in both the Caribbean and Europe. But European consumers generally eschewed jerky, except for the urban poor, who could also be made content with a dollop of cartilaginous jelly reduced from the boiled shinbones of cattle. Given the reduced purchasing power of this market, the price of beef jerky on European markets did not compensate for the costs of its shipping. The most powerful Argentine and Uruguayan ranchers soon invested in technological innovation, seeking to meet demand more efficiently. This meant partnering with European investors, who provided capital and know-how, beginning with the spread of railroads through the Argentine and Uruguayan pampas in the 1850s–1870s. The rail network included lines that ran nearly to the Brazilian border, to capture some of the Brazilian supply. Technological innovation continued with methods created in Fray Bentos, Uruguay, designed to render and export "meat extract," a thick, bottled paste of concentrated beef stock. Meat extract was easily shipped, and was enthusiastically adopted by European consumers eager for the flavor and protein of meat but unable to afford fresh beef.

Fray Bentos, along with similar plants on the Argentine side of the Uruguay River, became leaders in exporting canned, corned beef, using a combination of local and foreign investment, technological innovation, shipping efficiency, and marketability. By the time the nineteenth century drew to a close, early refrigerated plants and rail cars made possible large-scale transshipment of frozen beef for the first time. These enterprises depended on favorable policies from the Argentine and Uruguayan governments, where ranchers exercised great power. The relative proximity of Montevideo and Buenos Aires also favored these producers.

Despite geographical similarity on the Brazilian side of the border, the development of a beef-exporting industry played out differently, lagging behind border rivals. The owners of the salting plants of the small city of Pelotas had always been wealthier and more powerful than the ranchers themselves. They relied almost entirely on African and Afro-descendant slave labor until the 1880s. With their capital heavily invested in slaves, they tended to increase production through labor exploitation, rather than technological innovation.

In contrast to the ranchers of Argentina and Uruguay, the salt-plant owners of Pelotas held little power in their national capital. As a result, Brazil's imperial government and the Republican government that followed it tended to formulate policies that helped coffee producers in Rio de Janeiro and Sao Paulo, rather than southern ranchers. Rail networks in southern Brazil paled in comparison to those across the border, and Brazil was slower to adopt methods like canning and refrigeration. In consequence, production and profitability boomed in Argentina and Uruguay, and lagged in Brazil.

The nature and possibilities of rural life were similar in these three countries. But the more enduring commitment to slavery on the part of Brazilian landowners, and their position farther out on the periphery of national and Atlantic economies, made them less likely to seek innovation. Even when facing similar circumstances, local elites in Latin America might pursue different courses, with significant consequences.

Mexican and Peruvian Haciendas

Although earlier historians believed that haciendas were a holdover from medieval seigniorial estates that existed primarily to lend social prestige to an elite family, today's scholars reject this interpretation. Instead, they argue that haciendas were capitalistic enterprises, designed to generate profits by selling their products in local, national, or international markets. Some elite families, especially those who sold high-demand products abroad, were extremely wealthy and enjoyed opulent lifestyles. Other **hacendados** in remote, isolated regions serving a small market lived only slightly better than their employees. Size mattered, but was not paramount. Rich haciendas needed not only land but also adequate sources of water and labor. Poor haciendas lacked one or more of these necessities.

≡ **Mexican Hacendados.** These two hacendados are in charge of their rural world. As the *patrones* (bosses of the hacienda), they controlled a very patriarchal society where they, as the hacendado, wielded absolute authority. Their rich clothing and their fine horses differentiated them from the rags worn by the peon laborers on their estate. When hacendados visited their estates, they stayed in their large houses, but most often hacendados were absentee landlords. However, in poorer regions throughout Latin America, the social divide between patrón and peon was much smaller.

With some exceptions, the elite in early republican Mexico and Peru descended not from the conquistadores, but rather from entrepreneurial Spanish immigrants who arrived at the end of the eighteenth century. These ambitious immigrants, often successful merchants, won social acceptance because of their growing wealth. Because their riches could reinvigorate the languishing fortunes of poor but distinguished elite families, many fathers found these immigrants to be worthy suitors for their daughters. In turn, the immigrants gained access to an established and influential network of families, which opened up additional business prospects. These kinship alliances proved invaluable in hard times, such as during the wars of independence. In addition to blood relatives, the elite also used the fictional relationship of *compadrazgo* (godfatherhood) to expand their networks of friends and family.

The Sánchez Navarro family of northeastern Mexico personified many of these generalizations. The founders, a priest and his brother employed as a government official and tax collector, began purchasing property in the 1770s. The priest's nephew inherited the sheep ranch and grabbed more land at low prices during the troubled years after independence. His two sons, Jacobo Sánchez Navarro and Carlos Sánchez Navarro, purchased an enormous neighboring estate in 1840, creating the largest **latifundia** (great estate) in all of Latin America. Their hacienda stretched over 16 million acres, larger than the combined US states of Connecticut, Massachusetts, Rhode Island, New Jersey, and Delaware.

Despite all this acreage, the arid land and distant marketplace yielded only modest profits. Elder brother Jacobo remained on the estate, while Carlos, a lawyer, managed the political affairs of the family in Mexico City. There, he enjoyed the high life: European clothes, a coach, the best schools for his children, a full wine cellar, and box seats at the prestigious Iturbide Theatre. Jacobo, meanwhile, lived under much more modest circumstances in the countryside of the state of Coahuila. Like many typical great estates of this era, the Sánchez Navarro latifundia lasted three generations, amassing lands in a first generation, exploiting them in the second, and beginning to lose grasp on them through divided inheritance in the third. Spanish laws of inheritance required the division of property between all children, including daughters, and the postindependence abolition of entail (a holdover from medieval privilege preventing creditors from seizing property from select elite families) contributed to the relatively short duration of elite status for many families. Fortunately for the Sánchez Navarros, in a singular instance of sibling heirs, Jacobo and Carlos agreed to hold the land jointly. Spanish law protected the property rights of women, including widows. This legal requirement also benefited the Sánchez Navarros. When Jacobo and Carlos were young and inexperienced, their mother Apolonia ran the latifundia successfully. Even after her sons took over the business, she remained a forceful partner behind the scenes until her death.

The Sánchez Navarro's hacienda required a hierarchy of employees, ranging from an administrator who kept the books and reported directly to Jacobo, to several *mayordomos* (overseers) who supervised daily operations and more numerous foremen who in turn managed the work of the *vaqueros* (cowboys), skilled workers like blacksmiths, and peons. While the hacienda's main business was to produce medium-quality wool for mills in Puebla and Veracruz, it also raised foodstuffs such as wheat, corn, and sugar for local consumption. Because the family could never use all of its land, it leased plots to tenant farmers as well.

In the long run it was not the laws of inheritance that proved the undoing of the Sánchez Navarro latifundia, but rather Mexico's turbulent political situation. Like most successful elite families, the Sánchez Navarros navigated troubled political waters by having relatives and friends in both the Liberal and Conservative parties, at least until the 1850s. Carlos Sánchez Navarro befriended General Santa Anna during the Mexican War, and asked the president for a political favor during Santa Anna's final term in 1852. Long unhappy because the Sánchez Navarro properties straddled the border of the states of Coahuila and Zacatecas, which meant paying taxes to two jurisdictions, Carlos asked Santa Anna to move Coahuila's border southward in order to incorporate their entire hacienda. Santa Anna happily obliged, in exchange for a huge bribe. This well-publicized episode forced the family squarely into the Conservatives' camp, which did not stand them in good stead during the War of the Reforma and the ensuing French intervention. Benito Juárez ultimately confiscated the Sánchez Navarro estate, forcing Jacobo and Carlos to spend years in exile and poverty.

Sheep haciendas in the Peruvian province of Azángaro, located on the high plains near Lake Titicaca, contrasted with the modest grandeur of the Sánchez Navarro lands. Only a few small towns existed in the entire province, which limited the elite's market opportunities. To keep haciendas operating during the impoverished years of the early republic, hacendados from Azángaro needed a secondary source of income as a bureaucrat, an army officer, or as a politician. As in the Bolivian case discussed earlier in this chapter, because of the downturn in the economy, the rural poor enjoyed more autonomy during these years as the elite did not attempt to expand their landholdings.

Peruvian Market at Sicuani. This Sunday market, deep in the Peruvian Andes, provided an opportunity for local people to exchange goods. The clergy encouraged the development of Sunday markets in larger communities, hoping to draw indigenous people from surrounding rural areas to Mass before the market opened. This strategy often backfired because markets began early, and the sociability of the market often took precedence over Mass. As this image demonstrates, women have dominated these markets from colonial times to the present.

ECONOMICS AND COMMODITIES

Foreign Travelers in Andean Marketplaces

Almost every foreign traveler visiting the Andean nations during the early nineteenth century commented on the unique marketplaces they encountered in cities and towns. Once a week, often on Sundays, indigenous people would bring their wares to the central plazas found in most urban areas. Vendors typically arrived early in the morning to set up their produce for sale. Markets were arranged differently, but usually larger ones sold a variety of products including animals, fruits and vegetables, spices, prepared food, and handicrafts.

Indigenous and mestizo vendors, almost exclusively women, dressed in colorful ponchos, dark skirts, and hats typical of their region. While men helped transport goods to market and sold animals on its outskirts, the marketplace itself was the domain of women. In an era when primitive transportation made shipping fresh fruit nearly impossible, the variety of produce available astonished travelers; in addition to familiar items such as oranges, apples, pears, and melons, markets in highland Ecuador sold tasty fruits then not obtainable in the United States or Europe such as bananas, pineapples, passion fruit, tree tomatoes (*tamarilla*), *naranjilla* (a tart little orange), papaya, and (soursop).

Elsewhere in the market women sold shawls and ponchos woven from cotton and wool as well as other handmade goods. The smell of local delicacies, including soups, stews, fried pork, and *cuy* (guinea pig) as well as the ever-present *chicha* (corn beer) drew throngs of the hungry and thirsty (but few foreigners) to a different corner of the market. While customers also tended to be female, no self-respecting elite woman would venture into such a public space; the cook or some other servant shopped for household necessities.

Foreigners were simultaneously bemused and perplexed when purchasing items at these markets because of basic cultural misunderstandings. For example, one American botanist visiting Colombia in the 1850s set off to Bogotá's marketplace to purchase a ball of string to tie his specimens together. His hosts told him precisely how much he should pay. When he found the correct vendor at the market, she (noting the doctor was a foreigner) quoted double the normal price. Instead of bargaining with her as locals would have done, the botanist turned on his heels and stalked away, searching vainly in the market for another string seller. Meanwhile, the vendor's daughter followed him throughout the marketplace, holding the ball of string. Only when he appeared ready to abandon the marketplace altogether did she offer him the string at the regular price. He found this behavior mystifying, but his Colombian hosts simply laughed.

- Why do you think Andean marketplaces were primarily the domain of indigenous women?

Elite houses, like *campesinos'* huts, were constructed from adobe, with the luxury of a wooden door instead of a cowhide covering the entrance and wooden floors instead of dirt. More affluent hacendados had some furniture, silverware, and possibly a chapel. Here the gap between rich and poor was relatively small.

Nevertheless, sharp social distinctions between the *patrón* (hacendado) and the *peón* required that each know their place. In this paternalistic society, peons owed great deference to the elite owner, whom they reverentially referred to as *taita* (little father). His word determined right or wrong, and his mayordomo doled out rewards or punishments accordingly. On the occasions of a great holiday, the patrón would sit in front of the estate building while his peons filed by, each proffering a gift (like a chicken) to a foreman, who would hand it to the mayordomo, who in turn offered it to the hacendado. This ceremony reaffirmed the paternalistic hierarchy of the hacienda. In return, the patrón would provide each of his peons and tenants with a gift of cloth and a feast with copious amounts of alcohol. This long-standing Andean reciprocal relationship was designed to maintain harmonious bonds between the social classes, the elite and the peon.

Urban Life in Lima

Like their counterparts throughout Latin America, Peru's elite relished the urban lifestyle. In contrast to the predictable, even tedious, rhythms and routines of the country estate, Lima offered the excitement of frequent social gatherings and cultural entertainment like theater. Elites lived luxuriously in Lima; the largest of their urban homes could occupy a full city block. Family life centered around a patio or two located in the middle of the home, where scented flowers and gurgling fountains offered repose. Fortress-like walls deadened the cacophony of sounds from the street made by peddlers offering their wares, beggars crying for alms, and wooden carts rumbling along the cobblestones. Elites also believed that wives, mothers, and daughters should largely remain within the protected inner sanctum of the home, avoiding the risks and dishonorable associations of the public street.

From the time of the conquest until the twentieth century, Lima's elite families lived near the city center, the Plaza de Armas. For example, one of conquistador Francisco Pizarro's most loyal comrades-in-arms, Jerónimo de Aliaga, built his palatial residence a half-block from the government palace. Sixteen generations later Aliaga's descendants still live in this home. Residing downtown gave the elite access to the centers of political power and entertainment and separated them from those they deemed the "dangerous classes" of the urban poor.

Moving away from the center of the city, the neighborhoods grew poorer with increasing percentages of indigenous people and Afro-Peruvians. The urban poor and even some members of the downwardly mobile elite and middle classes struggled to make ends meet during the inflationary Age of Guano beginning in the 1850s (chapter 3). In the absence of banks or credits cards, cash-strapped members of the elite and middle class could pawn expensive items at the national pawnshop to maintain social appearances. To feed their families, the poor often hawked their meager goods for credit or cash at

≡ **A Cockfight.** Cockfighting, an inexpensive sport available to indigenous people, was one of the few forms of excitement available in smaller towns. Two people loosed their roosters (fighting cocks) with metal spurs tied to one leg onto each other, sometimes to fight to the death, sometimes until one cock dominated. Bystanders could place wagers on their favorite and cheer. Fights seldom lasted more than five minutes. Although cockfighting has been banned in the United States and many other countries because of the cruelty of the sport, it is still popular and legal in Mexico, Cuba, and the Andean nations.

pulperías (corner grocery stores) infamous for gouging their customers with high interest rates.

During the Age of Guano, President Ramón Castilla used some of Peru's new riches to revitalize Lima. A new railroad connected Lima to its port city of Callao. The city planners took the controversial step of tearing down the protective colonial walls, which critics claimed could expose Lima to a scourge of bandits and highwaymen. But expanding the city limits relieved the housing congestion caused by Lima's growing population. New construction that the elite deemed undesirable, such as the modern, progressive penitentiary designed to rehabilitate criminals, could be located on the outskirts of the city, far from the homes of the **gente decente** (the elite people, also sometimes called the *gente de razón*, in contrast with *los de abajo*, a phrase popularized by Mexico's famous author Mariano Azuela, who used the term as the title of his 1915 novel about the Mexican Revolution). Elite politicians nervously worried about crime rates in these neighborhoods, including the recently formed Chinatown.

Following the model of redesigned Paris and Vienna, Lima's urban planners replaced meandering colonial streets with wider boulevards and larger plazas. Gas streetlights and iron plumbing served the best neighborhoods near the Plaza de Armas, providing modern conveniences that encouraged the elite to remain in their colonial-era homes. People from the growing middle sector of society, which included lawyers, doctors, notaries, businessmen, students, and certain artisans, settled in neighborhoods near the elite. Artisans who crafted products that attempted to compete with European manufactured imports, such as textiles and leather goods, occupied the most ambiguous social position of these middling groups. The end of the guano boom signaled an economic downturn, and dwindling resources spelled the end to Lima's first steps toward creating a modern urban space.

Conclusion

Over the course of the nineteenth century, even as each Latin American nation experienced its own distinctive struggle to survive and cohere, everyday life across these nations gradually became more similar. Port cities like Havana, Veracruz, Cartagena, Rio de Janeiro, and Buenos Aires had similar institutions, similar social distinctions, and similar modes of sociability. Capital cities, such as Mexico City, Lima, Santiago, and Bogotá, developed analogous political factions, political party networks, and modes of organization. Even rural areas,

TIMELINE

1845–1867
Slave trade ends in
Brazil and Cuba

1854–1866
Abolition of tribute in
the Andean nations

1863–1886
Era of popular republicanism in Colombia

1850–1879
Limited beef exports
(jerky and corned beef)
from Argentina to Europe

1863–
Beginnings of
urbanization in Lima

where greater local differences survived, faced similar conflicts of the erosion of collective lands and the increasing transition from subsistence farming to market-oriented agriculture.

At the same time, everyday life throughout the region became more complex. The citizens and would-be citizens of these struggling Latin American nations filled an increasing number of roles, interacted with a greater range of institutions and offices, and faced a growing number of choices. As the larger patterns governing life throughout the region became more similar, distinction and differentiation within each society increased. Latin Americans, like their counterparts around the world, stumbled toward modernity.

KEY TERMS

abolition 146	gente decente 183	maroon societies 155
altiplano 153	hacendados 178	rurales 172
centrales 157	ingenios 158	Ten Years' War 160
colonos 150	latifundia 179	
folk Catholicism 165	Mambises 160	

1866–1874
Creation of Liberal land legislation in Bolivia

1879–1890
Seizure of indigenous communal lands in Guatemala and El Salvador

1868–1878
Ten Years' War for Independence in Cuba

1886–1888
Abolition of slavery in Cuba and Brazil

Selected Readings

Balmori, Diana, and Stuart Voss. *Notable Family Networks in Latin America.* Chicago: University of Chicago Press, 1984.

Bayly, Christopher. *The Birth of the Modern World, 1780–1914: Global Connections and Companions.* Oxford: Oxford/Blackwell Press, 2004.

Bell, Stephen. *Campanha Gaúcha: A Brazilian Ranching System, 1840–1920.* Palo Alto, CA: Stanford University Press, 1999.

Childs, Matt C. *The Aponte Rebellion in Cuba and the Struggle against Atlantic Slavery.* Chapel Hill: University of North Carolina Press, 2006.

Dean, Warren. "A Slave Autograph: São Paulo, 1876." *Luso-Brazilian Review* 7, no. 1 (1970): 81–83.

Hall, Carolyn, and Hector Perez-Brignoli. *Historical Atlas of Central America.* Norman: University of Oklahoma Press, 2003.

Harris, Charles H., III. *A Mexican Family Empire, the Latifundio of the Sánchez Navarros.* Austin: University of Texas Press, 1975.

Helg, Aline. *Our Rightful Share: The Afro-Cuban Struggle for Equality, 1886–1912.* Chapel Hill: University of North Carolina Press, 1995.

Howard, Philip A. *Changing History: Afro-Cuban Cabildos and Societies of Color in the Nineteenth Century.* Baton Rouge: Louisiana State University Press, 1998.

Jacobsen, Nils. *Mirages of Transition: The Peruvian Altiplano, 1790–1930.* Berkeley: University of California Press, 1993.

Klein, Herbert S. *Haciendas and Ayllus: Rural Society in the Bolivian Andes in the Eighteenth and Nineteenth Centuries.* Palo Alto, CA: Stanford University Press, 1992.

Lauria-Santiago, Aldo A. *An Agrarian Republic: Commercial Agriculture and the Politics of Peasant Communities in El Salvador, 1823–1914.* Pittsburgh, PA: University of Pittsburgh Press, 1999.

McCreery, David. *Rural Guatemala, 1760–1940.* Stanford, CA: Stanford University Press, 1994.

McGillivray, Gillian. *Blazing Cane: Sugar Communities, Class and State Formation in Cuba, 1868–1959.* Durham, NC: Duke University Press, 2009.

Murray, Pamela. *Women and Gender in Modern Latin America: Historical Sources and Interpretations.* New York: Routledge: 2014.

Pérez, Louis A., Jr. *Cuba: Between Reform and Revolution.* 3rd ed. New York: Oxford University Press, 2006.

Pérez, Louis A. Jr. *Winds of Change: Hurricanes and the Transformation of Nineteenth-Century Cuba.* Chapel Hill: University of North Carolina Press, 2001.

Rogers, Thomas. *The Deepest Wounds: A Labor and Environmental History of Sugar in Northeast Brazil.* Chapel Hill: University of North Carolina Press, 2010.

Sanders, James E. *Contentious Republicans: Popular Politics, Race, and Class in Nineteenth Century Colombia.* Durham, NC: Duke University Press, 2004.

Sanders, James E. *The Vanguard of the Atlantic World: Creating Modernity, Nation, and Democracy in Nineteenth-Century Latin America.* Durham, NC: Duke University Press, 2014.

Smith, Benjamin T. *The Roots of Conservativism in Mexico: Catholicism, Society and Politics in the Mixteca Baja, 1750–1962.* Albuquerque: University of New Mexico Press, 2012.

Viotti da Costa, Emília. *The Brazilian Empire: Myths and Histories.* 2nd ed. Chapel Hill: University of North Carolina Press, 2000.

PART TWO

Progress and Modernization: Commodities, Railroads, Neocolonialism, Race, 1875–1929

By the 1860s, Latin Americans reflected on their frustrated attempts to forge cohesive modern nation-states after independence. In many respects, Simón Bolívar's pessimistic words—"We have ploughed the seas"—seemed almost as apt in 1870 as they had when he spoke them in 1830. Although the doctrine of liberalism promised a new age of unparalleled prosperity for Latin America, the persistence of divisive issues tempered this idealism by the mid-nineteenth century. Optimism was renewed in the 1870s as the concepts of positivism and social Darwinism began to influence Latin American intellectual culture. Although these promised progress, they had disturbing implications for those who were not part of the educated, urban classes—particularly for people of indigenous or African ancestry. In Part II, we explore the vision that inspired elite and middle-class political leadership between the 1870s and 1929. This vision brought about dramatic changes, not always for the better, to the vast majority of people living in Latin America.

As discussed in Part I, liberals and conservatives fought about the nature of the national government throughout the middle of the nineteenth century. (Note: when describing sets of ideas and political tendencies, we use lower-case for liberal and conservative. When describing specific political parties, we use upper-case Liberal and Conservative). Most Latin American nations had Liberal and Conservative Parties in the mid-to-late nineteenth century. (In some nations, those names varied, such as in Argentina and Uruguay, where liberal parties changed names multiple times). Liberals favored granting greater power to individual states and the legislative branch of government, and protecting the civil liberties of free, property-owning men. Conservatives preferred a strong national government with a powerful president or caudillo who would preserve order by restricting some personal freedoms. Fatigued by incessant civil wars, Liberal parties in places like Colombia and Mexico finally came to believe that only by establishing political order (and curtailing individual liberties in the process) could a state modernize, a goal consistent with the philosophy of positivism.

During the age of progress and modernization, beginning approximately in 1875, maintaining political order did not mean maintaining the status quo.

Instead, liberals sought to encourage foreign investment and to promote economic development, with costs and benefits. Although foreign capital nurtured growth on a scale unimaginable in the early nineteenth century, it also increased direct foreign intervention in Latin America. International investors, particularly those from the United States, aggressively protected their investments. In several instances, the US military occupied vulnerable countries that had defaulted on debts, especially in Central America and the Caribbean. The United States also used force to achieve strategic goals, such as the construction of the Panama Canal.

Foreign investment accelerated technological innovation in Latin America, particularly in transportation and communication. A network of railroads overcame the topographical impediments that had isolated remote areas from each other and from national capitals. Steam locomotives moved passengers from the interior to the capital, and soldiers to rebellious provinces, and carried products to ports and markets. Other technological inventions, such as the telegraph, eased communications and directly facilitated the growth of the export economy.

Liberals espoused free trade, although with significant limitations. Latin American elites rarely accepted the principle of payment of taxes as a civic responsibility, and fought to evade taxes or keep them low in comparison to North America or western Europe. Even taxes on imported luxury goods remained minimal. Because of this reluctance to pay taxes even in the most prosperous of times, much of the state's revenue derived from taxes paid on exports. Foreign investment, therefore, became increasingly necessary as it paid for infrastructural improvements that made large-scale export possible.

The export sector became the engine that drove Latin American economies. Every nation had at least one product (usually an agricultural commodity, such as coffee, bananas, or beef) that it marketed internationally. More fortunate nations had more than one. Flourishing exports encouraged elite and middle-class consumers to purchase foreign-manufactured goods at reasonable prices. While Latin American artisans lost ground, the few nations that had nascent industries used selective tariffs to protect these businesses, such as Mexico's domestic textile industry. A new consensus in favor of modernization based on liberal principles of free trade and export-led development prevailed among Latin America's elite, but not without local variations and inconsistent application.

Liberals also tended to prevail in debates about the Catholic Church's status. Liberals secularized seminaries and schools, eliminated the Church's *fueros*, or special legal privileges, and expropriated huge tracts of Church-owned properties. This occurred earlier in some nations (Mexico, Colombia) than others; Peru and

Ecuador, for example, did not restrain special privileges and powers of the Catholic Church until well into the twentieth century. Despite the dwindling wealth and influence of the Church as an institution, however, Latin Americans as a people remained highly religious. Popular Catholicism (and popular religion in general) gathered strength in the late nineteenth and early twentieth centuries, particularly in rural areas. When threatened with suppression by authorities, leaders of popular religious sectors would protest and even rebel.

European and US ideas about education, urban beautification, women's role in society, labor organization, the arts, and popular culture all appealed to Latin American elites in the latter part of the nineteenth century. These cultural influences were especially visible as Latin Americans borrowed from European aesthetics to plan and design majestic capital cities. Buenos Aires, Mexico City, Santiago, and even Guatemala City all attempted to model themselves, with varying degrees of success, after Paris. These issues are discussed in detail in chapter 6.

But the age of progress and modernization had devastating consequences for the poor, for subsistence farmers, and for indigenous groups, as we shall see in chapter 7. The subsistence farmers that characterized much of rural Latin America found their situation deteriorating. Liberal plans to expropriate common lands for sale, and the exploitation of indigenous people as cheap labor for commercial agriculture and industry, all served to worsen the living conditions of the rural poor. Believers in the new liberal consensus based on export agriculture accepted these as the costs of creating prosperous modern nations. For the elite, the material gains of modernization in the growing capitals of Latin America justified the sacrifice of local customs and traditional ways of life.

Many historians regard this as Latin America's gilded age—a time when an export commodity boom generated dizzying wealth for some and Latin America's major capitals took on Parisian flair. But it was a gilded age marked by growing inequality. Pressing social and environmental questions remained unanswered. Would working people share in the fruits of progress? Would increasing urbanization offer rural peoples beacons of opportunity or result in squalor for the migrant poor? Would the hard-fought legal rights won by former slaves and indigenous people translate into better conditions? Or would emerging ideas of scientific racism lead to new kinds of social marginalization? Would new opportunities for women in the workplace change understandings of gender? Finally, would the revival of the export economy have unexpected environmental consequences? These questions and more confronted Latin Americans between 1870 and 1930.

5

Progress and Modernization: The Elite's Strategy, 1870–1929

Global Connections

During the late nineteenth and early twentieth centuries, the North Atlantic nations (western Europe and the United States) exercised their maximum influence over the remainder of the globe. Politicians measured progress in terms of scientific and technological advances as well as increased material wealth. North Atlantic business leaders became fantastically rich by exporting manufactured goods to the entire world. To facilitate this flow of products, European nations recast existing legal institutions such as sole proprietorships or partnerships into modern business corporations and banking systems that allowed fortunate entrepreneurs to accumulate untold wealth. Social position depended less on land ownership and inherited status and more on entrepreneurial acumen.

Technology, especially modernized systems of transportation and communication, made much of this material progress possible. Simultaneously, growing prosperity allowed for the rise of a consumer culture. To be sure, not all people living in the North Atlantic world shared equally in the prosperity. Europe experienced the greatest number of emigrants in its history, mostly to the United States, Canada, and southern Latin America. Despite this trend, the material progress created by Europe and the United States motivated much of the rest of the world to emulate the North Atlantic model of economic development.

This brave new world of progress and modernity had minimal influence in China, where political leaders felt little need to adopt Western ways, at least in the short term. China's Confucian culture favored tradition and rejected westernization. In the 1870s, for example, the Chinese government tore up railroad tracks that had been laid by an enterprising group of Chinese businessmen.

Westernization met with a more positive response in Russia and Japan. As latecomers to industrialization and modernity, both nations required active government intervention in the process of modernization in order to catch up with the North Atlantic states. After emancipating the *kulaks* (peasants legally bound to work on great estates, much like the peones who worked on Latin America haciendas) and liberalizing legal codes, the Russian czar ordered the construction of the Trans-Siberian Railroad in the 1880s. He encouraged foreign investors to build steel foundries and textile plants and decreed high tariffs to protect these fledgling industries. Once opened to westernization in the 1850s, Japan embraced modernization even more readily. The Meiji government played a major role: building railroads, creating banks, and providing capital to industry. More than any other Asian country, the Japanese adopted Western fashions and purchased products

≡ **The Rambla at Mar del Plata, Argentina.** Latin American elites quickly adopted the late nineteenth-century European practice of taking holidays, either at the shore or in the mountains, to escape the heat of the city during the summer months. By 1910 Mar del Plata in Argentina became fashionable for elites and the new middle class in part because of its accessibility from Buenos Aires. City planners constructed a lengthy boardwalk where visitors, dressed in all their finery, could promenade before dinner and take in the fresh salt air.

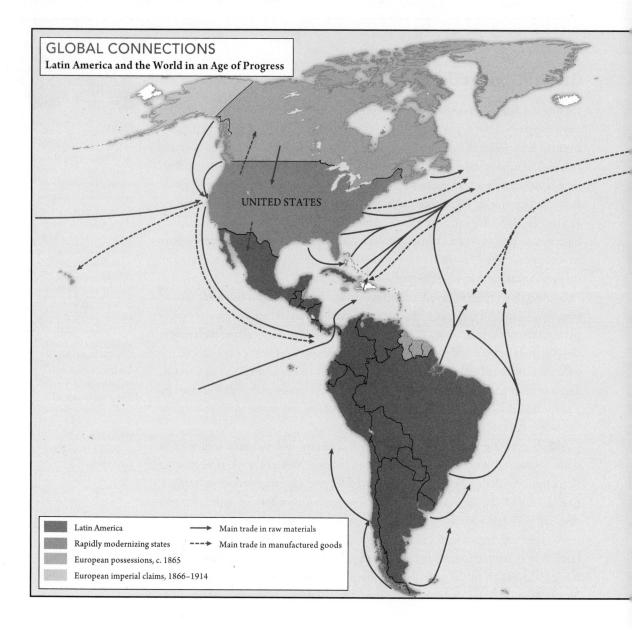

GLOBAL CONNECTIONS
Latin America and the World in an Age of Progress

Latin America
Rapidly modernizing states
European possessions, c. 1865
European imperial claims, 1866–1914

→ Main trade in raw materials
╌╌▶ Main trade in manufactured goods

promoting new technologies of hygiene, like the modern toothbrush. Nevertheless, many Japanese debated the long-term consequences of modernization on traditional religion and culture.

Like the Japanese imperial circle, elites in Latin American enthusiastically embraced progress as a panacea for all that had gone wrong in the postindependence era. For these Latin Americans, progress equated with material wealth, readily observed in such technological advances as the bright lights of western European and

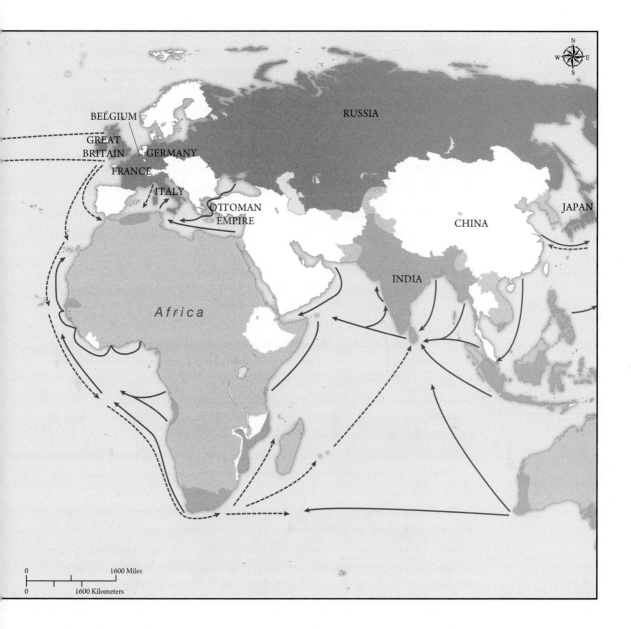

US metropolitan areas, where electrification illuminated and extended the day for city dwellers. A significant number of Latin Americans had seen the transformative nature of progress firsthand, often as a result of the "Grand Tour" of Europe that put the final touches on the educations of the sons of the elite.

Latin Americans seized on the French intellectual Auguste Comte's socioeconomic philosophy of positivism, interpreting it as a set of guidelines leading infallibly to progress. This chapter explores these guidelines followed by the elite and their technocrats and assesses the political and economic results of the program for progress and modernization. The model created by these economic technocrats (explored in this chapter) notably transformed the nations of Argentina, Brazil, Mexico, Chile, Uruguay, and Cuba. Although policy makers in other Latin American countries believed in the same general principles of positivism, local circumstances limited the degree of material progress that they could attain.

Philosophy and Principles of Modernization: Positivism and Social Darwinism, 1870s–1900s

After a midcentury Conservative interregnum, the Liberals returned to power across Latin America in the final decades of the nineteenth century. During the final third of the century, Latin American Liberalism was updated and transformed by two new potent philosophies that had seized the popular imagination in Europe, positivism and social Darwinism.

The Ideas behind Positivism and Social Darwinism

Auguste Comte, the French philosopher who developed **positivism**, argued that society reaches its pinnacle when it arrives at the last of three sequential phases: first the religious, then the metaphysical, and finally the "positive" stage of development. In the positive stage, according to Comte, a society has evolved to its fullest potential when it allows itself to be governed by infallible scientific principles and by the complete rejection of artificial limitations (such as religion) or such abstract political concepts as freedom of speech, for example, that had constrained it in the past. For Comte, one could measure progress in tangible ways such as professional security forces, railroads, opera houses, broad urban boulevards, and well-regulated rural areas.

Positivism appealed to modernizers throughout Latin America, but became particularly influential in Brazil. During the final two decades of the Brazilian Empire, a generation of Brazilian positivists used their own interpretation of Comte's doctrine to challenge slavery, monarchy, and the power of the Catholic Church. Miguel Lemos, who had studied with Comte in Paris, went so far as to found a positivist church in Rio de Janeiro, dedicated to the cult of order and progress as a religion. Lemos's church was influential among military officers and journalists—two sectors of society with growing influence in national politics. Meanwhile, the Brazilian engineer Benjamin Constant split with Lemos and founded a more pragmatic Positivist Society, similarly influential among military officers. In 1889, these officers played a decisive role in terminating the weakened Brazilian Empire and inaugurating the first Republic of Brazil. Its motto, *Ordem e Progresso* (Order and Progress), was emblazoned on the new Brazilian flag, where it remains today.

Positivism remained a powerful influence among urban technocrats in the late nineteenth and early twentieth centuries. Positivists established a modern conception of indigenous autonomy. Positivist tracts argued that Brazil's indigenous population deserved respect and "fraternal treatment" not because they were innocent souls awaiting Catholic evangelization but because they were "the rightful owners of the lands they occupy." Positivist military officers and civil engineers in the early twentieth century advocated peaceful outreach to previously uncontacted indigenous groups in the Brazilian Amazon, and for the establishment of tracts of land reserved for semisedentary indigenous habitation. Although these policies were all too frequently ignored in the rush to exploit new resources, they did begin to establish a framework for indigenous rights.

The other social philosophy that deeply influenced Liberalism in the late nineteenth century was **social Darwinism**. In 1859, the English naturalist Charles Darwin published *On the Origin of Species,* in which he argued that species on earth developed through the process of "natural selection," or evolution over time through random mutations. Although Darwin's work offered both a clear, accessible explanation as well as significant evidence based on observations he had made in Ecuador's Galápagos Islands, he was not the first scientist to put forth the idea. The English scientist and political theorist Herbert Spencer had previously reached similar conclusions.

It was Spencer who coined the phrase "survival of the fittest" to describe the effects of biology on human behavior, and concocted a theory of the evolution of societies, which he called social Darwinism. Positing that some humans are born more fit for survival than others, Spencer argued that the "procreation of the unworthy" was detrimental to society. Although Spencer was not directly a part of it, such thinking augmented the rise of eugenics and "scientific racism," a set of theories developed in the late Victorian era that attempted to prove the superiority of certain races and ethnicities (especially white, Anglo-Saxon) over others (black, indigenous, or mixed-race).

Positivism and Social Darwinism in Latin America

Latin American liberals enthusiastically embraced these new philosophies, as they reinforced the hopes for modernity and progress that had long been the liberal hallmark. In some respects, it may seem surprising that Latin American liberals endorsed social Darwinism, since its racist, geographically deterministic thinking placed even the liberal elites themselves (descendants of southern, not northern, Europeans), well down the pecking order of racial hierarchies. The mixed-race, indigenous, and black majorities of their nation's populations fared even worse in this schema.

For Latin American liberals who feared that their nations were already woefully far behind in the march toward progress, social Darwinism and positivism seemed to provide both diagnosis and prescription. The Latin American implementation of positivist remedies tended to the pragmatic, with an almost formulaic response to modernization. The prescription began with the creation of political order by centralizing governments and professionalizing the military and the police. Order, in turn, would encourage private investors from the United States and Europe to provide funding for new infrastructure and the development of the export economy. Railroads and other new technologies would enable the Latin American nations to deliver export products to markets abroad and link remote rural villages to national capitals and ports, and the resulting prosperity would encourage a wave of immigrants to make the arduous journey to new homes in Latin America. Latin America could then recapitulate the process of modernization that had occurred in the United States, Japan, and Western Europe.

The Quest for Order, 1870s–1900s

Latin Americans in the 1870s understood that they needed to establish political and economic stability before they could experience material progress. As Colombian president Rafael Reyes (1904–1909) succinctly stated, "Material prosperity rests on the establishment of confidence abroad." With few exceptions, the earlier national histories of Latin American nations were fraught with military and political conflicts, leading to dire consequences for their economies, as well as to chaotic political and social conditions. These elements of discord needed to be tamed. By the 1870s, most governments had discarded extreme liberal federalism in favor of a strong, centralized, and authoritarian government as the best means to achieve stability.

Argentina under the Liberals

For more than a generation, Buenos Aires liberals (those who advocated free trade between the port of Buenos Aires and Europe, who professed ideals of individual rights and education, and who tended to hail from powerful families linked to international trade) identified Juan Manuel de Rosas as the scourge of the nation, the diabolical force obstructing rational reform and progress. But when Rosas was finally driven from power in 1852, his ouster came at the hands of fellow caudillo and erstwhile collaborator Justo José de Urquiza. Urquiza made some liberal reforms, including the abolition of slavery and the drafting of a national constitution that balanced legislative, executive, and judicial powers (at least in theory).

Urquiza also subsidized European immigration to Argentina, a wave of immigration that would transform Argentina over the next half century.

But Urquiza was not a liberal: He was a provincial strongman, and the Buenos Aires liberal elites deplored his rule. Domingo Faustino Sarmiento, the leading intellectual of the Buenos Aires contingent, lambasted the president in the press (which, in comparison to much of the region, was relatively free and vibrant). Roused by Sarmiento, Buenos Aires rejected Urquiza and split with the rest of Argentina. The Buenos Aires liberals won the ensuing contest of wills and finally came to national power with the ascendancy of Bartolomé Mitre to the presidency in 1862. After defeating Urquiza's supporters, Mitre simply named himself president. The opposition was too fragmented to resist.

Sarmiento himself succeeded Mitre as president in 1868. This period marked the high point of Argentine liberalism, revealing both its power and its contradictions. Railroads (largely built and financed with British capital) and public schools became the key symbols and the decisive tools of Sarmiento's strategy for liberal nation-building. The former promised the ability to tap the resources of the Argentine interior, harnessing them in the service of domestic and international commerce. The latter promised to liberate the creative energy of the individual, securing the prosperity of future generations.

The rapid expansion of the railroad made commercial agriculture in distant regions highly profitable, such as sugar production in Tucumán. And Sarmiento's emphasis on building schools and training teachers established a model for subsequent administrations, eventually making the Argentine population among the best educated in the hemisphere. But these achievements were not universally beneficial. The arrival of the railroad (as was the case throughout Latin America) created losers as well as winners by stimulating expropriation and enclosure of previously accessible lands, and enriching export-oriented producers at the expense of subsistence farmers.

It was the indigenous population of Argentina that was most directly harmed by these initiatives. The growth of the railroad intensified pressure to drive Indians off open lands in the service of commercial ranching and agriculture. Sarmiento's handpicked successor, Nicolás Avellaneda, took these implications to extremes. In the late 1870s, Avellaneda's minister of war, Julio Roca, executed a **Conquest of the Desert** that amounted to a war of extermination against the indigenous population of southern Argentina. Roca's "Conquest" followed the North American model of displacement, reduction, and extermination of native peoples. It established the domination of the Argentine nation-state over the remote province of Patagonia, at an enormous social cost.

Mexico under Porfirio Díaz

Porfirio Díaz was the best-known military hero of the War of the Reform and the battle of Cinco de Mayo. Díaz presided over Mexico during a 34-year period (1876–1911) marked by both successes and failures. During the *Porfiriato* (the period of Díaz's rule), Mexico overcame the three most burdensome legacies of the mid-nineteenth century: acerbic political debates between Liberals, Conservatives, and their respective military allies; a moribund economy encumbered by foreign debt; and the loss of national pride resulting from the seizure of one-half of its national territory by the United States. The Porfiriato, however, was also marked by the dispossession of communitarian and small farmers and the concentration of capital. For all these reasons, the Porfiriato was among the most transformative regimes in Latin American history.

Using a pragmatic combination of patronage (handing out jobs to both cronies and rivals), the conciliation of enemies, and occasional brute force, Díaz by 1884 had become the indispensable patriarch of the Mexican state, backed particularly by the elite and the middle class. He held power until he was overthrown in 1911. The apparent political stability of the Porfiriato relied in part on Díaz's broad *camarilla* (political network), far larger than that of any of his political predecessors. It included veterans of recent military conflicts, liberals from diverse factions, local caudillos, and even some pardoned collaborators of Emperor Maximilian. Contemporaries noted that Díaz possessed political skills unmatched by any other Mexican politician of the nineteenth century.

Porfirio Díaz was widely quoted as saying that Mexico needed "*poca política y mas administración*" (less politics and more administration). To that end, he acted as the arbiter of all disputes: between rival political factions in elections;

≡ **Porfirio Díaz and the Aztec Calendar Stone.** The first generation of historians writing about Porfirio Díaz and his positivist followers lambasted the dictator because his policies purposefully disadvantaged indigenous people. Current writers acknowledge that the Porfirians' attitudes toward indigenous people were far more complex, as this image demonstrates. Díaz and the intellectuals of the Porfiriato were fascinated by the achievements of pre-Hispanic cultures, particularly the Aztecs. Here Díaz had his portrait taken with the Aztec calendar stone, arguably the most famous pre-Hispanic carved monument. The regime also financed archeologists who explored ancient sites like Teotihuacan. Díaz unabashedly identified with the glories of Mexico's indigenous past, while simultaneously disparaging contemporary indigenous people who had, in the opinion of the científico elites, "degenerated" from their glorious ancestors.

between laborers contending with their employers; and between **campesinos** (rural people) fending off the claims of encroaching hacendados. As Mexico prospered in the 1880s and 1890s, Díaz had plenty of state money to spread around. Díaz was antidemocratic but not personally corrupt: he accumulated power but not necessarily wealth. He was living in modest circumstances when forced from office in 1911. Many officials and businessmen surrounding him, however, took advantage of their privileged status to take bribes from foreign investors and Mexican capitalists and secure lucrative contracts for themselves. To enforce his political will, Díaz constantly expanded his camarilla by exercising considerable control over the "election" of governors and the choice of their *jefes políticos* (district administrators). While Mexico's regions remained distinct in many ways, the Porfiriato saw Mexico centralized as never before.

The **Pax Porfiriana** (Porfirian peace) was in many ways a grand illusion. Certainly Mexico experienced fewer rebellions than it had during the previous half-century. Díaz took the sting out of the divisive conflict between Church and State by reconciling with the clergy. This peace and stability depended on myths fabricated about the dictator, the effectiveness of his army, and the ferocity of rural police in curbing dissent. Porfirian legislation, the *Ley Fuga* (Law of Flight), permitted authorities to shoot prisoners if they attempted to escape, which an astonishingly large number attempted to do. Although in reality the rural police (the *rurales*) were frequently ill-disciplined, their effectiveness resulted in part from the legends spread about their cruelty in dealing with dissenters. On one such occasion, a rurales patrol that captured a group of rebellious villagers allegedly buried them in sand up to their necks, and proceeded to play a polo match on the newly constructed pitch. Although likely apocryphal, the story was one example of how Díaz effectively used his formula of *pan o palo* (literally "bread or stick," as in "carrot or stick") to reduce dissent.

Less visibly, creating stability also meant paying back foreign bondholders to achieve a positive credit rating for Mexico. At the beginning of Díaz's first term, tensions with the United States remained high because of the unpaid debt and the frequency of cross-border raids by Apache and Comanche indigenous groups on Texas border settlements. Díaz took strong measures to appease the United States by sending troops to the border and by making regular debt payments, winning diplomatic recognition and US friendship by 1880. Prompt payments to European creditors during the following decade gave those governments similar confidence in the Díaz regime. International investors viewed Díaz as a reliable partner, and deemed Mexico to be creditworthy as long as it remained under his rule.

Díaz also implemented new legislation designed to promote financial stability and growth. The Commercial Code of 1884 allowed banks and other financial institutions to incorporate as *sociedades anónimas*, or S.A. (the Spanish equivalent of "Incorporated," or Inc.). This reduced risks for investors because as shareholders they enjoyed limited liability. That is, if the business failed, the shareholders did not risk their personal assets. This innovation encouraged venture capitalists to back riskier, but potentially more lucrative, enterprises. Further legislation ended tariff barriers between Mexican states, creating a truly national economy for the first time.

Díaz's minister of finance, José Yves Limantour, implemented a number of laws (most importantly a protective tariff) to encourage foreign and Mexican investment in light industry, which resulted in Mexico becoming the most industrialized Latin American nation during this period. In 1905, Limantour made the ultimate symbolic gesture to demonstrate Mexico's conformity with international economic principles by adopting the gold standard to stabilize the value of the peso against the dollar and the British pound. By the final year of the Díaz dictatorship, Mexico's treasury held a surplus of 74,000,000 pesos.

As a result of these reforms, those sectors of the Mexican economy directly linked to international investment boomed. As chapters 6 and 7 demonstrate, however, traditional campesinos and industrial workers bore the costs of that growth, as international investment transformed agriculture and demanded growing profits from mines and factories.

Creating the Modern Latin American Military: The Case of Chile

Mexico was hardly alone in its preoccupation with order and progress. To ensure stability, elite politicians throughout Latin America sought to professionalize their national armies. By creating a modern, European-trained officer corps and equipping their forces with the most technologically advanced weaponry, the modernizers reasoned that the state could permanently defeat the troublesome regional caudillos. Equally important, the notion of a professional army meant limiting the military's function to protecting the nation against foreign invasion and the elected government against internal rebellions. In theory, professionalization implied subordination to civilian authorities. A professional army would also engage in a civilizing mission, drafting all citizens for a stint of military service, thereby providing the enlisted men with both the basics of education and a sense of national identity.

Chile became the first Latin American nation to professionalize its armed forces, a process speeded by fears of a border conflict with Argentina. In 1886, the Chilean government hired the Prussian (German) General Emil Körner to provide

≡ **Military Cadets Parading in Rio de Janeiro.** In the age of progress and modernization, centralization in part meant that the national government would acquire a monopoly of military force to eliminate the dangers posed by provincial militias and caudillos. To accomplish this end, governments throughout Latin America created military academies (like West Point and Annapolis) and hired foreign army officers from Germany, France, or the United States to train the cadets at these academies. Even in Brazil, whose oligarchical regime was more decentralized than were governments elsewhere in Latin America, the state trained cadets and professionalized the armed forces. In addition to curbing caudillos, elite leaders hoped that professionalization would teach officers to refrain from intervening in matters political.

technical and scientific training to Chile's military. Körner immediately revamped Chile's military academy, revising the curriculum to emphasize recent developments in tactics, military science, and cartography as well as basic general education classes. Thirty-six other German officers joined Körner as faculty members at the academy. For advanced training, Körner sent the academy's best students to Germany. Finally, following the Prussian model, Körner unified the army's command structure, eliminating the decentralized system that had created rivalries, jealousies, and confusion during the War of the Pacific (chapter 6).

Chile set the tone for the rest of the region. By the turn of the century, most Latin American nations had engaged military expertise from Germany or France to professionalize their armies. Professionalizing the military was yet another example of a scientific solution devised by the elite leadership to a problem that had plagued postindependence Latin America. In theory, professionalizing the military meant moving power from the hands of the personalized armies that were accountable to an individual caudillo to one in which the military was accountable to the nation-state. For positivist leaders in the late nineteenth centuries, the powerful militaries of European nations such as France and Prussia seemed to offer templates for a new type of modern military forces.

Unfortunately, in practice, military professionalization produced rather different outcomes than those predicted. Professionalized Latin American officers came to believe that they alone represented the nation's true interests, and that irresponsible and often corrupt civilian politicians were to blame for national woes. Many of these officers went so far as to become antidemocratic, certain that only the military could resolve social disorder, economic recession, and other national problems.

Chile experienced fewer long-lasting interventions by the professionalized military than most other Latin American nations, at least until 1973 (chapter 10). The short-lived Revolution of 1891 marked the first successful military coup in Chile since 1830. Ironically, it was General Emil Körner himself who violated his own teachings about military subordination to civilian authorities when he played the key role in the events of 1891. After a falling out with the elected president, Körner surreptitiously agreed to advise the president's foes in the Parliament, ensuring that they would win.

The professional military overstepped its bounds again in the 1920s, when Chile faced another crisis. Nitrates, valuable for use as fertilizers and in the manufacture of munitions, had made Chile prosperous during the age of progress. World War I, however, saw the collapse of the Chilean nitrate market. When Atlantic naval warfare prevented desperate European combatants from importing this commodity, vital for the production of munitions, their scientists invented synthetic substitutes. By 1920, synthetics had squeezed the more expensive Chilean natural nitrates out of much of the marketplace. Chile's parliamentarians quarreled among themselves and proved unable to address the growing social and economic problems. As one of the Parliamentary presidents, Ramón Barros Luco (1910–1915) had notoriously claimed, "There are two types of problems: those that solve themselves and those that have no solution," a maxim that seemed increasingly true as time wore on.

In 1925, the newly elected president, Arturo Alessandri, begged to differ, taking on two seemingly intractable problems: strengthening the executive branch and legislating social reforms. Parliament balked. The military divided, with senior officers (conservative generals) favoring Alessandri's removal from office and the maintenance of the status quo, and junior officers (younger and of lower rank) demanding the enactment of concrete social reforms as well as constitutional reform.

In 1925 the junior officers prevailed under the leadership of Colonel Carlos Ibáñez del Campo. They forced parliament to pass a number of labor and other social reforms, and to adopt the more centralized Constitution of 1925. Ibáñez stepped in and ruled until the worsening economic consequences of the Great Depression forced him from office in 1931. Even in Chile, then, the idea of professionalizing the military as a means of guaranteeing order and stability proved to be only partially successful. A highly professionalized military served as a guarantor of stability in periods when political elites established consensus among themselves. Those same professionalized armed forces, however, could become a source of volatility in periods when consensus broke down.

Foreign Investment, 1870s–1900s

Elite political leaders understood that domestic capital was inadequate to fund the infrastructure and development projects necessary to achieve modernization as defined by the North Atlantic liberal economic model of development. Once the five Latin American nations experiencing the most rapid growth (Argentina, Brazil, Mexico, Chile, and Uruguay) achieved stability, and the global economic crisis known as the Panic of 1873 (one of the most serious global economic recessions of the nineteenth century) subsided, foreign investors targeted these countries, along with the Spanish colony of Cuba, as viable investment opportunities. For their part, Latin Americans understood that massive expenditures like railroad construction could not be funded by domestic capital alone. Foreign surplus capital and Latin America's promise for profits constituted a marriage made in heaven, or so it seemed to many contemporaries.

Foreign Investment in Mexico

The case of Mexico's investment strategy deserves our attention not only because Mexico received more foreign capital than any other Latin American nation except Argentina but also because of the manner in which Díaz and his ministers of finance handled the risks associated with opening the country to US capital. US investors responded to Díaz's guarantees of stability by pumping $1.3 billion into Mexico, and British investors added nearly a billion more. Capitalists in France and the growing economy of a newly united Germany made considerable investments in Mexican manufacturing.

Díaz and his advisors (called the **científicos,** or scientists, because of their scientific, positivist approach to governance) particularly welcomed capitalists who were interested in providing technologies and expertise that would modernize the export economy and provide tax revenues to the state. With these capital investments, foreigners made possible the construction of expensive infrastructure, especially railroads to connect the resource-rich interior to modernized ports. Interest in Mexico's products spiked because of the country's presence at World's Fairs in Paris (1889) and Chicago (1893), which whetted foreign appetites for Mexican goods and in turn encouraged additional investment.

Much of the Mexican population, in turn, thirsted for new consumer items. While the elite and some members of the middle class preferred imported European-made luxuries like fashionable clothing from Paris, ordinary Mexicans consumed products such as domestically produced cigarettes, beer, and inexpensive clothing. The Mexican foreign minister, Limantour, and the científicos encouraged domestic manufacturing by enacting a tariff that raised prices on certain foreign goods (like the aforementioned products) by 70 percent. Patents (legal structures that protect an investor's right to profit from his own inventions or ideas) protected foreign technological inventions (like mechanical cigarette-rolling machines) used in Mexico. Limantour also granted tax subsidies to guarantee the profitability of these enterprises. Consumption of domestic goods, like Mexican-made machine-rolled cigarettes, boomed. By 1910, the French-owned El Buen Tono factory in Mexico City sold approximately 5.2 billion cigarettes a year. Its flashy advertising covered urban walls and illustrated newspapers. El Buen Tono even employed a man to walk around the fashionable districts of Mexico City sporting a suit with flashing lights advertising its products.

Porfirio Díaz's dilemma was how to secure US investment dollars while fending off economic domination by the United States. Díaz took the bold step of encouraging US investment in three railroads connecting Mexico City to the border, arguing that the resulting benefits of trade would outweigh the potential risk of the US annexing more Mexican territory. Other North American investors held controlling interests in Mexican mines near the border, including the valuable copper mines that provided the raw material necessary to make the copper wire required by expanding electrical networks.

At the same time, Díaz and Limantour sought to balance US investments with British capital as a means of limiting Yankee influence. Well-heeled Englishmen financed the railroads that ran east and west across Mexico, and Díaz's British friend, Weetman Pearson, won a concession for the most lucrative oilfields in Mexico. Other British investors financed the electrification of Mexico City and constructed and operated the streetcars in the capital. By playing US and British investors against one another, Díaz and Limantour sought to protect Mexican national interests. Despite these efforts, the British ultimately could not compete with the United States in its own backyard. By 1910, US investors in Mexico surpassed all others, often acting with a sense of entitlement that alienated Mexican citizens.

What was the balance for Mexico and for Mexicans? Díaz's opponents argued that "Mexico was the mother of foreigners and the stepmother of Mexicans," implying that Díaz had sold out national interest in favor of foreign investors. But the facts of Porfirian development are more complex. Foreign investors reaped great profits, but Díaz and Limantour took precautions to restrain and channel foreign capital and to regulate the investments of large conglomerates. (For example, Mexico purchased the controlling interest in its railroads in 1906, creating the Mexican National Railway). Such measures guaranteed that foreign investors could not willfully impose their own conditions in Mexico. No observer of Mexico could deny that foreign capital paved the way for Mexico's economic growth in the latter part of the nineteenth century. At the same time, not all Mexicans benefited from that growth, and some suffered its negative consequences—an inequity that set the stage for future turmoil.

British Investment in Argentina

British investment in Argentina grew exponentially in the 1870s and 1880s, especially in railroads and other industrial concerns. This sharp spike in foreign direct investment brought both benefits and risks for Argentina. British capital enabled the expansion of Argentine infrastructure and freed domestic capital for investment in land and agriculture. Argentina's economy grew, and its captains of commerce, industry, and agriculture acquired fortunes. At the same time, international investors were inherently skittish and had both the ability and the inclination to withdraw capital whenever Argentine prospects looked shaky.

In the 1880s, Argentine banks borrowed heavily from British lenders in order to finance domestic industrialization. Many of these projects, such as the construction of major rail lines and a water network for Buenos Aires, would take years to complete. But the loans had fixed interest rates requiring short-term payments. The spiral of British investment and Argentine borrowing reached a crisis point in 1890. Argentine borrowers, strapped by a temporary decline in growth rates, defaulted on loans to the powerful Barings Bank of London. Barings nearly collapsed, threatening to take down the London financial establishment along with it. While emergency collaboration from other British banks saved Barings, Argentina suffered a crippling recession. With the British connection suddenly disrupted, the Argentine economy stalled, leading rapidly to unemployment and poverty. Brazil and Uruguay, caught in the ebb of the same financial wave, suffered similar effects. The Southern Cone nations emerged from this financial crisis more slowly than did Barings. The 1890 crisis offered a bitter reminder that, while British and Argentine interests might temporarily align, they could just as easily diverge.

ECONOMICS AND COMMODITIES

The Department Store

Consumer culture flourished during the age of progress and modernization. For many Latin Americans living in major metropolitan centers, the department store represented one of the most tangible and positive manifestations of the new materialism and modernity. Modeled after department stores in New York, London, Paris, and other major European and US cities, Latin American department stores catered to the new consumer culture and offered the most sought after items of the late nineteenth century: clothing and furniture. No longer limited by colonial sumptuary laws, which had restricted sales of fine material goods to the elite, consumers of all backgrounds could now purchase high-quality clothing or furniture if they had sufficient wealth. As with many cultural manifestations of the era, including fine arts, sports, and other forms of popular culture, Latin Americans derived the core of their ideas about department stores from European and North American inspiration while providing their own unique cultural twist.

In Mexico City, French investors constructed the *Palacio de Hierro* (Iron Palace) department store. This edifice used the modern architectural technique of iron-frame construction (reminiscent of the Eiffel Tower) in a four-story building on a fashionable street near Mexico City's central plaza, the Zócalo. Enormous plate glass windows titillated window shoppers with dreams of purchasing the fashionable merchandise available within the store. Inside the Palacio de Hierro, stunning marble staircases invited prospective customers to climb to the upper levels of the building, which housed higher-grade textiles, furniture, and luxurious decorative pieces.

The department store challenged a number of Latin America's long-held social conventions. First, because the department store was an elegant, enclosed space catering primarily to elite and middle-class customers, women from these classes refused to abide by the colonial social norm requiring them to be accompanied by a male relative in a public space. By 1900, a majority of the customers in department stores were women. Shopping became a leisurely and refined activity, an outing for women unwilling to remain confined at home. Second, Mexican department stores eventually adopted the practice of tagging every

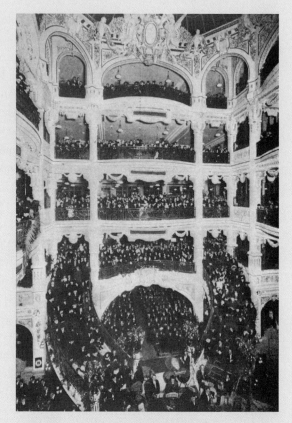

≡ **A Department Store in Buenos Aires.** Department stores epitomized the increased consumer commercialism associated with the age of progress. Based on western European and US models, department stores marked a dramatic transition from open-air markets and the small shops of the early nineteenth century. Department stores could offer a broad array of dry goods, often imported, from clothing to jewelry to furniture. Buenos Aires, which had the largest elite and middle class in South America, naturally had the wherewithal to support a glamorous department store like this one in the photograph. The elite and the middle class, including women shopping alone, patronized department stores for the newest and most fashionable products. Holding a position as a department store clerk elevated a person to middle-class status.

item with a fixed price, a break from the social ritual of bargaining prevalent at open-air markets. Contemporary economists argued that the endless haggling over a few pennies deterred other sales by occupying too much of the salesclerk's time. (How much more comfortable would Dr. Holton have felt in a Porfirian department store than he did the Bogotá open-air market described in chapter 4!). Third, department store employees were well-dressed, often bilingual men who could converse more or less as social equals with their customers; again, this was quite different from the rural marketplace, which was dominated by indigenous women. In short, the department store was a microcosm of the values of the age, showing off a glittering abundance of goods and offering proof of the success of modernization and progress.

- How does the creation of the modern department store fit in with positivist goals and ideals?

Scholars have debated whether British influence in Argentina constituted an "informal empire," one built on mercantile credit and political influence rather than gunboats. The influence of British bankers never approached anything like actual control over Argentine politics, which remained rambunctious and unpredictable throughout the long period when England remained Argentina's favored trading partner. That said, for most of the nineteenth century British capital and Argentine development were inseparable, and the British held the upper hand in that relationship.

Products for Export, 1870s–1920s

Foreign capitalists did not invest money in Latin America out of benevolence. They knew that the passengers purchasing tickets for the new railroads would not provide sufficient profits to pay dividends. Rather, railroad entrepreneurs understood that the transport of large quantities of freight to market (and the land concessions railroads received) would make the difference between profit and loss. Other foreign investors became involved in the extraction and production of the commodities being exported. Consequently, during the age of progress and modernization, nearly every Latin American nation specialized in at least one valuable product for export that would satisfy market demands in the United States or Europe.

Beef and Wheat in Argentina and Uruguay

Soaring beef and wheat production in Argentina between 1873 and 1910 laid the foundation for that country's extraordinary growth in this period. The invention of refrigerated rail cars and ships in the last quarter of the nineteenth century transformed the market for beef exports. British consumers continued to rely on the Argentine canned beef described in chapter 4, but they also clamored for frozen beef, as did consumers across the North Atlantic. The consequences in Argentina were enormous, as wealthy exporters rushed to fence and control previously open frontier land, converting the pampas into intensive ranchland.

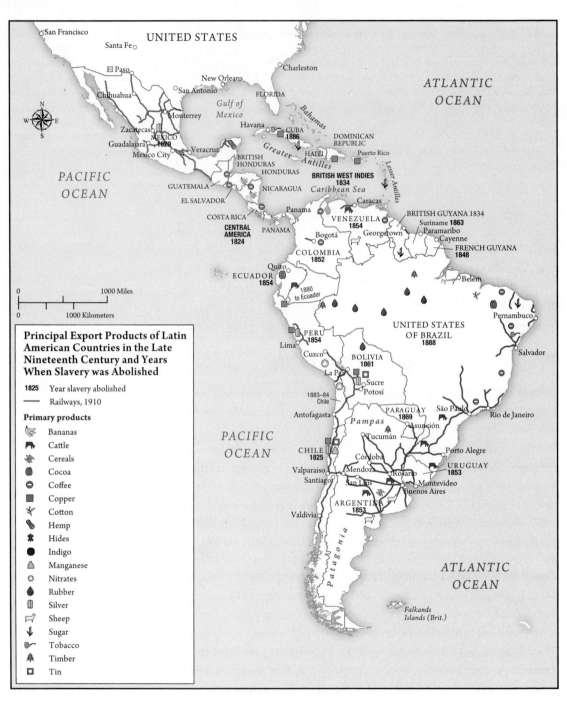

Principal Export Products of Latin American Countries in the Late Nineteenth Century and Years When Slavery was Abolished

1825   Year slavery abolished
——   Railways, 1910

Primary products

🍌	Bananas
🐂	Cattle
🌾	Cereals
◐	Cocoa
⊖	Coffee
■	Copper
🌿	Cotton
🪢	Hemp
✱	Hides
●	Indigo
△	Manganese
○	Nitrates
🌢	Rubber
▯	Silver
🐑	Sheep
⬇	Sugar
🌱	Tobacco
🌲	Timber
▢	Tin

≡ **MAP. 5.1**

The transition from free range to fenced land required greater land management, and landowners sought to rotate the alfalfa consumed by cattle with other grains like wheat, in order to maintain soil fertility. The subsequent boom in wheat exports, as a result, complemented rather than competed with King Cattle. Britain was again the primary consumer, a relationship that changed land and labor patterns on both sides of the ocean. Unable to compete with low-cost imported grain from the pampas, farmers in Cambridgeshire and Sussex gave up and moved to town. The large landowners of the Argentine hinterland, meanwhile, relied heavily on immigrant tenant farmers, who raised wheat in one location for several years, then moved on when landowners returned to alfalfa. Unlikely to acquire agricultural land of their own, these tenant farmers sought to save enough to forge a life in the city or to return home to their country of origin. Argentina's agricultural boom thus contributed to urban growth both in London and in Buenos Aires (as well as Newcastle and Rosario, for that matter).

Geographically akin to the Argentine pampas and the plains of southern Brazil, Uruguay's interior offered the country its best prospects for a lucrative export product. After decades of partisan struggles between Liberals (Colorados) and Conservatives (Blancos), a negotiated power-sharing arrangement in 1870 brought a modicum of stability to Uruguay. British investors responded to this stability with investment in a rail network connecting the Uruguayan interior to the port of Montevideo. British businessmen befriended their Uruguayan colleagues and intermarried with members of the Uruguayan elite, forming a cozy society of entrepreneurs.

Access to international markets transformed Uruguayan ranching life. No longer did lean livestock herded by gauchos roam the open range. After 1880, large landowners fenced their spreads and introduced pedigreed Hereford cattle and Lincoln sheep that would command a better price in the marketplace. In 1904, British investors underwrote the costs of the construction of the first refrigerated meat-packing plant in Montevideo, allowing Uruguay's exports to mimic Argentina's earlier shift from hides and beef jerky to the more profitable refrigerated chilled beef and mutton. So important were these beef and mutton exports to the Uruguayan economy that the president's cabinet included a minister of stock-raising!

Banana Cultivation and Its Consequences

The introduction of the banana to cultivation and consumer culture in Central America during the late nineteenth and early twentieth centuries transformed both the economy of the region and the diets of ordinary people throughout the Western Hemisphere. The banana was not native to the Americas. The fruit's origins are most likely in southern China or Southeast Asia, but its propagation in the

Pacific and Africa predate the age of discovery. It grew wild in Africa, from which the Portuguese brought it to the Brazil in the sixteenth century. It later was introduced during the colonial period in the Caribbean, where Spanish settlers used the fruit as food for slaves and other workers. The perishability of the fruit and a lack of consumer market for it outside of where it was grown, however, meant that bananas would not be cultivated and exported on a large scale until the invention of the refrigerated ship in the late 1860s. New multinational corporations, like the United Fruit Company, arose to cultivate, export, and market the fruit.

The industry developed in tandem with new demand for the commodity: They were virtually unknown outside of the region even in 1876, when the writer Jules Verne described the banana as "a fruit as healthy as bread and as succulent as cream" in his novel *Around the World in 80 Days*. That same year, ordinary North Americans encountered the banana firsthand at the Centennial World Exposition in Philadelphia, where the banana was touted as a salutary food that came "in its own sanitary wrapper."

The banana originally perplexed fruit-naïve North American consumers. Even the fruit's ripeness was confusing, since it arrived in stores looking deliciously green but was meant to be eaten when it had gone soft and "freckled," as a banana's brown spots are called in the industry. The United Fruit Company (UFCo) hired the author Frederick Upham Adams to write a fawning account of the company's work in Central America which also offered banana-based recipes designed to appeal to the American palate. His suggestions included dishes that have since become favorites, such as banana bread, banana cake, and fried bananas; but he also offered peculiarities such as spiced bananas, gelatin of bananas, banana croquettes, and (most provocatively) bananas with bacon and ham. Within a short time, the banana was well on its way to becoming the most widely-consumed tropical fruit in the world.

The development of the commercial banana industry is intimately tied to the late nineteenth-century developments in transportation and globalization that would transform northern Latin America's relationship with the world at large, and especially with the United States. As early as the late 1870s, small-scale local banana growers in Central America and Jamaica would sell bananas to steamship owners, who, having delivered manufactured goods abroad, did not wish to return home with empty vessels. In 1885, Lorenzo Dow Baker founded the Boston Fruit Company, which eventually became the largest and most influential foreign company in Central America, the United Fruit Company (now Chiquita). Despite the dominance of UFCo, other North American fruit concerns, most notably Standard Fruit (now Dole), also invested heavily in developing the tropical fruit industry in Central America (especially Honduras, Costa Rica, Guatemala, and Panama), as well as in Jamaica, Colombia, and Ecuador.

Between the 1880s and 1930s, the fruit companies (which produced not just bananas but also pineapples and palm oil) transformed the lowland coasts of Honduras, Guatemala, and Costa Rica. Because these "hot lands" were sparsely populated, usually not developed, and often legally available as "terrenos baldíos," or public lands, the fruit companies bought up huge tracts at bargain prices, often thanks to generous government incentives. They cleared, drained, and cultivated this land. The resulting banana plantations were enormous, incorporating many thousands of acres of land.

The fruit companies were vertically integrated and self-sufficient industries, meaning that they built and paid for the railways, ports, schools, clinics, telegraph lines, housing, public health programs, and provided the steamships they needed for their own enterprise and employees. Thus they fulfilled the dreams of the positivist leaders of the host countries and simultaneously made the banana plantations outposts of "modernity," segregated both by enterprise and geography from the rest of the country.

≡ **A Banana Plantation in Costa Rica.** Plantations dominated export agriculture especially during the late nineteenth century. Plantation life affected Central American nations more heavily than elsewhere in Latin America because banana producers like the United Fruit Company played a disproportionate role in national politics. This image of a banana plantation portrays the social separation that existed on plantations. Contrast the comfortable home of the plantation manager on the left side of the photograph with the barracks-like quarters for the workers on the right side. Not only is the manager's home larger, but it has windows and hence greater ventilation to provide comfort for the foreign manager living in a tropical climate.

The vast influence of the banana companies extended far beyond simple economic influence. This gave rise to a local nickname for UFCo as "**el pulpo**" (the octopus) for its extensive and multitentacled reach. The derisive term "banana republic," used to describe a small, unstable Central American country that was regularly subject to political upheaval, derived from the fruit companies' perceived ability to influence and even overturn national governments in Central America.

This was actually the case in Honduras, a country with a small and ineffectual national elite, where competing banana companies in the early twentieth century supported rival political parties and regularly affected the outcome of national elections. So acrimonious was this competition that each large company established its own virtual "capital," Tela, for UFCo, and La Ceiba, for Standard Fruit, both located on Honduras's Atlantic coast. In 1911, the president of UFCo, Samuel Zemurray, successfully financed an American adventurer and mercenary soldier named Lee Christmas to invade and briefly take over La Ceiba in order to help overthrow Honduras's elected president outright in favor of a politician more favorably disposed to UFCo's corporate interests.

Unlike coffee cultivation, which produced wealth for local elites, the banana industry mainly enriched its foreign investors, although some collateral economic benefits did accrue to small local producers who sold to the *fruteros* (fruit companies). The banana workers themselves also benefited somewhat; although they worked under harsh conditions, they earned better wages than did their campesino counterparts. While fruit companies wielded influence and power that served the interests of the corporations far more than those of the host countries, they brought ports, railroads, and paved roads to Central America, an investment in infrastructure that is still in use today. The fruit companies effectively shortened the distance between the United States and Central America, as ships, products, ideas, and people freely traveled between New Orleans (where UFCo was based) and the thriving fruit plantations.

Bananas and the Environment

The emergence of banana plantations on the north coast of Honduras transformed its tropical lowland environment, once a pristine ecological zone comprising beaches, mangrove swamps, and stands of palm and hardwood trees. When the market for bananas first emerged in the United States, local producers established small farms near streams or the single railroad that ran through the north country in order to ship their fruit to port. The arrival of large corporations like the UFCo and its competitors after 1900 dramatically increased the environmental impact on the land.

Although the idea of "taming the tropics" enjoyed considerable popularity among the proponents of progress, by cutting down forests the companies eliminated the

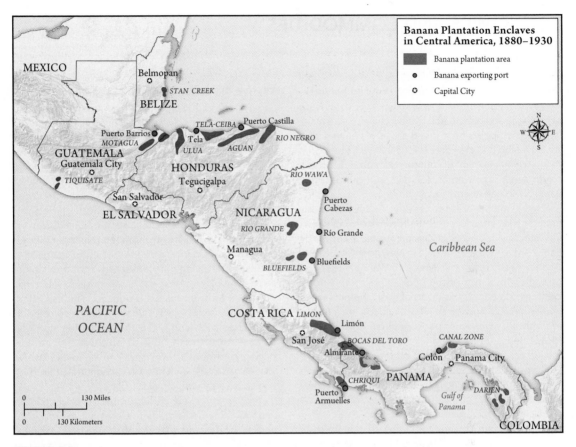

Banana Plantation Enclaves
in Central America, 1880–1930

- Banana plantation area
- ● Banana exporting port
- ✪ Capital City

MAP. 5.2

land's protective biodiversity. Deforesting the land (more than 50,000 acres in Panama's Colón District alone) created one set of problems, rechanneling surface water another, with less visible but equally profound consequences. By draining swamps, the plantations reduced the natural habitat for flora and birds. Although irrigation ditches, dikes, and canals attempted to control the naturally occurring water, the process also increased the likelihood of flooding during the rainy season. Altering the terrain had human consequences as well. When UFCo pulled out of the Colón region in 1932, they removed valuable infrastructure, like metal bridges, which left the villagers who remained in the region struggling to get their products to market over the now larger and deeper streams.

By 1900 both shippers and consumers of bananas agreed that the most desirable of all varieties was the Gros Michel. This banana, with its sweet taste, bright yellow peel, and thick skin, was less vulnerable to bruising during shipment. But

ECONOMICS AND COMMODITIES

Chicle

Chewing gum was largely unknown to Americans until the nineteenth century. Although chewing on something without the intention of swallowing it dates back across time and culture (the Greeks chewed tree resin, while archeologists have found a wad of chewed bark tar in Finland that may date back 5,000 years or more), the modern invention of chewing gum is credited to a North American inventor, scientist, and businessman named Thomas Adams.

In the mid-nineteenth century, Adams, curiously enough, was introduced to the raw material of chewing gum by Mexico's disgraced Antonio López de Santa Anna, who sought exile in New York City (where Adams lived) after the Mexican War. Santa Anna brought with him a gooey pitch, or sap, from tropical trees. He hoped this material might be processed into a durable substance that could be manufactured into, say, wheels or boots. Indigenous people in Mesoamerica (Mexico and northern Central America, the Aztecs and Maya) chewed on the resin from several types of trees to freshen their breath and clean their teeth. The Nahuatl name for this chew was *tzictli* (meaning "sticky"), which transliterates into Spanish as *chicle* (now the Spanish work for "gum.")

Farther south, the rubber trees of the Amazon produced a similar latex-like resin that forest dwellers called "chiclete," and also chewed. ("Chiclete" also means "gum" in Portuguese). But while the gum-like substance of the Amazon eventually proved enormously valuable as the base substance from which to make rubber (a lucrative commodity after the invention and the mass popularization of the automobile), the sticky sap that came from Mexico, Guatemala, and Belize could be processed only into a much more prosaic product: chewing gum. Although Adams was not the "inventor" of modern chewing gum per se, he was the first to import and sell it, in 1869.

Chicle has a neutral taste, so Adams added flavors. The first, in 1877, was a licorice taste that he called "Black Jack." Soon after, he introduced another flavor based on fruit and sugar that he called "tutti-frutti." His invention of the gum machine, where artificially colored and flavored balls of gum could be had for a penny, popularized the candy, which was cheap, readily accessible, and traveled easily. By the time of Adams's death in 1905, the customer base for chewing gum, sold by his company, American Chicle Company and its close competitor, Wrigley Gum Company (founded in 1891), already numbered in the millions.

As is often the case in the history of commodity chains, the chewing gum industry did not result in the same level of success in countries in which chicle was produced as it did for the producers. The harvesting of chicle by hand, which involved using a machete to chop crosshatches into the trunks of trees and wait for the sap to slowly "bleed" out, was tedious, low paying, and risky. It took many trees spread over a vast area (usually owned by an absentee landlord) to constitute a salable harvest.

In Guatemala, the chicle business took a bad turn in 1952. When an agrarian reform bill expropriated unused lands owned by the Wrigley Gum Company (by then, the only gum producer that purchased Guatemalan chicle), the company discontinued the Guatemalan arm of its business, leaving the *chicleros* (chicle harvesters) unemployed. Only a massive intervention on behalf of the chicleros on the part of the Guatemalan revolutionary government averted disaster. In the 1960s, however, most candy manufacturers switched to cheaper synthetic rubber to make chewing gum, and the market for Mesoamerican chicle dried up.

- How do ordinary commodities such as chewing gum, bananas, or coffee) create important transnational linkages?

the consequences of this monoculture (the cultivation of a single variety of a plant) were to be devastating. As the Irish discovered when they depended on a very few varieties of the potato as their principal food source, instead of the many varieties grown in the Andes, the spread of blight or other pathogen for which the chosen variety has no immunity can have a catastrophic result. This is especially in the case of an organism like bananas, which are all clones of one another (rhizomes) and so equally vulnerable to disease.

In the case of the Gros Michel, not only did the continuous harvesting and planting of this single variety result in declining soil fertility, but the plant proved vulnerable to a bacteria called *F. oxysporum*, known locally as the Panama disease. The bacteria spread rapidly from plantation to plantation, transported by canals, ditches and worker's feet, and caused the plants to wilt and not bear fruit. Although UFCo's scientists attempted to find a cure, they failed. UFCo's only solution, then, was to abandon the north coast plantations, cut down virgin forest elsewhere and start anew, this time with a new type of banana, the Cavendish, the smaller, more delicate banana that we consume today. In their wake, they left a severely damaged environment and a destitute population, many of whom soon migrated to the new plantations in search of employment.

Railroads and Other Technologies, 1870s–1900s

For Latin Americans who had traveled abroad, nothing more clearly differentiated their societies from those of western Europe and the United States than the absence of technology back home. Technological advances, especially in the fields of transportation and communication, had transformed the North Atlantic nations just as the Industrial Revolution changed the nature of commerce. No wonder, then, that policy makers worked to entice foreign investors to fund the transfer of North Atlantic technology, and especially railroads, to Latin America.

Railroads in Brazil and Mexico

Brazil offers a clear example of the economic transformation created by the expansion of railroads in the second half of the nineteenth century, as well as of the limits of that transformation. Through the 1860s, the paucity of railroads and the expense and uncertainty of overland transport were the greatest inhibitors of the development of the Brazilian interior. Railroad expansion in the 1870s and beyond unleashed a cascade of economic growth. It facilitated agricultural production hundreds of miles from the Atlantic coast, directed toward both domestic and export markets. The western half of the province of São Paulo, for example, eclipsed Rio de Janeiro as the nation's leading region for coffee cultivation. The railroad created savings on transport costs, which coffee planters reinvested into expanded production, capturing much of the growing global market for coffee.

In the short term, this expansion reinforced Brazilian dependence on slavery, as coffee planters in São Paulo sought to guarantee their labor force by purchasing slaves from the Brazilian northeast, where sugar fortunes were declining. This domestic slave trade proved insufficient to meet rising demands for labor, however, and planters in western São Paulo turned to transatlantic and even trans-Pacific free labor (that is, paid, rather than enslaved labor). Planters subsidized immigration of southern European and Japanese workers. The railroad thus played a role in the transition to free labor—but only after first intensifying slavery. Similarly, the savings produced by the railroad facilitated the growth and diversification of domestic markets. Finally, while the direct environmental impact of the railroad was limited, its indirect environmental impact was enormous, as it opened up new lands to intensive agriculture.

To further complicate this picture, most of the rail lines were foreign-owned, predominantly by British investors. Foreign capital investment proved vital to overcome the relative scarcity of domestic capital in the mid-nineteenth century. Foreign rail magnates did not have free rein: until its demise in 1889, the Brazilian Empire played an important role in distributing rail-line concessions and in setting freight rates. Imperial administration tended to impose limits on the profits of foreign investors, prodding reinvestment in domestic development. The Brazilian Republic, founded in 1889, went a step further, expropriating and nationalizing some of the foreign-owned railroads.

State intervention, however, did not always protect the vulnerable, as evident in the notorious case of the Madeira-Mamoré railroad. This quixotic venture, backed by North American capital, cut a rail line through hundreds of miles of Amazonian rainforest in the first decade of the twentieth century. Thousands of workers, many of them migrant laborers brought in from Caribbean islands, perished along the way. The same North American capitalists subsequently backed another rail line between São Paulo and Rio Grande do Sul in the Brazilian south. Construction of this railroad entailed expropriation of communities of small farmers, triggering a popular revolt. It took the Brazilian army four years to crush this Contestado Revolt, so named because of the "contested" nature of the lands in question.

Rail development in Argentina, Uruguay, and Chile followed a similar pattern. Argentine lines expanded rapidly enough to draw off cattle exports from both Uruguay and southern Brazil, using the production of neighboring countries to fuel Argentine growth. In all of these nations, by the early twentieth century rail was understood to be both the key to national economic development. Those who controlled the railroads seemed to control their country's future.

Ideally, railroads in Latin America served dual purposes: to unify the country physically and to transport goods and passengers more rapidly and less expensively. As the most celebrated technology of the nineteenth century, the railroad had caught the attention of Mexican policy makers as early as the days of Santa Anna. But Mexico's lack of stability prevented much from being accomplished for two generations. At the beginning of Porfirio Díaz's first term, Mexico possessed but one 400-mile railroad linking the port of Veracruz to Mexico City. During the early Porfiriato, the pace of railroad construction exploded, becoming the foremost of economic activities.

Díaz dismissed the traditional xenophobic policy concern that constructing railroads to the United States could facilitate a new Yankee invasion of Mexico. Instead, he entered into public/private partnerships with three groups of US investors to construct lines from Mexico City to the border. Completed in 1884, the **Ferrocarril Central Mexicano (FCM)** ran through the center of the nation, stopping at important cities like Guanajuato and Torreón before connecting with a US line in El Paso, Texas. The **Ferrocarril Nacional Mexicano (FNM)** went through Zacatecas and Monterrey before joining a US line in Laredo, while the third (and less significant) railroad ended in Nogales, Arizona. British investors concentrated their efforts in central and southern Mexico. By the end of the Porfiriato in 1911, Mexico boasted about 15,360 miles of track. Did this rail system further Mexico's progress and growth?

Porfirians clearly believed that railroad construction benefited the nation. Because Mexico lacked navigable rivers, such as those in Great Britain and the United States that had helped to transport goods during the early stages of the Industrial Revolution, Mexico had no alternative in this era but to build railroads to provide modern, cheap, and efficient transportation and to stimulate development in places that previously had experienced little economic activity. Railroads also contributed to political stability by allowing the government to dispatch troops or the rurales to distant parts of the country. Finally, railroads contributed to national unification. All but six state capitals enjoyed rail service to Mexico City (although rarely to one another).

Many of northern Mexico's small towns became important cities after the advent of the railroad. Land adjacent to rail lines gained in value and was frequently absorbed by neighboring haciendas. This had positive consequences for new owners, who planted crops or ran herds for market, and negative consequences for indigenous people who lost title to their land. The FNM hauled both coal and iron ore to Monterrey, laying the foundations for the steel industry there. Other mining centers sent minerals like copper to the United States. Railroads had hauled a mere 150,000 tons of goods in 1876. By 1911, the quantity had risen exponentially to 14,000,000 tons. Nevertheless, as chapter 7 explores, there were negative aspects to railroad construction in Mexico as well.

CULTURE AND IDEAS

The Chá Viaduct, São Paulo

In the last quarter of the nineteenth century, São Paulo grew from a secondary city into the hub of a coffee-exporting powerhouse. The city outgrew its colonial hilltop setting, as new residential neighborhoods blossomed on the other side of a steep valley. In 1877, Jules Martin, a French lithographer who made his career in São Paulo, planned a viaduct spanning the valley in order to facilitate urban transport. Local landowners, including titled nobility of the Brazilian Empire, opposed the plan, because it encroached on elite properties. Not until the demise of the empire in 1889 could the plan move forward. A private corporation imported the iron structure directly from Germany and finally inaugurated the Chá Viaduct, which opened in 1892.

The corporation charged a toll of three vinténs to cross the viaduct, about the price of a small bunch of bananas. This was enough to keep the urban poor from crossing the bridge from outlying districts to the heart of São Paulo's cosmopolitan downtown, but it did not trouble the rising merchant class. To the surprise and consternation of both the corporation and local government, however, low-wage workers proved eager to cross the bridge in order to enjoy the new downtown public spaces, and protested the toll. In 1897, ceding to popular pressure, the municipal government expropriated the viaduct, compensated the private corporation, and eliminated the toll.

The Chá Viaduct became the growing city's public place to see and be seen. On weekdays, trolleys crossing the span shuttled the clerks of new merchant houses to work and back. And on Sunday afternoons, workers and the sons of coffee barons alike took to the viaduct for their *footing*, or social promenade (an English loan-word which shows the high esteem for British cultural influence in São Paulo).

The Chá Viaduct encapsulated many of the trends of the late nineteenth and early twentieth centuries: urban growth, foreign capital and technological expertise, the decline of an old oligarchy, and the rise of an urban merchant class. It was also typical of many prominent urban reforms of this period in that it was initially intended to benefit the elite, but was ultimately appropriated for broader use. Its elegant but sturdy iron trelliswork seemed to declare the promise of the modern in this city at the vanguard of Latin American modernization.

- What does the Chá Viaduct tell us about understandings of urban planning and investment in the age of progress and modernization?

Railroads in the Andean Nations

The Andean nations (Colombia, Ecuador, Peru, and Bolivia) continued to experiment with elite-dominated governments rather than resort to dictatorships. As a consequence, civil wars interrupted their paths toward stability at times. The leadership of the Andean nations fully subscribed to the universal Latin American desire for progress and modernization. Specific circumstances in the four republics, however, limited the degree to which each could fulfill these objectives. All achieved greater stability between 1875 and 1930 than ever before. For example, after the devastating Thousand Days War (1899–1903), President Rafael Reyes, a great admirer of Porfirio Díaz, created a stabilizing coalition between his Conservatives and some Liberals, whereby the latter put down their guns in exchange for seats in Congress and a share of positions in the bureaucracy. That political compromise curbed significant violence in Colombia until 1946. Ecuador's much less bloody Revolution of 1895 brought the Liberals to power until 1925, during which time they generally maintained the peace while undoing most of the proclerical measures of Gabriel García Moreno and his followers.

By the turn of the twentieth century, Peru had created a durable, aristocratic republic that lasted until the rise of dictator Augusto Leguía in the 1920s. During these decades Bolivia—a country that had undergone more coups d'état than it had years of independence—experienced a mere three civil wars among its elite parties; conflicts that transferred power from the Conservatives to the Liberals and then to the Republican Party. As occurred elsewhere, the achievement of relative stability in the four republics led to some foreign investment, much of it directed toward constructing railroads over the extremely challenging topography.

Ironically, the largest and wealthiest of the Andean nations, Peru and Colombia, employed the least imaginative and least effective strategies for maximizing the potential benefits of railroads. Peru's lines were never intended to further national unity but rather to connect highland regions producing export products to the nearest port. Peru's attempt to construct a railroad from the port of Callao through the steepest part of the Andes to the mines at Cerro de Pasco drove the nation into bankruptcy in 1875.

A decade later, in 1886, Peru leased all of its railroads to the British W. R. Grace & Company on the condition that they complete the lines and pay off remaining debt owed to British bankers. Even then, Peru's railroads never turned a profit and transported freight almost exclusively. Colombia's railroads did nothing more than transport its most important product, coffee, to nearby ports. Financed by a US indemnity for the seizure of the Panama Canal Zone and additional US investment dollars during the 1920s, Colombians built a number of short railroads, the most important of which ran from the coffee-rich hills of Antioquía through the state's capital city, Medellín, and then to the coast.

Ecuador's Liberals envisioned the country's railroad project primarily as a means to promote national unity and secondarily to contribute to the movement of products and labor. The railroad would benefit the highlands by providing speedier access to coastal markets for its agricultural products (potatoes, dairy

≡ **La Oroya Railroad Bridge in Peru.** Geographical obstacles, particularly mountains, hindered the construction and use of railroads in much of Latin America. Because railroads can neither ascend nor descend steep inclines (a 4 percent grade is the maximum) skilled engineers developed a series of techniques to circumvent this problem. Each of these alternatives added to the cost of building railroads. Tunnels drilled through mountains obviated some of the problems, as did iron bridges like the one portrayed here stretching across deep canyons. Other techniques like switchback tracks also served as means to allow a train to continue along a track at as level a grade as possible. To climb from the port of Callao at sea level to more than 14,000 feet high in the Andes required many spectacular bridges. While in some countries railroads were designed to geographically unite the nation, in the case of Peru and many other Latin American nations, the railroads only served to bring products to ports.

products, and wheat) while providing coastal cacao plantation owners with workers fleeing the poor wages paid on highland estates. The nation's principal export product, cacao, grew in the region around the port of Guayaquil and was transported there by boat; hence the railroad project had nothing to do with marketing cacao. Liberal President Eloy Alfaro, nicknamed the "Old Battler" because of his many attempts to overthrow Conservative regimes as well as his experiences as a fighter for liberal causes in Central America and for Cuban independence, entered into a public/private partnership with the US businessman Archer Harman in 1897 to complete the railroad from Guayaquil to Quito, linking the country's two largest cities.

The daunting changes in altitude from the coast to the mountains made the construction phase of this project one of the most challenging in global railroading history. The Guayaquil to Quito Railway (commonly called the G & Q), faced obstacles from the outset. Ecuador's moist volcanic soil was prone to landslides in the rainy season, and indigenous people proved unwilling to labor on the project (because it disrupted the agricultural season) even for the high wages Harman offered. The government attempted to compel indigenous people to build the railroad through a labor draft, but the attempt failed when many indigenous laborers fled for home. Harman then imported 4,000 Jamaicans to complete the trickiest phase of the project, building the roadbed up the long, steep slope known as the "Devil's Nose" from the town of Sibambe to Alausi in the sierra. Finally, the G & Q steamed into Quito in 1908. Later in the century, the government built connecting lines to Ecuador's two other principal cities. Although the G & Q rarely turned a profit, it did physically unite the country.

Bolivia's railroads not only linked together the country's major cities (La Paz, Sucre, Potosí, and Cochabamba) but also delivered the country's principal export, tin, to the Chilean ports of Arica and Antofagasta, and to the Argentine border. Once a nuisance byproduct of silver refining, tin's new importance in modern manufacturing provided Bolivian governments with significant revenues for much of the twentieth century. Despite the wisdom of Bolivia's leaders in achieving the maximum utility for its railroads, important hurdles hindered their usefulness.

The most critical involved the difference in gauges (the distance between tracks) between Bolivia and Argentina. Argentina used the relatively wide standard gauge system, while Bolivia (and many other Latin American nations) built with narrow gauge rail, which facilitated construction and operation in mountainous terrain. Bolivia's narrow-gauge railroad going south and east required that shipped goods be unloaded at the border and then reloaded onto standard-gauge Argentine trains, increasing the cost of transportation. In short, having less investment capital and more difficult terrain to traverse than Mexico, Argentina, or Brazil, the Andean nations' experience with railroads met with more limited success. Air transport and paved highways would ultimately prove a better solution.

Refrigeration and Other Technologies

Although the railroad most dramatically influenced growth and modernization in Latin America, other technologies invented in the North Atlantic nations contributed as well. Improvements in communications often paralleled upgrades in transportation. First tested successfully in 1844, Samuel F. B. Morse's telegraph quickly spread across the United States, and a decade later, appeared in Latin America. Telegraph promoters found that stringing lines along the side of cleared railroad beds simplified their task. Not only did the telegraph (and soon the telephone) transmit business orders but it also contributed to Latin America's increasing

≡ **A Frigorífico in Uruguay.** The invention of frigoríficos (chilled meat plants) in Argentina, Uruguay, and southern Brazil after 1880 revolutionized the meat exporting industry. Beef and mutton could now be stored in refrigerated spaces and then shipped on refrigerated ships to European markets. To improve their chances in an international market, ranchers had to improve the quality of their stock until today many consider Argentine grass-fed beef to be the finest in the world. Because of this rapidly expanding market, Argentina, Uruguay, and southern Brazil became significantly more prosperous in the age of progress than they had ever been previously. In addition, frigoríficos were considerably more hygienic than saladeros.

stability after 1875. Local officials could wire the capital about bandits in their jurisdiction, or even more importantly, alert the government to the first stirrings of political dissent. As business ties to western Europe and the United States deepened, the transatlantic cables linking the three continents together significantly facilitated the transmittal of commercial orders. Less spectacular than the railroad, the new modes of communication nevertheless significantly aided the growth of the Latin American economy.

The invention of ammonia compression refrigeration greatly broadened prospects for prosperity for Argentina, Uruguay, and southern Brazil. In previous decades these cattle-raising regions had limited international markets: Ranchers sold hides to Europe to be fashioned into shoes and other leather products, and sent salted beef to slave-owning societies like Brazil and Cuba. In 1877, however, two ships, *Le Frigorifique* and the *Paraguay*, each equipped with ammonia compression refrigeration, loaded chilled beef and mutton aboard and successfully transported the cargo to London. Soon meat-packing plants dotted the shores of the La Plata River, as Buenos Aires and Montevideo became major exporters of chilled beef and mutton to feed the appetites of the British for fresh meat. Argentina and Great Britain would remain close trading partners until World War II interrupted the relationship.

Immigration, 1870s–1900s

Most members of the elite establishment, particularly those influenced by social Darwinism and positivism, believed that the influx of European immigrants was vital to transform and modernize Latin American society. Many members of the elite subscribed to racist ideas that northern European immigrants, especially Germans, made more desirable workers and citizens than did indigenous peoples, mestizos, and those of African descent. Among some policy makers, this was sometimes referred to as "whitening the population." In the opinion of the elite, only hard-working, thrifty, white immigrants, could push Latin Americans along the path to progress.

Immigration in the Southern Cone

At least four million people emigrated to Argentina between 1870 and 1930, with well over one million arriving between 1901 and 1910. They came in especially large numbers from Italy, Spain, eastern Europe and the eastern Mediterranean. Most of them arrived impoverished, particularly in the late 1870s, when the Argentine government heavily subsidized immigration. They tolerated the grueling,

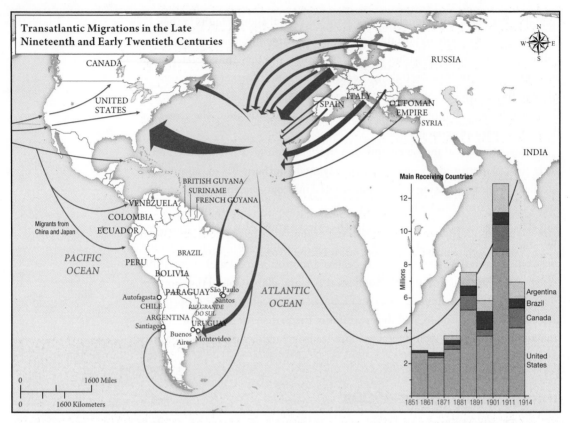

Transatlantic Migrations in the Late Nineteenth and Early Twentieth Centuries

MAP. 5.3

uncertain life of tenant farmers in the interior, and then tended to move to Buenos Aires or cities in the interior as soon as they had saved enough to survive and look for work. As *frigoríficos* (refrigerated meat-packing plants) and flour mills grew in size and number in the riverine corridor stretching from Buenos Aires to Rosario, immigrant labor served their needs and built up the surrounding, densely populated urban neighborhoods.

Nearly half of the immigrants came from Italy. Dockside neighborhoods in Buenos Aires became so heavily Italian that they transformed the language: *lunfardo*, a local dialect blending Spanish and Italian, was the language of everyday life in dockside neighborhoods like La Boca. Jewish immigrants from eastern Europe, in many cases refugees from early twentieth-century Russian pogroms, were admitted in large numbers but faced greater linguistic and cultural barriers to success in Argentina. These barriers only strengthened the resilience of their community networks, however.

Migrants fleeing the collapsing Ottoman Empire on the eve of World War I, particularly from Syria and Lebanon, responded in parallel ways to similar challenges. Across Latin America, these former Ottoman subjects were called *turcos*, or Turks, despite the fact that most spoke Arabic or French rather than Turkish. Although some were Muslim, most were Christian (although Orthodox rather than Roman Catholic). They created a merchant network with its own credit operations in urban outposts throughout Argentina and beyond, including regions far from the Southern Core, such as Honduras, which became home to many "turco" immigrants.

These immigrant streams transformed Argentine demographics in particular, making it a nation of cultural, linguistic, and religious diversity. As long as economic growth and the demand for immigrant labor continued, Argentina could accommodate that diversity without extensive internal conflict. When times grew tough, immigrants were often blamed for urban crime and labor agitation.

≡ **A Multilingual Policeman in Buenos Aires and the Hall for Immigrants.** The annual arrival of hundreds of thousands of immigrants in Argentina in the late nineteenth and early twentieth century posed many issues for Argentine society, especially in the port city of Buenos Aires, where most immigrants ultimately resided. First, immigrants were welcomed into the House of Immigrants, where newcomers were taught about Argentine customs in an attempt to incorporate them into society. In this particular photograph, immigrants are watching a movie about life on the pampas, where the elite hoped they would migrate to become laborers. In addition, the city created a special multilingual police force to assist immigrants. These officers wore badges on their arms to tell foreigners which languages they spoke (in this instance Spanish, English, Turkish, French, and Arabic). Officers like the one portrayed here could iron out cultural difficulties, intervene in disputes, and of course arrest troublemakers regardless of their place of origin.

Immigrant populations made up a smaller proportion of the national population in Uruguay than they did in Argentina, but followed similar patterns. Italian, Jewish, and Syrian and Lebanese immigrants to Montevideo played similar roles to those of their cousins across the Rio de la Plata estuary in Buenos Aires. By the late nineteenth century, Montevideo was already assuming the personality it would retain throughout the twentieth century, smaller than Buenos Aires yet similarly cosmopolitan.

The same immigrant groups arrived in large numbers in Brazil, particularly at Santos, the port of São Paulo. Italian immigration to the southern state of Rio Grande do Sul and to the southeastern state of São Paulo, created burgeoning Italo-Brazilian colonies. In the early twentieth century, planters in western São Paulo also recruited laborers from Japan. Both southern European and East Asian immigrants to rural Brazil often faced exploitative labor and miserable living conditions. Not surprisingly, many of them moved to the growing city of São Paulo as soon as they got the chance, creating vibrant Italian neighborhoods and a bustling Japanese neighborhood at the core of that city. Although immigration to Brazil was less momentous on a national level than it was in Argentina, it proved decisive in shaping the burgeoning metropolis of São Paulo.

Like positivists elsewhere in Latin America, Chilean intellectuals endorsed immigration as a means of modernizing their society. Liberals such as Benjamín Vicuña Mackenna believed that immigrants could replace the Mapuche on the lands in southern Chile, and thereby forestall possible Argentine expansionism into this disputed territory. With Gatling guns and a modern army, Chile forcibly subdued the Mapuche and pushed them further south or onto reservations. Nitrate mine owners in the north also sought immigrants who became skilled workers in technical positions.

In general, intellectuals believed that immigrants would modernize the country and improve national culture and the population through race mixture. Elites often described this as a process of **blanqueamiento** ("whitening;" **embranquecimento** in Brazil), an ideal that seems shockingly racist to modern sensibilities, but one that was frequently espoused in elite publications in Latin America's age of progress and modernization. This ideology of whitening was made manifest in social and economic structures that denied opportunity to Afro-descendant and indigenous citizens while facilitating European immigration.

The Chilean government was so eager to encourage immigration in the 1890s that it subsidized many immigrants' ocean voyages and placed no restrictions whatsoever on individuals seeking to emigrate from Europe to Chile. European immigration to Chile remained modest (about 85,000 individuals) compared to the masses that arrived in Argentina, in part because of the arduous ocean voyage around Cape Horn in the years before the construction of the Panama Canal. Despite their relatively small numbers, immigrants had a significant impact in Chile.

Unlike Argentina, where most immigrants took up residence in urban areas, immigrants to Chile settled either in the far north or the far south, distant from the national capital, Santiago. British migrants worked as managers or foremen at the northern nitrate mines, or took other middle-class jobs in nearby cities like Antofagasta, while immigrants from Peru and Bolivia performed the difficult physical labor in the nitrate pits. In the dense forests and lakes region of the far south, an area bearing resemblance to Switzerland or the Bavarian Alps, German immigrants tilled the soil, creating prosperous farms and populating quaint towns like Valdivia. There, and in other similar communities, immigrants operated tanneries, breweries, and furniture-making factories. These thriving settlements became the envy of many native-born Chileans.

The immigrants' success eventually worked against them, arousing nationalistic feelings among the next generation of Chilean intellectuals. Instead of being the laborers that Chilean intellectuals wanted, many of these immigrants (especially the second generation) became middle-class businessmen, engineers, teachers, shopkeepers, and even owners of light industry in Santiago. Chileans argued that their own nationals were equally competent to serve in many of these roles, but that immigrants received preferential treatment because of their status as Europeans. Other critics blamed working-class immigrants in urban areas for spreading ideas like anarchism, socialism, and syndicalism, accusing them of fomenting social discontent and urban problems. Some discussions turned ugly: Jews, the Chinese, and "Turks," many of whom owned successful businesses, were called parasites and worse. Even the once-admired Germans in southern Chile were now described as clannish and aloof. As a result of this growing nationalistic sentiment against immigration after World War I, the Chilean government ended its subsidies to immigrants and withdrew its recruiting agents from Europe.

Immigrants and Race

Although elite policy makers preferred European immigrants, they quickly learned that these foreigners, just like indigenous people and those of African descent, refused to perform certain types of particularly unpleasant labor. Only people fleeing the worst economic conditions would take such jobs. All too often, the laborers who committed to these jobs were duped by stories of wealth or encouraged to sign misleading contracts. The noxious, dusty, hazardous guano pits (where the excrement of seabirds was harvested for fertilizer), the treacherous landslide-prone roadbeds of the railways in the Andes, and hot, exhausting work on disease-infested Central American banana plantations or Brazilian coffee farms were often left to Asians from China and Japan and Afro-descendant workers imported from the British Caribbean.

Chinese laborers were recruited by middlemen in China—often lured by false or misleading promises and contracts—in the nineteenth and early twentieth centuries to work abroad. Many Chinese laborers initially came to Peru in the 1840s to work in the guano pits of the Chincha Islands, on sugar plantations on the north coast or on the railroad projects high in the Andes. In almost every instance, recruiters from Peru signed the workers, perhaps a grand total of 90,000 of them, to lengthy contacts of indentured servitude, which paid terribly low wages to offset the cost of the expensive trip across the Pacific. Once in Peru, workers found themselves housed in shanties, working long hours, and eating little more than rice. Almost no women accompanied these workers, and no other Peruvians spoke their language, leaving them isolated. A fortunate few found themselves contracted out as household servants or artisans in Lima, where conditions were significantly better. Not surprisingly, once the term of the enforced labor contract ended, many of the Chinese workers in the guano pits or on the plantations joined their countrymen in the capital.

By 1890, a distinctive Chinatown had emerged in Lima, centered on Capón Street near the municipal market in the heart of the old city. Chinese immigrants made their living as shoemakers, dressmakers, launderers, and grocery store owners. Popular *chifas* (Chinese restaurants) drew all classes of Lima residents to their tables. Some Chinese-born merchants made fortunes importing goods (such as furniture, rice, and pottery) from their homeland for neighborhood customers, but also sold porcelain objects and other luxury items to Lima's elite. Most people lived in crowded tenements (like the poor in any nineteenth-century city) where disease, crime, and opium dens flourished. Because Chinese workers competed with other Peruvians for jobs, and because they tended to isolate themselves, they were the victims of occasional riots. In 1910, for example, many were driven from their neighborhood. Peru began to regulate the number of Chinese immigrants in 1900 and adopted an official policy of exclusion in 1930 with the passage of a statute that barred further Chinese immigration. This statute remained in effect until the 1960s.

Japanese immigration to Brazil began later (the first Japanese immigrants arrived at the Brazilian port of Santos in 1908) but would quickly become as influential as Chinese immigration to Peru. By 1908, the Italian immigration that had transformed the demography of the state of São Paulo in the last quarter of the nineteenth century had slowed. Coffee planters in western São Paulo sought a new source of inexpensive immigrant labor. Japan was in the midst of its own traumatic transition from a semifeudal state characterized by local, subsistence-oriented agriculture to a modern, Western-oriented industrializing economy, a process that uprooted rural populations.

Japanese and Brazilian political officials initially agreed that this population provided an ideal solution to São Paulo's needs. Well-publicized campaigns and subsidized voyages lured thousands of Japanese to São Paulo's coffee lands, a migrant stream intensified by World War I. By 1930 there were well over 100,000 Japanese immigrants (in Japanese, *issei*, or first generation) and Brazilian-born descendants of Japanese immigrants (in Japanese, *nisei*, or second generation) in São Paulo—a population that would grow to 1.5 million over the next century. (These subsequent generations of Japanese-Brazilians are known in Japanese as *sansei*, or third generation.) Today, there are more people of Japanese ancestry in Brazil than in any other country outside of Japan.

Most of the early arrivals found that life in the coffee zone was precarious and difficult. Some endured, gradually finding ways to farm their own lands, contributing to the diversification of agricultural production in São Paulo in the first half of the twentieth century. Others fled the coffee plantations, settling in the city of São Paulo and in smaller towns throughout the state. They formed mercantile networks, taught children in Japanese schools, and published newspapers in Japanese. The neighborhood of Liberdade in downtown São Paulo became known as a hub of Japanese-Brazilian commerce and culture.

Japanese-Brazilians faced prejudice and discrimination. The Brazilian political theorist Oliveira Viana suggested that the Japanese immigrants were "like sulfur: insoluble," by which he meant that they could not be stirred into Brazil's melting pot. At the same time, white elites in Brazil often stereotyped Japanese-Brazilians as the more positive alternative to Brazil's Afro-descendant population, exemplifying the qualities of industriousness that descendants of African slaves supposedly lacked. These stereotypes became self-fulfilling prophecies, as Japanese-Brazilians found access to credit, education, and employment often denied to Afro-Brazilians. The Japanese-Brazilian population thus played a key role in the economy and culture of Brazil's most prosperous state, and an important symbolic role in the understanding of Brazilian national identity.

In the last quarter of the nineteenth century, Afro-Caribbean people migrated to coastal Central America in fairly large numbers. Because local people tended to be reluctant to work in the hot, pestilent lowlands, the banana companies induced black laborers from the Caribbean with the promise of relatively high wages to come and work on the plantations. American plantation managers favored banana workers from British Caribbean colonies such as Jamaica, as they already spoke English.

The benefits of working on a banana plantation, which typically included company-provided housing, schools, some sort of healthcare, access to religious services, and often a company store—were significant enough to lure large numbers of Caribbean immigrants. But it was not an easy life; the hard manual labor in a disease-prone climate was challenging, and the banana bosses, many of whom came from the US South, typically did not treat the Afro-Caribbean migrant workers humanely. This furthered the enclave-like quality of the plantations, where English, not Spanish, was most likely to be spoken by both foreman and crews, and where Afro-descendent banana workers would often find themselves isolated not just by language but also by skin color in their newly adopted countries.

Elite Women in the Age of Progress, 1870s–1900s

The age of progress offered modest opportunities for elite and middle-class women to redefine motherhood because of the era's emphasis on scientific thought. In addition, elite women found new opportunities in the public sphere for philanthropic service, while still operating within traditional patriarchal norms. These elite women did their good deeds while continuing to perform their patriarchal roles as wives and mothers. Despite being bound by their acceptance of the limitations imposed by patriarchy, these elite and middle-class women became more visibly active in society in the years between 1870 and 1910.

Social Motherhood

As the ideas of positivism became more pervasive in the latter part of the nineteenth century, the ideal of motherhood shifted away from that of a devout woman whose primary role was to indoctrinate her children with Christian values, to a mother who also taught her offspring more secular notions such as civic virtue and frugality. Young elite and middle-class women now sought more educational opportunities themselves, especially in practical subjects such as mathematics, science, and hygiene, to teach them to become better mothers. While this represented an expansion in certain kinds of opportunity for women, positivism still saw their roles as restricted almost completely to the traditional "woman's realm" of home and family.

"Scientific motherhood," the thinking went, would equip women to manage and run their household. "Modern" women were expected to manage expenses, raise healthy children by properly preparing nutritious meals, keep a clean and respectable home, and breastfeed their babies instead of entrusting them to mixed-race wet nurses. When late nineteenth century women became more involved in charitable organizations, they stepped into the public sphere as a logical extension of their roles as mothers.

During the colonial era, the Catholic Church had provided the vast majority of educational and social services in Latin America. The ascendancy of the Liberal position in the debate about the social role of the Catholic Church now made Liberal governments responsible for these programs. (Their inability to pay for these programs, in fact, constituted one of the arguments that Conservatives had made against secularizing Church property, as the Church traditionally funded schools, hospitals, charitable projects for the poor, and more.) Given the relative poverty of most of the Latin American nations, it fell to magnanimous private individuals, often women, from the elite class to form and lead charitable organizations. Further, the values of the late nineteenth century encouraged women to play a civic role, which legitimized greater activity in the public sphere. Elite men did not feel threatened by this new role for their wives because elite women worked as unpaid volunteers, an activity that did not diminish the reputations of their husbands as good providers.

Although many charitable organizations existed throughout Argentina, the largest and best known of all was the Society of Beneficence in Buenos Aires, founded by Bernardino de Rivadavia during his presidency in 1823. By the latter part of the nineteenth century elite women had taken over the management of the institution as an expression of social motherhood. Over the years, the Society's orphanage took care of many foundlings. Supervising the orphanage thus allowed elite women to indulge their maternal instinct outside the home. (Elite women did not perform the bulk of the labor, of course: Poorly paid wet nurses and servants fed the babies and cared for older children.) Elite women could take satisfaction from philanthropic work, leave the confines of their home while maintaining their honor, and enhance their reputations within their social circle.

As immigrants poured into Buenos Aires in the latter nineteenth century, the Society found itself overwhelmed. Illegitimacy rates soared during this era, and many children were abandoned. Poor women, unable to care for their offspring, would entrust a child or two to the orphanage so that they could continue to work and support the remainder of their family. In addition to the orphanage, the Society operated a hospital, a reform school for juvenile delinquents, and workshops where children and youths could learn trades. Girls learned to cook, to sew, do laundry, and make jam, while boys learned carpentry, shoemaking, and baking. After 1900, the Society received public funding to help it with its work, but financing remained problematic because of the sheer number of the needy. By 1930, the presence of so many homeless youths led to increased calls for a welfare state to take care of the disadvantaged.

New Roles in Education and Healthcare

Increased educational opportunities for certain Latin American women in the latter part of the nineteenth century opened new doors for employment. Although the social ideal for elite women remained family life and motherhood, circumstances such as early widowhood sometimes required some elite women to fend for themselves. For the elite and middle class, educational training provided additional opportunities. In Argentina, women gained the legal right to admission to universities in 1880. Numbers matriculating at the university remained small, however, as no secondary schools for girls existed until 1905. Those who managed to obtain a secondary school degree and gain admission to the university pursued professional careers as doctors and lawyers, and a significant number became outspoken feminists. (Their lives are discussed in

TIMELINE

1870–1920s
Immigrants flow into Latin America, especially Argentina

1884–1907
Mexico's positivists author prodevelopment legislation

1876–1911
Porfirio Díaz is Mexico's dictator

1884
Mexico begins expanding its railway network

chapter 6). Most middle-class women gaining admission to secondary schools chose a curriculum preparing them for primary school teaching (many of these women also were in the vanguard of feminism) or selected a commercial curriculum that taught them the clerical skills necessary to seek work as white-collar employees in the service sector.

Conclusion

Latin Americans born before 1870 and still living fifty years later were astonished by the dramatic changes that they had seen during their lifetimes. The new liberal, positivist ideas just coming into vogue in 1870 had evolved into concrete "scientific" policies that emulated steps that the North Atlantic states had previously taken to achieve material wealth, progress, and modernization. By 1870, the Latin American elites had generally reconciled their differences regarding the divisive issues that had prevented the emergence of modern nation-states in the first five decades following independence.

By agreeing on a centralized form of government, the new states delivered a crushing blow to regionalism and caudillismo. While the language of liberalism (such as federalism, individual liberties, and free trade) prevailed, the elite had largely accepted the conservative form of government and tariffs high enough to provide some income to the state. At the same time, Liberals had successfully disestablished the Roman Catholic Church even while Latin Americans' adherence to popular religion demonstrated their devotion to the faith. In short, the Latin American elite finally achieved enough consensus to allow for some stability.

1886
Emil Körner begins professionalizing Chile's army

1908
Ecuador completes the Guayaquil-Quito railroad

1904
Refrigerated meat-packing plant opens in Montevideo

Stability enticed investors from western Europe and the United States to sink their excess capital into modernization projects that brought much needed technology, especially railroads, to Latin America. Foreigners also invested heavily in mines or agricultural enterprises that produced highly profitable niche products for export. While some of the still-struggling nations relied on a single export product, the more successful countries (Argentina, Mexico, Brazil, Chile, and Uruguay) offered a broader spectrum of goods to international markets. Latin America's growth signaled to impoverished southern Europeans and East Asians that opportunity existed in Latin America, and millions of immigrants from those regions responded by flocking to Argentina, Uruguay, and Brazil.

For Latin American nations in this era, progress and modernization provided many benefits, particularly to a rising merchant class. The more candid among the elite, however, recognized that the benefits of material prosperity had not been shared equitably. Attempts to encourage European immigration had in many cases deepened racial inequity. In places like Mexico, Guatemala, and the Andean nations, the indigenous populations had little or no share in the benefits of modernity. Afro-Brazilians and Afro-descendant inhabitants in the Caribbean and surrounding region likewise were marginalized from the benefits of export-led growth. Modernization also threatened the environment. While the elite believed that these socioeconomic issues would be resolved by education and with the passage of time, the political leadership turned its attention to the more imminent question of the looming presence of the North Atlantic powers. This growing uneasiness is the subject of the next chapter.

KEY TERMS

blanqueamiento/
    embranquecimento   228

campesinos   201

científicos   205

Conquest of the
    Desert   199

el pulpo   214

Ferrocarril Central
    Mexicano (FCM)   219

Ferrocarril Nacional
    Mexicano (FNM)   219

Pax Porfiriana   201

positivism   196

social Darwinism   197

Selected Readings

Beatty, Edward. *Institutions and Investment: The Political Basis of Industrialization in Mexico before 1911.* Stanford, CA: Stanford University Press, 2001.

Blum, Ann. *Domestic Economics: Family, Work, and Welfare in Mexico City, 1884–1943.* Lincoln: University of Nebraska Press, 2009.

Bunker, Steven B. *Creating Mexican Consumer Culture in the Age of Porfirio Díaz.* Albuquerque: University of New Mexico Press, 2012.

Chomsky, Aviva. *West Indian Workers and the United Fruit Company in Costa Rica, 1870–1940.* Baton Rouge: Louisiana State University Press, 1996.

Clark, A. Kim. *The Redemptive Work: Railway and Nation in Ecuador, 1895–1930.* Wilmington, DE: Scholarly Resources, 1998.

Cohen, Rich. *The Fish That Ate the Whale: The Life and Times of America's Banana King.* New York: Farrar, Straus and Giroux, 2012.

Garner, Paul. *Porfirio Díaz.* London: Pearson's Education, 2001.

Nunn, Frederick. *Yesterday's Soldiers: European Military Professionalism in South America, 1890–1940.* Lincoln: University of Nebraska Press, 1983.

O'Conner, Erin E. *Mothers Making Latin America: Gender, Households, and Politics since 1825.* Malden, MA: Wiley Blackwell, 2014.

Soluri, John. *Banana Cultures: Agriculture, Consumption, and Environmental Change in Honduras and the United States.* Austin: University of Texas Press, 2005.

Summerhill, William. *Order against Progress: Government, Foreign Investment and Railroads in Brazil, 1845–1913.* Stanford, CA: Stanford University Press, 2003.

Striffler, Steve, and Mark Morberg, eds. *Banana Wars: Power, Production, and History in the Americas.* Durham, NC: Duke University Press, 2003.

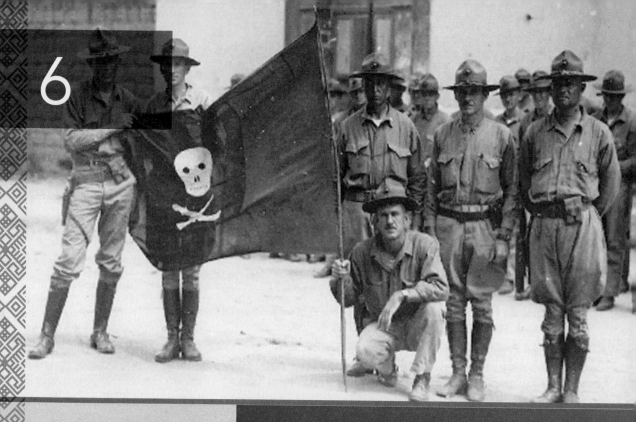

6

Worlds Connecting: Latin America in an Imperial Age

Global Connections

If the nineteenth century had, as some quipped, "entered on horseback and left on a train," the world at the start of the twentieth century was smaller and more connected than ever before. This connectedness was due in large part to the second wave of European imperialist expansion (also referred to as the "New Imperialism"). During the so-called Pax Britannia, when Great Britain dominated vast expanses of the world during the reign of Queen Victoria (1837–1901), British explorers, bureaucrats, missionaries, and businessmen, (with the help of the Royal Navy, the world's most modern military force at the time), expanded England's influence over the globe. At the apex of the British Empire, when it was said that the "sun never set on the British flag," much of the world remained or fell under British economic or political dominance. Wherever they went, the British brought the latest in technological innovation (the locomotive, paved roads, telegraph lines, electric lights, and efficient mail systems, to name a few) that made empire possible.

Beyond the British Empire, other European powers were also expanding their geopolitical grasp. Europe, and to some extend the United States, carved China (still under the leadership of the now weak and ineffective Qing Dynasty [1644–1912]) into economic and political "spheres of influence," effectively making the Chinese resentfully subservient to Europe. Britain and other European countries took part in the "Scramble for Africa," creating new colonies (such as Kenya, Cameroon, the Belgian Congo, Tanzania, Senegal, and the Ivory Coast, among others) between the 1870s and 1890s. Even the Netherlands, which had already established a significant presence in southern Africa as well as some of the smaller Caribbean islands (including Curaçao, Aruba, and St. Maarten) extended its footprint in the late nineteenth century by establishing its authority over most of what is today the country of Indonesia. Eastern Europe was not immune from European colonial incursions, as evidenced by the Austro-Hungarian Empire's growing expansionist ambitions in the Balkans in the last decades of the century.

But it would be the United States, not Great Britain or any other country of Europe, that would dominate the twentieth century, particularly in Latin America. Any number of factors conspired to make this so. Simple geography, of course, was paramount; from the beginning of the new century the United States would begin to take seriously its self-appointed role as "regional policeman" to the Americas. Improvements in communications and transportation, the decline of British interests

≡ **US Marines with Flag Captured from General Augusto Sandino's Troops in Nicaragua.** The incessant US interventions in the Caribbean and Central America between 1903 and 1932 provoked nationalistic responses wherever US troops landed. The best-known such response occurred in Nicaragua, where General Augusto Sandino rebelled and eluded capture until after the Marines departed in 1933. The frustrated Marines could do no more than capture a flag from one of Sandino's detachments, which they proudly display here.

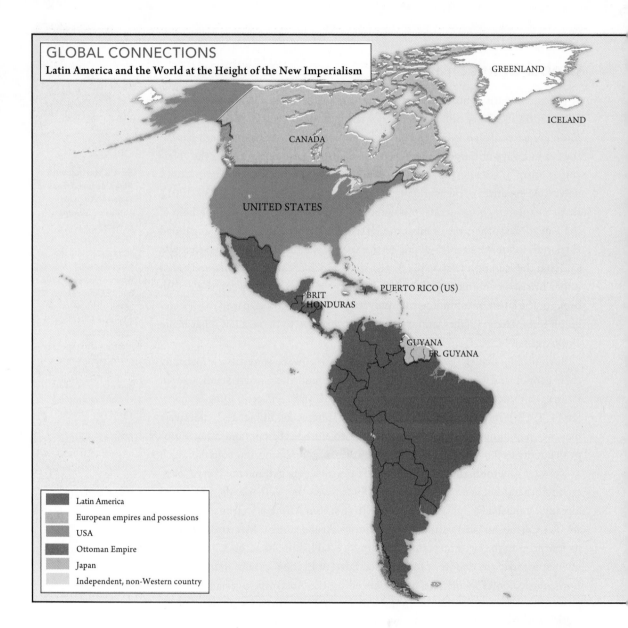

GLOBAL CONNECTIONS

Latin America and the World at the Height of the New Imperialism

GREENLAND

ICELAND

CANADA

UNITED STATES

PUERTO RICO (US)

BRIT HONDURAS

GUYANA

FR. GUYANA

Latin America

European empires and possessions

USA

Ottoman Empire

Japan

Independent, non-Western country

in the region, the emergence of the United States after the Spanish-American War of 1898 (also referred to as the War of 1898 or the Spanish-Cuban-American War), and the rise of a new type of global capitalism based on commodity chains (which closely linked raw materials to production and then to world markets and consumption), would all bring the two regions closer together, both for better and

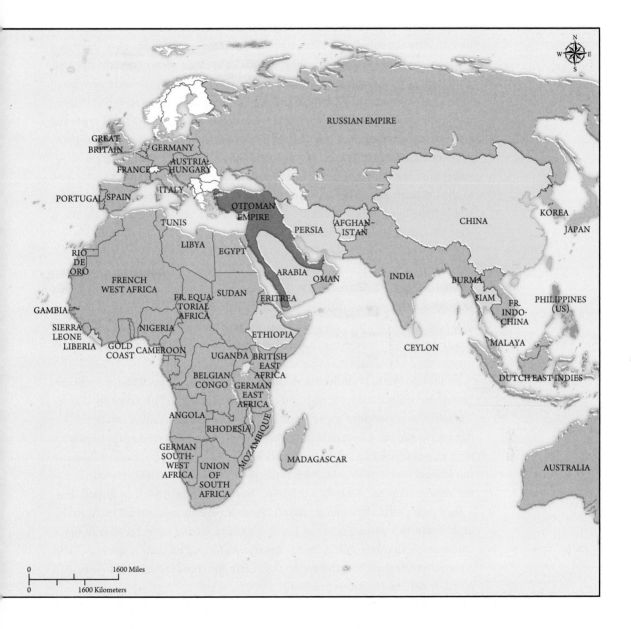

for worse. This was the dawn of the "American Century," when the United States would rise to its full status as a global superpower. It would be both Latin America's blessing and its curse to be in that superpower's backyard.

It is not surprising that US foreign policy toward Latin America evolved along-side increased financial investment in the region by US corporations, most of which continued to be involved in extractive industries and transportation. These investments are sometimes referred to as business imperialism: they improved infrastructure and facilitated export-led growth, albeit sometimes in ways that undermined local sovereignty and domestic development. By the early decades of the twentieth century, US interests in Latin America were substantial, particularly in the circum-Caribbean area, meaning the islands and mainland that border the Caribbean. Because many, if not all, of these countries were perceived to be politically or financially unstable, leaving them vulnerable to intervention from imperialist European nations, the United States claimed for itself the right to intervene in the domestic affairs of Latin American nations. In this role, the United States would be willing and able to intervene, ostensibly to restore order, but always in ways that served its own interests.

Where convenient, the United States justified intervention on the basis of a putative imperative to protect American lives and property. In practice, this often meant that the US military acted in the service of US corporations with investments in Latin America. The involvement of the US Marines in the Spanish-American War signaled their readiness to serve as the enforcers of the United States' political and economic interests in Latin America. The stage was set for the era of US intervention and expansion in Latin America.

By the late 1920s, US influence in Latin America was profound. North American know-how and capital had produced the infrastructure and investments that integrated the region into global capitalist networks. Ships sailing under the US flag transported raw materials from Latin America and returned again brimming with manufactured goods. Latin American elites began to send their children to the United States to be educated, while poor children in neighborhoods across the region adopted "America's pastime," baseball. Latin American leaders burnished their political discourses to suit North American audiences. American English began to surpass French as Latin America's second language of commerce and cosmopolitanism. While North Americans topped off their mugs with Latin American coffee, middle- and upper-class Latin Americans filled their homes with North American consumer products.

But this relationship was asymmetrical. Throughout the region, people, both rich and poor, powerful and powerless, chafed against what they perceived to be Yankee arrogance and entitlement. The occupations of various countries by the US Marines, sometimes for years at a time, sowed deep seeds of bitterness. US cultural imperialism (the assumption that the North American way of life was innately superior to the Latin American) insinuated itself into the psyche of Latin Americans. There, it created a sense of resentment and inferiority that would endure for decades to come.

The Growing Presence of the United States in Latin America, 1890s–1920s

The Spanish-American War of 1898 heralded the arrival of the United States as a global power in possession of an overseas empire. During the ensuing three decades, the US profile south of the Río Grande became dramatically enlarged, much to the discomfort of Latin Americans. This new age of imperialism was in many ways a continuation of the crusading spirit of the Manifest Destiny of the 1840s and 1850s. Particularly for the smaller nations of the Caribbean and Central America, the growing presence of the United States in their region threatened their security and even their independence.

The Cuban Independence Movement of 1895

The Pact of Zanjón ending the Ten Years' War in 1878 provided an illusory peace. Although Spain promised reforms granting Cuba greater autonomy, the system of governance changed little in practice, disappointing the planters and other elite members of the Liberal Party. With the revival of the sugar economy in the 1880s, planters pushed smallholders off their farms, including many Afro-Cuban veterans of the Ten Years' War. As a consequence, some of the veterans and other displaced persons opted to become bandits: robbing planters or holding them for ransom, and sometimes sharing their spoils with the poverty-stricken rural populace.

Many of the economically better-off advocates of independence left the island after the Ten Years' War and sought exile abroad, especially in the United States, where the emigré author José Martí emerged as the leader of the **Cuba Libre** (Free Cuba) movement. Recognizing that the separatists needed a broader, civilian-led coalition that included Cubans of all races, Martí created the Cuban Revolutionary Party (PRC). The PRC organized recruits from among Cuban workers living in the United States, raised funds, and promoted the cause of an independent Cuba among the non-Cuban US population. At the same time, Martí expressed to his colleagues his wariness of US policy makers, who for generations had harbored dreams of annexing Cuba as part of America's Manifest Destiny.

By 1895, Martí managed to forge a shaky alliance between Cubans who held three very different opinions about the island's future. One opinion favored annexation to the United States, because this would guarantee the continuation of the export-driven economy. A second opinion favored Cuba's becoming an independent republic. Finally, a third group called for social revolution that would end the plantation economy and redistribute small plots of land to farmers.

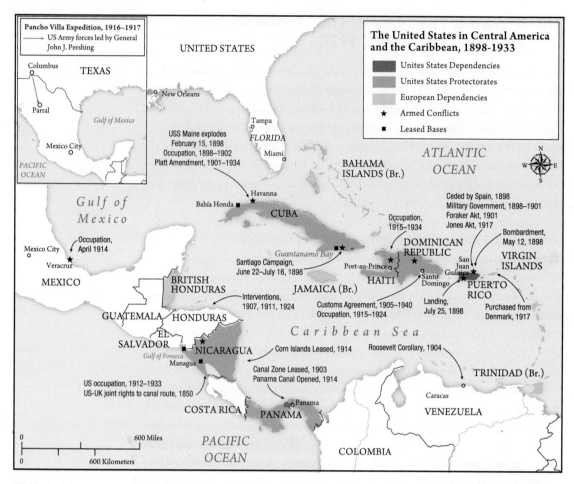

Pancho Villa Expedition, 1916–1917
→ US Army forces led by General
John J. Pershing

UNITED STATES

TEXAS

Columbus

Parral

Gulf of Mexico

New Orleans

Mexico City

PACIFIC
OCEAN

USS Maine explodes
February 15, 1898
Occupation, 1898–1902
Platt Amendment, 1901–1934

Tampa

FLORIDA

Miami

**The United States in Central America
and the Caribbean, 1898-1933**

☐ Unites States Dependencies

☐ Unites States Protectorates

☐ European Dependencies

★ Armed Conflicts

■ Leased Bases

BAHAMA
ISLANDS (Br.)

*ATLANTIC
OCEAN*

Gulf of
Mexico

Bahía Honda ■

Havanna
★

CUBA

Occupation,
1915–1934

Ceded by Spain, 1898
Military Government, 1898–1901
Foraker Akt, 1901
Jones Akt, 1917

Bombardment,
May 12, 1898

Mexico City

Occupation,
April 1914

Veracruz

MEXICO

BRITISH
HONDURAS

Guantanamo Bay

Santiago Campaign,
June 22–July 16, 1898

■★

Port-au-Prince

DOMINICAN
REPUBLIC

Santo
Domingo

San
Juan

Guánica ★

HAITI

JAMAICA (Br.)

VIRGIN
ISLANDS

PUERTO
RICO

GUATEMALA HONDURAS

Interventions,
1907, 1911, 1924

Customs Agreement, 1905–1940
Occupation, 1915–1924

Landing,
July 25, 1898

Purchased from
Denmark, 1917

EL
SALVADOR

Gulf of Fonseca

Managua ■

NICARAGUA

Caribbean Sea

Corn Islands Leased, 1914

Roosevelt Corollary, 1904

TRINIDAD (Br.)

US occupation, 1912–1933
US-UK joint rights to canal route, 1850

Canal Zone Leased, 1903
Panama Canal Opened, 1914

Panama

Caracas

VENEZUELA

COSTA RICA

PANAMA

0 ____ 600 Miles

0 ____ 600 Kilometers

*PACIFIC
OCEAN*

COLOMBIA

≡ MAP. 6.1

Martí also persuaded General Máximo Gómez, one of the military heroes of the Ten Years' War, to participate in this multiracial insurgency, a coalition difficult to create before the abolition of slavery in 1886. With the urging of Martí and the PRC, Cubans in the eastern part of the island rose up in February 1895, initiating the resumption of the war for independence under the leadership of Afro-Cuban general Antonio Maceo. In May, Martí sailed to Cuba with a small group of volunteers, but was almost immediately killed in battle. In one of his last letters, Martí again warned his countrymen about the dangers of a potential alliance with the United States. Without Martí's leadership, the fragile alliance of those who wanted to separate Cuba from Spain dissolved.

By January 1896 the rebels had invaded the western part and occupied stretches of rural land throughout the island. The separatists enjoyed the popular support of the rural poor, and conducted guerrilla campaigns in the countryside, burning fields of sugar cane and dozens of mills. As General Gómez put it, "blessed be the torch." Gómez's strategy appealed to many of the rank-and-file Afro-Cuban insurgents, for whom years of enforced servitude had instilled a deep desire for an end to the plantation economy. Even the battlefield death of General Maceo in December 1896 did not daunt the enthusiasm of the Afro-Cuban fighters.

Spain's Conservative Party, now in the majority in the Spanish Parliament, sent General Valeriano Weyler to extinguish the Cuban independence movement. Weyler brought shiploads of reinforcements, perhaps as many as 200,000 men. (This was a remarkable number, considering that Spain was also fighting against an independence movement in the Philippines, half a world away.) Weyler decided that only brutal tactics would squelch the Cuban revolt. He embarked on a campaign of terror, burning peasant villages and laying waste to crops and livestock. He forcibly relocated campesinos, perhaps as many as 300,000 people, to confined camps, where they languished and starved under the eyes of Spanish troops. These were the world's first concentration camps, and earned the general the nickname "Butcher Weyler" in the US press. The camps lacked adequate food and water, and disease spread rapidly in their cramped conditions. Estimates suggest that 25 percent of the people held in these camps perished, with numbers ranging between 90,000 and 170,000 civilian deaths in all.

Although Weyler appeared to have a numerical advantage in terms of troops, these figures proved deceiving. As in the case of the Haitian revolution of 1793, European soldiers lacked immunities to tropical diseases like malaria and yellow fever. Soon nearly half of Weyler's forces had fallen ill. By October 1897, Spaniards had wearied of war, and new parliamentary elections returned a Liberal cabinet that recalled General Weyler. After his departure, the Spanish army controlled the major cities, while the separatists dominated the countryside. Many historians believe that the Cubans would have triumphed given a little more time. But they did not get it: instead, US President William McKinley decided to send the battleship the USS *Maine* to Havana's harbor to protect American interests.

The US Intervention and the Spanish-American War

In 1898, the United States intervened in Cuba's war for independence from Spain, and did so because of long-standing US interests in Cuba. During the 1895 rebellion, the United States sought to displace Spanish influence on the island by extending sympathy and aid to Cuban rebels fighting for their independence. Meanwhile, American tabloid journalists like William Randolph Hearst and Joseph Pulitzer publicized the atrocities

NAVAL OFFICERS THINK THE MAINE WAS DESTROYED BY A SPANISH MINE.

≡ **Destruction of the Ship *Maine* Was the Work of an Enemy.** William Randolph Hearst and Joseph Pulitzer, rivals in the newspaper business, dueled each other for years trying to increase circulation by publishing provocative articles and political cartoons. Both sensationalized the ongoing war for Cuban independence, highlighting the brutalities committed by the Spanish general Valeriano Weyler and his policy of herding Cuban civilians into concentration camps. This particular article blames the Spanish government for the explosion of the USS *Maine* and the deaths of 258 sailors. These pieces whipped up public opinion, at least in New York, and provided popular support for the US intervention into Cuba in 1898.

committed by General Weyler, both to sell newspapers and to move Americans to action in favor of Cuban liberation from Spanish rule. When the USS *Maine* blew up in Havana's harbor on February 15, 1898, Hearst accused the Spanish of planting explosive mines in the harbor. The real cause of the explosion was never determined, and may have resulted entirely from internal causes. Nonetheless, outraged US citizens accepted Hearst's explanation and demanded retribution. McKinley asked Congress for a declaration of war, and tens of thousands of US volunteers responded enthusiastically to his call. More cautious voices in Congress insisted on a limitation to long-term involvement. In April 1898, they passed the Teller Amendment, guaranteeing Cuba some form of independence at the conclusion of the conflict. US strategic interests, however, proved more important than humanitarian concern in determining US involvement and its aftermath.

The ensuing "splendid little war" (as one diplomat termed it) began in East Asia, due to the foresight of Undersecretary of the Navy (later President) Theodore Roosevelt. Left in charge of the Naval Office for one day when his boss took a vacation, Roosevelt ordered Admiral George Dewey to arm the Asian squadron and prepare to take on the Spanish fleet in the Philippines. A quick cable to Admiral Dewey after the passage of the Teller Amendment put the plan into action, resulting in a complete US victory in Manila Bay on May 1, 1898. But this was no victory for the Filipinos themselves. After the Americans took possession of the Philippines, guerrilla fighters, and then the Philippine Republic as a whole, began fighting for the removal of foreign troops and for genuine independence of the Philippines. By the time the American

Theodore Roosevelt and the Rough Riders. Many of the early narratives about the US intervention in the Cuban War for independence were shaped by the larger-than-life personality of Theodore Roosevelt. Though a civilian, he organized a group of volunteers called the Rough Riders from all walks of life to join him on this decidedly imperialistic venture, a cause Roosevelt heartily embraced. Roosevelt's charge up San Juan Hill received considerable play in the US press and catapulted him into the vice-presidency in the election of 1900. Roosevelt and his admirers celebrated the charge up San Juan Hill, while downplaying the role that Afro-Cubans played in the long struggle towards independence.

military occupation of the islands ended in 1902, between 200,000-250,000 Filipinos had died in the struggle for national independence.

Back in the Caribbean theater, despite confusion, mismanagement of logistics, and at times inadequate supplies, an enthusiastic throng of volunteers and 25,000 US regular troops landed in eastern Cuba near the city of Santiago. Two hard-fought battles sealed the fate of the Spanish empire in Cuba. The best known of them, that of San Juan Hill, proved decisive. Theodore Roosevelt, now a colonel in command of a group of volunteers made up of college athletes, cowboys, and East Coast outdoorsmen who styled themselves the Rough Riders, charged through clouds of gun smoke and withering rifle fire to take the strategic blockhouse at the top of the hill. US commanders limited the Cuban insurgents to providing auxiliary support by doing reconnaissance, digging trenches, and preventing Spanish reinforcements from reaching the scene of the battle. A few days after the battle of San Juan Hill, the US Navy destroyed the remainder of the Spanish fleet outside Santiago harbor, effectively ending the military campaign. In all, bullets took the lives of 400 US soldiers and sailors while another four thousand men perished as a result of tropical disease and of food poisoning from improperly canned food.

The Treaty of Paris confirmed the status of the United States as an overseas imperial power. Spain transferred title to the majority of its remaining colonial empire (Cuba, Puerto Rico, Guam, and the Philippines) to the United States. The United States turned the Philippines and Puerto Rico into US colonies. In so doing, the United States projected its growing influence not only over Latin America, but also East Asia. The Teller Amendment, however, prohibited the United States from annexing Cuba and placed limits on its military occupation there.

Cuba under the Platt Amendment, 1899–1934

US involvement changed the meaning of the war. Instead of independence from Spain on their own terms, Cubans found themselves living under US military occupation from 1899 to 1903. US control over Cuban political affairs in the wake of the war would prolong those effects. Cuba fell under US domination, as the US effectively chose Cuba's political leaders and controlled its administration until 1934. This relationship well served US interests, but not those of Cuba.

The Platt Amendment, passed by the US Congress in 1901 and incorporated into Cuba's new constitution soon thereafter, provided the juridical rationalization for this arrangement. The amendment granted the United States the right to intervene in Cuban affairs at any time and for any reason. It also required Cuba to cede land for a US naval base at Guantánamo, an arrangement codified in 1903 with a ninety-nine-year lease. (By the time this lease officially expired in 2002, the United States was using Guantánamo as a prison for captives in the twenty-first century war on terror.) In return, the United States eliminated tariffs on Cuban sugar, a gesture that enriched Cuban planters and US investors without improving opportunities for humbler Cubans.

The United States disbanded the Cuban army that had fought for independence and created in its place the Rural Guard, which functioned as a police force protecting the interests of rural landowners. This reinforced the importance of sugar exports as the lifeblood of the special relationship between Cuba and its ostensible protector. With the Rural Guard minding the store, US forces temporarily withdrew. They soon returned. The 1906 Cuban presidential election failed to play out according to plan, leading to political disputes accompanied by popular rebellion. US Marines landed in force to quell the uprising and install the Nebraskan judge Charles Magoon as governor of Cuba. The full-fledged US occupation during Magoon's three-year term marked the political nadir of Cuba under the Platt Amendment. Cubans reviled the Marines as occupiers and lampooned the portly Magoon as greedy. Magoon and the Marines withdrew in 1909, returning Cuban administration to the hands of US-approved intermediaries.

In the meantime, Afro-Cuban veterans of the war for independence founded the Partido Independiente de Color, or PIC, a political party advocating for equal citizenship and access to public benefits for Cubans of African ancestry. The PIC challenged official state policies and elite cultural rhetoric suppressing racial identification in Cuba. The party gathered momentum in eastern Cuba, where Afro-Cuban veterans and their families faced increasing land pressure, driving them off small farms. The Cuban regime passed legislation outlawing racially defined parties in an attempt to block the PIC. This marginalized the PIC from official politics, contributing to greater pressure. In 1912, PIC members joined an armed uprising against the state in eastern Cuba. The regime cracked down with extreme prejudice, killing thousands of black citizens in the process. The massacre gave the lie to the official discourse of colorblind citizenship, but also revealed the risk of race-based mobilization.

US tutelage prevented the emergence of candidates who opposed the interests of US investors, ensuring that Cuban politics would remain highly circumscribed through the 1920s. A rapid decline in sugar prices in the second half of that decade threatened the US-Cuba relationship. The Platt Amendment was nearing its demise.

In the meantime, while the United States delayed Cuban political change, the island's economic and social transformation continued. The US Army Corps of Engineers built a modern system of roads in Cuba, and US missionaries established a network of primary schools. Perhaps most significantly, it was during the US occupation that a key collaboration between two epidemiologists, the Cuban Carlos Finlay and the American Walter Reed, proved that mosquitoes are the vectors for malaria and yellow fever. Thanks in part to this important medical breakthrough, Havana grew rapidly in the first decade of the twentieth century, and became more than an export hub. Light industrial enterprises such as breweries and textile factories emerged, employing growing cadres of urban wage earners. These workers, in turn, patronized the beer gardens that served as the laboratory for new forms of Cuban popular music. Fledgling Havana recording companies both typified light industrial growth and served to record Afro-Cuban musical forms like the *son* and the *danzón* for the first time. While political demands could be temporarily contained, Cuba's popular vitality could not.

By the late 1920s, nationalist resentment of Yankee intrusion grew stronger, particularly among the urban, industrial sectors that had grown in recent decades, and in the Cuban Army. With the backing of the US Department of State, President Gerardo Machado attempted to contain this growing pressure by distributing political perquisites to three different political parties. But this still left many Cubans alienated by the *Machadato*, or Machado presidency. The economic crisis of the Great Depression led to a rapid decline in the price of sugar, threatening Cuba's export sector. In the early 1930s, urban professionals, women's groups, and university students joined forces in an underground resistance against Machado. A revolutionary junta in New York sought to organize and direct their collective efforts.

Over the course of 1932–1933, Machado strengthened the military in an attempt to bolster his administration. But this had the unintended effect of creating a separate power only nominally restrained by civil authority. Machado was trapped between growing civil resistance and a restive military, as members of the revolutionary junta protested both Machado's corruption and the unaccountable military.

In May 1933, the United States sent Ambassador Sumner Welles to Cuba in an attempt to forestall violent revolution by ushering Machado out peacefully while brokering a negotiated transition. When Machado refused to leave, Cuban workers went on strike, alienated as much by Welles's intervention as by Machado's recalcitrance. Bus drivers started the strike in late July, and it quickly spread to teachers, journalists, and tobacco workers. The Cuban Federation of Labor called for a General Strike on August 5. As the Cuban economy shut down, Machado's rule became untenable, and he fled the country on August 12. The military stepped in to restore order, preventing the General Strike from turning into broad-based popular rebellion.

One month later, the military ceded power to a civilian government, which formally abrogated the Platt Amendment and rejected US intervention. The new administration proposed a raft of ambitious political and social reforms, but had little opportunity to put these into effect. In January 1934, Army Chief of Staff Fulgencio Batista, acting with the backing of Ambassador Welles, overthrew the civilian government and imposed a more conservative administration. Batista remained the real power behind the presidency for the next twenty-five years. The reformist ambitions of the 1933 General Strike, meanwhile, were largely suppressed, returning in different form in the 1959 Cuban Revolution that toppled Batista.

The Roosevelt Corollary and "Dollar Diplomacy," 1900s–1920s

Following the Spanish-American War, the United States was indisputably a world power, with an industrialized economy that required sources for raw materials and markets for manufactured goods across the world. Latin America, in particular, fell within the US sphere of influence both by virtue of its proximity and because of the long history between the United States and the region. At the same time, the small, somewhat unstable, and often indebted countries of the Caribbean Basin (Central America, the Caribbean, and Venezuela) were, from a US perspective, vulnerable to falling under the influence of other nations, particularly Great Britain and Germany. These concerns intensified in the years leading up to and including World War I.

Articulating the Roosevelt Corollary and Dollar Diplomacy
Several of the small countries of the Caribbean basin had taken out large loans from foreign lenders to pursue positivist dreams, few of which had panned out. By the early twentieth century, they discovered themselves indebted beyond their ability to pay. To prevent intervention on the part of lender nations to recover the loans, President Theodore Roosevelt initiated his policy known as the **Roosevelt Corollary** to the Monroe Doctrine. While the Monroe Doctrine had passively warned European powers to keep their hands off Latin America, the Roosevelt Corollary actively affirmed that the United States would assume the role of hemispheric policeman. The Corollary justified US intervention in Latin American nations to guarantee the repayment of loans from European creditors. Roosevelt's successor, William Howard Taft, announced his policy of **Dollar Diplomacy** that not only allowed US intervention to secure the payment of foreign debts but also protected and encouraged US business interests in the circum-Caribbean region. There was a catch, of course: The United States would fund collecting these debt payments by sending in troops and occupying a nation's customs houses in order to collect duties, enforce order, and protect US financial interests.

The initial US intervention into the Dominican Republic in 1905 offers a prime example of Roosevelt's interventionist policy. As debts mounted and European creditors threatened the Dominican government, Roosevelt sent in forces to take over the customs house. Revenue collectors paid 55 percent of all taxes to the foreign creditors and provided 45 percent to the Dominican government, reducing the foreign debt from 40 million dollars to 17 million dollars in two years and restoring democratic government to the republic by 1907. When debt issues recurred and Dominican politicians refused to agree on a solution acceptable to the United States, President Woodrow Wilson intervened in 1916 and imposed a military government.

Although the US military did manage to repay debts and build roads and schools, the occupation government favored sugar interests over small farmers. Military occupation provoked resentment and rebellion, which—from the US perspective—justified continued occupation. When the United States withdrew in 1924, they left behind a police force made up of US-trained Dominicans to maintain order—an order that served the interests of the sugar export sector, not the general population. This force ultimately facilitated the rise of General Rafael Leónidas Trujillo, who would rule the Dominican Republic like a personal fiefdom from 1930 to 1961.

The Panama Canal and the Conquest of the Tropics

The dream of an interoceanic canal linking the Atlantic and Pacific Oceans reached far back, but not until the mid-nineteenth century did that dream became an imperative. US acquisition of vast new territories in the West, the discovery of gold in California in 1848, the development of a US Navy and merchant marine after the end of the American Civil War, and the emergence of the United States as an industrialized economy in the second half of the nineteenth century all underscored the need for a canal, which would allow a single American fleet to patrol both oceans. The 1869 completion of the Suez Canal, a sea-level waterway, which allowed direct travel between Europe and South Asia, further fueled aspirations for an American-controlled transoceanic canal.

Because Central America was located at the narrowest point between North and South America, it offered the most logical location for such a canal. Nicaragua, not Panama, first seemed to potential canal builders to be the ideal location, given the presence of a promising water route via the Rio San Juan (Nicaragua's border with Costa Rica) and then through Lake Nicaragua, thus necessitating the construction of an actual canal only through the thin strip of land that separated Lake Nicaragua from the Pacific Ocean.

With the construction of a canal in mind, the British in 1841 took over the small Nicaraguan town of San Juan del Norte (renaming it Greytown). In 1850, Britain signed the Clayton-Bulwer Treaty with the United States, which would have allowed both nations nonexclusive use to a Nicaraguan canal if one were built. As mentioned in chapter 3, during the 1850s, the American transportation magnate Cornelius Vanderbilt established the Accessory Transport Company to move travelers across Nicaragua in anticipation of the construction of a canal. Around the same time, the United States signed the Bidlack Treaty (1848) with New Granada (Colombia, of which Panama was a province), allowing the United States a transit right-of-way across Panama.

The Nicaragua route was preferable, given its closer proximity to the United States (the route from New York to San Francisco, for example, was around 500 miles and two days of travel longer via Panama), and also due to the lower incidence of tropical disease. But the Panama route ultimately prevailed. The rise of US hegemony in the region coupled with the decline of British interest in Central America, the understandable reluctance of Nicaragua's liberal president, José Santos Zelaya, to negotiate with the United States for a canal, and the influence of special interests in the US Congress all colluded to bring the canal to Panama. One complication was that Panama was not an independent nation, but the northernmost province of New Granada (the country that was renamed Colombia in 1886). The push for a canal across the Panamanian isthmus would change that.

A group of New York financiers had already backed construction of a railroad across the isthmus, completed at great human cost in 1855 (at the tail end of the California Gold Rush). In 1876, Ferdinand de Lesseps, the French builder of the Suez Canal, gained permission from the government of New Granada to construct a sea-level canal. De Lesseps's company struggled for years to construct a canal, but disease and the swampy Panamanian terrain doomed the venture. By 1889, at least 20,000 laborers had died working on the canal, and the French abandoned the project.

By the first years of the twentieth century, Phillippe Bunau-Varilla, an investor in the French canal company, lobbied members of the US Congress to go forward with a canal in Panama. To do so, he had to draw their enthusiasm away from Nicaragua, which Bunau-Varilla accomplished in part by presenting every member of Congress with a Nicaraguan stamp that featured an alarming image of an erupting volcano. The accession of Theodore Roosevelt to the US presidency in 1901, sealed the deal, as Roosevelt believed that an interoceanic American canal would be both in the US strategic interest and a "bully" demonstration of North American technological prowess.

With strong encouragement from Roosevelt, in June 1902, Congress passed the Spooner Act, which allowed for the purchase of the land and viable machinery for $40 million from the French company. In early 1903, the United States signed the

Hay-Herrán Treaty, which was to permit the construction of a canal in Colombian territory. When the Colombian Senate failed to ratify the treaty, pleading for more time to deliberate the decision, an impatient Roosevelt complained that dealing with them was as futile as "trying to nail currant jelly to a wall." The United States resolved to move forward with or without Colombian support. Shortly thereafter, the United States aided and abetted a separatist movement for Panama's independence. This separatist movement succeeded on November 3, 1903. Construction of the canal began a few months later, in 1904.

The construction of the Panama Canal took ten years, and was a spectacular technological feat that helped to define the "American Century." The infeasibility of a sea-level canal was solved by a series of ingenious locks that allowed sea vessels to be elevated and travel across wide gradations of terrain from one ocean to another. The use of immigrant laborers from all parts of the world (Chinese, South Asians, and especially Afro-Caribbean workers) introduced multiple cultures and languages to Panama, a new nation that would find itself both racially divided and also cosmopolitan from its inception. Thousands of laborers of African descent emigrated from Caribbean islands such as Jamaica, St. Vincent, and St. Kitts, drawn by the promise of well-paid construction work. Even so, nonwhite workers often found themselves subject to mistreatment and discrimination at the hands of their white bosses. For example, black canal laborers were paid on one scale (the "silver scale") while white workers received their wages on the "gold scale."

The *Ancón*, the First Ship through the Panama Canal. Even with the threat of disease reduced, the construction of the interoceanic canal posed significant engineering difficulties, in part because of the need to elevate ships through a series of locks to a height of 85 feet, where they sailed into Lake Gatún and then entered a second series of locks that allowed them to descend 85 feet to the other ocean. President Theodore Roosevelt had played a major role in the achievement of Panamanian independence with the policy objective of promoting US commerce and facilitating the movement of the US Navy from the Atlantic to the Pacific in times of war. Fittingly, then, the SS *Ancón*, was the first vessel to navigate these locks through the canal.

As a newly independent country, Panama was also defined by internal colonialism, thanks to the US-controlled Canal Zone established in 1903 (a territory that reached for five miles on either side for the length of the canal, excluding Panama City). For all intents and purposes, the Canal Zone functioned as an English-speaking strip of the United States across the middle of Panama's sovereign territory.

Above all, the Panama Canal represented what some have called the "Conquest of the Tropics," in the sense that it was new medical technology that made this "Wonder of the Modern World" possible. Many, if not most, of the biomedical and epidemiological innovations that made the Panama Canal feasible were borne of the epidemiological catastrophes that had occurred during the Spanish-American War only a few years earlier. Two diseases in particular, malaria and yellow fever, had been the bane of the tropics for centuries, not only in places like Panama and Cuba, but in subtropical US cities such as New Orleans or Charleston, where thousands of people might die in a single summer epidemic. These diseases had doomed the French canal company and limited the development of many tropical coastal cities up until this time.

Following the conclusive identification of the mosquito as the vector for these tropical diseases during the US occupation of Havana, the US Army introduced mosquito eradication programs to Panama in 1904. This comprehensive and innovative program included the draining of standing water or covering it with kerosene, the widespread spraying of insecticide in the streets Panama City and the Canal Zone, the quarantine of malaria and yellow fever patients, and the administration of prophylactic quinine to workers along the canal route. By 1906, both malaria and yellow fever had virtually disappeared from Panama.

The US Occupation of Haiti, 1915–1934

The US occupation of Haiti from 1915 to 1934 was a another classic case of "Dollar Diplomacy." Although US economic interests in Haiti were not extensive (Haiti's only major cash crop at the time was coffee, and foreign financial investment on the island was modest) US strategic interests were substantial. Since Haiti's independence in 1804, the republic had gone through a series of tribulations, including dictatorial and abusive government, regular confrontations with the Dominican Republic and extreme poverty. All of these problems were exacerbated by Haiti's enormous, unpaid financial debt to France (a lingering consequence of the terms of Haitian independence).

In 1908, Haiti fell into near anarchy, as widespread violence broke out between regional warlords and informal militias known as *cacos*. In early 1915, a pro-US strongman named Jean Vilbrun Guillaume Sam became president of Haiti and promised to restore order. Within a few months of taking power, however, Guillaume Sam ordered the killing of 167 political prisoners, an act that provoked the populace to rebel and kill Guillaume Sam himself. In response, US President Woodrow Wilson sent the Marines to restore order to Haiti.

The US occupation of Haiti (which became a "**protectorate**" or a de facto colony of the United States) fell under the usual mandate to protect lives and property. But there were also larger strategic concerns at stake. A small but economically

≡ **Port-au-Prince in 1916.** Haiti's principal port became the headquarters of the US forces of occupation. Although the US claimed that their occupation (which lasted from 1916 to 1930) would benefit Haitians, local residents hardly agreed. Nationalists sparked a number of uprisings over the years that kept the Marines on constant patrol. In addition, the US occupying forces displayed considerable racism toward the Haitians, even prohibiting the president of the country from joining the social club that white officials formed.

influential German population lived in Haiti at the time, and, at the dawn of World War I, the United States was concerned that Germany might take advantage of the nation's chaos to establish a military base in the Caribbean. To preempt such a prospect, the US military set up an occupation government, overseeing public works such as road and bridge building, agricultural improvements, the introduction of basic public health services and primary education, and a reformed customs service. But military engineers subjected Haitian workers to forced labor in order to build these projects. In 1915, the United States installed a friendly president (Philippe Sudré Dartiguenave), and US lawmakers, including then Assistant Secretary of the Navy Franklin Delano Roosevelt, crafted a new Haitian constitution—with virtually no input or assistance from Haitian lawmakers themselves.

In 1919, while the United States was distracted by the final throes of World War I in Europe, a series of rebellions against the occupation broke out across Haiti.

Over the course of a few months, the Marines and their newly established constab-ulary force, the Garde d'Haiti, killed thousands of Haitian civilians in the process of suppressing these rebellions. While US Marine records state that around 3,200 "natives" were killed, Haitian historians estimate that as many as 15,000 Haitians may have died. US Marine Brigadier General George Barnett wrote, "I think this is the most startling thing of its kind that has ever taken place in the Marine Corps, and I don't want anything of the kind to happen again." Despite this atrocity, the US occupation of Haiti remained in place until 1934, and the US-trained Garde d'Haiti continued to enforce repressive order long afterwards.

Augusto Sandino and the US Occupation of Nicaragua, 1909–1933

Despite the long reign of Liberal President José Santos Zelaya (1893–1909), Nicara-gua remained a highly factionalized country divided between Liberals and Conser-vatives, with instability and sometimes violence between the two parties. In 1909, Zelaya was ousted in a coup during which government troops executed two US mercenary soldiers fighting for the Conservatives. This incident marked the begin-ning of US "gunboat diplomacy," in which the United States sent warships to patrol the coast of Nicaragua, both for the protection of US citizens and as a warning. It also precipitated the first, if brief, deployment of US Marines to Nicaraguan shores.

In 1912, the Marines returned to Nicaragua a second time, this time to protect American lives and property during a period of political upheaval. The installation of an American-approved Conservative leader, Adolfo Díaz, to the Nicaraguan presidency set off a decade of US-sanctioned rule, supported by the off-and-on presence of US troops. In 1914, the United States and Nicaragua forged a more formal relationship via the signing of the Bryan-Chamorro Treaty (not approved by the US Senate until 1916), which granted the United States the rights to any canal built in Nicaragua in perpetuity, a renewable ninety-nine-year option to establish a naval base in the Gulf of Fonseca, and a renewable ninety-nine-year lease to the Great and Little Corn Islands in the Caribbean. For these substan-tial concessions, Nicaragua received $3 million, a small amount even by early twentieth-century standards. The Bryan-Chamorro Treaty effectively reduced Nicaragua to a US protectorate.

In 1927, another major struggle broke out between Liberal forces and US-backed Conservative elements in Nicaragua, again provoking the return of the Marines. Shortly thereafter, all the belligerents (save one) signed onto the US-brokered Tip-itapa Agreement, which called for disarmament, free elections, and the creation of a national constabulary force. The agreement presumed that a Liberal leader would become Nicaragua's next president. Only Liberal commander Augusto César Sandino, a peasant, autodidact, and ardent nationalist, held out against the Tipitapa Agreement. As a young man, he had worked in Mexico's oil fields, where he found inspiration in the Mexican Revolution. In comparison with Mexico's robust revolution, he was ashamed that Nicaragua was, in his words, a nation of **vendepatrias**—sellouts. Along with two hundred of his men, Sandino refused to give up as long as US Marines remained present on Nicaraguan soil.

Thus began the Sandino Rebellion, which pitted Sandino's small guerrilla army against both Nicaraguan federal troops and the US Marines for nearly five years. Sandino's forces, hidden in the remote northern mountains of Las Segovias, waged war through guerrilla attacks and the word-of-mouth circulation of impassioned nationalist proclamations. At one point, Sandino taunted the US forces: "Come, you band of morphine addicts, come to kill us on our own land: I will await you." His words inspired rural Nicaraguans, who supported Sandino and took up arms to join him in his firefights with the Marines. "The sovereignty of a people cannot be disputed," Sandino famously said. "It is defended with a gun in the hand."

Despite their concerted efforts, neither the Marines nor the Liberal army were able to defeat Sandino. In January 1933, after the election of Liberal Juan Batista Sacasa to the Nicaraguan presidency, the United States withdrew the Marines from Nicaragua in keeping with the President Franklin Delano Roosevelt's new Good Neighbor Policy. This policy emphasized cooperation and non-intervention in the Americas, rather than protection of US lives and property. True to his word, Sandino swore his allegiance to the new president and laid down his arms.

But the calm was short-lived. In February 1934, Sandino was ambushed and assassinated by members of the Nicaraguan National Guard. As elsewhere in the region, this new national constabulary force had been established and trained by the United States. Anastasio Somoza García, head of the National Guard, would found a family dynasty that would rule Nicaragua with a heavy hand until 1979, when they themselves were overthrown by an insurgency, the Sandinistas, who carried Augusto César Sandino's name.

Territorial Readjustments and South American Imperialism, 1878–1929

During the latter part of the nineteenth century, Peru and Bolivia also fell victim to the expansionist aims of a more powerful state. This time, however, the aggressor was another Latin American nation, Chile, whose people are sometimes referred to by their South American neighbors as the Yankees of South America, because of their imperialist aggression during the nineteenth century. Although after independence the South American nations had generally agreed to respect the boundaries fixed during colonial times, flexible frontiers existed in sparsely settled places like the Amazon basin and the Atacama Desert. Because that desert region failed to yield mineral wealth during the colonial period, the precise location of the border between the three countries did not much matter. Circumstances would change in the 1860s.

Events Leading to the War of the Pacific

The War of the Pacific, in which Chile fought Peru and Bolivia, not only resulted in important territorial readjustments but also enhanced senses of national identity and patriotism in all three countries. Rivalries between the three nations over territory and trade began shortly after independence and intensified three decades later, when Chilean miners ventured into the ill-defined portions of the Peruvian and Bolivian Atacama Desert to dig sodium nitrate for export to Europe and the United States for use both as fertilizer and as an ingredient in dynamite.

Tensions between the three nations escalated further in the 1870s. Peru planned to monopolize the nitrate deposits to replace the now-depleted guano as its primary export. Bolivia, lacking the technology and population to exploit its coastal nitrate reserves, granted generous concessions to Chilean mining entrepreneurs in exchange for taxes on the mined products. Based on Bolivia and Peru's experiences from the 1830s during the days of the Confederation of the Andes (see chapter 2), both feared Chilean aggression and entered into a not-so-secret mutual defense pact in 1873. Leaked information about the treaty, Peru's attempts to assert a monopoly over the nitrates, Bolivia's decision to increase taxes on mining, and the overall mistreatment of Chilean miners led to the outbreak of war in 1879.

Conflict and Resolution

Despite possessing relatively modern military technology, such as breech-loading rifles, Gatling guns, ironclad warships and torpedoes, Peru and Chile both relied on traditional tactics (frontal assaults and ramming vessels) in the war, negating the potential advantages of the modern equipment. Bolivia was totally unprepared for the fight. Plague and severe drought wiped out the potato and wheat crops in that country, leading to severe shortages of food. Administrative incompetence exacerbated these difficulties, leaving Bolivia incapable of fielding a decent army. Peru and Bolivia both relied on conscripted indigenous soldiers supported by their **rabonas**, or female camp followers, who served as cooks, laundresses, nurses, lovers, and occasionally as combatants. Although Chile's soldiers were only

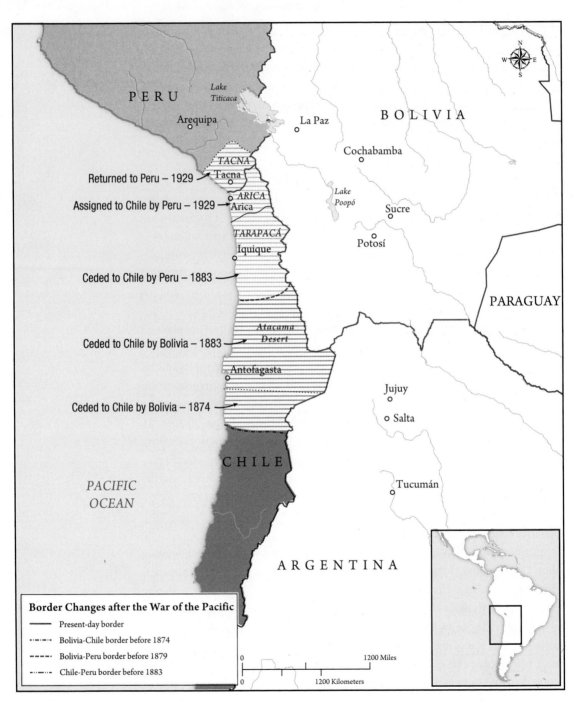

Returned to Peru – 1929

Assigned to Chile by Peru – 1929

Ceded to Chile by Peru – 1883

Ceded to Chile by Bolivia – 1883

Ceded to Chile by Bolivia – 1874

PERU

Lake
Titicaca

Arequipa

TACNA

Tacna

ARICA

Arica

TARAPACÁ

Iquique

Atacama
Desert

Antofagasta

CHILE

PACIFIC
OCEAN

BOLIVIA

La Paz

Cochabamba

Lake
Poopó

Sucre

Potosí

PARAGUAY

Jujuy

Salta

Tucumán

ARGENTINA

Border Changes after the War of the Pacific

———— Present-day border

–·–·–·– Bolivia-Chile border before 1874

– – – – Bolivia-Peru border before 1879

–··–··– Chile-Peru border before 1883

0   1200 Miles

0   1200 Kilometers

 MAP. 6.2

slightly better trained, their officer corps generally proved superior to the Peruvian and Bolivian commanders.

Previous conflicts in the 1830s had taught both Peru and Chile that victory depended on control of the sea. Tactically, both navies attempted to entrap their adversaries in narrow harbors and sink as many ships as possible. The naval battles also provided each nation with its most important war hero, Admiral Miguel Grau of Peru, and Captain Arturo Prat of Chile. Grau commanded Peru's the *Huascar*, an ironclad, or steam-propelled wooden ships with iron or steel cladding. The *Huascar* cornered Prat's smaller wooden vessel in Iquique's harbor on May 21, 1879. When the *Huascar* rammed the Chilean ship, Prat courageously leaped aboard the enemy vessel, sword at the ready, until rifle fire cut him down. His ship sank but never lowered its colors, making him a national hero.

Grau's opportunity for heroics came five months later. His raids on Chilean ports had destroyed so much shipping that Chile's president ordered his fleet to destroy the *Huascar* at all costs. Trapping the ironclad in port, Chilean ships raked the *Huascar* at close range, disabling its steering mechanism. A second round of shells obliterated Admiral Grau, leaving only his memory, his shoes, and a few teeth behind, and forcing the crippled *Huascar* to surrender. Grau's remarkable skill and courage earned him the honor of becoming a war hero in Peru.

Chile decisively won the conventional land campaign. Having control of the sea, Chile landed troops and soon took Peru's three nitrate provinces, Tacna, Arica, and Tarapacá, as well as Bolivia's coastal strip. In order to secure victory and extract a favorable treaty, Chile next occupied Lima, and then attempted to subdue the Peruvian interior. Outraged by the abuses of the Chilean soldiers, mixed-race and indigenous Peruvians rose in defense of their homeland. The war dragged on until the end of 1883.

The 1883 Treaty of Ancón, ending the War of the Pacific, gave Chile control over Peru's three nitrate provinces. In a separate treaty Bolivia ceded its entire coastline. During the 1920s Peruvian dictator Augusto Leguía would negotiate to regain Tacna while abjuring forever all rights to Arica and Tarapacá. Citizens of both Peru and Bolivia harbored deep and enduring resentment against Chile after the war. In the short term, Bolivia's dismal performance in the War of the Pacific damaged the reputation of caudillos and convinced civilians to form Conservative and Liberal parties that provided stability for the first time in Bolivia's history.

Chileans, for their part, took from the war a sense of military preeminence in South America. Chile also derived enormous mineral wealth from the annexed territory, as the new provinces yielded vast copper reserves. The War of the Pacific formalized the three nations' borders in the vast Atacama Desert while at the same time contributing to a growing sense of national identity in each.

Foreign Capital, the Automobile, and New Sources of Energy, 1900–1920s

The arrival of the automobile age opened new opportunities for foreign corporate investors to exploit additional Latin American products. The international demand for "Tin Lizzies" (Ford's affordable Model T) created an insatiable thirst for gasoline refined from petroleum. Prior to the invention of the automobile, petroleum had little significance other than as an ingredient in patent medicines and as a machine lubricant. Another commodity, natural rubber, originally used for waterproof galoshes, now became the raw material necessary for the production of tires. Foreign corporations competed with one another for the rights to extract these products, which were often found in obscure, out-of-the-way locations that up until that time had largely escaped the ravages of extractive industries.

Petroleum in Venezuela

Since the presidencies of independence hero José Antonio Páez, Venezuela had fallen under control of a series of military dictators. General Juan Vicente Gómez, who seized power from a former comrade in 1908, was no exception. In certain respects, Gómez exemplified the age of progress and modernity: He centralized the government, professionalized the army, eliminated regional caudillos, adopted the positivist slogan "**Paz y Trabajo**" (Peace and Work), paid off the foreign debt, built a modern highway system, and encouraged foreign investment. And he did so by allowing positivist advisors and close family members to determine policy while he preserved stability by instituting a tyrannical regime.

Gómez and his cronies were hardly admirable leaders; Gómez himself allegedly fathered seventy-four children with thirty-three different women. Nepotism ran rampant in the regime; brothers, cousins, his many sons, and the entourage from his home province of Táchira held most of the important political positions and left office with enormous sums of money squirreled away in overseas bank accounts. Gómez terrorized his opposition, spreading the legend that he possessed supernatural powers enabling him to discover plots against his government. Student leaders like Rómulo Betancourt, Raúl Leoni, and Rafael Caldera, who became the core of Venezuela's democratic leadership in the 1960s, all fled their native land for exile during the 1920s.

Until Gómez's time, Venezuela was best known for exporting coffee and cacao. By 1935, however, Venezuela had become the second-largest oil producer and the leading oil exporter in the world. Encouraged by the regime's stability, the largely British-owned Royal Dutch Shell group began drilling for petroleum in and around

Lake Maracaibo. From the outset the operation proved highly profitable because of the huge deposits under the lake and because the company could easily and inexpensively ship the crude oil to the Dutch islands of Aruba and Curaçao for refining. By the 1920s, Venezuelans became fully aware of the treasure that lay within their grasp, and so Gómez's government began to regulate and tax the oil industry more heavily.

The new laws tried to encourage further petroleum exploration while simultaneously maximizing revenues for the government. The company fought reforms, but eventually reached a satisfactory accord with Venezuela, in part because US oil companies like Standard Oil of New Jersey (which later became Exxon) were now competing with Royal Dutch Shell for concessions in Lake Maracaibo. Eventually, the companies and the Gómez government agreed that Venezuela would receive 15 percent of the profits, although this figure would increase over time. Production rose from 6,000 barrels a day in 1922 to 425,000 barrels a day in 1935. Likewise, the country's revenues soared from approximately $360,000 (US) a year to $8,480,000 during those same years. Ordinary Venezuelans migrated to the Lake Maracaibo region (Zulia state) because they could earn about $1.50 a day by working in the oilfields, a sum that far exceeded the standard agricultural wage of 25 cents a day paid elsewhere in the country.

Despite the revenue windfall, oil production had a number of unfortunate consequences for Venezuela. The internal migration caused labor shortages in the cacao- and coffee-producing regions, and oil production inflicted heavy environmental damage in the Lake Maracaibo region. The primitive means used for extracting petroleum and the negligence of foreign corporations caused local communities innumerable hardships and changed their way of life. Pipeline breaks and errant sparks routinely caused fires, burning homes and inflicting casualties. Communities could no longer draw water from the lake because of the pollution, and wells drilled in the middle of the lake sometimes produced gushers, which spread oil until they could be capped. The Venezuelan government proved unable to enforce regulations against multinational corporations. No longer was Lake Maracaibo the pristine location that had so reminded its discoverers of Venice, Italy, that they named the country for it.

Oil and Environmental Disaster in Mexico

Mexico produced even more oil than Venezuela during the early twentieth century. As in Venezuela, the Mexican oilfields were located in sparsely occupied, relatively pristine tropical lands, in this instance along the shore of the Gulf of Mexico in the northern extremes of Veracruz state. There, during the latter part of the nineteenth century, the struggle for land between hacendados and indigenous farmers

≡ **An Oil Gusher at Tampico, Mexico.**
The "Age of the Automobile" opened new export opportunities for countries like Mexico and Venezuela, both of which would become among the largest petroleum producers in the world by 1930. Petroleum geologists relied on local people to direct them to tar pits from which petroleum oozed, but drilling technology remained an inexact science and safety standards were nonexistent in the early twentieth century. Such limited technology often led to the accidental creation of gushers like this one at Tampico. When the drill tapped into a field of oil under tremendous pressure, the freed gases caused petroleum to explode through the drill holes with a roar that sounded like a volcano. Gushers like the one in Tampico spurted for weeks, sometimes longer, and polluted nearby streams, poisoning drinking water for animals and humans alike.

had slowly tipped in favor of the former, but the wet, densely forested region filled with poisonous snakes and toxic vegetation proved less than ideal for cattle ranching. The arrival of two petroleum entrepreneurs, the American Edward Doheny, the founder of the Huasteca Petroleum Company, and British engineer Weetman Pearson, the owner of El Águila Oil Company, would dramatically change the manner in which land was exploited in the Huasteca region.

Doheny, fresh from his triumphant discovery of "black gold" in California, had heard rumors about "bubbling springs of oil" in the Huasteca region and determined to investigate the tales—which proved accurate. After purchasing about 40,000 acres of ranchland as the centerpiece of his operations, he dispatched geologists to work with local indigenous people to map the precise locations of additional seepages, or tar pits. Because indigenous people owned many of these tar pits on their lands, Doheny and Pearson employed identical strategies to maximize the acreage they controlled. Both decided that it would be more efficient to lease these lands rather than to purchase them outright. Initially, both ranchers and indigenous smallholders willingly agreed to the oil companies' terms; not only did the rental money supplement their income, but the terms of the leaseholds also permitted them to continue to raise their crops or run cattle on the land.

This favorable situation changed when the drilling began. Soon both Doheny's and Pearson's investments paid off handsomely. The lands within the so-called Golden Lane, a half-moon shaped strip, contained a veritable ocean of oil. Within ten years each of these men had earned millions of dollars from Mexican oil. Because of their connections with influential businessmen and public officials, the oil entrepreneurs were able to convince Mexican railroad companies to convert their locomotives from coal to oil, and Mexico City and many other municipalities modernized their urban landscapes by paving streets with asphalt.

As in Venezuela, oil drilling in Mexico led to innumerable accidents and spillages. Drilling through the surface rock released the hot oil captivated under intense pressure, causing "gushers" that resulted in enormous environmental damage. The grimmest case occurred at El Águila's

SOCIAL UPHEAVAL

Conflict between Elites and the Popular Class

The modernizing policies of the age of progress deepened the divide between elites and the poor, sometimes resulting in instances of violent clashes and social upheaval. For example, beginning on the Thursday of the week before Easter (*Semana Santa*, or Holy Week), church bells that normally rang incessantly throughout Latin America went silent in commemoration of Jesus's crucifixion. On Saturday, the bells resumed ringing in a joyous anticipation of Easter, while simultaneously marking the beginning of the popular festivals, unsanctioned by either Church or State, known as Judas burnings. Papier maché figures of Judas Iscariot filled with food, coins, and fireworks exploded, showering spectators with treats to celebrate the death of Christ's betrayer. Often these figures bore a striking resemblance to unpopular politicians, bureaucrats, clergy, or perhaps some fat cat from the elite, as members of the popular class lampooned high society. In Mexico, Porfirio Díaz attempted to ban Judas burnings, but with limited success, only managing to exile them to the suburbs of the capital city. Even today in Guatemala, boys carry homemade effigies of Judas from door to door and ask for donations in a Holy Week version of trick-or-treat.

Opposition to elite and middle-class sports like bicycling presented another opportunity for members of the popular classes (*los de abajo*) to protest modernization and occasionally demonstrate their disdain through violence. Following the introduction of the "safety bicycle" (one with two equal-sized wheels) into Mexico in 1891, elite- and middle-class riders contended with pedestrians and oxcarts for space on Mexico City's streets. The newfangled European and US-manufactured gadgets drew the ire of the popular classes, who often attempted to unseat the "white devils" by tossing rocks as they rode by. The city council attempted to restrict riders to certain locations, but the dictator intervened and revoked the ordinances.

The modernizers' victory led to profound changes in society. First, because the elite modernizers thoroughly admired US popular culture, they seized on Theodore Roosevelt's mantra that physical exercise promoted good health, contributing to the formation of cycling clubs and weekly outings all over the country. Bicyclists demanded improved roads, leading to the asphalt paving of major thoroughfares. To promote safety, new traffic regulations protected the riders. Perhaps most importantly, young elite and middle-class women participated in the bicycle craze as well. Since their matronly chaperones rarely knew how to ride, these young women enjoyed greater freedom from social restraints than ever before as they donned their risqué trousers to partake of healthy exercise with their male companions.

Dos Bocas well on July 4, 1908. After work for the day finished and the men were relaxing, they suddenly smelled sulphur, heard the surface rock crack, and saw the drilling rig and other equipment disappear into a huge sinkhole. Then the well blew, shooting crude oil into the sky, which then fell like rain onto the workers. Some of the crude landed on embers, causing an explosion within the well and sending fire and smoke high into the atmosphere. Ships miles away on the Gulf of Mexico could see the flames. The fire burned for 57 days before extinguishing itself. An unknown number of firefighters and soldiers died attempting to put out the blaze. In all, the Dos Bocas fire consumed about 400 million gallons of crude oil and remains the largest oil spill in human history. The surrounding landscape, particularly the mangrove forests, never recovered.

While blowouts created the most spectacular environmental damage, other oil industry practices altered the landscape dramatically. In addition to increasing fire dangers and the loss of habitat for wildlife, pollution of various types poisoned both land and sea. The oil that routinely spilled into the Pánuco River particularly hurt the poor, who used the river for drinking water and bathing. Those who lived close to the oilfields complained about the unhealthy odors that made breathing difficult. Meanwhile, the wealthy US and British families dwelling in suburban compounds in port of Tampico, lived much as they had at home, playing golf and tennis, drinking bottled water, and remaining oblivious to this situation. Crude oil sank to the bottom of the river, where it killed off oysters, shrimp, and crab that constituted the livelihood of local fishermen. Sticky oil ruined the once-pristine white sand beaches. Leaking pipes spilled oil periodically, as did improperly capped wells no longer used for production. Poor Mexican laborers and their families faced the brunt of the environmental consequences of large-scale oil production.

The Rubber Industry and Fordlândia

Through the early nineteenth century, indigenous populations of the Amazon basin possessed a natural monopoly over rubber, as rubber trees grew nowhere else. They tapped the trees, extracted the latex, and cooked it, using the resilient skin to make waterproof pouches. As long as external demand for rubber remained low, there was little threat to disturb that natural monopoly, and by extension the indigenous lifeways that surrounded it. But in 1839, the American engineer Charles Goodyear improved the process for vulcanizing rubber, yielding a durable, flexible material capable of withstanding extreme temperatures. And in the late nineteenth century, the bicycle became a basic tool of urban transportation, spurring the invention of pneumatic rubber bicycle tires. The automobile followed quickly thereafter. Demand for rubber skyrocketed, and the Amazon basin would never be the same.

Caboclos, or mixed-race, tappers and contractors moved in, either pushing indigenous groups further into the rainforest or incorporating them into a growing mixed society. Tappers established proprietary trails through the forest, connecting rubber trees they claimed the right to tap. They cooked the latex into rough balls and carried them down to the river, where they turned them over to the contractors who had advanced them money or goods. The contractors then sold the rubber in the Amazonian cities of Manaus and Belém, from where it was exported to North America or Europe and used to manufacture tires or in other industrial applications. Foreign commercial agents established their own operations in Amazonian port cities, seeking to guarantee their supply.

Caribbean Sea

From Venezuela,
1859 and 1905

From Colombia, 1907

From Ecuador, 1904

Amazon R.

*ATLANTIC
OCEAN*

From Bolivia,
1867 and 1903

From Paraguay, 1872

From Argentina, 1895

*PACIFIC
OCEAN*

From Uruguay, 1851

Brazilian Territorial Expansion Since 1830

Brazil in 1830

Territory acquired after 1830

0   1200 Miles

0   1200 Kilometers

☰ **MAP. 6.3**

≡ **A Brazilian Rubber Gatherer.**
Brazilian *seringueiros* (rubber gatherers) lived along the Amazon River network. After the discovery of vulcanization in the 1830s, rubber found limited global uses (like for galoshes) and these independent workers could meet the demand. Because natural rubber trees grew at a distance from one another, the seringueiros traversed through miles of jungle daily, gathering the sap that had dripped into buckets placed under the gashes that the seringueiros made in the trunk. Their independent lifestyle changed with the coming of the automobile, as the demand for rubber dramatically increased. Now contractors took over the business, reducing the seringueiros to debt peonage.

As long as rubber trees grew only in the Amazon, Brazil retained something close to a monopoly on this export trade. Tappers in the Bolivian and Peruvian regions of the Amazon basin were slower to take advantage of the trade, and needed to export through Brazil and pay Brazilian customs taxes once they did. When Bolivia tried to play a larger role, Brazil exercised its leverage, annexing a large swath of Bolivian rainforest in 1903. This near monopoly in a period of escalating demand produced the short, frenzied Amazon Rubber Boom. The grandiose Amazon Theatre in Manaus, a luxurious opera house inaugurated at the height of the boom, brought the world's premier opera singers to the rainforest and exemplified the aspirations and excesses of the rubber boom.

The seeds of the rubber boom's demise had already been planted, however. To be precise, they were planted in the British Royal Botanical Gardens, by a British botanist who had carried (or smuggled, from Brazil's perspective) thousands of rubber-tree seeds back to London in 1877. By the late 1880s, British planters were establishing rubber tree plantations in the colonies of Ceylon and Malaysia. By the early twentieth century, British Asian production had undercut Amazonian production. Prices fell even as demand spiked, and Brazilian contractors could not compete. Manaus and Belém fell into depression as the economy shrank. Many tappers reverted to subsistence gathering or filtered into the cities, where they lived in humble shacks on stilts above the river.

In the late 1920s, the American automobile manufacturer Henry Ford attempted to revive Brazilian rubber fortunes and to secure control over a stable supply in the Americas. From his headquarters in Detroit, he oversaw creation of Fordlândia, a rubber plantation city. Fordlândia was meant to reproduce a North American town, with white picket fences and Protestant religious services. Brazilian workers, however, were vigilantly supervised and pushed to extremes in a mad attempt to impose order on what was once pristine rainforest. The Amazon struck back: native tree blight and Amazonian insects attacked the densely packed trees of Fordlândia, repeatedly wiping out the harvest. Rubber plantations, which had flourished in Malaysia, proved ecologically impracticable in the Amazon. Only in World War II, when Axis powers effectively cut off Asian production from consumers in the Western Hemisphere, did Brazil's rubber production resume its prominence, and then only temporarily.

The Latin American Reaction to US Aggression, 1890s–1920s

By the end of the nineteenth century, most Latin Americans had little positive to say about the United States. Whether it was because of the swaggering, loutish behavior of US sailors at liberty in Latin American ports, US workers lording it over Latin American laborers in their own countries, the smug superiority of US businessmen, or the imperialist tendencies of US foreign policy, Latin Americans understandably resented their neighbors from the north. Long forgotten was the admiration Latin Americans once felt for the United States during the wars for independence. Scholars often refer to this understandable resentment as Yankeephobia, or fear and loathing of the United States.

The Baltimore Affair

Anti-US attitudes should perhaps have been less prevalent in a nation like Chile, the South American republic most geographically distant from Washington. Nevertheless, the relatively minor scuffle between US naval personnel and Chileans that erupted in Valparaíso harbor in October 1891 threatened to broaden into a major conflict, largely because of the United States' bullying posture and the virulent Yankeephobic sentiments so commonplace in Latin America during the latter part of the nineteenth century. The so-called *"Baltimore* Affair" occurred in the aftermath of a diplomatic miscue during which the US minister (a representative from the State Department, lower in rank than an ambassador) had weighed in on the side of the losing faction during the Revolution of 1891, which unseated an unpopular autocratic president and resulted in the establishment of Chile's parliamentary republic (1891–1925).

Shortly after parliament deposed the president, the captain of the USS *Baltimore* granted one hundred members of his crew shore leave in Valparaíso. The sailors behaved as seamen traditionally did when at liberty in port: They flocked to the bars and got roaring drunk, they picked fights with the Chilean patrons of those establishments, and they offended Chilean men by flirting with their female companions (they likely offended the women, as well). Soon the police arrived and jailed forty US sailors and two Chileans. Unfortunately, just before the authorities arrived, two American seamen were killed.

The US State Department responded more aggressively than necessary to the incident. With only the most perfunctory of investigations, US authorities blamed the Chileans for the fray and demanded a significant sum to reimburse the Americans for their losses. Some American tabloid journalists even urged the United States to go to war. Chile's more thorough investigation laid the blame squarely on the shoulders of the Americans. Eventually, cooler heads on both sides prevailed. Chile agreed to pay restitution to the families of the two deceased sailors, released the prisoners to the custody of the captain of the *Baltimore*, and closed the incident.

Chilean legends about the diplomacy that ended the *Baltimore* affair are even more important than the facts. Chileans still believe that the United States required Chile to order one of its naval vessels to lower its flag as a form of apology to the United States. Allegedly, once the Chilean flag hit the deck, the ship's commanding officer committed suicide in protest. In truth, Chile did not lower its flag, and no officer committed suicide. The very existence of the story, however, demonstrates the pervasiveness of Yankeephobia even in a distant land like Chile where the possibility of US intervention was remote (at least in the 1890s).

Latin Americans Reflect on the Yankee Menace

Latin American intellectuals responded to US imperialism in the region with formative works that would shape understandings of US-Latin American relations for decades. Alarmed by the United States' frequent military occupations and commercial exploitation, Latin American authors crafted responses ranging from subtle allegories to forceful denunciations.

Haiti's Dantès Bellegarde enjoyed considerable stature both nationally and internationally because of his distinguished reputation as a professor of law, a stint as minister of education, and his service as the nation's diplomatic representative to France, the United States, and the League of Nations during the 1920s and 1930s. Bellegarde wrote two books and delivered several lectures about the injustices of the US occupation of Haiti beginning in 1915, the reality of which fell far short of its purported reasons for intervention on humanitarian grounds.

Bellegarde's restrained prose in his 1929 book *L'Occupation Américaine d'Haïti* (The American Occupation of Haiti) pointed out that the US occupation was entirely self-serving. As Bellegarde charged, the United States had violated international law by sending in the Marines. Not only had Haiti not suspended debt payments, but it had signed the Hague Convention of 1907, which provided that in the case of default, any debt questions would be submitted to arbitration. While US President Woodrow Wilson's humanitarian excuse for intervention in 1915 had been the assassination of former Haitian president Guillaume Sam, Bellegarde pointed out that at the same moment, a mob in the southern United

States had dragged a black man accused of a crime from jail and burned him alive in the town's public square, and that lynchings of blacks were widespread in the Deep South. As Bellegarde noted, the US occupiers were overtly racist; the president of Haiti himself was denied admission to the American Club in Port-au-Prince. In short, Bellegarde argued, the United States was scarcely in a position to make a moral or humanitarian argument in favor of intervention. Bellegarde also carefully demonstrated that United States occupation had not improved Haiti's economic situation, and had created a structure of dictatorship precluding the emergence of democracy.

Rafael Reyes, an Amazonian explorer, distinguished soldier, and diplomat, had served as the president of Colombia from 1904 to 1909 in the aftermath of the loss of Panama. Reyes was eventually forced from office by popular resentment because of his willingness to negotiate with the United States. In the aftermath of his term, Reyes traveled throughout the Americas and penned a book titled *The Two Americas* (1914) in which he strongly criticized the United States but nonetheless recognized the necessity of deepening US-Latin American economic ties. Reyes agreed with his fellow Latin Americans that the United States should forgo military occupation and treat Latin Americans fairly. He noted that US interventions in Central America constituted a "moral wrong" and violated international law in a number of ways. He argued that the United States had casually disregarded its treaty with Colombia, had not negotiated in good faith, and had sent warships that prevented him (then in charge of the army) from landing troops in sovereign Colombian territory. Thus, Reyes asserted, "the US is responsible for the unease and apprehension which inspires all Latin American countries." Nevertheless, Reyes's book accepted the inarguable preeminence of the United States in the region, and argued for the promotion of US-Latin American friendship and cooperation.

The famed Argentine writer and socialist Manuel Ugarte was more suspicious of US intentions. During the second decade of the twentieth century, he became passionate about the dangers of US imperialism and embarked on several speaking tours around the Americas to gather material for his book, eventually published as *The Destiny of a Continent* (1925). Ugarte argued that Latin America was vulnerable to further interventions because it lacked the unity necessary to deter the United States, and called for greater Pan-American cooperation. Since the early nineteenth century and the failure of the Congress of Panama (chapter 2), Pan-Americanism, the idea that the independent nations of the Americas shared military, diplomatic, and economic interests, had inspired rhetorical adherence and draft policies but little real cooperation. Ugarte envisioned a stronger

CULTURE AND IDEAS

Soccer in Argentina, Uruguay, and Brazil

The emergence of soccer (called football or *futbol* everywhere but the United States) in Buenos Aires, Montevideo, and São Paulo was an excellent example of the nature and limits of "informal empire." Young men from the British Isles brought soccer to each of these cities in the last decades of the nineteenth century. In Buenos Aires and Montevideo, schoolteachers at elite private schools serving the British expatriate community used the game to cultivate the manly virtues of spirited competition and fair play among their pupils. British railway engineers and merchants created their own teams. Buenos Aires had a fledgling expatriate soccer league in 1891, and Montevideo soon followed.

Charles Miller, son of a British father who had married into São Paulo's coffee-planting elite, brought the game to that city in 1894. Miller had attended prep school in Britain and returned to São Paulo eager to share the game. The British expatriate community was smaller there than in Buenos Aires or Montevideo, making it hard to form teams at first. But by the close of the nineteenth century expatriate German teams were challenging Miller's squad.

Local residents first envied and then emulated the modern sporting habits of the British expatriates. Teams of young Argentines, Uruguayans, and Brazilians formed to take on the British squads. The famed Buenos Aires clubs River Plate and Boca Juniors were both founded in the first years of the twentieth century, drawing on the talents of Italian and British immigrants at first, but soon tapping local boys as well. The Uruguayan clubs Nacional and Peñarol were founded about the same time, with Nacional drawing at first on local elites and Peñarol on immigrant railway workers. These new rivalries quickly attracted growing crowds, helping both to spread awareness of the game and turn it into a spectator sport.

In Rio de Janeiro, meanwhile, Oscar Cox, a Swiss-Brazilian educated at an elite school in Lausanne, Switzerland, returned with an enthusiasm for the game. Cox founded the Fluminense club in 1902. Membership was limited to the upper crust of Rio de Janeiro society. But soon competing clubs followed, drawing on less privileged local talent. By the end of the first decade of the twentieth century, soccer had already made its transition from British expatriates to local elites to the urban population more generally. Local players continued to use English terms (like "corner" and "penalty") but put their own spin on the game. This transition would become complete in the next decade, as poorer immigrants and Afro-Brazilians, Uruguayans, and Argentines brought soccer to the humblest and scrappiest neighborhoods. The quick, inventive game developed there challenged and ultimately outstripped the traditional British style of play.

- When and how did football make the transition from British game to Brazilian, Argentine, or Uruguayan game? Is this a case of the apprentice superceding the master?

Pan-Americanism, in which Latin American nations would have leverage to constrain the United States.

In 1880, Chile and Colombia had proposed a gathering of Latin American states to create an informal Pan-American union, but the ongoing War of the Pacific prevented the meeting from happening. US Secretary of State James G. Blaine latched onto the idea but hijacked it to include the United States as a member of the Pan-American Union to expand US influence in hemispheric affairs. During his second term as secretary of state, Blaine organized the First Pan-American Conference, held in Washington, DC, in 1889. He proposed that the organization have two objectives: to promote diplomatic arbitrations to minimize future wars in the

Americas (this proved acceptable) and to create a customs union between all the nations of the Americas that would have the effect of granting the United States more favorable access to Latin American markets (this was not accepted). Blaine's Pan-American Union, (now the Organization of American States) continues to exist and function in Washington, DC.

Ugarte noted that he first became aware of the dangers of US imperialism during a visit to Porfirian Mexico, where he perceived metaphorical "chains of gold" binding Mexicans through loans that guaranteed the majority of profits to US businesses. A second tour of the region in 1910 opened Ugarte's eyes even wider to the extent of US influence. When US Secretary of State Philander Knox simultaneously undertook a good-will tour through Central America and the Caribbean, Ugarte was denied permission to speak in Guatemala, Nicaragua, and Venezuela because those countries' leaders thought his anti-US words might offend the Colossus of the North.

On the other hand, Colombians welcomed Ugarte, who perceived the seizure of the Canal Zone as the first step in a new wave of US imperialism in South America. As he said, "Now that the Panama Canal is open, the imperialist shadow is falling towards the South." When Ugarte arrived in Ecuador, his fears of further US adventurism were confirmed by rumors that the government intended to sell the Galápagos Islands to the United States. Even the US attempt to sanitize the port of Guayaquil and prevent the spread of yellow fever worried Ugarte. While officialdom throughout South America remained blind to the potential danger from the United States, Ugarte found that the younger generation heeded his words. Even though Ugarte's vision of the need for a more assertive Latin American–dominated Pan-Americanism did not come to pass, another generation in the 1950s would more aggressively critique US actions in the hemisphere.

The Formative Years of Middle-Class Feminism, 1900–1930

The widespread influence of western European and US ideas about modernization also created the impetus for changes in gender relations and encouraged the advance of feminist thought and action in Latin American. Urbanization, the influx of European immigrants, and the growth of the middle class dramatically altered expectations about women's patterns of behavior and rights. Feminist activists centered their activities on redressing three areas of obvious gender inequality: the legal limitations on married women's property ownership rights and their ability to manage their own wages, the legal restrictions married women faced within their families, and the inability of any woman to vote.

Changing Social Behavior: The "Woman Question"

During the age of progress and modernization, Latin Americans became concerned with several social questions, one of which was "the woman question" and its overt challenges to patriarchy. Marriage remained the most popular choice for most modern middle-class women, whose nuclear families tended to be smaller in size than had traditionally been the case in Latin America. Middle-class women practiced birth control and even occasionally resorted to abortions. The Catholic Church condemned both practices, and the latter was illegal and dangerous.

In the United States, the birthrate had fallen by half between 1800 and 1900, and upper- and middle-class Latin Americans followed this trend. While birth control remained expensive and unreliable and abortions usually illegal and always dangerous, middle-class and elite families used both these measures of birth control to reduce the size of their families. Having fewer children, reformers argued, would allow parents to spend more time with each individual child, producing a better-educated and healthier younger generation. These modern women also sought, although they did not always achieve, greater happiness and equality in their marriages and a greater understanding of sexual intimacy and pleasure.

Many young women, even the most socially conservative, saw no reason to live confined to the home like their mothers and grandmothers. As increasing numbers of women earned secondary school degrees, they opted for careers as elementary school teachers or as white-collar workers in service industries. By 1900, over 40 percent of US college graduates were women, and while the percentage remained much lower in Latin America, educational opportunities for women significantly increased in the early twentieth century. Because of the expanding commercial and industrial sectors in cities, educated single women and widows found employment as typists, sales clerks, receptionists, telephone operators, and other professions seen as suitable for women.

Soon social norms changed so that middle-class married women could join the world of work, and not just to earn extra spending money. They sought employment to supplement their family's income when financial circumstances became tight. Such contributions often meant the difference between survival and starvation, even though female workers earned less than their male counterparts in professions such as sales clerk or primary school teacher. Particularly in the 1920s, women's disposable income helped to create a decade of conspicuous consumption.

≡ **A Normal School for Women in Uruguay.** The age of progress and modernization offered women more occupational opportunities outside of the home than had ever been available to them previously. Women tended to enter those professions that were closely related to their traditional nurturing roles: teaching their children and nursing family members. By the end of the nineteenth century, normal schools (teachers' colleges) like this one in Uruguay made their appearance in most Latin American countries. The government hired these women to teach in the new, public, state-funded primary schools for the most part. Women also played increasingly important roles in healthcare facilities.

Seldom in human history has such a steep generational gulf arisen between daughters and mothers. The modern city offered young women many more opportunities to interact with strangers in the public sphere. Not only did streetcars transport women to work, but they also provided women access to department stores and places of leisure. Glossy magazines such as Brazil's *Revista Feminina*, published from 1914 to 1927, opened middle-class women's eyes to trends in fashion and beauty as well as more serious subjects like the feminist movement in Europe and the United States and managing family finances. Hollywood films also exposed Latin American women to new fashion directions. Younger women abandoned the full-length dresses, whalebone corsets, and high collars of their mother's generation and replaced them with daring "flapper" styles, makeup, and bobbed hair.

Women frequented tearooms, opera houses, movie theaters, public parks, and even the beach, where they could meet eligible men far from any chaperone's disapproving eyes. Spectator sports gained a new popularity; among elite and middle-class women, an afternoon at the racetrack became a common social outing, while poorer women favored more affordable soccer matches. Deportment changed radically; young women even smoked cigarettes in public. At the beach, Brazilian females wore French-style swimsuits, which exposed bared arms and only extended halfway down the thigh. Sensual dances like the foxtrot, the Charleston, and the tango replaced the stately waltz of an earlier generation.

Paulina Luisi: Feminist and Physician

Although changes in fashion signaled new attitudes, feminist activists wanted more; they sought gender equality. Many of the early feminists were professional women: doctors, lawyers, and social workers, like Paulina Luisi, Uruguay's first female physician. The daughter of immigrant parents, Luisi earned her medical degree despite facing considerable obstacles. Not only did her professors hold her to higher standards than her male counterparts but also her classmates harassed her in unsubtle ways. On one occasion, she found the severed penis from a laboratory cadaver in the pocket of her lab coat. As class ended, she pulled it out and nonchalantly asked her colleagues: "Did one of you lose this?" After graduation, Luisi opened a successful practice, specializing in gynecology and obstetrics.

Luisi founded the two principal feminist organizations in the country, the National Women's Council and the Women's Suffrage Alliance. She represented Uruguay at the First Women's Conference in Buenos Aires in 1910, and subsequently served the Uruguayan government as a representative to the League of Nations and on numerous international commissions, including one designed to end "white slavery" (prostitution). At the same time, Luisi spoke at gatherings of the Socialist Party, in part because it supported women's suffrage, a cause dear to her heart. Because she wanted to maintain her useful political connections with the Colorado (Liberal) government, however, she never joined the Socialist Party. In 1932 Uruguay became one of the first Latin American nations to grant women the vote. Although Luisi and other early feminists had made considerable progress for women's rights, they were still constrained by patriarchy. A new women's movement would seek greater equality in the future.

The Quest for Married Women's Property Rights in Argentina

While the Liberal anticlerical legislation of the nineteenth century made marriage a civil contract rather than a religious sacrament, the legal doctrine of **patria potestad** (where the man of the house wielded absolute authority over his wife and children) remained in place. This principle subordinated the wife to the husband and gave him the right to control the property she brought into the marriage as well as her earnings thereafter. Patria potestad prevented a wife from being a party to a lawsuit and also granted the husband the sole right to oversee the person and property of their children. In essence, married women legally were treated like children.

By the end of the nineteenth century, however, as more women entered the workforce, both Liberals and members of the new Socialist Party in Argentina sought to rectify the legal inequities facing married women. Socialists focused their attention on measures designed to protect working women and children. Liberals argued that women's work benefited the nation as well as themselves, and believed that women should control their own financial circumstances. Argentine feminists of both genders followed the lead of progressive legislatures in both the United States and Great Britain, which had passed a series of Married Women's Property Acts to secure these rights for women.

In Argentina, the first generation of feminists—many of them professionals like Luisi—published magazines highlighting the illogic of treating married women like children under the law. Feminist organizations, such as the *Liga Feminista*, organized international conferences and created proposals for remedial legislation. Since women could not vote or serve in the legislature, sympathetic men, including the internationally renowned legal scholar Luis María Drago and several Socialist congressmen, brought reform proposals. Initially, these efforts failed to gain much traction. Over time, however, public opinion shifted, and in 1926 the Argentine Congress passed Law 11.357, nicknamed the "Law of Women's Civil Rights."

Argentina's legislation was the first law to protect the property rights of married women in all of Latin America, and had no equivalent in some countries until recently. The milestone Law of Women's Civil Rights of 1926 gave married women the same property rights as men. For the first time in Latin America, married

CULTURE AND IDEAS

Protestant Missionaries

Beginning in the last decades of the nineteenth century, Protestant missionaries from the United States began to establish their churches across Latin America. Unlike many areas of the world where missionaries worked, such as Asia and the Middle East, Latin America was already Christian, albeit Catholic. Nevertheless, US Protestant missionaries constituted active agents of the United States, as the nation to the north dramatically increased its cultural, political, and economic presence in the region at the turn of the twentieth century.

Generally speaking, US missionaries at this point came from mainline denominations, such as the Presbyterians, Methodists, and Baptists, as well as from a series of nondenominational "faith missions" that began to establish missions in Latin America around the same time. The primary object of all missionaries was to evangelize, but most US missionaries of this era also conceived their task as to enlighten, educate, and improve the lives of the people with whom they worked. Many missionaries, such as the Presbyterians, understood their mandate as one to help "civilize" local people through education and other similar kinds of projects. Literacy projects were especially important to missionaries, since being able to read the Bible constituted a key element of salvation.

Others saw their religious message as linked to the spreading of North American culture and values. It is little wonder that positivist and Liberal governments, though secular, typically welcomed missionaries, more for their economic projects than for their religious message. Even positivist leaders, however, believed with the missionaries that there was a strong linkage between Protestant religion and personal responsibility and productivity. By the early years of the twentieth century, there were few Latin American countries without schools, clinics, and hospitals established, paid for, and run by North American missionary organizations.

Cuba offers a particularly good case study. In the year following the end of the Spanish-American

≡ **Cover of McGuffey's Reader**

War, no fewer than twenty-eight different Protestant denominations initiated work on the island. Because Cuba seemed to offer an ideal laboratory for the creation of a "new" type of Latin American citizen—educated, democratic, and inculcated with North American, Protestant values—missionaries raced to establish schools designed to imbue young Cubans with these characteristics. They quickly produced Spanish translations of uplifting teaching materials, such as the American classroom standard *McGuffey's Eclectic Reader* and the sentimental but morally enriching story of a noble horse, *Black Beauty*. In those pages, Cuban children could absorb Aesop's fables, learn about George Washington and the cherry tree, and practice their reading on short stories about maple sugar production in New England. They also promoted Cubans' already palpable love of American baseball to new generations of young men—perhaps one of their most lasting contributions to the island.

The legacy of Protestant missionaries from the United States to Latin America during this period is mixed. Certainly, from the perspective of the missionaries' main goal, evangelization, they were not successful, at least not during their lifetimes. Latin Americans remained resolutely Catholic for most of the twentieth century. On the other hand, the effects of

mission-sponsored projects, such as the schools, clinics, maternal health, nutrition, and linguistic projects, were substantial and enduring. Across the continent, mission schools educated a generation of future Latin American statesmen and intellectuals. Mission-run hospitals introduced modern medical technologies into many Latin American countries and in some places remain premier medical centers to this very day. It is fair to say that the cultural influence of US Protestant missionaries exceeded their religious impact in Latin America in the early decades of the century.

- Would you think of US Protestant missionaries to Latin America as agents of modernization and progress, or of cultural imperialism?

women gained control over their earnings and also gained a juridical personality, meaning that they themselves could be plaintiffs or defendants in lawsuits. Married women also retained control of property that they had brought into the marriage. In short, the statute enabled women to exercise many civil legal functions and by using the language of equality, paved the way for eventual women's suffrage in Argentina.

The Role of the United States during South America's "Roaring Twenties," 1920s

Toward the end of the age of progress and modernization, US businessmen and corporations expanded their interests beyond Mexico, Central America, and the Caribbean, and began to penetrate into South America, long the domain of British, French, and (to a lesser degree) German investors. While the European nations rebuilt themselves following the devastation of World War I (1914–1918), US investors expended significant quantities of capital in the Andean nations whose agricultural products soon graced US tables and whose mineral wealth quickened the pace of US industrial growth. The "Roaring Twenties," as the decade was called in the United States, represented the last hurrah of the elite republics in Latin America, even though the elite would continue to play a disproportionate role in politics, economics, and society in Latin America after 1930.

The United States and the "Roaring Twenties" in Colombia

Two of the Andean nations, Colombia and Peru, achieved new heights of prosperity during the decade of the 1920s. Ten years earlier, Colombia began to recover from the twin nightmares of the loss of Panama and the devastating Thousand Days War (1899–1903), which cost over 100,000 lives. The victorious Conservatives agreed to share congressional seats and bureaucratic jobs with their Liberal rivals in order to promote stability and maintain the elite-managed political system. A new and valuable cash crop, coffee, greatly improved the country's economic fortunes. Grown on small farms and some estates clustered on the hillsides of the departments of Antioquía and Caldas, Colombian coffee gained a reputation for excellence unequaled elsewhere in the world. A second cash crop, bananas, grew on the Caribbean coast, although most of the profits from this enterprise flowed into the coffers of the North American United Fruit Company (UFCo).

During the 1920s, Colombia's economic position brightened further. The United States paid $25 million to Colombia for the loss of Panama, and US investors flooded the country with money, bringing total US investments from $30 million at the beginning of the decade to $280 million by 1929. In fact, US investments in Colombia grew at a faster rate than in any other Latin American country. In addition to having a stable government and offering valuable products for market, Colombian leaders won the confidence of Wall Street bankers by promising to accept technical financial advice from expert US economists, specifically the team led by the renowned Princeton professor Edwin W. Kemmerer. To demonstrate fiscal responsibility and creditworthiness, Kemmerer suggested to each Latin American nation he visited (Colombia, Ecuador, Peru, Chile, and Bolivia) that they adopt the gold standard, create a national bank much like the US Federal Reserve system, and balance their budgets. Colombia generally followed the script, although like the other Andean nations showed little commitment to maintaining balanced budgets.

The influx of borrowed cash led to a phenomenon known as the "Dance of the Millions," as investors funneled money into building railroads, modernizing harbors, and laying out asphalt roads. Unfortunately, a good deal of the remainder of the money was spent on expanding the size of the bureaucracy and providing jobs for cronies of Conservative and Liberal politicians. By the time of the Wall Street crash in October 1929, Colombia's foreign debt reached about $200 million. Although Colombia remained true to Kemmerer's policies longer than did most other nations, the Depression ended Colombia's age of progress and development by 1932.

Despite the increased well-being of coffee producers, other members of the elite, and the growing middle class, not all Colombians benefited from the Dance of the Millions. In November 1928, the most horrific strike in Latin American history broke out when banana workers at the United Fruit Company protested low wages, the lack of healthcare, and the exorbitant prices of everyday necessities at company stores. The Colombian army, acting at the behest of the UFCo and the US State Department, cut down striking workers with machine-gun fire. In the aftermath of the strike, estimates of the dead ranged from 410 (the army's version) to about 1,500. (Colombia's most famous novelist, Gabriel García Márquez, later captured the drama of these events in his novel *One Hundred Years of Solitude*.) Although the company soon agreed to improve workers' lots by opening up hospitals, schools, and improving wages for its employees, the United Fruit Company's exploitation of its workers provided a prominent example for nationalists critical of the role of US capital in Latin America.

The "Roaring Twenties" in Peru

On paper, Peru's potential for modernization during the "Roaring Twenties" far exceeded that of Colombia. For eleven years (1919–1930) the dictator and successful entrepreneur Augusto Leguía provided political stability while enjoying a modicum of popularity among all sectors of the population. Peru's export-led economy consisted of a diverse portfolio of agricultural products (sugar, cotton, wool) and minerals (copper and silver) that avoided the pitfalls of monoculture so commonplace in smaller Latin American nations. As cotton and sugar prices fell throughout the decade, US-owned corporations (such as the Cerro de Pasco Copper Company and the International Petroleum Company) came to play a more dominant role in the economy. The landed elite did well, converting their assets into banking and other business enterprises. Leguía voluntarily embraced many of Kemmerer's reforms, including a central reserve bank, and in addition, brought in US experts to modernize agriculture, the military, and the educational system. Foreign debt ballooned, however, from a mere $12 million at the beginning of his administration to a staggering $124 million by 1931. While exports expanded, domestic manufacturing flatlined, an indication of the export-led nature of Peru's economy in the "Roaring Twenties."

Like the Colombians, Leguía spent much of the foreign loans on public works' projects such as roads, ports, and railroads. To a greater degree than the

Colombians, Leguía dedicated funds to improving the urban environment as migrants from the countryside flocked to Lima in search of a better way of life. The old city walls disappeared, and water and sewer services expanded throughout the city. New parks and open spaces graced the modernized city even as the elite fled to suburbs such as Miraflores. Again like the Colombians, Leguía expanded the national bureaucracy fivefold during his eleven years in office. Prefiguring the governmental philosophy that would emerge after 1930, he believed that "the State is . . . the most efficacious agent for carrying out the beautiful work of human solidarity."

Nevertheless, as Peru's economic situation worsened in 1929, Leguía came under fire because of his subservience to the United States, his repression of critics, and perhaps most importantly, the notorious corruption of his son Juan and other members of the administration. As a result, the military removed Leguía from power in August, 1930 and held him in prison, where he died soon after from a lack of medical attention.

Conclusion

The first decades of the twentieth century were a time of rapidly growing, if wildly unequal, interdependency between Latin America and the United States. It was a period that fostered both great resentments and great prosperity. Nowhere is this more visible than the automobile industry: The popularization of the Model T, the car that put America on wheels, was possible because of the ready availability of Brazilian rubber. While it lasted, but only while it lasted, the rubber boom

TIMELINE

1889
French canal project in Panama fails

1895
Cuba's second war for independence begins

1899–1902
First US Occupation of Cuba

1901
Passage of the Platt Amendment

1879–1883
War of the Pacific

1891
The "Baltimore Affair" in Chile

1898
The Spanish-American War (also known as The War of 1898)

1899–1934
Era of Dollar Diplomacy in Latin America

made the Brazilian Amazon rich. When the boom passed to Asia, which produced rubber more cheaply, the US automobile industry continued to thrive, while the Brazilian rubber industry—unlinked from the commodity chain—sunk back to near-subsistence levels.

The "Dance of the Millions" that took hold in places like Colombia, Peru, and Cuba during the 1920s also represented the best of this partnership between North and South, as high prices for Latin American raw materials produced unprecedented wealth and a frenzy of spending among those sectors of the population—always a small but influential minority—who had been able to make the most out of the new global capitalism. Soon, however, the dance would slow, as the forces of economic depression and popular dissent—the voice of the majority who had benefited less, or not at all, from neocolonialism and the new world system—would drown out the song of early twentieth-century "progress."

KEY TERMS

Business imperialism   242   Paz y Trabajo   262   vendepatrias   258

Cuba Libre   243   patria potestad   277

Dollar Diplomacy   251   rabonas   259

1904
US begins construction of Panama Canal; canal completed in 1914

1915
US occupies Haiti for strategic reasons

1927–1934
The Sandino revolt vs. US occupation in Nicaragua

1903
Panama's independence and treaty with US for Canal Zone

1906
Yellow fever and malaria eradicated from Panama

1922–1935
Venezuela becomes major oil producer with US and British capital

Selected Readings

Brands, H. W. *The Reckless Decade: America in the 1890s.* Chicago: University of Chicago Press, 1995.

Besse, Susan K. *Restructuring Patriarchy: Modernizing Gender Inequality in Brazil, 1914–1940.* Chapel Hill: University of North Carolina Press, 1996.

Coatsworth, John. *Central America and the United States: The Clients and the Colossus.* New York: Twayne Publishers, 1994.

Conniff, Michael. *Black Labor on a White Canal, Panama, 1904–1981.* Pittsburgh, PA: University of Pittsburgh Press, 1985.

Diaz Espino, Ovidio. *How Wall Street Created a Nation: J.P. Morgan, Teddy Roosevelt, and the Panama Canal.* New York: Four Walls Eight Windows, 2001.

Ehrick, Christine. *The Shield of the Weak: Feminism and the State in Uruguay, 1903–1933.* Albuquerque: University of New Mexico Press, 2005.

Farmer, Paul. *Haiti: After the Earthquake.* New York: Public Affairs, 2011.

Ferrer, Ada. *Insurgent Cuba: Race, Nation, and Revolution, 1868–1898.* Chapel Hill: University of North Carolina Press, 1999.

Gobat, Michel. *Confronting the American Dream: Nicaragua under US Imperial Rule.* Durham, NC: Duke University Press, 2005.

Grandin, Greg. *Fordlandia: The Rise and Fall of Henry Ford's Forgotten Jungle City.* New York: Metropolitan Books, 2009.

Heinl, Robert Debs, Nancy Gordon Heinl, and Michael Heinl. *Written in Blood: The Story of the Haitian People, 1492–1995.* Lanthan, MD: University Press of America, 2005.

LaFeber, Walter. *The Panama Canal: The Crisis in Historical Perspective.* Oxford: Oxford University Press, 1989.

López, Alfred J. *José Martí: A Revolutionary Life.* Austin: University of Texas Press, 2014.

McBeth, Brian S. *Juan Vicente Gómez and the Oil Companies in Venezuela, 1908–1935.* New York: Cambridge University Press, 1983.

McCullough, David. *The Path between the Seas.* New York: Simon and Schuster, 1999.

McGuiness, Aims. *Path of Empire: Panama and the California Gold Rush.* Ithaca, NY: Cornell University Press, 2008.

Otovo, Okezi. *Progressive Mothers, Better Babies: Race, Public Health, and the State in Brazil, 1850–1945.* Austin: University of Texas Press, 2015.

Pérez, Louis A., Jr. *Cuba between Empires: 1878–1902.* Pittsburgh, PA: University of Pittsburgh Press, 1983.

Ramírez, Sergio, compiler, and Conrad, Robert Edgar trans. *Sandino: The Testimony of a Nicaraguan Patriot, 1921–1934.* Princeton, NJ: Princeton University Press, 1990.

Reyes, Rafael. *The Two Americas.* London: William Heinemann, 1914.

Santiago, Myrna I. *The Ecology of Oil: Environment, Labor, and the Mexican Revolution, 1900–1938*. New York; Cambridge University Press, 2006.

Schmidt, Hans. *The United States Occupation of Haiti, 1915–1934*. New Brunswick, NJ: Rutgers University Press, 1971.

Schoultz, Lars. *That Infernal Little Cuban Republic: The United States and the Cuban Revolution*. Chapel Hill: University of North Carolina Press, 2009.

Smith, Peter. *Talons of the Eagle: Latin America, the United States, and the World*. New York: Oxford University Press, 2013.

Tone, John L. *War and Genocide in Cuba, 1895–1898*. Chapel Hill: University of North Carolina Press, 2005.

Ugarte, Manuel. *The Destiny of a Continent*. New York: AMS Press, 1970.

Weinstein, Barbara. *The Amazon Rubber Boom, 1850–1920*. Stanford, CA: Stanford University Press, 1983.

7

Progress and Its Discontents, 1880–1929

Global Connections

Across the globe, the age of progress and modernization at the end of the nineteenth century and the start of the twentieth almost exclusively benefited the highly educated, those with capital to invest and those with new products to bring to expanding markets as we saw in chapter 5. But modernization imposed costs on the poor and the peripheral, on those driven off subsistence lands or subjected to exploitative labor. And those costs provoked discontent and mobilization, which is the subject of this chapter.

Ideas of democracy became more powerful than ever, including in places where they had made little headway earlier. In China, for example, Western-educated Sun Yat-Sen led the Chinese Revolution of 1911–1912, initiating a democratic government there until provincial warlords seized control. And reformers in the declining Russian and Ottoman empires pressed for reform, demanding expanded political rights and representation.

Political leaders tried to contain growing discontent by restricting suffrage, requiring literacy, property, gender, and even racial (in the US South) qualifications for voting. New "reform" laws enabled middle-class males to vote but continued to exclude the majority of citizens. And aristocratic institutions, such as Great Britain's House of Lords, continued to exercise preeminence over more democratic bodies. When threatened with popular unrest in the streets or in the factories, the increasingly powerful centralized states of the early twentieth century resorted to repression.

Living standards rose, reflected in longer life spans and greater average height. But the divide between urban and rural also grew starker, as rapidly advancing cities seemed to leave the countryside behind. Inequality within cities also grew, as impoverished migrants uprooted from traditional rural subsistence settled into tenement houses or precarious self-built housing. The bustling economy allowed the middle class to partake of the material and cultural benefits of urban life. For the vast majority of the migrants from rural areas, the poverty of privation, and disease awaited them as they toiled in menial jobs. Many turned to radical ideas like anarchism and socialism, challenging the intensification of capitalism during the age of progress and modernization. These ideas spread to Latin America along with working-class immigrants, who arrived in the Southern Cone in large numbers from Spain and Italy at the turn of the last century.

≡ **Maya Girl Playing with White Doll** This image portrays a young Maya girl from Yucatán, Mexico, playing with a white doll. Although it seems unlikely that her parents would be able to find a doll with indigenous features, the image also suggests the aspirational message of whitening that was so commonplace in the age of progress and modernization. The image is part of a much larger collection of Mexican photography that fits within the late nineteenth-century genre of *costumbrismo*, a desire on the part of artists and photographers to capture the everyday lives and occupations of the ordinary people of Mexico.

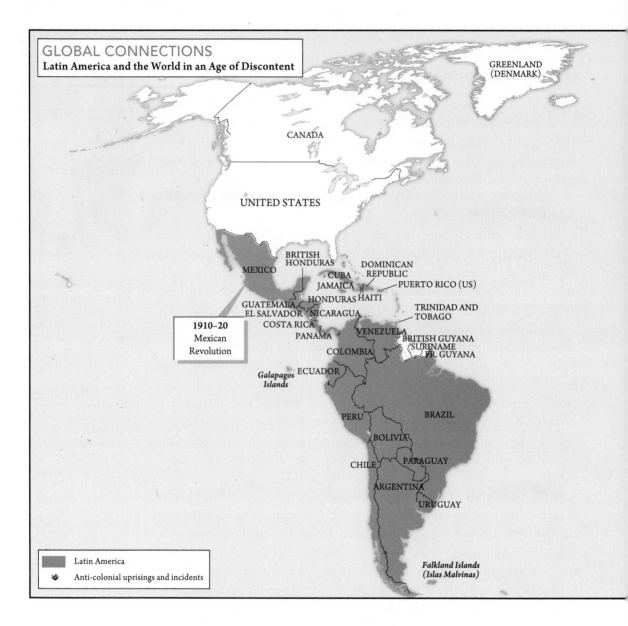

GLOBAL CONNECTIONS
Latin America and the World in an Age of Discontent

Fervent nationalism awakened passions in areas where once-mighty empires were receding, such as the Balkan Peninsula, the Middle East, eastern Europe, Cuba, and the Philippines. Across Europe and beyond, courtiers and intellectuals felt the pillars of the old regime crumbling. The violent nationalism that emerged during World War I not only destroyed a generation of European youth but also led to slaughter of tens of thousands of colonial subjects, hastening the decline of

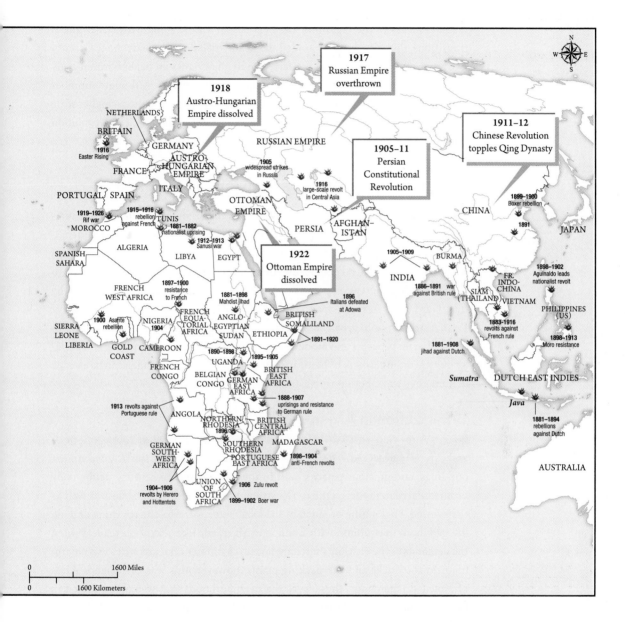

1918
Austro-Hungarian
Empire dissolved

1917
Russian Empire
overthrown

1911–12
Chinese Revolution
topples Qing Dynasty

1905–11
Persian
Constitutional
Revolution

1922
Ottoman Empire
dissolved

NETHERLANDS

BRITAIN
1916
Easter Rising

GERMANY

FRANCE

AUSTRO-
HUNGARIAN
EMPIRE

RUSSIAN EMPIRE

1905
widespread strikes
in Russia

1916
large-scale revolt
in Central Asia

PORTUGAL SPAIN

ITALY

OTTOMAN
EMPIRE

CHINA

1899–1900
Boxer rebellion

1919–1926
Rif war

1915–1916
rebellion
against French

TUNIS
1881–1882
nationalist uprising

PERSIA

AFGHAN-
ISTAN

1891

JAPAN

MOROCCO

1912–1913
Sanusi war

ALGERIA

LIBYA

EGYPT

INDIA

1905–1909

BURMA

1898–1902
Aguinaldo leads
nationalist revolt

SPANISH
SAHARA

1886–1891 war
against British rule

FR.
INDO-
CHINA

1897–1900
resistance
to French

FRENCH
WEST AFRICA

1881–1898
Mahdist jihad

1896
Italians defeated
at Adowa

SIAM
(THAILAND) VIETNAM

PHILIPPINES
(US)

1900 Asante
rebellion

SIERRA
LEONE

LIBERIA

NIGERIA
1904

FRENCH
EQUA-
TORIAL
AFRICA

ANGLO-
EGYPTIAN
SUDAN

BRITISH
SOMALILAND

ETHIOPIA

1883–1916
revolts against
French rule

1898–1913
Moro resistance

1891–1920

1881–1908
jihad against Dutch

GOLD
COAST

CAMEROON

FRENCH
CONGO

BELGIAN
CONGO

UGANDA

GERMAN
EAST
AFRICA

1890–1898

1895–1905

BRITISH
EAST
AFRICA

Sumatra

DUTCH EAST INDIES

Java

1888–1907
uprisings and resistance
to German rule

1881–1894
rebellions
against Dutch

1913 revolts against
Portuguese rule

ANGOLA

NORTHERN
RHODESIA
1896

BRITISH
CENTRAL
AFRICA

MADAGASCAR

GERMAN
SOUTH-
WEST
AFRICA

SOUTHERN
RHODESIA

PORTUGUESE
EAST AFRICA

1898–1904
anti-French revolts

AUSTRALIA

1904–1906
revolts by Herero
and Hottentots

UNION
OF
SOUTH
AFRICA

1906 Zulu revolt

1899–1902 Boer war

0   1600 Miles

0   1600 Kilometers

empires. Within Latin America, World War I precipitated the decline of British influence and strengthened the hand of the United States, with all of the risk and promise that relationship entailed.

The Mexican Revolution was one of the most consequential of the global crises of the early twentieth century. It demonstrated that the precepts behind Latin America's age of progress and modernization were flawed, and it inspired revolutionaries in the region for the next century. In keeping with larger global transitions, that Revolution sounded the death knell for, or at least the temporary knockout of, a liberalism that conferred individual rights on paper without truly including the disadvantaged in the construction of the nation. Although a number of Latin American nations would experience disturbances on a much smaller scale than Mexico's, in much of the region the wider effects of the Mexican Revolution remained subdued, at least until the global Depression of 1929.

Consequences of Urbanization, 1880–1920

Today, Latin America is one of the most urbanized regions on the globe, a phenomenon that began during the age of progress and modernization. Once the demographic movement from rural areas to cities began, much to the dismay of the elites who preferred provincial peoples and immigrants (most of whom were farmers) to remain in the countryside performing agricultural labor, nothing could stem the tide. Hard times in rural areas, coupled with the opportunities of the city, drove Latin Americans into urban areas in ever increasing numbers, an unintended result of the plan for progress and modernization. In urban areas, elite culture and popular culture often clashed. Urbanization transformed the Latin American landscape in numerous ways, both positive and negative.

Urbanization in Argentina

Buenos Aires vied with Rio de Janeiro for the title of the "Paris of South America," and certainly deserved it more. The broad central avenues, majestic government buildings, and gracious palaces built in the late nineteenth century deliberately recalled Parisian models. Due to the strong presence of British traders as well as the avowed Anglophilia of much of the local elite, however, the rhythms of daily life had more in common with London, with rituals like afternoon tea leavening the demands of the bustling merchant houses. A different Buenos Aires was emerging near the docks and the packing plants, however; this was the Buenos Aires of crowded tenements. These were the neighborhoods that welcomed the city's humble immigrants, and they echoed with Italian, Yiddish, Arabic, and Polish.

As in most Latin American countries, the Argentine capital was vastly larger and more economically powerful than any other city in the nation. In contrast to many of its neighbors, however, Argentina did nourish a handful of highly productive secondary cities, specializing in different economic sectors. Rosario, upriver from Buenos Aires, was home to the nation's largest meat-packing plants. Córdoba, to the west, became the center for industrial production; both cities would

Latin American Cities in 1910 with a
Population Exceeding 250,000

City with population of:

⊙ 250,000–500,000   □ 500,000–1 million

 MAP. 7.1

become hotbeds of labor activism. The small cities of Mendoza and San Miguel de Tucumán, at the foot of the Andes, both became hubs for agrarian production. The growth of these secondary cities helped propel urbanization in Argentina ahead of nearly any other Latin American country.

Urbanization in Uruguay

The Uruguayan capital of Montevideo grew into a bustling metropolis in the late nineteenth century. Uruguay presented the extreme example of urbanization during these years in Latin America, where one city dominated the life of the country. By 1900, Montevideo contained well over one-third of the nation's population. It played many roles: as the railhead for each of the three lines bringing cattle from the countryside, as the location of the *frigoríficos* (meat-packing plants) for processing cattle and sheep, as the center of banking and light industry, and as the cultural capital with museums and the famed Teatro Solís. In addition, the city housed the nation's only university and the majority of its public schools. Not surprisingly, more than half of the nation's physicians and most of the government bureaucrats resided in Montevideo. Both Europeans and rural Uruguayans flocked to the capital.

The architecture of turn-of-the-twentieth-century Montevideo demonstrated three growth spurts. The old colonial city, tucked away on a small peninsula, featured narrow, winding streets clustered around the cathedral and the *cabildo* (municipal council) building, still used as the seat of government in the years immediately after independence. By the 1870s, increased stability and economic prosperity allowed for a building boom in the "new city," which housed the Legislative Palace, modern department stores, theaters, banks, and public buildings like the National Library. Even a few squat (by today's standards) skyscrapers emerged.

The new city enveloped the few remaining colonial elite estates along the shores of the river. Finally, during the decade beginning in 1910, Montevideo's "newest city" sprung up among the beachfront on the La Plata River, becoming the preferred residential district for the city's elite and new middle class. But Montevideo was not entirely picturesque. Industrial neighborhoods were characterized by pollution, and the working poor crowded into unsanitary and flimsy tenement buildings.

The Old Republic and the Modernization of Rio de Janeiro

The foundation of the Brazilian Republic in 1889 stemmed from the exhaustion of the monarchy that preceded it. In the short term, the Republic did not substantially broaden the base of political power. Indeed, voting rights were more circumscribed under the Republic than they had been at the peak of the empire, and were limited to men of means. The national electorate shrank in the 1890s, even as the population grew. The transition to republican rule, however, did eventually make possible the formation of new political parties representing the aspirations of an emerging urban middle class, particularly in the state of São Paulo. (With the transition from empire to republic, the old provinces became new states.) As a result, the Old Republic was marked by vigorous jostling for political position in the core areas of the Brazilian southeast and by periodic flashes of more violent movements on the periphery of the northeast and the far south.

A flurry of ambitious modernizing projects accompanied the dawn of the twentieth century in Rio de Janeiro, particularly during the mayoral term of Francisco Pereira Passos (1902–1906). Pereira Passos was an engineer by training, and as the mayor of the national capital he was not elected but appointed directly by the president, and therefore had no popular electorate to consider. He seized the opportunity to redesign the city radically, clearing tenement blocks, cutting broad avenues

≡ **Avenida Rio Branco in Rio de Janeiro.** As government revenues improved during the age of progress, nations sought to enhance their international image by revitalizing urban areas, particularly capital cities. Frequently, city planners followed the model of Baron Haussmann, who had redesigned Paris with broad thoroughfares. Rio de Janeiro's makeover followed a similar pattern, as numerous tenements that had once housed the poor were torn down to make way for wide streets and glittering shopping areas on the Avenida Rio Branco. Broad streets also better accommodated modern modes of transportation, including trolley cars and automobiles.

through congested colonial neighborhoods, and constructing elegant public parks (whose use was limited in practice to wealthier citizens). Pereira Passos's reforms deliberately echoed those of Georges-Eugène Haussmann, an official in the administration of Napoleon III who had significantly reshaped the city of Paris into the "City of Light" a generation earlier. This "Haussmannization" of Rio neatly divided public opinion. Those who aspired to see Rio become the Paris of South America supported and praised the reforms, while those who were scrambling to make a life on the margins of the city felt (with good reason) they were being brushed aside.

Pereira Passos's initiatives created a grand axis at the heart of Rio, crowned by a public plaza, flanked on one side by the majestic National Library and the stately Academy of Fine Arts, and on another by the luxurious Theatro Municipal (itself a near replica of the Paris Opera House). These monuments were both symbolic and constitutive of Pereira Passos's ambitions: they were meant to elevate and civilize, while banishing the low and disorderly. The evictions and demolitions necessary for this project (termed the *bota-abaixo*, or "tear-down," by the press) provoked a popular backlash, particularly in the poor, crowded neighborhoods that were the mayor's first target.

Resentment of the demolition soon spilled over into other causes. Pereira Passos named the pioneering scientist Oswaldo Cruz as his director of public health and in 1904 empowered him to direct an ambitious, mandatory smallpox vaccination program for the entire population of Rio. Tenement-dwellers conflated the vaccine campaign with the *bota-abaixo* and resisted both as an intrusion of their homes and their bodies. For five days in November, 1904, a popular revolt took control of downtown, marked by attacks on government workers, barricades in the streets, and overturning of trolleys. The caustic journalist Nelson Rodrigues later described this as "a revolt in favor of smallpox," but the reality was more complicated. The humbler residents of Rio recognized that the mayor considered them obstacles to progress, rather than citizens.

At the same time, the Old Republic witnessed a flourishing of popular cultural vitality in the city, much of it centered on the new social spaces of cinemas and cafés. Pianist Ernesto Nazareth, along with a host of talented amateur and semi-professional musicians, was honing the intricate instrumental music known as *choro*. That music's syncopated rhythm and infectious melodies became the sound of the city in the first two decades of the twentieth century. The City Fire Department Band, a group that united black, white, and mixed-race musicians, became famous for its choro performances in downtown plazas. The band's demographic makeup mirrored that of both the department it represented and the audience it entertained, a mixture that typified the city's mercantile and civil service sectors.

Rio could be inclusive and accommodating at one moment, exclusive and forbidding at another.

From the vantage point of a Rio de Janeiro in the midst of tropical modernization, most of the rest of Brazil looked either retrograde or dangerously volatile. The north, in the midst of the rapid rise and precipitous fall of the Amazon rubber boom (chapter 6), seemed disconnected from the rest of the country. In the far south, a fratricidal civil conflict broke out early in 1893. This "Federalist Revolution" nominally pitted monarchists in favor of provincial autonomy against republicans in favor of centralized control. But it really boiled down to a movement by one segment of the landowning class to overthrow another. It took the military over two years to crush the revolt, and then only with great bloodshed.

On the national scene, only São Paulo seemed to be charging ahead more quickly than Rio de Janeiro. In a feat nearly unrivaled in Latin American development, the state of São Paulo turned coffee wealth into the basis for rapid domestic industrialization. By 1910, there were more miles of rail track in the state of São Paulo than in the rest of the country combined, linking an archipelago of bustling towns to the growing industrial hub of the city of São Paulo.

The Urban Environment and Public Parks

Rapid urbanization in the latter part of the nineteenth century convinced political leaders throughout the Western world to work to improve the urban environment. In addition to concerns about disease and the effects of the unpleasant hustle and bustle of crowded streets, healthcare professionals argued that urban dwellers needed fresh air and the pleasing sights and sounds of the countryside for their mental well-being. To solve these problems, planners created urban parks. Just as planners in Rio de Janeiro looked to Haussmann's boulevards for inspiration, planners in Mexico City looked to Haussmann's parks. Chapultepec Park in Mexico City was modeled in part on Haussmann's Bois de Boulogne.

During the postindependence era, Chapultepec Park and its castle became famous as the site of the exploits of the *Niños Heroes* during the final battle of the Mexican War (chapter 2). Later, the castle became the private residence of Emperor Maximilian and Empress Carlota, who enjoyed its seclusion from the colonial downtown and its spectacular views of Lake Texcoco and the nearby snow-capped volcanoes. Emperor Maximilian had workers clear the underbrush, plant new trees, and build a broad avenue (now called the Paseo de la Reforma) connecting the castle to the city center.

During Porfirio Díaz's administration, Chapultepec Park was transformed into a place the urban elite and the middle class could enjoy. The park quickly became

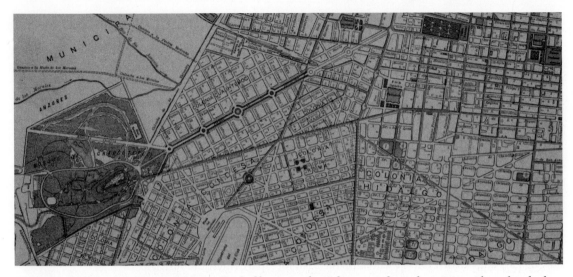

≡ **Mexico City Map, 1910.** By 1910, Mexico City had been transformed into a modern urban center with one hundred miles of electric trolley track connecting the colonial city (the area surrounding the National Palace including Alameda Park, top right), to the suburbs near Chapultepec Park, on the left. The latter offered thoroughfares where young men and women of the *gente decente* could ride newfangled bicycles, banned for years in the Historic District. Bicycles allowed young women to escape the sharp eyes of chaperones and experience more freedom than was possible in the postindependence years.

a showpiece of the Porfirian urban modernization project. As had happened in Paris, Chapultepec Park's location encouraged the elite to abandon their historic residences downtown and relocate in the wealthy suburbs around the park. Díaz's engineers extended the park's grounds, devised avenues for horse-drawn carriages and bicycles, and created narrower pedestrian promenades that led to gardens, statues, gazebos, lakes, fountains, and a fashionable café-restaurant that catered to the elite. A fence excluded those deemed undesirable (the urban poor) from the park, as did a gate that was locked after 7:00 p.m. Police were posted throughout the park to assure the privileged that only other members of the gente decente would share their space. Not surprisingly, Chapultepec Park, with its lit fountains and a spectacular fireworks display, played host to the glamorous Centennial Celebration of 1910, the last hurrah of the Porfiriato just before the Mexican Revolution erupted.

The Seamier Side of Urban Life in Mexico

The ideal of the city as the center of civilization and modernity was tested by the tide of people flowing into urban communities. Municipal officials took great pride in their efforts to modernize metropolitan areas, adding streetlights, parks, and sewer systems, at least in the fashionable neighborhoods. Since colonial times, Mexico

City's administrators had dreamed of draining Lake Texcoco, which flooded streets during most rainy seasons and occasionally caused catastrophic city floods. The lake became an even greater biohazard in the late nineteenth century as people dumped into it human and animal waste, dead carcasses, and household trash, contributing to the spread of water-borne diseases. Porfirio Díaz's city officials determined to use technology to drain the lake, and began construction on the Grand Canal.

Díaz's friend, the British investor Weetman Pearson, proposed a profitable contract for himself that gave his firm the responsibility for digging a wide, deep canal that would drain Lake Texcoco and Mexico City's other surrounding lakes and allow the water to flow through a tunnel under the mountains to a lower elevation. Pearson's company imported huge steam shovels called dredges that finally accomplished the long-desired result in 1900. When completed, journalists hailed the *Gran Canal* as one of the most remarkable engineering marvels of the Porfiriato.

Despite the optimism associated with the completed project, however, the canal had unforeseen environmental consequences. First, the Gran Canal lacked the capacity to contain all of the run-off that accumulated during the rainy season; as a result, many streets still flooded. Second, as one of the world's largest open sewers, the Gran Canal quickly became an example of urban blight in those places where it was visible. Finally, draining the lake caused the city's spongy soil to sink as much as 20 feet in some locations. For example, one of Díaz's most opulent projects, the Palace of Fine Arts, made of heavy Italian marble, today rests twelve feet below the level where it originally stood.

Crime became an increasing problem in the modernizing city. Travelers talked less now about hold-ups in rural areas than about pickpocketing and general larceny in the city. Elites expected crime rates to increase in the poorer neighborhoods as more refugees from rural poverty moved into cities. What surprised many well-heeled citizens, however, was that the new brand of criminals preyed on middle-class and elite consumer enterprises, such as the department store. These modern establishments kept their goods in glass cases, not on open shelves. To make a purchase, customers had to converse with clerks who presented the merchandise only if the customer passed the test of having the correct appearance, based on the racial profiling common in that age of scientific racism. New shoplifters, however, tended to be young, light-skinned women who flirted with the male clerk while their confederates stuffed untended goods into "kangaroo" pockets. And in 1891, a well-dressed French immigrant pulled off the largest jewelry store heist in Mexico City's history.

Female sex work, like so many aspects of urban life in Porfirian Mexico, also fell under greater scrutiny. In the name of science and discipline, improving hygiene and providing order became priorities in fashionable neighborhoods, where city councils regulated what they referred to as the "necessary evil" of prostitution. In Oaxaca City in southern Mexico, ordinances were passed controlling the activities of prostitutes. These women had to register with the authorities and have their photographs placed in official files, as well as be subjected to weekly medical examinations for venereal disease (a particularly intrusive example of the modernizers' preoccupation with promoting better hygiene). In addition, the city zoned brothels into "red-districts" on the outskirts of the city. Registered prostitutes paid taxes (another reason many women worked outside the system), which became an important source of municipal revenue. Brothels were organized along racial lines, with first- and second-class establishments housing lighter-skinned sex workers, while the women employed in less expensive brothels tended to be indigenous women from the local countryside.

Crime and Disease in Andean Cities

The rapid urbanization of Latin American cities heightened social tensions and created unforeseen negative consequences. While European immigrants flocked to Buenos Aires and Montevideo, Andean cities (like Lima in Peru, along with Quito and Guayaquil in Ecuador) mostly grew through internal migration. By 1920, some 63 percent of Lima's population came as a result of second-generation Chinese as well as Afro-Peruvian internal migrants fleeing their servitude in guano pits or on coastal sugar and cotton plantations. In Ecuador, similarly, indigenous families left behind exploitative conditions on haciendas in the highlands and sought improved employment opportunities in the bustling lowland city of Guayaquil.

These growing cities were divided into class-based neighborhoods in which the elite and middle-class individuals inhabited a very different world than did the poor. Lima's tenements, or *callejones*, were so crowded that as many as ten people sometimes slept in a single room. In Guayaquil, the poor constructed bamboo shacks on stilts in the city's low-lying outskirts, where they ran the risk of being flooded during the rainy season.

The urban poor generally lacked access to decent paying jobs. The lucky ones in Guayaquil found employment processing cacao or rice, or perhaps working in small factories making consumer goods like cigarettes and brooms. Others simply begged or stole. "Decent" women could find work as laundresses, seamstresses, cooks, or maids. Women who lacked opportunity were often forced into sex work, which allowed them to make a living, but cost them status and honor in the perception of the *gente decente*. High unemployment in crowded conditions contributed to the impression of poor urban neighborhoods as rife with disease and crime. Municipal governments responded with policies devised to emphasize hygiene and control.

At the turn of the twentieth century, Peruvian criminologists debated the causes of the spiking crime rate in Lima. Initially, the biologically based theory of the Italian criminologist Cesare Lombroso held sway, as his ideas coincided neatly with the scientific racism of the era. Lombroso believed that certain "degenerate races" (such as Afro-Peruvians, indigenous people, and the Chinese) were innately more likely to be "born criminals." Lombroso hypothesized that this was due to biological and genetic differences and deficiencies among the races.

Among the diagnostic tools of this scientific racism (a term used freely and without negative association at the time) was phrenology, the study of facial asymmetry and deformation of the skull, thought to indicate character, thought, intelligence, and emotions—one of several pseudosciences that predicted criminal behavior based on physical characteristics. By the dawn of the twentieth century, criminologists rejected these kinds of theories in favor of social explanations for crime. Poverty and exploitation, the new generation of social scientists argued, could lead people to criminal behavior. Even so, scientific racism remained prevalent well into the twentieth century not only in Latin America, but also in Europe and the United States. Eugenics, a pseudoscientific theory of racial evolution through improvement of human racial "stock," was particularly pernicious.

These theories informed the strategies of Lima's policy makers, who devised a two-fold strategy to address perceived urban ills. On one hand, hardened, dangerous criminals were imprisoned in Lima's modern penitentiary. To rehabilitate lesser offenders and improve the city's moral climate, urban reformers built more schools and attempted to curtail the consumption of alcohol through organizations like the National Temperance Society, founded in 1912. By applauding the qualities of the "honorable poor," the elite praised those people in the working class who rejected the criminal way of life and labored diligently at honest occupations.

While Guayaquil's elite also worried about the city's rising crime rate, they were more concerned about their city's appalling reputation as the "pesthole of the Pacific." Because Guayaquil was a busy port, diseases arrived regularly on ships from all over the world. The city's population grew from 25,000 in 1880 to 100,000 four decades later. Guayaquil lacked a working sewer system and even in the early twentieth century had only a limited potable water system. Because of the absence of adequate sanitation, water-borne diseases like dysentery and typhoid fever flourished.

≡ **Fighting Yellow Fever in Guayaquil.** Long known as the "Pest Hole of the Pacific" because of periodic outbreaks of fatal diseases such as malaria and yellow fever, officials in Guayaquil and other Pacific ports took advantage of the new scientific discoveries employed in Panama to combat disease. No longer attributing epidemics to miasmas (bad air), public health officials recognized that mosquito-borne diseases could be controlled by eliminating bodies of standing water. Because piped city water existed only in wealthy neighborhoods in Guayaquil in these years, most citizens kept fresh water in cisterns outside their homes. In this photo, officials are placing into the barrels fish that would consume the mosquito larvae. After resolving Guayaquil's perennial problems with disease, the city's population exploded in the early twentieth century, and today it is Ecuador's largest city.

Epidemics of yellow fever regularly swept through the population, as many doctors still labored under the theory that miasmas (infested air) caused illness. (The name of Argentina's capital, Buenos Aires, offers an indication of its founders' false hopes that this far-southern coastal city might offer some relief from the "males aires" that were thought to carry disease). As a result, doctors relied on special religious services, firing cannons in the air, and fumigating all mail from foreign countries as methods of ending the epidemics. (Such peculiar remedies sometimes took a long time to die out. As late as the 1930s, El Salvador's dictator, Maximiliano Hernández Martínez, ordered that all city lights be covered in red cellophane in order to purify the environment and fend off an epidemic of influenza).

Bubonic plague struck in 1908, and ravaged coastal Ecuador for the next decade. Both plague and yellow fever especially affected visitors and recent immigrants from the sierra who had acquired no immunities to these diseases. Finally, in 1919 the Rockefeller Yellow Fever Commission recommended placing minnows in the water barrels that sat alongside nearly every home in the city. The minnows ate the mosquito larvae and the epidemics finally came to an end, although a vaccine for plague was not developed until 1928.

The Rise of the Middle Class, 1890s–1920s

The "great acceleration" of the age of progress and modernization led to the emergence of new institutions and new forms of social life. Immigrants and rural people who migrated to urban areas took advantage of new opportunities to join the growing middle class. The nations where such changes occurred on a large scale witnessed a middle class that asserted its claims to civilization, self-worth, and modernity, its hopes of rising to positions of privilege and its fears of falling into the gritty popular classes. Public primary school systems, high schools, and universities expanded and now became an attainable goal for the sons (and, less often, the daughters) of shopkeepers and clerks. The fields of medicine, science, engineering, technology, and the law grew more professional, distinguished by credentials (like college degrees) and both defined and managed by representative associations. In some places, new political parties emerged to challenge the elite while simultaneously guarding against the claims of the rustic and urban "unwashed."

The Middle Class in Argentina

Argentina created the first extensive public education system in all of Latin America in the mid-nineteenth century. This system was never intended to accommodate all Argentines; the oligarchic liberal politicians who created these schools perceived organized education to be irrelevant for indigenous people, ranch-hands, manual laborers, and descendants of African slaves. Schools were intended instead to inculcate the values of civilization and patriotism in the children of the propertied classes. Even with their limitations and prejudices, however, these schools yielded a broader educated population in Argentina than elsewhere in the region.

Schools expanded in the late nineteenth century in order to prepare youth for the demands of commerce, law, and administration. Argentines came to understand that mastering an ever-shifting array of sums, and vocabulary was the key to economic success in a market society. Those immigrants who succeeded in rising to managerial positions believed that only schools and their credentials could guarantee social ascension for children. The demand for education consistently outpaced supply, particularly at the university level.

These institutions were decisive in the formation of a middle-class identity, based partly on the understanding that graduates, represented new model citizens.

≡ **President Hipólito Yrigoyen and His Middle-Class Constituents.** Although Argentina's oligarchic republic had brought the county and the elite incredible wealth (the country's GNP ranked among the highest in the world in 1904), not all Argentines had benefited equally from this prosperity. Yrigoyen formed a political party named the Unión Cívica Radical (Radical Party) to press for legislation to broaden suffrage by granting the vote to all males. The oligarchical regime relented in 1912, and in the ensuing presidential election in 1916, Yrigoyen swept to victory. Here Yrigoyen, surrounded by his middle-class followers, celebrates his triumph.

Ironically, that sense of identity became most coherent when universities failed to meet their students' expectations. In 1918, students at the National University of Córdoba, rebelled against their professors and administrators, accusing them of being tyrannical, outmoded, and beholden to religious instruction. Their demands set off a national movement, manifesting itself in Buenos Aires and numerous smaller cities. The students held public rallies and pressed national political authorities to intervene in order to modernize higher education. In June of 1919, they occupied the campus at Córdoba, shutting down the university.

The rebellious students demanded a host of reforms, beginning with autonomy and representation. They argued that universities should be free to create their own curricula; that students should have a key voice in determining those curricula; and that students should have a voice in selecting their professors. They demanded creation of new professional schools and updating of scientific academic programs.

And they demanded **docencia libre**, or academic freedom, to protect teachers and students who challenged the traditionalists.

Argentine President Hipólito Yrigoyen, the leader of the reformist middle-class Unión Cívica Radical Party that had swept to victory in the elections of 1916, sent in the army to clear the campus at Córdoba, the kind of action that often led to massacre when ordered against peasants or workers. Indeed, only months before, soldiers and police had brutally cut down labor demonstrators in the streets of Buenos Aires. In this case, however, Yrigoyen made sure the soldiers acted with restraint. And in the wake of the occupation, Yrigoyen issued a national decree granting virtually all of the student demands.

The university reform movement of 1918–1919 helped in the formation of an Argentine middle class, and also revealed its aspirations and assumptions. While its members craved progress, they also feared what would become of them if progress caught them unawares. Students benefited from the perception that their status placed them off-limits for police or military abuse, a privilege that allowed them forms of political action unavailable, at least in the short term, to workers. Savvy politicians, like Yrigoyen, began to cater to this sensibility rather than repress it.

The Middle Class in Peru

Peru's middle class differed from Argentina's largely in scale—it was much smaller—but like Argentina's, it also became a dynamic social and political force near the end of the nineteenth century. As in Argentina, the majority of Peru's middle classes dwelt in cities, especially Lima. Many of these urban dwellers worked as professionals (lawyers, doctors, and teachers) while the remainder held down white-collar jobs as department store clerks, bank and insurance company employees, and officials employed in the ever-increasing national, regional, and municipal bureaucracies. Although predominantly light-skinned, the literacy skills, professional status, and lifestyle of these **empleados** (white-collar employees) transcended race and allowed some mestizos and other ethnicities to join the middle class. Overwhelmingly male until 1930, these urban middle-class empleados emerged in increasing numbers as Peru prospered and the size of government grew.

Empleados identified with the elite or gente decente and looked down on working-class **obreros** (laborers). Like the gente decente, empleados disdained manual labor, the defining characteristic of obreros. For example, shop employees would defy their employers when asked to undertake a demeaning task, such as carrying a package in the street. Like the elite, they prided themselves in dressing well (sometimes beyond their means), and on their literacy, which enabled them to cast ballots in a nation with restricted suffrage.

Empleados saw themselves as educated, responsible, and trustworthy salaried employees, in contrast to the illiterate daily-wage earners who performed manual labor. In the era where a man had to wear a jacket and tie to walk around Lima's Plaza de Armas without being accosted by the police, empleados freely rubbed elbows with the gente decente in a location where obreros felt out of place. Theirs was essentially a male world, with only a few female empleadas working in the post office or the telegraph and telephone exchanges.

With the conclusion of World War I in 1918, Peruvians began debating the "social question," which had to do with the role of class in society. Naturally, the distinctions between empleados and obreros became integral to these discussions. Empleados found themselves caught between two worlds. On one hand, they embraced the values and the paternalism of the gente decente as well as their employers, and aspired to become just like them. On the other hand, they shared with the obreros a desire for higher earnings and greater job security. While unwilling

≡ **Telephone Operators in Montevideo.** The telephone, realistically affordable only to the elite and the upper middle class, also represented the modernization of the city. The job of telephone operator became the exclusive purview of women, largely because their smaller hands and manual dexterity were ideally suited for the task. Operating a manual switchboard required operators to plug the caller's cord into the intended recipient's connection and then unplug it when the call concluded. Working exclusively with other women and under the supervision of a woman also furthered the social goal of maintaining these women's honor outside of the home.

CULTURE AND IDEAS

The Redemption of Ham

The painting *The Redemption of Ham* by Modesto Brocos y Gómez presents a striking allegory of race in Brazil. A black grandmother, barefoot and wizened, raises her hands and looks to heaven in gratitude. A **mulata** mother holds her infant on her lap while the father, probably Portuguese, looks on. And the white infant, glowing with health, holds an orange.

Modesto Brocos was Spanish by birth but spent most of his career in Brazil, where he taught at the prestigious National Academy of Fine Arts. Academic paintings were meant to be interpreted allegorically, and this one portrayed purification of the race, with the family—suggesting the Brazilian national family—becoming lighter-skinned in each generation. The orange, a symbol of Christian purity, seems to proclaim the successful conclusion of a process of whitening.

The grandmother's bare feet and clothing suggest a slave origin. The father's clothing is that of a humble Portuguese immigrant, while the mother is dressed modestly in bright, graceful garments. The child's attire, like his skin, is whitest of all. The image conformed to the dominant racial understandings in late nineteenth-century Brazil—that the country's African inheritance was a burden, a stain that could only be cleansed (like the white laundry hanging in the background) through generations of intermarriage. The painting's title, referring to a biblical curse that Noah placed on his "dark" son, Ham, and his children, was understood in nineteenth-century Brazil to refer to those of African descent. Contemporary viewers understood that message and viewed the painting as a parable of whitening.

≡ *The Redemption of Ham.*

Modesto Brocos expressed the prejudices and anxieties of his time. But perhaps a coming reinterpretation of racial inheritance in Brazil, one that would reject the ideal of whitening, was lurking beneath the surface, demanding to be seen.

- Why does the mother point at the grandmother, as if into the past? Is the baby waving goodbye or gesturing fondly? Does the father look content or smugly insipid?

to unionize as the obreros were doing, empleados formed mutual aid societies that provided economic relief for members facing medical or funeral expenses. For the empleados, the moderate reforms of Augusto Leguía provided a partial solution. The Law of Empleados of 1924, which by definition excluded all obreros, required employers to give three months' notice before terminating an empleado, retirement pensions based on years of service, a life insurance policy, and workers' compensation.

The middle class in Peru, as elsewhere in Latin America, voiced a series of demands that would ultimately alter Latin American society. In most countries, the middle class urged governments to embrace economic nationalism and state-led development, especially after 1930, as a means for increasing government revenues that could be used for national development. In addition, political advocates for middle-class citizens demanded more access to public education for all children and a broader electorate that included illiterate males and (eventually women). Finally, the middle class, especially after 1930, often led the demand for greater social welfare benefits for the poor and a more equitable distribution of the nation's wealth.

Literary Visions and Transitions, 1870s–1920s

Latin American literature was a crucial arena for the formulation of ideas of nation, progress, and Latin American identity. The great Latin American novels of the nineteenth and early twentieth century did not merely reflect social and political transitions; they deeply informed collective understandings of what it meant to be Argentine or Peruvian or Brazilian, and what was necessary for uplifting those nations. Novelists, indeed, were often politicians; in Argentina, for example, during the mid-nineteenth century, Domingo Sarmiento, Juan Bautista Alberdi, and José Mármol each seemed to experiment in fiction with the ideas they hoped to put into practice as politicians. Even toward the end of the century, when literary authors began to think of writing as a full-time profession somewhat removed from the political arena, the literary imagination deeply shaped broader social understandings.

From Romanticism to Realism

Until the late nineteenth century, romantic nationalism was the dominant literary mode in Latin America. Throughout the hemisphere, novelists crafted stirring, melodramatic historical novels offering allegories of national foundation, the resolution of differences within the nation, and the marginalization of elements that could not be assimilated. Manuel de Jesús Galván's 1882 novel *Enriquillo*, considered the epic novel of the Dominican Republic, exemplifies the genre. The title character is an Indian prince at the time of the Spanish conquest, orphaned when bloodthirsty conquistadores slaughter his tribe. He is rescued and raised by Franciscans, who christen him Enrique, or, more colloquially, Enriquillo. But cruel Spanish overlords threaten his mestiza wife, Mencía. Enriquillo and Mencía run to the mountains, joined by other Indians fleeing subjugation. They successfully resist recapture, creating an idyllic community and eventually winning a concession of liberty from the emperor.

Mencía is the figurative mother of the Dominican Republic, assimilating and reconciling Indian and Spanish inheritance. Enriquillo embodies the inheritance of the courageous Indian. The friars, along with the distant emperor himself, represent the humanistic Spanish tradition, while the conquistadores show its obverse. Notable by their absence are Africans. Galván's vision of the nation thus offers a harmonious (if fictive) resolution of Spanish-Indian conflict, one far from the reality in Dominican history. By setting its allegory in the early conquest, before the rise of plantation slavery in Santo Domingo, it avoids touching on the Dominican Republic's African inheritance, leaving Africans out of the imagined Dominican family.

Similar novels emerged throughout Latin America in the second half of the nineteenth century, such as *Iracema*, by Brazil's José de Alencar, *Aves sin Nido* (*Birds without a Nest*) by Peru's Clorinda Matto de Turner, and *María*, by Colombia's Jorge Isaac. The particular dynamics of conflict and assimilation varied in each, but the elements of the romantic forging of the nation remained consistent.

By the late nineteenth century, new trends had emerged, challenging romantic nationalism. Naturalist novels, such as the Brazilian author Aluísio Azevedo's 1890 *O Cortiço* (*The Slum*), suggested that characters were destined to absorb the characteristics of their social environment, succumbing to the brutality that surrounds them. In the novel, João Romão, an ambitious Portuguese immigrant to Rio de Janeiro, builds a tenement house, seeking to claw his way out of poverty and into society by extracting the hard-earned coins of his tenants. Over the course of the novel, Romão's unhealthy tenement seems to infect the characters, starting with Romão himself, condemning them to shiftless idleness or treachery. Naturalism allowed new criticism of national failings, and also opened a path for more subtle explorations of social reality.

Joaquim Maria Machado de Assis is widely considered Brazil's greatest novelist, largely for the novels he wrote at the very end of the nineteenth century and the start of the twentieth. In contrast to previous works of Latin American fiction, these novels sharply delineate social customs, only to surprise or trouble the reader with indications of the narrator's unreliability. The result is a literary hall of mirrors, where—despite the clarity and vividness of the detail—the reader cannot be certain whether the image is "real," or the trick of a skewed perspective. This was not merely literary showmanship, but an exploration of artifice in Brazilian society. Most of Machado de Assis's narrators are upper-class men who are ultimately incapable of discerning truth from fiction, in part because nearly everyone around them seeks to please and accommodate them.

Of humble origins, Machado de Assis himself was the grandson of slaves; his father was a house-painter and his mother a Portuguese immigrant. Like many authors of his generation, he deliberately sought to professionalize and distinguish literature as a career. In 1896, he founded, and served as the first president of, the Brazilian Academy of Letters, dedicated to recognizing and stimulating national literary culture. The creation of this august society required the kind of social gamesmanship probed with such subtlety in his novels. In Machado de Assis's case, however, it also constituted a remarkably strategic trajectory of social ascension.

This professionalization of literature distanced new authors of the twentieth century from the romantic novelist/politicians of the mid-nineteenth, placing them within the broader professionalization typical of the emerging middle class. New authors were propelled on to greater experimentalism and provocation in subsequent years.

José Enrique Rodó and Antipositivism

In a number of Latin American countries, the once pervasive doctrine of positivism (chapter 5) was met with skepticism and even considerable criticism toward the end of the age of progress and modernization. The Uruguayan author José Enrique Rodó best captured the antipositivist spirit in his famous essay "Ariel," which eulogized classical western European culture and its values and protested against the materialism at the heart of positivism. Rodó's popular work won him international renown at the age of twenty-nine. As a famous intellectual, he corresponded with writers throughout the world, including Latin America's most famous poet of the era, Nicaraguan modernist Rubén Darío.

Rodó structured his essay in the form of a venerable professor's final lecture. The professor shares the wisdom gained over a lifetime with his students, encouraging them to be optimistic, noble, and generous as they assumed their future responsibilities as the leaders of Latin American society. Rodó used the three principal characters (Ariel, Caliban, and Prospero) from William Shakespeare's play *The Tempest* metaphorically. As Prospero, the all-seeing magician whose books provided him with access to the world's knowledge, Rodó dispensed his insights about the proper path that the new generation of Latin American political leaders should follow.

Rodó's essay cast the United States as Caliban, the ugly, vulgar half-man, half-beast, who embarks on a misguided adventure to overthrow Prospero's powers and seduce his innocent daughter. But like Caliban, the United States is not entirely evil, but rather is misguided and ignorant of what is important in life. Rodó conceded that North American civilization had contributed much to the world: its modern ideal of political liberty; its optimism, energy, and celebration of hard work; and its technological innovations. At the same time, Rodó criticized US utilitarianism and its broadly based democracy, which, in his opinion, led to mediocrity. Most importantly, he rejected US emphasis on materialism, which he believed to be totally inconsistent with Latin American values. Writing in 1901, Rodó decried the fact that North American ideas "are making impressive inroads in the minds of our leaders and also in the impressionable minds of the masses."

Instead, he urged, Latin Americans should resist the temptation to imitate the materialism of the United States. A society such as that of the United States, Rodó argued, left no enduring legacy. Instead, he encouraged Latin Americans to celebrate their creative aesthetic impulses, which would remain vibrant long after glittering modern cities turned to dust. Rodó believed that Latin Americans should pursue their traditional alliance with classical culture as personified by Ariel, the spirit that performed Prospero's bidding in humiliating Caliban and as a reward was granted freedom. For Rodó, Ariel represented everything affirmative about Western culture; spirituality, beauty, nobility and inspiration. Rodó's message was that Latin America needed to turn its back on the positivists and their crass materialism and realign itself with its traditional values.

Indigenous People and Liberal Rule, 1880s–1920s

Clearly, not all Latin Americans shared equally in the benefits of the age of progress and modernization. The vast majority of the rural poor, predominantly indigenous people or the descendants of enslaved Africans, experienced a decline in their standards of living as well as an erosion of their cultural traditions. While liberals believed that the free working of the marketplace would generate sufficient wealth to benefit everybody, in general those who had access to power and privilege enjoyed much better prospects than those who did not. To share the benefits of modernity with indigenous people, liberals sought to uplift the latter by educating them about the benefits of European ways and by eradicating their customs and traditions. Campesinos (rural people) resisted these efforts with varying degrees of success.

Indigenous People in Mexico

Porfirio Díaz's lengthy dictatorship promoting liberal positivist progress and development in rural areas (chapter 5) significantly altered the lifestyles and standard of living of many of Mexico's indigenous citizens, who were concentrated primarily in the southern portion of the country. Where export agriculture predominated, hacendados jockeyed with indigenous folk for control of land, water, and labor. Given the regime's proclivity to favor wealth creation over subsistence agriculture, hacendados generally won this battle. The controversies over land, water, labor, and

Indigenous People and Liberal Rule, 1880–1920

YUCATÁN
After 1900, the establishment of vast henequen plantations by the "Divine Caste" turns the local workforce into debt peons.

MORELOS
By 1910, large plantation owners possess half of the land in Morelos and increasingly exert control over the campesinos.

OAXACA
In response to a property tax imposed by the state in 1896, campesinos riot. The tax is repealed.

PERU
Increasingly exploited by *gamonales*, in 1915 campesino anger erupts into a small-scale rebellion. In the 1920s campesinos form protest groups that make demands directly to the Peruvian government.

BOLIVIA
Beginning in the 1880s, communal lands are increasingly seized by elites seeking additional land for cultivation. Aymara leaders plead in vain that they are not "savages," but their arguments fail to stop the seizures.

BAHIA
In Canudos, close to 30,000 followers of the renegade preacher Antônio Conselheiro are wiped out after a siege by military forces in 1897.

≡ **MAP. 7.2**

culture differed radically from state to state. Three examples should suffice to understand the conditions facing indigenous Mexican campesinos during the Porfiriato.

The best-known example of the fate of indigenous people in Mexico under Porfirian rule occurred in the southeastern state of Morelos (named for the hero of independence José María Morelos), famous since colonial times as a sugar-producing region. Modern technology dramatically altered the relationship between plantation owners and the Nahuatl-speaking indigenous villagers. A newly invented milling machine enabled owners to more than double the quantity of juice squeezed from a single stalk of cane, which in turn greatly increased the quantity of sugar available to satisfy the demands of the domestic market. Constructing a railroad that reduced the cost of transportation from the sugar producing regions around Cuautla to the rest of Mexico made Morelos's sugar competitive with that produced in the Caribbean. By 1910, Morelos had become the world's third most productive sugar region (after Hawaii and Puerto Rico). The planters' prosperity, however, came at the expense of the campesinos.

Because sugar became so profitable in the 1880s, planters not only purchased the state's public lands but also began to encroach on village communal property. Although villagers fought the planters in court, judges friendly to the planters dismissed such suits, consistently finding in favor of the planters. By 1910, large plantation owners possessed half of the land in Morelos, including the vast majority of the most fertile land. Political appointees quelled any further complaints, sending dissidents to labor camps or drafting them into the military. Hacendados also blocked villagers' access to water by acquiring all the land surrounding communities, making them virtual prisoners of the plantation. Without access to land or water, many campesinos had no choice but to take up residence on plantations as laborers, precisely the result planters wanted. Communities like Anenecuilco, the home of Emiliano Zapata, felt the futility of their protests and by 1910 elected new, youthful leaders to lead their struggle to regain village lands.

Further south, the many ethnicities that constituted the indigenous people of Oaxaca enjoyed greater success in protecting their land and water rights, but struggled to retain their cultural identities in the face of the liberals' onslaught to "uplift" the nation's poorest citizens. Because commercial agriculture mattered less in Oaxaca than in Morelos, 85 percent of the indigenous population continued to live in free villages or possessed small farms (called *ranchos*) in 1910.

Nevertheless, the state's modernizing liberal elite made a determined effort to change indigenous culture. First, the state government proposed creating rural schools to teach indigenous people Spanish and better acculturate them, although the government never had sufficient funds to build such schools or employ many teachers. More dramatically, the liberals wanted to modify indigenous behavior by forcing campesinos to participate actively in the capitalist economy. Thus, in 1896 the state passed a law imposing real estate taxes on properties worth less than 100 pesos, properties belonging to the poorest campesinos, which up to this point had been exempt from taxation.

In response, campesinos in a number of villages rioted, burning down town halls, destroying municipal records, and even beheading officials and gente decente. The homespun cotton breeches of the campesinos, contrasting with the tailored trousers of the gente decente, symbolized a larger class divide. "Death to all those who wear trousers!" became a rebel slogan. The state governor responded by sending in the army, but then revoked the hated tax to prevent further unrest.

Like their counterparts in Morelos and Oaxaca, many of the Maya of Yucatán suffered grievous exploitation because of the liberals' dogma of progress and modernization, especially after 1900. North American farmers coveted strong binder-twine for baling crops. They found the ideal solution in the rope processed from the fibrous leaves of the henequen variety of the agave cactus grown in Yucatán. The transformation of Yucatán's environment began with the new Porfirian legislation that permitted the future plantation owners, collectively referred to as the "Divine Caste," to claim both state-owned lands and the lands of the indigenous ejidos that lacked clear titles. Soon row after orderly row of henequen swallowed up much of the Maya villages' land, providing another dramatic example of the age of modernization's ability to conquer nature's extreme environments, in this case the desert.

The plantation owners adopted new technology, the steam-driven rasping machine, which removed the fiber from the henequen plant much more efficiently than when workers had previously had to comb the fiber by hand. To power this equipment, as well as the railroads that transported the henequen to port, required large quantities of wood. In addition, the plantations needed wood to construct housing for their laborers. The plantation owners used their cozy relationship with influential government officials to allow them to cut and gather wood from the nearby public lands, eventually deforesting hundreds of thousands of acres. Although a number of far-sighted individuals, including the richest member of the Divine Caste, Governor Olegario Molina, attempted to slow the destruction, the rush for immediate profits blinded his colleagues to the long-term value of conservation. Despite Molina's cautionary words and because of the henequen monoculture, Yucatán could no longer supply sufficient food for its growing population, requiring the government to import additional corn from the United States to feed the workers on the plantations.

Without any other means of survival, many Maya had no choice but to seek employment as workers on the henequen plantations, where they rapidly became debt peons because they had to make all their purchases at the *tienda de raya* (company store). Many haciendas issued pay in "script," a coinage that they produced themselves and which could only be spent on the hacienda itself. Needed year round to

COMMODITIES AND ECONOMICS

Brazil's Cacao Boom and Bust, 1870s–1930s

Sometimes new connections to global trade accelerate social transitions, while at other times these connections do the opposite, reinforcing social structures already in place, at least temporarily. The southern part of the state of Bahia, Brazil, during the cacao boom of the late nineteenth and early twentieth centuries was an example of the latter. The struggle to control the most fertile cacao lands reinforced the power of the "colonels," not actual military officers, but local strongmen capable of mobilizing armed loyalists. Brazil's prominence in the global cacao market intensified land wars between rival colonels, reinforcing hierarchy and social control in early twentieth-century Bahia.

French and German immigrants began cultivating cacao in southern Bahia in the mid-nineteenth century, but cacao export did not become highly lucrative until later in the nineteenth century, with the transplant of more robust varietals from Brazil's Amazonian region. In a growth curve that echoed that of coffee earlier in the century, Brazilian production helped fuel global demand, as chocolate went from luxury item to everyday treat for industrial workers.

Roads and infrastructure in the region remained poor, concentrating cultivation between the port of Ilhéus and Itabuna, thirty kilometers upriver. Laws intended to prevent accumulation of unproductive estates limited the size of new property claims and set differing prices for tracts suitable for cacao production and those only adequate for less lucrative purposes. But this merely intensified the land wars, as colonels pressured dependents to file claims, bribed local officials to register fertile land as unproductive, and hired *jagunços*, or armed men, to defend their stakes and harass rivals.

Conflict became particularly bloody in 1917–1918. Chocolate was often included in the rations of World War I soldiers, driving up consumption and prices. The global epidemic of the Spanish flu hit southern Bahia hard in 1918, killing off both cacao workers and some powerful colonels alike, disrupting local clans. And the injection of foreign capital into the local cacao trade raised the stakes for controlling land and men. Two rival clans battled over the most fertile tracts, resulting in hundreds of casualties.

The novelist Jorge Amado, himself the son of an Itabuna cacao-planting family, captured this period in his early works, particularly *The Violent Land* (1943), set during the 1917–1918 conflicts. Amado's portrayed the colonels as both barbarous and heroic, with their own skewed sense of ethics and propriety. The book deeply shaped broader perceptions of the region, to the point where it is difficult to unravel Amado's version from the deeper history.

Cacao in southern Bahia declined slowly at first, and then all at once. West African cultivation surpassed that of Bahia in quantity and efficiency, and Ilhéus went from boomtown to backwater. Then in 1989 the infamous witches' broom fungus spread in the Bahian cacao zone, destroying local cultivation. Only in the twenty-first century has Bahia begun to export cacao in volume again, albeit still at levels far lower than a century before.

- When do new connections to global trade spur modernization? When do they reinforce existing structure?

tend, harvest, and process the henequen, workers could never accumulate sufficient wages to pay off their obligations to the store and end their perpetual servitude.

Foreign journalists, most notably the American "muckraker" (a term for investigative journalists in the early twentieth century) John Kenneth Turner, exposed the abysmal conditions on Yucatán's plantations. Posing as a potential investor, he interviewed planters who confessed that indigenous Yaquis, imported to Yucatán from the northern state of Sonora, and other workers were virtual slaves and subjected to corporal punishment if they attempted to resist. In addition to employing the mechanism of debt peonage, planters ensured themselves of a permanent labor supply by providing healthcare, firewood, and guarantees of security and by arranging marriages between their workers. Many proud Maya resisted the routinization of plantation life, subverting its regimes through small, symbolic acts of resistance. Plantation owners punished these workers with whippings, giving rise to the paternalistic planters' phrase, "the Indian only hears with his buttocks." In some cases, plantation owners resorted to extreme corporal punishment, including cutting off a worker's ear, in order to, as planters' phrased it, castigate malingering or disobedient Maya laborers.

But Maya ears were not the only ones in play at this point. As liberal positivists gained Porfirio Díaz's ear during the last two decades of his administration, indigenous people consistently found themselves worse off than they had been a generation previously. Liberal policies treated land as a commodity, which led to two broad trends during the Porfiriato. First, all over the republic land was transferred from thousands of smallholders and communal holders to haciendas. Second, as a consequence of the emphasis on commercial agriculture, the real wages of rural workers declined. As result, Mexico for the first time in its history needed to import corn and other basic foodstuffs. Crushing village autonomy, pushing individuals off their **milpas** (small subsistance plots), reducing the status and autonomy of indigenous communities, and challenging the very existence of indigenous cultural traditions all tended to make the Porfirian regime seem both tone-deaf and illegitimate to rural peoples by 1910.

Guatemala

The wave of positivism and social Darwinism that spread across Latin America during the final third of the nineteenth century touched even the smaller countries. Although these two terms were rarely used explicitly in Guatemala, the ideas behind them deeply influenced the liberal government that returned to that nation in 1871 with a military rebellion that brought Justo Rufino Barrios to power. Becoming president in 1873, Barrios instituted what is known as Guatemala's Reforma.

This long run of liberal government and modernization ended with the expulsion of Guatemala's longest-serving president, Manuel Estrada Cabrera (1898–1920). Like Mexico, by the end of the nineteenth century positivist liberalism Guatemala brought increased foreign investment, improved infrastructure, the modernization of the capital and regional cities, and the integration of Guatemala into the global capital system. Much of this "progress" took place on the backs of poor campesinos and, particularly, the indigenous population, whom social Darwinists thought of as atavistic and valuable to the modern nation only as a source of cheap labor.

Barrios set his Reforma into action with modernity and liberal state-formation in mind. He continued the liberal practice of severely limiting the power of the Catholic Church; he oversaw the creation of a new Constitution in 1879, and his government established a system of public schools. José María Reyna Barrios, who continued his uncle's policies when elected president in 1892, ordered the composition of a *himno nacional* (national anthem) to help build people's allegiance to the reformed nation. With a positivist's concern for "order," Justo Rufino Barrios established a national police force and founded the country's first *escuela politécnico* (military academy) to train and professionalize a new national army.

As for the other mandate of positivism, "progress," Barrios set into place a project to clean up and modernize Guatemala City. Barrios and his successors aspired to model Guatemala City after Paris, complete with wide and orderly boulevards, elegant architecture, and cosmopolitan entertainments and novelties for a modern, urbane population. Manuel Estrada Cabrera, in particular, embraced the vogue of sophistication, even going so far as to try to establish a "cult of Minerva," the goddess of wisdom and the arts, in Guatemala. He initiated "feasts of Minerva" to celebrate accomplishments of students and teachers, and ordered that Hellenic-style "Minervan Temples" be built in large and small municipalities around the country.

Under the positivist liberal presidencies, "progress" took a tangible, material form. Justo Rufino Barrios, for example, introduced the first telegraph and railroads into Guatemala. His dream of a single railroad line that would link the remote indigenous highland and Guatemala's second city, Quetzaltenango, ultimately failed due to lack of money, but the tune "Ferrocarril de los Altos (Highland Railroad)" which commemorates this line, still remains one of the most popular songs in the repertoire of the Guatemalan marimba. Transportation and communications networks all dramatically expanded when Estrada Cabrera allowed United Fruit Company into Guatemala. As it did elsewhere in Central America, UFCo established large-scale fruit plantations on the Atlantic Coast, dredged out modern and efficient ports, and expanded railroad lines that linked the coast to the capital city.

By the positivist metric of "order and progress," Guatemala's liberal regimes between 1871 and 1920 were in many ways successful, but the social costs of these reforms were extraordinarily high. For indigenous campesinos, the continued expansion of coffee and other industrial agriculture came at the expense of

SOCIAL UPHEAVAL

Sex Workers and the Banana Plantations

In the early decades of the United Fruit Company's expansion in Central America, the majority of its workers came from the Caribbean, especially English-speaking islands such as Jamaica and St. Vincent. Most of the immigrants to the UFCo plantations were young men who, lured by the relatively high wages the plantations paid, came to Costa Rica and elsewhere in Central America with the plan to either work for a time and return home or to remain permanently. While some left families behind on the islands, many were single men. Large numbers of these immigrant banana workers eventually sought out paid female sexual companionship, and soon prostitution became rampant on the periphery of the banana plantations. In 1925, UFCo's Panama division slyly noted that "frequently there are small villages adjacent and many of the employees are drawn to places of amusement there."

In Guatemala and Costa Rica, prostitution was legal and sex workers in the cities were subject to regular (often invasive) health inspections and certifications. The same was not true of prostitutes in the banana enclaves, which were located far from the cities and were, in some sense, a world unto themselves. In his novel *Mamita Yunai* (1940), the Costa Rican writer and fierce social commentator Carlos Luis Fallas described the deplorable conditions under which these women worked, exhaustively serving men one after another in rudimentary shacks made of leaves and sticks. Many of these women were themselves immigrants from the Caribbean, also drawn to Central America by the promise of money from the banana industry, although local *ladinas*, too, coul[d] end up as prostitutes.

Because banana workers made more money tha[n] did workers in other industries, sex workers from th[e] Central Valley of Costa Rica would travel to Limón t[o] work around payday, where they earned nearly twic[e] as much as they did in the capital. Although UFCo di[d] not recruit sex workers directly, the company willingl[y] turned a blind eye to the practice, viewing prostitu[-]tion as a cost-free means of maintaining a docile labo[r] force. The US consul in Limón, Costa Rica (the prov[-]ince on the Atlantic Coast where the majority of th[e] fruit plantations were located) noted in a report t[o] his supervisors in 1925 that "Gross sexual immoralit[y] among the negroes and the lower class of 'Natives' is the rule, and the presence of loose women on th[e] farms is said to tend toward holding the laborers o[n] the farms and keeps them more contented."

Prostitution was not really cost-free, of course[.] Syphilis and other venereal diseases became wide[-]spread, and, although UFCo's medical facilities wer[e] among the best in Central America, the company wa[s] much more concerned with addressing health prob[-]lems that affected the industry's short-term profit[s] (such as malaria) than in dealing with syphilis, whic[h] could take years to show up in a worker. The healt[h] of female sex workers was even more precarious, a[s] their lives could easily be cut short by venereal dis[-]ease, botched abortions, or the miserable condition[s] under which they worked.

- How would sex work or other types of informal com[-]merce fit into the larger story of commodity chains[?] If sex work was considered illegal and immoral, wh[y] did UFCo turn a blind eye to its practice?

communally held lands, a strategy that accomplished the dual intent of converting indigenous lands into "productive" use and forcing indigenous people into the wage-based economies on the *fincas* (coffee farms). To assure that this happened, the Justo Rufino Barrios administration implemented a program called "*mandamiento*," (from the Spanish word, *mandar*: to order), a forced labor program whereby each town was obliged to provide a given number of indigenous workers for private agricultural labor and (less commonly) public works. Unlike neighboring El Salvador, where liberal government outlawed the holding of community property outright, Guatemala's leaders permitted native villages to retain a small amount of land so that people could minimally feed themselves, but not so much that they could remain isolated from the national project.

The mandamiento, as a coercive labor system, was designed to produce both economic and social results. Integration of Maya laborers into the capitalist economy was intended to introduce them to "civilized" and "modern" practices that would encourage them to abandon their traditional lifestyles, languages, religious practices, and culture. The result was not always as intended; in fact, the introduction of cash into indigenous community sometimes reinforced indigenous autonomy. For example, the *cofradias* (religious brotherhoods), which served to support community fiestas and identity, grew more influential when cash allowed for bigger and more extravagant fiestas, reinforcing local community and religious solidarity.

≡ **Workers on a Banana Plantation.** Because banana plantations were usually located in coastal areas with small indigenous populations, owners often had to import labor. In Central America, much of the workforce came from the Caribbean Islands, where workers already enjoyed some immunity to tropical diseases and also were accustomed to laboring under the boiling sun. Because plantations followed intensive agricultural practices, year-round workers had to make sure irrigation ditches were not clogged, weed unwanted growth around the banana plants, then harvest the fragile crop at the precise moment and transport it to a wharf for shipping. The photograph also depicts the social divide on a plantation, with the white overseer on the right and the four laborers of African descent on the left.

During the twenty-two-year regime of Manuel Estrada Cabrera, conditions for people in Guatemala, not only the rural indigenous, but lower- and even middle-class ladino and eventually even the planter class, worsened. A capricious and corrupt ruler, Estrada Cabrera expanded the power of the national police to include the repression of labor strikes and protests. He controlled elections and ruled largely by duplicity and graft. After an attempt on his life in 1907, he became more despotic and paranoid. He established a secret police force known informally as *"orejas"* (ears), terrorizing the rich and powerful as much as it did the poor and marginal. In 1920, the national assembly declared Estrada Cabrera mentally incompetent and removed him from office. His departure signaled the beginning of a brief period of relatively democratic government and social innovation in Guatemala. Estrada Cabrera's regime was notoriously immortalized in the novel, *El Señor Presidente* published in 1946 by Guatemala's Nobel Prize–winning author, Miguel Angel Asturias.

The Andean Republics

As was the case in Mexico and Guatemala, the indigenous people of the Andean region (especially in Ecuador, Peru, and Bolivia) experienced increased exploitation during the latter nineteenth and early twentieth centuries. Although Ecuador's Liberal Revolution of 1895 initially spent much of its time and energy passing anticlerical legislation, it eventually addressed the pressing problem of the nation's long-ignored indigenous peoples, some 40 percent of the population.

In addition to promoting progress and modernization, the increasingly active state attempted to reform the social and economic structure of the highland hacienda. By mandating public education for all Ecuadorians, Liberals hoped to incorporate indigenous people into the nation and eradicate indigenous language and culture. Without adequate funds to build rural schools, this effort failed. Likewise, Liberals addressed the problem of debt peonage—rural workers tied by law to haciendas because they owed money to the *patrón*. Nearly all of these people lived in the sierra. Liberals from the coast, representing the interests of investment bankers and cacao planters, sought to secure more labor for coastal cacao plantations by enticing workers from the sierra.

In 1918, statutes theoretically ended the permanent obligations of indebted tenants who traditionally owed their landlord four days of labor per week and full-time assignments during the planting and harvest seasons, while their wives and children provided free household service to the owner. The laws, however, were never enforced, because the landlords wielded so much political power locally. Only with the arrival of the military governments of the 1960s and 1970s would meaningful social change come to the highlands. Higher wages on the cacao plantations did induce a significant number of indigenous people to migrate to Guayaquil and its environs, but the lives of the rural poor in the highlands remained much the same until the 1960s and beyond.

The age of progress and modernization in Peru saw the growth of significant sugar plantations along the north coast and a wool export trade in southern highland Peru. Originally, north coast planters imported Chinese and Japanese laborers to work in the fields, but as these disillusioned workers fled to Lima or other cities to escape abuse, planters turned to the indigenous populations of the adjacent sierra for labor. There, land had become increasingly scarce as populations increased and haciendas expanded to satisfy the country's increased thirst for dairy products.

Local political bosses, called **gamonales** after the parasitic Andean plant that ultimately kills its host, plied impoverished campesinos with alcohol and promises of cash advances to lure them into signing contracts to labor on the hot, disease-ridden coastal plantations. Other individuals voluntarily migrated to the coast because these plantations paid much higher wages than those in the highlands. Conditions on sugar plantations varied; some resorted to debt peonage, while others took a more paternalistic approach by providing good housing, decent food, medical care, and a school for the workers' children in the hopes of creating a permanent labor force. Ultimately, paternalism failed, as highland indigenous laborers failed to reap sufficient rewards for their labor to justify remaining in the lowland plantations, resulting in a grinding cycle of labor migration.

In southern highland Peru in the wool-producing districts around Lake Titicaca, the indigenous population eventually had enough of the gamonales' land grabbing and exploitation. Initially, the army and police had suppressed hacienda strikes, which had become an increasingly common phenomenon throughout the Andean world. In 1915, the anger of the campesinos erupted into a small-scale rebellion, and they attacked both haciendas and their owners. During the 1920s campesinos formed protest groups that made demands directly to Peru's long-serving dictator, Augusto Leguía (1919–1930), who took indigenous complaints seriously. The government sent teachers and officials to the sierra, snatching power from the gamonales. Although indigenous people hated Leguía's reimposition of a labor draft (a system that had been used during the colonial period) to build roads, ultimately the roads allowed villages to develop weekly markets and gain economic independence from the gamonales.

The assault on collectively held land in Bolivia began when Conservative elite politicians passed the Disentailment Law of 1874, which divided indigenous

≡ **Rafael Reyes and Two Chilean Country Folk.** As part of his grand tour of the United States and Latin America, former Colombia president Rafael Reyes, a member of the elite and a positivist, spent time in Chile. This photograph captures his meeting with two Chilean cowboys and illustrates the contrasting life styles of the elite and poorer people. While President Reyes, like other members of the elite, is dressed in a European tailored suit, the cowboys wear the typical dress of the Chilean countryside. Yet many elite politicians like Reyes were also well known for their common touch, which he seems to exhibit here.

communal land into individual plots and allowed outsiders to buy the "unused" parcels that lay fallow for use in traditional rotational farming. In protest, Aymara community leaders filed lawsuits and lodged petitions with government officials. During the 1880s, however, the surveying continued, especially in the region around La Paz, where elites sought additional lands for cultivation. Led by Pablo Zárate Willke, the Aymara supported the Liberal Party's successful rebellion against Conservative rule in 1899, but to no avail. After their victory, the Liberals distanced themselves from their former indigenous allies and continued the seizure of communal lands. Aymara leaders pleaded in vain that they were not "savages," as the Liberals now claimed, but instead were worthy Bolivian citizens as descendants of the noble Inka. Their argument failed to persuade. Elite leaders differentiated the contemporary Indian from his more "noble" ancestors as a means of justifying the racial discrimination so common during these times.

Rural Conflict in Brazil: Canudos

The most emblematic conflict of the Old Republic came in 1896–1897 at Canudos, a settlement of several thousand inhabitants in the drought-stricken interior of the northeastern state of Bahia. The residents were fervent followers of a renegade preacher who called himself Antônio Conselheiro, a name that suggested his ambition to serve as *conselheiro*, or counselor, for his faithful. (His actual name was Antônio Vicente Mendes Maciel.) Why the highest powers of the Brazilian Republic felt it necessary to reduce Conselheiro's peaceful settlement to rubble and ashes with maximum prejudice against its inhabitants reveals much about the contradictions of that republic.

Conselheiro was a failed merchant in the 1870s when he heard the call to wander through the northeastern backlands building and repairing chapels, many of which had been abandoned as the rural population shrank. Along the way, he preached with charisma but without formal religious training; he also declared the imminent return of the legendary King Sebastian of Portugal, an event thought to signal the beginning of a period of justice and plenty. Conselheiro offered a message of redemption and renewal along with an austere and aesthetic lifestyle. He attracted a following of impoverished believers, who found in him both prophet and messiah.

Conselheiro's behavior fit into a common pattern in the northeastern interior (as well as other parts of Latin America), where ordained priests were scarce and itinerant preachers took their place, often combining Catholicism with apocalyptic mysticism in their sermons. The Catholic Church tolerated these preachers as long as their following remained small. When they challenged the Church or began to attract a larger following, the Church typically reprimanded them, even excommunicating them if they failed to reform.

Such was Conselheiro's fate in 1882, after he had become openly critical of a Church hierarchy he considered corrupt. By then, Conselheiro's flock—made up largely of former slaves, landless farmers and reformed criminals—had grown large enough to provoke the suspicions of landowners and government officials, who inherently distrusted any large gathering of the poor. But it was not until the declaration of the Republic and its attempt to assert authority in the dusty outback that Conselheiro became an outlaw and a wanted man. He condemned the Republic as an abomination and called for a restoration of monarchy. And he admonished his followers not to pay taxes, including the fee necessary to register a marriage with local government. He advocated instead "free love," apparently meaning by that not promiscuity but rather voluntary, private union, free of institutional intrusion. His detractors nonetheless perceived it as a threat to Church, state, and family.

Conselheiro and his followers first clashed openly with police in 1893, and thereafter resolved to find a remote place for a permanent settlement to avoid the harassment of the authorities. Conselheiro led them to a site he called Belo Monte (beautiful mountain), near the village of Canudos. Here, his flock multiplied, welcoming former slaves, the landless poor, and former backwoods bandits, who used their experience to defend Belo Monte. During its brief existence, Belo Monte (which the Brazilian media and history have more commonly referred to as "Canudos") became a self-sustaining, communitarian settlement.

The state government of Bahia, alarmed about the rumors of Belo Monte's growing population, sent an expedition to arrest Conselheiro in October of 1896. Before the soldiers reached Belo Monte, Conselheiro's followers routed them, forcing them to retreat. A second expedition, sent by the federal government, proved equally futile. Conselheiro's followers had established staunch defenses, and knew the terrain intimately. The Republic sent a third expedition, led by its most illustrious commander. Again, Belo Monte withstood the attacks. The military struggle laid bare a deep conflict between Belo Monte's hard-bitten residents and the disdainful officers, a conflict that could only end one way. A fourth expedition, boasting German-made artillery and thousands of soldiers, laid siege to Belo Monte. Most of Belo Monte's residents—including Conselheiro himself—died either from the shelling or from the starvation brought on by siege. Of the thousands of residents who had lived in Belo Monte, only a few hundred survivors remained when the Army finally took control of the settlement in October of 1897.

The journalist Euclides da Cunha accompanied the siege, and published a pioneering account of Belo Monte and its destruction. Da Cunha's *Os Sertões* (*The Backlands*) became one of the classics of Latin American letters. It reveals da Cunha's own evolution from disdain for the residents of Canudos to reluctant admiration. More deeply, the book suggests that, in its zeal to destroy Belo Monte, the Republic revealed its own tragic flaw—an inability to truly incorporate or even recognize the humanity of the poor.

Canudos was a singular epic, but at the same time one that fit into broader patterns throughout the region. In places like northern Mexico and the remote Andes, as well, radical religious mobilization emerged to threaten local hierarchy in the late nineteenth and early twentieth centuries. Where religious fervor was strong but the institutional Church was weak, where the claims of the state were grandiose but its ability to deliver services was minimal, the conditions were ripe for popular religious mobilization.

The Mexican Revolution: The Decade of Violence, 1910–1920

Before 1930, cracks in the success story of the age of progress and modernization developed in several Latin American nations, none more dramatically than in Mexico. Mexico's decade of violence between 1910 and 1920 raised a critical question: Did the Latin American states need to reject the entirety of the achievements of the age of progress and modernization, or could some of these achievements be preserved and reformed? The emergent Mexican state would provide the prototype for one of the options available to other Latin American nations in the decades following the Great Depression.

The Failed Transition from the Porfiriato

For many observers, Porfirian Mexico, at least superficially, exemplified the most stunning success in the age of progress; no other nation modernized so rapidly from such an inauspicious postindependence history as had Mexico. Those who had benefited from Díaz's policies (elites, foreign investors, and much of the expanding middle class) wanted to preserve those benefits beyond the dictator's lifetime. As Díaz aged (he turned 80 in 1910), Porfirian supporters worried about the future of their nation. Both influential Mexicans and foreigners hoped to persuade Díaz to retire in 1910 and act as the wise elder statesman by presiding over free elections, the crowning achievement for the person who had brought peace and prosperity to the once troubled nation.

To this end, US President Theodore Roosevelt and Secretary of State Elihu Root attempted to flatter Díaz by arranging for famed war correspondent James Creelman to write up a very complimentary farewell interview with Diaz. Creelman's 1908 article, which appeared in the American periodical *Pearson's Magazine*, highlighted Díaz's statement that because Mexico had matured sufficiently and was now ready for democracy, he would not run for reelection in 1910. Quickly, however, Díaz reneged on this promise. As he did not specify his choice for a vice-presidential running mate, a flurry of political activity unseen for decades resulted.

Díaz's silence about the vice presidency tempted ambitious individuals to offer themselves as potential running mates and provided a political opening. After a general with broad middle-class support stepped aside out of loyalty to the dictator, the vice-presidential field narrowed to the wealthy, courageous, but somewhat quirky hacendado Francisco I. Madero, who believed that the prediction of a Ouija board destined him to become president of Mexico. Madero immediately recruited a number of the general's civilian followers into his campaign. He penned a book titled *The Presidential Succession in 1910*, in which he argued for the importance of democracy and fair elections. Madero campaigned throughout the country, greeted everywhere by enthusiastic crowds, especially in the north. When the Anti-Reelection Party met in April 1910, it chose Madero as its standard bearer, even as he quietly negotiated with Díaz for a ticket on which he would serve as the latter's vice president. But Díaz refused to compromise, instead insisting that his unpopular sitting vice president be nominated on the Reelection Party ticket.

Against all odds Madero decided to fight back, seeking through armed force that which had been denied to him at the ballot box. For months beginning in November 1910, the outcome of battles provided leverage in the ongoing negotiations between Díaz and Madero. Although initially Madero's followers (the *maderistas*) suffered defeat after defeat, a revolutionary spark burned in the northern state of Chihuahua. Relatively few of the civilian politicians who had campaigned for Madero during the political fray actually took up arms. Instead, it was poor villagers, the rural campesinos, who aspired to regain land lost to greedy hacendados, who bore the brunt of the fighting against Díaz's army. While the rural maderistas could not win pitched battles, they weakened the administration with their raids against military outposts. These raids damaged federal prestige and demoralized the drafted soldiers fighting for the aged dictator.

Ultimately, Díaz's regime would collapse not because of a decisive military defeat but as a result of prolonged negotiations that intensified after the maderistas started winning battles in March 1911. Although most of the fighting took place in northern Mexico, a villager from the southeastern state of Morelos, Emiliano Zapata, soon personified campesinos' discontent with the inequities of the Porfirian land policy and joined Madero because of his vague promise to make reforms. After the battle of Ciudad Juárez in May 1911, Díaz capitulated and resigned, leaving a coalition of progressive Porfirians and civilian maderistas in charge. Díaz's recently appointed progressive minister of foreign relations ascended to the interim presidency in accordance with the Constitution of 1857. Because of the necessity for Madero and his civilian colleagues to resort to violence to secure political change which in turn had enlisted tens of thousands of other Mexicans with a more radical agenda into the revolutionary coalition, they and the moderate Porfirian reformers faced a daunting challenge as they assumed office in 1911.

From Reform to Revolution

Between 1911 and 1913, the civilian *maderistas* and progressive Porfirians attempted to direct the Mexican Revolution along a moderate reformist path that would also preserve the Porfiriato's positive achievements. Participants in this coalition agreed on several issues. They willingly offered concessions to urban workers, probably because most labor leaders focused on bread-and-butter issues rather than on ideological confrontations. The government regularly sided with workers who picketed peacefully for higher wages and better working conditions in traditional hotbeds of labor unrest, like the Orizaba textile mills. By way of contrast, workers who rioted and destroyed property faced police repression. Following European models, the regime created a Department of Labor to mediate disputes between workers and employers and also drafted Mexico's first workers' compensation statute and child labor laws.

In a similar vein, the government created the National Agrarian Commission to adjudicate village petitions for restitution of lands seized by hacendados during the Porfiriato. The Commission also began to devise a broader policy for the ultimate division of some estates. But the slow pace of the Commission hardly satisfied the demands of rural maderistas like Emiliano Zapata, who wanted the immediate restitution of village lands illegally seized without bothersome paperwork. The moderates, however, refused to tolerate extralegal invasions of estates by the rural poor, who tore down fences to plant their corn, beans, and squash and graze their cattle. Instead, the government encouraged governors to use the state militias to protect haciendas from rural invaders.

Moderates also hoped to reform society by expanding educational opportunities in order to bring indigenous people more fully into national life and to reform the behavior of the poor by passing legislation prohibiting drinking, gambling, and prostitution, reforms that were not well received by the intended beneficiaries. Moderates agreed that Mexico deserved democracy. Madero's slogan, "**Sufragio efectivo y no re-elección**" (literally "Effective Suffrage and No Re-Election," which people understood to mean "Count the Votes Fairly and End Boss Rule"), resonated not only with the elite and middle class, but also with villagers, particularly in the sierra, who were tired of Mexico City outsiders telling them what to do.

Despite broad agreement on policy, the governing coalition disintegrated. Although foreign journalists hailed the democratic elections of 1911 as the fairest since independence, to cynics and Porfirian progressives the results seemed skewed. Not only did Madero win the presidency with 95 percent of the vote, but his party's candidates won all of the gubernatorial elections. The opposition likewise could not fathom Madero's inability to restrain his rural followers and restore order. In the months after the civil war officially ended, many of the rural revolutionaries refused to demobilize or hand over their weapons. They preferred to remain on the army payroll, where they earned higher salaries, than they could as wage hands on haciendas. Zapata's forces, the most stubborn of all, were unwilling to lay down their arms until land redistribution took place. For the progressive Porfirians, the lack of order was sufficient cause to withdraw support from Madero.

For their part, civilian and rural maderistas also lost confidence in the president because he seemed too willing to compromise with the Porfirians. For many rural maderistas who had joined the revolution in order to regain their land, the pace of reform was agonizingly slow. When Madero seemed indifferent to their cause, several rural maderistas, and most importantly Emiliano Zapata, withdrew their allegiance from the regime. By early 1912, many of Madero's former supporters had had enough of him. Between the time of Madero's inauguration and the end of 1912, four other rebellions broke out and although the government defeated them all, it was clearly unpopular. In February, 1913, the final rebellion in Mexico City succeeded and placed General Victoriano Huerta in the presidency. Huerta deposed Madero and threw him in jail.

Perhaps it should not have been a surprise that an administrative neophyte like Madero, would fail, given the complexities of governance in the aftermath of the fall of Díaz. His assassination in February of 1913 was more shocking, and was one of the atrocities of the Huerta interregnum to provoke greater popular revolt. That uprising drove Huerta from office in July 1914. With all Porfirians now eliminated from office, would Mexicans be able to agree on a new course for Mexico?

Madero's death set new forces in motion, as the former maderistas broke into several factions, at war among themselves and with the old guard at the same time. A group calling themselves the Constitutionalists, led by northerners, sought to open the political system without extensive redistribution of wealth. The Constitutionalists, who were willing to tolerate limited land and urban worker reform in order to secure popular support, rejected massive expropriation of haciendas. In opposition to the Constitutionalists, Zapata and his followers insisted on the primacy of extensive land reform, and above all on the restoration and respect for commonly held village lands, timber, and water. Zapata allied temporarily with Francisco "Pancho" Villa, a quick-tempered one-time bandit who on one day could give a man an *abrazo* (bear hug) and the next order him to be shot. Villa, a northerner like the Constitutionalists, also favored redistribution of wealth, but not necessarily through restoration of communitarian village lands. He soon found himself locked in pitched battle with his erstwhile allies among the Constitutionalists.

The Constitutionalists' foremost general, Alvaro Obregón, turned the tide against Villa in April 1915. Having read the dispatches from the western front of World War I, Obregón adopted the tactics of trench warfare that were proving deadly on the battlefields of Europe. Holding a secure defensive position, Obregón's forces dug trenches, set up barbed wire barriers, and trained their machine guns on Villa's charging cavalry. Despite the bravery of the **villistas**, they proved no match for modern weaponry and modern tactics. General Obregón lost his arm in the struggle (it was shot off in the heat of battle), but won the war. In commemoration, the severed arm was preserved in formaldehyde and displayed in a monument honoring Obregón in Mexico City.

The Constitutionalist forces in 1919 treacherously ambushed Emiliano Zapata, killing the man who had become the symbol for the agrarian revolution. Although at this point the struggle against the Constitutionalists was hopeless, for many participants, the Revolution seemed to have a momentum of its own. In 1920, the final successful military campaign of the decade of violence installed Alvaro Obregón in the presidency.

≡ **Zapatistas in Arms.** The most profound example of the growing discontent with the values and policies of the age of progress and modernization occurred in 1910, with the outbreak of the decade-long Mexican Revolution. During the Porfiriato, particularly in regions that produced marketable crops, hacendados had expanded their estates at the expense of the rural poor. Emiliano Zapata and his country folk, shown in this photograph, joined the Revolution in 1911 to regain the land taken from them by hacendados and remained in arms for the entire decade, using weapons to assert their demand for agrarian reform. Today, Mexicans revere Zapata as the greatest hero of the military phase of the Revolution.

Perhaps the most important legacy of the decade of violence, other than the Constitution of 1917 discussed below, was the persistent image of its most famous icon, Emiliano Zapata. Already synonymous with rural revolution, by the 1930s he had become the symbol for social reform in general. Ceremonies commemorating the anniversary of his death, once confined to Morelos, spread to the nation's capital. His legend, now part of the core curriculum taught to primary school students, also became the subject of art, music, and popular books. Stories circulated that he had not been killed, that he had outsmarted his would-be assassins, and that he could be seen riding his white horse in the hills, waiting to defend campesinos should the need arise.

The Revolution produced both tangible and intangible results. More than one million people died fighting in the Revolution, and their sacrifice altered Mexican society forever. No longer did the poor have to scurry off sidewalks when the elite passed, or walk with their faces pointed toward the earth in a gesture of subservience. The lessons of the Revolution imbued participants with new nationalistic pride. Many women, known as the **soldaderas**, participated as soldiers in the Revolution, transforming traditional gender roles. Finally, the Mexican Revolution occasioned the mass internal migration of soldiers, breaking down regional barriers. Soldiers saw the world beyond their villages. Once peace arrived, they would take advantage of this new awareness to move to urban areas and seek opportunities to change their lives for the better.

Women at War: The Soldadera

The Mexican Revolution swept millions of people, including women and children, from their homes and uprooted their daily lives. Female camp followers, mostly poor women, had participated in warfare at least as far back as the religious wars of the seventeenth century. During the Mexican Revolution, however, large numbers of soldaderas played much more significant roles than did traditional camp followers. Because railroads offered greater mobility to the revolutionary forces, soldaderas pitched camp in unfamiliar locations, scoured the countryside for food, and prepared meals. Women also did laundry, nursed the wounded, buried the dead, and cared for their children. Because of the presence of so many women among Emiliano Zapata's revolutionaries, one observer described his forces as a "people in arms."

To a much greater degree than women had during the wars for independence, the soldaderas took on male roles and openly participated in military activities. Soldaderas spied on the enemy and procured munitions in the United States for armies fighting near the border. Allegedly a woman could smuggle several hundred rounds of ammunition under her skirt across the open border into Mexico. Only in 1913 did the US Customs Service employ female agents to search and arrest potential female smugglers. As the Revolution intensified, women played even more active roles in combat; some women fought so well that male commanders bestowed them with military rank as officers. As the fighting continued during the revolutionary decade, more and more women left their homes to participate.

One such woman was Manuela (née Oaxaca) Quinn, the mother of Hollywood film legend Anthony (originally Antonio) Quinn, an Academy Award–winning movie star from the 1950s through the 1970s. At the age of fifteen she followed her boyfriend and future husband into Pancho Villa's ranks. Unlike other commanders, Villa forbade the soldaderas from joining their men in battle. Instead, he relegated them to domestic chores: foraging for food, cooking, and doing laundry. According to an interview Manuela Quinn gave later in life, at night Villa's soldaderas sewed torn uniforms and cleaned guns while the men relaxed around the campfire. When Quinn became pregnant, Villa sent her home. She joined many other Mexican refugees fleeing the country because of the violence, ending up in California, where her husband eventually joined her. Unlike her husband, who romanticized the goals and ideals of the Revolution, Quinn remembered only the hardships and suffering imposed by life at the front.

Because so many soldaderas participated in the fighting, they have become iconic figures in popular culture and literature. In the most famous novel about the Revolution, Mariano Azuela's 1915 *Los de abajo* (*The Underdogs*), two soldaderas have prominent roles: Camila, the kind, gentle spirit kidnapped from her village by the rebel commander, and La Pintada, a masculine-acting cavalry officer who leads troops, ransacks homes, and takes several lovers before killing Camila in a jealous rage. Azuela's female characters represent the broad spectrum of soldaderas' experiences.

Popular culture's version of the soldadera is personified in the *corrido* (folk ballad) "La Adelita," a positive portrayal of the experiences of soldaderas. The ballad has many versions, but in all of them Adelita is pretty, virtuous, kind, and loyal to her man. In some versions she displayed great bravery and died in battle, while in others she so embodied the revolutionary spirit that soldiers took courage in the face of huge odds and achieved heroic victories. Unfortunately, despite the prominence of women in many revolutionary armies, with a few exceptions the post-Revolutionary Mexican government largely ignored women's issues.

The Constitution of 1917

The Constitution of 1917 came to represent the most tangible result of the decade of violence. The delegates who met in the fall of 1916 were not rowdy gun-toting generals, but rather well-educated middle-class civilians with a few military men, workers, and farmers sprinkled into the mix. Because Pancho Villa and Emiliano Zapata still maintained powerful armies and broad popular followings but were excluded from the deliberations of the convention, the delegates hardly represented all of the common-man participants in the Revolution. Few citizens within the Constitutionalist-held territory bothered to vote for these delegates, and most observers expected that the constituent assembly would merely rubber-stamp the interim president's draft document (which bore a marked resemblance to the 1857 constitution). Despite these assumptions, the delegates soon demonstrated that they had a mind of their own by drafting a more radical constitution that in at least four articles articulated most of the precepts underlying the popular revolution.

Although the draft reiterated many ideas of nineteenth-century liberal political theory such as the separation of Church and State, the delegates offered important new ideas. First, the Constitution of 1917 strengthened the powers allocated to the national government, or what social scientists refer to as the "State." Under the four radical provisions of the new constitution, the State could use its powers proactively to benefit its constituents, especially the poor who had been disenfranchised during the Porfiriato. Because many Mexicans resented the resumption of clerical influence that had occurred during the Díaz years, Articles 3 and 130 severely restricted the secular power of the Church. In addition to making marriage a civil ceremony and allowing states to limit the number of clergy within their borders, the articles declared that all education would be free, mandatory, and public. Banning parochial schools, while impractical for the near future, at least demonstrated the delegates' interest in making certain that modern Mexico would become a truly secular state.

The articles concerning land, labor, and subsoil rights proved even more transformative. Article 123 took the ideals of the Department of Labor initiatives of 1911 and opened the possibility of fuller implementation with the added muscle of the strengthened national government. In addition to mandating the eight-hour workday, guaranteeing the right to strike, and abolishing debt peonage, Article 123 allowed states to establish a minimum wage. Because Mexico was still predominantly an agricultural society, Article 123 affected relatively few people in the short term,

TIMELINE

1880–1910
Hacendados control increasing amounts of land in Mexico

1900
Uruguayan José Enrique Rodó publishes antipositivist essay "Ariel"

1917
Mexico adopts new Constitution embracing social reforms

1900
Engineers complete Mexico City's Gran Canal, draining nearby lakes

1910
Mexican Revolution begins under Francisco I. Madero

1918–1919
University reform movement in Argentina

but would remain a foundation of Mexican labor relations. Article 27, in contrast, had immediate implications on a grand scale. Recognizing that the ownership of land had a social purpose as well as an economic one, Article 27 empowered the state to expropriate haciendas (with compensation to the owner) and redistribute property to the landless, a provision that spoke to Zapata's constituents. The article also restored to Mexico the ownership of its subsoil resources, putting foreign oil corporations in particular on notice that continued drilling operations depended on the approval of the Mexican government. These four articles would allow the Mexican state to move in new directions, especially during the 1930s. The Constitution of 1917 also foreshadowed new directions that other Latin American states might take after 1930.

Conclusion

Historians have debated whether the age of progress and modernization, which ended in 1929 with the onset of the Great Depression, benefited or harmed the people of Latin America. Certainly the wealth generated was distributed unevenly. Order—foreign investment, technology, and the export-led economy—enriched the elite as never before. Prosperity enabled governments to redesign their cities using European models and allowed the elite and middle class to consume the fashions, the fine arts, and the literature of the broader Western world. An emerging urban-based middle class, expanded in the Southern Cone nations by European immigrants, shared in the elite's prosperity and (regardless of their race and ethnicity) did their best to emulate the lifestyles of the rich and famous. Women slowly but successfully began to assert their professional and personal rights.

This chapter, however, has emphasized the misfortunes of those who did not benefit from the economic prosperity. As José Enrique Rodó predicted, the contradictions implicit in the materialistic, capital-driven elite strategy would leave many people behind. The system encouraging profitable export agriculture in Mexico,

1919
Rockefeller Yellow
Fever Commission
cleans up Guayaquil

1924
Middle class gains
employee rights in Peru

1918–1919
University reform
movement in Argentina

1920s
Protests against land concentration begin in Peru

Central America, Brazil, and the Andean nations required landlords to encroach on and ultimately expropriate the land of villagers and smallholders, trapping ever-increasing numbers of the rural poor as laborers on the modernizing estates. For the vast majority of indigenous people and those of African descent who migrated to the glittering cities, hard lives awaited them. Squalid, cramped housing, unsanitary conditions resulting from a lack of clean water and sewage in the slums, and a shortage of jobs for unskilled laborers made their lives extremely difficult.

Despite all their travails, the poor retained their popular culture. Occasionally, popular elements successfully asserted themselves against the elite, as the Mexican Revolution demonstrated. In Latin America people followed the events of the Mexican Revolution closely, some with consternation, others with eager anticipation. For elites it was a dark portent of the possibility of violent revolution, which could be triggered when a new challenge emerged. That challenge would be the global economic depression of 1929.

KEY TERMS

docencia libre	303	milpas	314	soldaderas	328
empleados	303	mulata	305	Sufragio efectivo y no re-elección	325
gamonales	319	obreros	303	villistas	327

Select Readings

Aguirre, Carlos. *The Criminals of Lima and their Worlds: The Prison Experience, 1850–1935*. Durham, NC: Duke University Press, 2005.

Amado, Jorge. *The Violent Land*. New York: Knopf, 1965.

Armus, Diego. *The Ailing City: Health, Tuberculosis, and Culture in Buenos Aires, 1870–1950*. Durham, NC: Duke University Press, 2011.

Beezley, William H. *Judas at the Jockey Club and Other Episodes of Porfirian Mexico*. Lincoln: University of Nebraska Press, 2004.

Beezley, William H., and Linda Curcio-Nagy, eds. *Latin American Popular Culture: An Introduction*. Wilmington, DE: Scholarly Resources, 2000.

Blum, Ann. *Domestic Economies: Family, Word, and Welfare in Mexico City, 1884–1943*. Lincoln: University of Nebraska Press, 2009.

Brunk, Samuel. *The Posthumous Career of Emiliano Zapata: Myth, Memory, and Mexico's Twentieth Century*. Austin: University of Texas Press, 2008.

Chassen-López, Francie. *From Liberal to Revolution: Oaxaca, the View from the South, 1867–1911*. University Park, PA: Penn State University Press, 2004.

Drake, Paul W. *The Money Doctor in the Andes: The Kemmerer Missions, 1923–1933*. Durham, NC: Duke University Press, 1989.

Evans, Sterling. *Bound in Twine: The History and Ecology if the Henequin-Wheat Complex for Mexico and the American and Canadian Plains, 1880–1950*. College Station: Texas A&M University Press, 2007.

Hart, John M. *Revolutionary Mexico: The Coming and Process of the Mexican Revolution*. Berkeley: University of California Press, 1987.

Henderson, Peter V. N. *In the Absence of Don Porfirio: Francisco León de la Barra and the Mexican Revolution*. Wilmington, DE: Scholarly Resources, 2000.

Jacobsen, Nils. *Mirages of Transition: The Peruvian Altiplano, 1780–1930*. Berkeley: University of California Press, 1993.

Knight, Alan. *The Mexican Revolution*. 2 vols. New York: Cambridge University Press, 1986.

Kuenzli, E. Gabrielle. *Acting Inca: Identity and National Belonging in Early Twentieth-Century Bolivia*. Pittsburgh, PA: University of Pittsburgh Press, 2013.

McCreery, David. *Rural Guatemala, 1740–1940*. Stanford, CA: Stanford University Press, 1994.

O'Connor, Erin. *Gender, Indian, Nation: The Contradictions of Making Ecuador, 1830–1925*. Tucson: University of Arizona Press, 2007.

Parker, D. S. *The Idea of the Middle Class: White Collar Workers and Peruvian Society, 1900–1950*. University Park, PA: Penn State University Press, 1998.

Pineo, Ronn F. *Social and Economic Reform in Ecuador: Life and Work in Guayaquil*. Gainesville: University of Florida Press, 1996.

Putnam, Lara. *The Company They Kept: Migrants and the Politics of Gender in Costa Rica, 1870–1960*. Chapel Hill: University of North Carolina Press, 2002.

Reeves, René. *Ladinos with Ladinos, Indians with Indians: Land, Labor, and Regional Ethnic Conflict in the Making of Guatemala*. Stanford, CA: Stanford University Press, 2006.

Schenker, Heath. *Melodramatic Landscapes: Urban Parks in the Nineteenth Century*. Charlottesville: University of Virginia Press, 2009.

Wells, Allen, and Gilbert M. Joseph. *Summer of Discontent, Seasons of Upheaval: Elite Politics and Rural Insurgency in Yucatán, 1876–1915*. Stanford, CA: Stanford University Press, 1996.

Womack, John, Jr. *Zapata and the Mexican Revolution*. New York: Knopf, 1968.

Woodward, James. *A Place in Politics: São Paulo, Brazil, from Seigneurial Republicanism to Regionalist Revolt*. Durham, NC: Duke University Press, 2009.

PART THREE

The Call for Change: Twentieth-Century Transformations, 1930–1980

Latin America's transformation between 1930 and 1980 was so dramatic that one could say that this fifty-year period entered on a horse-drawn cart and exited on a rocket. Latin American governments turned away from the export-led development of the preceding decades, opting for nationalist policies that sheltered domestic industry. Policy makers recognized that the transition from an agrarian to a more industrial economy required a more inclusive political system, one that would incorporate mixed-race, indigenous, and Afro-Latin American people. A new generation of Latin American leaders realized that they could never achieve modernity if they continued to exclude the majority of their own populations from substantive political and economic participation. Intellectuals and policy makers came to understand that women, indigenous people, and Afro-Latin Americans needed to be included as full citizens of the nation, not just on paper, but in practice.

Members of the working class, meanwhile, pushed for inclusion from below, demanding a greater share of the economic profits that they generated, and a voice in the political decisions that affected their lives. The path to these goals was never smooth, nor could progress along it be controlled entirely by Latin Americans themselves. International challenges such as the global Great Depression, World War II and the onset of the Cold War profoundly shaped the context for Latin American transformation in the mid twentieth century.

In chapter 8, we explore Latin America's changes between 1930 and 1950. Beginning in 1929, the Great Depression reduced income from exports, hampering the ability to purchase imported industrial goods. Export troubles, however, offered Latin America an opportunity to industrialize. Initially, countries confined their manufacturing enterprises to light industry, such as soaps, beer and textiles. Eventually, larger nations like Mexico, Brazil, and Argentina expanded their efforts to heavy industry and produced durable goods like appliances, automobiles and steel girders.

This policy, known as import substitution industrialization, or ISI, had broad popular appeal. ISI dominated Latin American economic thinking until the 1970s. Because the focus of Latin American economics shifted from export agriculture to industrial manufacturing, the role of organized labor intensified. Labor organizations began as independent entities but often became closely affiliated with government. In particular, labor became central to several of the populist movements, where charismatic authoritarian leaders like Juan Perón and Getúlio Vargas organized broadly based, political parties that advanced the interests of industrial workers. In small nations like El Salvador, however, authoritarian dictators headed off such popular movements with violence.

In chapter 9, we turn to issues of race, class, and gender during the same chronological period. The racist viewpoints of the age of progress and modernization finally fell into disfavor. In their place Latin American intellectuals conceived of more inclusive societies that celebrated the contributions of mestizos, indigenous people, and Afro-Latin Americans. Mexico and Brazil led the way. Beginning in the 1920s, Mexican intellectuals argued that the mixture of Spanish and indigenous peoples, or *mestizaje*, had created a *raza cósmica*, or cosmic race, with unique cultural strengths. At the same time Mexicans sought to preserve and celebrate the indigenous roots of this cosmic race. Andean countries, particularly Ecuador and Bolivia, adopted the interest in mestizaje, while Peru, once the home of the great Inka Empire, championed the preservation of indigenous antiquities. Brazilians promoted the idea that they had created a racially blended tropical society where the color of one's skin no longer determined social status. Later generations would eventually challenge all of these assertions, noting the persistence of racism. But from the 1930s through the 1950s Latin American writers, musicians, and artists celebrated the culture of those who in the nineteenth century had been on the margins. Women, too, benefited from these changes as they gained a series of legal rights, including the right to vote, throughout the Americas.

Chapter 10 turns its attention to the revolutionary changes that began in the 1950s. Armed revolutionaries sought to overturn economic and social hierarchies that lingered from the colonial period. The first leftist governments of this era (Costa Rica, Venezuela, and Bolivia) embraced the democratic reformist principles that had been manifest in the Mexican Revolution. In doing so, they carefully avoided provoking the United States, whose government was increasingly wary of any reform that might suggest socialist sympathies or the influence of the Soviet Union. The Guatemalan Revolution of 1944 –1954, in contrast, awakened the antipathy of the United States, bringing about the regime's downfall.

When the leaders of the Cuban Revolution of 1959 embraced Marxist principles, confiscated US property without compensation, and set off other revolutionary insurgencies throughout Latin America and Africa, they ignited the deepest fears of the United States. In the early 1960s, the United States backed a failed invasion by Cuban antirevolutionaries, pushing the Cuban regime into deeper reliance on Soviet military support. The USSR, and the United States ratcheted up tension through a series of retaliatory measures that brought the world to the brink of nuclear war.

Meanwhile, during the 1960s, young people in most Latin American nations, found inspiration in the anti-imperialist ideas and guerrilla tactics of revolutionary icon Ernesto "Che" Guevara, and sought to spread revolution. Cuban socialism in the 1960s seemed to offer many Latin Americans an inspiring new political template. In most cases, those inspired by Cuba believed that the entrenched powers in their own countries would yield only to violent overthrow. During the 1960s, armed Marxist movements (most of them small and supported by Cuba itself), sprang up across Latin America. Anticommunists responded with harsh repression, initiating a cycle of armed conflict and counterinsurgency. The Cold War came to Latin America. Not all efforts to follow the Cuban example involved armed insurgency, it should be noted: when Chile attempted an electoral path to socialism in the early 1970s, the Allende government fell afoul of US Cold War policies, provoking a right-wing coup with the full support of the American CIA.

Chapter 11 examines the anticommunist response to revolutionary mobilization, which brought military governments to power across most of the region. US Cold War policies supported both moderate elected governments and authoritarian regimes in Latin America after 1945, depending on the circumstances. But as the Cold War deepened, military rule came to the fore. Brutal dictatorships emerged in Central America, the Caribbean, and the Southern Cone, often characterized by horrific "dirty wars"—extrajudicial assassinations, kidnappings, and torture—to eliminate alleged subversives, and to terrorize the civilian population into submission. By 1970, two-thirds of all Latin American countries were governed by military rule.

The United States also established new entities such as the Alliance for Progress (to promote economic development) and the School of the Americas (to train military officers in counterinsurgency tactics), designed to keep communism at bay. These strategies, particularly when applied by iron-fisted military governments, proved both effective and ruthless. In the 1960s nearly every Latin American country had given birth to a home-grown Marxist movement; but by the late 1980s, as the Cold War ended, only Cuba and Nicaragua were ruled by socialist or communist governments. By the end of the era, although some progress had been made in securing political rights for all Latin Americans and the expanding economy had allowed some urban Latin Americans a more egalitarian share of newfound prosperity, what had begun as a period of optimism ended on a dark note.

8

The Great Depression and Authoritarian Populists, 1930–1950

Global Connections

The Great Depression of 1930, the most consequential economic disaster in modern history, transformed economic and political institutions across the globe, contributing to the collapse of many of the underlying principles of the age of progress and modernization in Latin America. The Great Depression's effects reverberated outward from New York and eventually engulfed the entire world. US stock prices fell 85 percent, while one-quarter of all banks in the country failed. The unemployment rate jumped from 3.2 percent in 1929 to almost 25 percent in 1933, as the average family's real income (spending power) fell by one-half. Industrial production and sales slowed, resulting in massive layoffs of workers, whose employers could no longer turn a profit. Farmers let crops rot in the fields and poured their cows' milk on the ground because prices were so low they could no longer justify sending food to urban markets.

Europe soon followed suit. Already hampered by aging technology, British manufacturing, long the country's economic base, never fully recovered from the effects of World War I. Defeated Germany was forced to pay restitution for damages caused during the conflict and as a result experienced high inflation and unemployment in the 1920s and early 1930s. The unemployed tramped from city to city. Nations like Turkey and India, which relied heavily on agricultural exports, witnessed massive rural dislocation and poverty as overseas markets declined sharply. Those least affected by the global downturn were subsistence farmers in places like Africa, Asia, and Latin America. There, the rhythm of life hardly changed (at least for a time), until the prices for key agricultural products such as coffee, bananas, and sugar dropped so low that they affected even the most remote rural farmers.

To solve the economic crisis, many nations across the globe adopted protectionist policies, raising tariff barriers to give preference to locally produced goods. Such trade policies often went hand-in-hand with governmental incentives for domestic industrial growth and cultural emphasis on defining and celebrating the nation. In the United States, President Franklin D. Roosevelt's New Deal sponsored widespread public works projects to raise employment, implemented new government programs such as Social Security, and levied a universal income tax to pay for it all. Some criticized this comprehensive government agenda to provide for the common good as a type of socialism, but the New Deal may well have salvaged the United States from economic and political disintegration.

Germany and Italy undertook a different kind of political centralization, in the context of murderous regimes. In Germany in 1933, social and economic discontent

≡ **Guatemalan Dictator Jorge Ubico and His Popular Followers.** Surprisingly, many of the Depression-era dictators enjoyed a great popular appeal. Guatemala's long-term dictator, Jorge Ubico (1931 to 1944), is depicted here surrounded by hundreds of his indigenous followers. Ubico offered Guatemalans relief from the Depression by way of an extensive public works program. He built thousands of miles of roads (mostly dirt) that connected once-isolated communities to Guatemala City. Public works projects, including building projects in towns and provincial cities as well as Guatemala City, were also done mostly by hand labor, providing employment for many of the country's poorest citizens. Also very charismatic, Ubico also once famously stuck his head in a lion's mouth to demonstrate his courage.

339

led to the election of Adolf Hitler as chancellor. Hitler promised to restore Germany to its former greatness through the persecution of those he deemed not truly German, most notoriously Germany's significant Jewish population. In Spain, the economic crisis was largely responsible for the shift from monarchy to republic in 1931, a transition so controversial that it soon led to the Spanish Civil War (1936–1939), followed by a long period of authoritarian rule under General Francisco Franco.

These centralizing, xenophobic dictators became known as "fascists," a term first associated with Italy's Benito Mussolini, and later with Hitler and Franco. Fascism combined authoritarian government, persecution of outsiders, insidious state propaganda, and economic protectionism into a poisonous blend. The fascist regimes turned to extreme violence to rid their nations of the perceived threats of liberalism, anarchism, Marxism, and atheism. This included, for example, the repression of regional languages and ethnicities in Spain as well as the Nazi regime's rapid conquest of much of Europe. Fascism reached its genocidal brutality in the Holocaust, in which Hitler's Nazi regime systematically exterminated 11 million people, including 6 million of Europe's Jews and around 5 million others, including gay people, Roma, and those with disabilities. Franco's regime in Spain was less notorious but also virulently repressive. In the first two years of the regime alone, the government identified and eliminated more than 200,000 Spaniards as "enemies of the State." Nearly half a million more fled the country as political refugees; not surprisingly, many of these took exile in the former Spanish colonies of Latin America.

The left wing of the political spectrum produced its own responses to the tumult of modernization, in the form of socialism and communism. The leaders of the 1917 Russian Revolution, most prominently Vladimir Ilyich Lenin, drew on the work of Karl Marx and Friedrich Engels to envision a communist system in which all property would be owned in common and distributed according to each person's needs and abilities. In this ideal form, government would be led not by kings, autocrats, or elected officials, but by the people themselves, as a benevolent "dictatorship of the proletariat."

Even the USSR's revolutionary leaders, however, realized that this would take considerable social and economic restructuring, and their new Soviet Union could not fulfill the promise of true communism immediately. First, it needed to pass through a stage of socialism, characterized by state control over resources and production, as well as increasing state presence in education and cultural life. Marxist-Leninism, as the Soviet system was called, also created a "vanguard party" to assume state power on behalf of the proletariat, and which ruled through what Lenin called "democratic centralism." While Lenin described this as "diversity in discussion, unity in action," in practice, it meant that the Soviet Communist Party controlled all aspects of political and economic decision-making.

Economic crisis intervened, strengthening this tendency towards concentration of power and facilitating the rise of Josef Stalin as general secretary of the Communist Party Central Committee. Stalin became the de facto dictator of an increasingly tyrannical Soviet Union. By 1930, he had transformed the Soviet Union into a totalitarian dictatorship, enforcing strict collectivization and repressing religious and cultural minorities. In the early 1930s, as he attempted to reorient the Soviet economy from agricultural to industrial production, Stalin set into motion a series of disastrous economic reforms that plunged much of the Soviet Union into a catastrophic famine that killed millions between 1932 and 1933. In an attempt to redirect blame, Stalin ordered the large-scale purge of the purported "enemies of the Soviet working class," including members of the Communist Party, government officials, peasants, and the Red Army leadership. These he eliminated by sending them into internal exile in forced labor camps or by execution without trial or other due process of law. Some historians estimate that as many as three million Soviet citizens died between 1936 and1938 during Stalin's "Great Purge." Like Hitler, Stalin pursued political consolidation through mass state murder.

Centralizing reformers also emerged elsewhere around the globe. In Turkey, for example, Mustafa Kemal, later known as Atatürk ("Father of Turks"), ruled as an authoritarian reformer and attempted to transform the remnants of the former Ottoman Empire into a secular, modernizing state based on rationalism and pragmatism. During his presidency from 1923 to 1938, Kemal established the contours of the modern, secular Turkish state. He replaced Muslim law and customs with a Western legal code, adopted a Latin alphabet for the Turkish language so that it would be more legible to the West, and mandated the wearing of western-style clothing, including outlawing the use of the classic Turkish hat, the fez. He encouraged urbanization, subsidized industry, and put in place mandatory public education of Turkish girls and universal suffrage. His reforms, however, included what he called "Turkification," which meant the assimilation or elimination of non-Turkish elements in this country. To this end, Kemal sought to expel or repress internal minorities, such as Armenian and Greek Christians and the Kurds of southeastern Turkey.

Autocratic leadership emerged in Asia as well. The "Great Japanese Empire," as it called itself, was, technically led by the hereditary emperor, Hirohito, but in fact run by a prime minister, generals, and political advisors. At the beginning of the century, Japan's leadership had adopted the slogan "Enrich the Country, Strengthen the Armed Forces," and turned to the West as a model for industrialization and imperialism. Having already gained an important foothold in Korea, which was already a tribute state of Japan, Japan turned increasingly to militarism in the 1920s, seeking to establish itself as a world and colonial power in order to gain access to raw materials and markets.

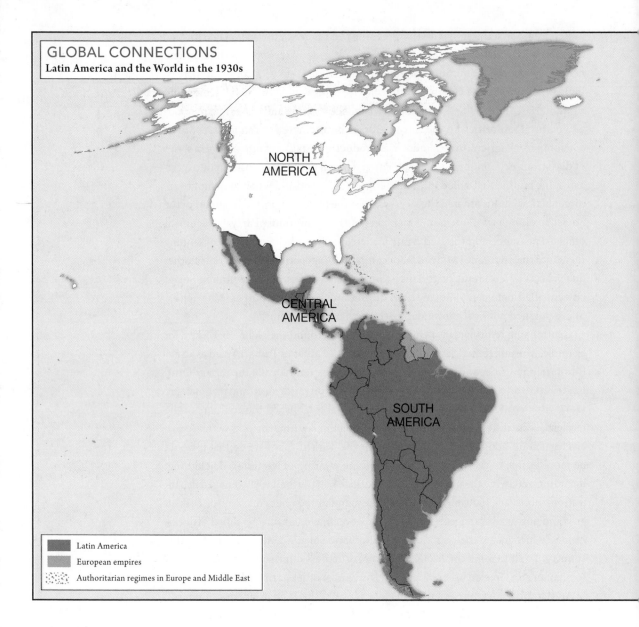

GLOBAL CONNECTIONS
Latin America and the World in the 1930s

NORTH
AMERICA

CENTRAL
AMERICA

SOUTH
AMERICA

Latin America
European empires
Authoritarian regimes in Europe and Middle East

Its large neighbor and long-time competitor, China, set squarely in Japan's sights of global ambitions. In 1931, Japan invaded Manchuria, and in 1937, the invasion and brutal occupation of Nanjing set off the Second Sino-Japanese War (the first had been in the 1890s). Japan shortly thereafter, in 1940, joined the Axis Alliance with Germany and Italy. In 1941, Japan attacked Pearl Harbor and went to war with

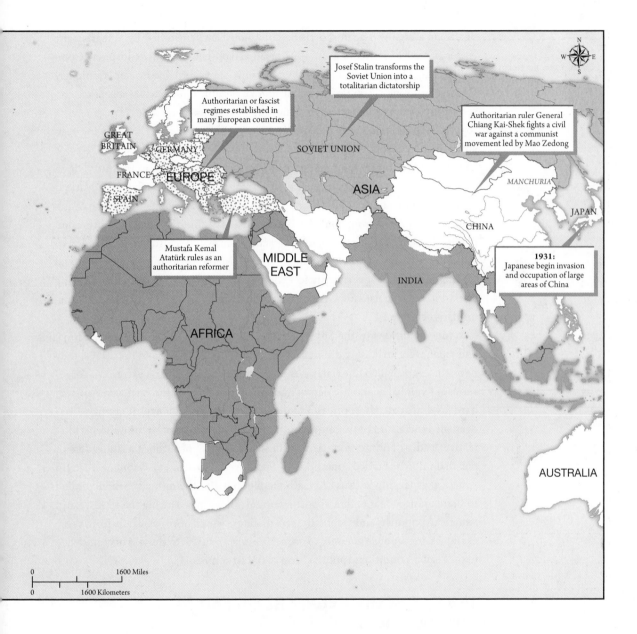

Josef Stalin transforms the Soviet Union into a totalitarian dictatorship

Authoritarian or fascist regimes established in many European countries

Authoritarian ruler General Chiang Kai-Shek fights a civil war against a communist movement led by Mao Zedong

Mustafa Kemal Atatürk rules as an authoritarian reformer

1931: Japanese begin invasion and occupation of large areas of China

GREAT BRITAIN

GERMANY

FRANCE

EUROPE

SPAIN

SOVIET UNION

ASIA

MANCHURIA

JAPAN

CHINA

MIDDLE EAST

INDIA

AFRICA

AUSTRALIA

0   1600 Miles

0   1600 Kilometers

the United States. During the Pacific War (as the Japanese refer to World War II, 1941–1945), imperial Japan would occupy vast portions of the Asia-Pacific regions.

Even aside from the hostilities with Japan, the situation in China in the 1920s and 1930s was complicated. There, the nationalist government of General Chiang Kai-shek replaced a democratic government with an authoritarian one in order to prosecute a civil war against a rising communist movement led by a charismatic leader named Mao Zedong. In 1927, Mao established the Soviet-inspired Communist Party in China (CCP) (although he would eventually develop a uniquely Chinese variation version of communism that became known as "Maoism"). In response to this threat, in April 1927, Chiang Kai-shek launched a series of massacres of suspected communists and sympathizers around Shanghai; over the following year, approximately 300,000 Chinese died in what came to be called the "White Terror."

Through strict military rule but also by promoting a program to unify China through encouraging Confucian values and moral discipline, Chiang's "Nationalist" government was able—barely—to retain control of China from Mao's communist forces throughout the 1930s and 1940s. But the defeat of both sides' common enemy, the Japanese, in the Pacific War in 1945, also spelled the downfall of the Chiang Kai-shek's regime. In 1949, Mao's forces took over China and Chiang moved his government to exile on the island of Taiwan, which Chiang ruled with an iron fist and with the intention to reclaim "Red" (mainland) China, until his death in 1975.

While conditions in the Soviet Union, Turkey, Italy, Spain, Germany, China, and Japan were strikingly different from that of Latin America in the 1930s, they nevertheless provided templates—though sometime violent and extreme—for responses to global economic depression. The Great Depression hit Latin America hard, as drastic drops in prices and demand for the region's export commodities deepened social and economic inequities and made the poor—now poorer still—restive, leading both to popular uprisings and the rise of authoritarian leaders to put them down. Franco's methods in Spain were particularly resonant in Latin America, especially within the Catholic Church and the military, which tended to share Franco's fear of liberalism and popular uprisings. During the 1930s, Latin American populists and Depression era dictators would borrow heavily from these examples, in response not only to economic crisis but also to the loss of confidence in the region's traditional political and social structures.

The End of the Export Boom and Its Consequences, 1929–1935

The collapse of the export boom for most Latin American products began even before the onset of the Great Depression and worsened for a few years thereafter. Those countries that relied most heavily on agricultural or mineral exports proved most vulnerable to the effects of the Depression. Exports fell by approximately two-thirds in the early 1930s because of a combination of the oversupply of commodities and declining prices. Reduced taxes from export earnings forced Latin American nations to spend more and more of their financial reserves to service their debts, until almost all defaulted on their loan payments.

Mineral Exporting Nations

According to statistics compiled by the League of Nations, Chile, the most successful of Latin America's mineral-exporting nations during the age of progress and modernization, suffered the most serious decline in export earnings of any country in the world as a result of the Great Depression. Despite the creation of synthetic substitutes during World War I, Chile's natural nitrates mined in the Atacama Desert still dominated the world market during the 1920s because of their competitive price. Likewise, Chilean copper had gained a decent share of international trade. But the oversupply of these two minerals during the Depression caused prices to plummet, such that by 1932, Chilean exports had fallen to one-sixth of their 1929 level, causing government revenues to sink to a mere 22 percent of their previous total. In the throes of bank failures, US lenders refused to extend further credit to Chile. Chile's dictator, Carlos Ibáñez del Campo, did his best to reverse the decline by creating the National Chilean Nitrate Corporation to purchase nitrates and prop up the market, but this strategy failed. By July 1931, workers, students, and members of the middle class rioted, forcing Ibáñez's resignation. To compound Chile's misery, the United States and Great Britain both enacted tariff barriers against foreign copper, thus crippling Chile's second-most important export. As a consequence, Chile defaulted on its debts. Only as World War II approached would Chile emerge from the shadows of the Depression.

Other mineral producing nations like Peru and Bolivia shared Chile's experiences. Peru's economic slide resulted from the decline of copper and silver prices, forcing production at the Cerro de Pasco mines to grind to a halt. Because Peru had cultivated a broader portfolio of exports than Chile, other products, such as cotton, somewhat offset the decline of mineral prices, allowing Peru to essentially recover by 1933. Unwilling to risk funds in risky US or European financial markets, Peruvian entrepreneurs instead invested in new mines that produced gold and zinc, both of which returned good earnings throughout the 1930s. The increased demand for cotton also offset some of the unemployment in the mining sector.

The market for Bolivia's tin also shrank, causing massive layoffs and unrest among the tin miners. While tin miners typically returned to subsistence agriculture, Bolivia's government had no easy answer for replacing its lost export earnings.

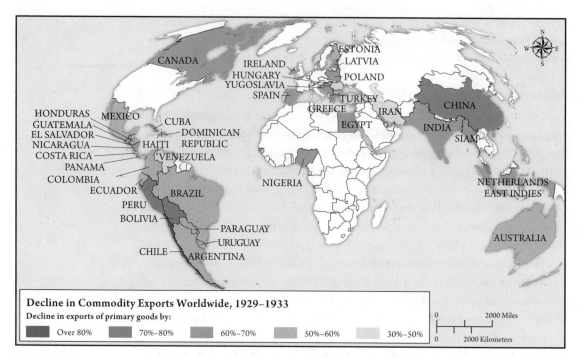

Decline in Commodity Exports Worldwide, 1929–1933

Decline in exports of primary goods by:

Over 80%	70%–80%	60%–70%	50%–60%	30%–50%	

0 ─── 2000 Miles
0 ─── 2000 Kilometers

 MAP. 8.1

Export Agriculture and the Depression

Next to Chile, Cuba suffered the most from the adverse effects of the end of the export boom, mostly because its economy, ever dependent on sugar production, was so closely linked to that of the United States. Because of the glut of sugar in world markets, in part caused by the revival of sugar beet production in Europe, sugar prices slumped to historic lows in 1929. Making matters worse, the United States, seeking to protect its sugar-producing territories of Hawaii, Puerto Rico, and the Philippines, imposed heavy tariffs on Cuban sugar, further depressing the price. Cane cutters and mill workers suffered from this sharp decline, as wages fell dramatically.

In Colombia and elsewhere, coffee cultivators also experienced the economic consequences of decreased demand and falling prices. Coffee cultivators had already formed the National Federation of Colombian Coffee Growers to urge the government to assist the troubled industry. The Federation's political leverage staved off complete collapse in the coffee sector, but not enough to diminish growing rural unemployment.

Only in Argentina did the traditional export-led system survive. Concerned about losing their traditional British market for beef and wheat, Argentina negotiated the Roca-Runciman Treaty in 1933, guaranteeing access to the British market, but only at reduced prices. In addition, the agreement allowed British investors to maintain their ownership of Argentine railroads, meat-packing plants, and utilities.

Everyday Life during the Depression, 1930–1940

These discussions of national economies, however, do little to illuminate what happened to individual people during the Depression. In most nations, as the historian Alan Knight informs us, "rural areas served as a sponge to soak up unemployment." For many of the displaced, however, the situation was dire. Within a four-month period after September 1930, about 46,000 Chileans fled the nitrate fields to find employment elsewhere in the country. The government created an agency to relocate the unemployed to places that actually had jobs. Sometimes the jobs proved so arduous and poorly paid that workers refused them. Often, however, the numbers of jobs were insufficient and the remainder of the unemployed simply wandered the streets looking for handouts and shelter. Those more fortunate found work in gold mining camps while others relied on new social welfare programs.

In Argentina, tenant farmers, rural laborers, and young people (like the future Eva Perón) left the poverty of the provinces for better prospects in urban areas, especially Buenos Aires. For long-time residents of the capital, especially the children of European immigrants, the 1930s continued to offer the opportunity to assimilate into the middle class. Estimates suggest that by 1945, nearly 48 percent of Buenos Aires's population had achieved middle-class status. These people lived healthier lives than the previous generation because of improved sanitation and greater access to potable water. Their children attended schools, raising the literacy rate in Buenos Aires to 87 percent by the end of World War II. Consumption increased as well. Argentines ate more beef than anybody in the world, flocked to American-made movies, and purchased more radios than ever before. For the middle class, the Depression was shallow and of short duration. Meanwhile, the poorest of the working class struggled to earn a living. Even though Argentina had the most developed manufacturing base in South America, these poor, unskilled workers (the **descamisados** who rallied to the Peróns) had no unions representing them. They faced high unemployment rates and were paid salaries lower than the cost of living. For them, the Depression was long and hard.

Although the end of the export boom obviously had negative consequences, it also offered new opportunities for Latin America. On the negative side, not only had global markets dried up but so also had the sources of loans that had fueled Latin America's explosion of public works projects in the 1920s. Workers suffered when they lost their jobs in mines or on plantations involved in the export trade, although by returning to the countryside they mostly avoided the tragedies of homelessness, hunger, and broken families all too commonplace in the United States and the industrialized world during the Depression. With some exceptions, urbanization slowed because the cities no longer promised opportunity. On the positive side, the Depression proved to be less severe and ended sooner than it did in the United States or in Europe. Part of the reason for Latin America's relatively quick recovery resulted from its new economic policy. With the end of the export boom and with factories closed throughout the industrialized world, Latin Americans now looked inward for a solution to the shortage of basic consumer necessities and found the answer in a more nationalistic economic policy.

Strategies for Change: ISI and Economic Nationalism, 1935–1960

Despite the disastrous decline in the export economy, the Great Depression opened up new opportunities. The reduced ability to purchase US and European manufactured goods improved prospects for Latin American industrialization. Almost all Latin American nations developed some form of light industry producing consumer goods for local markets. Almost all nations also engaged in a second innovative economic strategy—economic nationalism. But only the larger and more developed nations (Brazil, Mexico, Argentina, and to a lesser degree Chile and Uruguay) were able to enter the world of heavy industry (the production of durable goods) to any degree. The rise in domestic production spurred the development of improved transportation networks, which by the 1930s meant increasing the number of paved highways.

Light Industry

The combination of the downturn in export earnings coupled with the scarcity of foreign goods meant that Latin America's imports fell approximately 60 percent between 1929 and 1932. Faced with unreliable international suppliers, Latin Americans realized that promoting domestic industry would prove beneficial and profitable. Thus was born the concept of **import substitution industrialization,** or ISI. Early stages of ISI concentrated on light industry, such as textiles, packaged goods and pharmaceuticals, which required relatively little capital investment. In retrospect, this was considered the "easy" stage of ISI. Production of durable goods like automobiles, locomotives, steam turbines, petrochemicals and electronics, requiring greater capital investment and technological input, would constitute the "hard" phase of ISI, achieved only by a few of the Latin American nations

During the early stages of this process, producers targeted urban consumers of everyday items like clothing, shoes, cigarettes, and beer, and, for the more affluent

≡ **Highway Construction in Venezuela.** Jorge Ubico was scarcely the only Latin American leader to engage on extensive public works, especially road construction projects. In Venezuela, new oil revenue enabled dictator Juan Vicente Gómez (1908–1935) to begin an extensive road-building program in the early twentieth century as a means to tie remote communities to Caracas. Roads enabled workers to move to the new oilfields in Lake Maracaibo and Gómez to move the National Army into provinces to crush potential uprisings. The dictator also enjoyed formally opening new roads by racing a sports car the length of the highway.

members of society furniture, cosmetics, tires, and processed food. Each of these products could be made in small factories producing for the domestic market. The state contributed to the growth of light industries by erecting tariff walls against foreign imports. In Mexico, for example, the combination of these factors allowed El Buen Tono cigarettes and beer from the Cervecería Moctezuma to compete with cigarettes made by R. J. Reynolds, Inc., and beer from the Anheuser Busch Brewing Company.

Peru's national soft drink, Inca Kola, provides an excellent example of the forces at work that led to the success of light industry even in medium-sized economies. The founder of the company, a British immigrant named José Robinson Lindley, in 1910 opened a small store in Lima where he brewed his own soft drinks at the slow rate of one bottle per minute. As the popularity of his beverages grew, he introduced mechanization. To help celebrate the four hundredth anniversary of Lima's founding in 1935, he concocted a soft drink made from lemon verbena that he named Inca Kola. To foreign palates, the drink tastes like a viscous chemical brew resembling bubblegum or a sweet cream soda, but to Peruvians its nationalistic image spurred sales. The company's advertisements featured indigenous people and well-known locations, helping to swell its popularity. When Coca-Cola and Pepsi-Cola finally entered the Peruvian market, Inca Kola had already won the publicity battle. By 1970, as Peru's national drink, it controlled the largest share of the soft drink market. Even without tariff protection, Inka Kola became a successful example of light industry because it marketed its product with a patriotic name and nationalistic imagery.

☰ **Auto Mechanics School.** The original caption for this photo of an auto mechanics' school from South America, probably taken in the 1920s or earlier, reads, "The good repair man is always in demand and well paid. This class for auto mechanics offers opportunities for trainees to become well acquainted with the gas engine and all other features of automobile building and repairing." The wheels that the men are working on and the simple, nonautomated setting indicate that this photograph was taken when the automobile was a relatively new invention; the students in this photo would appear to be the beneficiaries of positivist policies that encouraged foreign investment and capital.

Brazilian Industrialization

In the first quarter of the twentieth century, industrial production in Brazil was characterized by a handful of light industrial enterprises, such as small-scale textile factories, scattered along the length of the Atlantic coast. A skeletal rail network, largely owned and operated by foreign entities, linked these enterprises to mining and agro-exporting concerns in the interior. By the 1940s, this landscape had been dramatically transformed. Industrial growth concentrated in São Paulo dominated and guided the national economy. São Paulo's economic emergence and the industrialization it led had substantial political, cultural, and environmental consequences that continue to shape modern Brazil.

A comparison of the careers of two early twentieth-century industrialists in Brazil, Percival Farquhar and Francesco Matarazzo, helps illuminate that transformation. Although Farquhar, an American rail titan, controlled a global portfolio of investments, he devoted the greatest part of his resources and energy to Brazil. Farquhar was the major investor behind the failed Madeira-Mamoré Amazonian Railroad and the controversial Contestado Railroad in the first two decades of the twentieth century. He also captained several more successful and less controversial projects such as major port reconstruction in Belém, the creation of streetcar lines and an electric network in Rio de Janeiro, and mining, railway, timber, and hotel investments throughout the country. Even before the onset of the Great Depression, Farquhar's ambitions raised concerns among federal officeholders worried about protecting Brazilian resources from foreign exploitation. By 1939 he had largely withdrawn from Brazil, as the federal government seized many of his holdings.

Matarazzo was also a foreigner, born in Italy, but in contrast to Farquhar he became a Brazilian citizen. In 1888, he arrived in Sorocaba, a cattle-trading outpost in the interior of São Paulo, as an impoverished immigrant. Together with his brothers, he built a powerful conglomerate with connections to nearly every sector of the economy of São Paulo. He diversified from early mercantile enterprises into light industry, such as soap and textile factories, and later invested in heavy industry, including an oil refinery and the modernization of the port of Santos. The Matarazzo holdings also included banking, shipping, metalworking, and paper-mills—a strategic asset for wielding influence over local newspapers dependent on cheap newsprint. By the 1930s, Matarazzo was perceived not as a foreign exploiter but as the face of modern São Paulo.

Like Farquhar, Matarazzo's vast economic leverage aroused the concern of an expanding federal government in the 1930s. But in contrast to Farquhar, Matarazzo was too intimately connected to every aspect of São Paulo's economy—to say nothing of its political and social elite—to expropriate. As a result, Matarazzo's iconic career did not typify a stage that Brazil passed through on the way to industrial modernity, but instead constituted the fabric of that industrial modernity.

Heavy Industry in Mexico

Only a few Latin American nations were able to undertake the transition to the heavy industrialization or the "hard" stage of ISI, one that required investment capital, advanced technology, adequate supplies of skilled labor, and a large consumer base. The high costs of heavy industry required significant state investment. Governments created development banks to lend money at low interest rates to industrial entrepreneurs. Such policies flourished in larger nations that also had universities and technical institutions that could offer research and development facilities.

Mexico provides a clear example of the power of ISI during World War II and beyond. In 1940, President Manuel Ávila Camacho shifted post-revolutionary economic strategy from land reform to industrial growth. Ávila Camacho and his successor, Miguel Alemán, used state intervention to subsidize both production and consumption, fueling the growth of a Mexican middle class linked to the PRI (Partido Revolucionario Institucional, or Institutional Revolutionary Party) and the federal government. The 1941 Law of Manufacturing Industries and the 1946 Law for Developing New and Necessary Industries, for example, provided tax exemptions and high tariffs that protected vital Mexican industries. As a result of these policies, heavy industries such as cement, iron, steel, and chemicals flourished, and Mexico experienced an admirable growth rate of roughly 6 percent per year.

Laws barring foreign investors from owning more than 49 percent of any Mexican business forced foreign capitalists to work with Mexican partners in order to gain access to this growing market. As elsewhere in Latin America, assembly plants (including the Ford Motor Company) led the way. As Mexican technology improved, Mexican auto assembly plants bought fewer and fewer US-made parts, replacing them (even engines) with locally made substitutes. Other factories produced complete tractors, radios, refrigerators, stoves, and other electrical appliances. In addition to consumer durables, Mexican plants manufactured fertilizers, which in turn made land more productive and helped to feed the increasingly urbanized population. Dams built from Mexican cement provided irrigation and expanded the amount of land under cultivation. While industry prospered, industrial growth in Mexico did not result from centralized planning and direction as occurred in the Soviet Union. Instead, regional industrial interests in Monterrey, Puebla, and Mexico City jockeyed for favors from the government and fought over policies as each attempted to benefit their own particular businesses.

By 1970, while Mexico had clearly eclipsed almost all other Latin American industrial societies, with 95 percent of all light consumer items produced locally and a good percentage of heavy industrial products made nationally as well, not all Mexicans had benefited equally. Extreme poverty characterized the lives of many Mexicans, especially the unskilled new arrivals to urban areas. To many observers, the development of industry left the countryside behind.

The Expropriation of the Oil Industry in Mexico: Economic Nationalism

Far more emotionally stirring as a tool of economic nationalism than ISI, the expropriation of foreign-owned property aroused the patriotic sentiments of Latin Americans. The best-known instance of this second form of economic nationalism occurred in Mexico on March 18, 1938, when Mexican president Lázaro Cárdenas seized the properties of US- and British-owned oil companies. Although a general of modest importance during the military phase of the Mexican Revolution, Cárdenas (who served as president from 1934 to 1940 and is often referred to as a left-leaning populist) gained stature as one of the country's greatest presidents because of his efforts to implement the social provisions of the Constitution of 1917.

Cárdenas's conflict with the foreign-owned oil companies began as a labor dispute. The oil workers' union felt emboldened by its partnership with the government and pressed for higher wages and better working conditions. The companies refused. Neither side would budge. The contract dispute went before Mexico's Federal Board of Conciliation and Arbitration, which essentially endorsed the union's position. The oil companies appealed to the Mexican Supreme Court to reverse this finding and simultaneously urged President Franklin D. Roosevelt to intercede diplomatically on their behalf. Roosevelt, in what many regarded as the test case for the Good Neighbor Policy, refused to intervene. When the Mexican Supreme Court upheld the Federal Board's finding, the companies refused to accept its decision. The oil workers then threatened to walk off the job at midnight, March 18, 1938.

But President Cárdenas preempted the strike by expropriating both British and US petroleum interests two hours before midnight, to the immense joy of a national radio audience. Cárdenas argued that under Article 27 of the Constitution, subsoil rights belonged to the nation and that the Constitution empowered him to take this dramatic step. He had calculated well. Roosevelt did nothing to assist the oil companies and the British government was too preoccupied with the opening salvos of World War II to pay much attention to an oil dispute half a world away. Overnight, Cárdenas's political stock rose, as his countrymen congratulated him for declaring Mexico's economic independence.

ECONOMICS AND COMMODITIES

The Early Tourism Industry in Mexico

The recovery from the worst effects of the Great Depression allowed not only for the growth of light and heavy industry but also gave rise to a new economic activity that would become increasingly important in many Latin American nations: tourism. The recovery also meant that Latin Americans and people from the United States, Europe, and elsewhere now had the wherewithal to travel for pleasure. Discussions among Mexican officials during the late 1930s about the wisdom of promoting tourism proved quite decisive. Despite Lázaro Cárdenas's promotion of economic nationalism by expropriating US and British petroleum companies, his government simultaneously explored the possibility of encouraging US tourism to offset the loss of revenue from oil. Other officials feared that excessive numbers of foreigners would adversely affect Mexican culture. Ultimately, the government decided to encourage more tourism and embarked on the construction of a modern paved road linking Laredo, Texas, to Mexico City (the Pan-American Highway) that would convey more gringos to Mexico, lured by archeological ruins, historical colonial edifices, cosmopolitan Mexico City, and the sunlit beaches and tropical vistas of coastal resorts like Acapulco.

This once-remote community became Mexico's first state-developed tourist destination. Founded in 1523 and the center of the Spanish colonial empire's glamorous trade with East Asia, Acapulco in the 1930s bore little resemblance to the prosperous port it had once been. In 1947 President Miguel Alemán, who had overseen Mexico's growing tourist industry under the previous administration, proposed the rehabilitation of Acapulco's economy by planning and facilitating the construction of new hotels and exclusive villas for the wealthy along the western beachfront of the crescent-shaped bay, and by promising improvements (sometimes unfulfilled) like paved streets, potable water, and abundant electricity to draw tourists to the resort. To facilitate travel along the bay, the government built a paved ring road, the Calzada Costera, that transported tourists quickly to their destinations. More importantly, to appeal to international visitors, the government "cleaned up" the beaches by dispersing the colorful vendors who rented umbrellas and sold tasty treats and thirst-quenching beverages on the sand and replaced them with a building that housed shops and dispensed more sanitary food and drink.

To make room for additional ocean-front growth, Alemán's government expropriated the remaining shoreline belonging to campesinos, making this land available for hotel sites and subdivisions of vacation homes catering both to Mexicans and international visitors. When local people resisted the government's efforts, police enforced the expropriation order. On a more positive note, in contrast to Havana, Cuba, where US business interests controlled the hotels and casinos, Acapulco remained a Mexican-owned luxury resort that drew international movie stars and celebrities (John Wayne, Johnny Weissmuller, and Brigitte Bardot during the golden days of the 1950s, more recently Al Pacino and Sylvester Stallone) to enjoy the beach, fishing, good food, and the excitement of the cliff divers, who leaped from a platform to the water 130 feet below.

- How effective was the Mexican government's idea to offset financial setbacks by promoting foreign tourism? What drawbacks are there to encouraging international tourism?

In the wake of the expropriation, Cárdenas had no realistic alternative but to establish a national corporation, **Petróleos Mexicanos** (Pemex for short) to extract, refine, and market the oil. He originally hoped to use petroleum profits to lessen the blow caused by a new recession. But Pemex experienced a troubled launch. The international petroleum companies retaliated against Pemex by boycotting Mexican crude, refusing to sell Pemex replacement parts for broken refinery equipment, and declining to supply tankers to deliver Mexican oil to markets.

Expected profits soon turned into losses. The financial consequences of the retaliatory measures forced Pemex to lay off 25 percent of its workers. Trying to reimburse the US and British corporations for the fair value of their property also placed stress on the budget. In part because of these short-range costs associated with the oil expropriation, conservative voices in the ruling party's upper circle forced Cárdenas to choose a more moderate successor, Manuel Ávila Camacho, in 1940.

By 1946, Pemex had stabilized, controlling all activities from production to refining to marketing. But Pemex never earned huge profits because Mexico's leaders viewed it first and foremost as an engine for national economic and social development. Pemex produced petroleum products for the domestic market at subsidized prices. During the 1960s, the price of gasoline, natural gas, and petrochemicals remained frozen because each of them contributed to the growth of Mexico's heavy industry. Pemex also hired more workers than necessary to operate efficiently, thereby boosting employment in Mexico, effectively subsidizing the expansion of an industrial working class. Although Cárdenas's expropriation of the oil industry popularized this form of economic nationalism throughout Latin America, a good number of these nationalized companies would not turn a profit.

Urbanization and the Emergence of Labor Movements, 1900–1945

The intertwined processes of immigration, urbanization, and industrialization in the first few decades of the twentieth century facilitated the rise of urban labor movements in much of Latin America. Although the pace of immigration from Europe slowed to a standstill during the Great Depression, internal migrations from rural to urban areas continued and escalated rapidly in the 1940s. Many of these new migrants found work in the new industries, and as they did, they often became involved in the labor movement.

The Evolution of the Labor Movement

While workers in each city experienced their own particular struggles for a living wage and safe working conditions, those struggles generally conformed to several stages. Early labor movements were dynamic but diffuse, facing great challenges to coordination. Cooperation between one labor sector and another, such as textiles and transportation, was rare. Some of the most vocal labor activists of the early twentieth century considered themselves "anarcho-syndicalists," combining the absence of institutional organization of anarchism with the voluntary association of a syndicate, and pressing for greater worker control over production. But most workers were more interested in the fundamental concerns of decent pay for

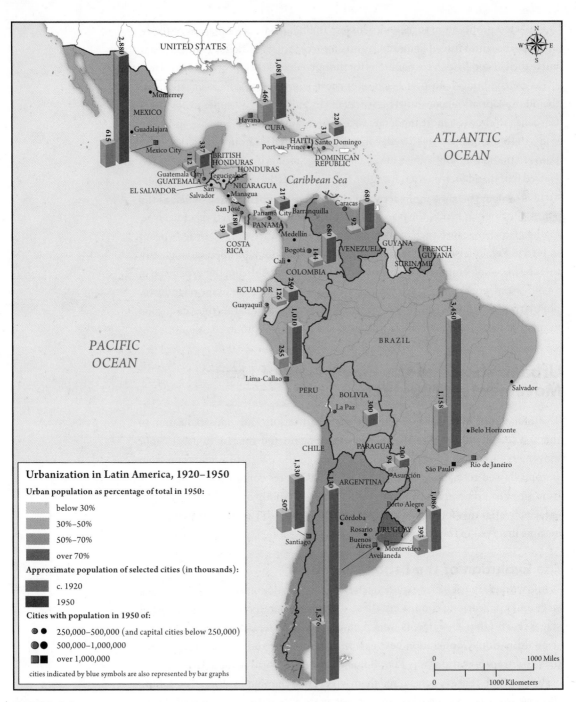

Urbanization in Latin America, 1920–1950

Urban population as percentage of total in 1950:

- below 30%
- 30%–50%
- 50%–70%
- over 70%

Approximate population of selected cities (in thousands):

- c. 1920
- 1950

Cities with population in 1950 of:

- ● ● 250,000–500,000 (and capital cities below 250,000)
- ● ● 500,000–1,000,000
- ■ ■ over 1,000,000

cities indicated by blue symbols are also represented by bar graphs

 MAP. 8.2

hard work than in direct worker management of factories. Anarcho-syndicalism tended to be more feared and reviled by politicians and industrialists than it was embraced by workers.

These limitations notwithstanding, early labor movements were characterized by "wildcat" strikes, undertaken without any official union representation. These usually provoked brutal crackdowns on striking workers and suppression of labor organization, with police and armed forces acting in the service of factory owners. The volatility of this cycle, however, helped persuade politicians, labor leaders, and industrialists that some kind of negotiated framework was preferable. As governments became more active in enforcing agreements, they served as the required mediating parties between workers and industrialists. In many places, this took the form of unions or cooperatives either sanctioned or directly created by governments, with membership required for workers, empowered to negotiate with entrepreneurs.

The result was a unionization that many workers criticized as being too "vertical," emphasizing institutional chains of command and connections to the government, rather than "horizontal" ties of cross-class solidarity. Vertical unionization, however, removed much of the volatility from labor negotiation, leading to impressive gains in working conditions and compensation. Every industrializing nation in Latin America, and even different cities within each nation, moved through these stages at different times and in different ways. But by the 1940s they began to create a landscape where industrial workers were part of the state rather than a potentially disruptive force outside it. Brazil, Argentina, and Mexico offer case studies of this progression.

Industrial Labor in Brazil

Industrial labor made its dramatic entrance into Brazilian politics with a general strike in São Paulo in 1917. This was not the first labor stoppage by Brazilian factory workers, but it was the first to galvanize workers across multiple sectors, shutting down production in most of the city and striking fear into the hearts of factory owners. The 1917 strike started in late June among textile workers long burdened by low pay and dangerous conditions. On July 9, police shot and killed a young shoemaker taking part in the demonstrations. His death provoked outrage, leading to the sudden expansion of the strike across multiple sectors, such as bottling plants and metallurgy factories. By mid-July, tens of thousands of workers were on strike.

Police arrested the most visible organizers, shuttling them from jail to detention center for months before trial. But the unraveling of the strike revealed tensions among workers as well. Leaders from several sectors formed a Proletarian

Defense League to present labor demands collectively. In the process, they lost some of the dynamism that had led to the rapid spread of the movement. But increasing organization helped lay the groundwork toward greater unionization over the next decade.

During the 1920s, the armed forces proved a hotbed of labor agitation. This was not exactly industrial labor organization—soldiers were not textile workers—but the similarities between uniformed service and factory work were clear to all. Like factory workers, rank-and-file soldiers were often subject to abusive authority and dangerous conditions for meager pay, with few opportunities for advancement. And junior officers, frustrated by a glass ceiling that seemed to limit the highest ranks to sons of the elite, proved most radical. In 1922, a group of young lieutenants initiated a rebellion in Rio de Janeiro, demanding reforms both within the army and more broadly. The first "Lieutenants' Rebellion" was quickly stifled, but was followed by a second, broader revolt in 1924. The army proved unsuccessful in completely quelling the second revolt, as a group of officers and enlisted men defied their commanders and broke away. This group spent two and a half years in the deep Brazilian interior, occasionally crossing and recrossing international borders. Led by the rebellious Captain Luís Carlos Prestes, this "Prestes Column" polarized political opinion in late 1920s Brazil, with many workers celebrating Prestes while elites abhorred him. The Prestes Column eventually wore down from exhaustion and disease, finally dissolving in February of 1927 near the Bolivian border.

As in most industrializing nations, the onset of the Great Depression in 1929 initially threw organized labor into disarray as jobs disappeared and living conditions deteriorated. But the repercussions of the Depression made clear the need for greater state intervention in labor relations. In Brazil, this recognition contributed to the rise and endurance of President Getúlio Vargas, discussed later.

Industrial Labor in Argentina

The emergence of a powerful organized industrial labor sector in Argentina did not parallel Brazil precisely, but ultimately arrived at a similar place. In February 1919, Argentine police and armed forces cracked down brutally on striking workers and labor demonstrators. The events had much in common with the São Paulo general strike of 1917, but featured even more aggressive suppression of labor activism—suppression that, in this case, took on virulent anti-Semitic characteristics, as repression of striking workers turned into persecution of Jewish immigrants. In the wake of this notorious **Semana Trágica**, or Tragic Week, however, President Hipólito Yrigoyen reached out to moderate labor organizers. Yrigoyen's party, the Unión Cívica

Radical, or Radical Civic Union, initiated early social welfare policies, providing some protections and improved wages to factory workers. Yrigoyen's ability to reconcile the demands of moderate industrial labor leaders with the aspirations of an emerging middle class enabled him to remain in power—either as elected president or the openly acknowledged power behind the office—from 1916 through 1930, when the stresses of the Great Depression laid waste to his fragile coalition. A junta seized power from Yrigoyen in a coup in September of 1930, beginning the Década Ínfame that ended with the rise of Juan and Evita Perón (discussed later).

The Regional Confederation of Mexican Workers and the Confederation of Mexican Workers

The emerging partnership between the Mexican state and national labor unions during the 1920s and 1930s enabled Mexican workers to use their political muscle to secure significant wage increases and other benefits. To be sure, the Mexican labor movement, initially led by individuals steeped in radical European ideas such as anarcho-syndicalism and socialism, predated the Mexican Revolution, but these foreign ideas dwindled in significance as Mexican labor grew closer to the state. When industrial workers formed "Red Battalions"—militias defending worker interests—and took to the battlefield in support of the Constitutionalists, they earned political leverage and seats at the convention that wrote the Constitution of 1917. The delegates' deliberations resulted in the inclusion of Article 123, at the time the most advanced statement of the rights of labor in the world, as an integral part of the Constitution. The pragmatic principles expressed in Article 123 became statutory law in 1931.

During the 1920s, the military hero of the Mexican Revolution, General Álvaro Obregón, and his colleague, General Plutarco Elías Calles, strengthened the Mexican state and began implementing some of the promises of Article 123. Placing Mexican labor in this esteemed position demonstrated the government's commitment to reform by opening up the possibility of favoring local workers at the expense of foreign, and particularly, US business interests. Described as the "great compromiser," President Obregón (1920–1924) defended labor's right to organize and strike. He encouraged the growth of a national union, CROM (the Regional Confederation of Mexican Workers) under the leadership of a former electrician named Luis Morones to the exclusion of other, smaller unions. In exchange for CROM's political support, Obregón created a cabinet post for labor, appointing Morones to the post. Although Obregón mandated the eight-hour workday and paid sick days for workers, he simultaneously resisted other concessions, consistently backing employers, rather than workers.

Calles, a close friend of Morones, was more receptive to labor demands. With Calles's support, Morones shifted towards a reformist approach modeled on the success of the American Federation of Labor (AFL) in the United States. Calles allowed CROM to secure new benefits such as limiting compulsory overtime hours, forcing businesses to provide sick and vacation pay, and requiring businesses to fund workers' compensation. In exchange, Morones guaranteed to minimize strikes. In the years before the Depression workers' real wages increased roughly 30 percent. But many Mexicans resented CROM's growing corruption. Morones's legendary taste for jewels, fancy cars, and luxurious mansions seemed inappropriate for the representative of the working people. In 1928, Calles dismissed Morones from his post in part because popular gossip implicated Morones in the assassination of President-Elect Obregón.

Under President Lázaro Cárdenas, Mexican labor achieved its greatest successes. A new national labor union, the CTM (Confederation of Mexican Workers), replaced CROM as one of the partners in Cárdenas's government. Led by the Marxist Vicente Lombardo Toledano, CTM won significant benefits for working men and women. Maintaining the role of the government as the arbitrator of all labor disputes, Cárdenas emerged as labor's great champion. Although Lombardo Toledano talked about moving the Mexican economy toward socialism, Cárdenas was unwilling to listen to such extremes. To keep Lombardo Toledano in check, Cárdenas refused to allow the CTM to organize rural workers and authorized the Mexican Communist Party (PCM) to organize the teachers.

While Cárdenas typically found in favor of labor in disputes the government adjudicated, he balanced labor's interests against those of agrarian workers, the middle class, and the military. Disillusioned, Lombardo Toledano became more involved with his attempt to organize a union of all Latin American workers. He ceded his role in CTM to one of his more moderate lieutenants, Fidel Velázquez, who later ousted Lombardo Toledano from the CTM because of his leftist political views. Velásquez, whose politics were closer to Morones's than Lombardo Toledano's, led Mexico's labor movement in an alliance with PRI until his death in 1997.

Gender and Labor in a Chilean Copper Mine

Gender roles in Chile's El Teniente copper mine reinforced patriarchy but simultaneously served to further working class solidarity. Owned by a subsidiary of US corporate giant Kennicott Copper, the El Teniente mine hired men exclusively in the early twentieth century to perform the difficult physical labor of extracting and refining ore. Nevertheless, single women also migrated to the nearby community, seeking employment as domestic servants, laundresses, cooks, and barkeepers.

These women earned so little money that they often supplemented their income by entering into informal and usually transitory unions with miners to make ends meet. The volatile combination of single men and women, alcohol, and playing cards led to an unreliable and disorderly workforce.

Mining itself reinforced this masculine culture, since it glamorized physical strength and male camaraderie. Workers often described the mine as a woman, one they penetrated and dominated. As a result of the social disorders and worker absenteeism, the copper company adopted the strategy of promoting domesticity as a means of securing a more stable labor force. These efforts paid off when the Great Depression made employment at El Teniente particularly desirable.

In addition to paying the men higher wages than available almost anywhere else in Chile, the Braden Copper Company offered significant benefits to traditional, legally married families, which included access to housing, soccer fields, a bowling alley, movies, schools, and a library. Most importantly, the family allowance—extra pay for workers with wives and children—encouraged cohabiting couples to marry, as did the threat of dismissal should the couple fail to do so. By paying the miners a decent wage, the company made possible the middle-class ideal of a male-led household that made for more reliable workers. Stay-at home mothers who ideally kept immaculate homes and practiced thrift could supplement their family's income by taking in laundry or by cooking delicacies like *empanadas* (meat pies) that her children could sell at soccer matches. Even the left-wing Popular Front government (1938–1952), a coalition of the middle-class Radical Party (like their Argentine counterparts), the Communist Party, and the Socialist Party encouraged the new form of patriarchy as a means to create a stable working class.

The company witnessed the negative consequences (from their perspective) of this paternalistic scheme during the three-week long strike in 1942. Women and children joined their husbands on the picket line, acting in solidarity with the unions. In addition to moral support, women led community meetings and cooked meals in communal kitchens for the entire community with food donated by sympathizers. As a result of the worker's solidarity and the Popular Front government's willingness to side with the unions and broker negotiations with the copper company, miners realized a 30-percent raise and a reduction of the cost of goods at company-owned stores.

The miners' subsequent strike in 1947 proved less successful. Not only did the politics of the Cold War encourage the Popular Front to favor Braden Copper, but the government did not want to endanger its principal source of revenue, the taxes derived from copper exports. As a result, the government ordered the army to disperse the strikers. Nevertheless, Chilean miners' unions have maintained their affiliations with the Communist and Socialist Parties to the present. But like the labor movements in Mexico, Argentina, and Brazil, the success of Chilean unions has always depended on the favor of the government in power.

Andean Populism, 1930–1955

Almost all of Latin America's governments fell to revolutions as a result of the Depression. The social stresses caused by the Great Depression brought a new political movement called **populism** into prominence, particularly in Argentina, Brazil, and the Andean nations. Populists were charismatic leaders with remarkable oratorical skills, but no consistent ideology. Instead, populist leaders sought to create a multisector alliance, usually including a strong component of organized labor, either urban or rural—sectors traditionally ignored in the Latin American political world. Populist strategies sought to link these previously disenfranchised sectors with some privileged insiders, like industrialist entrepreneurs or media, or at least their rhetoric did, since many populist plans did not always pan out as expected. Social and economic changes, such as increased consumerism, literacy, and opportunities for women, further energized the populist movement. By promising their constituents higher wages and a political voice, populists seemingly offered solutions to the grave crises of the 1930s and 1940s. This kind of populism emerged first in the Andean nations, then flourished in Brazil and Argentina.

Jorge Eliécer Gaitán of Colombia

In 1928, the Colombian army carried out a brutal massacre of banana workers on strike against the United Fruit Company. While the Colombian authorities sought to suppress coverage of the incident, the brilliant young mestizo attorney Jorge Eliécer Gaitán condemned the massacre and blamed it on corrupt political elites. Gaitán quickly emerged as the charismatic leader of a loose alliance of empleados, small business owners, and the urban poor, disparagingly called the *chusma* (the rabble). He served first as minister of education in a moderately reformist Liberal government in the 1930s, then briefly as minister of labor and mayor of Bogotá, building his support among the urban poor by extending utilities into poorer neighborhoods and constructing more schools. Colombia's political elite feared Gaitán's growing popularity, dismissed him as a demagogue, and worked to block any significant reforms of Colombian society.

Frustrated, Gaitán decided to run for the presidency in 1946. Unlike previous presidential candidates, he campaigned across the entire country, flying to the most remote departments (states) to meet voters and drawing crowds of up to

Latin American Countries with
Uninterrupted Elections, 1930–1945

Uninterrupted elections

UNITED STATES

Gulf of Mexico

MEXICO

Mexico City

Caribbean Sea

ATLANTIC
OCEAN

COSTA RICA

Caracas

VENEZUELA   GUYANA

Bogotá   Georgetown   Paramaribo

COLOMBIA   Cayenne

SURINAME   FRENCH
GUYANA

Quito

ECUADOR

PERU   BRAZIL

Lima

PACIFIC
OCEAN

La Paz   Brasilia

BOLIVIA

PARAGUAY

CHILE   Asunción

ARGENTINA

URUGUAY

Santiago   Buenos Aires   Montevideo

N
W   E
S

500 Miles
500 Kilometers

Miami   ATLANTIC
BAHAMAS   OCEAN

Havana   DOMINICAN   San Juan
CUBA   REPUBLIC

Guantánamo   HAITI   Santo   PUERTO
Domingo   RICO
JAMAICA   Port-au-Prince   (U.S.)

Kingston

MEXICO   BELIZE

GUATEMALA   HONDURAS
Guatemala   Tegucigalpa
San Salvador   NICARAGUA
EL SALVADOR

Managua

PACIFIC   San José   Panama   VENEZUELA
OCEAN   COSTA RICA   PANAMA
COLOMBIA

0   1200 Miles
0   1200 Kilometers

≡ **MAP. 8.3**

≡ **Haya de la Torre Speaking to a Crowd, 1931.** Víctor Raúl Haya de la Torre was a Peruvian politician, philosopher, and author who founded the American Popular Revolutionary Alliance (APRA), which included the poet and activist Magda Portal. Haya de la Torre called this system *Indo-Americanism,* a rejection of both US imperialism and Soviet communism, which he summed up as "Neither with Washington nor with Moscow! Only Aprismo will save Peru!" Although he initially earned his populist spurs by endorsing socialist economic policies and communal landholding, by the 1950s he opportunistically set aside many of its progressive, socialist ideals as APRA moved further and further to the political right.

30,000 people with his fiery, anti-oligarchic rhetoric. In proclaiming, "I am not a man! I am a people!" he cast himself as the embodiment of his followers' political will—perhaps the decisive component of populist strategy.

Gaitán lost the 1946 election but never stopped campaigning, proposing a series of economic and social reforms. In April 1948, just when his victory in the next presidential election seemed inevitable, he was assassinated. This ended Colombia's populist movement. Gaitán's murder seemed to eliminate any possibility of reformist compromise in Colombia, marking the decisive escalation of a wave of conflict first known as **La Violencia**, which would define Colombian politics for the next sixty-five years.

Populism in Peru and Ecuador

Víctor Raúl Haya de la Torre first emerged as a student leader in the 1910s, then went on to become Peru's most prominent populist politician in subsequent decades. Haya was instrumental in bringing the ideas of the Argentine University Reform movement of 1918 (La Reforma) to Peru's public university, San Marcos. In Lima, Haya organized tuition-free "Popular Universities" for workers and served as their negotiator during a strike during 1917 to 1918. His activism won him the enduring loyalty of labor and middle-class idealists in northern Peru, and the enmity of dictator Augusto Leguía, who sent Haya into exile two years later. Haya founded the populist American Revolutionary Popular Alliance (APRA) party in exile, and plotted his return. When Leguía's dictatorship fell, Haya returned to Peru and used his oratorical skills to increase his political following with nationalistic rhetoric aimed against foreign, especially US corporations. Observers described his rallies in religious terms: His followers sang a patriotic "hymn," waved white handkerchiefs, and clapped their hands rhythmically three times to his inspiring words.

Ecuador's José María Velasco Ibarra evoked a similar response. Like Colombia's Gaitán, Velasco Ibarra transformed his nation's politics through an energetic presidential campaign, crisscrossing the country to visit tiny villages in the 1931 election. The gifted orator ultimately proved more able to attract popular support than to govern. Although he won five presidential elections (infamously stating, "Give me a balcony and I will become president"), four of his five terms as president succumbed to military coups. Like his fellow populists, however, Velasco Ibarra successfully brought the unrepresented masses into national politics for the first time.

The Andean populists cracked open highly restrictive political structures, but were unable to implement successful reforms. Velasco Ibarra never lasted long enough in power to fulfill his many promises, and neither Haya nor Gaitán ever won the presidency. All faced a fundamental challenge that would be shared by populists throughout the region: how to reconcile the transformational mobilization of the popular classes they awakened with the interest-group compromises and loose coalitions on which their political success depended. The Andean populists faced further limitations because of the relatively weak industrialization of their nations. In countries with a stronger industrial base, organized labor soon emerged as the base for populist transformation.

Brazil's Populist: Getúlio Vargas, 1930–1945

Getúlio Vargas was an unlikely candidate to become the most influential Brazilian politician of the twentieth century. Born in 1882 in Brazil's remote south along the border with Argentina, far from the center of power, his family enjoyed local influence in the politics of the state of Rio Grande do Sul, but not on a national scale. But his term as governor of Rio Grande do Sul in the late 1920s happened to coincide both with the onset of the Great Depression and with momentous transitions in national politics. These domestic and international crises paved the way not only for Vargas's rise to national power but also for his emergence as a statesman of grand ambitions and deft abilities.

Vargas Comes to Power

Through much of Brazil's Old Republic, wealthy landowners in São Paulo and Minas Gerais dominated Brazil's senate and presidential cabinet, and by extension the presidency itself. Their cozy arrangement was known as "Café com Leite" ("Coffee with Milk"), referring to the coffee of São Paulo and the dairy production of Minas Gerais. But in the late 1920s, the Café com Leite machine broke down, paving the way for the first truly contested presidential election in a generation.

A coalition of interests in Rio Grande do Sul and Paraíba, in northeastern Brazil, nominated Vargas as presidential candidate in the election of 1930, mostly because he seemed an adequate compromise.

Vargas lost in an election marked by apparent voter fraud, albeit no more so than most elections in the Old Republic. Vargas's vice-presidential candidate, the Paraíban politician João Pessoa, was murdered in the wake of the election. Although the motive for the killing was apparently personal, not political, Vargas and his cohort used it to rally support for a coup. They called their movement the "Revolution of 1930," but at least initially it seemed more like a slight geographical expansion of political power than a social revolution. Vargas himself was from a landowning family, and did not seem interested in shaking up social hierarchies.

Vargas found himself governing in the midst of economic crisis. This propelled him to overhaul federal government, considerably expanding its powers. He created powerful ministries of labor, industry, and commerce, bringing the federal government into all sectors of the economy. Vargas also created a new ministry of education and health and overhauled the ministry of justice. He used these various ministries not only to carry out his administrative vision but also to bring potential opponents inside that administration, where he could supervise and discipline them. The ministry of education and health was liberal and humanist, while the ministry of justice was controlled by open sympathizers of fascist Italy. Vargas presided over these disparate ministries as if running separate experiments in government.

He did not hesitate, however, to crush those who could not be brought within the fold. In 1932, Vargas quelled a middle-class rebellion in São Paulo, and then imposed an interventor, or federally appointed governor, to maintain order. In 1935, Vargas crushed a quixotic communist uprising, the *Intentona*, or Great Attempt, led by Luís Carlos Prestes, the former leader of a renegade military column in late 1920s Brazil. Prestes had spent much of the early 1930s in exile, including a sojourn in the Soviet Union, where he adopted Marxist revolutionary principles. Vargas jailed the conspirators and deported Prestes's wife, the German communist Olga Benário Prestes, to Nazi Germany—the equivalent of a death sentence. And he used the uprising as an opportunity to suppress radical labor leaders, locking them in prison while he negotiated with moderate labor representatives who accepted his regime.

The Estado Novo

Following the communist revolt, in September of 1937 Vargas declared the inauguration of a dictatorship he named the **Estado Novo**, or New State. The Estado Novo deepened Vargas's control. He closed the federal congress, and symbolically burned Brazil's state flags—a gesture indicating the time had come for national unification over regional loyalty. Despite dictatorial control, however, Vargas continued to manage and constrain the fascist sympathizers within his own regime, rather than grant them power. In 1938, for example, Vargas suppressed a rebellion by the **Integralistas**—Brazil's homegrown fascist party. He then used that rebellion as a means to strengthen his own alliance with the United States and to purge fascist sympathizers from the Estado Novo.

None other than US President Franklin Delano Roosevelt, in a 1936 visit to Brazil, declared that the New Deal had been created by two men—himself and Getúlio Vargas. That remark testified to a real affinity between the two leaders, but it also was part of a delicate diplomatic dance. When the United States entered World War II, it eagerly sought to formalize a military alliance with Brazil. The northeastern coast of Brazil offered an ideal jumping-off point for the Allied effort to strike at Nazi positions in North Africa. And Brazil's natural resources, such as rubber and minerals, offered a vital alternative to supply chains cut off by the war in the Pacific.

Volta Redonda Steel Plant. Getúlio Vargas's bargain to get US funding and consultation for the creation of a steel plant at Volta Redonda in return for Brazil's contributions to the Allied war efforts in World War II was one of the populist dictator's most successful maneuvers. Volta Redonda powered Brazil's industrial growth for a generation.

Vargas, ever the canny strategist, held off on formal alliance until he extracted a substantial concession: US funding and technological input for the first steel plant in South America, built in the small Brazilian town of Volta Redonda. The steel plant was the key element in Vargas's industrial strategy, and was an engine of the Brazilian economy for decades.

Vargas's ministry of labor created a far-reaching system of government unions. Labor leaders within this system were sometimes derided as **pelegos**, a Brazilian term for saddle blankets, from the idea that they softened the domination of the industrialist rider over the horse of industrial labor. But this characterization was too strong–under the Estado Novo and beyond, industrial workers enjoyed both rising material fortunes and increasing political leverage. It was in this regard that Vargas had most in common with his fellow populists in the region. Vargas joined the Allies in their fight against dictatorships in Italy and Nazi Germany, but clung to dictatorial authority in Brazil. As World War II wound to a close in 1945, that contradiction became increasingly untenable. Vargas was finally removed from office in a bloodless coup in October of 1945, but he immediately began planning a return to power.

Damming the São Francisco

From the eighteenth century through the mid-twentieth, the São Francisco River was the symbolic lifeline of the Brazilian interior. One of only a handful of navigable rivers in this vast nation, the São Francisco winds northeast from its source in the mountains of Minas Gerais, through the arid hinterlands of Bahia and Pernambuco, forming the border between the impoverished states of Sergipe and Alagoas before spilling into the Atlantic. Throughout the 1700s, it served as the pathway to the interior for gold prospectors and settlers traveling from the northeast into the mining region. And well beyond that it inspired the grand plans of a host of would-be nation-builders who envisioned schemes to populate the interior and reorient Brazilian economic life.

☰ **Frans Post Painting,** *Cachoeira Paulo Afonso".*
Frans Post was a Dutch painter who visited Brazil in 1640 during the Dutch occupation of parts of northeastern Brazil. Post was one of the first European artists to capture the power and majesty of the Brazilian landscape. Three hundred years later, Brazilian engineers captured the power of this waterfall in a different way, establishing Brazil's first major hydroelectric plant, the Cachoeira de Paulo Afonso Hydroelectric Complex. Updated several times since the initial construction in 1948, it continues to provide electricity for much of the surrounding region, and is emblematic of Brazil's heavy reliance on hydroelectric power.

Until the mid-twentieth century, the São Francisco was used mostly as a conduit for small-scale cargo. Then in the early 1950s, during the second presidency of Getúlio Vargas, it was harnessed and transformed into a source of hydroelectric power through the creation of the Paulo Afonso Hydroelectric Complex, a series of dams above the Paulo Afonso Falls, deep in the interior of the state of Bahia. The Paulo Afonso dams had far-reaching consequences. Together with Vargas's creation of Eletrobras, a new state electric company, they marked the entrance of the federal government as the dominant player in Brazil's electric network. They facilitated urbanization in the impoverished northeast. And they set Brazil firmly on the path of hydroelectric development, a path that proved both a blessing and a curse.

In part through its exploitation of hydroelectric power, Brazil industrialized without the coal-burning pollution of many of its peers. Although the environmental costs of hydroelectric power were less immediate, however, they were equally inevitable. Brazil entered the twenty-first century with a fragile and overburdened electric network, hampered by periodic drought. And dependence on the São Francisco and other Brazilian rivers for hydroelectric power vastly altered the landscape around these enterprises, often subordinating the long-term sustainability of rivers to short-term political needs.

The Peróns: Argentine Populism, 1945–1955

In Argentina, the populism of Juan Domingo Perón had striking similarities to that of Getúlio Vargas. Like Vargas, Perón was an outsider from the provinces who rose to become his nation's most influential politician. Like Vargas, Perón's popular base depended above all on the support of industrial labor. Like Vargas, he pursued policies of industrialization, stoking domestic production and employment. But there were also important differences: Together with Evita, his second wife—a former actress and passionate advocate for the poor—Perón went well beyond Vargas in creating a cult of personality. Worshipped by their followers and passionately reviled by their opponents, the Peróns left a divisive political legacy.

Perón's Ascension to Power

In contrast to the civilian Vargas, Perón rose to power through the military. As a rising army officer, he conducted a fact-finding mission throughout the Axis powers of Europe during the early years of World War II, an experience that would later shape his strategy as president. The Depression years in Argentina became known as the *Década Ínfame*, or Infamous Decade (really a period of thirteen years), marked by suppression of civil rights, the erosion of social welfare policies, and a brutal crackdown on organized labor. In 1943, Perón joined a *junta* (a small, self-appointed group) of reformist officers, seizing political power and ending the Infamous Decade. Perón initially seemed to be a junior member of the new junta, accepting a position as the head of the National Department of Labor, up to then an insignificant branch of the federal government. But he proved an ambitious administrator, rapidly expanding the department and using it to intervene between workers and industrialists. Perón embarked on an energetic campaign of factory visits, shocking owners with his orders to improve conditions and wages—a strategy that won him the fierce loyalty of workers. He supplemented this charismatic appeal with organization, strengthening the pan-union **Confederación General de Trabajo** (CGT), or General Labor Confederation.

When an earthquake destroyed the city of San Juan in January of 1944, Perón led the government relief efforts, building a base within the junta through his distribution of infrastructural spending, employment and political alliance. At a benefit concert for the victims of the earthquake, the young actress Eva Duarte approached Perón and uttered the famous line, "**Gracias por existir, mi Coronel**"—"Thanks for existing, my Colonel." Perón, who had been widowed for several years, quickly became attached to Evita. She became first his mouthpiece, then his wife, and ultimately the embodiment of the inchoate political ideology of Peronismo.

By late 1945, Perón and Evita had proven a threat to the ruling junta, and in October of that year his fellow officers removed him from his post and threw him in jail. The CGT responded with one of the most famous demonstrations in Latin American history. On October 17, 1945, tens of thousands of Argentine workers walked from the distant industrial suburbs or took buses from outlying cities to the heart of Buenos Aires. They marched to the Plaza de Mayo, in front of the Casa Rosada, Argentina's presidential palace—a plaza previously reserved for the wealthy residents of Buenos Aires's city center. Perón's working-class and poor supporters, the *descamisados*, or shirtless ones (the origins of the name are obscure, but it is likely a reference to their humble work clothes), demanded that the junta release Perón, and vowed not to leave until he addressed the crowd. The junta acceded to these demands. Perón spoke to the descamisados in a speech broadcast on national radio. The junta's plan to sideline him had backfired utterly: He was now an unstoppable political force.

Flanked by Evita, Perón swept to power in presidential elections in 1946. He used his office to bring the CGT inside the machinery of the federal government and to expropriate and marginalize his opponents among Argentina's old oligarchy.

Evita Perón

Evita's importance in Perón's rise to power and in the expansion of his influence cannot be overstated. The power of the alliance between Juan and Evita transcended the political roles of president and first lady. Evita made a successful transition from a second-rate actress in radio melodramas to one of the most influential political orators in Latin American history. Her humble origins and her devotion to Perón spoke directly to a generation of Argentina's poor. Evita's radio speeches galvanized the descamisados, convincing them they were the heart and soul of Argentina and that their time had come. She did not hesitate to antagonize the old elite, deliberately snubbing society ladies in favor of more humble company. And from the moment of her meeting with Perón until her death from cancer in 1952 at the age of 33, she appeared not to rest.

Once Perón was elected, Evita overhauled the inadequate federal social welfare institutions of urban Argentina (see chapter 5). In their place, she created the Eva Perón Foundation and the City of Children, beneficent institutions designed to distribute welfare directly to individual recipients in Evita's name. She was known to sit at her desk for fourteen hours a day, receiving adoring supplicants who formed a long line, stretching blocks outside her office door.

As administrative policy, this strategy had obvious shortcomings. There was little institutional structure, and thus nothing that could be built on after Evita's departure. Her handouts were intended to be temporary help rather than to facilitate structural change. On the other hand, many new Peronistas experienced their meeting with Evita as a transformative moment, their initiation into a life of political relevance and activity. More quantifiably, Evita's foundation and her City of Children were economically unsustainable. They were made possible by the brief boom in export receipts following World War II. When European demand stabilized and profits fell in the early 1950s, the Argentine government could no longer pay for Evita's largesse.

By that time, Evita herself was dying of cancer. Her impassioned followers nearly succeeded in forcing Perón to put her on the ticket as the vice-presidential candidate in his 1951 campaign for reelection—an initiative demonstrating that Evita had become more popular than Perón himself. Debilitating illness prevented her from accepting nomination. Perón won reelection with Evita serving as his "Spiritual Leader of the Nation," a post she arguably continued to hold after her death in July of 1952.

Her continued influence, however, was not enough to sustain Perón or his administration. His second term was marked by rampant inflation, corruption scandals, dissension within the labor ranks, and the fraying of his coalition. With the opposition howling for vengeance, fellow officers ousted him in a coup in

≡ **Eva Perón Addressing a Crowd of Women.** Eva Perón, the wife of Argentina's populist leader General Juan Perón, did as much to popularize her husband and Perón's populist message as the general did himself. She was the regime's most valuable political asset. Evita, as she was affectionately called, came from humble origins herself, having worked her way up from a dancehall hostess and radio actress to First Lady of Argentina, and she related intimately to the needs and aspirations of Argentina's poor and working-class people. Eva Perón became a touchstone of the Perón administration; her autobiography, *La Razón de Mi Vida* (My Purpose in Life), was required reading in all Argentine schools. She also became an international celebrity, celebrated and sometimes ridiculed for her dyed blond hair and obvious raw ambition.

September of 1955. Like Vargas, Perón immediately began plotting his return—although his would be longer in coming and even more chaotic.

Both Vargas and Perón sought to remake their nations by implementing a strategy that combined economic, political, and administrative elements. Economically, they sought to supplant dependence on export agriculture with industrialization. Politically, as populists they described their followers as the true nation, and characterized political adversaries as internal enemies of that nation. Administratively, they sought to reorganize changing societies in discrete sectors, such as industrial labor, cultural producers, or industrialist entrepreneurs, and managed each of these sectors through hierarchical relationships.

This administrative strategy is often described as **corporatism**, from the Latin *corpus*, for body: In a corporatist administration, the state is a body, with the executive power at its head administering commands to the various limbs of organized social sectors. In Brazil and Argentina, this economic, political, and administrative strategy responded to the crisis of the global Great Depression and the Infamous Decade, and flourished in the brief boom following World War II. But corporatism could not survive new challenges in the mid-1950s and beyond. When that strategy unraveled, the limbs of the corporatist body began warring against one another, instead of cooperating.

Depression-Era Dictatorships, 1930–1945

The Great Depression struck especially hard in Central America and the Caribbean. There, fragile governments and dramatic social inequities between rich and poor threatened to crumble in the economic crisis. As the Depression progressed into the 1930s, elites turned to strongmen.

The Dictators

Unlike the caudillos of the nineteenth century, Latin America's Depression-era dictators were typically military men. By 1940, some of Latin America's best-known and sometimes most notorious leaders—Rafael Leónidas Trujillo (Dominican Republic), Anastasio Somoza García (Nicaragua), Jorge Ubico (Guatemala), Fulgencio Batista (Cuba), Maximiliano Hernández Martínez (El Salvador), among others—were firmly in power.

As in South America, the Depression-era dictators in Central America and the Caribbean typically kept dissent in check by employing a combination of carrot-and-stick measures. They monitored and controlled populations through spy networks and secret police. At the same time, they dispensed favors and benefits to build popular support. These included subsidies for basic foodstuffs, better access to healthcare, improved housing and education, and perhaps most importantly, a sense of enhanced recognition and enfranchisement.

This changed in the mid-1940s. World War II triggered economic growth in the Americas, bringing the Depression to an end and opening the door to new social movements. Latin American students, in particular, began to question the logic of fighting fascism in Europe while enduring authoritarianism at home. With the emergency of the Depression receding, Latin America's planters, businessmen, and military cohorts no longer needed the strongmen, and the dictators lost their key support. By the end of 1945, nearly all of them had fallen from power as a wave of democracy swept over the region.

La Matanza in El Salvador

Even before the Great Depression struck, the small nation of El Salvador was on the brink of crisis. Although the smallest Central American nation in terms of landmass, it was the most densely populated. For much of its history, El Salvador's rigid social pyramid has consisted at the top of a tiny elite, known as the "Fourteen Families"—enriched by family status and heavy investment in coffee cultivation—who owned most of the nation's arable lands and the means of production; the large base of the pyramid was composed of a vast indigenous and poor mestizo campesino class who worked the land for them. Liberal reforms in the second half of the nineteenth century had introduced coffee cultivation to El Salvador and dramatically increased the country's overall GNP. Coffee production had transformed El Salvador's once-modest aristocrats, catapulting the Fourteen

≡ **A Scene in El Salvador with a "Branch" Department Store.** In the years before the Great Depression and the Matanza, El Salvador experienced growing consumerism in rural areas. This photograph shows commerce at the village level in rural El Salvador. Local representatives from a department store in the capital in San Salvador offered basic merchandise in smaller communities. Although most people in El Salvador remained abysmally poor, market forces had reached into the countryside by the 1920s.

Families into great wealth and status as cosmopolitan international elites by the early twentieth century.

After 1882, the elimination of the indigenous communal land system and the commercialization of other campesino lands into coffee cultivation had turned traditional farmers into landless peasants, many of whom worked seasonally or permanently as *colonos* (resident workers) on the great coffee fincas. The vast discrepancies between rich and poor—a reality in nearly all Latin American countries at the time—was unusually acute in El Salvador. Even a US military attaché to El Salvador remarked on this. In 1931, he wrote to his superiors, "There is practically no middle class between the rich and the very poor.... I imagine the situation in El Salvador is very much like France was before its revolution, Russia before its revolution, and Mexico before its revolution.... A socialistic or communistic revolution in El Salvador may be delayed for several years, ten or even twenty, but when it comes it will be a bloody one."

Despite that gloomy prediction, however, El Salvador had enjoyed nearly a decade of reform and innovation during the 1920s, culminating in the election of a reform-minded engineer, Arturo Araujo, to the presidency in 1931. His timing was terrible: In a matter of months, the price of coffee collapsed. The military, with the strong support of the oligarchy, expelled Araujo in a coup. The leader of the coup, Maximiliano Hernández Martínez, immediately assumed the office of the presidency.

Martínez was as quirky as he was iron-fisted. A believer in reincarnation with a fondness for esoteric beliefs, he once ordered colored cellophane paper be put over street lamps in San Salvador as a prophylactic against disease. Among other things, Martínez stated that it was worse to kill an ant than a man because an ant could not undergo reincarnation. During his term of office, he also ordered that drums be beaten around the streets of the capital at 9:00 p.m. on certain evenings, accompanied by the shout, "Now is the time to conceive, gentlemen," reminding married couples of their patriotic duty to populate the country with useful citizens. Martínez was also a military hard-liner and avowed anticommunist, even at a time when international communism had a minimal presence in Latin America. These last qualities would precipitate the event that would ultimately define Martínez's presidency and the next several decades of Salvadoran history.

At this point, the gloomy prediction of the US military attaché came true. As the Depression wore on and the price of coffee continued to plunge, conditions worsened dramatically in the Salvadoran countryside, particularly in the coffee-producing sectors of the country and in the western part of the country. In addition to being the poorest region, it was also the most indigenous, inhabited by Nahuatl-speaking *Pipiles*, one of northern Central America's largest non-Maya indigenous populations. At the time, perhaps one-quarter of the Salvadoran population was indigenous.

As the economic crisis deepened, popular uprisings and protests broke out. Believing the moment ripe for a large-scale uprising, a small cohort of communists and social reformers from the capital began organizing in the western provinces, encouraging the local population to rebel. These urban leaders, led by a mestizo named Agustín Farabundo Martí, planned a major uprising for early in 1932. When Martí and some of his coconspirators were arrested and interrogated by Martínez's police, cadres in the countryside determined to detonate the uprising early, on January 22, 1932.

The pent-up rage of generations assured that the uprising was especially violent. The rebels killed perhaps as many as a hundred landowners and planters in and around the towns of Nahuizalco, Juayua, Apaneca, and Izalco; set buildings on fire; and forced elite women to perform humiliating acts, such as grinding tortillas—work normally done by their maids and the rebels' wives. But this short-lived, if brutal, rebellion was not the event now known as "**La Matanza**,"—the massacre. The Matanza, rather, was the Martínez's government's response to the uprising. He sent troops into the rebellious towns and ordered all conspirators, potential conspirators, and, indeed, virtually anyone with indigenous features, eliminated.

The results were horrific. By the end of March 1932, government forces had killed between 10,000 and 40,000 peasants, most of them indigenous. So brutal and comprehensive were the killings that cruel and terrifying rumors circulated about the slaughter—that dogs grew fat from consuming corpses and that unscrupulous salesmen sold human flesh in the market as beef. In response, survivors of La Matanza abandoned their Nahuatl language and Pipil dress and customs out of fear of further reprisals. The year 1932, as a result, marks the point at which El Salvador's indigenous population seemed to disappear, reduced through massacre and driven into hiding by state terror.

The Matanza's other outcome was precisely what Martínez and his supporters desired. The repression drove the communist movement in El Salvador so far underground that it would be many decades before it resurfaced again. Nor would any popular dissent, in fact, present a threat to El Salvador's repressive government. In fact, so proud was Martínez of his accomplishment of "saving the country" that El Salvador reputedly issued a postage stamp that featured an image of the hanging of Feliciano Ama, a Pipil political leader from Izcalco, during the 1930s.

SOCIAL UPHEAVAL

Rafael Leónidas Trujillo and the Parsley Massacre

General Rafael Leónidas Trujillo became president of the Dominican Republic in 1930 and remained either as chief of state or the power behind the throne until his assassination in 1961, making him the Depression-era dictator with the longest tenure. Trujillo, however, differed from his fellow dictators by an order of magnitude, thanks to his unbridled authoritarianism, his narcissism, and the cruelty of his rule. He eliminated all political parties except his own, of which he or one of his proxies was the sole candidate in elections for more than three decades. Even more significantly, he was ruthless toward all opposition. Those who opposed or even spoke negatively of Trujillo in private could expect to be arrested, imprisoned without trial, or even killed by his secret police, the Servicio de Intelligencia Militar (SIM).

One of the most notorious of many episodes in the long Trujillo regime involved his persecution of Haitians, which reached its culmination in October 1937. The history of rancor between the two countries ran deep. Haiti had occupied the Dominican Republic from 1822 to 1844, and the border between the two countries was poorly defined even in the 1930s. But because Haiti was a much more densely populated, poorer, and environmentally degraded country, many Haitians over the years had come to work as laborers in the Dominican Republic.

In one of his many efforts to build up support for his regime, Trujillo decided to scapegoat Haitians who lived on the Dominican side of the border, blaming them for the economic crisis and charging that immigrant Haitian workers posed security risks. On October 2, 1937, on the pretext that they were aiding and abetting his political enemies, Trujillo ordered the killing of Haitians living along the Dominican-Haitian border. Over the next five days, Trujillo's soldiers murdered thousands of Haitians and Dominicans of Haitian descent—estimates range from between 1,000 to as many as 20,000 lives lost.

The massacre became known as **"el corte"** (Spanish) or **"kout kout a"** (Kreyòl), both meaning "the cut," since many victims were killed by machete. But it is also called the "Parsley Massacre," to mark the way in

☰ **Rafael Leónidas Trujillo**

which Dominican troops differentiated between black Haitians and black Dominicans. The soldiers allegedly asked victims to pronounce the Spanish word for parsley, *perejíl*. Because French and Kreyòl speakers were usually unable to pronounce the word with the proper rolled Spanish r—in Kreyòl, "r" sounds more like the English "w,"—the mispronunciation of this single word could result in death. Although at least one prominent historian has recently suggested that the *perejíl* test is a historical myth, it is nonetheless a story that illustrates the terror of a very real and dark moment in Dominican and Haitian history—one that underscores the violent and capricious nature of Trujillo's rule.

- How did authoritarian populists exploit racial divisions and prejudice to consolidate their power?

The Good Neighbor Policy and World War II, 1934–1945

Both populists and Depression-era dictatorships benefited from a dramatic shift in US policy toward Latin America. When Franklin Delano Roosevelt (FDR) assumed the office of president of the United States in March 1933, the Great Depression had reached its nadir, with 1932 marking the year when joblessness, poverty, economic stagnation, and desperation reached its lowest point. Roosevelt would be the only US president to be elected to serve four terms, and his long tenure in office would mark an important shift toward liberalism that would define US policy for generations to come, especially within the Democratic Party.

The Good Neighbor Policy

Roosevelt's policies toward Latin America marked a dramatic departure from the past: They brought an end to direct US intervention in the region, they redefined US–Latin American relations in less asymmetrical terms, and they called for more reciprocal and equitable economic transactions between the Latin and North America. This remarkable rebooting of US–Latin American relations was called the **Good Neighbor Policy**.

FDR's new policies were based as much on the fact that the Great Depression made keeping US troops abroad a prohibitively expensive proposition as they were on ideology. Even so, the Good Neighbor Policy offered a sharp reversal of the interventionist strategy that had characterized US–Latin American relations since US President Theodore Roosevelt (FDR's cousin) had proclaimed the United States the region's "policeman," at the turn of the twentieth century. At that time, the United States had begun to discipline "unruly" Latin American nations with intervention and, often, occupation by US forces to "enforce order" and "protect American lives and property." Although US policy had evolved somewhat since the time of Theodore Roosevelt—President Woodrow Wilson, for example, argued for the recognition of the authority of Latin American governments on a "moral basis," meaning they could not have come to power by way of violence—the policy of intervention and occupation had remained intact. Even during the Wilson administration, US troops had seized and occupied the port city of Veracruz in 1914 during the early days of the Mexican Revolution, chased Pancho Villa fruitlessly through northern Mexico, and occupied Haiti, the Dominican Republic, and Nicaragua. As late as 1927, the US government sent a full contingent of Marines to fight the guerrilla leader Augusto Sandino in Nicaragua—an occupation that did not end until the Good Neighbor Policy required that US troops withdraw from Central America in 1934.

Three main elements defined the Good Neighbor Policy. The first, and most important, was the principle of nonintervention and noninterference in the domestic affairs of sovereign Latin American states. Second, the United States also pledged that it would be a "good neighbor" toward the Latin American republics—a promise that implied mutual respect and parity in diplomatic and economic relations between north and south. Finally, the United States promised to help create new economic opportunities in Latin America by way of mutually favorable reciprocal trade agreements and investment. In this way, the Roosevelt administration anticipated that the promise of improved economic conditions would help to pave the way for increased US investment in the region and a more favorable view of the United States in general.

The policy was so central to US interests that Roosevelt introduced the Good Neighbor Policy in his first inaugural address. "In the field of world policy," he proclaimed, "I would dedicate this nation to the policy of the good neighbor, the neighbor who resolutely respects himself and, because he does so, respects the rights of others, the neighbor who respects his obligations and respects the sanctity of his agreements in and with a world of neighbors." Roosevelt's secretary of state, Cordell Hull, stated the policy more succinctly. "No country has the right to intervene in the internal or external affairs of another," he explained.

The Good Neighbor Policy in Practice

The Good Neighbor Policy brought an end to all ongoing occupations in in Latin America by 1934 (Nicaragua, Haiti, Cuba, and the Dominican Republic). In each of these cases, the presence of US Marines was replaced by new, US-trained national constabulary forces (in most places called the "guardia nacional" or national guard). Their job mirrored that of the Marines, but with local troops: to keep order, protect private property, and, sometimes, to oversee elections. In each case mentioned above, the head of the national guard would eventually rise to hold authoritarian power— Nicaragua's Somoza family, in fact, would directly or indirectly rule the country from 1934 until 1979—but this was largely a case of unintended consequences. (Although perhaps not entirely: Roosevelt reputedly said of the head of the Nicaraguan national guard who became the long-standing, very pro-American president of Nicaragua, Anastasio Somoza, "He may be a son of a bitch, but he's our son of a bitch.") On a more positive note, the Good Neighbor Policy allowed for the peaceful negotiation of terms for the expropriation of foreign-owned oil fields in Mexico in 1938.

The Good Neighbor Policy had cultural aspects as well, since reciprocity is typically built on mutual respect. Until this point, both North Americans and Latin American based their perceptions of the other both on stereotypes and history:

many Latin Americans thought of Americans as overbearing and bombastic, while people in the United States sometimes imagined Latin Americans as indolent. In 1940, Roosevelt established the Office of the Coordinator of Inter-American Affairs (OCIAA), which, for all intents and purposes, was tasked with manufacturing propaganda in favor of the Good Neighbor Policy. For US cultural consumers, Hollywood played its part in producing positive images of Latin Americans in movies, including a vogue for rumba (both the dance and the music) and promoting the celebrity of the Brazilian movie star Carmen Miranda, along with the rising prominence of Cuban-born Desi Arnaz, later of *I Love Lucy* fame.

In Latin America, the Good Neighbor Policy sought to promote higher culture through translations of major American works of literature. The OCIAA (renamed the Office of Inter-American Affairs in 1945) also generated pro-American radio programing for Latin American consumption and encouraged the distribution of films and movies produced in the United States that portrayed American culture and values in a positive light. A pinnacle of warming relations was the 1939 World's Fair, held in New York, where a multitude of Latin American nations (including Cuba, Mexico, Nicaragua, Chile, Brazil, Argentina, and others) had an opportunity to showcase their countries, offering visitors from the United States windows on their cultures and societies that transcended stereotypes. These increased affinities became crucial when the United States entered World War II and ultimately persuaded nearly every country in Latin America to join the war effort on the Allied side.

The death of FDR in 1945 and the conclusion of World War II brought an end to the Good Neighbor Policy. But the strategy, by many measures, had been a success. In the eyes of many scholars, by 1945 Latin America was broadly supportive of US foreign policy. One historian has described the Good Neighbor Policy's efforts to encourage support for the United States by persuasion instead of by force as an "empire by invitation," one that brought the United States to an unprecedented level of world power.

TIMELINE

1926
Commodity prices begin to fall

1929 (October)
Wall Street crash in United States

1930
Getúlio Vargas initiates the modern Brazilian state

1933
Beginning of the Good Neighbor Policy

1927–1934
Sandino rebellion in Nicaragua

1930
Populist Leadership emerges in Andean nations

1932
La Matanza in El Salvador

Latin America in
The Second World War

- Declared war on Axis, Dec 1941
- Declared war on Axis, 1942–43
- Declared war on Germany and Japan, Feb 1945
- Declared war on Japan only, Feb 1945
- European colonies

 MAP. 8.4

1934
Lázaro Cárdenas legalizes the Communist Party in Mexico

1938
Cárdenas nationalizes foreign-owned petroleum assets

1945
End of World War II

1952
Eva Perón dies

1937
Getúlio Vargas leads Estado Novo in Brazil

1940s–1950s
Mexico, Brazil, and Argentina initiate heavy industry

1945–1954
Juan Perón in Power in Argentina

Conclusion

The Great Depression that began in 1929 brought great change to Latin America. Shedding their image as mere producers of primary products, the Latin American nations bounced back from declining export sales and embarked on a new era of import substitution industrialization (ISI). As such, countries partook of the heady doctrine of economic nationalism that had largely been absent during the Roaring Twenties. Most countries had the resources and markets to engage in light industrial production, supplying their citizens with a number of previously imported consumer goods. Nations with larger populations, more available capital, and more diverse resources could even produce durable goods, although after World War II, these nations needed to employ protective strategies to fend off international competition. For the first time, Latin American nations also expropriated foreign-owned property in the name of economic nationalism, the most visible legacy of the 1930s and 1940s.

The linkage between the Great Depression and the political changes often associated with the 1930s are a bit more tenuous. Almost every pre-Depression government collapsed in 1930. More active national governments became a permanent feature of Latin American political life, accelerating an earlier trend. Populist leadership in some ways revived the model of the charismatic caudillo, albeit now strengthened by the power of mass media. Previously underrepresented groups, particularly urban labor, played increasingly important roles in nations like Brazil and Argentina. Meanwhile, the Central American states, with the exception of a few spectacular popular uprisings, remained in the hands of right-wing dictators. Across the region, the growth of capital cities intensified, as Latin American began a shift from predominantly rural to predominantly urban.

KEY TERMS

Selected Readings

Anderson, Thomas. *La Matanza: El Salvador's Communist Revolt of 1932*. Lincoln: University of Nebraska Press, 1971.

Ashby, Joe C. *Organized Labor and the Mexican Revolution under Lázaro Cárdenas*. Chapel Hill: University of North Carolina Press, 1963.

Booth, John A. *The End and the Beginning: The Nicaraguan Revolution*. Boulder, CO: Westview Press, 1982.

Brown, Jonathan C., and Alan Knight, eds. *The Mexican Petroleum Industry in the Twentieth Century*. Austin: University of Texas Press, 1992.

Buchenau, Jurgen. *Plutarco Elías Calles and the Mexican Revolution*. Lanham, MD: Scholarly Resources, 2007.

Carr, Barry. *Marxism and Communism in Twentieth-Century Mexico*. Lincoln: University of Nebraska Press, 1992.

Derby, Lauren. *The Dictator's Seduction: Politics and the Popular Imagination in the Era of Trujillo*. Durham, NC: Duke University Press, 2009.

Drinot, Paulo, and Alan Knight, eds. *The Great Depression in Latin America*. Durham, NC: Duke University Press, 2014.

Gould, Jefffrey L., and Aldo Lauria Santiago. *To Rise in Darkness: Revolution, Repression, and Memory in El Salvador, 1920–1932*. Durham, NC: Duke University Press, 2008.

Grandin, Greg. *Empire's Workshop: Latin America, the United States and the Rise of the New Imperialism*. New York: Metropolitan Books, 2006.

Haber, Stephen H. *Industry and Underdevelopment: The Industrialization of Mexico, 1890–1940*. Stanford, CA: Stanford University Press, 1989.

Klubock, Thomas Miller. *Class, Gender, and Politics in Chile's El Teniente Copper Mine, 1904–1951*. Durham, NC: Duke University Press, 1998.

LaFeber, Walter. *The American Age: U.S. Foreign Policy at Home and Abroad, 1750 to Present*. 2nd ed. New York: Norton, 1994.

Lindo-Fuentes, Hector, Erik Kristofer Ching, and Rafael Lara Martínez. *Remembering a Massacre in El Salvador: Roque Dalton and the Politics of Historical Memory*. Albuquerque: University of New Mexico Press, 2007.

Niblo, Stephen. *Mexico in the 1940s: Modernity, Politics, and Corruption*. Wilmington, DE: Scholarly Resources. 1998.

Pike, Frederick B. *FDR's Good Neighbor Policy: Sixty Years of Generally Gentle Chaos*. Austin: University of Texas Press, 1995.

Schoultz, Lars. *Beneath the United States: A History of U.S. Policy towards Latin America*. Cambridge, MA: Harvard University Press, 1998.

Sharpless, Richard E. *Gaitán of Colombia: A Political Biography*. Pittsburgh, PA: University of Pittsburgh Press, 1978.

9

The Challenges of Modernity, 1930–1950

Global Connections

The sustained trauma of two world wars and a global Great Depression presented not only economic and political challenges but also cultural and ideological ones. How to make sense of a world that seemed to tear itself apart, one where old certainties crumbled in a moment? What to make of new technologies that both offered tremendous promise and unleashed unthinkable destruction? Authors, painters, and musicians tended to agree that modern nation-states presented one method for making sense of these changes; and in their work they defined, protected, or exalted their respective cultures. But they disagreed on what the nation-state meant, whom the nation included, and what kind of cultural works best depicted that nation. The cultural arena, as a result, was as hotly contested as the political one. Chapter 9, then, covers the same chronological period as chapter 8 (roughly 1930–1950) but instead emphasizes cultural formulations, including new understandings of race, class, and gender. We move geographically from north (Mexico and Central America) to south (the Andes and the Southern Cone).

In some ways, the cultural arena *was* the political arena. National governments understood that they needed to manage the production of culture in order to mold their citizenries. To that end, state cultural administration, in the form of museums, ministries of culture, and government propaganda, expanded dramatically. New mass media, including radio, the recording industry, and film were seen as especially vital and potentially insidious, as well.

These initiatives were common throughout the world. In the United States, Franklin Delano Roosevelt's "New Deal" responded to the Great Depression in part by putting artists on the payroll of the Works Progress Administration and charging them with documenting and defining a nation in transition. Image-making became a responsibility shared by every program and department: Roosevelt's Farm Security Administration, for example, became famous less for its efforts to provide material assistance to poor farmers than for its documentary photography, which revealed the face of rural poverty and resilience to the rest of America. In a more sinister example, Joseph Goebbels, Nazi minister of propaganda, oversaw a diabolical machinery of cultural production. The Nazi project was a controlled exercise in visual propaganda, exemplified by highly choreographed massive rallies that brought Hitler's words to millions of enthusiastic Germans. One of the most terrifying aspects of Nazi image-making is that many of the works remain unforgettably striking.

As noted in chapter 8, the example of Mustafa Kemal Atatürk in Turkey perhaps had more in common with the industrializing nations of Latin America. Atatürk

≡ **Indigenous Couple, Model, and the Stone of Twelve Sides.** Race and class in the Andean nations are vividly depicted in this image that contrasts the impoverished indigenous couple with the glamorous white fashion model. The couple's ragged clothing and sandals also contrast with the model's elegant dress and high heels. As was considered appropriate, the model has the sidewalk to herself while the indigenous couple are relegated to the street. To sharpen the contrast, the three are strolling beside one of the quintessential examples of fine Inca stonework—the stone of twelve sides—fitted without a drop of mortar into the middle of this wall of Emperor Huayna Capac's palace.

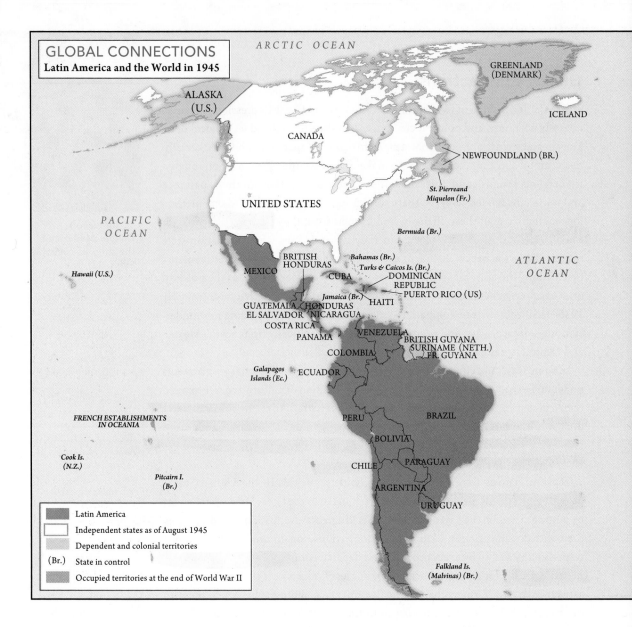

GLOBAL CONNECTIONS
Latin America and the World in 1945

ARCTIC OCEAN

GREENLAND
(DENMARK)

ICELAND

ALASKA
(U.S.)

CANADA

NEWFOUNDLAND (BR.)

St. Pierre and
Miquelon (Fr.)

PACIFIC
OCEAN

UNITED STATES

Bermuda (Br.)

ATLANTIC
OCEAN

Hawaii (U.S.)

BRITISH
HONDURAS

MEXICO

Bahamas (Br.)

Turks & Caicos Is. (Br.)

CUBA   DOMINICAN
           REPUBLIC
Jamaica (Br.) HAITI PUERTO RICO (US)

GUATEMALA HONDURAS
EL SALVADOR NICARAGUA
COSTA RICA
PANAMA

VENEZUELA
           BRITISH GUYANA
           SURINAME (NETH.)
COLOMBIA   FR. GUYANA

Galapagos   ECUADOR
Islands (Ec.)

FRENCH ESTABLISHMENTS
IN OCEANIA

PERU   BRAZIL

BOLIVIA

Cook Is.
(N.Z.)

Pitcairn I.
(Br.)

CHILE   PARAGUAY

ARGENTINA

URUGUAY

Falkland Is.
(Malvinas) (Br.)

Latin America
Independent states as of August 1945
Dependent and colonial territories
(Br.)   State in control
Occupied territories at the end of World War II

sought to create the foundations of a modern, secular nation through a vast program of economic development and cultural management. His strategies of expanding public education (for both boys and girls), sponsoring nationalist cultural expression while suppressing criticism from ethnic minorities, and stoking a propaganda machine that projected his own image as the icon of the modernizing nation bore many similarities to developments in Brazil, Argentina, and Mexico, for example.

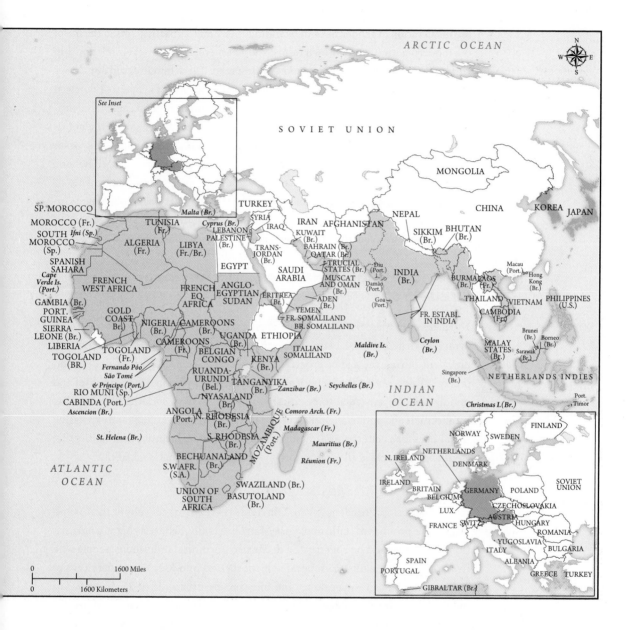

These experiments in cultural management resulted not only from natural growth and urbanization, which concentrated populations and made them more visible, but also of an expansion of the notion of citizenship. The rural poor, descendants of slaves, indigenous peoples, and impoverished immigrants—sectors formerly considered by many officeholders to be marginal—were increasingly understood as vital to the future of the nation. This expansion of citizenship entailed a reconsideration of gender, as understandings of women as participants in the life of the modern nation on their own terms, and not merely through their relationship with a father or husband, became more widespread. These impulses did not always take a positive direction: For example, the fascist government of Spain's Francisco Franco aggressively sought to eliminate minority languages and regional identities in favor of a single pan-Spanish identity, while on the other side of the political spectrum, the USSR's Josef Stalin pursued a similar goal by suppressing other nationalities and ethnicities under a common "Russian" rubric. But elsewhere, cultural management expressed itself as a dramatic expansion of citizenship to previously marginalized sectors of society. In particular, national governments increasingly came to understand that the expansion of suffrage and public education were part and parcel of the urgent demands of cultural administration.

New Ideas about Race in Latin America, 1920–1935

Nowhere were these transitions more apparent than in debates about the meaning of race. Even before 1930, Latin Americans had begun to confront the racist notions prevalent during the age of progress and modernization. Reformers understood that racist stereotypes dating back centuries and held by Latin American elites and middle class alike needed to be discarded before modern societies could evolve. Intellectuals and politicians, reflecting on their nations' past failures and expressing their hopes for a better future, now dreamed about a more inclusive community that would bring people of all races, colors, and creeds into the national family.

The Ideas about Mestizaje in Mexico

José Vasconcelos, President Alvaro Obregón's secretary of education, and his colleague the prominent anthropologist Manuel Gamio, believed that a single national culture could be constructed in Mexico once rural indigenous people who lived outside the mainstream became incorporated into Mexican society (essentially mestizo, Spanish-speaking, and increasingly urban). In 1925, Vasconcelos published his deeply influential book, *La Raza Cósmica*, in which he offered his vision of this more inclusive society. He argued that modern Mexico had been born from two cultures (Spanish and indigenous) that had melded together over four hundred years into a single mestizo culture. For Vasconcelos and Gamio, the process of assimilating indigenous people into this more inclusive culture, a process called **mestizaje**, would result in a uniform national identity. To their way of thinking, the mestizo took the best from both heritages to create a superior Mexican race. Both intellectuals agreed that promoting the assimilation of indigenous peoples into Mexican mestizo society, while simultaneously encouraging each ethnic group to preserve their cultural heritage, would ultimately benefit both Mexico and the long neglected elements of society.

Manuel Gamio, the scientific anthropologist, explained that in his opinion, material culture rather than biology explained the divide separating mestizos from indigenous peoples. While indigenous people ate maize and beans, drank pulque, lived in adobe huts, and spoke their own languages, mestizos preferred meat and European grains, drank beer, wore Western-style clothing, and spoke Spanish. Gamio and Vasconcelos pointed out that indigenous people passed for mestizos regardless of their biological parentage if they had assimilated and adopted mestizo markers and habits.

To "redeem" and assimilate indigenous people, Vasconcelos promoted education. He built a thousand rural schools, designed to educate a new kind of citizen who would be steeped in the values of the Mexican Revolution. Besides teaching young indigenous people Spanish and modern agricultural methods, Vasconcelos's rural schools inculcated nationalistic values by teaching students about Mexican history and its heroes, while requiring them to sing the national anthem and celebrate national holidays. Schools also dispensed moral lessons designed to reduce alcohol consumption and postpone teenage marriages, typical barriers to indigenous progress in the eyes of the reformers. By following this curriculum, the government hoped to "liberate" indigenous Mexicans from their traditional values while expanding their knowledge of the greater nation.

Indigenismo in Mexico

While many intellectuals agreed with Vasconcelos about the importance of mestizaje, they simultaneously endorsed the idea of **indigenismo**, the exaltation of indigenous cultures as a key component of Mexico's national identity. While most post-independence regimes before the Revolution had saluted the past glories of the pre-Hispanic Aztecs and the Maya, they uniformly disparaged what they believed was the poverty, ignorance, drunkenness, and laziness of contemporary Indians. Manuel Gamio and other indigenistas argued that Mexican culture should reflect the creativity of the rural popular classes. They asserted that the contributions of living indigenous people and their popular art to Mexican national identity must be celebrated, but on terms that prioritized the Mexican nation at the expense of local indigenous identities and culture.

To that end, a Mexico City newspaper sponsored a "Beautiful Indian" contest in 1921, won by a short, brown-skinned, dark-eyed, straight-haired young woman who would not have been allowed to compete in traditional Miss Mexico pageants. These intellectuals also spearheaded the drive to initiate an Exposition of

Popular Arts during the same year, exhibiting the clothing, jewelry, ceramics, and lacquered handicrafts of regional Mexican artisans. The interest in indigenous popular culture as a national expression exploded in the 1930s, and became commercially successful worldwide.

During the 1930s, indigenista reformers argued that advancing the cause of indigenous people and their art should focus on local cultures. By taking a less centralized and more locally sensitive approach to improving the lives of three million of Mexico's poorest citizens, these reformers hoped to rehabilitate indigenous people without removing them from their culture while simultaneously "improving" those cultures. Given the diversity of the indigenous population (Mexican groups spoke about 50 different languages), reformers abandoned the cookie-cutter approach to reform that had characterized educational policy in the 1920s. In 1933 the government also established **internados indígenas**, or Indian boarding schools, which focused on preserving local arts, crafts, and language while providing pupils with instruction in Spanish, hygiene, nutrition, and agriculture. At the same time, teachers in the federal rural schools proved willing to work with their communities to preserve community identity. With this more inclusive attitude and their willingness to assist with agrarian reform advocacy, the hostility to the federal schools and teachers that indigenous peoples had expressed in the earlier days of the indigenismo program significantly decreased.

The government also promoted unity by encouraging regional indigenous conferences where local community leaders could express their views. Indigenous communities petitioned the national government for tangible benefits such as schools, roads, bridges, and telephone lines, all of which incorporated once-isolated villages into greater Mexico. President Lázaro Cárdenas (1934-1940) was pleased to comply with these requests, not only because he genuinely believed in improving the lot of the rural poor but also because his nationalistic vision was essentially assimilationist. Under Cárdenas, while local interests were protected to a degree, the tangible successes of the indigenista project depended on funding from Mexico City. The more locally sensitive approach that some community leaders would have preferred would have to wait until later decades.

Indigenismo in Guatemala

Just to the south, in Guatemala, indigenismo played out very differently. Unlike Mexico, Guatemala was home to a majority indigenous population (predominantly Maya, though this ethnic group was differentiated by different languages and local customs). As in the three South American countries with indigenous majorities or near-majorities (Bolivia, Ecuador, and Peru), indigenismo, as both a national aspiration and an ideology, had both benefits and drawbacks. On the one hand, it promised to restore the rightful place of America's indigenous peoples in the national narrative and elevate their place in modern society. On the other, it denigrated their current culture and state of living as inferior to the preferred ladino template. In addition, indigenismo undertook to "elevate," "improve," and "modernize the Indian," but through assimilation—a high price for economic improvement that, for indigenous peoples, involved the abnegation of their ancient cultures. Last but not least, indigenismo pledged to bring full citizenship to native peoples—but this, too, came at high cost, at least for traditional elites and oligarchs, who feared that their voices and influence would be threatened by a newly empowered indigenous majority.

In Guatemala, indigenismo was often used as a way to blame the contradictions of national development on the presence of the nation's large native population. It engaged some of Guatemala's greatest minds during the period that ran roughly from the last decade of the nineteenth century until the 1930s, when it helped to define the policies of the Depression-era strongman Jorge Ubico. Elite Guatemalans believed their country to be on the cusp of becoming a modern and prosperous nation. In their view, however, the large indigenous majority was resistant to progress and blocked Guatemala's path to modernity.

Early indigenista thought in Guatemala predated Mexico's indigenista movement, surfacing first in the work of Antonio Batres Jáuregui, a member of elite Guatemalan European heritage, whose *Los indios: Su historia y su civilización* (1893) celebrated the golden Maya past. (Notably, most of the prominent indigenista writers were not themselves of indigenous background.) At the same time, Batres Jáuregui portrayed contemporary indigenous people as innately inferior, characterized by indolence, drunkenness, ill health, ignorance, and poverty. Subsequent indigenista writers made different claims for the cause of this purported inferiority, ranging from biological to historical and even phrenological explanations, but all agreed that contemporary Indian "degradation" (a common and recurring term-of-art in the literature) stunted the natural growth of the developing nation.

The indigenistas proposed assimilationist development, meant to "civilize" indigenous people (in the view of elites) and integrate them into national life. This translated into the improvement of Indians' material circumstances along expressly Western, mestizo lines. These included, among other things, education, *castellanización* (the use of Spanish in place of native languages), state regulation of labor, and improved basic public health.

Within the discourse of indigenismo lay a minefield of internal contradictions. For example, Miguel Angel Asturias, another rising intellectual and a scion of the

Guatemalan elite, referred to the indigenous population as the "national beasts." He questioned whether or not they were indeed capable of development, and, if so, whether their elevation from degradation would ultimately truly serve the good of the nation as a whole. In general, Guatemalan indigenismo assumed fluidity across ethnic and racial categories by essentially defining contemporary "Indianness" as a pathology to be cured by modernity's various remedies.

But before the cure could be exacted, elites needed to make a full diagnosis of the illness. Intellectuals such as Asturias undertook the process of diagnosis and prescription in his 1923 graduate thesis, titled *El problema social del indio* (The Indian Social Problem). Asturias's work turned indigenismo into the template of modernism in Guatemala during the early twentieth century. For Asturias, the diagnostic pathogens of "Indianness" included poor nutrition and hygiene, excessive work, premature marriage, and poverty. Alcoholism, in Asturias's judgment "most contributed to the degenerate defects" of the Indians.

In the short run, indigenismo in Guatemala produced a fresh variety of laws and regulations meant to forcibly modernize indigenous life. For example, the government forbade the use of indigenous languages in public discourse. It imposed new regulations on alcohol consumption and cracked down on the production of illegal homebrew, a staple of indigenous fiestas (and a vital component of Maya cultural life). The government made tentative forays into a few communities by introducing basic sanitary services, such as potable water and mosquito-eradication programs, as well as making some modest efforts at expanding public education to Maya children (although mainly only boys).

Unlike Mexico, where indigenismo encouraged a flourishing cultural productivity—the great muralists such as Diego Rivera and José Clemente Orozco, for example, visually rewrote Mexico's history—Guatemala's indigenismo generated only a modest creative outflow, specifically in literature. Guatemala's most heralded indigenista intellectual was Asturias himself, whose thinking on the "Indian problem" transformed rather dramatically over time. While never recanting his youthful explication of "**el problema indio**," Asturias nonetheless went on to write what remains one of Central America's most acclaimed novels, *Hombres de Maiz* (Men of Maize) in 1949; this book features an indigenous protagonist, Gaspar Ilom, and portrays a premodern indigenous community besieged by modernity and rapacious outsiders. Asturias later wrote a well-known poem to Tecum Uman, the last king of the K'iche' Maya, slain by the Spaniards while defending his people in 1524. For these and his other works, Asturias was awarded the Nobel Prize for Literature in 1967, the first Guatemalan and only the second Latin American to win this prestigious award.

Pan-Africanism, Negritude, and New Ideas about Blackness in Latin America

Just as indigenismo became a powerful set of ideas in much of Latin America, particularly in nations shaped deeply by indigenous ancestry, new understandings of blackness informed debates on race and citizenship, particularly in nations marked deeply by the experience of African slavery. Cuba's Partido Independiente de Color, suppressed through state-sponsored massacre in 1912 (as discussed in chapter 6) gave one strong indication of elite fear of the potential of such identification. For the next several decades, new understandings of blackness tended to emphasize the cultural importance of the African contribution to modern nations, as in the Brazilian case, discussed later in this chapter.

This emphasis on African cultural inheritance could be absorbed and even exploited by political elites in order to deny the existence of racism. But it could also be used by humbler citizens of African ancestry to demand greater access to civil rights and legal protections. In this regard, new ideas of blackness in Latin America drew on and contributed to broader international ideas of **Pan-Africanism** and negritude. Marcus Garvey (1887–1940), the foremost exponent of Pan-Africanist mobilization in the first half of the twentieth century, was born and raised in Jamaica, then worked for several years in Central America. Garvey's experiences working on a banana plantation in Costa Rica and as a newspaper editor in Panama shaped his understanding of the possibilities for political mobilization of Afro-descendant populations across national boundaries. Garvey later came to prominence as an activist in his native Jamaica and in the United States, where his outspoken advocacy of black economic and political mobilization put him at the center of debates on race and citizenship. Garvey's scheme for African American migration to Liberia, idealized as the foundation of a powerful, industrial nation, caused controversy across the political spectrum.

The idea of a symbolic return to Africa through voluntary migration did not attract much sympathy in Latin America. But the broader goal of transnational solidarity among Afro-descendant peoples did, informing debates in places ranging from Cuba and the Dominican Republic to Ecuador and Peru. These debates were transformed again in the 1930s and 1940s with the growing influence of the ideas of **negritude,** espoused by intellectuals from the French colonies of Martinique, Senegal, and French Guiana. Negritude drew inspiration from the Haitian Revolution, and blended ideas of Pan-African mobilization with Marxist understandings of structural oppression and the inevitability of revolution. Negritude, as well, became part of the political vocabulary of black Latin Americans. By the 1950 and

1960s, proponents of negritude in Latin America espoused black political mobilization, rejecting claims of colorblind citizenship and challenging elites to address the legacies and continued existence of racism.

Engagement with ideas of Pan-Africanism and negritude in Latin America was never a simple importation of foreign ideologies. Pan-Africanism and negritude, rather, were initially shaped in part by ideas and experiences emerging from Latin America. They found resonance there, and were in turn transformed again as they became Latin Americanized.

Cultural Nationalism: The Mexican Example, 1920–1955

As Mexico's Secretary of Education, José Vasconcelos oversaw a far-reaching project to promote secular nationalism rooted in belief in the power of la raza cósmica and the legacy of the Mexican Revolution. The artists who participated in this project turned 1920s and 1930s Mexico into an extraordinarily vibrant cultural legacy, one of the twentieth century's most vibrant anywhere.

Artists and the Development of Mexican National Culture

Two Mexican artists, Diego Rivera and José Clemente Orozco, gained international fame for the quality of their work in the 1920s. (A third muralist, David Siquieros, became quite prominent within Mexico itself). Cultural pilgrims from the United States—artists, writers, and historians—who spent time in Mexico and saw the artists' works went home and stimulated US interest in Mexican art. The first of these two artists, Diego Rivera (1886–1957), was (both literally and figuratively) a giant among his colleagues, standing six feet tall and weighing over 300 pounds. Rivera's acquaintances wrote that his enormous head, bulging eyes, and corpulent body made him resemble a huge frog (a noun he used to describe himself). Rivera reveled in the bohemian atmosphere of the era and indulged in sexual conquest as a form of creative license. Rivera's paramours included the sister of his third wife, Frida Kahlo. Flamboyant, charismatic, and full of energy, he dabbled in politics, and along with Kahlo joined the Communist Party. Rivera was later expelled from the party because of his unorthodox doctrinal beliefs and his friendship with capitalists like Henry Ford and John D. Rockefeller.

Rivera's precocious aptitude for drawing enabled him to enroll in the prestigious Academy of San Carlos at nine years of age. He then received a grant from Porfirio Díaz's government to study painting in Spain, a "Cortés in reverse" as one biographer described him. There Rivera sharpened his technique and befriended a number of important artists like Pablo Picasso. In 1921 he returned to Mexico, skilled in painting the fresco murals soon to be the trademark form of Mexico's cultural nationalism.

Meanwhile, José Vasconcelos had organized the Syndicate of Technical Workers, Artists, and Sculptors to further his project of promoting public art. Believing that art should serve a social function, he allocated significant sums to pay artists to paint murals with nationalistic themes in highly visible public spaces. Rivera and José Clemente Orozco shared Vasconcelos's vision and endorsed the idea that art should enrich the lives of the general public, not just private patrons. Rivera received commissions to paint prominent murals at the Ministry of Education building, the converted Chapel at Chapingo, and most importantly, alongside the stairway of the National Palace in the Zócalo, the heart of Mexico City.

Inspired by the vivid colors he saw during a visit to the Isthmus of Tehuantepec in southern Mexico, Rivera used them to contrast with the brown figures of workers and peasants whom he made the heroes of his paintings. Rivera defined true Mexicans as people of color. Each panel of his murals had a didactic purpose; often they compared the cruelty of evildoers (conquistadores, Spanish overseers, avaricious priests, and Porfirian gentry) to the glorified workers laboring in harmony in factory and field. Rivera began working on the extensive project at the National Palace in the 1930s and only completed the task in the mid-1950s. Here, he unveiled his interpretation of Mexico's history beginning with the idyllic pre-Hispanic cultures, the violence of the Conquest, the cruelty and excesses of the colonial period through the Díaz regime, concluding with the ultimate triumph of Revolutionary heroes like Emiliano Zapata, the workers, and peasants.

José Clemente Orozco (1883–1949), the second great muralist painter, remained in Rivera's shadow for most of his career. Having lost his left hand and some vision in a childhood explosion, Orozco faced physical obstacles that might have daunted a less determined individual. Perhaps because of his experience, his view of life (and hence his painting) was more pessimistic than Rivera's. His dark tones and occasional flashes of bright reds and white created startling visual contrasts. Orozco first won recognition as a great painter while living in the United States, when he displayed a series of somber drawings titled *The Horrors of the Revolution*. Later, the Jalisco state government commissioned Orozco's most famous murals in the state capital, Guadalajara. One striking mural shows independence leader Father Hidalgo, whose brown skin and white hair contrasts with his black coat and the flaming red eruption glowing behind him. Orozco's *Man of Fire* in the city's orphanage was the centerpiece of a series of painted vaults that depicted the history of the interplay of Spaniards and the indigenous people of Mexico. In all his murals, Orozco castigated corrupt and dishonest politicians, labor leaders, and bureaucrats. Like Rivera, he idealized campesinos and workers. Rivera and Orozco's art visually epitomized the message about Mexico's struggle for social justice for the indigenous people and national identity.

Frida Kahlo: Art and the Importance of Popular Culture

Frida Kahlo (1907–1954) expressed her cultural nationalism in a very different way. Born to a successful German immigrant photographer and his Mexican wife, Kahlo attended the best schools in Mexico City. As a young girl she overcame polio and a horrific streetcar accident during which a steel pole impaled her, fracturing her spine in three places and breaking her pelvis. She suffered tremendous physical pain throughout her adult life, requiring thirty-two surgeries in an attempt to relieve her misery. Painting distracted her during her lengthy hospital stays. In 1928 she met and married Diego Rivera, beginning a tumultuous relationship that would last until her death. Like Rivera and another great muralist, David Siqueiros, she joined the Communist Party. She willingly shared Rivera's bohemian lifestyle, taking lovers of both genders, including the famed dissident Soviet revolutionary Leon Trotsky. In the late 1940s she rejoined the Communist Party and remained a member for the rest of her life.

As she and Rivera traveled throughout the United States, Kahlo proclaimed herself a Mexican nationalist in part by the clothing she wore. As a mestiza, she identified both with the cultural nationalism project and also with the mestizaje policy of "uplifting" indigenous people. To that end, she dressed as a *"china poblana"* (a woman from the state of Puebla, who traditionally wore

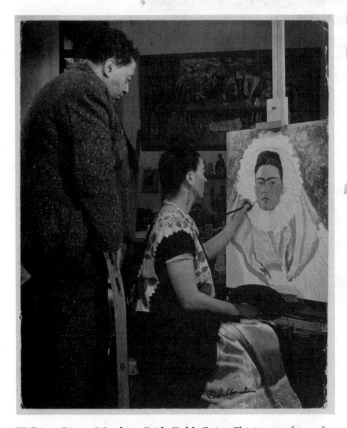

≡ **Diego Rivera Watching Frida Kahlo Paint.** This image of two of the greatest Mexican painters of the twentieth century captures them at a warm domestic moment. Even though their styles differed radically, Diego Rivera admired Frida Kahlo's work (he had encouraged her to study art when she was young), and the two were of similar minds politically, both affiliating at times with the Communist Party. Both also used their art to express themes of Mexican nationalism. Frida's admiration of the colors prevalent in flowers and clothing in southern Mexico inspired both of them.

ornate dresses in the colonial period), usually paired with long, Spanish-style gold earrings or other colonial jewelry. At times she wore an indigenous *rebozo* (a long garment worn around the head and shoulders) and at other times a lacy Spanish shawl. Typically, she wore her hair up in any one of a number of Mexican regional styles. Fashion editors in San Francisco, among other cities, celebrated her style.

More importantly, Kahlo's small, intimate paintings exemplified both Mexican cultural nationalism and the artistic spirit of the age. She did her best work in the late 1930s and 1940s, particularly her self-portraits, which simultaneously depicted her physical and emotional pain and the deep roots of Mexican culture. One example of the latter theme is *My Nurse and I*, in which Kahlo portrays herself as a mestiza baby at the breast of a very stern-looking indigenous wet nurse. Perhaps her best-known painting, *The Two Fridas*, also expresses her interest in mestizaje. One Frida has pale skin and is attired in a white European-style dress, while her counterpart has dark skin and is clothed in a Tehuana skirt and blouse. The two figures sit starkly alone, probably describing Frida's inner feelings about her (temporary) divorce from Rivera. Kahlo continued to paint similar scenes of illness but with nationalistic themes until her painful death. Although not as famous as the muralists in her own lifetime, Frida Kahlo's work gained greater influence and renown in the 1980s and beyond as a representation of feminism and of Mexican cultural nationalism.

Mass Media: Promoting Revolutionary Mexican Culture, 1935–1960

More disposable income among Mexico's urban population as well as increased literacy allowed Mexicans to take advantage of several new forms of popular culture, including movies and comic books. For both of these genres, the era from the late 1940s until the 1960s represented a golden age when national productions outsold imported popular culture from the United States. More importantly, these media helped to mold modern Mexican culture as a compromise between the secularism and modernity of the Revolution and more traditional values of family and religiosity.

The Golden Age of Cinema

During Mexico's "golden age" of cinema, movies became a vehicle to transmit ideas about national culture to broad audiences. During World War II Mexican cinema blossomed. Like Hollywood, the Mexican studio system of the 1940s used famous stars to woo viewers. Because movie tickets were so inexpensive, films reached broad audiences and spread cultural nationalism. The nation's most famous director, Emilio Fernández, nicknamed "El Indio," oversaw the production of several films that clearly expressed the indigenista message. Perhaps the 1944 classic

María Candelaria, which won prizes at the prestigious Cannes Film Festival, best exemplifies El Indio's interpretation of Mexico's cultural nationalism.

The plot of *María Candelaria* centers on an idyllic indigenous couple: María, played by the Hollywood legend Dolores del Río (in real life a light-skinned mestiza) and Lorenzo (Pedro Armendáriz). Set in the indigenous community of Xochimilco, the impoverished flower-seller María finds herself unable to repay the debt she owes the greedy mestizo storekeeper. He covets her pig, which she refuses to give him because she intends to sell it to pay for her wedding to Lorenzo. Rebuffed, the storekeeper shoots the pig in anger. To complicate the couple's lives further, María contracts malaria, and because they have no money, Lorenzo steals the curative drug, quinine, from the storekeeper, who has Lorenzo jailed for the crime. Meanwhile, a famed artist has noticed María selling flowers, becomes captivated by her beauty, and asks her to pose in the nude. Although she refuses, being desperate for money, she agrees to let the artist paint her fully clothed. In the finished picture the artist eliminates her clothes, and when the painting is displayed, the scandalized villagers call María a prostitute and stone her to death. Hearing about the danger María faces, Lorenzo breaks out of jail, but she is already dead. Heartbroken, he lays her corpse in a canoe surrounded by the flowers she loved so much.

This romanticized film glorified the beautiful landscape of Xochimilco's "floating gardens," one of the last remnants of pre-Hispanic agriculture, and portrayed its indigenous protagonists idealistically. *María Candelaria* also showed the contradiction implicit in the Mexican state's two expressions of cultural nationalism: indigenismo and mestizaje. While the government embraced mestizaje as a unifying ideal that would assimilate indigenous people into the national culture, individual artists like El Indio depicted not only the indigenous past but also more importantly his awareness of indigenous peoples' present reality. *María Candelaria* further heightened the ambiguities of Mexico's official cultural nationalism by identifying the mestizo store owner as the villain of the film.

Comic Books

During the concurrent golden age of comic books, that genre shared the ambiguous nature of Mexican cultural nationalism. On one hand, many comics depicted the new modernity of urban Mexico of the 1940s and particularly the modern woman, now frequently working outside of the home as a teacher, industrial worker, or doctor. Yet at the same time, graphic artists were aware of the need to placate conservative elements in society who denounced comics because of their alleged corrupting influence on the values of Mexico's youth. As a result, most comics sought a middle ground acceptable to the general public in order to escape the condemnation of the censorship commission. Comics rarely critiqued the government, which allowed them to operate as a voice of mild dissent. In the minds of these graphic artists contributing to Mexican national culture, these two complementary national cultures could coexist.

For example, the popular comic *Adelita* (the namesake of the heroine recollects the subject of Mexico's most famous corrido) depicted the adventures of two *chicas modernas* (modern girls). Along with her friend Nancy, a professional detective, Adelita wore suits to work, used makeup, met with men in public places, and undoubtedly planned to work after she married. Both endured melodramatic plot twists, losing a parent during the Revolution, being held prisoner by a mad scientist, but always escaping with their virtue intact. Like other modern women, they sought marriage partners with whom they shared an emotional attachment and common interests, as well as a strong sexual attraction. Yet the creators of comics made certain that these modern women shared their stage with more traditional women who valued family and faith.

Mexico's Practical Programs to Reform National Culture, 1926–1940

Mexican Revolutionary politicians also sought pragmatic measures that would incorporate indigenous people into the nation. These concrete changes would allow rural indigenous people to claim their equal and rightful place as citizens. Between 1920 and 1940, the postrevolutionary leadership experimented with several measures designed to create the "new revolutionary citizen." These policies, part pragmatic and part idealistic, sought to destroy the influence of what they regarded as the malevolent institutions responsible for rural "backwardness": the Catholic Church, the hacienda, and the *cantina* (neighborhood bar).

The Campaign against the Church and Its Consequences

Like nineteenth-century Liberals, many postrevolutionary leaders, and especially President Plutarco Elías Calles (1924–1928), focused their attention on the Catholic Church as the most potent enemy of the plan to incorporate indigenous people into the nation. Calles believed the clergy were dangerous because their objectives were diametrically opposed to that of the secular state. Unlike nineteenth-century liberals, who merely sought to reduce the wealth and the secular power of the Church, Calles felt that the Church's pervasive influence over rural peoples' minds posed the principal danger to the Revolution's message. While the government and its idealistic teachers used the Marxist language of class conflict to urge their students to struggle against the elites to achieve a new social order, the Church's alternative vision offered the possibility of defusing social tensions by suggesting, under the precepts of the papal bull **Rerum Novarum**, (1891) that laborers and property owners could work together in harmony under clerical guidance to create a better world.

Calles wanted to weaken the Church's cultural hold on rural peoples by using strident anticlericalism to free rural folk (in his rhetoric) from the shackles of obedience to parasitic priests. The plan called for teachers to substitute for the Mass secular activities such as celebrations of national holidays, performances of folkloric music and dances from all over the country, and the singing of patriotic songs. By teaching practical subjects like improved agricultural methods and better hygiene as well as Spanish, secular schoolteachers hoped to convince campesinos that they deserved more than a life of poverty on earth with the promise of a heavenly reward thereafter. In an ironic sense, the new schoolteachers, many of whom were women, acted like secular missionaries, teaching rural peoples new values. They purposely created the school as the "house of the people" in juxtaposition to the "House of God."

Many rural people (but not all) resisted the government's attempts to change their culture by beating and sometimes even killing teachers. In many cases, rural people viewed teachers as alien, intrusive, and untrustworthy outsiders. The growing hostility between the secular-minded and more religious folk escalated in 1926 when Mexico City's archbishop advised the faithful that they need not obey the anticlerical provisions of the Constitution. Calles took umbrage at this effrontery and ordered his governors to implement Articles 3 and 130 by closing parochial schools, limiting the numbers of priests within state boundaries, and restricting priests' ability to perform the sacraments publicly. Even more radically, Calles forced priests to register with the state governments just like all other professional persons and took away their right to vote. Within the states, anti-Catholic legislation went even further by prohibiting new priests from being ordained and even demanding that clergy be forced to marry—although most of these more outrageous laws never went into full effect.

In response, the Church went on strike, and no longer offered the sacraments. Although the hierarchy counseled compromise and many priests surreptitiously performed Mass, baptisms, and marriages, pious laypersons in states like Michoacán and Jalisco in Mexico's center-west region launched the Cristero Revolt (1926–1929), called **La Cristiada** in Spanish. Shouting "Viva Cristo Rey" ("Long Live Christ the King!") as they ambushed federal troops, executed teachers, and burned schools, the *Cristeros* (literally, "Christers"), proved impossible to crush despite the federal army's overwhelming superiority (and equally vicious counterinsurgency tactics, including the execution of priests and the stabling of horses in churches to desecrate them). Finally, US Ambassador Dwight Morrow brokered a compromise. The Cristeros laid down their arms in 1929 and Calles agreed not to enforce some anticlerical measures. Priests resumed offering the sacraments, but could only offer religious instruction at Sunday school and had to register with the government.

Although the Cristero Revolt demonstrated the persistence of popular religious culture in certain regions of Mexico, Calles and his successor, Lázaro Cárdenas, continued to attempt to create "rational" and modern rural people by using education to undermine the faith, or as they more colorfully put it, to end superstition and fanaticism. Cárdenas's "socialist education" initiative ran into snags because of the state's emphasis on building coeducational schools. Several prominent cases of teachers accused of sexual misconduct with students provoked widespread outrage. Parents and priests exploded in anger, awakening the possibility of a renewed Cristero rebellion. Cárdenas listened to the protests and, beginning in 1936, began to tone down anticlerical rhetoric in favor of a program that more clearly fit his priority, agrarian reform. Teachers, too, muted the message of socialist education and worked with the community on other projects of local interest as well. Nevertheless, the antipathy aroused by Cárdenas's socialist education program engendered distrust and hampered his efforts to enact agrarian reform. By 1940, the government had succeeded in creating a greater sense of inclusive cultural nationalism, but had failed to subvert the Catholic Church. It would take many decades until the Catholic Church and the government in Mexico fully reconciled. Mexico's population remained among the most devout in all of Latin America.

Destroying the Hacienda: The Agrarian Reform Program

Mexico's postrevolutionary leadership envisioned the attack on the hacienda and the redistribution of its land as a program for social justice that would promote greater egalitarianism. Agrarian reform was never intended to be a plan for economic development. Cárdenas's vision of the revolutionary citizen was based on his belief that impoverished rural Mexicans deserved a helping hand from the government, to redress the imbalance of property ownership that had occurred during the Porfiriato. This philosophy coincided with a grassroots demand for land and the ongoing activities of village revolutionaries who led local agrarian movements. The first two postrevolutionary presidents had soft-pedaled the implementation of agrarian reform, citing the tenuous economic situation in the 1920s following the decade of destruction and local resistance on the part of elites, the clergy and the owners of many small- to medium-sized farms. Cárdenas, however, placed a priority on agrarian reform and expanded the process of redistributing lands. Between 1935 and 1938, Cárdenas turned the teachers' youthful idealism in a different direction—encouraging villages to petition the government for land. Over the next three years Cárdenas redistributed roughly 43,730,000 acres (17,891,522 *hectares*) of land to Mexico's campesinos, largely in the form of collective *ejidos*.

Cárdenas was able to parcel out such large quantities of property in part because of the pent-up demand for land as well as the fact that he had created a successful national coalition with labor and campesinos during his presidential campaign. In addition, the legal process for land redistribution gave tremendous authority to the president. Once a local community petitioned for land, the document wound its way through the governmental bureaucracy until it was either approved or rejected by the president. While earlier chief executives had denied many petitions, Cárdenas did not, because he believed that a wholesale attack on the hacienda was the most effective way to transform rural society.

Agrarian reform advocates debated whether parcels should be granted outright to individuals (thereby raising the dangerous possibility that they could be sold) or that usufruct rights (the right to use the property with the title remaining in the hands of the nation) should be transferred to collective ejidos. Cárdenas favored the latter, not only as a means of guaranteeing that the property remained in indigenous hands but also because it took advantage of the economies of scale. In certain agricultural industries, ejidos could purchase a single piece of expensive equipment necessary to plant and harvest sugar, cotton, and henequen. The entire community could then share use of the machine.

The ejido program enjoyed mixed success. For example, with the help of teachers writing petitions, the Yaquis of Sonora received a large grant of ejido lands, thereby ending hundreds of years of resistance and conflict as they sought to regain their ancestral properties in the fertile Yaqui Valley. By invoking the statute that limited land ownership to a maximum of 250 acres in the state of Sonora, Cárdenas could confiscate the lands belonging to US companies and grant it to the Yaquis. Cárdenas relished the opportunity to finally incorporate the Yaqui into the nation, so he invested resources: building new housing, providing medical facilities, banning liquor, offering night classes, and introducing organized sports. The Yaqui absorbed some of these changes while rejecting others, and continue to assert their autonomy nearly a century later.

While many ejidos were successful at first, population pressures and land exhaustion took their toll. Other important ejidos also fell short of Cárdenas's expectations. His greatest hope was for La Laguna, a cotton-producing region in the north, which he converted into an enormous ejido in 1936. Despite large loans from the National Ejido Agrarian Bank, productivity declined by 1938. Campesinos complained that not everybody worked equally hard; some sought out the cushiest jobs or just loafed. As a result, many ejido members said that they preferred to receive individual plots. Others complained that they had been omitted from the redistribution of land, or that they had insufficient land to meet their family's needs. And La Laguna fared better than most ejidos because it had received such a massive infusion of government capital. By 1938, however, the combination of a recession and the cost of the oil expropriation (chapter 8) allowed more conservative elements within the Revolutionary family to force Cárdenas to retreat from the land redistribution program. Nevertheless, Cárdenas's radical experiment remained Latin America's most extensive land reform program until the implementation of the Cuban Revolution in the 1960s. In short, Cárdenas's agrarian reform was a huge social and political success, even if it did not resolve the problem of rural poverty.

The Campaign against Vice

Postrevolutionary Mexican reformers, like their Porfirian forebears, perceived the village cantina as a pit of vice. Their efforts to shut down such establishments recapitulated a long history of attempts to police indigenous morals, and to restrict indigenous citizens from indulging habits more likely to be accepted among the mestizo population, such as drinking, gambling, and adultery. Priests in the colonial period preached against such behaviors to no avail, as did their secular cousins during the age of progress and modernization. Reformers paternalistically agreed that only if the rural poor turned away from such excesses could they become industrious citizens thoroughly incorporated into the nation. Such analysis never considered that while this behavior in part represented ancestral cultural traditions, it was also a psychological response to the abusive conditions that rural, often indigenous, people experienced on a regular basis. Although the climate of the early twentieth century seemed favorable to the temperance movement (the United States passed the Volstead Act mandating Prohibition in 1919), the Porfirian Anti-Alcohol League won adherents only among the elite and the middle class, with little success spreading its message to a broader audience.

The burden of promoting the postrevolutionary campaign against vice fell to teachers

≡ **Pulque Drinker.** The original caption to this picture reads: "Salud and Pesetas: Health and Money," which is the Mexican toast whenever two or more are gathered together to drink a glass of pulque. The native Mexican Indians claim it as their ancestral beverage and it is drunk fresh and comparatively pure with no harmful results. Pulque, made from the maguey plant, tastes like harsh and less refined tequila. It was the drink of the poor, considered too indelicate a spirit for middle- and upperclass drinkers. The photographer here endeavors to create a folkloric, "typical Indian" tableau.

and women. In communities that supported secular teachers and land redistribution, Women's and Girls' Clubs did their best to speak out against alcoholism. Women volunteered to improve campesinos' health by giving smallpox vaccinations. Volunteers burned garbage, cleaned streets, and tidied their own homes in an effort to comply with the goals of revolutionary citizenship. Cárdenas tried to regulate the sale of alcohol, outlaw card playing, and prohibit cockfights, but depriving people of their favorite recreational activities met with no more success than did Prohibition in the United States. Although Cárdenas did more than any other president before him to transform campesinos into revolutionary citizens, in this matter he fell short. At this juncture the national government simply did not enjoy the power to transform the countryside, especially when governors and regional elites thwarted this vision. After 1940 the effects of modernization would bring greater change to Mexico's rural areas, but not always for the better.

Indigenismo and Mestizaje in the Andean Nations, 1928–1980

The appealing ideas of indigenismo and mestizaje quickly spread throughout other Latin American nations with large unincorporated non-European populations. As Mexican and Guatemalan intellectuals had hoped, their works inspired Latin Americans in the Andean nations to rethink old ideas about race and instead focus their discussions on culture. Disagreements arose between the adherents of the moderate ideals of mestizaje, who wanted to create an inclusive national culture (as in Mexico); and the proponents of the radical vision of indigenismo, who believed that the dire situation of indigenous people demanded fundamental changes in the economy as well as the protection of their separate and distinct identities.

Andean Mestizaje

Because mestizaje promised a way to promote an inclusive national identity, it dominated Andean intellectuals' discourse from roughly the 1920s to approximately 1980. By holding out a positive message for the future, mestizaje appealed to those who wished to abandon the racism of the age of progress. As in Mexico, the proponents of mestizaje preached the unifying principles of cultural nationalism. Perhaps Benjamín Carrión, the founder of the Ecuadorian House of Culture, said it best in 1928: "My Ecuador ... will powerfully feel the words of José Vasconcelos, the prophet ... of the warm territories." The ongoing discussion about mestizaje and indigenismo encouraged the Eighth Pan-American Conference to schedule an Inter-American Indigenist Conference in Mexico in 1940. At that well-attended meeting, each Latin American country agreed to establish a national institute to explore contemporary indigenous issues. Ecuador was the first country to authorize such an institute. The government chose an all-white membership led by the nation's most distinguished anthropologist to lead the initiative. Passionate in their belief that the conditions under which Indians lived and worked must be improved, these scholars and political leaders agreed that these objectives could only be achieved if indigenous people were assimilated into the national culture as Vasconcelos had urged. From 1943 forward, the Ecuadorian government's official policy promoted mestizaje as the most effective instrument for cultural nationalism.

Many Peruvians felt similarly. Because the populist Víctor Raúl Haya de la Torre had spent much of his time in exile during the 1920s working for José Vasconcelos in the Secretariat of Education, the *Alianza Popular Revolucionaria Americana* (APRA) embraced mestizaje. APRA's middle-class membership in Cuzco resurrected the ancient Inka celebration of Inti Raymi (the winter solstice), but in addition to showcasing the past glories of the empire, the festivities incorporated mestizo contributions to Peruvian culture as well as contemporary folklore and crafts. To crown the festival parade in 1945, indigenous people bore a litter carrying the "Inka," played by a tall, light-skinned mestizo. Meanwhile, scholars observing the official embrace of mestizaje posed some difficult questions about its reality in the Andean world.

Observing the demographic changes that had occurred since the 1890s, namely the influx of rural indigenous peoples into urban centers, scholars of race and culture asked themselves whether these former campesinos who had learned to speak Spanish, wore Western-style clothing, had some education, and perceived themselves to be part of the growing mestizo

≡ **A Peruvian Mestizo Family.** British mining engineer Reginald Enoch, who traveled through Peru with an eye to developing its mineral resources and building railroads through the cordillera, wrote several books about the country and captured many interesting images during his travels in the Andes. At a discussion on Enoch's work held at the Royal Geographic Society in London, one of the members, speaking of the pre-Hispanic Incas, declared his astonishment that "such a people would have been at the zenith of their powers at the time when the climatic conditions of the country must have been severer, certainly, than they are at present. I know something of the [contemporary] Andean people, but amongst them all, there are not people who could have risen to such heights of civilization. They are incapable of developing such intelligence as those as have shown by those who built the wonderful fortresses and building of which you have seen pictures tonight." This comment also reflects the attitude of the Peruvian elite in 1916.

population, were really mestizos or remained indigenous at heart. Although questions like this exemplified the ambiguity surrounding mestizos, for proponents of mestizaje, more education, better healthcare, and full legal protection would finally complete the process of the assimilation of indigenous people into the greater nation. Over the next few decades, the Ecuadorian Institute (as well as the governments of that country and Peru) proved more successful in studying problems than in delivering concrete benefits to indigenous peoples. Interestingly, the place of Afro-Andeans was ignored in all of these discussions.

Andean Indigenismo

For some indigenistas, the proponents of mestizaje missed the point because their solutions failed to address the greater problem of the economic inequities inherent in rural society. The most famous of these indigenistas, the Peruvian writer José Carlos Mariátegui (1894–1930), inspired radicals for generations. Born into a family too poor to provide him with a university education, Mariátegui began working as a journalist while a teenager and soon impressed his contemporaries with the brilliance of his writings. His poor health (tuberculosis and an amputated leg) made him an unlikely candidate for active service in any revolution, but he more than compensated for his inability to fight with his inspired prose.

Building on the work of the indigenista author Manuel González Prada, who argued that Peru had lost the War of the Pacific because of its failure to incorporate indigenous people into the body politic and thereby inspire them to take up arms in defense of the nation, Mariátegui offered new solutions based on the Marxist ideas he absorbed while exiled in Europe. Returning to Peru, Mariátegui stumbled in the political arena. He found that his awkward public speaking abilities and his lack of charisma left his Socialist Party unable to compete with the ebullient populist Víctor Raúl Haya de la Torre. Nevertheless, Mariátegui's profound ideas inspired leftist Peruvian intellectuals.

Mariátegui believed that Peru's Inka past had laid the groundwork for the country's Marxist future. Building his analysis on the (later disproven) beliefs of some contemporary French archeologists, he suggested that the Inka had created an egalitarian socialist state. For Peru's social revolution to take place, he argued, the indigenous people of the highlands would need to rebel against the hacendados, their feudal oppressors, as well as the bourgeois sugar planters and bankers of the coastal region who dominated Peruvian politics in the 1920s. Mariátegui published his ideas first in a newspaper and then in his influential book, *Seven Interpretive Essays on Peruvian Reality* (1928). While his work appealed to Peruvian leftists because it blended Inka traditions with Marxist thinking, the Communist International disavowed Mariátegui because he proposed that peasants, and not industrial workers, would lead the revolution. In the 1970s, the influence of Mariátegui's ideas would be revived as a cornerstone of the guerrilla group, the Shining Path.

Although neither Ecuador nor Bolivia produced a radical indigenista theorist like Mariátegui, both countries faced demands from grassroots activists assisted by local communist and socialist parties in the 1930s. In Ecuador, a series of strikes, protests, and marches on Quito highlighted campesinos' complaints about the conditions on haciendas. Governments used violence to quell these riots and strikes, blaming the rural unrest on the presence of communist agitators. Despite government opposition, indigenous people in both countries held congresses during the 1940s to propose structural solutions to the problems of rural peoples. In Ecuador the FEI (Ecuadorian Federation of Indians) met in 1944 and proposed agrarian reform and the recognition of the separate identity of indigenous people—the creation of a pluralistic society.

These indigenous conferences differed from prior gatherings not only because indigenous people provided the leadership, but also because they addressed national rather than local problems. In addition, these indigenistas aspired to change the socioeconomic structure of rural life and completely rejected the idea of mestizaje. Neither Ecuador nor Bolivia would contemplate these ideas in the 1940s. Although the FEI met with no success at this time, its platform favoring the preservation of unique indigenous cultures would be revived in both Ecuador and Bolivia in the 1980s.

≡ **Peruvian Policeman Pulling an Indigenous Boy by the Ear, 1920s.** Everything about this photo speaks of difference: the pale skin of the mestizo policeman contrasts with the dark skin of the indigenous boy, the policeman's pressed, woolen uniform and leather shoes with the boy's ragged, homespun clothing and bare feet, the relatively tall and strong policeman with the tiny, vulnerable boy. And the image shows us clearly the everyday violence of social hierarchy in 1920s Peru. The policeman looks impassively at the lens. What is in the boy's gaze?

Cholas in the Andes

While Andean intellectuals and policy makers extolled the virtues of mestizaje as a means for creating a unified national identity, their vision did not always comport with reality. These leaders believed that education would refashion indigenous people and mestizos into citizens who would willingly adopt the westernized habits these policy makers perceived as inherently superior. But many of the subjects of this discourse, particularly the independent-minded *cholas* (mestizas whose cultural traits closely resembled those of the indigenous) had no intention of conforming to the whites' ideal.

Cholas in the Marketplace

Cholas occupy an enigmatic place in Andean society. From colonial times to the present, these women have dominated public market places. Distinguishing themselves from other mestizos who donned European clothing and learned Spanish in order to pass as whites, cholas proudly retain much of their indigenous heritage, particularly their language and dress. The term chola itself is ambiguous: it takes on derogatory inflections in some cases, but can also be affirmed as a positive identity, particularly among female vendors in Andean marketplaces, who often proudly self-identify as chola. Speaking Quechua in Peru, Quichua in Ecuador, and Aymara in Bolivia, these market vendors sell mostly to household servants and members of the popular classes who come to the urban marketplace to purchase fresh vegetables, meat, *chicha* (an alcoholic beverage made from fermented corn) and other commodities. Dressed in their traditional brightly colored *polleras* (multilayered skirts), shawls, and distinctive headgear (Panama hats in Ecuador, white stove-pipe hats in Cuzco, and in La Paz bowler hats made at the Italian Borsalino factory), these women display their indigenous roots, albeit in a way also marked by Spanish inheritance.

Elite city-dwellers considered cholas to be disturbing figures for a variety of reasons. First, they believed that cholas should remain in the countryside rather than invading modern and white-dominated urban spaces to hawk their wares. They resented the presence of these women in central urban plazas, traditionally a space tacitly reserved for well-heeled citizens. Entrepreneurs rather than servants or employees, cholas refused to fit within the economic, racial, or gender hierarchy. To compound the insult to patriarchy, these women not only work outside the home but also dominate the urban marketplace, as both sellers and buyers, and defer to nobody, not even to the men who truck goods and the venders to and from the marketplace.

In La Paz, Bolivia from the 1920's through the 1940s, the elites passed a series of municipal ordinances attempting to control the behavior of cholas. City government banned cholas from streetcars and required them to be licensed by the "Hygiene Police." To acquire the license, the chola not only had to pay a fee, but also to strip naked in front of a health inspector who conducted an examination to make certain she did not have a venereal disease (just as they did for prostitutes). Outraged marketplace cholas demonstrated against the regulations and continued to wear their polleras and shawls in protest.

Cholas also inspire unease because of their disdain for many patriarchal expectations. Although some marry, many remain unmarried, seeing husbands as an unnecessary burden. For cholas, in contrast to the Peruvian elite, it was common and socially unremarkable to have children out of wedlock. Young children assist their mothers in the marketplace. Often an elder woman tutors a younger one in the best practices of displaying wares and retaining loyal customers. Historically, many market women began their careers as cooks, laundresses, and domestic servants for urban white families but because of the sexual abuse and exploitation they often experienced, traded their jobs for the more independent life of a marketplace chola.

ECONOMICS AND COMMODITIES

The Survival of Handicrafts: The Panama Hat

While larger and more developed Latin American countries took advantage of the propitious circumstances of the 1930s to industrialize, many indigenous people and mestizos in smaller nations relied on niche handicraft products to earn a living. Artisanal industries, like the "Panama" hats made in Ecuador, combined traditional handicraft skills (weaving) with light industrial work in factories (blocking and dyeing). Sold throughout northern South America, the lightweight fibers of Panama hats protected a wearer against the tropical sun's burning rays. Despite their Ecuadorian origin, Forty-Niners (gold miners heading for California) crossing the Isthmus of Panama dubbed them "Panama" hats and introduced them to the United States, where the name stuck. Sported by celebrities such as President Theodore Roosevelt, author Mark Twain, and Ecuador's own populist president, José María Velasco Ibarra, Panama hats made a high fashion statement between the 1890s and the 1960s from Hollywood's red carpets to the boulevards of Paris.

Grown on small coastal farms, *toquilla* palm fronds are cut, boiled (to increase suppleness), and bundled for sale to indigenous or mestizo craftspeople living in the two regions famed for Panama hats: select coastal communities and small towns near Cuenca, Ecuador's third-largest city. This was once a man's trade, but today women do most of the weaving to supplement their family's income. Coastal weavers specialize in the production of the famed *superfinos*, hats of such quality that they can be folded yet retain their shape and so tightly woven that they can hold water. According to legend, such fine hats (which take months to complete and command top dollar on the international market) can only be woven by the light of the moon because direct sunlight dries the straw and makes it brittle. Superfinos are then bleached to create a uniform white color. Today the weavers around Cuenca produce larger numbers of the lesser quality hats for local commerce.

While coastal workers are usually independent operators, the Panama hat business in Cuenca operates more like a light industry. Indigenous weavers from towns with mellifluous names like Biblián and Sigsig sell their wares to mestizo middlemen, who collect large quantities of hats to deliver to small factories.

≡ **Panama Hat Fabrication**

There, a few workers finalize the blocking and coloring processes. After the loose ends of straw on the hats are trimmed and tied together, an operator using a simple machine presses the hat to give it shape, and then the hat is pounded with a mallet to soften it. The hats are graded. Poorer quality ones, which retain their brown color, are sold to farmers, tradespersons, and workers all across South America. From earliest times, the Ecuadorian government promoted these hats by publishing brochures trumpeting the fact that "Panama hats are made in Ecuador" (usually to no avail). In recent decades, however, the whims of fashion (the ubiquitous baseball cap) and rigorous competition from Chinese paper knock-offs have diminished sales of Ecuador's Panama hats.

- Why did the Panama hat become a ubiquitous symbol of tropical flair? How does the history of the Panama hat typify or vary from patterns of Latin American cultural influence?

Indigenista Art and Literature in the Andean Region, 1940–1960

The Andean region has produced some of the most prominent and influential indigenista artists and authors. These Andean indigenistas of the mid-twentieth century explored social problems in stark detail. Unlike the Mexican muralists, Andean artists preferred working on canvas rather than on the walls of public buildings. For their part, Andean writers probed far more deeply into the conditions indigenous people faced than did their Mexican counterparts.

Andean Literature

Indigenista novels proffered clear messages and rarely offered any subtlety to their readers. Every character was readily identifiable as a hero or villain. Beautiful countryside and idyllic country people faced insoluble problems based on the all-too-common reality of exploitation by white hacendados and mestizo bureaucrats. Typically, the good characters struggled against all odds but almost inevitably failed. If the main protagonist and his fellow villagers did not die at the end of the novel, at the very least their way of life had forever been destroyed.

For example, the Peruvian novelist Ciro Alegría's *Broad and Alien Is the World* (1945) captures the quintessential rural problem, the conflict between the indigenous community and the hacienda for land and labor. Opening with a sunny description of a plentiful harvest and a joyous community enjoying their seasonal labors, the picture turns bleak when the neighboring white hacendado files suit in the local court claiming that the community lands belong to him. Although the community's wise mayor, Rosendo Maqui, retains legal counsel, his lawyer and the local bureaucracy sell out the community. When the presiding judge decides in favor of the hacendado, the resigned community members rebuild their homes on the poorer-quality lands located at a higher elevation that the judge has awarded them. Yet the hacendado is not satisfied. Needing more labor for his estate, he has Maqui arrested on a fabricated charge and convinces local authorities to send in the military to take the newly awarded land by force. In the end, community members must choose either between working on the estate, or fleeing to rubber plantations in the jungle, where only disease, poverty, and death await them.

Two additional well-known indigenista novels depicted different problems that indigenous people faced. Jorge Icaza's *The Villagers* (1934) examined the exploitation of resident tenants on Ecuadorian haciendas. In this instance, the evil landlord forces his tenants to work on a highway, requires entire families to harvest his crops, and insists that indigenous wives act as household servants, all without pay. To make matters worse, while the men toil on the road project, he rapes one of his tenant's wives. Corrupt local officials and the priest abet the landowner in these nefarious deeds. When the tenants finally rebel, the hacendado calls in the military, which crushes the rebels and forces them off the hacienda to starve on their own.

Peru's José María Arguedas's *Yawar Fiesta* (1941) investigates the cultural clash between indigenous lifeways and that of the dominant white/mestizo class. In the novel, a political appointee from Lima comes to the highlands and decides to "civilize" the bullfight traditionally held to celebrate Peru's independence. Despite the protests of the community, he builds a bullring and hires a professional matador from Lima to fight the bull. Most of the elite submit to the official's will, but one recalcitrant landowner coerces his workers to capture and bring to town the fiercest bull from the wild. When the bull proves so ferocious that the professional flees the ring, drunken Indians leap in to replace him, waving their ponchos and ultimately killing the bull in the traditional way, by blowing him up with dynamite.

≡ **Modernity Meets Tradition.** Modernity meets tradition in this 1920s image of a motorcyclist traversing the plaza of an Andean village. The dapper motorcyclist is attired in European fashion and rides an imported machine—it appears to be a US-made Indian brand motorcycle, ironically enough. The Peruvian flag adorns his handlebars. The arrival of the motorcycle in this village was possible only because Peruvian dictator Augusto Leguía (1919–1930) had embarked on extensive road-building projects in the highlands, albeit with conscripted indigenous labor. Humbler villagers look on or make their own way across the plaza's rough stones, or lean against its aging walls.

These stark reminders of the plight of the poor caught the attention of Andean governments, which sporadically legislated during the early twentieth century against unpaid labor both for tenants and their families and outlawed the beatings that often accompanied disobedience. These laws, however, were rarely enforced. Despite the gruesome picture painted by indigenista authors, many campesinos chose to remain in the countryside. In an insecure world, haciendas offered a safety net, a certainty of provisions in hard times. Because of the scarcity of rural labor, many campesinos could negotiate decent deals for themselves, or failing that, seek employment at a neighboring hacienda. Indigenous people felt a religious and cultural tie to their rural homelands, which contained sacred landscapes and access to important rituals. Others would abandon the countryside to seek better lives for themselves and their families in urban areas.

Andean Visual Arts

Two decades after the Mexican muralists splashed onto the international art scene, Andean painters picked up their brushes to express their own version of indigenismo. No longer interested in depicting the quaint costumes and customs of Indians, the indigenista artists explored the daily travails that indigenous people faced. Two Ecuadorian painters excelled at capturing these images. Eduardo Kingman produced grim scenes of emotionless indigenous laborers hauling ice from Mt. Chimborazo or working in road gangs. One of his most moving works, *Los Guandos* (1941), depicts a group of campesinos collectively bearing heavy loads on their shoulders as they descend a mountainside. A faceless overseer mounted on a huge white horse whips them pitilessly. Kingman's better-known compatriot, Oswaldo Guayasamín, himself of indigenous heritage, painted more abstractly. Brought to the attention of the US art world by Nelson Rockefeller in 1943, Guayasamín received a grant to study in New York, where he met José Clemente Orozco and became interested in fresco painting. Thereafter, he produced a number of public murals as well as his most famous work, *The Trail of Tears* (1952). Like Kingman, Guayasamín drew attention to the terrible suffering indigenous people experienced as the underclass of Ecuadorian society.

While no Peruvian painter matched the skill of Guayasamín or Kingman, Martín Chambi, born into an indigenous family in a small town outside Cuzco, produced breathtaking documentary photographs of Andean society. When his father took a job as a laborer with a British mining company, the young boy tagged along and befriended the company's photographer, who showed him the rudiments of picture taking. As a teen, Chambi moved to Arequipa and apprenticed with a well-known photographer. By the 1920s, Chambi had established his studio in Cuzco, where he became part of the growing indigenista cultural movement. Chambi's clientele included both the rich and the poor. Besides society weddings and grand fiestas, he also photographed humble campesinos in their homes, a woman selling chicha in her hut, as well as portraits of typical indigenous faces. He was among the first individuals to photograph Machu Picchu, the famed Inka site. Like Frida Kahlo, Chambi's work almost disappeared when the indigenista movement lost popularity, only to be rediscovered in the 1970s.

This first generation of indigenista novelists and painters proved more formidable in the artistic and literary world than they did in political circles. Their call for social justice awakened the consciences of some Andean politicians and intellectuals to the need to create a more inclusive society. But like Vasconcelos and most Mexicans of this era, Andean intellectuals felt uncomfortable dismissing the entire Spanish heritage, and thus preferred the more moderate message of mestizaje.

☰ **Andean Villagers Drinking Chicha, 1920s.** This multigenerational group of villagers has gathered to drink chicha, homemade fermented corn beer. Everything about the image seems to suggest deep indigenous tradition, from their dress and their way of sitting on their heels to their bare feet, simple earthenware, and rough-hewn walls. The unseen modern hand here is that of photographer Martín Chambí, an indigenous photographer who learned his craft taking pictures for a mining company, and became one of the most perceptive documentarians of a changing Andean world.

For them, the binary division of Andean society into the world of the whites and the world of the Indian seemed like a false dichotomy. Although modest reforms would attempt to alleviate some of the most dire conditions indigenous people faced, it would take a post-1980s indigenous movement led by indigenous people themselves to press for social and economic justice.

Land Use in Southern Chile, 1925–1960

Chile's frontier south of the Bío Bío River remained in the hands of indigenous people until the latter half of the nineteenth century. As in the US West, the Chilean southern frontier, once incorporated into the nation, became the object of intense interest among people anxious to take advantage of its natural resources. Beginning in the 1880s, several groups of Chileans hotly contested the rights to the use of the land and its resources.

Early Efforts to Control Forest Usage

Before Spaniards arrived in the 1530s, the Mapuche people hunted and planted crops in Chile's far south, using the swidden (slash and burn) method to clear small portions of the forest and then replicating this process as needed when soils became depleted. Although the Mapuche successfully fought the invading Spaniards to a draw in the sixteenth century, the invention of the Gatling gun in the 1860s enabled the Chilean army to defeat the Mapuche and resettle the survivors on reservations. Initially the government aspired to populate the south with German immigrants, but the results were discouraging (about 40,000 Europeans in all came to Chile). As a result, three Chilean groups fought over the ownership of the remaining land: members of the elite, whose individual and dubious claims extended to as much as 740,000 acres; throngs of the landless poor like the *inquilinos* (tenant farmers) and day laborers from the Central Valley and the north; and the remnants of the Mapuche, who argued that their reservations were too small to permit them to maintain their way of life.

All three groups duplicated the Mapuche method of clearing land. By burning the forest, the charcoal remnants stimulated the production of nitrogen, which enriched the soil. For a few years, the massive burns succeeded in making southern Chile the breadbasket of the country before soil depletion set in. In the meantime, some of the elite established logging operations with marginal profitability because dense undergrowth and heterogeneous varieties of trees, some not commercially useful, increased the cost of doing business. Small sawmills primarily produced primarily ties for railroads, but also made doors, window frames, and parquet flooring for housing. Bark stripped from *linge* trees was used in the tanning process.

In 1910 the national government attempted to gain control of this Wild West–like frontier region by appointing Federico Albert as the head of the newly created Forestry Department. He attempted to end the practices of burning and clear-cutting forests by setting aside state-owned public lands as forest reserves. Individuals or companies could apply for licenses to cut wood in these forests and receive subsidies to replant the land in fast-maturing, exotic species like the Monterey pine (from the US Northwest) and the eucalyptus (from Australia). Such homogeneous forests would in the future prove much easier to log than Chile's natural woodlands. Thus, the Forest Department's initial program promoted sustainable management of the forest reserves and allowed the government to regain control of the forests, preventing unauthorized settlement by landless workers.

Peasant Protest and Forestry Development

After the Great Depression devastated the nitrate market, the Chilean government looked to the southern forest region to replace its lost export earnings. As a result, it enforced the Forest Law of 1925, which clarified land use policy. These regulations spelled out the manner in which companies could acquire logging licenses, and (more importantly) enclosed the forest reserves and denied the poor (the inquilinos and the Mapuche) access to them. Forest guards were hired to protect the reserves, which caused considerable protest. The explosive situation led to a revolt by the inquilinos in the area of Ránquil in 1934 that the police repressed with several casualties.

Meanwhile, the governments of the 1930s and 1940s proceeded with their plans to allow large landowners to reforest the area around Concepción with Monterey pine and eucalyptus to arrest soil erosion and lay the foundation for an expanded forestry industry. These pine plantations required large tracts of land and a great deal of capital, much of which came from government subsidies. During the Popular Front years (1938–1952) the government loaned three million pesos to the forestry companies. In addition, civil servants and other small investors were encouraged to put money into the corporations as a hedge against inflation. This public-private partnership bore fruit in the 1940s, as Chile exported significant quantities of pulp, paper products, and plywood to its South American neighbors. The pine plantations also produced the lumber for an expanding housing industry in Santiago to accommodate the city's swelling population. The quantity of land dedicated to the managed forests grew from 345,950 acres in 1946 to 617,800 acres by the 1960s.

Chile's decision to dedicate its southern forests to commercial purposes had a number of consequences. By replacing many native tree species with just two exotic species, forest managers reduced biodiversity, which increased the possibility of disaster should an infestation occur. Excluding the poor from the forests only heightened the disequilibrium of Chilean society, as jobs in the forestry industry were not numerous enough to provide employment for all those displaced from farming. On the positive side, the pine plantations did halt soil erosion and moderated climate change as more normal rainfall patterns reestablished themselves in southern Chile. Yet this decision made in the 1930s to dedicate the southern frontier to commercial logging would continue to plague recent governments from the Allende administration (chapter 10) to the Pinochet dictatorship (chapter 11) and beyond.

New Understandings of Race in Brazil, 1930–1960

Like Mexico and Guatemala, Brazil faced an urgent need to reconsider legacies of racial domination. In Brazil, however, these questions focused less on the indigenous population and more on the inheritance of African slavery. Descendants of African slaves made up approximately half the population of the nation in the 1930s, and African cultural legacies were inextricably embedded in every part of Brazilian daily life. Until the early twentieth century, Brazilian elites tended to think of the Afro-descendant population as a burden on the nation, and of African cultural influence as, at best, a colorful peculiarity, if not a source of embarrassment. The challenges of modernity, impelling the reconsideration of limits of citizenship and the meaning of national culture, required reevaluation of these prejudices.

Brazil's most influential social theorist of the early twentieth century, Francisco de Oliveira Viana, argued that Brazil would be saved from the pernicious demographic effects of centuries of African slavery by a slow but steady process of *embranquecimento*, or whitening. Oliveira Viana praised miscegenation (race mixing), but only in the service of whitening: In his understanding, black traits— and indeed black citizens—would gradually disappear, to Brazil's benefit. This was the dominant understanding in the first three decades of the twentieth century, at least.

In the late 1920s and early 1930s, a new social theorist, Gilberto Freyre, emerged to upend this conventional wisdom. In a series of publications, most notably the 1933 *Casa Grande e Senzala* (literally *The Big House and the Slave Quarters*, and published in English as *The Masters and the Slaves*), Freyre argued that the African demographic and cultural inheritance was a source of Brazilian strength, perhaps the nation's most vital resource. Freyre emphasized the ways in which Portuguese culture and Brazilian social structure favored sexual relations between Portuguese and African, slave owner and slave. Freyre acknowledged the violence and exploitation inherent in this system, but argued that it nonetheless produced a vibrant demographic and cultural mixture, defined by intimacy and paternalism. In Freyre's view, this enabled Brazil to balance antagonistic tendencies. Freyre's views often come across as offensive to current readers, but they held enormous power in the 1930s, in a Brazil struggling to balance its dreams of modernizations with the reality of a legacy of slaveholding. Freyre's vision became Brazil's dominant understanding of race.

Less well understood—but perhaps equally enduring—was Freyre's defense of social hierarchy. Freyre's vision was at once radically provocative and deeply conservative. As a scion of the sugar-planting aristocracy of Pernambuco, Freyre was not advocating social leveling. Quite the opposite: his argument was that Brazil was defined by its flexible and intimate patriarchy, one in which domination and submission were all part of the extended family. He hoped that system could be saved from the crisis of modernity, not superseded. In contrast to Oliveira Viana, who looked favorably on immigration and urbanization, Freyre feared these forces would erode all that made Brazil distinctive and vital. Freyre himself later retreated to a familial estate, living his own life in a kind of facsimile of nineteenth-century Brazilian society. The multiple, conflicting strains of Freyre's thought largely set the terms for debates on race and nation in 1930s Brazil, and continue to compel and challenge critics and scholars nearly a century later.

Freyre's work has often been characterized as a defense of Brazilian "racial democracy," but that phrase never appears in *Casa Grande e Senzala*, and it was not an idea he looked on with favor. The phrase "racial democracy," rather, grew out of larger reconsiderations of race in Brazil, and attempts to contrast racial mixing in Brazil with a stark color line in the United States. Such comparisons often deliberately underestimated enduring racism within Brazil, and have been soundly debunked. But the common use of the phrase, from the mid through the late twentieth century in Brazil, does hint at deeper aspirations within Brazilian society. Freyre's socially conservative, patriarchal vision of Brazilian culture was contested by more hopeful visions of inclusion and expanded citizenship. Getúlio Vargas's Estado Novo included watered-down versions of Freyre's theories of demographic and cultural mixing in its propaganda. The virtue of this oversimplification was that it allowed for multiple understandings and uses of those theories. By the end of the Estado Novo, theories of whitening were understood as outmoded, celebration of African cultural and demographic influence had become dominant, and the true meaning of citizenship, for descendants of slaves and slave owners alike, remained up for grabs.

CULTURE AND IDEAS

The Maracanaço

July 16, 1950: The Brazilian national team takes the field at Rio de Janeiro's new Maracanã Stadium to face the *Celeste*, the Uruguayan squad, in the final game of the World Cup. Brazil has played masterfully in its recent games, destroying Sweden 7–1 and Spain 6–1. Given the results of the prior matches, all it needs is a tie to win the championship. Tens of thousands of fans in the stadium and millions more listening on the radio are eagerly expecting coronation. When Brazil scores first, they can nearly taste the victory.

A team seen as the embodiment of Brazil's emergence into the first rank of world nations is minutes from proving its superiority. The Brazilians came into this World Cup convinced that they had invented a better way of playing soccer, the **jogo bonito** (beautiful game). In keeping with the new celebration of Afro-Brazilian cultural inheritance, they point to the influence of brilliant black Brazilian players, such as Leonidas da Silva, a star of the 1938 World Cup, in developing a tricky and creative—and uniquely Brazilian—style of play.

And then Uruguay comes back, evens the score, and makes the winning goal. Brazil has no response. Uruguay is the champion. The Maracanã falls silent, and the nation goes into shock. The next day, among tears and recriminations, Brazilians seek a scapegoat. Many point to Moacir Barbosa, the Brazilian goalkeeper. Some go so far as to suggest that he failed under pressure because he was black.

The road to cultural transformation is not smooth. The impassioned celebration of national cultural identity has its own kind of heartbreak. The Maracanaço and the sentiments around it embody the frustrated aspirations of Brazil and its contradictory racial thought.

- Why did the World Cup defeat to Uruguay cause Brazilians to agonize over much larger questions of national identity? How did race figure into perceptions of the strength and vulnerability of the Brazilian side?

Women and the Quest for Equal Voting Rights, 1929–1960

During the post-1930s era, women's organizations, in conjunction with sympathetic male politicians in most countries, took up the fight for suffrage. While some historians have viewed the successful outcome of the battle for the vote as an important advance for women, others have viewed the results as simply "the modernization of paternalism." The increasing numbers of women participating in the workforce as well as their active participation in international conferences slowly altered societal perspectives about appropriate gender roles.

Suffrage in South America

Pan-American feminism brought together women's rights activists across the Americas in the 1920s and 1930s. Leaders such as Paulina Luisi of Uruguay and Bertha Lutz of Brazil stitched together a coalition of reformers throughout the

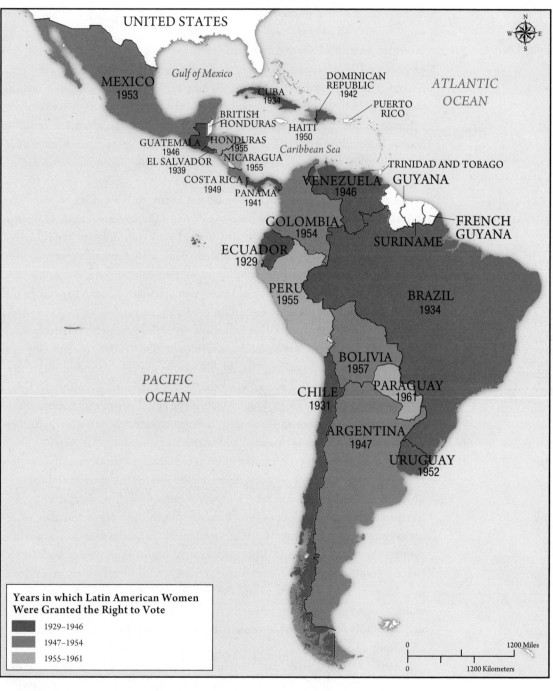

UNITED STATES

Gulf of Mexico

MEXICO
1953

*ATLANTIC
OCEAN*

DOMINICAN
REPUBLIC
1942

CUBA
1934

PUERTO
RICO

BRITISH
HONDURAS

HAITI
1950

GUATEMALA
1946

HONDURAS
1955

Caribbean Sea

EL SALVADOR
1939

NICARAGUA
1955

COSTA RICA
1949

TRINIDAD AND TOBAGO

VENEZUELA
1946

GUYANA

PANAMA
1941

COLOMBIA
1954

FRENCH
GUYANA

ECUADOR
1929

SURINAME

PERU
1955

BRAZIL
1934

*PACIFIC
OCEAN*

BOLIVIA
1957

PARAGUAY
1961

CHILE
1931

ARGENTINA
1947

URUGUAY
1952

**Years in which Latin American Women
Were Granted the Right to Vote**

- 1929–1946
- 1947–1954
- 1955–1961

0   1200 Miles

0   1200 Kilometers

≡ **MAP. 9.1**

hemisphere. Leaders in each country faced their own struggles, and when they came together in international congresses they often disagreed about tactics and priorities. South and North American leaders, in particular, often parted ways, emphasizing different combinations of social and political priorities. South American leaders often understood that they could only achieve real advances by couching their claims in traditional language of honor and purity. These differences and disagreements notwithstanding, Pan-American connections were vital in enabling leaders in South America to overcome local opposition, pressing for women's suffrage and other reforms and gradually strengthening the claims of women for full and independent citizenship.

The push for suffrage paralleled but did not mirror the entrance of women into the wage-earning workforce. In both the city and the countryside, poor women had always been working, although the kind of work they did may have changed with time. But in industrializing cities like São Paulo and Montevideo, women were increasingly earning hourly or monthly wages, as textile workers, schoolteachers, and clerical staff. Modern, industrial employment facilitated claims to suffrage and reforms based on the requirements of the modern woman.

By way of contrast, in socially conservative Andean cities with relatively small populations of women wage earners, reformist leaders tended to emphasize the ways in which women's suffrage would allow them to preserve and fulfill the traditional familial roles in a changing world. Perhaps surprisingly, although women's movements tended to grow more vigorously in industrializing nations, these movements did not necessarily achieve suffrage more easily or earlier than their counterparts in nations with a small industrial base.

Indeed, suffrage was sometimes more acceptable in countries with low percentages of women wage earners, because elite politicians understood that the only women likely to use the franchise were relatively well-to-do and white, unlikely to overturn social hierarchies. For example, the first nation in Latin America to grant women's suffrage, in 1929, was Ecuador, where in practice, only white property owners could vote. The conservative coalition in power understood that by granting wealthy women suffrage they would thereby strengthen their own electoral position. Indians and the poor remained excluded. As a result, Ecuador's voting population remained a tiny fraction of its national population for decades. Only in 1978 did the franchise expand to include illiterates and hence all women and men.

Bolivia offers a similar case. This impoverished, landlocked nation allowed women to vote in 1938, relatively early by Latin American standards, but it limited that vote to literate women of means. Only in 1952 did Bolivia grant universal suffrage. Early suffrage, then, did not always mean a real expansion of democracy or even a strengthening of women's citizenship. Uruguay and Brazil presented a different model of early suffrage, one where well-organized and relatively broadly-based women's movements achieved suffrage after years of activism. Here, too, middle-class women who failed to grasp fully the challenges faced by female factory workers led these movements. But this should not obscure the achievements of these activists, who helped force open the electorate in these nations, yielding more inclusive democracies.

In Brazil, Bertha Lutz and the organization she led, the Brazilian Federation for Feminine Progress, seized on the opportunity presented by the so-called Revolution of 1930 to press for greater rights. Getúlio Vargas, in turn, recognized in the Federation for Feminine Progress the kind of organization that would be wise to incorporate into his populist strategy, rather than marginalize. Pressed by the Federation, Vargas opened the possibility of women's suffrage in 1932, then appointed Lutz to the government commission drafting a new constitution. At Lutz's insistence, the 1934 Constitution granted women's suffrage.

In Uruguay, the 1917 Constitution theoretically allowed for the possibility of women's suffrage, but required a two-thirds majority vote in the legislature to enact the measure. Paulina Luisi (chapter 6) pushed for approval, building support through dissemination of her feminist magazine, *Acción Feminina*. Despite this steady pressure, Uruguay still had not enacted women's suffrage by the early 1930s. A renewed wave of reformism in that decade laid the groundwork for final approval in 1934. Even then, the Constitution of 1934 limited the franchise to citizens born in Uruguay, deliberately excluding the nation's large immigrant population, both male and female. Despite Argentina's early feminist movement, women did not receive the vote until 1947. Although popular stories attributed this success to Evita Perón's activism, in fact she did not speak out in favor of suffrage. The bill originated in the legislature, Juan Perón signed it, and then handed the document to Evita, thereby allowing her to take credit for the achievement.

Mexico Belatedly Joins the First Wave of Feminism

Despite specific outpourings of support for feminism during Mexico's great Revolution of 1910, the quest for legal rights and the ability to exercise suffrage stalled for decades. From the outset of the fighting, women played significant roles including that of soldaderas (chapter 7). Others served the cause as civilians. For example, the precocious Hermila Galindo de Topete became the private secretary to a revolutionary president and edited the journal *Mujer Moderna* (Modern Woman), which espoused radical feminist ideas, all before she turned seventeen. In Yucatán, two revolutionary governors hosted feminist conferences during the early phase of the revolution, which served as useful forums for debate. But this localized support for feminism waned in the 1920s when President Calles and his anticlerical colleagues feared that conservative women's reverence for the Catholic Church and support for the Cristero rebellion would derail the government's interest in building a secular society.

Although Lázaro Cárdenas expressed no particular interest in women's issues during his presidential campaign in 1934, once freed from the influence of Calles, he rallied to the idea of including women in his coalition of laborers and campesinos in the national political party. At first he sought women's collaboration in his moral campaign to curb alcoholism, to rein in gambling, to promote better hygiene (a phrase which often was an oblique reference to family planning), and to advance education. Soon women's organizations, ever increasing in number, pressed him to move forward on political issues. But many of Cárdenas's supporters balked largely because party regulars feared that women would vote incorrectly (against the revolutionary party). As one congressman bloviated during the debate, "If they (women) obtain their object, we shall have the Archbishop of Mexico as President."

By 1936 Cárdenas had persuaded his colleagues that women should be allowed to vote in party primaries. He even promised women's suffrage in national elections. Congress dutifully passed the constitutional amendment expanding suffrage, and all twenty-eight state legislatures ratified it. But Congress never certified the votes of the states (as the US electoral college does) to finalize the process because Cárdenas's political party (soon to be renamed the PRI—the Institutional Revolutionary Party) feared that its more conservative rival PAN (National Action Party, founded in 1939), whose popular candidate already appealed to pro-Catholic and probusiness elements, would sweep the female vote and win the election of 1940.

Feminist organizations like the Mexican Women's Alliance persisted, and after World War II ended, domestic issues regained their importance. Along with others, the Mexican feminist Amalia Castillo Ledón encouraged the United Nations to endorse the idea of equality for men and women. The feminists made headway with the PRI leadership by arguing that women would bring into the party and national politics feminine and maternal virtues, including their commitment to education and improving health. In addition, Castillo Ledón and the sitting president, Adolfo Ruiz Cortines, were long-time friends. By 1953, PRI party leaders confidently predicted they could win the female vote. PRI spokespersons carried the debate in Congress in favor of women's suffrage. Thus, the amendment passed allowing women to vote in national elections in 1958.

Popular Culture and the Spread of Modern Ideas, 1930–1960

Deeply influential tomes like Gilberto Freyre's *Casa Grande e Senzala* or José Vasconcelos's *La Raza Cósmica* may have revealed the deep matrix of cultural transformation in Latin America's modern nations, but relatively few Latin Americans were reading them. Authors like Freyre and Vasconcelos achieved much of their influence through indirect dissemination of their ideas. The market for *any* books, particularly dense, literary works, remained tiny even in Buenos Aires, Latin America's most bibliophilic city.

The Sources of Cultural Images

So where did ordinary Latin Americans absorb and express cultural images and ideas? From comic books and illustrated popular magazines, accessible even to those with limited literacy, and passed hand-to-hand among multiple readers. Popular literature ranged from newspapers targeted at the urban working class to public broadsides to traditional popular chapbooks, such as the *literatura de cordel* (inexpensive pamphlets often displayed at county fairs) of northeastern Brazil. All these forms grew in popularity in the middle decades of the twentieth century, as literacy spread and printing became more accessible. Popular films were also widely accessible, shown first in luxurious movie palaces, then passed along months later to humbler, peripheral moviehouses.

Above all, Latin Americans listened to radio and to recorded popular music. Even those who could not afford a radio or a record player could listen at a friend's house, at a local corner store, or in a downtown plaza. As a result, the latest popular music had a currency in midcentury Latin America that no other art form could match. And popular music turned out to be an ideal form for inquiry into the content and meaning of national culture. In the industrializing nations of Latin America, emerging recording and radio industries nurtured the growth of specific popular forms that became imbued with sentiments of national identity.

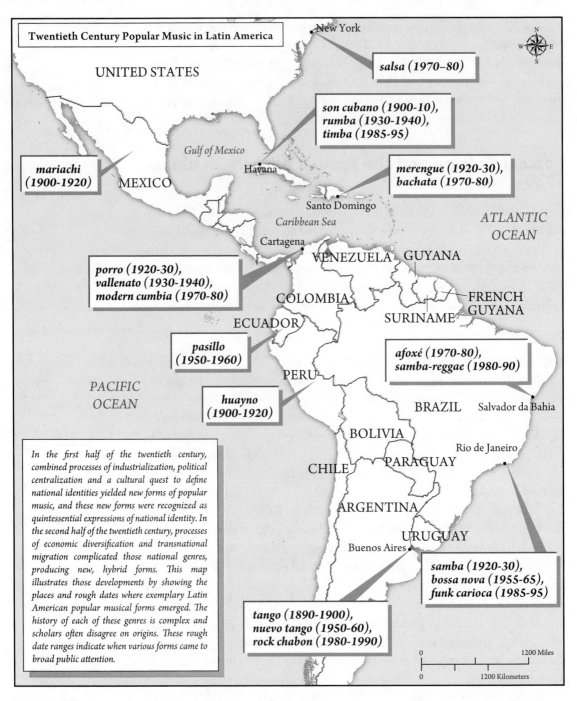

Twentieth Century Popular Music in Latin America

UNITED STATES

New York

salsa (1970–80)

son cubano (1900-10),
rumba (1930-1940),
timba (1985-95)

Gulf of Mexico

Havana

mariachi
(1900-1920)

MEXICO

merengue (1920-30),
bachata (1970-80)

Santo Domingo

Caribbean Sea

ATLANTIC
OCEAN

Cartagena

porro (1920-30),
vallenato (1930-1940),
modern cumbia (1970-80)

VENEZUELA GUYANA

COLOMBIA

SURINAME

FRENCH
GUYANA

ECUADOR

pasillo
(1950-1960)

afoxé (1970-80),
samba-reggae (1980-90)

PERU

PACIFIC
OCEAN

huayno
(1900-1920)

BRAZIL Salvador da Bahia

BOLIVIA

Rio de Janeiro

CHILE

PARAGUAY

In the first half of the twentieth century,
combined processes of industrialization, political
centralization and a cultural quest to define
national identities yielded new forms of popular
music, and these new forms were recognized as
quintessential expressions of national identity. In
the second half of the twentieth century, processes
of economic diversification and transnational
migration complicated those national genres,
producing new, hybrid forms. This map
illustrates those developments by showing the
places and rough dates where exemplary Latin
American popular musical forms emerged. The
history of each of these genres is complex and
scholars often disagree on origins. These rough
date ranges indicate when various forms came to
broad public attention.

ARGENTINA

URUGUAY

Buenos Aires

samba (1920-30),
bossa nova (1955-65),
funk carioca (1985-95)

tango (1890-1900),
nuevo tango (1950-60),
rock chabon (1980-1990)

0   1200 Miles

0   1200 Kilometers

MAP. 9.2

Each of these new national forms offered opportunities to reflect on and debate those sentiments.

Argentina and the Tango

Tango as a dance and a musical form emerged from the dockside bars of Buenos Aires in the late nineteenth century. The basic rhythmic cell of the music, one that seems to propel bodies in motion, was common to several Afro-Atlantic forms. In tango, that rhythmic cell was combined with the plaintive sounds of the *bandoneón*, a small button accordion, and melancholy lyrics sung in a minor key. The songs were often about tragic love, or about knife-fights in the *arrabaldes*, rough, vacant lots on the outskirts of town, celebrating gritty urbanism.

With the foundation of recording studios and then radio stations in Buenos Aires in the first three decades of the twentieth century, producers began searching for content, and tango was the logical choice. It could be played by a variety of ensembles, from a simple trio of voice, guitar, and bandoneón to full band. The studios began cranking out records and distributing them throughout Argentina, and then throughout South America. The radio stations expanded their broadcasting reach, and set the tone for imitators farther afield. Within a few decades, tango went from being a marginal form of a few dockside neighborhoods to being Argentina's popular music.

The golden-voiced tango singer Carlos Gardel became the first Latin American popular cultural superstar of radio, recording and film, instantly recognizable and beloved throughout the Spanish-speaking world. Although not Argentine by birth, he was already hailed as a national treasure by the late 1920s, and his tragic death in an airplane accident in 1935 affected Argentines as a national tragedy. Many of the tangos that Gardel made famous, particularly in his final years, sketched the conflict and anguish of the Infamous Decade in masterful strokes.

Tango was, and is, an art form deeply shaped by African influence. But the superstardom of the white Gardel largely erased that African inheritance—a process that typified the marginalization of Afro-Argentines themselves—and a kind of deliberate amnesia about their contributions to Argentine culture. Tango embodied the triumphs and contradictions of Argentina.

The Brazilian Samba

Samba's emergence and consolidation followed a similar trajectory to that of tango a decade or two later. Samba emerged from house parties in a working-class, racially mixed neighborhood of downtown Rio in the late 1910s. It was then embraced

≡ **Men Dancing the Tango in Uruguay.** Tango emerged from the dockside bars and brothels of Buenos Aires and Montevideo in the late nineteenth century. Men vastly outnumbered women in these environs, in part because the immigrant populations from southern Europe arriving in these cities in the late nineteenth century were predominantly male. It was common for men to dance tango with one another, even as the lyrics of the emerging genre celebrated heterosexual seduction. Tango flourished in the semirural outskirts of the cities on both sides of the Rio de la Plata basin, as well, as this photograph, taken outside Montevideo, indicates. The attire and the snapshot style suggest this photo is from the 1920s or '30s, demonstrating that the practice of men dancing tango with one another remained common even as the musical form became the staple of the music industry in both Montevideo and Buenos Aires.

most fervently by the mostly black residents of a few downtown favelas—hillside neighborhoods of self-built, precarious housing. In that context, it gained the reputation of rogue music of sensual delight. When recording and radio producers began searching the city for performers in the 1920s and early 1930s, they turned to samba. As those studios and stations gained power and influence, they made samba Brazil's national popular music.

As with tango, the first superstar performer of the Afro-Brazilian genre of samba was a white man, Francisco Alves, who purchased the sambas of black favela composers and signed his own name as a collaborator—a common practice at the time. Alves's trajectory echoed that of Gardel, from humble background to multimedia stardom, right down to his tragic death, in this case in an automobile accident. In contrast to Gardel, however, Alves was never seen as the embodiment of samba. Instead, in the midst of Getúlio Vargas's regime, with its emphasis on mixing and the celebration of Afro-Brazilian cultural inheritance, samba was understood as originating from Rio's black, favela population.

This made it the perfect forum for claims and debates about the meanings of race in Brazil. Those included relatively celebratory claims of mixed-race national identity, such as Ary Barroso's famous "Aquarela do Brasil" (1939), which lovingly described Brazil as a *mulato inzoneiro* (mulatto rascal), or wily man of mixed racial ancestry. But they also included deep, ambiguous portraits of racial inequality in Brazil, such as the sambas of Geraldo Pereira, a black composer from the favela of Mangueira. Samba, as a result, became a idiom not just to celebrate Brazilianness, but to probe its shortcomings.

Son and Rumba in Cuba

No nation in the world has wielded the per capita musical power of Cuba, a tiny island that has accounted for an outsized proportion of global popular music. Long before the invention of the gramophone, Cuba was already a fertile laboratory for musical styles, one that influenced practices throughout the Atlantic world. But the foundation of recording studios and radio stations on the island in the first decades of the twentieth century intensified that influence and stimulated rapid growth in the music itself.

The first genre to consolidate as the preferred form of the new media was *son*, usually performed by a small ensemble featuring vocals, guitar, bongó drum, and clave (wooden sticks beaten together). This relatively minimal orchestration could be recorded in the low-fidelity studios of the period, and came through clearly on single-microphone radio broadcasts. Son's syncopated rhythmic groove made it easy to dance to, and the lyrics told emotionally resonant stories of migration from the country to the city, reflecting the roots of the music itself.

In the 1930s, glitzy and sensuous Havana nightclubs catering to international tourists proliferated, and recording techniques became more sophisticated.

Both of these transitions favored the turn to larger ensembles, playing up-tempo dance music, leading to the emergence of several new variants of *rumba*. Rumba had traditionally been a sacred music of Afro-Cuban worship, performed only on conga drum and vocals. The new nightclub styles of rumba, such as *guaracha* (an Afro-Cuban genre with syncopated rhythm and comical lyrics popular between 1930 and 1950), featured ensembles of seven instruments or more, including brass, strings, and percussion. It was in the 1930s Havana that rumba became the basis for much of the dance music that still dominates Spanish American tastes today.

Recognition of African cultural inheritance in son and rumba followed a middle path between the relative erasure of Argentine tango and the institutionalized celebration of Brazilian samba. African cultural presence in Cuban music was far too predominant to erase, and was tangible in the Yoruba and Congo-influenced lyrics of many rumbas, as well as in the drums and rhythms themselves. But while dancers, performers, sex workers, and audiences often embraced an exotic idea of Afro-Cuban sensuality, many Havana nightclubs remained effectively segregated, and black Cubans themselves rarely saw the profits of Cuba's lucrative music industry.

Similar accounts tell the story of Colombian *porro* and *vallenato*, Mexican *son jarocho* and *bolero*, or Dominican *merengue* and *bachata*. In all these cases, the expansion of new national recording industries facilitated the consolidation of new musical forms and imbued them with sentiments of national identity. This was among the most momentous cultural transitions in twentieth century Latin America.

TIMELINE

1921
Beautiful Indian Contest in Mexico City

1925
José Vasconcelos publishes *La Raza Cósmica*

1926–1929
The Cristero Revolt in Mexico

1928
José Carlos Mariátegui's publishes *Seven Essays on Peruvian Reality*

1929–1945
Diego Rivera paints murals about conquest on walls of National Palace

1925–1935
Carlos Gardel popularizes the tango

Conclusion

The comparison may be unfair, but it is difficult to escape the conclusion that Latin America nations met the cultural challenges of modernity more successfully than their political and economic challenges. The art, music, and literature created in Latin America in the 1920s through the 1950s remains an endless source of meaning and fascination. In those decades, cultural reflection served as a way of explaining political and economic crisis, but it also served grander ambitions, those of explaining the modern nation to itself.

In the process, cultural production—much of it emanating from the bottom up, rather than being orchestrated from the top down—deeply informed and at least in some cases strengthened the expansion of the citizenry. Those who were once marginal moved closer to the center, literally and figuratively. The dreams and aspirations that kindled this process could not be fully realized. But even their symbolic expression had the power to shape the imagination of generations to come.

KEY TERMS

indigenismo 389	La Cristiada 400	Pan-Africanism 393
internados indígenas 390	mestizaje 388	problema indio 392
jogo bonito 418	negritude 393	Rerum Novarum 400

1938
Cárdenas's broad-scale redistribution of land to ejidos ends in Mexico

1939
Frida Kahlo paints *The Two Fridas*

1941
Ciro Alegría writes *Broad and Alien Is the World*

1944
Ecuador's House of Culture founded

1958
Women vote in Mexican presidential election for first time

Selected Readings

Asturias, Miguel Angel. *Men of Maize: A Modernist Epic of the Guatemalan Indians.* Pittsburgh, PA: University of Pittsburgh Press, 1995.

Bantjes, Adrian A. *As if Jesus Walked on Earth: Cardenismo, Sonora, and the Mexican Revolution.* Wilmington, DE: Scholarly Resources, 1998.

Boyer, Christopher R. *Becoming Campesinos: Politics, Identity, and Agrarian Struggle in Post-Revolutionary Michoacán.* Stanford: Stanford University Press, 2003.

Butler, Matthew. *Popular Piety and Political Identity in Mexico's Cristero Rebellion: Michoacán, 1927–29.* Oxford: Oxford University Press, 2004.

Dawson, Alexander. *Indian and Nation in Revolutionary Mexico.* Tucson: University of Arizona Press, 2004.

De la Cadena, Marisol. *Indigenous Mestizos: The Politics of Race and Culture, Peru, 1919–1991.* Durham, NC: Duke University Press, 2000.

Delpar, Helen. *The Enormous Vogue of Things Mexican: Cultural Relations between the United States and Mexico, 1920–1935.* Tuscaloosa: University of Alabama Press, 1992.

Henderson, Peter V. N. *The Course of Andean History.* Albuquerque: University of New Mexico Press, 2013.

Herrera, Hayden. *Frida: A Biography of Frida Kahlo.* New York: Harper & Row, 1983.

Klubock, Thomas Miller. *La Frontera: Forests and Ecological Conflict in Chile's Frontier Territory.* Durham, NC: Duke University Press, 2014.

López, Rick A. *Crafting Mexico: Intellectuals, Artisans and the State after the Revolution.* Durham, NC: Duke University Press, 2010.

Mannham, Patrick. *Dreaming with His Eyes Open: Diego Rivera.* New York: Alfred A. Knopf, 1998.

McCann, Bryan. *Hello, Hello Brazil: Popular Music in the Making of Modern Brazil.* Durham, NC: Duke University Press, 2004.

Miller, Marilyn Grace. *Rise and Fall of the Cosmic Race: The Cult of Mestizaje in Latin America.* Austin: University of Texas Press, 2004.

Needell, Jeffrey. "The Foundations of Freyre's Work: Engagement and Disengagement in the Brazil of 1923–1933." *Portuguese Studies* 17, no. 1 (2011): 8–19.

Olcott, Jocelyn. *Revolutionary Women in Postrevolutionary Mexico.* Durham, NC: Duke University Press, 2005.

Rubenstein, Anne. *Bad Language, Naked Ladies, and Other Threats to the Nation.* Durham, NC: Duke University Press, 1998.

Stepan, Nancy Leys. *The Hour of Eugenics: Race Gender, and Nation in Latin America.* Ithaca, NY: Cornell University Press, 1992.

Soto, Shirlene. *Emergence of the Modern Mexican Woman: Her Participation in Revolution and Struggle for Equality, 1910–1949.* Denver: Arden Press, 1990.

Vaughan, Mary K. *Cultural Politics in Revolution: Teachers, Peasants and Schools in Mexico, 1930–1940.* Tucson: University of Arizona Press, 1997.

Weismantel, Mary. *Cholas and Pishtacos: Stories of Race and Sex in the Andes.* Chicago: University of Chicago Press, 2001.

10

Revolution and Reform in Latin America, 1950–1980

Global Connections

In the aftermath of World War II, global politics took a sharp turn towards Cold War. Although the victorious Allies created the United Nations in 1945 as an institution to peacefully resolve future international disputes, a deep fracture soon emerged between the United States and Western Europe on one hand and the Soviet Union and its Eastern Bloc satellites on the other. The US bombing of Japan to end World War II in 1945 had ushered in a new atomic age, making the stakes of a showdown between East and West extraordinarily high. No longer were the old political considerations of geography, sovereignty, and nationalism the only geopolitical issues on the line. After Hiroshima and Nagasaki, the very future of humanity was in play.

The ideological divide between the democratic West and the communist East both influenced and clouded perspectives on events happening in the so-called developing world. This included Latin America. Although China also turned to communism under Mao Zedong in 1949, its internal orientation, as compared to the Soviet Union's expansionist policies, meant that China—preoccupied with its own restructuring of its ancient culture and society—played only a minor role in Latin American affairs in this time period.

While the two superpowers (the United States and the USSR) squared off, political actors across the globe sought to achieve their own ends through strategic alliance with one or the other party, or tried to chart a careful course between them. The war had successfully brought an end to the fascist threat in Europe and Asia. But at the same time, it led many people around the world to recognize that they did not share in the benefits of liberal capitalism. The decades following World War II would witness the rise of a variety of local uprisings and movements— some nationalistic (such as the partitioning of India and Pakistan), some anticapitalist (including the majority of the Marxist-inspired revolutions in Latin America described in this chapter), and many of them anticolonialist (including those in Africa and Southeast Asia). All of these "Third World" movements were shaped in part by the Cold War. The United States supported those movements that were prodemocracy and procapitalist, and the Soviet Union aided those that endorsed socialism, and tended to ally with the nondemocratic Eastern Bloc. In all cases, however, local conditions transformed the meaning of the struggle between the superpowers.

Europe's weakness after World War II opened opportunities in places like Africa and Southeast Asia for the emergence of new anticolonial and nationalist movements, with local leaders emerging to demand independence from European

≡ **Fidel Castro and Camilo Cienfuegos enter Havana, Cuba, January 1959.** Along with Fidel Castro, Ernesto "Che" Guevara, and Raúl Castro, Camilo Cienfuegos was a member of the 1956 *Granma* expedition, which launched Fidel Castro's armed insurgency against the government of the Cuban dictator Fulgencio Batista. After heading to the Sierra Maestra mountains to launch a guerrilla assault, the rebels all grew beards—something very unusual for men to do in the 1950s—for which they became known as "*los barbudos*" (guys with beards). Cienfuegos became one of Castro's top guerrilla commanders, and after the triumph of the revolution was named head of the Cuban armed forces, but he died in a plane crash before the year's end.

GLOBAL CONNECTIONS
Latin America and the World in the Age of Decolonization

control. Within the British Empire, India initiated the decolonization process, as Mahatma Gandhi led hundreds of thousands of peaceful protesters demanding that the British quit India. The Partition of India in 1947, however, which divided Muslim-dominant Pakistan from largely Hindi India, was both extremely violent and disruptive to tens of millions of South Asians; the religious and geographic tensions that the Partition exposed would anticipate many of the geopolitical difficulties

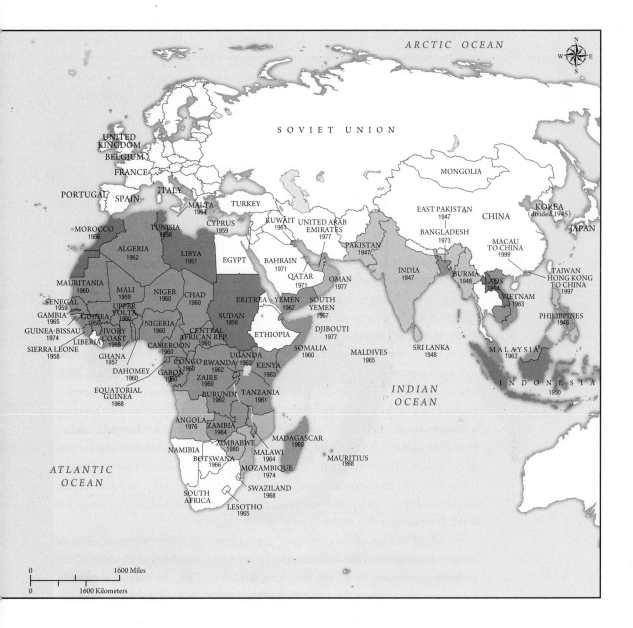

that would emerge much later, in the early twenty-first century. In Africa, the British yielded more willingly except in colonies like Kenya and Hong Kong, economically productive regions where significant numbers of expatriates lived. In Kenya, where British settlers in the so-called White Highlands owned more than 25 percent of Kenya's best tea-producing land, the fighting lasted ten years before Jomo Kenyatta's party prevailed. Kenya won its independence from Great Britain in 1963.

The French, having suffered painful subordination to the Germans during World War II, sought to hold onto their colonies more stubbornly than did the British. But eventually their grip loosened over Indo-China (Vietnam, Laos, and Cambodia) and Algeria, all places where French expatriates lived in large numbers and where French language and culture had set deep roots. Although the concepts of nationalism and decolonization were common threads in these developing world independence movements, several of them also employed the language of Marxism, communism, and socialism. The Algerian War (1954–1962), characterized by fierce guerrilla warfare by "national liberation groups," a ferocious counterinsurgency by the French army that included the use of torture and campaigns against civilian noncombatants, and large-scale human rights abuses committed by both sides, in many ways served as a template for the Cold War armed conflicts that would emerge in Latin America in the coming decades.

The tide of decolonization inspired leaders of the Latin American left, who saw their nations as economic colonies of the United States. This perceived economic "dependency," they argued, undermined their ability to govern themselves, especially when their national interests did not match those of the imperious neighbor to the north. In the immediate post-World War II years, democratic socialist movements emerged in a handful of countries that managed to coexist successfully within a context of North American geopolitical and economic interests. But this balance largely came to an end with the Cuban Revolution, which also began as a democratic socialist movement. Cubans began to use Marxist language and to form close ties to the Soviet Union in the early 1960s. In the United States, the loss of one nation after another in the 1950s to the Eastern Bloc—all of Eastern Europe, north Vietnam, and northern Korea—was enough to convince policy makers that so-called Third World countries would fall like dominoes to communism if not directly contained.

Within US policy circles, there was little effort to distinguish the nuances of left-wing politics. US politicians, diplomats, and officers tended to view any movement or government that advocated land reform or flirted with expropriation of foreign-owned property as a communist threat. This lack of discernment led to tragic outcomes, as the United States was prone to react with violence against reformist and revolutionary administrations alike. As John Peurifoy, US ambassador to Guatemala in the early 1950s, put it when questioned whether Guatemalan president Jacobo Arbenz was a communist despite his claims of being a nationalist: "If it walks like a duck and it quacks like a duck, it's a duck."

For the Latin American left, meanwhile, the Cuban Revolution (1953–1959 were the years of the Revolution's insurrection) changed everything. In the short term, at least, Cuba gave leftist radicals a victory, demonstrating that a ragtag group of revolutionaries could defy US domination and move toward socialism, given the proper circumstances. As a result, Cuban-inspired rebels across Latin America set out to produce those circumstances, in homegrown versions of armed revolutionary movements. Given the context of the Cold War, each of these inevitably triggered a heavy-handed response from the United States or its local allies. The Cold War integrated Latin America into world geopolitics to an unprecedented degree, as the showdown between the two great superpowers played out in a grim and destructive series of proxy wars—wars in which neither local actors nor international allies truly controlled the outcome. Both chapter 10 and chapter 11 detail the events of the period from roughly 1950 to 1980 as Latin America became even more closely entwined into the global Cold War struggle.

Latin America Follows Mexico's Path to Reform, 1948–1980

Not all of Latin America's shift to the left resulted from Cuba's influence, as less radical forces were also at work. Postrevolutionary Mexico's apparently successful reordering of society as well as the ideas of Víctor Raúl Haya de la Torre's American Revolutionary Popular Alliance (APRA) movement (chapter 9) inspired a generation of Latin American intellectuals and politicians, who sought to bring similar structural changes to their own countries. The reformers intended to broaden political participation, introduce agrarian and labor reform, and use the tool of economic nationalism to rid themselves of foreign corporate exploitation.

The Bolivian National Revolution of 1952

In the 1930s, Bolivia experienced military humiliation at the hands of its weak neighbor, Paraguay, in the Chaco War (1932–1938). In 1932, Bolivia sent troops into the sparsely settled, swampy, Paraguayan-controlled Chaco Boreal region in the hopes of gaining access to the Atlantic via the Plata River system. But the masses of ill-prepared indigenous troops failed in their attempt to assault well-defended Paraguayan positions. Bolivia experienced an ignominious defeat as Paraguay advanced, gaining the majority of the disputed territory.

With national pride shattered, middle-class Bolivians and military reformers sought to jettison the elite political parties and redefine the nation. What better example to follow than Mexico's stable regime? The Lázaro Cárdenas administration in Mexico appeared to represent a viable model for Latin America's democratic left, achieving a rare combination of representation, social reform, and stability.

(Peru's APRA party promised many of the same goals but never achieved power until the 1980s). These social reforms included among other things, the redistribution of land, the defense of workers' rights, and economic nationalism—the expropriation of foreign-owned property under certain circumstances (see chapters 8 and 9 for the specifics).

The economist Víctor Paz Estenssoro and a cohort of like-minded reformers founded the National Revolutionary Movement (MNR) political party in the early 1940s. To broaden MNR's appeal, Paz and his colleagues reached out to tin miners, the largest unionized group of workers in the country. Paz won the presidential election in 1951, but the military, perceiving him as a dangerous radical, refused to let him take office. In response, the tin miners' union, some 130,000 strong, joined forces with the MNR to overturn the unpopular military government. The three-day revolution, which cost 600 lives, profoundly marked Bolivia for the remainder of the twentieth century.

The revolutionaries wrote a new constitution inspired by the Mexican Constitution of 1917, which enfranchised both illiterates and women. In the ensuing election, Paz and the MNR triumphed in a landslide. Immediately, the MNR government enacted reforms. Because tin was the country's most profitable export, not surprisingly President Paz Estenssoro used his executive powers to nationalize the properties belonging to four large international mining corporations (including the one controlled by the Bolivian Simón Patiño, who preferred life in Paris to his sumptuous mansion in Cochabamba). To replace foreign ownership and to market the tin, Paz created a national corporation, COMIBOL (Mineral Corporation of Bolivia).

The MNR used these revenues from tin exports to increase miners' wages, in one instance by 250 percent in a single year. The MNR also passed safety legislation to improve working conditions and reduce the high incidence of silicosis. In addition, the MNR paid compensation to the expropriated foreign corporations. That proved a wise decision, convincing the United States that the MNR was reformist and not communist. It also made Bolivia eligible for foreign aid. (As we shall see, Bolivia, which is landlocked and far from the United

≡ **Bolivian Ore Carrier.** The original caption reads, "The country is the great tin reserve in the world," writes Frank G. Carpenter of the *Washington Star* on July 12, 1914, in his story on how the Panama Canal will open up trade with Bolivia. "It has been sending its tin ore through the Straits of Magellan to England, where the metal has been smelted and refined, and sent across the Atlantic Ocean for the making of tin plates. The tin ore will now probably come to us direct, and a smelting industry may grow up to handle it." The writer makes no comment on the man who is carrying the ore, who is using the same technology to transport metal ore from mines as his ancestors would have been likely to use in Bolivia's great silver mines of Potosí in the sixteenth century.

States, and with relatively little US investment, was less vulnerable to direct US intervention than Guatemala, where the Arbenz administration would be overthrown for similar reforms).

Despite the prominence of the tin miners' union, the MNR leadership knew that the vast majority of Bolivians earned their livelihood through agriculture. Under

☰ Bolivian Peasants Receive Deeds from MNR. The Nationalist Revolutionary Movement (*Movimiento Nacionalista Revolucionario*, MNR), founded in 1941 by Víctor Paz Estenssoro, was the first political party with widespread support in Bolivian history. Its membership included intellectuals, white- and blue-collar workers, and indigenous campesinos. The party took power in a coup in 1952 and retained the presidency until 1964; the period is known as Bolivia's National Revolution. The MNR's program of reform was modeled on Mexico, but took its efforts many steps further; the MNR government instituted universal suffrage, increased social spending, temporarily reduced the size of the armed forces, created a peasant militia, and nationalized Bolivia's mines. The MNR also created a Ministry of Peasant Affairs, which organized campesinos into syndicates. In 1953, the MNR passed a comprehensive Agrarian Reform law, which granted land titles to landless campesinos, as we see in this photo. Because of political divisions within the MNR, Paz Estenssoro's third term ended abruptly when he was overthrown in a military coup in 1964. His only allies at the end were the armed campesinos, who proved no match for the military.

the Agrarian Reform Law of 1953, the MNR redistributed land to resident peons on haciendas simply by giving them title to the small individual plots (two to five acres) they already worked and allowing them to engage in subsistence agriculture or to produce for local markets. Further, the agrarian decree exempted from expropriation "productive" medium-sized properties, thereby assuring a reliable source of food for urban populations. Already existing collectives, called *ayllus* or *comunidades* in Peru and Bolivia, became inalienable, providing legal protection to indigenous peoples. Other landless folk were encouraged to colonize unoccupied land on the eastern slopes of the Andes. As in Mexico, agrarian reform proved a social, if not an economic, success.

By the end of the decade, however, MNR's promises unraveled, largely because tin exports earned insufficient revenue to build schools, hospitals, and other infrastructural and social requirements. As a result, the MNR had to lay off substantial numbers of tin workers and close inefficiently managed mines. With the revolution running out of gas, the military intervened in 1964 and removed Paz from office. Nevertheless, the Bolivian National Revolution of 1952 had significantly improved the lives of many of the country's poor and disadvantaged.

The Venezuelan Democratic Revolution

In the decades prior to the Cuban Revolution, the United States looked with favor on another administration of the democratic left, that of Venezuela. Rómulo Betancourt, exiled from Venezuela in the 1920s because of his radicalism, returned in 1935 to found the AD (Democratic Action) party. The party collaborated with young military officers to seize power in 1945. The coalition wrote the Constitution of 1946, creating a centralized, activist state. The new constitution broadened suffrage to include all men and women over the age of 18, provided rights for labor unions, and empowered the national government to expropriate private property, including foreign petroleum interests, all reminiscent of the Mexican Constitution of 1917. Although a decade-long military dictatorship interrupted the implementation of the constitution, when democracy returned in 1958 the civilians reached an accord that allowed democracy to take root.

To cement this agreement, Betancourt, Rafael Caldera (the leader of the recently formed Christian Democratic or COPEI party) and other important national power brokers met at Caldera's estate to work out the Pact of Punto Fijo, which confirmed Venezuela's firm commitment to capitalist development and democracy. The political parties agreed to share government jobs (while excluding all communists from such posts), to hold fair elections, and to support whichever candidate won. Church officials accepted a compromise that allowed them to maintain control of parochial schools and receive a governmental subsidy to pay clergy and maintain churches. The military (except for the former dictator) received a blanket amnesty for the abuses that it had committed during the ten-year dictatorship. With the accord in place, Venezuela finally entered the family of democratic nations.

As in Bolivia, the democratic left's ability to make necessary reforms and create greater egalitarianism depended on the state's control over natural resources. Venezuela's economic well-being depended on oil, and thus on Venezuelan relationships with foreign oil companies. Beginning with the Petroleum Law of 1943, the government negotiated an increasingly larger percentage for itself of the oil profits extracted by the big three oil companies, Gulf, Shell, and Exxon (all based in the United States and the United Kingdom). The government's cozy relationship with the oil companies proved a major benefit in the 1960s, when oil producers competed for markets and a glut of oil kept prices low. Instead of outright expropriation as Mexico had done, the Venezuelans implemented "consensual" nationalization. Knowing that they lacked the managers, engineers, technology, refining capacity, and tanker fleet to manage the industry profitably, the AD government created a holding company, the Venezuelan National Petroleum Company, Incorporated (PDVSA), under which the three international corporations continued to operate. The PDVSA also undertook the task of exploring new oilfields and gradually claimed an ever larger share of oil profits, ultimately nationalizing oil in 1975. The Big Three oil companies, however, continued to reap profits from Venezuelan operations by branching into the new petrochemical industries.

Meanwhile, the AD and COPEI governments agreed that they should "sow the petroleum" and implement policies to encourage agricultural productivity as well as distribute oil's proceeds for other broad social purposes. Oil workers, located mostly in the Lake Maracaibo region, became the primary beneficiaries of AD's largesse, gaining hefty wage increases over the years. Other workers also fared well, because, as in Mexico, all unions operated under the umbrella of a national union allied with AD. The federal government invested in health care and education, giving Venezuela low infant mortality and high literacy by regional standards. Venezuela's economic success created a significant urban middle class, which, like labor, tended to be strong supporters of the Punto Fijo pact and the two political parties at its center.

While labor unions and the middle class prospered, the AD and COPEI generally neglected the rural poor. During the 1960s the AD government expropriated some properties belonging to the family of the former dictator Gómez and other disgraced generals, but this redistribution affected a mere 118,000 families, most of whom gained about 6 acres of land in individual plots. Instead of redistributing the fertile land near Caracas, the Venezuelan governments encouraged the landless to move south and colonize the open *llanos* (plains). As elsewhere in Latin America, this colonization scheme failed for environmental reasons, as thin soils, flooding, and a lack of roads made it unviable for small-scale, market agriculture. By 1979, Venezuela was importing some 70 percent of its basic food necessities.

During the 1970s, the democratic left's policy to use oil revenues to foster social change turned sour. Soaring demand for petroleum after the successful oil embargo of 1973 provided OPEC (the Organization of Petroleum Exporting Countries, founded by a Venezuelan oil minister, Juan Pablo Pérez Alfonso in 1960) with the historic opportunity to manipulate prices upward. The youthful and energetic AD president Carlos Andrés Pérez crafted a policy designed to remake Venezuela as an industrial nation using the principles of import substitution industrialization (ISI). Ruling by decree, he initiated a number of large-scale projects: steel mills, a petrochemical industry, oil refineries, and ship building. Awash in petroleum money and foreign loans, the temptation to expand the bureaucracy, create patronage jobs, and skim profits became too great. Before Pérez's plans came to fruition, the international economy collapsed and oil prices plummeted, leaving Venezuela with massive debts. Although AD and COPEI managed to weather the political fallout until the late 1990s, corruption did irreparable damage to both parties' reputations. Worse, the oil revenues had largely been squandered. Despite the presence of so much black gold, the poor found themselves increasingly economically strapped.

José Figueres and the Costa Rican Revolution

By the beginning of the twentieth century, tiny Costa Rica had begun to diverge politically from its neighbors and to forge its own path. Although its economy still lay primarily in the hands of coffee planters and US-owned fruit companies, the nation's small size, both geographically and demographically, helped its history unfold in a distinct direction. Costa Rica developed a different national self-concept, one that envisioned the small country as an exceptional nation in the region—peaceful, democratic, hard working, modest, and egalitarian.

This imagined exceptionalism had clear racial implications, as nationalists lauded Costa Rica's purported ethnic homogeneity, a coded way of suggesting that it was not burdened by the large indigenous or Afro-descendant populations of its neighbors. Despite the fact that some of these elements were demonstrably untrue—for example, the large population of Afro-descendant banana workers legally confined to live in the far-Atlantic province of Limón, the short dictatorship of a general by the name of Federico Tinoco in 1919, and obvious inequities in power and wealth that the coffee industry had produced—Costa Rica's national myth served it well, over time becoming something of a self-fulfilling prophecy.

During the first half of the century, two important figures helped lead Costa Rica toward the destiny it envisioned for itself. The first, Jorge Volio Jiménez, a former priest and general, in the 1920s guided the Costa Rican legislative assembly toward codifying social support in favor of the poor, with the aspiration to elevate Costa Rican society across the board. Although Volio himself had a military background, he is credited with formulating one of Costa Rica's guiding mandates: that it be a democratic country with "more teachers than soldiers." The second, Víctor Sanabria, an influential Catholic bishop (in a devoutly Catholic country), strongly advocated that the Church be a spokesman for its people's temporal as well as their spiritual well-being. Sanabria was the influential proponent of legislation that strengthened workers' rights and other social guarantees in the 1940s.

Although not without some significant social dislocations and rising tension, Costa Rica's social contract sustained it through the Great Depression. It was the only Central American country not to fall under the sway of a dictator during this volatile period. Early in 1948, however, this positive trajectory was interrupted by a highly contested presidential election, where the losing side accused the winner of having won by fraud and expelled him in a coup—a series of events that directly violated the principles of democracy and the deeply held values of Costa Ricans.

But this deviation did not last long. On March 12, 1948, a key ally of the contested winner—a philosopher, farmer, and political dynamo named José "Pepe" Figueres, along with his supporters (primarily made up of students, businessmen, tradesmen, and farmers), led a revolt to overthrow the provisional government. After forty-four days of fighting, much of which took place

≡ **José Figueres.** José Figueres led the National Liberation Movement (MLN) and served as president of Costa Rica from 1944 to 1948 and again from 1953 to 1958. *Ticos* still remember him today as the framer of modern Costa Rica's successful democratic-socialist republic. During his presidency, Costa Rica abolished its army, implemented basic social welfare legislation, enfranchised women and black citizens living on the Atlantic coast, nationalized banks, elevated the political and social status of rural workers, and sealed in Costa Rica's long-standing commitment to democratic rule. In 1981, Figueres remarked in an interview about his presidency, "In a short time, we decreed 834 reforms that completely changed the physiognomy of the country and brought a deeper and more human revolution than that of Cuba."

in the normally tranquil streets of the capital, San José, some two thousand people had died. Figueres took over as provisional head of the country by late April, and remained in that role until the nation could hold free elections.

Figueres remained a highly influential figure in the nation for decades to come and served as president himself twice, once in the 1950s and again during the 1970s. It was Figueres—whom *ticõs* (a fond nickname for Costa Ricans) affectionately called "Don Pepe"—who set into motion the many new laws and regulations that marked the beginning of what is called Costa Rica's "Second Republic." Among other things, Don Pepe introduced full suffrage for women and full citizenship for Afro–Costa Ricans, established presidential term limits and created an independent electoral tribunal to oversee future elections. He also abolished the Costa Rican army, thus assuring that the nation would never again be subject to a military coup. As an additional benefit, because Costa Rica no longer maintained an expensive military, government funds were available for social investment, such as free public education (up to and including graduate and professional school) and quality free universal healthcare, two of the hallmarks of Costa Rican society today.

Figueres also nationalized the banks and insurance companies, a move that paved the way for state intervention in the economy. Although a democratic socialist, Figueres was not a Marxist, as he demonstrated by outlawing the Costa Rican Communist Party in 1948—a prudent gesture that also assured that Don Pepe would not run afoul of the United States in the Cold War era. In 1949, the legislative assembly promulgated a new Constitution that permanently codified all these reforms.

By the bloody standards of many other parts of the world, Costa Rica's 1948 civil war was hardly "revolutionary" in the sense that it did not represent a break with the past, but rather offered an affirmation of its historic path. Even so, Costa Rica's brief civil war remains a pivotal moment in Costa Rica's historical trajectory. The legacy of Figueres and Costa Rica's emphasis on social equality remains alive in the country, which has maintained scrupulously democratic and nonviolent political transitions since 1948. Even during the 1980s, when the rest of the isthmus was embroiled in deep violence, Costa Rica was able to stay the course of peace.

Guatemala's Ten Years of Spring, 1944–1954

In October 1944, Guatemala's Depression-era dictator, Jorge Ubico, resigned from office. Students, reform-minded junior military officers, and members of the planter class who had become discontent with his authoritarian rule had demanded his departure. Because such a wide coalition demanded change, Ubico's ouster marked the beginning of a decade of dramatic social, economic, and political reform entirely unprecedented in Guatemala, a decade that came to be called the Guatemalan revolution, or the "Ten Years of Spring." Guatemala's experiment with social and economic reform, which bore many similarities to the MNR and AD revolutions, would fall victim to one of Latin America's pivotal Cold War crises. The US-sponsored intervention that ended this experiment served as the template for subsequent interventions, in places like the Cuba, the Dominican Republic and Chile (and indeed as far away as Vietnam). In Guatemala, the Ten Years of Spring and its aftermath would be remembered as a broken dream and opportunity lost, followed by decades of violence and terror.

Arévalo and Spiritual Socialism

In the beginning, the strongman Ubico's resignation brought a feeling of widespread optimism. Leading the vanguard of change was Juan José Arévalo, a university professor and critic of Ubico, who had spent years of exile in Argentina. Elected president in December 1944, Arévalo called his agenda for reform "spiritual socialism." His government wrote and adopted a new constitution in March 1945, proclaiming a social-democratic revolution. Under this constitution, the government pledged to pay more attention to the grievances of middle- and lower-class Guatemalans and to begin to restrict the privileges of the largest landowners, including foreign capitalists. The constitution gave more Guatemalans a voice in the political system, granting women the right to vote for the first time. It also provided for free speech and freedom of the press and allowed previously banned labor unions and political parties to organize.

While Arévalo's spiritual socialism was strongly anticommunist, it did emphasize an unprecedented sense of cooperation and concern for the common welfare. During his five-year term, the government established an advanced system of social security and passed a labor code to protect workers' rights and benefits. He encouraged the growth of urban labor unions and popular participation in politics, including in the rural areas where most people lived. Perhaps most importantly, the government heavily emphasized basic literacy for rural people and higher education for urban dwellers, and implemented improved programs in basic public health.

For the first time, Maya people joined rural campesino unions, giving them a new stature and voice in national affairs. Guatemala became a founding member of the United Nations in 1945 and the Organization of American States in 1948. Arévalo's reforms were moderate and gradualist, but nonetheless alarmed the traditional planter class. A particular concern for planters and business interests (as well as the Catholic Church) were Arévalo's pro-labor policies, which seemed to threaten their own interests and which also seemed poised to alienate the United States.

The Arbenz Administration

Even with this opposition, Arévalo managed to complete his term. His successor in 1951, Colonel Jacobo Arbenz Guzmán, a reform-minded army officer, had helped to lead the 1944 revolt against Ubico. Where Arévalo had been a man of rhetoric, Arbenz was a man of action, and the revolution moved sharply to the left during his administration. Arbenz's most revolutionary act, a land reform law known as **Law 900**, passed in June 1952. This law attempted to take unused or underused agricultural land from large property owners and give it to landless rural workers. For the most part, coffee fincas owned by rich and powerful Guatemalans fell outside this law. Instead, it took direct aim at the huge banana plantations of the US-owned United Fruit Company (UFCo). These holdings were an obvious target for land reform, both because of their foreign ownership and because much of UFCo's land was unplanted, both to keep the price of bananas relatively high and to prevent the spread of banana disease from one field to another.

Law 900 approved the taking of 91,000 hectares (225,000 acres) of UFCo lands, offering compensation based on the stated tax value of the property that the company, though it had been happy to pay taxes based on these estimations, considered inadequately low for purposes of compensation. The government also distributed some 162,000 hectares (400,000 acres) of government-owned land to rural residents. Meanwhile, Arbenz allowed the Communist Party to organize, and he added a few leftist labor leaders to his advisers. These were the measures that alarmed Ambassador Peurifoy and the rest of the US government.

The Covert Operation in Guatemala

United Fruit's propaganda campaign against the Guatemalan revolution strongly influenced the US government. Timing was everything; in 1938, Lázaro Cardenas successfully nationalized Mexico's oil industry without US intervention, but in the Cold War era, even the expropriation of banana fields in a small country provoked fears of spreading communist revolution. It did not help Arbenz's case that many prominent men in the US government were lawyers for major shareholders in UFCo—including President Eisenhower's brother, the US Secretary of State, and the head of the CIA. Even more importantly, Guatemala was the first place in Latin America where the newly formed Central Intelligence Agency (CIA) covertly assisted in overthrowing a sovereign government. It was the CIA that organized, augmented, and mobilized domestic opposition into a counterrevolutionary force. With such oversized firepower against it, the Arbenz government was doomed.

In June 1954, a group of CIA-trained and supported Guatemalan exiles, commanded by Colonel Carlos Castillo Armas, invaded Guatemala from Honduras. This group, known as the National Liberation Movement (MLN), was small and not

SOCIAL UPHEAVAL

A Pro-Arbenz Agrarian Reform Poster

This poster informs viewers about the benefits of the Guatemalan agrarian reform program. More specifically, Law 900 redistributed unused land of sizes greater than 224 acres to local peasants, while compensating landowners with government bonds. Land from at most 1,000 estates was redistributed to about 500,000 families—one-sixth of the country's population. The goal of the legislation was to move the Guatemalan economy from feudalism to capitalism. Although in effect for only eighteen months, the law was both controversial and popular among the rural poor, and it had a major effect on the Guatemalan land reform movement.

≡ **A Pro-Arbenz's Agrarian Reform Poster.**

especially competent—at one point, for example, they fired on schoolboys on a playground, mistaking them for Guatemalan soldiers. The support of the CIA, however, eventually assured their success. The Guatemalan army refused to resist the invaders, and Arbenz resigned on June 27, 1954. A military government replaced him and disbanded the legislature. Castillo Armas became president and ordered the arrest of all communists, setting off a wave of violence that would soon take Castillo's own life (he himself was assassinated in 1957). The 1954 coup sowed the seeds of a bloody armed conflict that would ravage the country for nearly thirty-six years.

The Cuban Revolution, 1959–1989

On January 8, 1959, Cuban rebels led by Fidel Castro, Ernesto ("Che") Guevara, Camilo Cienfuegos, Raúl Castro, and others triumphantly entered the capital city of Havana. Deliriously jubilant crowds welcomed them. They cheered wildly for the young militants' success in driving out the detested dictator Fulgencio Batista, who the previous evening had boarded a flight to the Dominican Republic. With this victory, the Cuban Revolution—and what would soon become Latin America's first and by far its longest-lasting socialist regime—began. The impact and influence of the Cuban Revolution, both real and perceived by hostile governments, would transform the political landscape of Latin America for the rest of the twentieth century.

The Batista Regime and Its Overthrow

In the years prior to the Revolution, Cuba was a nation where the lives of poor rural laborers (*guajiros*) and urban casino workers contrasted dramatically with those of the many foreign tourists who regularly visited Havana to drink, gamble, and party. The country sank into a morass of corruption, and the downward spiral seemed to generate one catastrophe after another. In 1951, the popular politician Eddy Chibás was so overcome with despair that he committed suicide, shooting himself during his weekly radio show in 1951. (Chibás's suicide was driven by personal as well as political reasons, but was largely understood as an act of political despair.) In 1952, Fulgencio Batista, a former military man and president from 1940 to 1944, seized power during a hotly contested election. Batista promised stability, but delivered corruption and violence.

This was a marked decline for both Batista and Cuba. During his previous administration, Cuba produced its 1940 constitution, one of the most progressive in the Western Hemisphere: It granted extensive rights to labor, and mandated social services and political liberty for its citizens. In the 1940s, Cuba boasted a free and boisterous press, a flourishing civil society, and one of Latin America's largest middle classes. Its university nurtured an open, vibrant student culture that produced intellectuals and activists, including the young Fidel Castro. Cuba's infrastructure and public health were among the strongest in the region.

Economic challenges, inequality and political corruption, however, led to a rapid downturn in the late 1940s, exacerbated by Batista's return to office. He suspended the 1940 Constitution, took kickbacks and facilitated the local operations of the North American Mafia, which did a booming business in gambling and prostitution in Cuba. He resorted to censorship, false imprisonment, torture and extrajudicial assassination in a vain attempt to silence dissent. Many Cubans determined that revolution offered the only solution.

The former law student Fidel Castro, along with other students including his younger brother, Raúl, was among those who ardently opposed Batista. Shortly after Batista seized power, they devised a plan to foment a nationwide revolt.

On July 26, 1953, Castro and a group of about 140 student dissidents commenced an attack on the Moncada army barracks in Santiago de Cuba, both to steal weapons and to alert the Cuban populace to the opposition. The attack was a tactical disaster from the start—student rebels were no match for trained military men, and most of the young invaders were either captured or shot on the spot.

Fidel and Raúl Castro and the other surviving rebels were put on public trial. Realizing that he had no chance of being exonerated for his part in the attack, Fidel Castro spoke in his own defense, using the opportunity to denounce the Batista regime. His speech was lengthy and persuasive (setting a precedent for Castro stemwinders after Batista's ouster). It ended with the line, "History will absolve me." Although sentenced to fifteen years in prison, copies of his "History will absolve me" speech circulated clandestinely during his imprisonment. By the time Batista released the Castros and the other Moncada raiders during a general amnesty in 1955, Fidel Castro had become a nationally recognized figure and a hero not only to many poor Cubans, but even to many members of the middle class.

The former prisoners traveled to Mexico to regroup and plan the next step in the revolution. Mexico's own revolutionary past made it a congenial home for radical exiles from all across Latin America, , including an idealistic young Argentine medical doctor, Ernesto "Che" Guevara, who allied with the Cubans. Guevara encouraged the Cubans to frame their rebellion not just in terms of the overthrow of Batista but also in favor of a Marxist revolution. ("Che" is an Argentine slang word, similar to "hey," or "dude;" it was the Cubans who gave Ernesto Guevara the nickname that would follow him to the grave). With their energies redirected, the Castros and around eighty other men, formed the 26th of July Movement in honor of the failed barracks raid. They sail for Cuba in a small boat called the *Granma*, hoping to set off a popular uprising.

The rebels were thrown off by a storm and landed near Cuba's second largest city, Santiago, in southeastern Cuba, far from Havana. To escape Batista's troops, they fled to the remote Sierra Maestra Mountains, where the local population lent them support. There they grew the beards that would become their visual trademark, and planned further attacks on the government. In February 1957, a *New York Times* reporter named Herbert Matthews paid a visit to the rebels (now popularly known as the **barbudos**, meaning "guys with beards"). Matthews published a series of favorable reports, describing the rebels as altruists who wished to bring democracy to the island and justice to the poor. In addition to giving the 26th of July movement excellent publicity, Matthews's articles also put Cubans on the alert that the rebels were alive, well, and a viable force against the hated Batista regime.

By late 1958, many of Cuba's various other opposition groups had thrown in their lot with the Castro's 26th of July movement, and rebel forces were able to liberate most of the island. At the end of the year, Batista, losing the support he had enjoyed until the bitter end from the United States, conceded defeat, and fled. On January 9, 1959, Castro's forces entered Havana to joyous acclaim. Just like

≡ **Fidel Castro Entering Havana Applauded by Massive Crowds.** On January 1, 1959, Fidel Castro and his band of revolutionary supporters, officially known as the 26th of July Movement, entered the capital of Cuba to widespread enthusiasm and support from nearly all sectors of Cuban society. The corrupt former president, Fulgencio Batista, fled the country with much of the national treasury the same day. At the time, many Cubans anticipated that Castro would demonstrate a strong commitment to democratic government and implement widespread social reform. Upon taking the capital, Fidel delivered the kind of electrifying and lengthy speech that would become his signature, and at the end, white doves of peace were released. When one landed on Mr. Castro, perching on a shoulder, the crowd erupted, chanting: "Fidel! Fidel!" But it would not be long before many Cubans would become increasingly disenchanted with the new regime.

that, the Caribbean's playground for the rich and decadent and workhouse for the poor transformed itself into a laboratory for revolution.

Fidel Castro and the Early Days of the Cuban Revolution

Many Cubans believed that Castro would restore democracy and civil rights to them, and popular sectors enthusiastically participated in the early growth of the revolutionary state. But the regime did not hesitate to suspend civil rights of political opponents. As was to be expected, the regime consolidated power by purging Batista's followers. More alarmingly, the regime also soon persecuted erstwhile allies deemed insufficiently revolutionary. They organized show trials for Batista's inner circle and executed purported war criminals. The Castro government soon began to expropriate private property—first from landlords, and then from landowners—and convert it into government holdings. Upper-class and then many middle-class Cubans began to flee the island for what they anticipated would be temporary exile in nearby Miami, Florida. There they would form a Cuban community in exile that worked zealously, if unsuccessfully, to subvert and undermine the Castro regime for the next half-century and beyond.

Back in Cuba, the revolutionary regime secured the impassioned support of the poor and working classes, and for good reason. The expropriation and reconstitution of large private farms into cooperative, government-owned farms, the equal distribution of basic consumer goods and food, and the opening of new opportunities, constituted a dramatic redistribution of wealth, lifting tens of thousands of Cubans out of poverty. This redistribution benefited Cubans of color, in particular. Symbolic defiance of the United States also earned the Castro's administration avid popular support in its early years.

Che Guevara's Marxist influence notwithstanding, there is no evidence that Fidel Castro was a communist at the time he took power in January of 1959. His aspirations to overthrow a corrupt dictator and expropriate foreign holdings were similar to those of any number of Latin American nationalist revolutionaries. In the context of the Cold War, however, Castro's defiance of the United States inevitably provoked that superpower's hostility, pushing Castro's regime into the camp of the other superpower, the Soviet Union. Castro endured a humiliating trip to the United States in 1960, when US government officials snubbed him and declined to meet with the Cuban delegation. Blaming ill treatment from the United States and crediting favorable overtures from the Soviet Union, Fidel formally proclaimed himself a Marxist-Leninist in December 1961.

CULTURE AND IDEAS
The Iconography of Che Guevara

This famous image of Ernesto Guevara has taken on a life of its own in popular culture, appearing so ubiquitously that celebrities from Johnny Depp to Madonna to Bart Simpson have been seen wearing the image. It long ago lost its power to shock. One scholar has called the Che photo "the quintessential postmodern icon signifying anything to anyone and everything to everyone." It was not always so: During the Cold War, in some places the mere possession of this (or any other) photograph of Guevara could be enough to earn the owner punishment, imprisonment, or worse. When the photo was taken, however, it embodied the aspirations, promises, and the dangers of revolution. Photographer Alberto Korda did not even identify the image as Guevara himself, but simply labeled it "*guerrillero heróico*" (heroic guerrilla fighter). In fact, this image captures a very different Che than do most of his other photographs, where, instead of striking a noble gaze, he looks either fierce and stern-faced, or disheveled and laughing.

This picture probably became so well known because the bearded Che looks beatific and inspirational, almost Christ-like. The connection is not made overtly, as Cuba was officially an atheist nation from 1959–1992, and Guevara himself took a dim view of Christian pacifism. "In fact," he once said, "if Christ himself stood in my way, I, like Nietzsche, would not hesitate to squish him like a worm." Yet as most

≡ **Korda and His Photograph of Che Guevara.**

Latin Americans at the time were Roman Catholics, the visual association with Jesus carried powerful, if subconscious, connotations. The famous photograph remains the iconic image of the Cuban revolution. The ability of the regime to shift the iconography of the Revolution to Che—forever young, forever revolutionarily pure—helped to assure its longevity. Fidel Castro, his brother Raúl, and the Revolution itself, in contrast, gradually became more aged and ossified.

- How and why did Che Guevara—an Argentine doctor—become as much a symbol of the Cuban Revolution as Fidel Castro? Why did this photograph become a global popular icon?

The Cuban Revolution Enters the Cold War

Cuba represented the United States' worst nightmare—a communist nation ninety miles from the Florida Keys, with an aggressive, intelligent leader at the helm. With the Cuban Revolution, the United States lost its key partner in the sugar trade, US companies lost their properties to expropriation, and Cuba opted to process Soviet heavy crude oil in defiance of the United States. Cuba had once been a subservient client state of the United States, a role it vigorously rejected after Castro took power.

The United States instigated multiple assassination attempts against Fidel Castro in the early 1960s. In April 1961, the United States tried to overthrow the Castro regime using the same technique that had been so successful in Arbenz-era Guatemala just a few years earlier—the training and deployment of formerly privileged expatriates bent on overthrowing the leaders who had threatened their social and economic position. A poorly trained and ill-equipped group of Cuban expatriates landed at Playa Girón in the Bay of Pigs, attempting to overthrow Castro. Popular loyalists of the revolutionary regime successfully fought off the invaders until Castro's forces arrived, killing or capturing them all. The Bay of Pigs invasion dealt an enormous defeat to the United States, discrediting the new administration of President John F. Kennedy. It also handed Cuba an unparalleled symbolic victory against the Revolution's most avid opponent.

In 1962, the Soviet Union took advantage of Cuba's client-state status to place long-range nuclear weapons in Cuba, pointed directly toward the United States. Although President Kennedy deftly negotiated a successful and peaceful resolution to this **Cuban Missile Crisis** with the Soviet Union, the crisis marked the most dangerous moment of the Cold War. The Cuban Missile Crisis provided the United States with justification to tighten the trade embargo it

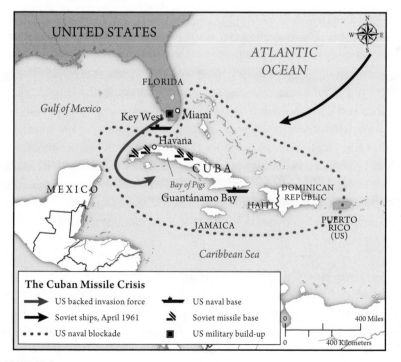

≡ **MAP. 10.1**

had placed on Cuba in 1960. The embargo contributed to decades of hardship and privation for the Cuban people. It also served as an excuse on which the Cuban government has been able to blame its own failings. Yet for well over fifty years the embargo failed to fulfill its purported objectives of weakening the Castro regime. (Indeed, the embargo outlived Fidel Castro himself, who died on November 25, 2016.)

The Cuban Revolution at Home

During the mid-1960s, Che Guevara, the revolution's great theorist, set forth the model of the New Socialist Man: the well-educated, healthy, and egalitarian avatar of Cuban socialism. In the regime's understanding, fulfilling this model required cleansing the nation of those who defied this standard. During the 1960s the regime imprisoned *lacra social* (social scum)—political dissidents, antirevolutionaries, devoutly religious people, and homosexuals—in camps. Ordinary *compañeros* (comrades) found themselves under the continued scrutiny of "neighborhood defense committees," which determined people's access to foods, jobs, and other revolutionary amenities based on their political compliance. Cuba's lack of civil rights and economic opportunity outside of the system forced many thousands of people to leave the island, risking death and exile to establish new lives elsewhere, most commonly in South Florida.

During these same years, however, the revolution achieved lasting accomplishments that made it the model for the Latin American revolutionary left for decades. Cuba made available to its people nearly universal access to social benefits such as free, quality education, and cradle-to-grave healthcare. The long-term effects of Cuban social programs dramatically improved many of the nation's key social indicators (educational attainment, childhood mortality, and life expectancy), placing Cuba on a level closer to Europe than to most of the rest of Latin America. Even today, after years of economic decline and privation, Cuba's literacy and life expectancy rates are among the highest in the Americas, exceeding those of the United States in both categories. Generations of Cuban doctors have provided essential and quality healthcare to much of the Third World at low or no cost at all to recipient nations.

Exporting the Cuban Revolution to Africa and Latin America

From the beginning, Cuba was interested in exporting revolution, and the government actively sponsored rebel movements throughout Latin America during the 1960s and 1970s. After Che Guevara's death in Bolivia (discussed later), Cuba pulled back slightly from aggressively promoting revolution in Latin America and shifted its gaze to Africa, where it sent thousands of troops during the 1970s. There, the Cuban government provided support to national liberation movements such as that of the Marxist Popular Movement for the Liberation of Angola (MPLA), to Nelson Mandela's antiapartheid African National Congress in South Africa, and the *Frente de Libertação de Moçambique* in Mozambique. The apex of Cuban involvement in Africa took place in Angola in the 1970s and 80s, where, against the odds, Cuban and MPLA troops defeated local adversaries allied with white South African army forces, which enjoyed better weapons, training, and CIA support. Cuban involvement was vital to Angola's consolidation of independence in the late 1970s, and to the MPLA's victory over South African-backed rivals.. Over the course of a little more than a decade, Cuba ultimately ended up giving military, medical, strategic, and other aid to seventeen African nations.

These efforts bolstered Cuba's reputation as a leader in the Non-Aligned Movement (NAM), a group that had been founded in the early 1960s by leaders from India, Indonesia, and Egypt in order to promote the interests of nations that were allied neither with the United States or the Soviet Union. (In practice, some of these nations, like Cuba itself, were indeed allied with the Soviet Union.) Cuba continued to play a leadership role in the NAM through the 1980s.

During the 1980s, Cuba reasserted its position as a model for rebel movements and Latin American leftists. For those on the Latin American left, the Cuban Revolutions triumphs in healthcare, education and Third World leadership outweighed its failings in terms of human rights violations, large-scale outmigration and rationing of goods and services. Cuba offered travel money and scholarships to young leftists from other parts of Latin America to study on the island or in the Soviet Union, while the deployment of Cuban doctors to underserved rural parts of Latin America offered a demonstration of the revolution's achievements.

Yet opposition to Cuba from ardently anticommunist governments in nearly every country meant that Cuba would never enjoy the same kind of influence in its own backyard as it did in Africa, for example. This was in no small measure because the United States, acting as self-appointed hemispheric policeman, did everything in its power to prevent it. Within Latin America, only in Nicaragua and on the tiny island of Grenada did Cuban-supported rebels ultimately succeed in helping to bring leftist governments to power.

CUBAN REVOLUTION (1953-1959)

FSLN GUERRILLAS (1961-1977)

"TEN YEARS OF SPRING" (1944-1954) FRENTE ARMADO REVOLUCIONARIO (1962-1967)

JOSÉ "PEPE" FIGUERES AND THE CARIBBEAN LEAGUE (1948)

BOLIVIAN NATIONAL REVOLUTION (1952-1964)

MONTONEROS (1970s)

TUPAMEROS (early 1960s– early 1970s)

Revolutionary Groups in Latin America, 1950s–1970s

≡ **MAP. 10.2**

ECONOMICS AND COMMODITIES

The Ten-Million-Ton Harvest

In December of 1969, Fidel Castro officially inaugurated a campaign his regime had been planning for six years—the quest to harvest ten million tons of sugar in 1970. Castro put everything he had into the effort, massively increasing sugar cultivation, importing new machinery from the Soviet Union, and creating a Ministry of the Sugar Industry to oversee the efforts. Above all, he counted on the volunteer efforts of tens of thousands of Cubans, calling for them to take to the fields in order to cut cane. He led the efforts himself, and news photographs showed him in the fields, machete in hand. Men, women, students, schoolteachers, soldiers, athletes, and civil servants followed his example. The goal was to prove the merits of Cuban organization and agroindustrial might, and also of revolutionary virility and voluntary spirit.

Economically, the **Ten Million Ton Harvest** marked a direct about-face from the ISI strategy of 1959–1963. Recognizing the failures of ISI on a small island, Castro returned to Cuba's historic comparative advantage, its agricultural fertility. But reversing course made clear that Cuba's sugar industry faced great challenges. Nearly all of the island's sugar mills were outmoded. And many Cubans had seen the Revolution as their chance to get out of the cane fields.

The imported Soviet machinery failed to function well in Cuba's tropical heat. The volunteer workers made matters worse: City folk looked down on cane-cutting as unskilled labor. Experienced cane-cutters knew how to cut quickly and close to the ground, lopping off dead stalks and leaves in the process, maximizing sugar yield. Inexperienced workers, unused to backbreaking labor, cut too high, leaving the best sugar in the ground, and padding weight totals with brittle stalks and leaves. And the Ministry of the Sugar Industry often could not get tractors to the fields to carry the cane to the mills, leaving the cut stalks to dry in the sun.

The campaign for the Ten Million Ton Harvest yielded fewer than eight million tons. But the longer-term consequences were more significant: the campaign deepened the dependency of the Cuban economy on sugar, neglecting other agricultural enterprises. It also deepened dependence on Soviet technology and subsidies. Many Cubans were temporarily inspired by the volunteer effort but disillusioned by the plan's shortcomings. There was at least one positive consequence: An ensemble of young musicians took the name for their band from a variation of the propaganda slogan for the campaign, "*Los Diez Millones Van*" (The Ten Million Go). The son band Los Van Van became one of Cuba's most-enduring and beloved institutions. The Revolution had its shortcomings, but Cuban culture remained unstoppable.

- Why was the Ten Million Ton Harvest such a decisive campaign for the revolutionary regime?

Aging Populists and Leftist Opposition in the Southern Cone, 1954–1970

In the 1950s, the corporatist administrations of South America faced rising demands in a period of falling income. Industrial labor, privileged both symbolically and materially under Vargas of Brazil and Perón of Argentina, simultaneously demanded wage increases that would keep step with inflation and sought to increase their political leverage. Other sectors sought the same protections granted industrial labor, or raised cries of panic when wages of machine operators threatened to rise to middle-class levels, endangering social privilege. The corporatist administrative structure turned into a battleground of entrenched interest groups, unable to compromise.

At the same time, the populist fervor of Getulismo and Peronismo guaranteed that these would remain potent political forces for decades to come. As a result, when the shock waves of the Cuban Revolution reverberated across South America, their effects were impossible to discern from the crisis of corporatism. This turmoil gave rise to strange, local hybrids of revolutionary Marxism and Peronism, and to particular strains of Cold War paranoia. The death of Getúlio Vargas and the exile of Juan Perón were prelude to the military coups and guerrilla wars that followed in the 1960s and 1970s. Uruguay, sandwiched between these behemoths, could not help but be torn apart in the same ways.

The Return of Getúlio Vargas

Five years after being ousted from the presidency in the coup of October 1945, Getúlio Vargas returned triumphantly to the national scene in 1950, winning the presidential election handily. He quickly discovered that the administrative machinations he had honed during the dictatorship of the Estado Novo did not work in the rambunctious democratic arena of the 1950s. The opposition press exposed corruption within his administration. Industrial labor remained nominally loyal but far from subservient. And falling export receipts made it more difficult to grease the wheels of import substitution industrialization. By mid-1954, Vargas was a pale shadow of the galvanizing leader of the early 1940s. His resignation from office seemed inevitable.

Then on August 24, 1954, in one of the most dramatic exits in Latin American political history, Vargas shot himself in the heart. His followers saw his death as martyrdom at the hands of **entreguistas**, or sellouts—those they accused of selling the country cheap to foreign interests. Vargas's shocking suicide turned the political tide in Brazil. The outpouring of affection for Vargas guaranteed the election of Juscelino Kubitschek, a politician within the Getulista machine, to the presidency the following year.

Kubitschek made his mark with the construction of a new capital at Brasília, deep in the interior of the country. This initiated a new stage in state-led economic development, allowing for plentiful distribution of jobs and contracts. Kubitschek adapted Vargas's corporativist administration to a new model of technocracy, ostensibly refining the science of government on Brazil's high central plains. Once the capital was inaugurated in 1960, Kubitschek's successors faced the same kinds of difficulties experienced by Vargas in the early 1950s: rising demand and fewer resources to distribute. Jânio Quadros, elected president in 1960, renounced office after eight months in an unsuccessful attempt to force Brazil's Congress to yield to his will. Quadros's vice president, João Goulart, assumed the presidency in the midst of crisis in September of 1961.

Goulart and the Unraveling of the Getulista Coalition

Goulart had been Vargas's closest political protégé and was widely identified with Getulista machine politics—and that machine had broken down. Industrial labor leaders demanded wage hikes to counteract inflation. And in the rural Northeast, a labor leader named Francisco Julião mobilized the Ligas Camponesas, or Peasant Leagues, a federation of rural cooperatives and landless farmers. Inspired in part by the Cuban revolution, Julião and the Peasant Leagues demanded land reform—particularly the breakup of unproductive large estates in the northeast and their distribution to landless farmers. Other Brazilians, particularly members of the urban middle class, rural landowners, and industrialists, saw the Cuban Revolution as an abomination and feared its influence on Brazil.

Getulista and anti-Getulista positions thus overlapped with pro- and anti–Cuban Revolution positions. The factionalization was evident in every sector of Brazilian society, but two would become most decisive, the Catholic Church and the armed forces. Several Brazilian archbishops, such as Dom Helder Câmara, ardently favored land reform and the redistribution of wealth. These priests were the forerunners of a doctrine that became known as liberation theology, emphasizing social justice over individual spiritual transformation. An older guard of conservative clerics opposed these reformist bishops. Members of both factions expected political leaders to pay heed.

The armed forces were similarly divided. It bears remembering that Luís Carlos Prestes (chapter 8) had been a military officer, and that revolutionary communism, as well as more moderate social reform, had long found adherents within the Brazilian Army. Most senior officers, however, feared the spread of Marxism, both within their own ranks and more broadly in Brazilian society. As the turbulence of the Goulart years increased, even moderate senior officers became wary of revolutionary activity within Brazil and impatient with the vacillating Goulart. Early in 1964, these officers prepared to intervene and remove Goulart from power, confident of the support of the US government for their initiative.

Perón and Peronism: From Exile to Return

In Argentina, Perón reached a similar impasse in the mid-1950s. After Evita's death, he was unable to assuage the diehard Peronists, who loved Evita more than they loved Perón himself. His opponents grew ever more vitriolic, and found abundant evidence of political corruption to stoke their outrage. Perón's decrees became increasingly erratic, alienating both the Catholic Church and the armed forces. Perón had initially risen to power as an officer, but by 1955 he had lost military support, and navy officers rose in open rebellion. Peronist factions rioted in response, looting churches in downtown Buenos Aires. In September of 1955, a military junta ousted Perón and claimed power. Perón fled into exile, making his way to Spain.

The faction that had seized power was virulently anti-Peronist, banning any iconography or literature praising the former dictator or his wife. But Peronism remained deeply rooted among many Argentines, particularly industrial laborers. This led to a curious phenomenon: adherence to Peronism in the ranks of industrial labor deepened even with Perón in exile. But what *was* Peronism, without Perón or Evita to determine its content? Individual labor leaders disputed the movement's true meaning. One of them, Augusto Vandor, conceived of himself as more Peronist than Perón himself. Vandor and his allies built their own factions within the general labor federation of industrial workers. The split within industrial labor was not between Peronist and anti-Peronist, but between followers of Vandor and followers of Perón. Meanwhile, operating even more deeply in the shadows, a cohort of ruthless operators linked to José López Rega, Perón's personal secretary, prepared to move against all other claimants to the throne.

The Montoneros and Urban Guerrillas in Argentina and Uruguay

As in Brazil, the influence of the Cuban revolution further complicated the situation in Argentina, as left-wing radicals organized covert revolutionary factions. Several of these factions combined a revolutionary adaptation of the speeches and iconography of Evita with Marxist theory, resulting in a uniquely Argentine hybrid, guerrilla Peronism. The *Movimiento Peronista Montonero*, for example, better known as the **Montoneros**, believed in violence as a catalyst to revolution and as a purifying political act. As with many revolutionary factions, they wielded that violence as frequently against rivals on the left as against adversaries on the right, and perhaps with greater vengeance. The Montoneros attacked Peronist labor unionists and moderate student leaders as often as they did military officers.

In this chaotic context, a quick series of military coups failed to cut down on the number of kidnappings and car bombings, much less bring order to Argentine politics. Students and labor leaders joined forces to demonstrate against the military government in the industrial city of Córdoba in May of 1960, suffering violent reprisal from the government. They rose again a year later. By 1972, pressure for a return to democratic elections had grown, allowing for the return of Perón from his long exile.

If Vargas's most iconic moment was his suicide, Perón's was his return to Argentina. Each of the factions believed it held the key to Peronism, and that Perón would endorse its claim to the mantle. By the time Perón prepared to land at Ezeiza Airport outside Buenos Aires on June 20, 1973, sentiments were at a fever pitch. Over three million Peronists from mutually antipathetic factions gathered to meet him. Before Perón could land, López Rega's men opened fire, turning the triumphal return into a bloodbath, killing more than a dozen and injuring hundreds of student demonstrators and Montoneros.

The Ezeiza massacre played into Perón's hands in the short term, as it forced the resignation of the sitting president, paving the way for a special election that brought Perón back to power. Isabel Perón, the aging leader's third wife, served as his vice president and a symbolic replacement of Evita. But in the longer run the massacre demonstrated that the splits within Peronism could not be reconciled, either by Perón or López Rega. The same kinds of guerrilla attacks and violent civil conflicts that had plagued Argentina for years marred Perón's second presidency. When Perón died of a heart attack in 1974, Isabel Perón assumed the presidency, becoming the first female head of state in Latin American history. But it was the sinister López Rega who influenced her leadership, orchestrating a series of disastrous economic measures and political reprisals. Soon the officers returned, more violently than ever.

Tiny Uruguay could not help but be buffeted by the same tides that rocked Argentina and Brazil. The **Tupamaros**, a revolutionary faction similar to the Montoneros, emerged in Montevideo in the late 1960s, and waged catastrophic violence over the next several years. The Tupamaros took their name from Túpac Amaru, the eighteenth-century leader of an indigenous revolt in the Andes. In contrast to their namesake, the Tupamaros were urban guerrillas, and many of their members were white, middle-class, radicalized former students. In 1970, they kidnapped and killed the CIA agent Dan Mitrione, in an apparent attempt to provoke overt US involvement in Uruguay, triggering greater crisis. The United States continued to operate behind the scenes rather than openly, but the Tupamaros may have gotten more than they bargained for. A military-backed coup of 1972 brought to power a junta dedicated almost entirely to the aggressive eradication of the Tupamaros. They would effectively wipe out the organization, with a massive number of contingent civilian casualties.

Ernesto "Che" Guevara's Misadventure in Bolivia, 1967

Ernesto "Che" Guevara, having become restless with his position as Cuba's minister of industry and the failure to create ISI, decided to resign his office and rededicate himself to furthering the global social revolution. First, he left the island nation to aid communist guerrillas in the Congo. When that revolution failed, he returned to Cuba determined to start a new revolution in Latin America.

The Expeditionaries in Bolivia

Ernesto Guevara picked Bolivia as his target in part because of its location in the heart of South America, which could then, he believed, become a base for continent-wide revolution. In addition, he thought that because of the Bolivian campesinos' reputation as the poorest and most exploited people in continental South America, they would be most receptive to his call for change. After recruiting a total of about fifty Cubans and volunteers from other Latin American countries, including a few Bolivians, and learning a bit of Quechua, the disguised Guevara traveled to Bolivia in early 1967.

From the outset, the guerrillas experienced unanticipated setbacks. Guevara had chosen to start the campaign in the remote southeastern corner of the country. Unfortunately for the expeditionaries, the indigenous people there spoke Guaraní, not Quechua. Unlike in Cuba, where the Communist Party had assisted Castro's forces, the Bolivian Communist Party followed Moscow's dictates and avoided any contact with the guerrillas. The indigenous people and the tin miners felt little kinship with the foreign invaders, in part because they identified strongly with Bolivia's popular mestizo president, General René Barrientos, and in part because their situations had improved because of the MNR revolution. Not a single campesino or tin miner joined Guevara.

In the spring, the Bolivian army discovered a cache of Che's maps and plans, which made the guerrillas relatively easy to locate. Finally, the expedition ran short of food, forcing them to steal from the local campesinos, which hardly endeared them to the very people for whom they were supposed to be fighting. In short, Che could never establish the *foco* (base camp) that was crucial to his strategy (as the Sierra Maestre Mountains in Cuba had been for the Castro Revolution). The combination of these factors condemned the expedition to failure.

Che Guevara's Capture and Death

By September, the guerrillas were in trouble. A campesino informed the army about the band of foreign men traipsing through the countryside, and the army killed one-third of the guerrillas in a shoot-out. To make matters worse, Che ran out of his asthma medication. On October 8, 1967, the Bolivian army wounded the rebel leader in a gun battle and captured him alive. Despite the CIA's requests to keep him alive for further questioning, the next day President Barrientos issued the order to execute Che Guevara. Thus, counterinsurgency tactics and Che Guevara's poor strategic choices enabled the Bolivian army to end the career and the life of the world's most famous revolutionary icon.

Salvador Allende and Electoral Socialism in Chile, 1970–1973

Chileans preferred the ballot to armed revolution as the means to achieve greater social egalitarianism. Following the model of European socialist and communist parties, Chile's two leftist parties had long competed in national elections. Both socialists and communists exercised considerable influence, especially during the Popular Front era (1938–1952), when they formed part of the governing coalition. During the Cold War years, the Chilean left increasingly came to believe that they could achieve meaningful change by following the peaceful "Chilean Path to Socialism."

The Chilean Presidential Election of 1970

Chile's democratic tradition remained strong after 1945. Its broadly based democracy enjoyed high rates of participation (around 80 percent of the electorate). Because of the number of parties competing, only rarely did the leading candidate win an outright majority. But—in keeping with the Constitution of 1925—Chile's Congress routinely awarded the nation's highest office to the candidate with the plurality of votes. The multiparty system meant that a successful executive had to create a working coalition in Congress. In 1964, a moderate member of the Christian Democrat party, Eduardo Frei, won the presidential election outright. Because he represented the type of anti-Communist reformism that the United States admired, his administration received considerable foreign aid. He implemented modest agrarian reform programs and negotiated to increase Chile's share of the profits generated by the US-owned copper corporations.

Frei's reforms notwithstanding, by 1970, many Chileans believed that their government had not pursued economic nationalism with sufficient fervor. Critics on the left rallied behind the medical doctor Salvador Allende, the candidate of the Popular Unity (UP) coalition, comprising socialists, communists, and other assorted Marxists. During his forty years in politics, Allende had served as minister of health in the first Popular Front government, implementing programs to improve safety conditions for workers as well as school lunch programs for poor children. As a senator, his signature achievement had been a bill creating Chile's national healthcare system. Nobody doubted Allende's commitment to socialism, but he also enjoyed the good life, as demonstrated by his wardrobe of forty silk suits and a fine home in the suburbs. Allende's lifestyle seemed to illustrate that socialism meant prosperity, not austerity.

The election of 1970 marked his fourth run for the presidency; on each previous occasion he had won a slightly higher percentage of the vote. This time, Allende eked out a narrow victory with 36.2 percent of the votes, compared to 34.9 percent for the conservative and 27 percent for the Christian Democrat. While Cubans applauded the results (Allende had been friends with Fidel Castro for over a decade), the United States feared that the democratic election of a socialist to the presidency set a dangerous precedent. What followed in the month after the election demonstrated the United States' interest in meddling in Chilean politics.

The CIA plan had two tracks. The first track required the active participation of President Frei to subvert the Chilean electoral process and call for new elections. Because Frei was a firm believer in the constitutional process, the administration of US President Richard Nixon quickly recognized that this track would fail. The second track authorized the CIA to identify military personnel willing to carry out a coup, with the full support of the United States, to prevent Allende from being inaugurated.

The plan's success depended on the removal of Commander-in-Chief General René Schneider, who had already signaled his belief that Allende should take office. The conspirators bungled Schneider's kidnapping, murdering him in the process, and with this failure the Nixon administration backed off the second track. Instead, using covert methods, the United States sought to weaken the Allende administration and build up the opposition by funding the country's conservative newspaper and providing money to opposition political parties.

Allende's future depended on his ability to manage the Chilean road to socialism. He faced three obstacles. First, his election victory via a slim plurality, rather than a majority, gave him a weak mandate for broad social and economic change. Second, he struggled to hold together the fractious UP coalition, which ranged from radicals like the Movimiento de Izquierda Revolucionario (MIR) (Revolutionary Movement of the Left), to moderate reformers. Third, and perhaps most decisively, he faced the subversion and antipathy of the Nixon administration and the CIA.

Allende's Controversial Policies and Their Consequences

Allende moved slowly on the most important issue touching Chile's economic future: the nationalization of the US-owned holdings of the Kennicott and Anaconda copper companies, including the El Teniente mine. Even legislators outside Allende's coalition (largely the Christian Democrats) supported this act.

When Allende finally decreed the expropriation in July 1971, what particularly upset the US government and the copper companies was Allende's rather cavalier attitude (from the North American point of view) about compensation. Arguing that the two companies had exploited Chile and earned "excessive profits" over the years, Allende offered no compensation for the mines.

In addition, the UP government decreed the expropriation of other foreign-owned and Chilean companies: banks, steel mills, coal mines, and most notably, the Chilean subsidiary of the US-owned IT&T, the latter in part as retaliation for its role in funneling CIA money to UP's political opponents in the election of 1970. As the socialization of the economy proceeded, even small, Chilean-owned businesses came under government control. Eventually some members of Allende's inner circle thought he had gone too far. As Allende's ambassador to the United States, Orlando Letelier, quipped to a Socialist colleague: "One day we will learn . . . (that the government) . . . has taken over roasted peanut carts on street corners!"

Agrarian reform, begun modestly during the Christian Democratic administration, escalated during the Allende years. Whereas the Christian Democrats had expropriated approximately 20 percent of Chile's large haciendas before 1970, the UP government confiscated and collectivized all farms in excess of 200 acres. In some cases, landless farmers took reform into their own hands and invaded smaller farms without governmental authority. The MIR encouraged these land invasions, and urged workers to take over factories, expel management, and control production.

Rapid, unplanned takeovers and invasions exacerbated economic turbulence. Allende declared a price freeze on agricultural products and immediate wage increases as part of his plan to redistribute wealth. During his first year in office, real wages increased by roughly 22 percent as Allende strove to create a nation of "socialist consumers." But such a dramatic transition would cause enormous economic disruptions.

To expand government programs, especially in the fields of education and healthcare, UP hired more government employees. These programs cost more money than the Treasury received in revenue, resulting in deficit spending. To compound these economic difficulties, international copper prices declined. By 1972, inflation reached 140 percent and the country's GDP (gross domestic product) contracted. Low fixed prices for milk and meat made it counterproductive for farmers to ship these products to market only to sell them for a loss. Many slaughtered their cattle and sheep instead. Store shelves were bare. To pay for the costs of the new state employees and programs, the government began printing more money, stoking inflation. In short, Allende's attempt to rapidly socialize the economy severely damaged the Chilean economy.

The United States' covert policy of exerting economic pressure did not help. The administration used its influence to delay loans from international lenders such as the World Bank and the Inter-American Development Bank. When Allende decreed a moratorium on debt payments in November 1971, these banks had an economic justification to reject loan applications. Most telling was the withdrawal of US foreign aid, which had proved so important to the Frei administration. The Soviet Union did not offer financial assistance. Chile presents a fascinating case of the changing nature of the Cold War, no longer a war between two global superpowers, but now more dramatically confined within the Western Hemisphere.

The Coup of September 11, 1973

Chile's middle class had long since abandoned Allende, as his extreme measures alienated Christian Democrats and other moderates. Allende responded by ignoring Congress and implementing many of his reforms by decree. As early as December 1971, about five thousand middle-class housewives led the first "March of the Empty Pots," banging spoons on cookware as they marched through Santiago's streets protesting the empty shelves in the city's grocery stores. Shopkeepers refused to open their stores periodically because price controls meant they operated at a loss. Long-distance truckers proved to be the regime's most consistent small-business opposition. Faced with the government's plan to nationalize the trucking industry, in October 1972 these small businessmen refused to haul produce to Santiago and other cities. The truckers' strike created shortages in urban areas and a drag on the economy. MIR militants attempted to respond to the strike by commandeering vans to deliver food to the city, which only intensified growing opposition to Allende.

Historians have for decades debated the role that the CIA played in the coup that overthrew Salvador Allende on September 11, 1973. There is no doubt that the CIA and the United States' Secretary of State Henry Kissinger were closely involved. But the key organization and leadership came from within Chile, primarily from military officers, backed by the business sector and opposition politicians.

The Chilean Congress had become increasingly frustrated with Allende's refusal to implement approved constitutional amendments limiting his power. In May of 1973, the Supreme Court agreed with Congress, noting that there had been a "constitutional breakdown." Allende had proven incapable of controlling the revolution from below. Land and factory seizures upset the middle class and the military warned that the MIR was importing and storing Cuban weapons on the outskirts of Santiago, preparing for guerrilla war. This led to a split in the officer corps. Many officers believed that the professionalized forces should uphold the constitutionally elected government under any circumstance, while others came to believe that only a military coup could save the nation.

In September, another "March of the Empty Pots" demonstrated Chileans' increasing dissatisfaction with the direction of the regime. A renewed truckers' strike created such dislocation that Allende publicly admitted that only four days' worth of provisions remained on store shelves in Santiago. Senior officers in all four branches of the armed services gave their backing to a military coup.

On September 11, the navy rebelled and took control of the port of Valparaíso, while army units marched on *La Moneda*, Chile's historic presidential palace. By midmorning, tanks surrounded La Moneda, but rather than surrender and go

≡ **Salvador Allende's Broken Glasses after His Suicide.** These glasses belonged to Salvador Allende, Chile's socialist president from 1970 to 1973. He was wearing them when he committed suicide on September 11, 1973, as General Augusto Pinochet's forces bombed the presidential palace in the CIA-supported coup that brought about seventeen years of right-wing military rule. For some time analysts debated whether Allende was assassinated in the course of coup by the Chilean Armed Forces, or if he had taken his own life during the siege of the La Moneda Palace, the seat of government. In May 2011, a Chilean judge authorized the exhumation and autopsy of Allende's remains. A team of international experts examined them and concluded that the former president had shot himself with an AK-47 assault rifle. On September 11, 2012, the thirty-ninth anniversary of Allende's death, a Chilean appeals court unanimously upheld the trial court's ruling, officially closing the case.

into exile with his family, Allende decided to fight to the bitter end. Early in the afternoon the air force strafed the Palace, and army units burst into the building, capturing those who wished to surrender and fighting those who resisted. One of the last of Allende's friends to leave the building heard a shot as he neared the exit, ran upstairs, and found that the president had committed suicide, using an AK-47 given to him as a present by Fidel Castro.

For years conspiracy theorists believed that the coup's architects assassinated Allende, but a 2011 inquiry exhumed Allende's body and confirmed that he had taken his own life. Allende's failure to achieve the peaceful path to socialism resulted from his attempt to do too much too quickly, his inability to maintain the unity of his coalition, and because of the considerable economic pressure exerted by the United States.

Latin America's Third Way: Authoritarian Reformers in Peru and Ecuador, 1967–1980

In a few places, Latin American military officers offered a third type of government, one they believed would do more than ineffective democracies to create egalitarian societies. While most military regimes in this time frame repressed leftist reformers and revolutionaries (see chapter 11), a few such regimes believed that by fiat they could dictate significant structural remakes of Latin America's society and economy. These Andean authoritarian reformers of the 1960s and 1970s employed executive power much as had occurred in the dictatorships of Juan Perón and Getúlio Vargas, but because they governed much less industrialized states, their policy objectives differed.

The Military and Economic Nationalism

In both Peru and Ecuador, the military seized power against the backdrop of failed democratic regimes. Like Venezuelans, Peruvians had high hopes in the 1960s of developing a two-party system (one of which was APRA, the Popular American Revolutionary Alliance discussed in chapter 8) where both parties stood for moderate change. Unfortunately, the parties did little to justify this confidence; they neither corrected social problems nor provided order. Marxist guerrillas led by the radical intellectual Hugo Blanco demanded agrarian reform and gained some traction in the *sierra*, which unnerved many Peruvians. As a result, in 1967 General Juan Velasco and fellow reformist officers, who had been trained at the military academy to be not only guardians of national security but champions of social change, seized power. Influenced to some degree by the idea of "Inca socialism" and Indo-americanism" advanced by Haya de la Torre, they sought to offer solutions where the civilians had failed. Velasco himself came from a modest background (he once worked as a shoeshine boy) and thus seemed a likely champion of the underprivileged.

Implementing economic nationalism increased the popularity of authoritarian left regimes. General Velasco began with easy targets: the US-owned oil company, the Cerro de Pasco Copper Company, and the vast W.R. Grace sugar plantations and other holdings. Initially Velasco refused to compensate these foreigners for nationalized properties, which caused profound repercussions. In addition to attracting an immediate hostile reaction from the US government, the failure to compensate frightened off potential investors, both foreign and domestic. Velasco attempted to extend Peru's territorial waters from three miles to two hundred miles in defiance of traditional international law in order to close the valuable fishing grounds of the Humboldt Current to trawlers from foreign nations.

Eventually General Velasco extended his nationalization program to include large sectors of Peruvian-owned businesses. By 1975 the government controlled 25 percent of the Peruvian economy. By eliminating foreigners and oligarchs from their dominant role in business, the government hoped to encourage small-scale investors to establish new companies. This never happened, as Velasco's reforms continued to alienate potential entrepreneurs and thus failed to stimulate economic development. Many of the nationalized companies that remained in government hands proved marginally profitable or operated at a loss, which defeated the policy objective of generating revenues for use in other social programs.

Ecuador's populist, perennial president, José María Velasco Ibarra, a charismatic public speaker and a magician on the campaign trail, had on several occasions already proven his inability to govern wisely. During his previous presidencies he quarreled with friends, jailed or exiled his enemies, and tried to gloss over his failures to enact meaningful social change by distracting the electorate with expensive public works projects (such as roads, bridges, and canals) that did provide some employment but left the government helplessly in debt. By the time of Velasco Ibarra's fourth and fifth elections (never consecutive), his electoral margins had grown razor-thin, and when on both occasions he tried to replicate the same failed policies, the military removed him from office and took charge (1963–1966, and 1972–1979).

The Ecuadorian military's modest proposals for economic nationalism generally worked better than did Peru's more extreme approach. The Ecuadorian military created a national oil company to compete with Texaco and other giants (and which did an equally destructive job polluting the Amazonian rain forest), joined OPEC, and operated a moderately successful national airline, among other state-owned enterprises. Modest industrialization based on ISI principles commenced. As in Mexico in 1938, the acts of economic nationalism led to outbursts of popular jubilation. The military officers used petroleum income to build schools and hospitals, dramatically improving Ecuador's literacy rate and the availability of healthcare services. Newly found revenues and borrowed money enabled the government to hold down food prices and subsidize the cost of other services, but at the price of some unforeseen economic consequences that needed to be resolved in the 1980s.

Agrarian Reform and Policies Affecting Other Sectors of Society

General Velasco's agrarian reform program successfully dismantled much of Peru's traditional landholding pattern, whereby roughly 1 percent of Peru's population owned 76 percent of the land. By decree on Independence Day, 1969, Velasco limited coastal estates to 120 acres and highland haciendas to 75 acres. Overnight, expropriated coastal plantations became sugar and cotton cooperatives worked by the former tenants. Redistribution in the sierra occurred at a much slower pace despite special courts designed to transfer titles quickly. There, residents could choose between individual plots or forming collectives. The reform resulted in 38 percent of Peru's land being redistributed. Unfortunately, as had occurred in Mexico, many of the poorest campesinos received no land, and others received plots of less than seven and a half acres, the minimum needed to provide a decent living.

By using dictatorial powers, Velasco's government did create remarkable structural changes in the Peruvian countryside, reducing patriarchy and allowing campesinos to assert their newfound rights. But the agrarian reform measures did not lessen poverty in rural areas, largely because the government had little practical expertise in managing agricultural enterprises and even less money to pour into rural investments. For example, the government failed to provide necessary technology, education in up-to date farming methods, or make available low-cost fertilizer that would have made small plots viable. As a consequence, food production declined.

Ecuador's more modest agrarian reform program functioned in the sierra as an incentive for estate owners to modernize agriculture rather than as a program to redistribute land. Limiting highland estates to two thousand acres challenged estate owners to dedicate their land to profitable export crops like flowers and broccoli, while the impoverished campesinos received the poorer-quality land on the less fertile mountain slopes. The military also encouraged campesinos to form cooperatives to increase their standards of living, with mixed results. Ecuador's statutes also outlawed the demeaning and nearly fuedal unpaid tasks that campesinos had been required to do for estate owners, such as household chores or having the entire family work for free during the harvest. In coastal regions, the military encouraged campesinos to invade and occupy lands formerly owned by the UFCo.

Both Peru's Velasco and the Ecuadorian authoritarian reformers paid limited attention to other sectors of society, particularly labor unions, businesses, and the urban poor. Although labor reform had been at the core of the Perón and Vargas administrations in Argentina and Brazil respectively, neither General Velasco nor the Ecuadorian military governments made much of an effort to woo union members. In both cases, the military governments understood that unions already owed their allegiance to other parties.

Businessmen did not like the authoritarian reformers. General Velasco's Industrial Reform Act of 1970 alienated entrepreneurs because it required companies that had more than six employees to grant those employees a role in management. The act also required these "medium-sized" businesses to give workers 50-percent ownership rights. Both these provisions created a disincentive to growth, as they discouraged small businesses from hiring more than five employees. In marked contrast, Ecuador's military government won plaudits for its social spending, which dramatically increased the size of the middle class. Granted, many of the new members of the middle class worked for the government or in the large nationalized businesses, but as long as the country was flush with oil money the strategy seemed to offer a positive social result.

General Velasco also failed to connect with the urban poor, a growing segment of Peruvian society. He charged a new government agency, SINAMOS (the National System for Support of Social Mobilization), with the mission of assisting the urban poor and especially the growing squatter communities. Although many squatters received titles to the lands they occupied, the government simply could not keep pace with the growth of these settlements. Demands for better housing, employment, social services, electricity, water, and schools exceeded the government's ability to fund these necessities. When Peru's economy collapsed in the late 1970s in the midst of the global recession, Velasco's military successor simply turned off the spigot of funds for these social programs. While Velasco's authoritarian reforms had changed Peru's socioeconomic structure, in the short run they failed. In fact, in 1980, 75 percent of Peruvians were poorer than they had been when Velasco took power.

Ecuador did slightly better. Despite the oil revenues, the generals borrowed heavily from international bankers to fund the growth of the middle class and provide subsidies for the urban poor. When the bubble burst in the late 1970s, the military had no choice but to turn governance back to civilian parties. The military returned to the barracks and returned Ecuador to civilian rule.

CULTURE AND IDEAS

Bob Marley and Reggae in Latin America

Bob Marley flashed like a shooting star across the firmament of global popular culture. He was practically unknown outside Jamaica in 1972, became one of the world's most recognizable icons by 1976, and died from cancer at age 36 in 1981. In the course of that progress from meteoric rise to tragic early death, he transformed global popular music, making Jamaican *reggae* the rhythm of resistance, infusing aspirations for radical transformation around the world, not least in Latin America.

By the mid-1970s, Marley's dreadlocked, spliff-smoking image—carefully cultivated by his photographer and confidant Esther Anderson both to embody his Rastafarian beliefs in sacred natural growth and to appeal to disenchanted youth—was emblazoned on posters from Buenos Aires to San Juan, Puerto Rico. He seemed to embody not only a new approach to blackness but also a vision of Third World rights in defiance of superpowers.

Reggae emerged from the same Afro-Atlantic sources that had given rise to Latin American genres like Brazilian *samba*, Cuban *son*, and Colombian *porro*. It had both the accessibility of familiar rhythmic and melodic elements and the allure of a foreign sound that had emerged from the poorest neighborhoods of Kingston, Jamaica, to capture the world's attention. Reggae in Spanish and Portuguese soon became common, often accompanied by images of Marley and other Rasta icons. Covers of Marley hits, like Gilberto Gil's *"Não Chore Mais"*—a version of "No Woman, No Cry,"—rose up the Brazilian and Spanish American charts.

Marley's visit to Rio de Janeiro in March 1980 cemented the bond between the reggae superstar and his Latin American public. Footage of Marley in a local soccer jersey, scoring a goal in a pick-up game with the composer Chico Buarque, confirmed the similarity between Jamaican and Brazilian sensibilities. Marley's appearance in Zimbabwe a month later had a similar resonance, a sign of increasing popular cultural connections across the Global South.

By the time of his visit to Rio, Marley was already weakened by cancer, and he died a little over a year later. By that time, reggae and its association with "uprising" (the title of Marley's last album) was entrenched. In the Dominican Republic, Puerto Rico, and Cuba, Spanish-language reggae doubled-back to Jamaican dancehall, the genre that had preceded reggae, producing the blend known as *reggaetón*. In the first decade of the twenty-first century, reggaetón galvanized dance floors around the world, a fascinating example the cyclical nature of cultural influence.

- Why did Latin American youth in the 1970s identify with Bob Marley? In what way was his music and Rasta lifestyle an embodied form of resistence?
- Was reggae a foreign import to Latin America, or was it already Latin American by virtue of its Caribbean origins?

The Revolution in Latin American Literature, 1950s–1980s

During the 1960s three Spanish American novelists became internationally renowned for the quality of their works of fiction. These writers initiated the "Latin American Boom," the explosion of Latin American literature onto the international literary scene. Whereas earlier generations of Latin American writers had addressed national issues, the writers of the boom era appealed more broadly because of their universally relatable themes. Each of the three best-known writers befriended Fidel Castro, initially championed his Revolution and advocated for leftist if not Marxist solutions to Latin America's social ills. In addition, each author adopted the revolutionary literary style of magic realism, the juxtaposition of fantasy against reality.

The Authors

Gabriel García Márquez (1927–2014), the winner of the 1982 Nobel Prize for Literature, was the first to gain international acclaim. As a child, his parents and grandparents regaled him with tales about his birthplace (which he renamed Macondo in his most famous novel) and their families' lives interwoven into the context of Colombian history. These realistic stories, much embellished with magical flights of fancy, became the framework for his greatest novel, *One Hundred Years of Solitude* (1967). After studying law, García Márquez became a journalist and a short-story writer. Dispatched as a reporter to Paris, he soon met other Latin Americans and began to think of himself less as a Colombian and more as a Latin American.

When Fidel Castro overthrew Fulgencio Batista in 1959, García Márquez volunteered to go to Cuba to head Castro's news agency, which he ran from Bogotá. In 1962 he moved to Mexico City to write novels, but experienced a horrendous case of writer's block. Suddenly inspired on the way to a family vacation in Acapulco, he raced back to Mexico City, where he completed his masterpiece. After the stunning success of *One Hundred Years of Solitude*, García Márquez wrote other acclaimed novels and continued to embrace leftist causes until his death.

As the son of a Mexican diplomat, Carlos Fuentes (1928–2012) enjoyed a privileged existence as a child. Because he spent his early years in Argentina, Brazil, Chile, Panama, and Washington, DC, as well as Mexico, Fuentes (like García Márquez) viewed himself as a Latin American rather than simply a Mexican national. Trained as a lawyer at Mexico's leading university, Fuentes quickly traded his desk job at the Foreign Relations Ministry for work as a journalist and a short-story writer. While furthering his education in Europe, Fuentes befriended intellectuals from several countries. As a result, Fuentes's writings, like those of García Márquez, also employed the stylistic devices commonly used by contemporary US and European writers.

A voracious reader, Fuentes steeped himself in the works of William Faulkner, Franz Kafka, and Fyodor Dostoevsky as he sought to portray universal themes in a Mexican setting. His most productive years during the 1960s drew inspiration from the Cuban Revolution. Castro's success so enthralled him that on January 2, 1959, the day after the rebels took Havana, Fuentes and a few other Mexican intellectuals boarded a plane to interview Fidel. Fuentes wrote prolifically for the remainder of his life. His best-known novel, *The Death of Artemio Cruz*, was first published in 1962.

The youngest of the "Big Three" Boom authors, Mario Vargas Llosa (b. 1936) spent his youth in Bolivia before his middle-class family returned to Peru. During his final year of high school, he began working at a newspaper and then entered San Marcos University to study law. At age nineteen he shocked his family by marrying his aunt Julia (his uncle's former wife), his elder by more than a decade. His escapades during these years became the plot for his humorous novel *Aunt Julia and the Scriptwriter* (1977). After winning a short story contest, Vargas Llosa and his wife moved to Paris, where, like Fuentes and García Márquez, he became acquainted with influential literary figures. He spent the next eleven years in France writing some of his most famous works, including *Conversation in the Cathedral* (1969).

Vargas Llosa initially shared his two colleagues' enthusiasm for the Castro revolution and visited the island to meet the great leader. Like Fuentes, Vargas Llosa became disillusioned with Castro because of his human rights abuses, especially after 1971, when the dictator imprisoned the poet Heberto Padilla for his critical comments about the regime. Vargas Llosa became more conservative politically through the years, nearly winning the presidency of Peru in 1990 on a center-right ticket. In 2010 he won the Nobel Prize in Literature.

Their Best-Known Novels

Part of García Márquez's appeal to audiences worldwide resulted from his use of popular stylistic conventions of modern literature, such as stream-of-consciousness, a technique that allowed him to enter the minds of his most important characters in order to understand their psychological motivations. For example, *One Hundred Years of Solitude* details the inner loneliness of each of the members of the Buendía family as they struggle through the numerous nineteenth-century civil wars between Liberals and Conservatives and the violent suppression of the banana workers' strike in 1928. At the end of the novel, all the remaining members of the family are swept away in a windstorm, isolating them permanently from their community and country.

García Márquez's other best-selling work, the more accessible *Love in the Time of Cholera*, strikes a more optimistic tone because it suggests a cure for loneliness—love. The novel portrays a story of patience: a young man, spurned by his teenaged love whose family insists she marry someone from a higher class, persists in his affection and ultimately reunites with her after she is widowed and they are both in their seventies. As in García Márquez's other works, he richly develops each major character. The novel also resonates because of its thoughtful, sophisticated

≡ **Gabriel García Márquez at Work on His Novel *One Hundred Years of Solitude*.** Gabriel García Márquez, arguably the most famous and internationally known novelist from Latin America is seen here working on a draft of his most famous book, *One Hundred Years of Solitude*. Based on a lengthy span of Colombian history, García Márquez used very modern techniques, such as magical realism, to capture the ambiance of life in a rural community in Colombia in much of the nineteenth century. García Márquez wrote several other important novels, such as *Love in the Time of Cholera* and *The General in His Labyrinth*, that deepen readers' understanding of Latin American history.

discussion about race and class in nineteenth-century Cartagena. Once again, García Márquez interprets Colombian society and history in a complex way that related to international audiences.

One of Fuentes's most intriguing novels, *The Death of Artemio Cruz*, offers great insights into human psychology and a biting critique of the post-1940 Mexican Revolution. Fuentes, who wrote much of this novel while living in Castro's Cuba, described the novel as one of lost vision. Several different characters serve as narrators at different points of the story. The novel begins with Revolutionary General Artemio Cruz on his deathbed, reminiscing about his life. Cruz held high ideals during the decade of fighting, but given the opportunities to enrich himself after 1940, makes the decision to jettison those ideals. At the same time he betrays his wife by having two serious affairs, destroying his family in the process. On his deathbed Cruz realizes he could have made other choices that would have left his ideals intact. He dies thinking about his son Lorenzo, killed while fighting for his principles during the Spanish Civil War of the 1930s.

Critics generally agree that Vargas Llosa's *Conversation in the Cathedral* is his most profound and complex novel. Although the title implies that the conversation takes place on holy ground, in reality the Cathedral is a seedy bar. There Santiago Zavala, a journalist and the son of a prominent politician-businessman, sits with his father's former chauffeur, a black man named Ambrosio Pardo, who also worked for the ousted dictator's chief of security. The two discuss the question: "At what precise moment has Peru screwed itself up?" The dialogue provides thorough documentation of the misdeeds of Peru's dictator in the 1950s, but more importantly, describes how political corruption and influence-peddling ruin individual lives. Nevertheless, the novel offers no definitive answer to the question originally posed, either on a political or personal level, leaving the reader struggling with ambiguity. Like García Márquez and Fuentes, Vargas Llosa produced thoughtful and revolutionary novels that popularized Latin American fiction globally.

Conclusion

The winds of change swept over Latin America in the middle decades of the twentieth century, as Latin American revolutionaries strove to redress the gross inequities that existed between rich and poor. Initially the revolutionaries followed the democratic Mexican constitutional model, implementing programs of agrarian reform to redistribute hacienda land to campesinos, strengthening labor unions'

TIMELINE

1944
Guatemala embarks on its "Ten Years of Spring"

1948
Costa Rica's revolution

1952
Land reform Law 900 goes into effect in Guatemala

1954
CIA assists in overthrow of Jacobo Arbenz in Guatemala

1959
Fidel Castro leads the Cuban Revolution to victory

1961–2006
Fidel Castro becomes Latin America's dominant communist figure

1961–1964
Quadros and Goulart enact reforms in Brazil

1962
Cuban Missile Crisis

rights to organize and bargain collectively, and adopting strategies of economic nationalism to diminish the influence of foreign-owned enterprises in favor of state-controlled corporations. But in the years after World War II, some people living in the developing world and Latin America came to see the Mexican model as inadequate to contend with the challenges of dependency, liberal capitalism, and the legacy of colonialism.

The Cuban Revolution intensified these conflicts even as it offered a different set of solutions. To Latin Americans opposed to the Revolution, the Cuban form of government was familiar—a dictatorship. The all-powerful state, however, took on a new dimension with its ownership of virtually everything: sugar plantations, small farms, mills, and businesses large and small, expropriated to further social egalitarianism. Although the average Cuban remained desperately poor—in large part because of the US embargo and its implacable opposition to this socialist regime—even the poorest Cubans gained access to a level of education and health-care benefits unavailable elsewhere in Latin America. As leftist revolutionaries looked to Cuba for inspiration, right-wing conservatives prepared their own hard-line reaction, as discussed in chapter 11.

KEY TERMS

barbudos   449

Cuban Missile Crisis   453

entreguistas   458

Law 900   446

Montoneros   460

Ten Million Ton Harvest   457

Tupameros   461

1967
Che Guevara attempts a revolution in Bolivia

1960s–2000
Latin American boom in literature

1970
Allende elected president in Chile

1967–1975
Juan Velasco's authoritarian revolution in Peru

1969
Emergence of urban guerrillas in Argentina and Uruguay

1973
Allende is overthrown by Augusto Pinochet, with help from the CIA

Selected Readings

Bell, John Patrick. *Crisis in Costa Rica: The 1948 Revolution.* Austin, TX: Institute of Latin American Studies, 1971.

Chase, Michelle. *Revolution within the Revolution: Women and Gender Politics in Cuba, 1952–1962.* Chapel Hill: University of North Carolina Press, 2015.

Coronil, Fernando. *The Magical State: Nature, Money, and Modernity in Venezuela.* Chicago: University of Chicago Press, 1997.

Ewell, Judith. *Venezuela: A Century of Change.* Palo Alto, CA: Stanford University Press, 1984.

Garrard-Burnett, Virginia, Mark A Lawrence, and Julio E Moreno, eds. *Beyond the Eagle's Shadow: New Histories of Latin America's Cold War.* Albuquerque: University of New Mexico Press, 2014.

Gleijeses, Piero. *Conflicting Missions: Havana, Washington, and Africa, 1959–1976.* Chapel Hill: University of North Carolina Press, 2002.

Harmer, Tanya. *Allende's Chile and the Inter-American Cold War.* Chapel Hill: University of North Carolina Press, 2011.

Kinzer, Stephen, and Stephen Schlesinger. *Bitter Fruit: The Story of the American Coup in Guatemala.* Expanded ed. Cambridge, MA: David Rockefeller Center for Latin American Studies, 2005.

Kinzer, Stephen. *The Brothers: John Foster Dulles, Allen Dulles, and Their Secret World War.* New York: St. Martin's Griffin, 2014.

Kornbluh, Peter. *The Pinochet File: A Declassified Dossier on Atrocity and Accountability.* New York: The New Press, 2003.

Nichols, Elizabeth Gacksetter, and Kimberly J. Morse. *Venezuela.* New York: ABC-CLIO, 2010.

Molina, Ivan. *History of Costa Rica.* 2nd ed. San José: Editorial Universidad de Costa Rica, 2007.

Rabe, Stephen. *Eisenhower and Latin America: The Foreign Policy of Anti-Communism.* Chapel Hill: University of North Carolina Press, 1988.

11

Counterrevolution in Latin America, 1960–1980

Global Connections

The confrontation between the First World (the United States, Western Europe, and Japan) and the Second World (the Soviet Union, China, and Eastern Europe) continued during the 1960s and 1970s. The Western powers were determined to protect their ideals of individual liberties, democracy, and liberal capitalism against what they viewed as the false but seductive promises of communism: egalitarianism, full employment in a state-run economy, and rapid modernization through industrialization. The United States did not hesitate to support repressive dictatorships in order to stifle socialist movements—and often interpreted even moderate reformist movements as socialist. Both sides attempted to expand their influence into the newly independent nations of Southeast Asia and Africa. The Soviets crushed attempts by Hungarian (1956) and Czechoslovakian (1968) governments to liberalize their regimes, while the United States defended its interests in "its own backyard," Latin America.

The United States enjoyed advantages of technological superiority and military resources, but at the time, the two superpowers seemed evenly balanced. In Vietnam, the United States learned an important lesson in humility, failing to squelch a nationalistic unification movement led by Ho Chi Minh. Ho had led an independence movement against the French (1945–1954), which resulted in the formation of two Vietnams, a communist north and a democratic south. When Ho Chi Minh and his allies in South Vietnam resumed the struggle, the conflict became a Cold War proxy war, with the Soviet Union and China assisting the North, while the United States, Australia, and South Korea aided the South. Despite overwhelming air power and the sacrifice of 59,000 American lives, the United States could not overcome the determination of the nationalists. After massive US internal opposition to the war, the United States withdrew its troops in 1975, and South Vietnam surrendered to the North.

In Africa, as new nations emerged from long colonial histories, national leaders advocated for greater pan-African unity. But the Cold War complicated these efforts. In 1961, the new nations divided into two blocs: the Casablanca Group (Egypt, Ghana, Morocco) called for nonalignment during the Cold War, while the Monrovia Group (Liberia, Ivory Coast, Nigeria) preferred to maintain close ties with the West. Alliance with the West brought many advantages. Former British colonies gained membership in the Commonwealth. The French Community offered fewer advantages but punished the one former colony, Guinea, that refused to join by removing its railroad lines and telephone systems.

≡ **General Augusto Pinochet of Chile.** Augusto Pinochet epitomized the brutal right-wing dictatorships that seized power across much of Latin America in the 1960s–1970s. Pinochet emerged as the most powerful and remorseless member of a junta that overthrew a democratically elected government and murdered thousands of Chileans in the name of imposing counterrevolutionary order.

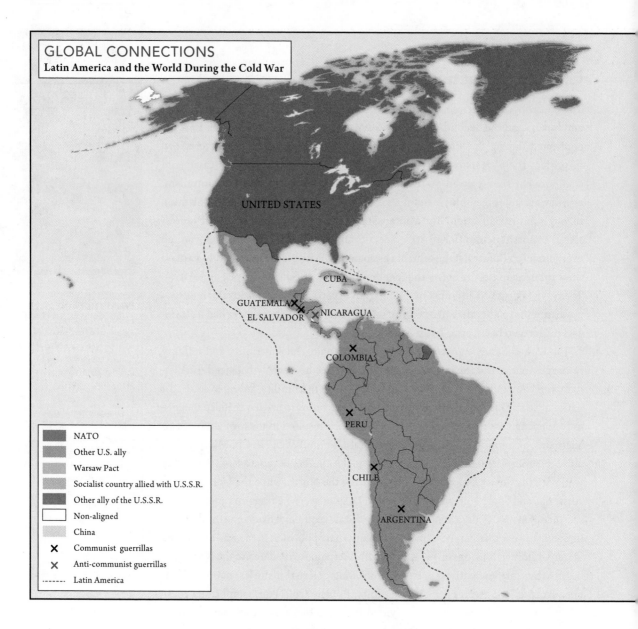

GLOBAL CONNECTIONS
Latin America and the World During the Cold War

UNITED STATES

CUBA

GUATEMALA
EL SALVADOR NICARAGUA

COLOMBIA

PERU

CHILE

ARGENTINA

NATO
Other U.S. ally
Warsaw Pact
Socialist country allied with U.S.S.R.
Other ally of the U.S.S.R.
Non-aligned
China
✖ Communist guerrillas
✖ Anti-communist guerrillas
------ Latin America

Under the pressures of the Cold War, many African experiments with democracy devolved into single-party systems and then into military dictatorships. In the Congo, for example, protracted civil war and regional divisions led to the rise of General Joseph Mobutu in 1964. Mobutu ruled erratically and vindictively until his death in 1997. Because he steadfastly opposed communism, the United

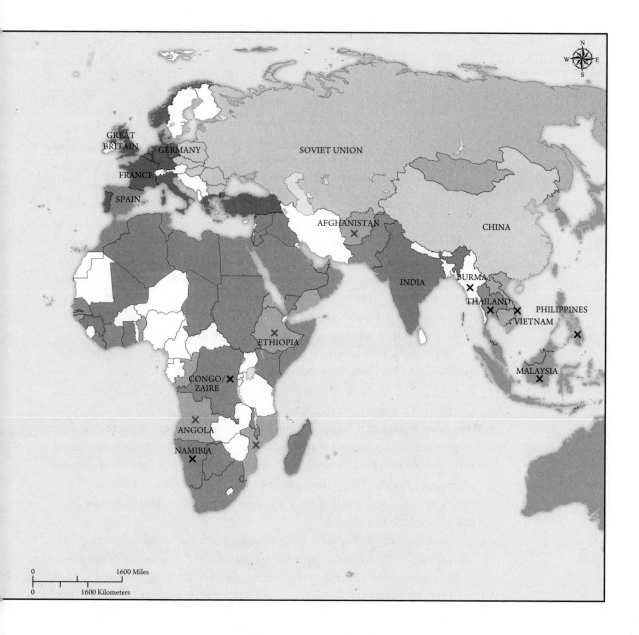

States and the West continued to overlook his abuses. In Latin America, as well, the United States tolerated and even supported authoritarian abuses in the name of anticommunism.

"We need to go up the hill before they come down." This was one mantra for anticommunists in Latin America from the 1960s through the 1980s. These reformers argued that they needed to relieve the poverty of Rio de Janeiro's hillside squatter settlements—as well as those of Caracas, Medellín, or Lima—in order to forestall the political radicalization of their residents. The implication was that if conditions were not improved, in the opinion of government officials and entrenched elites—*they*—those whom outsiders viewed as the undifferentiated, faceless poor—would descend in massive numbers and wage violent revolution. In the immediate aftermath of the Cuban Revolution, these fears were palpable among the propertied classes, and even more so among foreign policy advisors. Hardline anticommunists cared less about reform than about eliminating the "red menace of communism" by any means necessary, including state-sponsored violence against their own populations. When faced with revolutionary Marxist threats, and even with modest reform efforts, governments across Latin America developed new repressive mechanisms designed to silence dissent and clear the political field of any **dirty wars**. Military dictatorships seized power and used violence to enforce it.

In all these ways, Latin America prefigured broader global trends. Supporters of the Cuban Revolution viewed global revolutionary guerrilla movements of the 1960s and 1970s as brushfires promising to merge in one great, transformative blaze. Che Guevara, overjoyed to see the US military mired in Vietnam in 1967, called for "two, three, many Vietnams." Many Vietnams—or many Cubas—were exactly what conservative military officers feared. Like Che, they saw the potential for revolution everywhere; but unlike Che, they looked on that possibility with apocalyptic horror rather than hope. And they acted preemptively to forestall revolution, even if it meant inflicting state-sponsored violence on the citizens of their own nations. In Latin America, these tendencies came to define a generation, as a linked network of military regimes cast a shadow over the hemisphere.

This chapter covers the same chronological timeframe as does chapter 10, but tells the story of the forces that opposed revolutionaries. It begins with a discussion of the dual strategies that the United States employed between 1960 and 1980 to combat the perceived threat of communism in Latin America: first, the Alliance for Progress intended to improve the material well-being of Latin Americans and lessen the allure of communism; and second, the National Security Doctrine, designed to equip and train Latin American militaries to protect their nations from domestic communist threats. From there, our discussion moves from south to north discussing the responses undertaken by authoritarian regimes to confront the revolutionary groups described in chapter 10.

The Alliance for Progress, 1961–1972

The **Alliance for Progress** opened a new era of inter-American cooperation at a level not seen since the Good Neighbor Policy of the 1930s. The Alliance represented an optimistic approach to block what seemed to be the unstoppable advance of socialism, communism and anti-American sentiment throughout the region. But the Alliance was not a paternalistic program conceptualized and paid for by the United States. Latin American democratic leaders had initiated the discussion about a region-wide aid program even before President John F. Kennedy took office in 1961; although the Alliance for Progress was a US initiative, these Latin American democratic leaders would help to shape its goals and objectives.

The Creation of the Alliance

The absence of any major initiative in US–Latin American policy after World War II disappointed Latin Americans. Almost all Latin American countries had sided with the Allies during the war. In the late 1940s, the United States's Marshall Plan poured billions of dollars into rebuilding Europe, including the defeated Axis powers of Germany and Italy as well as Japan. But none of this aid went to Latin America. Presidents Truman and Eisenhower told their Latin American allies to be patient, insisting that rebuilding Western Europe and Asia took priority because of the imminent threat of the Soviet Union's Cold War expansionism. But by the end of the 1950s, many Latin Americans felt betrayed. Students, in particular, expressed vehement displeasure. When Vice President Richard M. Nixon took a "goodwill trip" through Latin America in 1958, crowds spat on him in Lima and swarmed his limousine in Caracas, nearly overturning it before his driver sped to safety.

Brazil's President Juscelino Kubitschek proposed a multilateral (that is, involving the governments of several countries) "Operation Pan-America," which encouraged the United States to increase its financial aid to Latin America. Other Latin American democratic leaders (including Venezuela's Romulo Betancourt and Costa Rica's José Figueres) chimed in with their support. The Organization of American States (OAS), proposed the creation of an Inter-American Development Bank, to fund infrastructural, social and educational projects in Latin Amerca. The Eisenhower administration adopted the plan in 1959, with the strong support of then-Senator John F. Kennedy. Congress offered low-interest development loans to Latin American governments through the new bank. Kennedy's election to the US presidency in late November 1960, ushered in a new era of US–Latin American relations. Articulate, charismatic, handsome, and Catholic (a characteristic crucial to his appeal in Latin

America), the newly inaugurated President Kennedy announced that he intended to make improved relations with Latin America a priority of his "New Frontier." In March 1961, he delivered an impassioned speech to the assembled Latin American diplomatic corps, outlining a "Marshall Plan for Latin America," called the Alliance for Progress. The Alliance was built around two principles: to provide financial aid to assist economic development in Latin America and social justice for free peoples living under democratic governance, and to prevent other nations in the Americas from following in the footsteps of the Cuban Revolution.

Kennedy and his advisors believed that prosperity and socioeconomic structural reforms would create a larger middle class that would in turn strengthen democracy. Representatives from all Latin American nations together with the United States hammered out the details in the **Charter of Punta del Este** (Uruguay) in August 1961. Che Guevara, who attended the conference as Cuba's delegate, predicted that the Alliance would fail, and was not completely incorrect in that assessment. But US's chief spokesperson carried the day with an impassioned defense of the project.

The Charter's goals and objectives allowed each nation to propose specifics in its individualized development plan (a decision that proved to be both the Alliance's greatest strength and also its greatest weakness). The parties to the Charter promised economic growth, an end to adult illiteracy, an elementary school education for every child, affordable and decent housing for all, moderate agrarian reform measures, and support for non-Communist labor unions. Each nation pledged to reexamine and revise its tax policies. Traditionally, taxes in Latin America had been regressive, meaning that the poorest members of society shouldered the bulk of the tax burden, instead of progressive, where the wealthy and middle classes would pay a greater share. The nations also agreed to establish national planning agencies, as the OAS and the region's most famous economist, Argentine Raúl Prebisch, had recommended.

A number of these proposed policies, especially agrarian reform and tax reform, hit hard at Latin America's elite. Ultimately, their resistance would inhibit the ability of even the most progressive governments to fulfill the goals of the Charter. As national governments determined the spending priorities, Alliance funding ended up reflecting the prerogatives of national elites. In Nicaragua, for example, where the Somoza family controlled both the presidency and the Guardia Nacional, most funds went to the military; in Costa Rica, by contrast, Alliance funds supported educational and social welfare programs.

The United States agreed to provide upward of twenty billion dollars of loans and grants over the decade. President Kennedy created the US Agency for International Development (USAID) under the joint auspices of the Department of State and the White House. He and his key advisors played a hands-on role, working directly with Alliance staff. In addition, complementary initiatives like the Peace Corps, which enlisted volunteers to help the impoverished all over the globe, contributed to the development and humanitarian objectives of the Alliance for Progress.

The Alliance's Successes and Failures

The Alliance for Progress enjoyed some successes, but in the long run its objectives were subordinated to the use of funding as a political tool in the Cold War battlefield. Four nations received the vast majority of the Alliance's money: Chile, Brazil, the Dominican Republic, and Colombia. In Chile, funding helped defeat Salvador Allende's presidential bid in 1964 and shored up Eduardo Frei's democratic left government thereafter; in Brazil, the monies largely flowed after a right-wing military regime overthrew a government that favored ambitious land reform. Brazilians joked: "The Alliance for Progress must be working . . . we're getting a better class of dictator." In the Dominican Republic, the funds were only awarded in large amounts after the US Marine invasion of 1965 prevented a leftist from being elected president. In Colombia, the government did enact many of the proposed socioeconomic reforms consistent with the Charter of Punta del Este.

Some of the Alliance's most innovative objectives, particularly the desire to spark structural changes in Latin American society, proved overly ambitious. While the Alliance's proponents declared it to be the Latin American equivalent of the Marshall Plan, the comparison was not altogether apt. Latin America was less developed and lacked Europe's financial infrastructure and credit mechanisms. The Charter encouraged industrialization, but Latin American industrialization lagged far behind Europe's and that of Japan. Finally, and perhaps most importantly, the Marshall Plan had provided 90 percent of its aid in the form of grants, which did not have to be repaid, while the members of the Alliance received 70 percent of its funds as long-term interest-bearing loans. Many Latin Americans felt shortchanged once again.

The Alliance's support for health and sanitation projects helped lower mortality rates and raise life expectancies. In the short term, ironically, that success made it more difficult to generate economic growth exceeding population growth. Population growth also complicated efforts to provide schooling for all children through the elementary grade level. Nor could governments reach the goal established for adequate housing, as rural peoples facing extreme poverty crowded shantytowns on the outskirts of metropolitan areas. In El Salvador, for example, coastal piedmont lands were converted into cotton cultivation to serve a thriving new textile industry subsidized by Alliance initiatives. But the number of rural poor displaced by the new agricultural scheme was greater than the number of jobs that the new factories provided. Because excessive population growth stretched resources, US policy makers did provide funding for the first family-planning programs, distributing condoms and birth control pills, the latter a breakthrough new medical technology.

Even democracy—the Alliance's loftiest goal—failed to take root. Local militaries ousted many of the region's elected leaders beginning in the 1960s, the Alliance for Progress's prime years. The United States preferred to fund military regimes rather than face the threat of Cuban-inspired Marxist revolutions flaring up across the continent. After Kennedy's assassination on November 22, 1963, President Lyndon B. Johnson diminished emphasis on Latin America as his administration focused more on the problems of Vietnam and the costs of reforms designed to reduce poverty within the United States. Johnson supported funding for rural electrification programs and rural infrastructure development in Latin America, and promoted regional trade efforts like LAFTA (Latin American Free Trade Association), but these efforts were modest in comparison to the early years of the Alliance for Progress. As support for democracy fell by the wayside, so did many of the proposals for meaningful socioeconomic reforms.

While most Latin American aid recipients passed modest agrarian reform legislation, they often failed to implement those initiatives. In other cases, governments lacked the resources to offer farmers fertilizer, irrigation systems, and agricultural services necessary to make small farms viable. Agrarian programs nonetheless contributed to a **Green Revolution** in the 1960s, thanks to the introduction of pesticides and fertilizers and the introduction of new agricultural commodities, such as new vegetable hybrids. Guatemala, for example, diversified agriculture, after long emphasis on coffee and banana exports. But neither the Alliance for Progress nor local governments had the will to address land concentration. In nations like Guatemala and El Salvador, the planter owned the vast majority of their nation's productive agricultural lands. El Salvador's elite "Fourteen Families," for example, owned more than 80 percent of the arable land. (In reality, there were more than fourteen interlinked, extended families even in El Salvador's narrow elite, but the popular term indicates the concentration of wealth.) The campesinos who worked the land owned little of it themselves.

These shortcomings notwithstanding, the Alliance for Progress made important contributions before its demise in 1972. For the first time, smaller Latin American states received the technical assistance (including trained economists and adequate statistical data) necessary to develop their own economic planning programs. Investments of billions of dollars dramatically improved the region's infrastructure. Facilities constructed in partnership with the Alliance

≡ **Peruvian Schoolgirls Receive Milk from USAID.** Peruvian schoolgirls in the early 1960s line up for milk provided by USAID. The poster behind them reads, "From the American people to Peruvian schoolchildren." Particularly in its early stages, USAID set out to combat the perceived threat of communist subversion by offering reformist programs to populations likely to be targeted by radical movements—particularly the urban and rural poor of Latin America. The glass of milk was intended as tangible evidence that close alliance with the United States offered a more reliable path to development.

bettered the lives of hundreds of thousands of people. Potable water and sewer projects systems expanded into shantytowns and rural areas, making conditions there more livable, and miles of new roads enabled people to bring products to market. USAID excelled at funding the construction of thousands of infrastructure projects such as schools, healthcare facilities, hydroelectric plants, irrigation systems, markets, slaughterhouses, and bus terminals. While the Alliance for Progress did not prove to be the transformative approach to Latin American relations that President Kennedy had hoped, on a smaller and practical scale it made tangible improvements.

The National Security Doctrine, 1960–1980

The **National Security Doctrine** was both an ideology and a policy initiative that emerged in response to the Cuban-inspired armed guerrilla movements of the 1960s. Although it first took shape under the Brazilian military government, its strong anticommunist directives and methods were developed with the assistance of and in accordance with US foreign policy and quickly spread to other countries in Latin America's Southern Cone and beyond. As a philosophy, the National Security Doctrine proposed military solutions for the "defense of democracy" in the "struggle against communism."

The Workings of the Doctrine

In the post–World War II period, the United States and most Latin American nations had signed a series of treaties that paved the way for increased cooperation between the militaries of the United States and Latin America. The most important of these was the 1947 Inter-American Treaty for Reciprocal Assistance (known as the **Rio Treaty**). The Rio Treaty provided not only for US military intervention in Latin America, but also for reciprocal aid in the case of "any armed military attacks on any Latin American State" and in prevention of "threats of aggression against any of them." In the context of the Cold War, the signatories on all sides understood that these treaties were pacts against "communist aggression" above all else.

Among the most important results of these agreements was the growth in US support for Latin American militaries in the 1960s, combined with a dramatic increase in the political authority of those militaries. Latin American militaries began to redefine themselves no longer as mere "defenders" of the national interest, but as *definers* of what that interest might be, all within the context of the Cold War.

The National Security Doctrine called for the development of new definitions and methods appropriate to the perceived global emergency of communism and guerrilla war. The doctrine posited that this global threat could only be met by extraordinary responses. These might include irregular warfare, harsh counterinsurgency, the suspension of civil and constitutional rights and free elections, surveillance, the definition of a nation's citizens as "internal enemies of the state," extrajudicial killings, and military control of government with suspension of elections. The defining precept of the National Security Doctrine was that communism represented the quintessential threat to national survival, and must be eradicated to save the nation. The corollary was that National Security Doctrine defined nearly all threats to existing hierarchies as "communist" or "socialist" and therefore subject to elimination as the price of freedom.

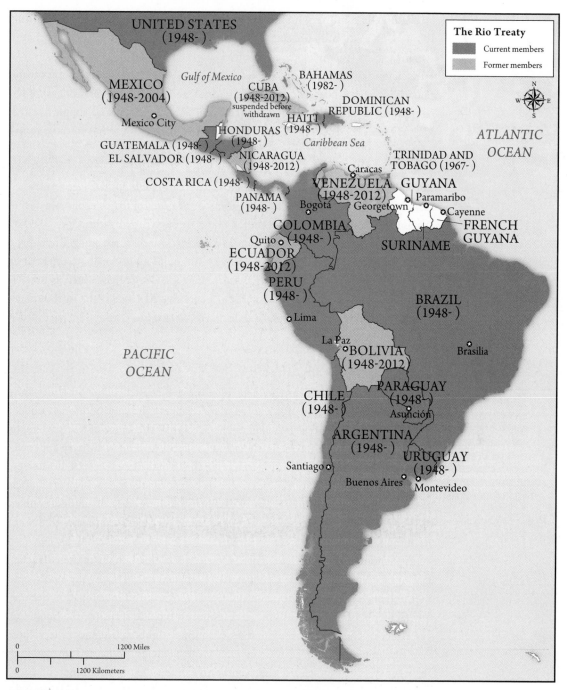

UNITED STATES
(1948-)

Gulf of Mexico

MEXICO
(1948-2004)

Mexico City

BAHAMAS
(1982-)

CUBA
(1948-2012)
suspended before
withdrawn

DOMINICAN
REPUBLIC (1948-)

HAITI
(1948-)

HONDURAS
(1948-)

Caribbean Sea

ATLANTIC
OCEAN

GUATEMALA (1948-)
EL SALVADOR (1948-)

NICARAGUA
(1948-2012)

TRINIDAD AND
TOBAGO (1967-)

COSTA RICA (1948-)

PANAMA
(1948-)

Caracas

Bogotá

VENEZUELA
(1948-2012)

GUYANA

Georgetown

Paramaribo

Cayenne

FRENCH
GUYANA

COLOMBIA
(1948-)

SURINAME

Quito

ECUADOR
(1948-2012)

PERU
(1948-)

Lima

BRAZIL
(1948-)

La Paz

BOLIVIA
(1948-2012)

Brasilia

PACIFIC
OCEAN

CHILE
(1948-)

PARAGUAY
(1948-)

Asunción

ARGENTINA
(1948-)

Santiago

URUGUAY
(1948-)

Buenos Aires

Montevideo

The Rio Treaty

Current members

Former members

0   1200 Miles
0   1200 Kilometers

≡ **MAP. 11.1**

The Brazilian military implemented the National Security Doctrine following the nation's 1964 military coup. This marked a change in military rule in Latin America, away from personalist rule by a single commanding officer and towards bureaucratic rule by a cohort of deliberately bland but often deadly military technocrats. Over the next five years, one Latin American government after another adopted the National Security Doctrine, with the approval and support of the United States. By the mid-1970s, more than two-thirds of Latin American countries were under military rule.

The National Security Doctrine made Latin American militaries responsible not only for security but also for national development. Military governments across the region undertook a wide variety of projects to foster economic development. With support from the United States through organizations like USAID, military governments in places such as Central America, introduced new programs to improve agricultural productivity and build up national infrastructure. In South America, military governments undertook vast projects, such as Brazil's Trans-Amazonian Highway and Chile's "Economic Miracle"—the introduction of neoliberal ultra-free-market capitalism. All were understood to be part of the anticommunist struggle.

The School of the Americas

The National Security Doctrine depended on well-trained Latin American militaries, and the United States wanted assurance that those armed forces understood the doctrine's objectives and methods. One of the terms of the Rio Treaty was a provision that allowed for thousands of Latin American military and technical personnel to attend training courses in the United States or in US territories. Beginning in 1946, Latin American officers began to take courses at Fort Gulick in the Panama Canal Zone. By the 1970s, the US military described these courses as the School of the Americas. In 1984, the School of the Americas moved to Fort Benning, Georgia.

The School of the Americas offered a variety of courses, many of them concentrating on counterinsurgency campaigns, or "special war." During the 1960s, new methods such as surveillance, nontraditional warfare, and interrogation became key elements of the curriculum. In response to outside scrutiny, the School of the Americas added required courses on human rights and democratic values. The fundamental focus of the curriculum nevertheless remained on counterinsurgency training against the communist threat. Many thousands of Latin American officers passed through the School of the Americas' training programs, some completing multiyear certificates and others participating only in short-term courses for a month or two. Virtually every noteworthy National Security Doctrine–era military officer in Latin America participated in the School of the Americas, including some of the most egregious human rights violators. (In 2001, the School of the Americas—which became the object of considerable controversy and protest when it moved to Fort Benning—changed its name to the Western Hemisphere Institute for Security Cooperation. The new name reflects the new global concerns with drug trafficking and global terrorism, rather than the previous focus on anticommunism.)

A National Security State: Guatemala in the 1960s

The overthrow of Jacobo Arbenz in 1954 and the end of Guatemala's "Ten Years of Spring," marked the beginning of decades of violence, starting with the government's purge of leftists and downward spiral of suspended civil rights, assassination, and terror. Although the military had not defended Arbenz against the coup, he had supporters within the ranks. Those individuals, along with students and labor and peasant leaders who had supported his reform movement and the democratic process, began to organize themselves clandestinely in opposition after his overthrow. Their initial impulse had been to restore reformist government, but once the Castro revolution succeeded, these dissidents turned to Cuba as their model for revolution.

General Miguel Ydígoras Fuentes had usurped power in 1958 after the assassination of the incumbent, Colonel Carlos Castillo Armas. On November 13, 1960, a group of left-wing junior military officers at the national military academy led a revolt against the Ydígoras Fuentes government. The army put down the uprising decisively, and the coup plotters fled to rural eastern Guatemala, a region known as *el oriente*. There, they and their supporters established an armed guerrilla movement called the MR-13 (Movimiento Revolucionario 13 de Noviembre) taking their name from the date of the initial uprising.

The MR-13 soon joined forces with several other opposition groups. These included the Guatemalan Workers' Party (PGT, by its Spanish acronym), a radical student organization, and another small affiliated armed group. These merged together under a single umbrella organization, the Frente Armado Revolucionario (FAR), in 1962. The FAR and its constituent groups conducted insurgent activities against the government in the oriente and in the capital, Guatemala City.

If Cuba's abrupt turn to Marxist-Leninism had caught the world by surprise, the emergence of a communist rebel movement in Guatemala seemed imminently predictable. Both the Guatemalan and US governments feared that Guatemala might well be the next "domino" to fall to communism. (The untested domino theory assumed that once one nation turned to communism, it would influence its neighbor to follow suit, just like dominoes lined up next to one another.) The Ydígoras government took draconian action. Shortly after the FAR inaugurated its first hostile actions, the president ordered troops to the oriente. He suspended the constitution and imposed an emergency remission of basic civil liberties. Hardline military officers considered these gestures insufficient, and in 1963 they replaced Ydígoras in a military coup. They introduced a National Security Doctrine military government that would rule Guatemala almost without interruption until 1986.

The FAR did not limit its activities to the oriente. It also engaged in urban actions, including bombings, bank robberies, and kidnappings. The FAR was also responsible for the 1968 assassination of US Ambassador John Gordon Mein in Guatemala City. In return, the United States sent technical aid and personnel to Guatemala to assist in surveillance and modern military counterinsurgency, including new weaponry and military hardware. With US assistance, Guatemala established a comprehensive network of internal intelligence, including the National Police and their greatly feared urban hit squad, *Comando Seis* (Command Six).

In November 1965, with the help of US advisors, the Guatemalan army launched **Operación Limpieza** (Operation Cleanup), an urban counterinsurgency program in Guatemala City. This coordinated the activities of all of the country's main security agencies (including the army, the judicial police, and the national police) in both covert and overt antiguerrilla operations. Those targeted in the counterinsurgency operations were labeled as subversives, and subject to forced disappearance, torture, and death. In the second half of the 1960s a new extralegal form of counterinsurgency emerged in Guatemala, a model that would soon be replicated in many other parts of Latin America, including Argentina and, most notoriously, in neighboring El Salvador. "Secret groups" of "concerned citizens"—often guided and supplemented by members of the security forces—took the law into their own hands, forming paramilitary groups that threatened, kidnapped, and killed supposed subversives, leaving their bodies in public places as a warning to the general public. Guatemala originated these infamous "death squads," a noxious phenomenon that spread through much of Latin America during the 1970s. These groups, whose members were presumably known to both the Guatemalan government and the US Embassy, operated with impunity. One well-known Guatemalan death squad, known as the "White Hand," made its mark on or near its victims with an eponymous handprint, leaving notes and identifying fingerprints without fear of arrest or prosecution. Counterinsurgency thus turned to terror as a means of keeping a fearful population in line.

In 1967, the Guatemalan military, given carte blanche to defeat the guerrillas "by any means necessary," launched a devastatingly effective counterinsurgency campaign in the oriente, which by March 1968 nearly wiped out the guerrillas. The counterinsurgency campaign also killed 3,000–5,000 campesino noncombatants. In all, the defeat of the FAR cost some 15,000 Guatemalan lives—including rebels, soldiers, and many ordinary people, between 1966 and 1968. So brutal was the campaign that it earned its leader Colonel Carlos Arana Osorio the nickname, "The Butcher of Zacapa" (Zacapa is a province in the oriente), and won him enough credibility with the Guatemalan military that they selected him to serve as Guatemala's president from 1970 to 1974.

Like other National Security Doctrine states, however, the Guatemalan military government of the 1960s also attempted to foster economic development. Ideally, such development would bring enough material improvement to ordinary people's lives that they would not be lured into support for communism. In tandem with USAID, the government helped implement new agricultural technologies, such as the use of fertilizers and the introduction of new commodity crops to supplement income for producers of Guatemala's basic food, maize, and to enhance productivity on the small-scale farms around the country. With help from the Catholic Church, the government also opened new lands for settlement and agricultural cooperatives in a remote section of the country close to the border with Mexico.

All of these efforts had the desired effect in the short run. Agricultural productivity of Maya and ladino farmers increased, as did the nation's population rate; this was Guatemala's "Green Revolution." At the same time, the introduction of other types of technology—paved roads deep in the countryside, trucks and buses that connected villages to the cities and to jobs on coastal plantations, transistor radios that brought news and the Spanish language to Maya communities, and, for many, increased contact with capitalist consumer culture—brought new opportunities and expectations. What did not change were Guatemala's deep social inequities, its authoritarian and antidemocratic government, and institutionalized violence.

SOCIAL UPHEAVAL

Death Comes to a Beauty Queen: Rogelia Cruz Martínez

Rogelia Cruz Martínez was a young woman whose trajectory from beauty queen to student activist to guerrilla cadre to her death at the hands of Guatemala's security forces took less than a decade. Cruz, the product of a respectable, middle-class urban ladina upbringing, was crowned Miss Guatemala in 1959. She participated in the Miss Universe pageant in Long Beach, California, that same year, and although she did not win the pageant, she won fame and admiration in Guatemala—a country that takes its beauty pageants very seriously.

After her "reign," Rogelia Cruz enrolled in San Carlos University (USAC), Guatemala's oldest public university, where she took classes in architecture. Here, she became exposed for the first time to student politics. Student activism is, generally speaking, much more engaged in Latin America than in the United States, especially at the public universities, where students use their college years to cultivate political positions and alliances. During the volatile mid-1960s, when Cruz attended USAC, Guatemala experienced an armed revolutionary movement, the suspension of the constitution, and the iron fist of military government—including the disappearances and deaths of what would eventually be hundreds of university students. This environment galvanized her activism. She joined several revolutionary cells, including a group called the Patriotic Youth Workers' party, covertly allied to the Guatemalan Workers' Party and later the FAR. Through these contacts, Cruz became convinced that only revolution would transform Guatemala. Cruz began handing out revolutionary pamphlets, then turned to more ambitious actions, including assisting with the transportation of weapons and of people from one covert location to another. In 1965, she was arrested and held briefly for possession of arms. In this way, Cruz became identified as a "subversive."

≡ **Rogelia Cruz Martínez.**

In November 1967, Rogelia Cruz was initially arrested for a traffic violation, then quickly released. Shortly thereafter, however, members of the National Police, acting through a death squad, seized Rogelia Cruz. She "disappeared" on January 11, 1968. Her body, showing signs of horrific sexual assault, mutilation, and torture, turned up in Guatemala City the next day. She was twenty-five years old.

With her death, the security forces sought to drive home the point that no one who "betrayed the nation," not even a beloved beauty queen, was immune from the iron fist of the National Security state; the wheels of state-sponsored terror turned for all. Rogelia Cruz became an icon of the revolution on Guatemala's left, one of the most public "martyrs" of the first-wave guerrilla movement. Like so many "disappeared" people who came after her, she left behind none of her own words or records with which to speak for herself.

- How does the story of Rogelia Cruz Martínez embody the complexities of the conflicts of the region in the 1960s? How does her story complicate your understandings of the Cold War?

The Brazilian Military Dictatorship, 1964–1974

As Brazil's political landscape became increasingly turbulent early in 1964, President João Goulart attempted to rally popular support by swinging to the left. In early March of that year, he claimed powers to expropriate private land, seize critical industrial works, and implement "base reforms" that would raise taxes on the wealthy and redistribute wealth. Middle-class residents of Rio de Janeiro, São Paulo, and other major cities responded with massive rallies calling for Goulart's ouster. Senior officers, acting with the approval of the US Embassy, prepared to seize power. Goulart desperately tried to encourage enlisted soldiers to resist any potential coup.

The Lead-Up to the Coup

Both sides seemed to agree that some kind of military action was almost inevitable. Both had numerous examples from recent history to draw on, as the armed forces had intervened in political crisis in the Revolution of 1930, in the 1937 creation of the Estado Novo, in the initial removal of Vargas in 1945, and in the struggle over his succession in 1955. High-ranking officers had grown accustomed to seeing themselves as the referees of Brazil's political process, intervening to stop the mayhem, then temporarily withdrawing from the action once civil violence had abated.

This time would be different, however—more so than anyone could have imagined in March of 1964. Once the military stepped into power, a combination of anticommunist paranoia, guerrilla violence, overconfidence in military administration, and sheer hunger for power conspired to keep it there. The armed forces seized power on March 31, 1964. They would not leave until the 1980s, departing in a series of slow and reluctant steps. In the meantime, Brazil was transformed in enduring ways.

Dictatorship in the Name of Democracy

Goulart, his more radical brother-in-law Leonel Brizola, and a diverse array of left-wing radicals and reformers were dismayed by the ease with which the military seized power. Goulart called for resistance from enlisted men, but it did not materialize. Many civilians supported the coup, and few of those who opposed it were foolhardy enough to challenge the soldiers rolling their tanks through the streets of Brazil's major cities. Goulart, Brizola, and dozens of left-wing activists and politicians fled Brazil. Over the next several years, they would be followed by thousands more: in many cases voluntarily, in others an exile imposed by the military regime. The long odyssey of the exiles deeply marked Brazil. Many returned only after the regime finally declared political amnesty, in 1979.

The United States immediately recognized Brazil's military government and moved to provide strategic assistance to the generals. The military junta that seized power in 1964 initially planned to purge radicals, protect private property, oversee democratic elections in the near future and step down. But some officers decided a return to civilian rule was less desirable than initially anticipated, a decision made easier with the financial backing of the US government.

The junta conducted a cautious experiment in electoral politics by permitting gubernatorial elections in 1965, from a tightly circumscribed list of candidates. The results of even these dubious elections demonstrated that the regime's preferred candidates were not likely to win open elections. The officers responded by outlawing all existing political parties, and channeling legal political activity into two new parties, the centrist Movimiento Democrático Brasiliero (Brazilian Democratic Movement, or MDB) and the conservative *Aliança para a Renovação Nacional* (Alliance for National Renovation, or ARENA). Observers joked that these were "the party of yes, and the party of yes, sir!" Military governance began to take on a life of its own.

Soft and Hard Dictatorship

The military regime did not shut down congress but hollowed it out, governing instead through a series of seventeen Institutional Acts, which overrode the Constitution and were deemed beyond appeal. The first and second Institutional Acts, decreed shortly after the coup, legitimized military rule and gave the military control over presidential elections. The third, decreed in 1966, did the same for gubernatorial elections. General Humberto de Alencar Castelo Branco, who served as the military-imposed president of Brazil from April of 1964 through 1967, governed within these Institutional Acts. Under Castelo Branco, the regime largely refrained from political censorship of the press, allowed student and labor political organizations to continue their activities, and put those accused of crimes on trial in civilian courts.

Throughout these early years, however, a hardline contingent within the regime agitated for more aggressive cleansing of the political arena. When the regime outlawed existing political parties, Brazil's remaining left-wing radicals went underground and formed revolutionary factions, several of them with direct links to the Cuba. By the late 1960s, these underground factions were engaged in guerrilla activity like bank robberies and kidnappings. This activity caused hardline officers to demand greater leeway to pursue alleged subversives. In 1967, they forced

Castelo Branco from power and brought General Artur da Costa e Silva, a more aggressive anticommunist, to the presidency. Costa e Silva's administration soon decreed the most infamous of all the Institutional Acts: **Institutional Act Five**. This Act suspended habeas corpus, giving the regime the power to arrest and imprison civilians without warrant. The Act also gave the regime the power to shut down Congress, remove politicians from office, and intervene directly in state and municipal governments.

Under Institutional Act Five, Brazil moved definitively from what Brazilians called *ditabranda* to *ditadura*—from "soft" to "hard" dictatorship. The new style was marked by the secretive arrest and torture of political opponents, the beginning of an extensive and capricious program of press censorship, and a ratcheting up of military power and corruption. Several subsequent Latin American military dictatorships would go through a similar evolution, as the failure of initial coercive measures led to a push from within for a hardline stance. In all these cases, the intolerance of dissent and the willingness to rule by force allowed more virulent hardline repression to emerge and dominate.

At the same time, the decree of Institutional Act Five demonstrated at least a nominal adherence to the rule of law. This epitomized what scholars often describe as the "bureaucratic authoritarianism" of Latin American dictatorships. Even at its most violent, the Brazilian regime did not burnish a cult of personality, and sought to portray its rule as technocratic—merely carrying out the duties of the modern, scientific administrative state. To that end, the regime greatly expanded the number and powers of existing cabinet ministries—a strategy that tended to increase opportunities for government corruption. Even as the regime oversaw an extensive network of torture, the officers in charge continued to think of themselves as fulfilling the law.

This fiction was often hypocritical, but it did impose some restraints. The Brazilian military regime was brutal but, unlike some of military dictatorships that would emerge in Spanish America, not bloodthirsty. The best estimates suggest that the regime killed somewhere between 350 and 400 political adversaries. Many thousands more were imprisoned and tortured by the regime, including Dilma Rousseff, who decades later would serve as Brazil's elected president from 2011 to 2016. This is an abhorrent total, but one significantly lower than comparable cases. In neighboring Argentina in the 1970s, where the regime operated outside the fictive constraint of law, consequences were even more dire, and deaths numbered in the many thousands. Farther north in Central America, the number of those killed by military governments would range from the tens of thousands to hundreds of thousands.

≡ **Trans-Amazonian Highway.** The building of the Trans-Amazonian Highway in the late 1960s and early 1970s was typical of the grandiose projects of Brazil's military government, undertaken with inflated expectations of short-term economic benefit and out of largely misplaced security concerns, with little regard for environmental protection.

The Trans-Amazonian Highway: Threatening the Rainforest Environment

Like other adventurers in the Amazonian region, technocrats in the Brazilian military dictatorship looked at the vast rainforest as a blank slate awaiting their handiwork. And like other adventurers, they would discover that the forest is more easily admired than tamed. The dictatorship's plans had tremendous consequences for the forest, most of them unintended.

In 1972, the regime inaugurated a 2,500-mile highway—a rough dirt road, really—from the Atlantic coast of northeastern Brazil deep into the heart of the Amazonian rainforest. The idea was to provide a pathway for the migration of impoverished, landless northeastern farmers into the rainforest, in hopes that they would clear their own land and turn the untilled jungle into productive agricultural land. The military regime not only opened the highway, at massive cost and logistical difficulty, but also divided up much of the adjacent land in neat grids and distributed it to migrating farmers.

The road quickly proved to have devastating environmental consequences. The plots did not conform to any features of the land, the soil did not support cultivation, and the farmers of drought-stricken northeastern Brazil could not cope with the rainforest. The result was slash and burn deforestation. The **Trans-Amazonian Highway** cleared the way for the construction of illegal logging roads and other destructive extractive industries. Regime technocrats saw this as positive in the short run, believing it would lead to settlement and production. Instead, it led to destruction, desertification, and renewed migration. The enduring effects of the Trans-Amazonian Highway continue to be felt in ongoing deforestation in the region.

Argentina, Uruguay, and the Dirty Wars in the Southern Cone, 1970s–1980s

As in Brazil, the Argentine military had grown accustomed to intervening in domestic political disputes, removing civilian presidents in 1930, 1943, 1955, 1962, and 1966. An initial ouster of the civilian president was followed by two internal coups, replacing one military leader with another, each failing to impose order on fractious Argentina. The disastrous Peronist interlude of 1973–1976 only convinced anti-Peronist hardliners within the military that more drastic measures were necessary.

The Dirty War Begins

When Juan Perón died in 1974, his widow, Isabel, rose to power, but proved unable to mediate between competing Peronist factions. Political violence escalated, provoking military takeover in March of 1976. Argentina's officers had attempted relatively restrained military rule in the late 1960s with no success. This time, they turned immediately to violent repression. In contrast to Brazil, they did not bother with any pretense of rule of law, kidnapping and murdering civilians they deemed subversives with no figment of legal cover. The willful erasure of people turned "disappear" into a transitive verb, as in "the military regime pursued a strategy of actively *disappearing* thousands of civilians," and turned "disappeared" into a noun ("**desaparecido**"), as in "the memory of the *disappeared* continues to haunt Argentina."

Dirty Wars in South America

BRAZIL
350-400 political adversaries killed, 1964-1985

BOLIVIA
approximately 500 disappeared, 1971-1978

PARAGUAY
approximately 3000 political murders, 1954-1989

CHILE
over 3,500 executed or disappeared, 1973-1900

URUGUAY
approximately 200 political opponents disappeared, 1973-1976

ARGENTINA
at least 10,000 disappeared, 1976-1983

≡ **MAP. 11.2**

As a result, the Argentine military regime of 1976–1983 was arguably not "bureaucratic" in the same way as its Brazilian counterpart to the north. It may still be considered "bureaucratic-authoritarian," however, as the junta in power avoided any cult of personality and governed behind an impassive mask. General Jorge Rafael Videla, head of the junta that took power in 1976, had already earned a reputation for untrammeled political cleansing in his pursuit of left-wing guerrillas in the Argentine interior. Videla had shown a willingness to stop at nothing in his efforts to uncover and eliminate revolutionaries hiding in the mountains.

As the Argentine head of state, he brought those tactics to the nation at large, treating groups as disparate as rock musicians, moderate student leaders, psychiatrists, and advocates for women's rights as dangerous subversives. He diligently studied the tactics of repression employed elsewhere, using interrogation techniques honed by British officers in Northern Ireland, for example. He worked to secure his own regime by cultivating alliances with the Brazilian and Paraguayan regimes to the north and Chile to the west, and attempting to engineer regime change in Bolivia. The resulting collaboration, named Operation Condor, was a net of espionage and persecution cast across the southern cone of South America.

While the Brazilian regime pursued a policy of state-led industrial development and the Chilean dictatorship adopted free-market reform, Videla's regime cast about wildly for an economic path, trying unsuccessfully to eliminate industrial subsidies without laying off workers. The Argentine junta pinned both its political and economic hopes on hosting the World Cup soccer tournament in 1978. The result was the most harrowing tournament in the history of the game, and certainly one of the most dubious: The regime used open intimidation and—in all

≡ **Argentine Junta.** The military junta that overthrew Isabel Perón and seized power in 1976 embodied the term "bureaucratic authoritarianism." Whereas dictators of an earlier era became the objects of cults of personality, the bureaucratic authoritarians cultivated the lack of personality. They hid behind thick glasses, avoided looking at the camera, and read directly from the script to suggest they were just going about the difficult business of beating back communist insurgency. Meanwhile, they carried out a brutal campaign of virulent and often indiscriminate repression.

likelihood—covert operations to guarantee the results. Argentina's hollow victory brought temporary propaganda benefits at home but failed to deliver any lasting economic benefit.

Victims and Survivors

As Argentina's World Cup champion team hoisted its trophy on the field, torture and disappearance continued to escalate. The army, navy, and air force each maintained secret networks of facilities for interrogation and extermination. Many of the victims were buried in unmarked mass graves. Others were given heavy sedatives, then loaded into cargo planes, flown over the Atlantic and dumped into the ocean. Reliable figures on casualties are impossible to ascertain, but 10,000 is a conservative estimate for the number of Argentines murdered by the regime.

Many of the victims were women, some pregnant. The military detained pregnant women secretly until they gave birth, and then disappeared them, their babies adopted by members of the Armed Forces or their allies. The fate of these children, some of whom would be raised, unbeknownst to the orphans, in the families of the military officers who had murdered their own parents, became one of the most haunting legacies of the dictatorship. It also proved to be one of the causes of that regime's downfall. While the military hunted down and persecuted into submission radical activists, political leaders, and any youth suspected of countercultural opinions, a group of humble grandmothers gathered in the Plaza de Mayo, a public space outside the presidential palace, to press the regime for answers. They carried photographs of their disappeared children and grandchildren, and became known as the *Abuelas*, or **Grandmothers, of the Plaza de Mayo**. The regime initially dismissed them as crazy, and dispersed them with force, but they kept coming back. Their patient, dignified insistence laid the groundwork for the construction of a network of survivors, and the gradual compilation of irrefutable evidence of torture and disappearance.

The Grandmothers called on the Catholic Church for support, with inconsistent response. The Argentine Council of Bishops had supported the junta from its inception, and only gradually and hesitantly began to acknowledge its abuses. A strong right wing within the clergy did not balk even as the evidence mounted. At the same time, liberation theologians were among the regime's first victims, and many priests acted to protect the persecuted at great peril to their own lives. One figure caught in the maelstrom was Father Jorge Mario Bergoglio, Provincial Superior of the Society of Jesus in Argentina. Bergoglio helped save several potential victims from the regime, working for their safe passage out of Argentina. Following the end of the regime, however, some accused Bergoglio of not having

☰ **Abuelas Protesting in the Plaza de Mayo.** The famous Mothers and Grandmothers of the Plaza de Mayo honed one of the most effective tactics of resisting bureaucratic authoritarian regimes. They marched in front of the presidential palace with photos of their disappeared loved ones, demanding answers. Their humble, insistent protest made clear to all Argentines, and then to the world, that the victims of the regime were not dangerous radicals but everyday families. Even after the regime fell, they continued to march, demanding a full accounting of the tragedy of the disappeared—one that ultimately took decades to achieve

done enough, particularly in the case of two Jesuits who were arrested and tortured soon after the coup. These conflicting accounts exemplify the murky history of disappearance and resistance more generally. Bergoglio, for his part, made no secret of the way in which the period scarred him and shaped the humility with which he approached his elevation years later as Pope Francis (see Chapter 12).

As has so often been the case in South American history, events in Uruguay closely paralleled those in Argentina. Uruguayan implementation of an aggressive strategy of arrest and torture of political prisoners by a military regime preceded that of Argentina. Juan María Bordaberry, president of Uruguay from 1973 to 1976, was ostensibly a civilian leader, but one imposed and closely supervised by a military junta. Under Bordaberry, the Uruguayan Armed Forces carried out a brutal dirty war against Tupamaro guerrillas and anyone suspected of sympathizing with them, engaging in widespread censorship, torture, and the elimination of all political opposition. In the mid-1970s, Uruguay had more political prisoners than any nation in the world, so much so that one study later found that every family in the country had a relative who had been imprisoned, tortured, or "disappeared." The legacy of torture and survival, as a result, has marked Uruguay as deeply as it has Argentina.

Augusto Pinochet and the Dirty War in Chile, 1973–1990

Chile presented a different variation on the bureaucratic authoritarianism of the period. It was marked by the same rhetoric of technocracy as the Brazilian case, but in Chile, the regime turned to free-market economics rather than state-led developmentalism as their recipe for national economic growth. (As in Brazil, short-term gains were impressive, while longer term growth was more uneven.) In contrast to both the Brazilian and Argentine cases, however, Chile's regime did produce a cult of personality, one celebrating General Augusto Pinochet.

Pinochet Suppresses the Left and Imposes Order

As the ranking member of the most powerful branch of the armed forces, General Augusto Pinochet consolidated power in the months following the September 11, 1973, coup against President Allende. Pinochet's regime had two purposes: to excise what he and his allies viewed as the "cancer" of Marxism, and to revive the Chilean economy.

Although some members of the original junta wanted a quick return to democracy, Pinochet and others believed that only a lengthy dictatorship would undo the effects of the Allende administration. Pinochet took steps to become the sole leader of the junta, first naming himself the supreme chief of the nation, then promulgating a constitution in 1980 and having himself elected president by a yes-no plebiscite. A "Yes" vote meant Pinochet would continue in office; a "No" vote would have ended his regime. With Pinochet in control, "No" was an impossibility.

As his first priority, Pinochet promised a war without mercy against the forces on the extreme left. The military rounded up and detained roughly 35,000 suspected leftists (including 25 US citizens), herding them into the National Stadium and into prisons. Teams of police interrogated the suspects and in many instances tortured them in order to learn the names of any of the suspect's associates. During the first three months of the dictatorship, DINA (the Directory for National Intelligence–essentially the secret police) jailed many people, exiled others, and executed approximately 1,260 individuals.

Among those captured and killed in those early days was Víctor Jara, a well-known singer-songwriter, poet, actor, and political activist. Shortly after the coup, Jara was arrested, detained, and shot; his body was dumped in a shantytown outside of Santiago. His murder, in the word of one historian, transformed Jara into a "potent symbol of struggle for human rights and justice" for those killed during the Pinochet regime. The murders in the National Stadium included at least one US citizen, the journalist Charles Horman. The story of this journalist and documentary filmmaker and his death became the subject of the director Costa-Gavras's 1982 Cannes Film Festival Prize–winning *Missing*. Many others were disappeared. The reign of terror created a climate of fear. In Santiago, witnesses reporting seeing bloated corpses floating down the Mapocho River, a scene replicated elsewhere. Many of the disappeared were buried in unmarked graves.

DINA undertook a sweep of Marxists around the country in what came to be called "the Caravan of Death," searching for and then executing leftists. The military was particularly aggressive in its pursuit of the MIR, executing almost all of the organization's leadership as well as about 235 followers by 1977. A second wave of murders thereafter was more methodical, as the regime sought to extirpate all Chilean Marxists, whether inside or outside the country. The regime's death toll would ultimately rise to the tens of thousands, as discussed in chapter 12.

Human rights advocates from around the world began to scrutinize DINA's activities. But few among the broader US public paid attention to Chile until the September 21, 1976, assassination of Orlando Letelier, Allende's former ambassador to the United States. Letelier had been imprisoned and tortured immediately after the coup, then released into exile in the United States in 1974. Two years later, he was living in Washington, DC, working at a foreign policy think-tank. One September morning, a member of DINA's paid assassins attached a bomb to the undercarriage of Letelier's car. Letelier and two young American policy consultants were in the car when the bomb exploded as they drove down a Washington, DC street. The explosion severed Letelier's legs just above the kneecap, and he bled to death within minutes. One of his young American co-workers died, as well. An FBI investigation quickly pointed the finger at Pinochet's hitman, who had already killed other opponents of the regime. The incident showed that Pinochet was willing to bring his campaign of violence into the heart of the US capital in order to eliminate his enemies. The scandal forced Pinochet to close down DINA, but soon another secret police force bearing a different acronym harassed communists and other leftists throughout the remainder of Pinochet's reign. All totaled, estimates suggested that the military tortured about 28,000 civilians, executed around 2,279, and disappeared another 1,298. As many as 200,000 Chileans may have fled their country for exile before Pinochet was forced from power in 1988.

≡ **Orlando Letelier's Bombed Car.** The murder of Orlando Letelier in Washington, DC, in September 1976 demonstrated that the Pinochet regime would not hesitate to carry out bombings on US soil to destroy its enemies. Letelier was a former Chilean ambassador to the United States, and a victim of the Pinochet regime. As a refugee in the United States, he became an influential opponent of the dictatorship. Chilean secret service agents, operating on direct orders from Pinochet, used a car bomb to kill Letelier, along with the young US policy consultant who happened to be in the passenger seat. Letelier himself had been a political moderate. His murder made clear to many US citizens that the Pinochet regime was not a stable US ally defending the continent against communism, but a dangerous tyrannical dictatorship.

Pinochet, Neoliberalism, and the "Chilean Miracle"

The US government was aware of the Chilean regime's human-rights abuses, including the assassination of Letelier within blocks of the White House. But the United States continued to support General Pinochet for two reasons: its continued fear of radical revolution in Latin America and its enthusiasm for Chile's free-market economic reforms. Pinochet and company rapidly opened the Chilean economy from a state-controlled system characterized by socialist reform to one that was market-oriented and globally integrated. The generals believed that by adopting neoliberal policies they would be able to reduce inflation and eliminate the black market and food shortages prevalent during Allende's final year. They paid down the foreign debt and eliminated price controls on food and other essentials, but these measures alone failed to improve the economy. In 1975, Pinochet appointed civilian technocrats like Finance Minister Sergio de Castro to his cabinet to extricate the country from the economic chaos. As students of Milton Friedman, the innovative but controversial Nobel Prize–winning University of Chicago economist, de Castro and the other "Chicago Boys" recommended adopting strict neoliberal principles. This strategy of removing government subsidies and price controls became known as "economic shock therapy." The idea behind it was that eliminating government interference would allow the free market to restore prosperity.

Neoliberalism shrank the government's role in the economy by adopting four specific measures. First, the government sold off many state-owned businesses to private investors (the government held onto the lucrative copper mines). Privatization allowed the government to reduce its payroll dramatically, as roughly seventy thousand state employees were fired during the first eighteen months of the initiative. As the government reduced its expenses, unemployment surged. The government undid Allende's land expropriation and returned property to private hands. The government broke up agricultural collectives and distributed the land to its former members as individual plots. These small plots often proved unviable, leaving their new owners no choice but to sell them to larger landowners.

Second, the government repealed banking regulations. Deregulation permitted the banks, now returned to the private sector, to set their own interest rates, encouraging foreign investment. Absent regulation, three large conglomerates soon dominated the banking industry. These unregulated, large conglomerates eventually proved vulnerable to overextension and collapse.

Third, the government embarked on a program of austerity, reducing public spending on social programs such as the subsidies for transportation and housing that the Allende government had provided to the poor. According to the Chicago Boys, these subsidies not only burdened the treasury but also distorted the marketplace. Overall, the government reduced its expenditures by about 50 percent. Although these measures to balance the budget contributed to Chile's 8-percent annual growth rate and a decline in inflation from 370 percent a year to a manageable 9 percent, they took the greatest toll on those who could least afford it.

Fourth, Chile reduced its tariffs from 94 percent to 10 percent. This facilitated import of foreign manufactured goods, allowing for greater competition in the marketplace. The Chicago Boys argued that ISI had outlived its usefulness. Relatively free trade made Chilean exports more competitive, allowing Chile to capitalize on its comparative advantage in copper, fruits, seafood, and forest products. Heavily subsidized domestic industries, like textiles, in contrast, could not compete in the new environment. Chile's neoliberalism benefited investors and consumers (especially the elite and the middle class) but disadvantaged the country's poorest folk and organized labor.

The economy continued to grow until the recession of 1982. Pinochet took advantage of the **Chilean miracle** to write a labor code that debilitated the union movement by limiting collective bargaining and the right to strike. He also reformed the pension system (Social Security) by allowing individuals to manage their own accounts. Over the long run, this would theoretically produce significantly more income for social security recipients but also exposed these small investors to much greater risk. Many nations, including Mexico and Peru in Latin America, attempted to copy this Chilean model, often with disastrous results.

Economic Collapse, the Recovery, and the Path toward Democracy

Like many other Latin American nations, Chile experienced an economic collapse in 1982, caused in the Chilean case by declining copper prices and rising petroleum costs. At the same time, some of the flaws of extreme neoliberalism became apparent. Unregulated banking did not always lead to competition and efficiency, as neoliberal theory suggested. In many cases it led to consolidation and corruption, as the large conglomerates that controlled the private banks lent money to speculative enterprises in which they owned an interest. As a result, GNP fell in 1982 and unemployment reached 30 percent. Wages fell further.

Pinochet fired de Castro the following year and placed Chile on a more pragmatic and moderate neoliberal path with the approval of the International Monetary Fund, the lender of last resort. The government continued to privatize state-owned businesses but bailed out the banks and implemented some regulations to prevent the speculative excesses of the conglomerates. The Chilean economy grew again after 1986 at a rate of 7.7 percent. The return to prosperity weakened the political opposition and reduced pressure on Pinochet to step down.

Chileans continue to debate the merits of Pinochet's economic policies. For conservatives, Pinochet's economics saved Chile from Allende's disasters and laid the groundwork for contemporary Chile's impressive economic growth rate—one of the highest in the hemisphere. Those on the political left emphasize that the modest growth of the Pinochet years primarily favored the wealthy and middle classes. More importantly, they observe that Pinochet achieved neoliberal reform at catastrophic cost: seventeen years of dictatorship, marked by persecution, torture, assassination and a pervasive climate of fear. Was modest growth worth the price?

Human-rights observers and victims of the regime continued to expose Pinochet's abuses. Pressure gradually mounted on Pinochet to cede power. The

Constitution of 1980 granted him an eight-year term of office, and the dictator had agreed to hold a "Yes-No" plebiscite in 1988 to choose whether he should continue in office until 1996. Under President Jimmy Carter (1977–1981), the US had supported democratization in Latin America, including Chile. Pinochet had largely ignored Carter's protestations. The inauguration of Ronald Reagan in 1981 temporarily eased pressure on Pinochet. But by the second half of the 1980s, even the Reagan administration began to counsel Pinochet to make the transition to democracy, as Brazil and Argentina had recently done. Meanwhile, Chile's Christian Democrats, moderate Socialists, and Communists debated their options. While the Christian Democrats and Socialists agreed to participate in the planned referendum, a number of the Communists believed that assassinating Pinochet was the only solution. In September 1986, a group of communists ambushed Pinochet's motorcade as he returned to Santiago from his vacation home in the mountains. His driver skillfully escaped the ambush, although several members of Pinochet's escort were killed. Pinochet responded with another wave of violent repression, strengthening the Christian Democrat and Socialists' resolve to organize a peaceful, electoral campaign to vote "No" against Pinochet's continuance in office.

Women's Participation in the Pinochet Regime

Both right-wing and leftist women's groups played important roles during the Pinochet regime. Pinochet counted women among his most ardent political supporters. Women from all socioeconomic groups had participated in the March of the Empty Pots as well as the massive demonstration of September 5, 1973, that had contributed to the collapse of Allende's presidency. Pinochet's government rallied female support by evoking traditional themes of feminine purity, modesty, and domesticity. The regime promoted the ideal of the traditional woman who loved family and nation above all else.

After the coup of 1973, Pinochet and his wife, Lucia Hiriart de Pinochet, persuaded women, particularly officers' wives, to serve as unpaid volunteers, enabling the regime to cut massive numbers of paid social workers and family counselors from the government's payroll. While this service arguably helped to ameliorate social problems, it did so by perpetuating stereotypes of women as selfless nurturers who needed nothing themselves while diminishing the ranks of organized labor.

Women's political activities during the Pinochet era were sharply curtailed. Even the women's organization that had helped to oust Allende, Feminine Power (PF), was disbanded after the coup. Politics opened up to all Chileans, however, when the economy soured in 1982. Women who had supported Allende formed the Women for Life (MPLV) to protest the disappearance of their loved ones, the general atmosphere of terror, and the collapsing economy. The PF reappeared as a pro-Pinochet group especially after the economy rebounded and the date of the 1988 plebiscite approached. Both of these groups gained great influence because of their gendered approach to politics. Both organizations prided themselves on being less partisan and vitriolic than the male-dominated parties and as a result enjoyed success. For example, in 1983 the MPLV assembled ten thousand people in Santiago to protest the dictator's human rights abuses. Meanwhile, much to her surprise, Pinochet's wife had little luck organizing a "Yes" vote on her husband's behalf in the 1988 plebiscite. By a small margin, women voted "No" to Pinochet's continuation in office. This transition exemplified and proved pivotal in the plebiscite. The "No" vote triumph. Pressed from all sides to acknowledge the legitimacy of the results, Pinochet began making plans for gradually stepping away from power.

Mexico: From Economic Miracle to Dirty War, 1950–1964

Early observers of Mexico's post-1940 progress outdid one another praising the "Mexican miracle." Not only did the country's economic project fuel the highest growth rate in all of Latin America, but the Institutional Revolutionary Party (**PRI**) appeared to have fulfilled its promises to deliver both political stability and social justice. By the 1960s, however, some political scientists questioned whether single-party rule could be truly democratic, since the PRI had never lost the presidency or a single gubernatorial election. More recently historians have agreed that the early assessments of development and social justice also ought to be tempered.

The Institutional Revolutionary Party and Dominant Party Politics

Given the populist coalition that Lázaro Cárdenas had assembled in the 1930s, the broadly based PRI's sustained popularity over the next three decades seemed reasonable. Labor unions, campesinos, party bureaucrats, the military, and even businessmen enjoyed a home in the party. Voters showed overwhelming support for the PRI in regular elections. In 1958, for example, the party's charismatic presidential candidate, Adolfo López Mateos, swept to victory with 90 percent of the popular vote. But as more and more citizens questioned the openness of the electoral process, López Mateos proposed reforms to guarantee opposition parties that earned a certain percentage of the popular vote a few seats in the Congress. Despite the reform, PRI remained the dominant majority until the late 1980s. How was this possible?

First, the president possessed extensive powers: He initiated legislation, could remove elected officials from office, and served as the ultimate dispenser of patronage jobs. Barred by the constitution from seeking a second term, he chose his own successor by means of *"el dedazo"* (the tap on the shoulder) from among his inner circle. He exercised similar powers in the choice of governors and other high officials. Nomination by PRI was sufficient. As Mexicans joked, their political process was more efficient than that of the United States because they knew for a year in advance of the election the identity of their next president. The PRI members passed over in one round remained loyal because they hoped to secure office in the next election cycle.

As the dominant party, PRI enjoyed access to overwhelming financial resources to fund its campaigns. Not only were public employees expected to contribute to the PRI but so also were publicly owned corporations such as the giant petroleum company Pemex. Tax revenues from the national treasury also poured into the PRI's coffers. For campaign donors, contributing to opposition parties made no sense because their candidates could not win elections and return favors. While campaigning, PRI politicians not only hired bands, printed posters, and flooded the airwaves with their message but also fed people at rallies and promised new public works to benefit local communities. Opposition parties, like the fiscally conservative National Action Party (PAN), were painted as being too ideological. Because of these overwhelming advantages, PRI generally did not need to resort to fraud or repression to win elections—although it was willing to do so when necessary. As labor leader Fidel Velázquez cynically stated: "We arrived here with bullets and they are not going to remove us with votes." Until the opposition parties could move closer to the center and gain a larger share of campaign resources, they would struggle to compete with PRI.

Early Opposition to the Institutional Revolutionary Party

Statistically, Mexico's economic miracle appeared to have accomplished the twin goals of expanding economic growth while simultaneously keeping the Revolution's social promises. Between 1950 and 1968, growth was among the highest in the world (6.5 percent per year on average), spurred primarily by industrial production (chapter 8). After World War II ended and the United States, Japan, and European nations resumed exporting industrial goods, Mexico used direct state intervention to protect its domestic market. In addition to tariffs, the government issued import licenses to limit any retailer's ability to purchase foreign-made goods for resale in Mexico. Mexican products dominated the marketplace largely because of these artificial restraints.

The government simultaneously required manufacturers to lower their cost of production, which meant reducing workers' wages with the complicity of the Confederation of Mexican Workers (CTM) union bosses. In lieu of wage increases, the pragmatic Fidel Velázquez convinced workers to accept nonmonetary benefits such as pensions, housing, healthcare benefits, and greater job security. During the late 1940s, dissident unions seceded from the CTM and formed independent, more militant organizations. Led by the 75,000-member railroad workers' union, petroleum workers, and telephone workers, these organizations protested inflation, the devaluation of the peso, and corporate attempts to change work rules, all of which threatened to reduce workers' incomes. In 1948, the government intervened in union operations, capitalizing on dissension among union leaders and charges of corruption, to replace the dissidents with pro-PRI union leaders.

Diminishing union independence made labor PRI's junior partner. Most of these unions rejoined CTM, and Fidel Velázquez's leadership remained unchallenged for nearly fifty years. For the most part, labor refrained from strikes during the postwar period and remained loyal to the PRI. Railroad workers bucked the trend, striking in 1958 and 1959, winning wage increases and benefits. When they threatened to strike for a third time, however, the PRI dispatched the army to arrest union leaders, several of whom served lengthy prison sentences. Striking workers were fired, and the government forced the remaining rank-and-file back into the CTM.

Increased agricultural productivity contributed to the Mexican economic miracle and helped to resolve some of urban labor's economic concerns. As elsewhere in the region, this growing productivity stemmed in part from a "Green Revolution," in this case one funded by a collaboration between the Mexican government and the Rockefeller Foundation. Scientists encouraged farmers to use hybrid seeds, chemical fertilizers, herbicides, and pesticides to improve crop yields. The foundation encouraged Mexico to train its own agronomists, a profession that grew so popular that by 1980 over forty thousand undergraduates took degrees in the field. As the first developing nation to benefit from the Green Revolution, Mexico stood on the forefront of agricultural technology. During the 1950s and 1960s, annual agricultural yields increased 4.6 percent, outstripping the population gain. The country became virtually self-sufficient in wheat production and nearly reached that goal for maize. By 1970, however, the government admitted that the Green Revolution had only partially succeeded, as the country once again began to import 20 percent of its cereals.

The shortcomings of the Green Revolution were closely related to the growing dissent in the countryside. First, because of efficiencies of scale, the technology benefited wealthy large-scale producers much more than campesinos. Haciendas received more government loans and technical assistance, which enabled them to produce greater quantities of food. More controversially, haciendas could now produce more fresh food for export to the United States. Smallholders, whether as individuals or members of ejidos, defaulted on loans and often resisted using the new technologies. As campesinos grew poorer, they either migrated to cities or left Mexico for farm work in the United States. The PRI's State Food Agency, designed to subsidize the cost of food for urban dwellers, furthered the favoritism shown to large producers because it too depended on the efficiencies of scale. The agency used food distribution to maintain popular support for the PRI. Although Mexico had grown economically at an astounding rate, the benefits of growth had not been equitably distributed, leading to growing unrest in the 1960s and 1970s.

A few campesinos determined to resist and force the government to live up to the legacies of Emiliano Zapata and Lázaro Cárdenas. Rubén Jaramillo, for example, was a campesino and Methodist pastor who had fought briefly for Emiliano Zapata. Jaramillo began to raise questions about the PRI's broken promises to the rural poor in the 1940s. During the 1950s and 1960s, he initiated three guerrilla campaigns in the mountains of the state of Morelos and twice ran for governor on an independent leftist ticket to protest Mexico's new direction. Defeated and pardoned each time, Jaramillo and some of his followers invaded an abandoned ejido in 1962 and petitioned the government to validate their claim to it. The government had other plans for the property, however, and allocated the land to cattle ranchers, large-scale coffee and avocado producers, and influential individuals interested in creating a resort community. On May 23, 1962, the army swooped down on Jaramillo's home, captured him, his wife, and three children, and executed them all. The episode horrified Mexico's left (author Carlos Fuentes even attended Jaramillo's funeral) and demonstrated that the PRI was willing to repress even those who claimed to uphold the ideals of the Mexican Revolution. Jaramillo's fate would serve as a harbinger of things to come during Mexico's dirty war.

The Dirty War in Mexico, 1964–1974

Although less notorious than the dirty wars that took place in Central America or the Southern Cone, Mexico's PRI government also used force against regime opponents and innocent civilians during the 1960s and 1970s. As independent labor leaders, teachers, and students questioned whether PRI's leaders had betrayed the ideals of the Revolution, the government felt the necessity to respond to this new opposition by engaging in repressive tactics. When the military and police used force to curb dissent, they created the precise situation that they hoped to avoid: armed opposition to the regime.

Rural Protests

During the 1960s and 1970s a relatively small number of rural teachers and students attempted to emulate the tactics of the Cuban Revolution by creating a secure focal point in the countryside (a foco) from which they could proselytize the countryside. Although the military quickly suppressed the first such effort in the state of Chihuahua, insurrections in southern Mexico proved more durable. In the state of Guerrero, Genaro Vázquez's and Lucio Cabañas's groups robbed banks and kidnapped wealthy businessmen to finance their revolutions, but had much less luck recruiting campesinos between 1968 and 1974. Vázquez died in a fiery automobile crash in February 1972, while Cabañas was killed in battle at the end of 1974.

During these counterinsurgency campaigns, the Mexican army showed no compunction about using terror as a tactic against the civilian population. In some instances, suspects were buried alive, tossed from helicopters into the Pacific Ocean, or forced to drink gasoline and then lit on fire. Although the statistics are very unreliable, as many as 3,000 people disappeared in Mexico during the 1960s and early 1970s, and another 7,000 may have been kidnapped and tortured. Because of the US concern about Marxists in Latin America, the Mexican government could freely purchase armored vehicles and advanced military equipment from Washington. Many in Mexican society tacitly approved of this repression. Would popular sentiment be as forgiving if the government turned its guns against students from the elite and middle classes?

The Tlatelolco Massacre

The most visible example of Mexico's dirty war occurred when the Mexican army and police opened fire on student demonstrators in Tlatelolco Plaza in Mexico City on October 2, 1968, and revealed the full repressive power of the PRI. The episode began innocuously enough as a scuffle between two groups of students from rival high schools in late July 1968. Like some industrial labor leaders and rural protesters, students had expressed growing dissatisfaction with the PRI since the 1950s. The students demanded greater participation in the governance of the Instituto Politécnico Nacional (IPN), the largest vocational training institution in the country, which enrolled many students from poorer families, and more government financial support for scholarships and facilities, including new dormitories. What dismayed the authorities was the level of violence, which exceeded the usual rambunctious behavior that accompanied student protests.

The government significantly overreacted to a second day of student brawls. Instead of sending in a few policemen, the minister of the interior opted to call out the *granaderos*, the riot police, who beat up and jailed a number of the demonstrators. Because of the granaderos' excessive violence, other students, particularly those from the National Autonomous University of Mexico, joined the marches. In August and September, both male and female students held massive demonstrations with between 150,000 and 200,000 participants, joined by faculty, intellectuals, and UNAM's rector, Javier Barrios Sierra.

With the Olympics less than a month away, President Gustavo Díaz Ordaz (1964–1970) determined to end the disturbances through violent repression. One of the student marches had planted the red and black Communist flag in the Zócalo (Mexico City's central plaza), an act that offended many Mexicans. Díaz Ordaz and many government officials mistakenly believed that an international

☰ **Soldiers Forcibly Cut a Student's Hair after Tlatelolco Massacre.** Mexican soldiers forcibly cut a student's hair in the wake of the Tlatelolco Massacre. On October 3, 1968, Mexican police opened fire on a crowd of demonstrators in Tlatelolco Plaza, killing hundreds. The gruesome incident revealed profound schisms in Mexican society; between rebellious youth and more conservative older generations; between those who continued to believe that the ruling Institutional Revolutionary Party was a guarantor of social peace and those who regarded it as cloaked authoritarianism; between middle-class students and working-class soldiers. Security forces attempted to restore order through symbolic acts, like cutting of the long locks of detained students. But the genie of popular protest could not easily be put back into the bottle.

CULTURE AND IDEAS

Popular Music, Mexican Youth, and the Counterculture Movement

During the 1960s and early 1970s, popular music served as a vehicle of protest worldwide, whether against a government's repressive tactics or as a broader protest against society's traditional values. Mexico's popular culture scene certainly fit this pattern. Initially known as "the Wave," the counterculture movement began in the mid-1960s with middle-class teens and young adults emulating the appearance of the Beatles and the Rolling Stones. Men grew their hair long and shaggy; women abandoned the gloves and hairsprayed bouffants their mothers wore and proclaimed their liberation with short skirts and long, straight hair. Both genders adopted the omnipresent blue jeans and wore sandals to identify with the indigenous poor (as well as with North American backpackers). Defenders of traditional family values objected that one could differentiate young men from women only through the presence or absence of facial hair.

The massacre at Tlatelolco in October 1968, intensified young peoples' sense of alienation from the PRI regime and society in general. United by their love for the new international music critical of society and the "establishment," middle-class and working-class students joined to form a broader counterculture movement. Encouraged by the arrival of scores of US and Canadian hippies, sharing a common disgust with contemporary political and social mores and embracing the allure of international youth culture, Mexican youth began "dropping out" and taking drugs, particularly the *hongos*, or small, hallucinogenic mushrooms growing in Oaxaca's mountains. Rumors that the international rock stars John Lennon and Jim Morrison

had secretly journeyed to Oaxaca to partake of the magical mushrooms encouraged foreign and Mexican hippies alike to hitchhike throughout the country in search of the fungus.

The countercultural movement also encouraged freer sexual behavior. The idea of "free love," however, made fewer inroads in Mexico than in the United States and Europe because most university students, particularly young women, continued to live at home while studying rather than enrolling at distant campuses. For middle-class students, the counterculture movement allowed them to assert greater independence from their families than had traditionally been the case.

As in the United States, defenders of traditional family values blamed popular music for the irreverence of teens and college students. After 1968, Mexican popular showed the increasing influence of psychedelic rock, blending Spanish and English lyrics. No wonder that Carlos Santana, who moved from Jalisco, Mexico to the United States in the early 1960s and who sang in both languages, was the most popular vocalist of this Chicano Wave. The height of the movement took place at an outdoor concert in 1971. Much like Woodstock, huge crowds, estimated at 200,000, attended the event. Cultural nationalists decried the foreign influence. But the music spoke to a new generation of Mexicans, increasingly skeptical of the PRI and its hold over Mexican politics.

- What were the meanings of rock music to young Mexicans in the 1960s and 1970s? Why was this so powerful?

communist conspiracy was behind the student movement. As the protests continued, the government took control of the UNAM and IPN campuses to deprive students of their organizational headquarters. In response, rioters burned over eight hundred buses, some trolleys, and six police cars, while the granaderos clubbed students and engaged in other acts of brutality.

A few days later, on October 2 and just ten days before the start of the Olympics, between 10,000 and 20,000 protesters gathered in the Plaza of Three Cultures (Tlatelolco), surrounded by members of the army, to listen to speeches from student leaders. Suddenly, helicopters flew overhead, flooding the crowd in bright light as military personnel armed with submachine guns and the granaderos opened fire. Although the government later claimed that agitators initiated the shooting, eyewitness accounts dispute this allegation. Later evidence indicated that the order to fire was given by the Minister of Defense himself. Somewhere between 300 and 500 people died in the massacre, and more than 1,300 students were arrested. The government managed to keep the massacre out of the media temporarily; the day's headlines instead focused on the preparation for the Olympic Games. But even harsh censorship could not prevent news of the massacre from spreading, provoking revulsion and backlash. Many Mexicans saw the Tlatelolco massacre as a defining moment, the key event that marked the death of the PRI's legitimacy.

Conservation and National Parks in Latin America, 1964–2000

The news from Latin America during the 1960s and 1970s was not all dismal or filled with horrific stories of violence and death. These decades also marked the intensification of efforts to preserve the natural environment in several Latin American countries. The publication of American conservationist Rachel Carson's *Silent Spring* in 1962 brought international attention to the vulnerability of the earth's environment, helping to inspire and bring to the surface a global environmental movement. Some Latin Americans became advocates for the preservation of locations threatened by development. As a supplier of primary products to world markets, Latin America's natural resources had long been exploited without demonstrating much restraint for conservation. Inspired by increasing global concerns about protecting natural treasures, a few Latin American nations stepped up their efforts to set aside pristine sites and unique natural habitats for national parks.

The National Park System in Costa Rica

Costa Rica's small indigenous population and lack of mineral wealth minimized exploitation during the colonial period. Even the expansion of the coffee industry during the nineteenth century had done relatively little damage to the environment because most production took place on small farms. Only during the twentieth century did more intensive commercial activities (banana plantations, cattle ranches, hardwood logging) begin to threaten Costa Rica's extensive forest areas. Even before the emergence of the conservation movement in the 1960s, foreign scientists and a few Costa Rican biologists praised the country's flora and fauna—the small nation is home to 5 percent of the planet's biodiversity, a density unmatched by any other place in the world—and did their best to prevent the extinction of its zoological population. This land-use debate required Costa Rican policy makers to decide whether to continue to commit to short-term agricultural prosperity at the expense of the remaining forests or to engage in long-term conservation of the nation's unmatched—but also at that time unmonetized—natural resources.

Fortunately, the advocates of conservation won the debate and passed the Forestry Law of 1969. This law created the National Park Service and outlined regulations that restricted further deforestation. The statute also provided guidelines and rationales for the creation of national parks in areas of breathtaking scenic beauty, in locations containing rare or endangered biological specimens, and in spots where important historical events had occurred. In all cases, the National Park Service had to compensate previous owners (often squatters) for the value of their land, which meant from the outset the agency had to engage in fundraising. In addition to international donations, the Costa Rican government consistently committed generous funding. Among other things, the advocacy of popular multiterm president José Figueres and his wife contributed to the success of the conservation project. As a result of this law, today about 28 percent of Costa Rica's land surface is protected by the National Park System.

Three of the country's most visited parks provide good examples of each rationale for protection. Poás Volcano, in close proximity to San José, is well known for its breathtaking beauty. Visitors can overlook the crater rim and view (and smell)

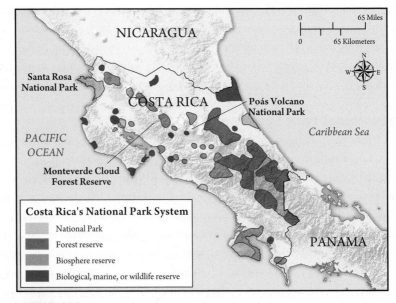

≡ **MAP. 11.3**

the sulfurous bubbling cauldron of lava below. First opened in 1972, the more remote Monteverde Cloud Forest Biological Reserve, poised along the Continental Divide, is home to an incredibly biologically diverse cloud forest. Monteverde's moist winds encourage the growth of a variety of orchids and other bromeliads and provide the habitat for rare birds like the quetzal and the bell bird, as well as the near-extinct *sapo dorado*, the "golden toad." Further north, Santa Rosa National Park in Guanacaste province, the site of the successful Costa Rican defense of their country against the filibuster William Walker in 1856, contains one of the two remaining lowland dry tropical forests in the world, and is home to many unusual mammals, turtles, and trees.

Despite these valiant efforts, Costa Rica's parks face threats because of their very success. A surplus of visitors, while bringing in revenue, frightens animals, tramples plants, and degrades the very biodiversity tourists come to see. In 1973, for example, Monteverde had 300 visitors; by 1995 the number had climbed to 50,000, despite a tooth-rattling road that limits traffic up the "green mountain." Tourists also demand more comforts, whether luxurious beach hotels that generate massive quantities of sewage or better roads to remote locations like Monteverde. As one park guide noted, "People come here to enjoy the rainforest, but then they want their cup of coffee. They don't realize that you have to cut down forest to grow coffee."

Costa Rican President Oscar Arias, who was awarded the Nobel Peace Prize in 1987 for helping to end the Central American crisis (chapter 12), encouraged the National Parks Service to shift its emphasis from conservation to sustainability during the 1980s. Recognizing that his country's rapidly increasing population could threaten the conservation program, Arias encouraged the Parks Service to think about human needs by employing people to work in sustainable enterprises by serving as park guides or working on reforestation projects. In Santa Rosa Park, for example, workers planted seeds from typical dry tropical forest trees to reforest the region once stripped bare by a cattle ranch owned by Nicaraguan dictator Anastasio Somoza.

By the 1980s, average Costa Ricans understood the value of ecotourism, and tourism began to replace export agriculture as the small country's main source of income. Revenues from tourism in 1997 exceeded the monies earned from both coffee and banana exports. When proposals surfaced in the early 1980s during the economic downturn to carve off portions of the national parks and sell them to rice cultivators, riots erupted in the streets of San José. As a result, Costa Ricans have committed to make this valuable resource sustainable so as to continue to attract tourists. Today, Costa Rican students from the primary grades to the university are well versed on environmental issues and a number of the country's institutions of higher education have outstanding biology programs. As a result of these efforts,

Costa Rica is often held up as an example to other Latin American nations because of its sensible environmental protection policies.

The Galápagos Islands: Darwin's Laboratory

Ecuador's Galápagos Islands remain the premier conservation tourist destination in all of South America. Located 621 miles from the South American coast, the archipelago's isolation has allowed birds, amphibians, and reptiles to evolve free from natural predators (mammals—especially humans). Moreover, each of the islands is located a sufficient distance from its neighbor that it evolved distinctive species or subspecies. For example, the flightless cormorant that lives only on portions of Fernandina and Isabela Islands lost its ability to fly because the plentitude of marine life near shore meant that it merely needed to flop into the water, grab its meal, and climb out.

Although Ecuador took possession of the Galápagos in 1832, three years before Charles Darwin's memorable visit, the government used it primarily as a prison colony. Whalers presented the greatest threat to the survival of the islands' most famous and unique inhabitants, the giant tortoises. Stopping at the islands for water and food during the lengthy Pacific fishing season, sailors captured the huge tortoises and stored them in the holds of their ships, where they provided fresh meat for months. International organizations and some far-sighted Ecuadorians eventually became concerned about the ecological fate of the islands. In 1959, the government declared 97 percent of the archipelago (that portion not settled by Ecuadorians) to be a national park. The Charles Darwin Foundation shortly thereafter funded its research station on Santa Cruz Island. The Foundation's dual mission is to explore the Galápagos's biology and assist in the conservation effort.

In 1972 about seven thousand visitors undertook the difficult ocean journey from Guayaquil to the islands. Well aware that the Galápagos attracted tourists interested in ecotourism, the government replaced the islands' old World War II airport on Baltra Island in 2012 with a new facility advertised as the world's first "green" airport. Increased human traffic produced a dilemma similar to Costa Rica's: the importance of tourist revenue to a poor country versus the necessity of preserving the environment. Most foreigners elect to see the islands on modest-sized cruise ships that house, feed, and transport visitors to preselected sites daily. This arrangement minimizes impact on the islands but leaves very little revenue in the hands of the people of the Galápagos. Other visitors, many of whom are Ecuadorian, choose the less expensive option to book small hotels in one of the archipelago's towns and take day trips, also with park guides. This system, however, places more pressure on the land because of increased waste and some occasional criminal activity.

≡ **The Giant Tortoises of the Galápagos Islands Protected by the Darwin Research Center.** The giant tortoises of the Galápagos Islands are prime examples of the need for conservation programs in Latin America. Lumbering, ungainly beasts, the tortoises proved convenient sources of food for whalers and other passers-by in the nineteenth and early twentieth century, almost driving them to extinction. Fortunately, interested conservationists, both international and Ecuadorian, stepped up and as private individuals began the conservation effort, which the Ecuadorian national government has underwritten since the 1960s. As with the Costa Rican National Park system, Ecuador has shown that preserved natural habitats not only are good for the environment but also bring wealthy ecotourists in droves, helping the national economy.

More serious threats come from Ecuadorian migrants, especially fishermen, who moved to the islands during the 1990s to take advantage of the Galápagos's relatively prosperous economy. Many of these fishermen dove for sea cucumbers, a marine animal bearing a striking resemblance to the vegetable and highly sought after as an aphrodisiac in the Asian market. When the government attempted to restrict fishing, the fishermen rioted and threatened the biologists at the Charles Darwin Center. In response to the clash, the government passed (and generally has enforced) the 1998 Special Law for the Galápagos, which extended the Park's maritime protection to a 40-mile limit around the entire park. The statute allowed permanent residents—but not the illegal transients—the right to fish and prohibited the large-scale industrial harvesting of marine life. A combination of the diminution of the number of fish and a rise in tourist dollars has convinced the remaining fishermen that obeying the legislation makes sense for the long-term benefit of the islands.

Invasive species like feral goats and donkeys and plants like blackberries and guava also threaten native Galápagos species. Recently scientists have used herbicides to try and control the spread of these invasive plants. More aggressive methods have successfully reduced the feral animal population, which had essentially destroyed the habitat on Pinta Island, the home of the famous giant tortoise nicknamed "Lonesome George." On Isabela, where the feral goat population posed a similar threat, the Park Service used helicopters, sharpshooters with automatic weapons, and Judas goats (specially trained goats that would coax feral goats out into the open) to kill about 140,000 goats in 1998. Today, native growth again flourishes on Isabela and the tortoise population has recovered.

As in Costa Rica, even though the Park Service and the government try to preserve the unique habitat of the Galápagos, the pressure on the land remains. In 2015 Ecuadorian President Rafael Correa outraged locals by imposing further restrictions on the islanders' economic activities. To reduce the quantity of wildlife killed by vehicles, he reduced the gasoline subsidy and limited the number of automobiles that could be imported. Local authorities have been instructed to crack down on illegal immigrants. By requiring a fifteen-day interval between visits to ecologically sensitive sites, Correa's new laws lessen damage to the most popular tourist landing places. Like Costa Rica, Ecuador realizes that to maintain a sustainable environment in the islands it must balance tourist and conservation interests with those of the local population who need to earn a decent livelihood.

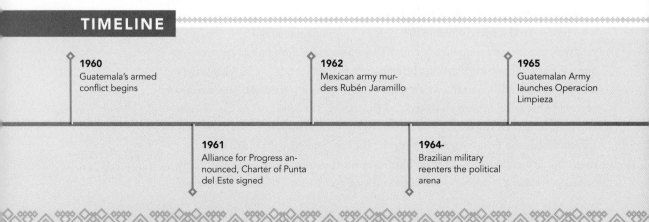

TIMELINE

1960
Guatemala's armed conflict begins

1961
Alliance for Progress announced, Charter of Punta del Este signed

1962
Mexican army murders Rubén Jaramillo

1964-
Brazilian military reenters the political arena

1965
Guatemalan Army launches Operacíon Limpieza

Conclusion

The stirrings of radical reform described in chapter 10 provoked violent reaction and counterrevolution. The United States led the onslaught against the perceived communist menace, first by proposing the Alliance for Progress, designed to promote democracy and encourage social reforms with significant funding, and second by pursuing a strategy called the National Security Doctrine that offered strategic training and military assistance to Latin American governments fighting domestic communists. By the mid-1970s, the National Security Doctrine predominated.

By that time, two-thirds of the Latin American nations were under military rule. A view from the Straits of Magellan northward would have revealed a dark picture, especially in the Southern Cone nations. Argentina, Brazil, and Chile each experienced brutal authoritarian rule, marked by political arrests, torture and assassination. Ultimately, the military's attempt to cloak these excesses by trumpeting their economic achievements failed. In the meantime, however, the flames of the Cold War rekindled in Central America, where citizens suffered perhaps the harshest responses to the events of the late Cold War, as the next chapter will reveal.

KEY TERMS

Charter of Punta del Este   486

Chilean Miracle   510

desaparecido   501

dirty wars   484

Grandmothers (*Abuelas*) of the Plaza de Mayo   504

Green Revolution   488

Institutional Act Five   499

Neoliberalism   509

Operación Limpieza   494

PRI (Institutional Revolutionary Party)   512

Trans-Amazonian Highway   501

1968
Mexican government massacres students : Tlatelolco square

1969
Costa Rica passes Forestry Law

1972
Construction of Trans-Amazonian Highway begins

1973
Pinochet regime executes approximately 1,260 opponents, more to follow

1975
Chile begins its neoliberal experiment

1976
Argentina's military takes over and begins the dirty war

1976
Allende's former ambassador Orlando Letelier assassinated in Washington, DC

Selected Readings

Alegre, Robert F. *Railroad Radicals in Cold War Mexico: Gender, Class, and Memory.* Lincoln: University of Nebraska Press, 2014.

Aviña, Alexander. *Specters of Revolution: Peasant Guerrillas in the Cold War Countryside.* New York: Oxford University Press, 2014.

Evans, Sterling. *The Green Republic: A Conservation History of Costa Rica.* Austin: University of Texas Press, 1999.

Fietlowitz, Marguerite. *A Lexicon of Terror: Argentina and the Legacies of Torture.* New York: Oxford University Press, 2011.

Gillingham, Paul, and Benjamin T. Smith, eds. *Dictablanda: Politics, Work and Culture in Mexico, 1938–1968.* Durham, NC: Duke University Press, 2014

González, Victoria, and Karen Kampwirth, eds. *Radical Women in Latin America: Left and Right.* University Park: Pennsylvania University Press, 2001.

Jonas, Susanne. *The Battle for Guatemala: Rebels, Death Squads, and US Power.* Boulder, CO: Westview Press, 1991.

Keller, Renata. *Mexico's Cold War: Cuba, the United States, and the Legacy of the Mexican Revolution.* Cambridge: Cambridge University Press, 2015.

Middlebrook, Kevin J. *The Paradox of Revolution: Labor, the State, and Authoritarianism in Mexico.* Baltimore: Johns Hopkins University Press, 1995.

Muñoz, Heraldo. *The Dictator's Shadow: Life under Augusto Pinochet.* New York: Basic Books, 2008.

Ochoa, Enrique C. *Feeding Mexico: The Political Uses of Food since 1910.* Wilmington, DE: Scholarly Resources, 2000.

Padilla, Tanalís. *Rural Resistance in the Land of Zapata: The Jaramillista Movement and the Myth of the Pax PRIísta, 1940–1962.* Durham, NC: Duke University Press, 2008.

Pensado, Jaime M. *Rebel Mexico: Student Unrest and Authoritarian Political Culture during the Long Sixties.* Stanford, CA: Stanford University Press, 2013.

Rabe, Stephen G. *The Most Dangerous Area in the World: John F. Kennedy Confronts Communist Revolution in Latin America.* Chapel Hill: University of North Carolina Press, 1999.

Stern, Steve J. *Remembering Pinochet's Chile: On the Eve of London, 1998.* Durham, NC: Duke University Press, 2004.

Taffet, Jeffrey F. *Foreign Aid as Foreign Policy: The Alliance for Progress in Latin America.* London: Routledge, 2007.

Tinsman, Heidi. *Buying into the Regime: Grapes and Consumption in Cold War Chile and the United States.* Durham, NC: Duke University Press, 2014.

Treacy, Mary Jane. "Killing the Queen: The Display and Disappearance of Rogelia Cruz." *Latin American Literary Review* 29, no. 57 (2001): 40–51.

Valdés, Juan Gabriel. *Pinochet's Economists: The Chicago School in Chile*. Cambridge: Cambridge University Press, 1995.

Winn, Peter. *Victims of the Chilean Miracle: Workers and Neoliberalism in the Pinochet Era, 1973–2002*. Durham, NC: Duke University Press, 2004.

Zolov, Eric. *Refried Elvis: The Rise of the Mexican Counterculture*. Berkeley: University of California Press, 1999.

PART FOUR

Old and New Ideas, the Search for A Middle Ground, 1980–2016

The 1970s through the early twenty-first century witnessed new manifestations of old patterns of inequality but also rising hopes for change in Latin America. While these patterns varied throughout the region, these decades can usefully be seen as three sequential (if partially overlapping) stages. The first stage, the late Cold War in the 1970s and 1980s, saw local players taking advantage of the struggle's final chapters to advance their own interests. The second stage, the rise of neoliberal policy prescriptions in the late 1980s, witnessed the application of "new solutions" to long-standing economic problems. While these new policies brought growing prosperity for the middle classes and a new wave of consumerism, neoliberalism also brought increasing inequality. By the 1990s, political coalitions based on identity politics and populist responses to neoliberal prescriptions had emerged. The third phase saw the growing prominence of transnational networks, along with conflicts over scarce and extractive resources that began in the first decade of the twenty-first century. These networks intensified the debate about both the importance and vulnerability of connections to global markets.

The turbulence of the late Cold War (chapter 12) shocked both Latin Americans and external observers. In South America, guerrilla movements became increasingly untethered from the global competition between superpowers that had defined the early Cold War. Colombia's FARC (Revolutionary Armed Forces of Colombia), for example, looked to drug trafficking and kidnapping as revenue streams while continuing to cling to vast swaths of territory and recruiting impoverished rural youth. The right-wing militias that emerged to combat the FARC developed their own connections to the lucrative drug traffic, even as they identified the most notorious traffickers as their sworn enemies. Indeed, profits from the hemispheric drug trade became the one common thread linking revolutionaries, reactionaries, and profiteers alike.

In Peru, a different type of guerrilla movement emerged. Most of the region's revolutionary armed groups in the 1960s–1980s looked to "foco" theory for inspiration, believing that small guerrilla bands could inspire and draw on the solidarity of local populations to topple regimes. Peru's *Sendero Luminoso* (Shining Path), in contrast, emerged from a Maoist breakaway faction of Peru's Communist Party. Sendero's leader, Abimael Guzmán, preached a horrifying message of violence, proclaiming that mass civilian casualties—particularly among the Quechua-speaking highland peasants in the region where Sendero based itself—were necessary to achieve the revolution's triumph. Sendero Luminoso had more in common with Cambodia's brutal Khmer Rouge, another Maoist movement that used mass execution as a tool of terror, than with other Latin America guerrilla movements. The poorly trained Peruvian security forces sent to eradicate the movement often harbored deep hostility toward the highland indigenous population. Nearly seventy thousand people died in Peru's civil wars of the 1980s, the great majority of them indigenous highland residents. Most of those died not as soldiers fighting either for the state or the Shining Path but as innocent civilian victims executed by both of these groups.

Central America, meanwhile, was wracked by different manifestations of the late Cold War. Leftist Sandinistas toppled Nicaragua's dictatorial Somoza regime in 1979, only to find themselves embroiled in a decade-long civil war against the *Contras*, a reactionary coalition trained and funded by the United States. El Salvador, Guatemala, and Honduras suffered repercussions as heavy-handed military regimes advanced bloody counterinsurgency campaigns not only against leftist guerrilla groups but also against civilians thought (correctly or incorrectly) to support the insurgents. As in Colombia and Peru, these regimes relied heavily on death squads to carry out extrajudicial assassinations and massacres to impose state terror, particularly on the rural and indigenous poor. Grisly tales of unspeakable inhumanity became commonplace. These repressive mechanisms, ostensibly enacted to fight off a communist revolutionary threat, took on a grim logic of their own, eliminating dissent through violence in regimes characterized by grotesque inequality.

These wars reached their endgame in the same years that South American nations like Brazil, Argentina, Chile, Uruguay, and Paraguay emerged from long dictatorships. Even the "perfect dictatorship" of Mexico's PRI found itself under increasing pressure to reform from both the left and the right, leading to greater openness and electoral competition. As a result, the late 1980s and 1990s witnessed a period of new democratic beginnings across Latin America and a lessening of revolutionary violence (with the notable exception of Colombia, where connections to drug trafficking prolonged the conflict between the FARC and the state until 2016).

By the late 1980s and early 1990s, neoliberal policy prescriptions came to dominate political discussion (chapter 13). The rhetoric of free trade, open markets, and reduced government spending stifled any alternative, at least in the short term. The Cold War struggles and the hyperinflation crises of the 1980s had buried most Latin American governments in debt, leaving them powerless to resist conditions imposed by lenders like the International Monetary Fund and the World Bank. The neoliberal Washington Consensus (chapter 13) did bring renewed foreign direct investment to Latin America—but often at the price of rising inequality, environmental destruction, and weakened sovereignty. While neoliberal policies enabled significant numbers of Latin Americans to join the middle class, they also triggered a reaction, as a new generation of populist politicians sought to appeal to the many left behind by neoliberal growth.

The new populists (chapter 14) found themselves entering a very different electoral arena from the one their predecessors had faced in the mid-twentieth century. The corporatist politics of the 1950s, which linked class-based sectors in a coalition, had fractured and could not be reassembled. Instead, new identity-based movements, which framed an understanding of social inequalities around identity based on race, gender, and identity rather than class conflict, jockeyed for position. Indigenous and Afro-descendant movements challenged the ostensibly race-blind constructions of citizenship of an earlier era, demanding new ways of understanding national belonging. Both LGBT and women's groups challenged traditional gender hierarchies. These new actors required political parties to reconsider their strategies and their networks of alliances.

Identity-based movements often looked to transnational networks for support and inspiration, transcending national boundaries that had largely defined popular movements of previous generations. Indigenous movements in Ecuador and Bolivia began to find common cause and forge alliances across borders and even across continents. A transnational environmentalist movement became one of the most successful in changing political conversations throughout the region, with particularly dramatic consequences in nations like Costa Rica.

At the same time, the trend toward transnational networks had its dark side. Demobilized units of the armed forces, right-wing militias and former guerrilla bands in Central America evolved into armed protection rackets for hire, extorting profits and reaping a toll of casualties. The deportation of Central American gang members from US cities like Los Angeles facilitated the growth of offshoots of these organizations in cities like San Salvador in El Salvador and Tegucigalpa in Honduras. In many cases, these were the US-raised children of Salvadorans, Guatemalans, and Hondurans who had fled the Central American conflicts of the 1980s, bringing that violence full circle.(Epilogue).

The Washington Consensus of the 1990s weakened under these new pressures. But the real importance of connections to global markets persisted. Popular movements, new populists, and transnational networks alike found themselves alternately buoyed and buffeted by the tides of global commerce. And new political actors struggled to articulate a political vision that could transcend what often seemed to be the winner-take-all logic of the marketplace.

12

The Late Cold War in Latin America, 1970s–1990

Global Connections

As the long Cold War continued, a series of proxy wars in Asia, Africa, and Latin America threatened global peace. The late 1970s and 1980s marked a new phase, one of increasing entropy. By the 1980s, rogue subnational groups made connections and asserted their influence transnationally, making the old binaries of the earlier Cold War era obsolete. Extensive military funding from one of the superpowers to an armed group did not necessarily mean ideological alliance: both the superpowers and the diverse groups they funded acted opportunistically to maximize short-term advantages, often with unanticipated long-term consequences.

Although the United States and the USSR entered the 1980s apparently on an equal footing, over the decade the Soviets clearly lost ground. The Soviet invasion of Afghanistan in 1979 triggered an uprising by Islamic groups collectively called the *mujahideen*. Although the Soviets committed almost 110,000 troops to the struggle, by 1989 the mujahideen, assisted by financial and military aid from Pakistan, the Persian Gulf states, and the United States, forced the Soviets to withdraw from Afghanistan. Failure in Afghanistan would be one of the factors that would soon bring down the Soviet Union.

Second, the USSR expended significant resources during the 1970s and 80s in a proxy war in Angola, where, along with Cuban volunteers, it defended the ruling *Movimento Popular de Libertação de Angola* (Popular Movement for the Liberation of Angola or MPLA) party against US- and South African–backed rebels.

In the mid-1980s, President Ronald Reagan abandoned the United States' forty-year-old containment policy toward the Soviet Union in favor of a more aggressive strategy. Specifically, he initiated the Strategic Defense Initiative (Star Wars) designed to shield the United States from incoming Soviet missiles carrying nuclear warheads. The required increase in military spending was in part designed to force the USSR to ratchet up its own spending, leading it into bankruptcy. Reagan argued that the Soviet Union's state economic planning had failed, that the quality of social services and healthcare had declined, and that the Eastern Bloc was already seeking loans from the West. Fortuitously for his policies, the price of oil, the Soviet Union's principal source of hard cash, fell precipitously in the 1980s.

The Soviet Union's new leader after 1985, Mikhail Gorbachev, demonstrated his own interest in ending the Cold War. He met with Reagan on four occasions and brokered an arms deal with the United States. Gorbachev promised structural reforms, such as granting Eastern Bloc nations more autonomy. Gorbachev's intended his reforms to respond to growing dissent against Soviet rule in the Eastern

≡ **Dirty War in El Salvador**. Soldiers search bus passengers along the Northern Highway. Public buses were regularly stopped at checkpoints or randomly stopped by security forces during El Salvador's armed conflict, in search of purported guerrillas or potentially subversive material. Passengers who were thought to be suspicious were typically taken away by the police or soldiers; many became *desaparacecidos*, disappeared persons, who did not return from their travels alive. Photographer Susan Meiselas captured the harrowing Central American conflicts of the 1980s in a series of unforgettable pictures, including this foreboding image.

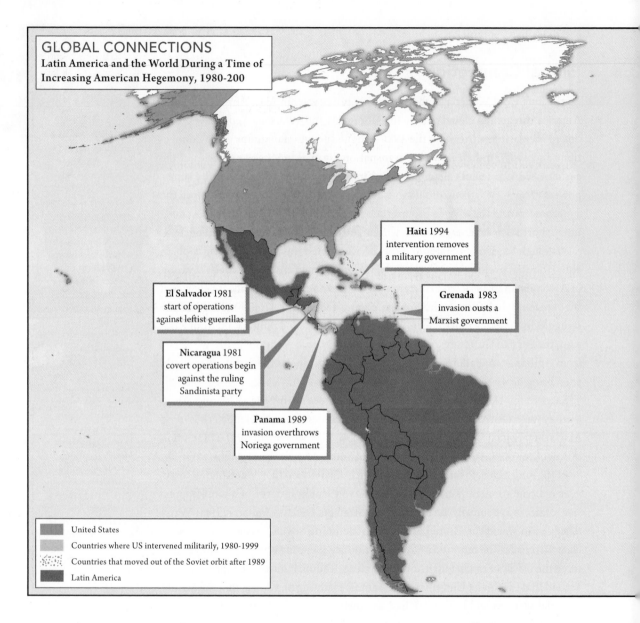

GLOBAL CONNECTIONS
Latin America and the World During a Time of
Increasing American Hegemony, 1980-200

Haiti 1994
intervention removes
a military government

El Salvador 1981
start of operations
against leftist guerrillas

Grenada 1983
invasion ousts a
Marxist government

Nicaragua 1981
covert operations begin
against the ruling
Sandinista party

Panama 1989
invasion overthrows
Noriega government

- United States
- Countries where US intervened militarily, 1980-1999
- Countries that moved out of the Soviet orbit after 1989
- Latin America

Bloc. Instead, his policies took the USSR in an unexpected direction, as the Eastern Bloc nations quickly pressed for greater autonomy.

By the time Reagan delivered his challenging words in West Berlin in 1987: "Mr. Gorbachev, tear down this wall," most of the Eastern Bloc nations were ready to secede from the Soviet Union. On November 9, 1989, the Berlin Wall did come down, and the Soviet Union and the Eastern Bloc it had once controlled with an

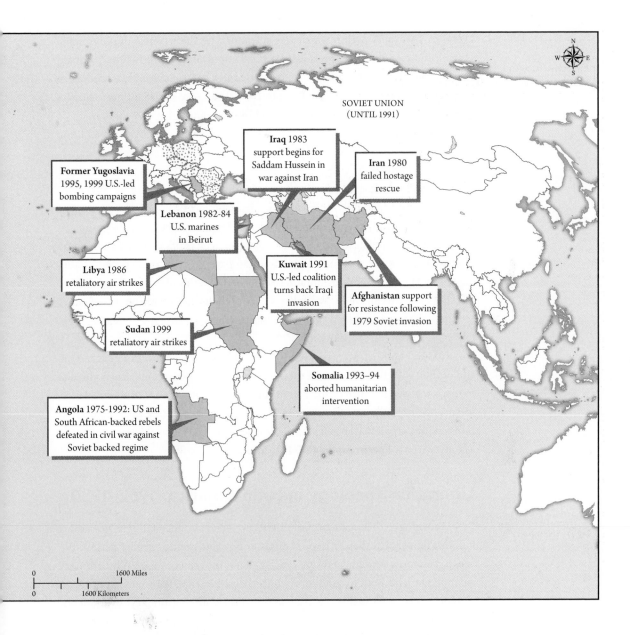

SOVIET UNION
(UNTIL 1991)

Iraq 1983
support begins for
Saddam Hussein in
war against Iran

Iran 1980
failed hostage
rescue

Former Yugoslavia
1995, 1999 U.S.-led
bombing campaigns

Lebanon 1982-84
U.S. marines
in Beirut

Libya 1986
retaliatory air strikes

Kuwait 1991
U.S.-led coalition
turns back Iraqi
invasion

Afghanistan support
for resistance following
1979 Soviet invasion

Sudan 1999
retaliatory air strikes

Somalia 1993–94
aborted humanitarian
intervention

Angola 1975-1992: US and
South African-backed rebels
defeated in civil war against
Soviet backed regime

0   1600 Miles

0   1600 Kilometers

iron hand were no more. As we see in this chapter, the collapse of the Soviet Union profoundly affected Cuba, while the loss of Eastern Bloc imports damaged the revolutionary cause in Central America. After 1989, Latin America's remaining revolutionaries were on their own.

The Late Cold War was hot in Latin America, which witnessed some of its highest levels of violence in the late 1970s and 1980s. These years were particularly brutal in Central America, which was subsumed by the violence of proxy wars. During his two terms as president of the United States (1981–1988), Ronald Reagan sought to use US power to extirpate all signs of perceived Soviet influence in the Western Hemisphere. The **Reagan Doctrine** called for US military support for revolutions within the Soviet sphere of influence, and aggressive suppression of left-wing radicalism in the Americas. This turned Central America into a killing zone, as US-backed regimes used the anticommunist struggle as a pretext to amass weapons and power.

In South America, guerrilla movements unmoored from waning Soviet influence went off on wildly different tangents. Colombia's FARC (Revolutionary Armed Colombian Forces), originally an idealistic Marxist guerrilla group, digressed from the revolutionary path to engage in drug trafficking and kidnapping in order to fund its operations. Peru's Shining Path, in contrast, asserted its allegiance to Maoist communism, rather than the Soviet model. In the case of the Shining Path, this meant the willful massacre of thousands of inhabitants of Peru's remote indigenous highlands in a perverse attempt to cleanse the region in preparation for communist revolution.

All of these conflicts were part of a "long decade" between the mid-1970s and the end of the 1980s that was among the most contentious periods in Latin America's modern history. Because of the extraordinary levels of state-sponsored violence, torture, kidnapping, and disappearances that took place during these confrontations, many commentators referred to Central America's late Cold War conflicts as a continuation of Latin America's "Dirty Wars."

Liberation Theology in Latin America, 1962–1980

Before turning to the conflicts of the 1980s, we need to understand the grassroots mobilization that reshaped Latin American popular politics in this period. Because grassroots movements were exactly that—movements started by ordinary local people and built around local concerns rather than some abstract foreign ideology—they represented a particular threat to right-wing military governments' power and often dubious authority. This left even peaceful reformist movements vulnerable to militarized crackdown and retribution. One prominent influence in grassroots mobilization was liberation theology, a social interpretation of the Gospel in the Catholic Church (and adopted by some ecumenical denominations) that advocated "a preferential option for the poor," and took a strong stance against oppression and injustice. **Liberation theology** both mobilized a generation of ordinary Catholics to social action—causing fierce retribution on the part of their governments—and redirected, at least for a time, the focus and energies of Latin American Catholicism from the mid-1960s until the 1980s.

The Crisis in the Catholic Church and the Reforms

The Roman Catholic Church clearly needed a new infusion of energy at midcentury because it had lost much of its traction, even in Latin America. Although nearly all Latin Americans self-identified as Catholics in the 1950s and early 1960s, many were nominal or indifferent members. Increasing numbers of people had begun to leave the Church altogether for other religious options (such as Protestantism or Afro-Caribbean practices). Others found themselves drawn to secular alliances, especially new left-wing political movements that conflicted with the conservative social values espoused by traditional Church teachings. A generation of idealistic young Latin Americans seemed more eager to invest their passion and faith in utopian political ideologies than in the "Holy Mother Church."

As early as the late 1950s, the Church found its temporal power greatly reduced, the number of young men joining the clergy plummeting, and its authority over the faithful increasingly challenged. Hostile forces associated with the modern world (such as communism, secularism, urbanization, and demographic changes) pulled people away from traditional lifestyles and worldviews. The last straw was the Cuban Revolution, which brought an avowedly atheist government to power in Latin America for the first time. The Revolution threatened to end the Church's hegemony in one of the most profoundly Catholic regions in the world.

In the aftermath of—and partly in reaction to—the Cuban Revolution, Pope John XXIII convened the Second Vatican Council in October 1962. The object of the Second Vatican Council (Vatican II) was to reclaim Catholicism's moral and temporal authority by reasserting its relevance in the modern world. While some historians have dismissed Vatican II as a shrewd "membership retention strategy," it did far more by bringing the Church back into the daily lives of ordinary people in Latin America to an extent not seen since the colonial period.

Between 1962 and 1965, the Council set a new direction for universal Catholicism that brought it directly into the fray of the social and political turmoil of the mid-twentieth century. The most important of these changes included a substantially increased role for the laity; an emphasis on Bible reading and reflection over formulaic ritual; increased accessibility to the sacraments, especially by abandoning Latin as the language of Mass and replacing it with modern, local languages; a conciliatory attitude to ecumenism; and, perhaps most importantly,

≡ **A Christian Base Community in Nicaragua.** Members of a Christian Base Community in Solentiname discuss scripture by the shore of Lake Nicaragua. In 1966 Ernesto Cardenal, a priest and poet, founded a lay monastery on the largest island of an archipelago of thirty-eight islands named Solentiname in Lake Nicaragua. Instead of delivering the customary sermons on the gospel, Cardenal conducted dialogues with the people, sometimes in church at Sunday Mass or in a thatched hut opposite the church used for meetings and the communal lunch after the Mass. The campesinos applied the Bible readings to their daily lives, struggles, and, in time, to the oppression by the Somoza regime, which they came to understand to be the result of "structural sin." Solentiname became the foremost of all the Christian Base Communities (CEBs) that sprang up across Latin America and Central America. It was a living embodiment of Liberation Theology. From 1979 to 1987, its founder, Ernesto Cardenal, served as minister of culture for the Sandinistas.

a renewed emphasis on the Church's role in the problems of the secular world.

This last element captured the interest and enthusiasm of many clergy in Latin America, who believed that Vatican II signaled a dramatic new conceptualization of the Church's relationship with the poor. In 1968, Latin America's bishops convened the Second General Episcopal Conference (CELAM) in Medellín, Colombia, where they called for the specific application of Vatican II to the region. Three elements in particular stood out from the bishops' documents on poverty and the Church: the call for social justice, the call for equality, and the call for an articulation of what the bishops called a "preferential option for the poor." Among other things, this mandate required the formation of intense Bible study organizations called **Christian Base Communities** (CEBs), led by ordinary people who would read and apply scripture to their daily challenges. This concientización (consciousness-raising), which would help the poor take control of their lives in the quotidian world, was the essence of what came to be known as "liberation theology."

The Effect of Liberation Theology

Liberation theology had a galvanizing effect throughout Latin America. It not only brought thousands of the faithful to a newly informed understanding of their beliefs but also encouraged them to take social action for the very first time. It is hard to overstate the significance of the strong position taken at the Medellín conference, not only for the Catholic Church, but also for ordinary Catholics all over Latin America. As the US journalist who first introduced these ideas to a popular American audience observed in 1980: "Medellín was one of the major political events of the century. . . . It shattered the centuries-old alliance of Church, military, and rich elites."

Liberation theology profoundly affected the Catholic Church across Latin America. While it was a Peruvian priest, Gustavo Gutiérrez, whose book *A Theology of Liberation: Perspectives* (1971) gave the movement its name, it would be Brazil that produced some of its most noted theologians and practitioners. One of the most influential was Paulo Freire, whose *Pedagogy of the Oppressed* (1970) offered a methodology for providing education to empower the poor.

Nowhere did these ideas have more effect than in El Salvador, Nicaragua, and Guatemala. In each of these countries, armed leftist movements, many of them influenced and supported by revolutionary Cuba, formed at roughly the same time as the emergence of liberation theology. Guerrillas in all three nations planned to overthrow repressive governments. The movements varied considerably in their specific ideologies and alliances, but virtually all of them sought to bring about a more equal distribution of resources (especially land) long held by the elites and foreign interests. Soon, these two powerful forces—liberating Catholicism and popular armed movements—would identify common ground. They were linked not so much by ideology or methodology as by a shared understanding about the roots of injustice and inequality.

Where Marxist guerrillas might blame dependency, exploitation, and capitalism, liberationist Christians decried "structural sin" and "institutionalized violence." Yet a common concern with the welfare of the poor would eventually make Catholic activists and Marxist guerrillas strange allies in Central America. The convergence of interests between the guerrillas and liberation theology–inspired Catholics (*catequistas*)—local priests and nuns, alongside campesinos whose consciousness had been raised through participation in the CEBs—would eventually cause governments in all three of these nations to label "radical Catholics" as communists and make them the targets of repression, persecution, or even assassination.

By the late 1960s and 1970s, some Catholic activists and the clergy who worked among them had indeed come to admire armed revolutionary movements and vice versa, although suspicions between the Christians and Marxists, many of whom were atheists for ideological reasons, remained high for some time. Many lay Catholics and clergy also drew the line at the use of violence in the armed movements. Instead, they maintained a practice of liberation theology built around a "development" orientation that provided peaceful social services, such as running soup kitchens and clinics for the poor. Even so, the CEBs in particular familiarized some people with the goals of the armed movements, and Catholic student groups helped introduce many middle- and upper-class students to the harsh realities of poverty for the first time. Many of these young people became involved in social action issues, including support for guerrillas (even to the extent of joining them as armed combatants).

In Nicaragua, activist Catholics played a pivotal role in the **Sandinista insurrection** that overthrew the rapacious Somoza dynasty in 1979. Some priests in Central America and elsewhere eventually moved toward the revolutionary path, believing that this provided a last chance for meaningful societal change and wishing to "follow their flock where they went." However, bishops and cardinals higher up in the Church hierarchy rarely offered support for liberation theology, which they tended to regard as dangerous and divisive. One extraordinary exception was El Salvador's Archbishop Óscar Arnulfo Romero, who came to take a strong and outspoken stance against violence, and government violence against campesinos in particular. Romero's progressive views led to his tragic death: a gunman assassinated him on March 24, 1980, while he was in the act of celebrating Mass.

Archbishop Romero may have been the best known, but he was just one of many hundreds of Christians killed for their dedication to the poor in Latin America, and Central America in particular, between the late 1960s and the early 1990s. In Guatemala, for example, nearly thirty Catholic priests were assassinated during this period, and the intensity of the military's counterinsurgency campaign targeted Catholic catequistas so directly that some historians have called that period a "holy war." Liberationist priests and catequistas also played active roles

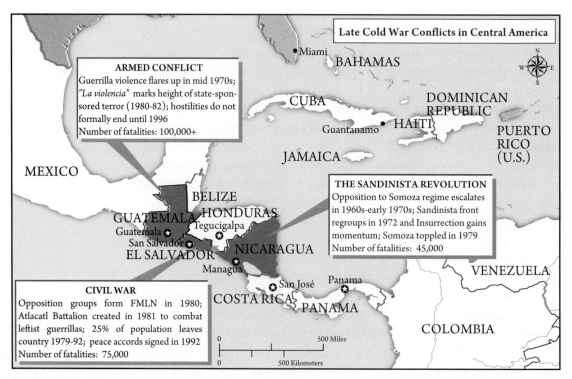

Late Cold War Conflicts in Central America

ARMED CONFLICT
Guerrilla violence flares up in mid 1970s; *"La violencia"* marks height of state-sponsored terror (1980-82); hostilities do not formally end until 1996
Number of fatalities: 100,000+

THE SANDINISTA REVOLUTION
Opposition to Somoza regime escalates in 1960s-early 1970s; Sandinista front regroups in 1972 and Insurrection gains momentum; Somoza toppled in 1979
Number of fatalities: 45,000

CIVIL WAR
Opposition groups form FMLN in 1980; Atlacatl Battalion created in 1981 to combat leftist guerrillas; 25% of population leaves country 1979-92; peace accords signed in 1992
Number of fatalities: 75,000

≡ **MAP. 12.1**

in El Salvador, Nicaragua, Argentina, Chile, Peru, and Brazil, where priests and prominent theologians helped to develop new ways for the Church to embrace the poor.

The price of liberation, however, ultimately proved too high for the Vatican, especially after John Paul II assumed the office of the papacy in 1978. Pope John Paul II's experience as a Catholic living in communist Poland had convinced him that Marxism and Christianity were inimical to one another. His views directly contradicted a prominent sign in Managua, Nicaragua, in the early 1980s that declared, "Between Christianity and Revolution there is no contradiction." Between the large number of Catholics—numbering at least in the thousands—who died for their beliefs at the hands of their own governments and the Vatican's withdrawal of support for the movement, liberation theology slipped into the background of Catholic social thought and action in the late 1980s.

The Sandinista Revolution in Nicaragua, 1972–1995

Nicaragua was ruled by a single family, the Somozas, from 1934 to 1979. Although during brief interludes other men sat in the office of president, the Somoza family remained the power behind the throne. Its patriarch, Nicaragua's Depression-era dictator Anastasio ("Tacho") Somoza García, initially came to power after having served as head of the National Guard following the assassination of Augusto Sandino (an event orchestrated by Somoza in 1934). Anastasio Somoza García ruled Nicaragua nearly single-handedly until his assassination in 1956. Somoza was succeeded by his two sons: first the elder, Luis Somoza Debayle, who served as national leader until his death from natural causes in 1967, and then the younger, Anastasio ("Tachito") Somoza Debayle, who assumed power after his brother's passing and remained firmly in place until a national uprising, led by the leftist Frente Sandinista Liberación Nacional (FSLN or Sandinistas), overthrew him in July 1979.

The Continuing Somoza Dynasty

The Somoza dynasty used its vast political power to take over Nicaragua's economy for the family's private benefit. The extended Somoza family and their cronies owned not only almost all of the nation's best agricultural land but also the national airlines, the nation's merchant marine fleet, the only concrete factory in the country, the only pasteurizing dairy, and the nation's only automobile dealership (Mercedes-Benz, a Somoza family favorite in a poor country where most people could not afford a car at all). Under Tachito, political freedom and civil rights reached a new low point as he commonly deployed the National Guard (*la guardia*), which he headed, to enforce his will capriciously and brutally around the country. After more than three decades of Somoza family rule, Nicaragua in the 1970s registered some of the most appalling social indicators of any country in the Americas—the average life expectancy was only 53 years and less than half of its people were literate. But despite the Nicaraguan peoples' fear and distaste for the dynasty, the Somozas' strong anticommunist outlook assured the regime's long-term support from the United States.

A devastating earthquake struck Nicaragua on December 23, 1972, killing tens of thousands of its citizens and almost completely destroying the capital city of Managua. The earthquake made an already bad situation intolerable, as Tachito's greed and lack of concern for the quake's victims assured that the nation's full recovery would be, at best, years in the making. This fear proved well founded when the media exposed the fact that Tachito had sold blood plasma donated to help earthquake victims on the international market for his own financial gain. These revelations, combined with Somoza's 1978 order to assassinate the newspaper editor Pedro Joaquín Chamorro, the scion of a prominent Nicaraguan family who had published the information about the blood plasma sales, pushed the Somoza regime past the boundaries of decency for even his supporters in the small Nicaraguan middle and upper class. Popular opposition to the regime escalated into violence throughout the 1970s.

The Sandinista Revolution and the Aftermath

Student activists Tomás Borge and Carlos Fonseca Amador sought to galvanize opposition to the Somozas by founding an organization they called the **Sandinista Front**, taking their name from Augusto César Sandino, the nationalist hero of the 1920s. Borge and Fonseca were arrested, along with many dissidents, following the assassination of Tacho Somoza in 1956. After his release from prison, Fonseca traveled to the Soviet Union; he also avidly followed the progress of Castro's 26th of July Movement and the successful insurrection against Batista. Using Cuba as a model, Fonseca and Borge established the Sandinista Front (FSLN) in the early 1960s. Their goal was the ending of the Somoza dictatorship and the establishment of a revolutionary government, modeled on Cuba, in its place. Throughout the 1960s and into the 1970s, confrontations between the National Guard and the Sandinistas played almost exclusively to the state's advantage. On several occasions, the National Guard almost succeeded in wiping the Sandinistas out completely. In 1976, Fonseca was killed in a confrontation with the National Guard.

After the 1972 earthquake the Sandinistas began to regroup and to modify their approach. They sought to incorporate emerging sectors of dissent, which by that time included not just Marxist revolutionaries and labor unionists but also radicalized Christians, businessmen, women, and even some members of the Nicaraguan upper class who had previously accepted the Somoza regime. The Sandinistas looked to the Cuban experience as a model, with the hope of adopting beneficial Cuban innovations while jettisoning bad ones. They also adjusted their message and objectives to include a broader array of players and ideologies. The fact that the Insurrection (the popular name for the uprising to oust Somoza) could rally people of divergent political views against Somoza in many ways assured its success. Activist priests and radicalized church people played a significant role in the Insurrection, helping to bring what might otherwise have been an unpalatable revolutionary idiom to ordinary Nicaraguans.

The Insurrection was a bloody affair. Some 45,000 Nicaraguans were killed between 1972 and 1979, as the National Guard brutally attempted to quell opposition through violence against the general population. It took the death of an American television reporter on June 20, 1979, at the hand of National Guardsmen for the United States to finally withdraw its support from the Somoza government. On July 17, 1979, Somoza fled the country and the Sandinistas assumed power.

The Sandinista Government and Its Opposition

The Sandinistas envisioned themselves as "new" socialists, guided not just by directives of classical Marxism and the Cuban Revolution but also by radical Christianity and Scandinavian democratic socialism. They were informed by the failures of earlier and more hardline leftist regimes, whose mistakes the Sandinistas did not wish to replicate. At first, the Sandinistas hoped to avoid alienating the United States, which had cast such a long shadow over Nicaragua's history and had proven hostile to every leftist government in the hemisphere.

At first, the broad governing coalition—the Junta of National Reconstruction, which included priests, businessmen,

Female Sandinista Miliciana de Waswalito. This photo portrays the "new Sandinista woman," it appeared on FSLN posters throughout the revolution, showing an idealized image of a very young Sandinista guerrilla, smiling while nursing an infant, and carrying a rifle over her shoulder. These were the qualities that the Sandinistas sought to project during their struggle to topple the Somoza dictatorship: youth, health, regeneration, optimism, and courage.

and Pedro Joaquin Chamorro's widow Violeta Barrios de Chamorro, along with Sandinista *comandantes*—seemed to promise an expansive, innovative, but also relatively moderate regime. Moreover, the Sandinistas' earliest reforms, including a massive literacy campaign, headed by a Jesuit priest, and an ambitious primary healthcare program, led by a woman, introduced new kinds of players into the social and political arena and were heralded both within the country and internationally. Even the Sandinistas' first forays into land reform—a contentious project in most countries—unfolded smoothly in Nicaragua, since most of the choice land in the country had belonged to the hated and now exiled Somoza family.

The Sandinista honeymoon did not last long, however, for two reasons. First, the new government's Marxist roots quickly began to show, as the Sandinistas began to radicalize their rhetoric, expropriate other privately held properties, accept Soviet aid, and import large numbers of Cuban doctors to help lead the healthcare program. This pivot to the left impelled the resignation of the more moderate members from the governing junta and frightened many of Nicaragua's business sector and upper class into exile.

Second, the 1980 election of Ronald Reagan to the US presidency signaled an abrupt end to the cautiously cordial relations that the United States (under President Jimmy Carter) and Nicaragua had enjoyed during the Sandinistas' first five months in power. Reagan, an old-school Cold Warrior, immediately recast the struggles going on in Central America within a Cold War framework. As part of the US strategy to confront the Soviet Union's interests in distant parts of the globe, the Reagan administration reconceptualized the Central American conflicts (in El Salvador and Guatemala as well as Nicaragua) as proxy wars within the broader Cold War. Nicaragua, to its detriment, found itself in the crosshairs of the superpower to the north.

In 1981, the Reagan administration initiated a covert project to overthrow the Sandinistas through the training and support of local troops, known as **contras** (meaning "against," or counterrevolutionary). The contras were eventually funded by a complicated and flagrantly illegal arrangement in which the United States sold weapons to Iran to pay for the contras in Nicaragua—the secret uniting of two completely unrelated political scenarios that, when revealed in 1986, became known as the "Iran-Contra scandal." Like the other two Latin American cases where the United States had attempted this tactic of manipulating overthrow from within (successfully in Guatemala in 1954, and unsuccessfully in Cuba in 1961), the covert insurgency drew from those sectors of the Nicaraguan population that opposed the Sandinistas. These included former Somoza supporters, former

National Guardsmen, and businessmen put off by the nation's business-unfriendly move to the left.

A less obvious source of vigorous opposition to the Sandinistas came from many of the indigenous and Afro-descendent residents of the Atlantic Miskito Coast, who resisted the Sandinistas less for their leftist policies than for the Sandinistas' desire to impose on these autonomous groups a "national" mestizo, Spanish-speaking culture. As in Guatemala in 1954 and in the Bay of Pigs invasion, money, training, strategic planning, and military support for the contras came from the United States—large numbers of US troops were stationed in readiness in nearby Honduras. These factors ultimately gave the contras their identity, their rewards, and their cohesion.

As one historian has wryly noted, "Reagan and the Sandinistas brought out the worst in each other," as the Sandinista decade—they would leave power in 1990—would come to be defined by both the contra war and shattered revolutionary dreams. During this period, the Sandinistas themselves became more heavy-handed and less able to cope with the challenges of running a country while at war. The *modus operandi* for the contras consisted largely of attacks on civilian populations and of planting landmines in the coffee fields of the northern mountains, where they hoped to disrupt the national economy by ruining the most important export crop. The landmines resulted in the death and dismemberment of many ordinary and largely apolitical campesinos, and, as the contras had hoped, did severely derail the economy. Anticipating the possibility of a potential invasion by the US military, the Sandinistas mobilized the country and instituted a wildly unpopular draft, which placed young men and women from poor families in harm's way. The dramatic escalation in the size of the Sandinista army fed unfounded US fears that the FSLN was providing aid to revolutionary groups in nearby countries and had plans to raid neighboring Costa Rica, a country with no army and a long history of border disputes with Nicaragua.

Some of the other Sandinistas' woes were self-inflicted. In 1983, a visit from Pope John Paul II resulted in a hostile encounter between the pope and Sandinista cadres. They attempted to drown out the papal Mass with revolutionary chants, forcing the pope to demand "*¡Silencio!*" from the altar, driving a wedge between the important sector of revolutionary Christians who had been among the Sandinistas' most ardent supporters. Under the Sandinistas, Nicaragua's fragile economy—now badly mismanaged—crumbled, resulting in worsening poverty and an increased lack of basic consumer goods, which the Sandinistas tried unsuccessfully to blame on the contra war. But even during the darkest days of the contra war, the Sandinistas continued to prioritize education and, as much as possible, healthcare. Those achievements remained a positive legacy.

As the United States continued to push for the overthrow of the Sandinistas, the Nicaraguan government turned increasingly to the Eastern Bloc (and, to a lesser extent, Cuba) for assistance and material goods. This, not surprisingly, seemed to support the US government's claims that Nicaragua had become a Marxist, Soviet ally state much like Cuba, and thus a foe of the United States. The new Sandinista national anthem, with lyrics by the Sandinista intellectual Tomás Borge and set to music by the great Nicaraguan composer Carlos Mejía Godoy, was staunchly anti-imperialist, with US observers reading anti-Americanism in verses such as:

Los hijos de Sandino	The children of Sandino
ni se venden ni se rinden	are neither sold nor defeated
luchamos contra el yankee	We fight against the Yankee
enemigo de la humanidad	Enemy of humanity

In February 1990, the Sandinistas held presidential elections. Despite the Reagan administration's constant drumbeat of accusations that the Sandinistas were antidemocratic, they had held a presidential election in 1984, which elected Sandinista former comandante and stalwart Daniel Ortega to office. Although the elections were legitimate by the letter of the law, they were clouded by the fact that the other viable candidates for the presidency—fearing an unfair fight—had withdrawn from the race just prior to the balloting. In the 1990 election, Ortega ran for a second term against Violeta Chamorro, the widow of the newspaper editor. Chamorro, a former Sandinista ally, enjoyed the support of the institutional Catholic Church, the exile community, and the many Nicaraguans who had become disillusioned with the regime over the previous decade. To the surprise of all involved, the Sandinistas lost the election. If the Reagan administration's goal had been to use the contras to destabilize the country enough to force an electoral defeat for the Sandinistas, then it had succeeded. Without dispute and without drama, Ortega turned over the reins of power to Chamorro. Nicaragua's decade-long experiment with revolutionary government came to an end.

Revolutionary Women in Nicaragua

Women played an active role in the Sandinista revolution, in part motivated by the FSLN's 1969 Manifesto. The Manifesto articulated specific rights for women, including expanded day care, extended maternity leave, improved working conditions for domestic servants, and increased educational and employment opportunities. In a country as poverty-ridden and traditionally Catholic as Somoza's

Nicaragua, such an advanced declaration of women's rights seemed quite remarkable. In addition, the sacrifices of brothers, fathers, and husbands at the hands of Somoza's National Guard encouraged women to take up arms for the Sandinistas in significant numbers. Ultimately, women constituted about 30 percent of the fighting force. A few, such as Dora María Téllez, achieved the rank of commander and led the 1978 assault on the National Palace in which the Sandinistas successfully took over the National Congress and held two thousand hostages for two days. Because of her medical training, Téllez eventually served as the minister of health in the Ortega administration (one of the very few women admitted to the inner circle) until she broke with the Sandinistas in the 1990s.

The life of Otilia Casco Cruz Téllez provides another example of women's participation in the Sandinista revolution. Taking a page from the Cuban Revolution's playbook, the Sandinista government rallied thousands of volunteers to teach poor peasants to read and provide basic healthcare (such as inoculations against childhood diseases) to the poor. Too young to participate in actual combat, Cruz took advantage of the educational opportunities available in the 1980s to train for a career in healthcare. Along with other volunteers, she went into the mountains and vaccinated children. Later, she became a specialist in herbal medicines, demonstrating such skill and dedication that the government sent her to Mexico City for further education.

Although the Sandinista government recognized that they owed a debt to the women who fought for the revolution, once in power, their enthusiasm for feminism waned. Although they rewarded women for their role in the revolution by endorsing the *Asociación de Mujeres Nicaraguenses Luisa Amanda Espinosa* (The Luisa Amanda Espinosa Association of Nicaraguan Women) during the revolution, this support did not translate into an expansion of women's basic rights under the Sandinistas.

≡ **Dora María Tellez.** Dora Maria Tellez was one of the foremost female comandantes in the Frente Sandinista de Liberación Nacional. A former medical student, she joined the Sandinistas in the late 1970s to help end the Somoza dictatorship When she was twenty-two years old, using the *nom d'guerre* Commander 2, she helped lead a daring operation on August 22, 1978, that occupied the Nicaraguan National Palace in Managua (home to the Nicaraguan National Assembly, in full session), capturing 1,500 civilian hostages. The FSLN ultimately gained the release of key Sandinista political prisoners and a million dollars in ransom money. When the Sandinistas assumed power after Somoza's fall, Dora María Tellez served as minister of health in the first Sandinista administration, initiating a public health campaign that won Nicaragua the UN Educational, Scientific, and Cultural Organization's prize for exceptional health progress. In 1995, she established the Sandinista Renovation movement, a short-lived political party formed to restore the values of the revolution. In 2008, Tellez went on a hunger strike to oppose the "dictatorship of Daniel Ortega," her former comrade-in-arms.

Many promises made to women in the Sandinista manifesto remained unfulfilled. The government blamed its inability to proceed further on the contra counterinsurgency, which diverted almost the entire budget to the military. Others less willing to accept this explanation noted that Daniel Ortega and a number of his cohorts opposed certain rights that women wanted, especially the right to an abortion.

The election of Violeta Chamorro in 1990 represented not the triumph of Nicaraguan feminism, but rather the restoration of a more traditional and Catholic vision of women's proper role in society. (Even so, she was the first woman in the Americas elevated to her nation's highest office in a free election). Budget cuts reduced spending for social programs, a move that particularly burdened women. Nevertheless, community-based organizations continued to press for new legislation to improve women's lives. For example, the Women against Violence Network, comprising a number of grassroots community organizations, met in 1995 to propose legislation that would make the domestic abuse of women and children a criminal offense. When the National Assembly initially ignored their draft Law 230, the Network presented it with a petition containing forty thousand signatures. The Network also organized a media blitz in support of the bill. As a result, it passed the National Assembly unanimously in 1996.

But the existence of a law does not always change human behavior. One of the first cases brought to light involved Daniel Ortega's stepdaughter, who claimed that he had sexually abused her since she was eleven years old. Despite her well-grounded allegations, a majority of Nicaraguans did not believe her. Nicaraguan women, like women in most Latin American nations, still faced a difficult journey to secure reproductive rights and the right to equal pay, among other issues.

The Cold War in El Salvador and Guatemala, 1970–1992

Two other Central American countries, El Salvador and Guatemala, also found themselves in the vortex of the late Cold War in the late 1970s and 1980s. In both countries, the roots of the crisis were basically the same: shocking discrepancies in wealth, profound inequities of landownership, deeply asymmetrical power relations between a tiny, wealthy oligarchy and the large disenfranchised campesino population, and long-standing government repression of efforts to bring reform to the system. In time, these conditions provided fertile ground for the formation of Cuban-inspired insurgencies committed to overthrowing their governments in order to bring Marxist revolution to each country.

Both countries already marked tragic events in their histories when efforts at change had met with repression and failure (recall El Salvador's 1932 La Matanza and the overthrow of Guatemala's Arbenz in 1954), but the Sandinista revolution in neighboring Nicaragua in 1979 imbued the armed movements in both countries with great hope for their own success. The Sandinista victory also upped the ante for El Salvador and Guatemala's military governments, both of which dramatically increased their counterinsurgency campaigns against dissidents and rebels. In both cases, the armed conflicts raged for years, killing many tens of thousands of civilians and forcing more than a million Salvadorans and roughly an equal number of Guatemalans to flee their own countries. In the end, each of these governments "saved the country from communism," but at a terrible price of violence, massive human rights violations, national trauma, and the diaspora of their people. The scale of the destruction would carry major ramifications for many decades to come.

El Salvador

El Salvador was the smallest but most densely populated country in Central America (and in all of Latin America at the time). Its agricultural base—where the oligarchical "Fourteen Families" owned almost all of the land—left the campesinos among the poorest in the region. During the 1960s, El Salvador had become a showcase for the Alliance for Progress, the US-funded initiative that encouraged foreign capital investment, promoted education, and pushed for modest land reform (chapter 11). A US technology giant (Texas Instruments, which at the time fabricated bombs for the Vietnam War) and companies involved in textile manufacturing invested heavily in the country but created few jobs suitable for a poorly educated population.

Nevertheless, in the early 1970s, El Salvador experienced a short-lived political opening and elevated new leaders with fresh ideas from outside the oligarchy and the military to office. José Napoleon Duarte, a cofounder of the pro-US, centrist Christian Democratic Party, proved to be the most dynamic of the reformers. Duarte, who had served as an effective mayor of San Salvador, ran for president in 1972. However, in a dramatic reversal, he was defrauded of his victory at the last minute. On the day of the election, as results were being reported, El Salvador's TV screens and radios suddenly went silent. Three days later, the government announced that the military candidate, Colonel Arturo Armando Molina, had won the presidency, and Duarte himself was nowhere to be found. Duarte would regain political influence in the 1980s and later serve as El Salvador's president. But the stolen 1972 election and the sense of national disillusionment it produced contributed directly to the rise of the country's guerrilla movement.

Another factor that destabilized El Salvador was the economic privation that began in 1969. Then, a four-day-long conflict with Honduras dubbed the Soccer (*Fútbol*) War—the proximate cause of the hostilities was a World Cup qualifying game between the two countries, though the underlying causes ran deeper—resulted in the permanent closing of the border to Salvadorans, who had long seasonally migrated as workers to the neighboring nation. This cycle of rising-and-dashed expectations so disheartened the people of El Salvador that the emergence of the armed leftist opposition in the early 1970s proved attractive to many. Although any number of small and divergent opposition groups emerged during this period (some armed and Marxist, many not), most converged under a single umbrella organization, the **Frente Farabundo Martí de Liberación Nacional** (Farabundo Martí Liberation Front, or FMLN), in 1980. Opposition to the government increased dramatically during the decade of the 1970s.

The Salvadoran civil war extended roughly from 1979 to 1992. On October 15, 1979, the Salvadoran military, fearing an uprising similar to the one that had brought the Sandinistas to power just a few months earlier, led a coup against the sitting president to strengthen military control over the presidency. Protests against military violence led to severe repression—including forced disappearances, torture, and extrajudicial killings—by the Salvadoran security forces and paramilitary death squads against activists, teachers, health providers, and church people mobilized by liberation theology. With this outburst of violence, the twelve-year fratricidal conflict began.

During the early years of the conflict, both sides engaged in kidnapping, disappearances, murders, and atrocities, although the government perpetrated most—perhaps as much as 95 percent—of the violence. In the capital of San Salvador, the scale of atrocity was such that ordinary people would regularly search the grounds of the city dump for the bodies of their "disappeared" loved ones, often to encounter precisely the grim discovery they feared. Firefights and conflicts in the countryside forced many to flee from their homes; women would describe traveling "on the *guinda*," a reference to the small wild cherries that they and their children scavenged to consume while they were fleeing violent military sweeps.

When voices of conscience dared speak out against military violence, the military quickly stifled them. The most prominent case was that of San Salvador's metropolitan archbishop Óscar Arnulfo Romero. Romero, whose popular weekly sermons were regularly broadcast around the country, became increasingly vociferous in his calls for human rights. Although Romero was not himself political, he grew increasingly sympathetic to liberation theology, and the difficult and polarizing conditions eventually forced him to take sides. By 1980, when right-wing terror had begun to reach a horrific crescendo, Romero called on members of the military and paramilitaries, whom he correctly understood to be the worst human rights violators, to cease obeying immoral orders. On March 24, 1980, only a few days after a sermon in which Romero ordered, "in the name of God, I beg you, I implore you, I order you: stop the repression," a death squad gunman assassinated him while he was celebrating the Mass. In El Salvador's highly polarized climate, even Romero's death was controversial, so much so that the government fired on and bombed the massive, grieving crowd that attended his funeral. Dozens of mourners were killed.

In December 1980, another assassination of church people occurred that spotlighted the role of the United States in the Salvadoran conflict. Four American Catholic churchwomen (three nuns and one lay missionary), who had been working with the rural poor, were raped and murdered by members of the El Salvadoran National Guard at a military roadblock while returning to El Salvador from a visit to visit their fellow nuns in Nicaragua. The military command apparently ordered the murders because the women had allegedly imported dangerous ideas. US Ambassador Robert White strongly protested the killings, to both the Salvadoran authorities and to the US government, which ardently supported the Salvadoran government and its military. The ambassador, however, lost his job for his outspokenness, and the crimes against the churchwomen remained, officially, "unaccounted for."

The Reagan administration reconfigured the Central American conflicts within the political matrix of the Cold War. Central America became a key battleground for the projection of the Reagan Doctrine, the administration's global strategy to undermine the Soviet Union. In particular, Reagan's Central America strategy applied the "symmetry

≡ **Portrait of Archbishop Romero with Devotee.** The assassination of Archbishop Óscar Arnulfo Romero while saying Mass in San Salvador on March 24, 1980, sent shockwaves throughout El Salvador and much of Latin America. During his life, Romero was a controversial figure, despised by right-wing conservatives for what they perceived to be his lack of condemnation of priests and parishioners whose conviction for Liberation Theology compelled them to support the FMLN. He was also deeply distrusted by the far left, including the FMLN, for his failure to condemn Catholics who were not enemies of the government. Above all else, Romero was consistent in his fierce and bold condemnation of violence committed by both sides of the armed conflict, a position that ultimately pushed the leader of a right-wing paramilitary group to order his murder. In the years since his death, Archbishop Romero has come to be seen as a champion for justice, for human rights, and for the poor and of the oppressed, not only in El Salvador but in many parts of the world. Despite long-standing opposition from some influential Salvadoran conservatives, Pope Francis declared him a martyr of the Church on February 3, 2015, paving the way for his beatification, which took place on May 23, 2015. As a beatified martyr (one step remains for his canonization to "saint"), he is now known in the Roman Catholic Church as *San Romero.*

doctrine" to El Salvador and Nicaragua. Subscribing to the theory that authoritarian regimes can be negotiated out of power but totalitarian regimes cannot, the United States chose to offer support to the Salvadoran government (which the US government perceived as authoritarian) in its war against the FMLN, while opposing the Sandinista regime (which the US perceived as totalitarian) through the funding and support of the contras. (As we shall see, Guatemala fell outside this model altogether.)

One particularly brutal and effective example of US support of the Salvadoran government was the creation in 1981 of the Atlacatl Battalion. Named for El Salvador's last indigenous ruler, the Atlacatl Battalion was an elite fighting force and rapid-response team to combat leftist guerrillas. Characterized by its nimbleness as well as its ruthlessness, the Atlacatl Battalion responded rapidly and directly to fast-moving guerrilla operations by using helicopters to deploy small-arms units to hot spots. The battalion, a central element of US tactical aid to El Salvador, was the first Salvadoran unit of its kind trained by US military advisers. Most of the Atlacatl Battalion officers trained at Fort Bragg, North Carolina, learning counterinsurgency techniques there.

Despite President Reagan's immense popularity in the United States, some Americans strongly opposed the US government's support for the Salvadoran government and Reagan's efforts to topple the Sandinistas. Solidarity groups formed in the United States around these issues, especially after the assassination of Archbishop Romero and the churchwomen, to draw attention to and oppose US policy. On December 11, 1981, the Atlacatl Battalion committed a particularly horrendous massacre of nearly all the villagers in a politically neutral village called El Mozote. One of the few survivors of the attack, Rufina Amaya, hid in a cornfield while she listened to the killing of her children and eight hundred other villagers. Although the Salvadoran government initially denied the massacre and the Reagan administration claimed US reporters had hyped up the story, it eventually became clear that the US-trained and sponsored Atlacatl Battalion had conducted the massacre. Even after such revelations, the United States retained its fierce commitment to the Salvadoran government, despite mounting public opposition in the United States.

The election of the respected politician José Napoleon Duarte to the Salvadoran presidency in 1984 did little to calm the situation. In November 1989, the FMLN launched a "final offensive" to take the capital city but failed to do so. In retaliation, the military ordered (and the Atlacatl Battalion carried out) the assassination of six Jesuit priests who had been involved in liberation theology, along with their housekeeper and her daughter. In a defiant mockery of the Jesuits as the "intellectual authors of insurgency," the soldiers bashed the priests' brains out of their skulls.

But eventually the people of El Salvador became exhausted by the war. The passage of time, the intervention of a series of pan–Central American peace talks brokered by Costa Rica known as the **Esquipulas Accords,** and the end of the Reagan Doctrine ultimately brought an end to the hostilities. In September 1992, all combatant parties signed a firm and lasting peace accord. The Atlacatl Battalion was dismantled in December 1992 as a requirement of the peace accords. At the ceremony where the government disbanded the battalion, El Salvador's president, Alfredo Cristiani, praised them with these words. "You served a transcendental mission in the armed conflict. You fought with mysticism, discipline, courage and valor.... You will always be remembered in the hearts of the Salvadoran people as heroes."

But remembered how? Approximately 75,000 Salvadorans had died during the twelve long years of the war. Many thousands also were forced to leave the country, seeking exile outside of El Salvador. Studies estimate that as much as 25 percent of the population left El Salvador between 1979 and 1992. Many sought refuge in the United States, where they congregated to locations that now have very large Salvadoran and Salvadoran-American populations, particularly Los Angeles and Washington, DC. Today, the FMLN functions as a legal political party, and two of its members have served as president of the republic.

Guatemala

As we have seen in chapter 11, Guatemala's armed conflict began in the early 1960s in the aftermath of the Arbenz overthrow and the rise of armed leftists' movements across Latin America. The struggle in Guatemala would last from 1960 until 1996—a thirty-six-year-long conflict between armed rebels and a powerful military counterinsurgency that ebbed and flowed throughout its duration. In Guatemala, unlike either Nicaragua or El Salvador, the conflict was complicated by class struggle, and also by deeply entrenched racial prejudices and mistrust. By the 1980s Guatemala's mestizo nation-state would frame its anticommunist counterinsurgency campaign against "internal enemies of the state," not only as a war against communism, but also against the nation's majority indigenous Maya population.

Guatemala's long period of violence (Guatemalans, unlike Salvadorans, rarely refer to this long period of violence as a "civil war," instead preferring the term "armed conflict") was ultimately the most deadly in the region. Although various sources contest the numbers killed, truth commission reports estimate that some 100,000 Guatemalans, mostly noncombatants and mostly Maya, died as a result of the armed conflict. This means that the Guatemalan conflict claimed far more lives than the more well-known Nicaraguan Insurrection and contra war and

Salvadoran conflicts combined. Curiously, the Guatemalan conflict attracted very little attention in the United States as it unfolded, in part because the United States did not give direct military aid to Guatemala because the previous Carter administration had withdrawn aid to Guatemala because of its egregious human rights record. Adding it to the equation perhaps would have upset the balance of Reagan's "Symmetry Doctrine," which defined US policy in Nicaragua and El Salvador.

The modern phase of the Guatemalan armed conflict flared up in the mid-1970s, when the guerrillas, who had been nearly annihilated by military campaigns in the late 1960s, began to reorganize. This time they based themselves mostly in the largely indigenous highlands, where profound economic inequities and ethnic prejudices contributed to the most grinding poverty in the nation. The Guatemalan altiplano (highlands) and a northern strip of territory called the Ixcán were also regions where some social innovation had begun, particularly the formation of cooperative settlements, many founded with the guidance of Catholic clergy influenced by liberation theology. By 1974, four principal left-wing guerrilla groups—the Guerrilla Army of the Poor (EGP), the Revolutionary Organization of Armed People (ORPA), the Rebel Armed Forces (FAR), and the Guatemalan Labor Party (PGT), an older political entity that dated back to the Arbenz era—established a presence in these areas as well as in the capital city and, to a lesser extent, in other parts of the country. These four groups recruited supporters, attacked government troops and facilities, and committed acts of violence and sabotage against both the military and powerful conservative civilians, such as coffee planters who mistreated their workers. Following the example of the FMLN in neighboring El Salvador, these organizations combined to form the Guatemalan **National Revolutionary Unity (URNG)** in early 1982.

One of the proximate causes for this upsurge in guerrilla activity was a devastating earthquake that rocked Guatemala on February 4, 1976. The quake had its epicenter in the predominantly Maya town of Chimaltenango—the gateway to the altiplano— killing thousands of people and destroying much of the country's already fragile infrastructure. Much like what happened after Nicaragua's earthquake, Guatemala's disaster disproportionately affected the poor. Guatemala's ultraconservative archbishop Mario Casariego unsympathetically opined on the night of the earthquake that God had punished a deserving nation by squashing it under His divine thumb. Government aid to afflicted areas was only somewhat more helpful. The earthquake set off a wave of discontent and despair that directly fed the cause of the guerrillas. More or less around this same time, indigenous leaders formed an organization called the Comité de Unidad Campesina (CUC) that began to marshal Maya and other rural support for radical change.

The Guatemalan guerrillas never could claim large areas of "liberated territory" as El Salvador's FMLN did. But like the FMLN, the URNG was inspired by the Sandinista victory in 1979. By 1980, the rebels had gained sympathy and support in the capital and in the altiplano, and even managed to take control of a small amount of territory in the remote and largely inaccessible Ixcán. Guatemala's military government responded brutally by permitting death squads and security forces to assassinate workers, students, teachers, union members, and others thought to be associated with the Left.

Under the presidency of General Romeo Lucas García (1978–1982), state-sponsored violence climbed dramatically upward. Residents of the capital city became accustomed to seeing dead bodies in the street, which were quietly collected each morning by firemen. The military began the intermittent massacre of villages where the guerrillas were thought to enjoy support. A 1978 massacre in the village of Panzós, where government troops killed scores of rural activists, organizers, and townspeople, marked the beginning of a dark period state-sponsored terror between 1980 and 1982 that Guatemalans refer to now as "**La violencia**." In January 1980, after rural CUC members took over and occupied the Spanish embassy in Guatemala City to protest repression and inequities, the Lucas government ordered the building and all thirty-eight people in it incinerated. (The Spanish ambassador is the only one who survived the ordeal, by escaping through a window). The burning of the Spanish embassy represented the moment where the Guatemalan people, who in the words of one scholar recognized "an act of profound disrespect on the part of the military," began to turn against the regime to an unprecedented extent.

In the face of mounting social discontent, on March 23, 1982, a triumvirate of three senior army officers, with the military's backing, overthrew Lucas García's hand-picked successor in a coup, bringing to power General Efraín Ríos Montt, a born-again Christian and career military man who became one of the most controversial figures in Guatemala's contemporary history. Ríos Montt, whose recent conversion to Pentecostalism had made him a darling of religious and political conservatives in the United States, ruled with an authoritative hand for seventeen months until he was expelled from office in a coup led by his own Minister of Defense.

Many Guatemalans were enamored with Ríos Montt's vision of a "New Guatemala," especially the residents of the capital, Guatemala City. Among other things, Ríos Montt withdrew government approval for death squad activity. He required every government employee to take a vow to "not rob, lie, or steal," and, in an unprecedented move, put an end (at least temporarily) to corruption on the part of government officials. Because the regime implemented harsh penalties against criminals, crime in the capital reached nearly unprecedented low levels. Each Sunday night, the general offered what were popularly called "sermons," in which he spoke of patriotic and morally edifying topics and urged Guatemalans to enter a new covenant between the governed and the government. In the cities, many citizens applauded Ríos Montt for his ability to restore order to their long-troubled country.

But as a military man, Ríos Montt fully embraced the ethos of the National Security Doctrine over benevolent Christianity. After briefly making an offer of amnesty (which was largely ignored), the military under Ríos Montt's authority launched a scorched earth campaign against the URNG and their supporters, real or perceived. In the altiplano, the army implemented a policy called "fusiles y frijoles," (rifles and beans), which offered rural villagers the opportunity to either accept military authority and protection or to suffer the consequences. (The "protection" offered sometimes involved involuntary relocation to "model villages"—hence

Guatemalan Kaibiles. The Kaibiles are the elite special operations force of the Guatemalan army, which specializes in counterinsurgency operations and jungle tactics. Greatly feared by many in the civilian population, the Kaibiles (who take their name from Kaibil Balam, an indigenous leader who outsmarted Pedro de Alvarado during the Conquest), were responsible for many of the atrocities committed during the counterinsurgency campaigns that took place during the period of the Guatemalan armed conflict known as "La Violencia" in the early 1980s. During this time, a government-ordered scorched earth campaign destroyed at least 440 villages, displaced more than a million, and killed as many as 100,000 people. Truth commission reports estimate that as much as 80 percent of the people who were victims of state-sponsored terror during this time were Maya.

frijoles, a household staple—in government-run camps under strict surveillance). The Ríos Montt government also created "civil patrols," units of men who guarded their villages and enforced government rule.

Those who refused military "protection" faced a violent and comprehensive counterinsurgency campaign intended to destroy not only the insurgency but also everything and everyone that might support it. During this period, from June 1981 to the end of 1982, Guatemala's *violencia* reached its nadir. By the government's own count, the army and the civil patrols eliminated some 440 villages, leaving more than a million children with no surviving parents. That dreadful toll does not begin to take into account the many massacres that took place on large fincas and settlements that fell outside the official census. The Guatemalan government also proclaimed the Maya people—ostensibly because of their support for the guerrillas—the "internal enemy of the state," a condition made all the worse by the guerrillas' late realization (or their failure to acknowledge) that their presence in the villages put innocent people in harm's way.

As a result of this toxic brew of Cold War politics and racism, Maya deaths constituted some 80 percent of the conflict's victims during La violencia. But by the government's reckoning, this was not too high a price; the scorched earth campaign had essentially wiped out the URNG as a military threat. Guatemala had, as government documents proudly noted, accomplished this without the help of the United States. So successful was the Guatemalan counterinsurgency campaign of the early 1980s that in military circles elsewhere in Latin America it became known as the "Guatemalan solution."

Despite his putative success, Ríos Montt was overthrown in a coup on August 8, 1983, and replaced by another general who served as Guatemala's last military president, eventually replaced by a freely elected civilian, Vinicio Cerezo, in 1985. As they did in El Salvador, the Esquipulas Peace Accords helped to pave the way to Guatemala's own peace plan, which ended hostilities in December 1996. But the legacy of the long armed conflict continues to loom large in Guatemala's public memory and conscience.

Ríos Montt remained a significant political figure for more than two decades, although his fortunes turned in 2013, when he was put on trial and convicted on charges of genocide and crimes against humanity—earning an 80-year sentence of which he served only ten days before the conviction was thrown out for "judicial irregularities." The national polarization that emerged around the Ríos Montt trial, with one side arguing across the public forum, *"Sí hubo genocidio,"* ("There was genocide") and the other, *"No hubo genocidio"* ("There was no genocide"), illustrates how a nation struggles when the public memory of a recent tragic history is still contested.

Like El Salvador, postwar Guatemala lives with the harsh realities of its peoples' diaspora to other nations, such as Mexico and the United States; also like El Salvador, extremely high rates of crime make life there almost more precarious than during the armed conflict. Democracy remains fragile, but Guatemalans have demonstrated their commitment to keeping it alive. When Otto Pérez Molina, a former field commander from the 1980s, was elected president in 2012, running on a platform of aggressive crackdown on crime, it seemed to be an example of the persistence of the old regime in a new guise. But in early September 2015, escalating popular protests against political corruption forced Molina's resignation. Such a response to public opposition would have been unthinkable in Guatemala only a few years earlier.

Guatemala has also come to grips with some of the missteps of the past. For example, the participation of indigenous people and of women in politics—elements specifically mandated by the 1996 Peace Accords—ranks among the highest of any country in Latin America. Maya culture and languages today receive much greater respect than perhaps at any point in Guatemala's history. The nation's economy has improved from the war years, thanks in part to increased tourism, industry, and remittances (money sent home by Guatemalans living abroad), and also because of illegal trade, especially narco-trafficking, for which Guatemalans are *not* thankful. Still, the cynical old axiom, "*de Guatemala a Guatepeor,*" (From Guate-bad to Guate-worse) no longer rings quite as true as it did in the past.

Cuba in the Special Period, 1989–2016

The fall of the Soviet Union in 1989 had a lasting effect on Cuba. At its peak, the Soviet Union had pumped an astonishing $4–$5 billion worth of aid (in all its forms) *per year* into Cuba. The demise of the Eastern Bloc left Cuba without a patron state for virtually the first time in its history. Since the 1960s, Cuba had provided sugar to the Soviet Union in return for its political loyalty (Cuba being the Eastern Bloc's best and most US-aggravating ally in the Western Hemisphere). In return for Cuba diverting almost all its agricultural lands into sugar production and in the face of the decades-long US trade embargo, the Soviet Union and the Eastern Bloc provided communist Cuba with almost all its basic needs. These included manufactured goods, food commodities, fertilizers and chemicals, medicine, agricultural machinery, educational materials, and petroleum and other fossil fuels.

The Economic Effects of the Special Period

Almost immediately following the dissolution of the Soviet Union, Cuba lost its oil allotments, which had become a major source of state revenue upon resale. Worse, Cuba could no longer fuel its agricultural and industrial production. Within months, Cuba lost 80 percent of its imports, 80 percent of its exports, and its GDP dropped by nearly 35 percent. The election of Castro ally Hugo Rafael Frías Chávez as president of oil-rich Venezuela in 1998 eventually offered some relief to Cuba's problems, but it did not solve them. The name that Fidel Castro gave this decade of crisis, "**The Special Period**," euphemistically suggested a manageable crisis of short duration. But, in fact, the Special Period marked the beginning of a new era of Cuban society and history that endures to the present day.

The Special Period foregrounded Cuba's most serious underlying economic and social problems and challenged many of the Revolution's indisputable achievements in medicine and education. Transportation and agricultural machinery shut down. The importation of tens of thousands of Chinese bicycles and the introduction of huge people-carrying buses (known as "camels") helped with transportation in Havana, but in rural areas, many returned to the use of horses and mules for transportation and for pulling tractors for which they no longer could obtain gasoline.

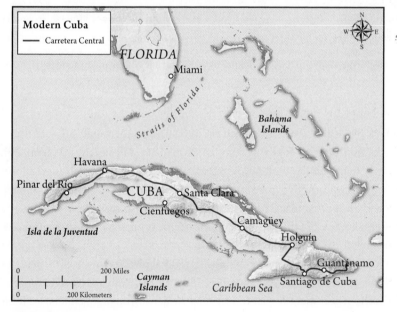

≡ MAP. 12.2

☰ **Street Scene in Havana during the Special Period.** Cuba's Special Period was a time of great deprivation, as Cuba suddenly found itself deprived of the Soviet subsidies that had buoyed the economy for decades. Residents adapted in myriad ways, some of which unexpectedly provided models for new kinds of environmental sustainability, such as urban farming using sophisticated, sustainable methods.

Because Cuba's economy relied on industrial factory-style sugar farming, the production of basic foods became an immediate and urgent problem. Cubans, already long familiar with rationing, watched in dismay as their food allotments continued to diminish in both size and variety. Medicine and medical supplies, formerly imported from the Eastern Bloc, became so scarce that it threatened to undermine one of socialist Cuba's greatest achievements, the internationally recognized healthcare system.

Cubans vividly remember the severe food shortages in the early years of the Special Period. In the scramble for nourishment, Cubans received permission from the government to plant individual gardens in abandoned lots, on rooftops, and in the yards outside the large Soviet-style apartment buildings in which many people lived. Rumors and urban legends abounded of terrible predations—the alleged consumption of animals at the national zoo, for example, or of family pets. At the very least, the austerity forced the average Cuban to exercise (by walking or biking) and to eat, out of necessity, a high-fiber, often vegan diet that actually improved Cuban health overall. Ironically, these everyday accommodations to a dire situation over time made Cuba a public health model for the rest of the high-starch Caribbean. In 2007, the *American Journal of Epidemiology* reported that in Cuba "during 1997–2002, there were declines in deaths attributed to diabetes (51 percent), coronary heart disease (35 percent), stroke (20 percent), and all causes (18 percent)." However, the report also noted an increase in morbidity among the elderly caused by malnutrition.

Indeed, the most radical transformation in Cuba of the Special Period was neither social nor political but agricultural. The end of Soviet-subsidized oil forced a rapid transition from large-scale, state-directed agriculture heavily dependent on petrochemical fertilizers and pesticides to local, dispersed organic production. Even after the failed Ten Million Ton Harvest of 1970, Cuban agriculture was characterized by monoculture and increasing reliance on chemicals and technology. In these respects, at least, state-directed socialist production mirrored developments in capitalist agribusiness elsewhere.

As we have seen, that mode of production came to a crashing halt in Cuba in the early 1990s. Forced to improvise, Cubans began growing their own food in backyard plots and vacant lots, roof gardens, and warehouses. Agriculture moved to the city—there was no gasoline available for trucking produce in from the country. As in any large-scale, uncontrolled experiment, failure rates were high, and nutritional well-being dropped precipitously in the early 1990s. But farmers shared knowledge with each other and with local researchers, and methods improved. Farmers honed practices of natural insect control, drawing on resources like the neem tree, whose crushed leaves deter insects, and deliberate attraction of aphid-killing wasps and beetle-destroying lion ants. By the end of the 1990s, nutritional outcomes exceeded those of many other Latin American countries, where rising agribusiness supposedly promised cheap and ample food. The leaders of Cuban innovation, like the farmer and agrarian scientist Fernando Funes Monzote, hailed the process as "agroecology," a sustainable mode of production that would survive political transition. Funes Monzote completed a PhD in ecological production in the Netherlands, returning to Cuba to found and develop Finca Marta, a model of sustainable agriculture.

Critics pointed out that throughout the Special Period and beyond Cubans remained heavily reliant on food imports for most of their calories. Agroecology, for all its merits, did not produce rice, a vital staple of the Cuban diet. Was Cuban agroecology the global model for post-petrochemical sustainable agriculture, as its practitioners claimed? Or was it a minor curiosity arising from a temporary period of political transition, as critics suggested?

Either way, by 2015 the future of Cuban agroecology as a source of food for most Cubans was in doubt. The phasing-out of the long US blockade once again makes petrochemical fertilizers and pesticides widely available. And the rise of expensive, tourist-oriented organic restaurants risks turning organic agriculture into the same kind of perquisite of affluence that it remains in much of the Western world.

Other Changes during the Special Period

The crisis of the Special Period provoked slow but dramatic changes in the Cuban economy and society and even glacial change in the political system. For example, the popular gardens that people planted to fend off starvation evolved over time into farmers' markets, which the government eventually permitted, even allowing individual farmers to keep some of their own profits—a mixed-economy strategy that marked a dramatic departure from the "all for one and one for all" communist approach. As people became increasingly disillusioned with everyday life on the island and began to seek new solutions to their malaise, the Cuban government slightly loosened its grip on organized religion. It began to tolerate the limited development of small Protestant "house churches" in individual homes, as well as the modest reexpansion of the Catholic Church on the island. This latter initiative gained momentum after the visit of Pope John Paul II to Cuba in 1998.

To bring in new sources of foreign revenue, the Cuban government invested heavily in tourism, permitting capital investment by foreign corporations. The vibrant tourism industry that resulted reintroduced Cuba's beaches and nightclubs to European, African, South American, and Canadian visitors who could freely spend their tourist dollars and euros to see for themselves why Cuba had so long been known as the "Pearl of the Antilles." Regrettably, one prominent aspect of the prerevolutionary vice industry, sex work, also returned during the Special Period, as young Cuban women (and some men) known as *jineteras/jineteros* (horseback riders) coped with the severe shortages and deprivations by selling sexual favors to foreigners.

Yet the Special Period brought little change to certain key areas of Cuban life, especially politics. Because the majority of Cubans had been born after the 1959 Revolution and therefore accepted the all-encompassing, cradle-to-grave communist system, even in the midst of the crisis they (for the most part) did not challenge the regime. Some dissent existed, but it was demonstrated in largely obtuse venues—in music, and in Cuban science fiction (a genre that is popular on the island to an extent that surprises many outsiders). The most dramatic dissent was the attempt by some Cubans to flee the island, risking the shark-infested waters of the Florida Straits on flimsy boats or inner tube rafts (*balsas*—the riders known as *balseros*) to seek the automatic asylum under the Cuban Adjustment Act that would greet them if they could successfully reach the shores of the United States.

For the duration of the Cuban Revolution, which as of this writing is in its sixth decade, prognosticators had predicted that the communist rule would end with either the overthrow or the death of Fidel Castro. But this turned out not to be the case. Even the strains of the Special Period did not impel Cubans to overthrow the regime they had grown up with. In 2006, an ailing Fidel Castro turned the reins of government over to his brother Raúl, with no interruption in the regime. Fidel Castro's death on November 25, 2016 had no immediate effect on the regime.

Under Raúl Castro, the top-down communist government has remained intact, but there has also been a gradual evolution in the restrictive economic and social policies that had defined the regime for more than half a century. Private enterprise has been cautiously expanded, the tourism industry nurtured, and restrictive US-imposed regulations limiting communications and visits of Cuban Americans to the island have been modified. Cubans now have some access to digital social media and, perhaps most significantly, the United States and Cuba reestablished diplomatic relations for the first time in many decades. Without a doubt, many of Cuba's problems endure—for example, political freedom in the country is virtually nonexistent, political prisoners sit in prisons without recourse, and the government is controlled by a seemingly uncontestable communist gerontocracy. But even so, the July 2015 reopening of the embassies of two antagonists after so many years—the US Embassy in Havana and the Cuban Embassy in Washington—seemed to promise the beginning of a new era.

The Sustainable Agricultural Movement in Mexico and Central America

During the 1980s and 1990s, a growing number of experts in countries other than Cuba were worried that the Green Revolution, originally advertised as a means to increase agricultural productivity to feed rapidly expanding and increasingly urban populations, had not fulfilled its promise. In Mexico, the nominal control of communal ejido lands by private landowners exacerbated the effects of the Green Revolution by encouraging the formation of large corporate agricultural entities in the country's most fertile lands, where owners could more efficiently make use of the green technology. In Mexico as well as in Guatemala, Honduras, and Nicaragua, poor subsistence farmers were pushed from their traditional smallholdings on fertile valley floors onto mountainous slopes so that the more productive agrobusinesses could use the flat terrain. Behind these efforts were not only the governments of each country but also USAID, which promoted increased agricultural productivity over land reform. Other stakeholders were the foreign producers of the modified seeds and agricultural chemicals that made the "Green Revolution" possible and which also promised to make these corporations sizable profits.

But the combination of profit-seeking agriculture with the Green Revolution had dire, unanticipated consequences. Monoculture damaged the environment. Cattle pounded the soil hard as bricks, making it impossible for it to absorb moisture, leading to erosion. Even in environmentally sensitive Costa Rica, the expansion of cattle ranching into the northern frontier area quickly decimated old-growth rain forests. Further, the profit motive encouraged large landowners to produce crops for export to US consumers, who demanded fresh fruits and vegetables year around. Because lands once farmed to raise crops for local consumption were now dedicated to exports, these Central American nations each ended up importing heavily subsidized US-grown staples to feed their populations. Despite the Green Revolution, many Latin Americans still went to bed hungry.

The marginal peasant farmers displaced to the hillsides felled trees to create fields and then employed the expensive (and ultimately counterproductive) technology of the Green Revolution on sloped surfaces. In Guatemala, farmers began to till land so steep that one Maya language developed a verb to describe the act of "falling out of" one's field. Crops produced with chemical fertilizers, herbicides, and genetically modified seeds produced diminishing returns when these bare, sloping fields, once covered with forest and shrubs, experienced topsoil runoff and landslides.

By 1972, one agronomist working for a nongovernmental organization (NGO) found a solution. Working in the community of Chimaltenango, Guatemala, the agronomist persuaded a few smallholders to risk a portion of their land to try his sustainable methods. Their early successes persuaded other villagers to follow suit. The result became known as the **campesino a campesino** (farmer to farmer) movement, which promoted sustainable practices that would hopefully lead to "food sovereignty." Farmers learned various practices (some of which dated back to early Mayan agriculture) to make farming on sloped surfaces viable. First, they reduced the angle of slopes by constructing terraces and contour ditches to reshape the land. Applying large quantities of mulch and raising velvet beans (a fast-growing ground cover) retained rainfall and prevented erosion. Reforesting portions of the slopes also minimized rainfall runoff. Knowledge of these various practices spread informally from village to village, as farmers, who had more credibility than foreign experts, voluntarily offered hands-on workshops to their neighbors.

In October 1998, Hurricane Mitch devastated Central America and especially Honduras, drenching the Atlantic coast with 75 inches of rain in five days and

CULTURE AND IDEAS

Latin American Baseball

Baseball, the quintessential "American Pastime," enjoyed considerable popularity among people of all political persuasions in the twentieth century throughout northern Latin America and the Caribbean. Its origins in Latin America are the subject of considerable debate. Although US soldiers (including, allegedly, the inventor of baseball, Abner Doubleday) may have introduced baseball into northern Mexico during the Mexican War, Cubans studying in the United States certainly brought the game home in the 1860s.

From there, the game spread to the Dominican Republic, Mexico's Yucatán Peninsula, Puerto Rico, and Venezuela. Esteban Bellán, who played briefly in the Major Leagues, in 1878 managed the first Cuban professional team, which became the nucleus of the (segregated) Cuban League. Following the conclusion of the Ten Years' War in 1878, Spanish officials attempted to reinforce Cuban cultural loyalty by encouraging attendance at bullfights, but patriotic Cubans instead chose baseball as a symbol of their struggle for freedom. The Cuban League (integrated after 1900) thrived until 1959, when Fidel Castro—who had once aspired to become a professional baseball player himself—outlawed professional sports in Cuba.

Meanwhile, Cubans introduced the sport to Yucatán during the Porfiriato. Early on, wealthy henequen planters organized teams, built diamonds, and provided uniforms and equipment for their squads. During the 1920s, the Revolutionary government, as a means of promoting the popularity of its socialist programs, encouraged workers and even campesinos to play baseball as a healthy form of exercise. So competitive were these teams that visiting Cubans joined the local nines. The teams from Yucatán even occasionally competed against stars from the US Negro League. Baseball spread to most rural parts of Yucatán as the government invested in ballparks everywhere so that Mexicans from all social classes could participate. Yet Yucatán baseball was not simply derivative of the US version. In addition to early innovations like using ten men in the field, local players flavored the games with the Yucatec Mayan language, using phrases like "Conex, conex, jugar béisbol" (Come on, let's play ball).

Because sugar refineries organized the first amateur baseball teams in the Dominican Republic, many Dominicans still refer to the game as "sugarball." During the 1950s, Dominicans developed a league structure and a regular schedule for the winter months, drawing both local talent and US players to the league. As a winter organization, the Dominican League flourished, sending stars like Juan Marichal (an eventual Hall of Famer), David Ortiz, and Vladimir Guerrero to the Major Leagues and providing employment and hope for many other young men seeking alternatives to cutting cane. The success of Dominicans who competed successfully with US players enhanced national pride. Although significant numbers of Dominicans still play in the Major Leagues today, the effects of free agency in the 1980s changed winter ball. High-salaried Dominican stars no longer wanted to play for small wages back home, nor did their employers want them to risk serious injury. Nevertheless, Dominican baseball remains truly Dominican, with its free-spirited style of play conducted in a festive atmosphere.

- Why has baseball (as compared to other imported sports) had such an effect on the people, especially in the Caribbean? What is it about this game in particular that would make it so accessible and popular?

wreaking havoc with the economic and demographic structures to such an extent that its effects still impact the country today. But the storm also provided scientists with an opportunity to test whether these sustainable agriculture methods yielded better results than did conventional farming. While the farmers still using Green Revolution technology experienced landslides and massive soil erosion, those practicing sustainable agriculture fared much better. Experts compared the soils and found that the land farmed with sustainable techniques had retained 30 to 40 percent more topsoil, more moisture, and more vegetation. As a result, the sustainable farms experienced far less erosion than the conventional farms. The remaining question that advocates of sustainable agriculture face today is whether these labor-intensive practices that have worked on small farms can be scaled up to a point where Central American nations can become self-sufficient in the production of food. The hardships Cuba faced upon the loss of industrial farming technology during the Special Period offered additional evidence of the value of sustainable agriculture.

The Late Cold War in the Andes, 1960–2016

Because of the actions of late Cold War guerrillas and their adversaries, two Andean nations, Colombia and Peru, experienced incredible levels of violence during the 1980s and 1990s. Even 170 years after independence, both nations had retained much of their traditional social structure. Colombia's elite had made only modest gestures toward agrarian and labor reform, while much of the top-down change implemented during Peru's authoritarian revolution of the 1970s had come undone because of the country's subsequent economic collapse. Leftist insurgents in each nation took advantage of popular discontent to undertake very different types of guerrilla campaigns.

The FARC and the ELN in Colombia

The late Cold War conflict between Marxist guerrillas and Colombia's government can be traced back to the 1940s, when an aspiring Liberal politician, Jorge Eliécer Gaitán, challenged the more staid members of his party (chapter 8). Gaitán proposed significant social changes, including an expansion of rights for labor unions, women's suffrage, and meaningful agrarian reform. After a term as mayor of Bogotá and a stint as a cabinet member, Gaitán seemed poised to gain the party's presidential nomination and win election to the highest office in the land when he was gunned down in the streets of Bogotá in 1948. Hearing the news of Gaitán's death, his partisans rioted and nearly burned the entire city to the ground but for a providential rainstorm, which doused the blaze. Thereafter, Colombia endured the bitter civil strife known as La Violencia (The Violence), which resulted in more than 300,000 deaths by the early 1960s.

By then, La Violencia had spawned two Marxist revolutionary movements inspired by Fidel Castro's successful revolution in Cuba. The larger group, the **Revolutionary Armed Forces of Colombia (FARC)** led by Manuel "Tirofijo" ("Sureshot")

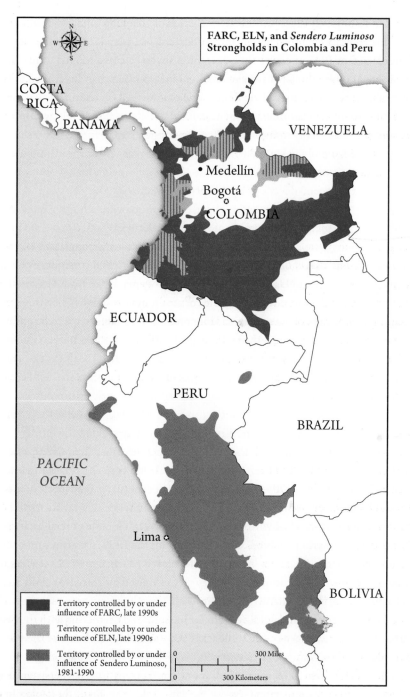

FARC, ELN, and *Sendero Luminoso*
Strongholds in Colombia and Peru

COSTA
RICA

PANAMA

VENEZUELA

• Medellín

Bogotá

COLOMBIA

ECUADOR

PERU

BRAZIL

PACIFIC
OCEAN

Lima ✪

BOLIVIA

Territory controlled by or under
influence of FARC, late 1990s

Territory controlled by or under
influence of ELN, late 1990s

Territory controlled by or under
influence of Sendero Luminoso,
1981-1990

0   300 Miles

0   300 Kilometers

≡ **MAP. 12.2**

Marulanda, dominated the southwestern portion of Colombia along its border with Ecuador. A campesino with little formal education, Marulanda first participated in La Violencia in 1947 and over time became a Soviet-inspired Marxist. Surviving a near-fatal bombardment of his encampment in 1964, Marulanda escaped to the eastern Amazonian region, where he remained as the FARC's nominal leader until his death from heart failure in 2008. Marulanda easily related to fellow campesinos and recruited many to the cause. As a result, the FARC evolved into a serious threat to the Colombian state during the late Cold War years. The FARC would eventually become Latin America's most intractable revolutionary movement, lasting into the second decade of the twenty-first century.

By the 1980s and 1990s, Colombia experienced one of world's highest rates of violent death. The total annual number of violent deaths in Colombia exceeded those of the notoriously violent United States, even though the US population was five times larger than that of Colombia. Even more horrifying was the manner in which people were killed. In addition to dismemberments by machetes, the FARC used its gruesome "necktie" signature (pulling the corpse's tongue through his slit throat) to create fear among the peasantry. With Colombia's army unable to quell the guerrillas, paramilitary forces joined the fray against FARC. The paramilitaries ratcheted up the violence, ultimately causing more deaths than the FARC itself. As elsewhere in the hemisphere, rightwing paramilitaries used anticommunism as a justification for suppression of moderate reformers and expropriation of valuable resources.

The second and smaller guerrilla organization, the National Liberation Army (ELN), controlled the northeastern region of the country along the border with Venezuela. At its peak in 1964, the ELN numbered no more than five thousand fighters, many of whom had been trained in Cuba. Initially the ELN lacked a leader with a magnetic personality like Castro's, though eventually they located one in Father Camilo Torres. The son of an elite family, a Catholic priest, and a highly regarded sociologist who had written extensively about Colombia's social problems, Torres joined the group in 1965. Unfortunately for the ELN, the army ambushed Torres and killed him during his first battle. Nevertheless, the ELN's leadership remained influenced by the liberation theology espoused by Torres for many years to come. By the late Cold War, however, the ELN adopted new tactics: kidnapping US oil executives and holding them for ransom, and partnering with the drug cartels to raise funds. After 2002, the ELN regained visibility because the group received covert assistance from Venezuela's socialist president, Hugo Chávez.

Political scientists have speculated about the reasons for the persistence of Colombia's guerrilla movement during the late Cold War. First, the Colombian electoral system had failed. Apathetic voters (only 40 percent of the population participated in presidential elections during these years) stayed away from the polls in droves. Liberal and Conservative party presidential candidates, many the sons of former presidents, failed to inspire enthusiasm. Because the Colombian army lacked the military might to win the civil war, the government attempted to negotiate with the FARC and the ELN from a position of weakness, not strength. The army and the FARC nominally agreed to an armistice in the 1990s, but the guerrillas took advantage of the temporary peace to secure more territory. Given their successes in the 1980s and 1990s, the optimistic FARC leadership believed that the insurgents had a chance to overthrow the weak Colombian state. Finally, despite the horrendous death rate, most of the violence occurred in rural areas, allowing the urban-based elite and middle class to ignore the bloodbath to some degree. When the guerrillas joined forces with the drug cartels in the late 1980s and the threat of violence increased further, however, Colombians demanded stronger action.

President Alvaro Uribe (2002–2006, and reelected 2006–2010) promised to take the offensive against the guerrillas as part of a new hardline peace policy. Elected on a law-and-order slogan but one with compassion (Firm Hand, Large Heart), the charismatic Uribe immediately dedicated more resources, with additional support from the United States' Plan Colombia initiative. The US president Bill Clinton included an economic aid package in his Plan Colombia as an attempt to curtail drug trafficking and remedy a host of other issues. With progress made against the drug cartels during the 1990s, Uribe proposed to use the funding to combat the guerrillas.

After the terrorist attacks of September 11, 2001, President George W. Bush added Colombia's guerrillas to the list of terrorist organizations and increased the aid package for Plan Colombia. Soon Uribe became one of the United States' closest allies in the "war on terror." For his part, Uribe coupled continuing negotiations with the guerrillas to a requirement that they agree to enter into a cease-fire. By increasing the size of the army from 120,000 to 180,000 soldiers, and the police force from 90,000 to 120,000 officers, the government had the ability to use overwhelming force to seize the offensive and advance into guerrilla-held territory. In addition to Plan Colombia's funds increasing the army's logistical support, US advisors trained the reorganized army in counterinsurgency tactics and helped with operational planning and intelligence gathering, which allowed the army to win most military engagements.

Simultaneously, Uribe proposed new legislation, the Law of Justice and Peace, which would establish the parameters for negotiations. From the outset, the government offered reduced sentences for those guerrillas who surrendered. Uribe first bargained with the paramilitaries (the AUC, or *Autodefensas Unidos de Colombia*) who held the weakest military position. After accepting a cease-fire, the AUC agreed to demobilize their soldiers on the condition that AUC members not be extradited to the United States because of pending drug trafficking charges.

Uribe agreed. Since AUC had never attempted to overthrow the government, the state could more easily compromise on this issue. The ELN, now a small group of between two thousand and five thousand insurgents, proved more resistant to Uribe's proposition. They agreed to remove some antipersonnel mines, but negotiations stalled for a number of reasons, such as ELN's belief that the government also needed to address social issues and because a number of its leaders still believed the guerrillas could defeat the government.

Talks with the FARC, who refused to agree to any cease-fire for years, went nowhere. Nevertheless, the army enjoyed considerable military success against them, rescuing high-value hostages like former presidential candidate Ingrid Betancourt, three US army officers, and a number of Colombian officials. In addition, the Colombian army crossed the border into Ecuador (without Ecuadorian permission) and killed FARC leader Raúl Reyes. With kidnapping and murder rates plummeting, no wonder Uribe enjoyed a 70 percent approval rating in 2010.

The Supreme Court, however, ruled that Uribe could not run for a third term, so his defense minister, Juan Manuel Santos, assumed Uribe's mantle. His Social Party of National Unity, comprised of both Liberals and Conservatives, won a huge majority in 2010 and a much smaller one in 2014, based on promises that Santos would continue Uribe's tough policies against the guerrillas. Despite heavy criticism about what were euphemistically called "false positives" (innocent civilians killed by the army and tallied as dead guerrillas to demonstrate the effectiveness of the military campaign), Santos made slow progress with the negotiations, persuading both the ELN and the FARC to sit down at the negotiating table in Havana, in sessions hosted by Cuba. In large part because of Cuban mediation, FARC agreed in September 2016 to lay down its arms and to form a political party that would compete in elections. When a national referendum rejected the deal, the parties returned to the table and hammered out an agreement that punished FARC members more severely and was in line with popular sentiment. The parties signed the agreement in November 2016. Colombia nevertheless continues to struggle with the challenges of creating a more just society in a nation of drastic inequality recovering from decades of war.

The Shining Path: The Scourge of Peru

Sendero Luminoso (the Shining Path), one of several splinter factions claiming the mantle of the Peruvian Communist Party, burst into public view in a gruesome manner in 1980. Residents of Lima awoke one morning to find dead dogs hanging from streetlamps bearing placards that read "Deng Xiaoping, son of a bitch," in apparent reference to the Chinese leader's recent capitalistic economic reforms in China. This strategy of hanging dogs, designed to terrorize urban dwellers, was a tactic once employed by Mao Zedong in China to symbolize the forthcoming death of tyrants. It also signaled the emergence of Peru's newest leftist insurgency, which would soon distinguish itself for its Maoist (as opposed to Cuban-style Marxist) ideology, its willingness to use extreme violence—even against peasants—to achieve its objectives, and the cultlike fervor that it inspired among its followers.

Earlier that year (an election year, following twelve years of military rule), the Shining Path had officially initiated its revolution virtually unnoticed, stealing and burning ballots and voter lists in the public square of the Andean town of Chuschi, in the department of Ayacucho. The Shining Path's egotistical leader, Abimael Guzmán, who frequently used the nom de guerre Presidente Gonzalo, drew ideological inspiration from Maoism as well as Peru's greatest radical intellectual, José Carlos Mariátegui, whose work argued that socialism in Peru should be built from the collective ownership of land and patterns of political relations practiced by the indigenous people.

Guzmán, the illegitimate son of a successful businessman, had become a philosophy professor and administrator at a regional university in the poor, largely indigenous provincial city of Ayacucho in southern Peru. Soon his "chilling charisma" (several of his students' characterization of him) enabled him to organize the highly disciplined Shining Path faction, into which he recruited faculty and former students, many of whom were now rural schoolteachers. Guzmán acquired the nickname of "Dr. Shampoo" because of his remarkable ability to brainwash his students. As a result, Guzmán and his pupils gained tremendous influence over many communities in the southern highlands of Peru.

During the 1970s Guzmán traveled to China, where the dogma of the Cultural Revolution profoundly influenced him. Demanding ideological purity from his compatriots strengthened party unity, but effectively separated the Shining Path from other Peruvian leftist groups. Unlike other Marxist organizations in Latin America, Sendero rejected the Cuban revolution as a model. Instead of creating a foco of devoted revolutionaries who would proselytize

Lima Policeman Cutting Down Dog Hung by Sendero Luminoso. During the 1980s, Peru fell into widespread violence, as major insurgent groups sought to take over the government and were met with harsh repression by the Peruvian military. The most notorious of these was Sendero Luminoso (Shining Path), a highly violent, Maoist-oriented guerrilla organization formed, organized, and directed by Abimael Guzmán, known to his followers as Presidente Gonzalo. Sendero Luminoso, which advocated a socialist-anarchist philosophy similar to that of the Khmer Rouge in Cambodia of a decade earlier, operated out of the rural province of Ayacucho. They terrorized, murdered, and massacred Peruvian soldiers and apolitical peasants alike. Despite the brutality of Sendero's presence, evinced in this photo by their killing and hanging dogs from Lima's street lamps, they attracted a passionate, even fanatical following among both some indigenous campesinos and also urban leftists. During Sendero's reign of terror, violence in the countryside became so endemic that one-third of the population sought relatively safety by immigrating into the capital city of Lima, putting pressure on the city's resources and completely transforming the city itself.

among the peasantry and bring them into the fold (as Castro had done), Guzmán believed in Mao's doctrine of "churning up the countryside"—destroying everything that predated his revolution in order to start anew. With the military in power during the 1970s, Guzmán had kept his Maoist organization underground, perfecting his plans. When democracy returned to Peru in 1980, Guzmán proposed to use Maoist tactics in rural areas before converging onto the cities with his forces and eventually taking over the national government. His wife and second-in command, Augusta de la Torre, convinced him that the time had come to take action, and so Sendero turned from planning to unleashing violence.

Armed with dynamite stolen from mines, Sendero cadres occupied rural communities and dispensed rudimentary justice with "popular trials" that offered the poorest campesinos an opportunity for revenge against their oppressors. In addition to killing local elites, Shining Path groups executed cattle thieves, drunks, and perpetrators of domestic violence as well as corrupt police officers and officials. In a reversal of typical revolutionary models of collectivization, the guerrillas broke up the unpopular cooperatives that the Velasco government had established and granted campesinos individual plots instead.

Particularly in the movement's latter years, women played an important role in the organization. At first, traditional patriarchy prevailed, as women were limited to tasks such as teachers of ideology and healers, but as the rebellion progressed they became as involved as men in military roles. In fact, young women (and young people in general) were often assigned some of the most brutal tasks, such as assassinating local officials and executing prisoners. Because of the lack of opportunity caused by the depressed economy of the 1980s, young people in search of their own identity were initially drawn to Sendero. When Sendero began recruiting children as young as eight into their ranks, however, many mothers resisted and no longer looked on the guerrillas favorably. Even so, for those who subscribed to its tenets, Sendero Luminoso instilled a deep, even fanatical loyalty, and "Presidente Gonzalo" acquired a nearly superhuman, mythic status to his many followers.

Initially, Peru's government believed Sendero to be a minor irritant. By 1983, however, Sendero actually seized territory in southern and central Peru. The army dispatched patrols into the mountain villages and killed those suspected of being Sendero sympathizers in actions much like the dirty wars concurrently taking place in El Salvador and Guatemala. Those who were not killed were sent to high-security prisons, where Sendero prisoners organized highly disciplined cadres and recruited heavily for their movement.

Back in the countryside, Sendero executed thousands of campesinos who they believed had betrayed their cause. The violence reached its peak in 1983 and 1984, with villagers torn between guerrillas and the army. When Sendero retreated to protect itself instead of defending the villages against the army, campesinos allied themselves with the military, recognizing that the Peruvian army possessed superior force. In addition, many villages formed self-defense committees that patrolled their communities to protect against Sendero's violent retribution. In this midst of this violence, the electorate chose the unknown political outsider Alberto Fujimori as president in 1990, rejecting author Mario Vargas Llosa, who had campaigned with a platform emphasizing economic liberalism.

The Shining Path embodied a number of contradictions that made its seizure of power at the national level ultimately impossible. Guzmán's dogmatic, uncompromising ideology held the party organization together, but his ruthless tactics against all who disagreed with his ideas prevented the formation of a broader, unified leftist coalition that might have achieved a successful outcome for the revolution. Sendero's insistence on the destruction of Peruvian society and starting afresh offered no pragmatic reforms that would have appealed to campesinos once their thirst for revenge against their oppressors had been satisfied. In fact, because most of Sendero's leaders were mestizo intellectuals, their espousal of extreme violence eventually led campesinos to equate them with *pistachos*, the white vampire-like bogeyman suspected since colonial times of killing indigenous people to carve them up and sell their fat.

At odds with Andean customs, Sendero killed senior village mayors and replaced them with youthful Senderistas. Guzmán's puritanical forbiddance of fiestas, drinking, and local rituals upended local customs. Sendero blew up bridges and roads and prevented villagers from getting their goods to markets, which meant that many families' standard of living worsened under Sendero rule. Tens of thousands of Peruvians fled to Lima to escape the violence; during the 1980s, sociologists estimate that up to one-third of Peru's total rural population relocated to the capital city. Between 1980 and 1990, violence forced at least 200,000 rural Peruvians from their homes, especially in the Sendero-permeated Ayacucho department.

As many as 69,000 Peruvians, most of them indigenous, died in the violence. A 2003 Truth and Reconciliation Commission attributed a slight majority of the deaths to the Sendero, ascribing most of the rest to the Peruvian military itself. Not only did Sendero's belief in an autonomous, self-reliant agricultural society without markets impoverish campesino families but it proved anachronistic in the late twentieth century. Finally, Sendero never appealed to labor unions, and in a society that had become increasingly urbanized, this failure limited their support in cities. Even in the barriadas (the vast shantytowns on the edges of Lima), Sendero lost even more favor when it violently attacked women's organizations that failed to follow the guerrillas' rules.

Clever detective work ended the Sendero's reign of terror in September 1992. Because Guzmán suffered from a medical condition that made living at high altitude difficult, authorities suspected that he was hiding somewhere in the sub-urbs of Lima. Tracking him down had proven difficult because few recent photo-graphs of him existed. Fortunately for the police, they knew that Guzmán suffered from a severe case of psoriasis, a skin disease that presents as an itchy red rash. A detective in the special police unit charged with finding Guzmán noticed an un-usual quantity of trash, including numerous tubes of an ointment specifically pre-scribed for psoriasis, outside a suburban dance studio. Shortly thereafter, Peruvian security forces captured Guzmán there without incident, along with his computer and Sendero's organizational archive.

≡ **Abimael Guzmán in Prison.** The jail cell of Manuel Rubén Abimael Guzmán Reynoso, also known as Presidente Gonzalo, the founder of Peru's violent armed revolutionary movement, the Shining Path (Sendero Luminoso). Guzmán, a former philosophy professor, was captured in May 1992 by Peruvian security forces, who found him in a Lima safe house after they discovered large numbers of tubes of a medication to treat psoriasis, a condition from which Guzmán was known to suffer, in the trash. After his arrest, Guzmán was sentenced to life in prison. His arrest and sentence did not bring Sendero Luminoso to an end, but did cause the group to splinter and retreat. Today, "Presidente Gonzalo" remains incarcerated in a maximum-security prison in Callao, the port of Lima, an area that Sendero Luminoso once dominated through terror and regular bombings.

SOCIAL UPHEAVAL

Mario Vargas Llosa Contextualizes the Shining Path

Peru's Nobel Prize–winning novelist and unsuccessful presidential candidate in 1990, Mario Vargas Llosa, explores Andean Peru's fascinating culture in his insightful novel, *Death in the Andes*. The novel is told from the perspective of two policemen from the coast, Corporal Lituma and his subordinate Tomás Carreño, who have been posted to the small town of Naccos to protect a crew building a road through the mountains from the Shining Path. Over the course of the novel, Lituma and Carreño's eyes are opened to contrasting experiences with violent death in the Andes, two forms of which are traditional and rational (once the two understand local culture) and the third of which (the methods of the Shining Path) is barbaric and irrational.

As the plot unfolds, Lituma explores a series of mysterious deaths in Naccos. Ultimately he discovers that a gang of drunken road workers, goaded on by a witch, sacrificed three of their colleagues to the *apu*, or mountain spirit, in order to guarantee the workers' safety. These three died just like sacrificial victims did in pre-Hispanic Incan times; feted and plied with alcohol and treated like a king for a night, before being slain on the mountain. In fact, the sacrifice succeeds in its purpose; all the workers mysteriously survive an avalanche that buries their camp. Other people from Naccos meet their deaths at the hands of a rampaging pishtaco, the pale-skinned bogeyman. The pishtaco had lured village women back to his cave, where he slit their throats and roasted them over a fire to extract their fat, used in contemporary times to make tractors run smoothly or as rocket fuel.

Vargas Llosa contrasts these traditional causes of unnatural deaths to the more ominous, chilling murders perpetrated by the Shining Path. Sendero strikes on several occasions during the course of the novel, casting a pall of fear among miners, road workers, police, and ordinary citizens. Sendero's soldiers seem immune to human feelings and are deaf to reason and logic. For example, Vargas Llosa conveys the cold, ruthless nature of a Sendero patrol following its seizure of the village of Andamarca. Immediately the town's officials and merchants, as well as former soldiers, thieves, drunks, and whores are placed on trial. Poor campesinos are offered the opportunity to seek revenge by testifying against those who exploited them, culminating in death sentences or severe beatings for most of the accused. In another instance, Sendero captures the environmentalist Señora d'Harcourt, who has refused a military escort as she travels into rebel-held territory to inspect a reforestation project designed to assist the poor. Her captors refuse to listen to any of her explanations about her scientific work or the benefits she has selflessly provided Peru over her lengthy career, and condemn her to a barbarous death by bashing in her head with stones. Vargas Llosa uses the novel to expose the senseless brutality of the Shining Path.

- How did the Shining Path's methods assist or detract from their revolutionary effort?

In custody, the once terrifying Presidente Gonzalo had no compunction about selling out his comrades. He provided names and addresses of his collaborators, who were immediately rounded up by the police. All of the principal leaders of the Sendero Luminoso received life sentences because of their brutal late Cold War rebellion.

Conclusion

The 1980s ended with the shattering of revolutionary dreams. In Central America, hundreds of thousands of ordinary citizens had died in the armed conflicts, all of which ended without solving the fundamental problems that had caused the guerrillas to take up arms in the first place. Nicaragua, the only nation in Latin America to even come close to approximating the Cuban experience, voted out its revolution in 1989 after a decade of US-backed resistance against the Sandinistas. Meanwhile, Cuba managed to retain most of its revolutionary principles, even during the troubled Special Period. In South America, while Marxist guerrillas fought on in Colombia, Peru's experience with Maoist guerrillas ended quite suddenly in 1992, in large part because the Shining Path seemed as intent on terrorizing the population it allegedly represented as it did on bringing down the Peruvian state.

And yet, peace did come to Latin America, and the Cold War finally came to an end. Whereas in the mid-1970s, two-thirds of Latin American countries were in the hands of military governments and suffering from some sort of armed conflict, by the mid-1980s, military governments were ceding power to freely elected civilian presidents in one country after the next. By the end of the decade, Argentina, Chile, Brazil, Bolivia, Uruguay, Paraguay, Guatemala, Nicaragua, Honduras, and El Salvador had all returned to civilian government. Unfortunately, as we shall see in the next chapter, the transition to civil society during the "lost decade" of the 1980s would create a new set of challenges for Latin Americans.

KEY TERMS

campesino a campesino   564

Christian Base Communities   538

contras   544

Esquipulas Accords   553

Frente Faribundo Martí de Liberación Nacional   550

La violencia   555

Liberation Theology   536

National Revolutionary Unity   554

Reagan Doctrine   536

Revolutionary Armed Forces of Columbia (FARC)   566

Sandinista Front (FSLN)   542

Sandinista insurrection   539

Sendero Luminoso (Shining Path)   570

The Special Period   559

TIMELINE

1979
Sandinistas overthrow Somoza dictatorship in Nicaragua

1980
Assassination of Archbishop Oscar Arnulfo Romero in El Salvador (March)

1980
Shining Path begins its revolution in Peru

1981
El Mozote massacre, El Salvador

1980
Ronald Reagan elected president of the United States

1980
Murder of American churchwomen in El Salvador (December)

1981
US-sponsored contra war begins in Nicaragua

Selected Readings

Angel, Adrianna, and Fiona Macintosh. *The Tiger's Milk: Women of Nicaragua*. New York: Henry Holt, 1987.

Berryman, Phillip. *The Religious Roots of Rebellion: Christians in the Central American Revolutions*. Maryknoll, NY: Orbis Press, 1984.

Danner, Mark. *The Massacre at El Mozote*. New York: Vintage Books, 1994.

Garrard-Burnett, Virginia. *Terror in the Land of the Holy Spirit: Guatemalan under General Efraín Ríos Montt, 1982–1983*. New York: Oxford University Press, 2010.

Grandin, Greg. *The Last Colonial Massacre: Latin America in the Cold War*. Chicago: University of Chicago Press, 2004.

Guillermoprieto, Alma. *The Heart That Bleeds*. New York: Vintage Books, 1995.

Isbester, Katherine. *Still Fighting: The Nicaraguan Women's Movement, 1977–2000*. Pittsburgh, PA: University of Pittsburgh Press, 2001.

Kline, Harvey F. *Showing Teeth to the Dragons: State-Building by Colombian President Alvaro Uribe Vélez, 2002–2006*. Tuscaloosa: University of Alabama Press, 2009.

MacQuarrie, Kim. *Life and Death in the Andes: On the Trail of Bandits, Heroes, and Revolutionaries*. New York: Simon & Schuster, 2015.

Palmer, David Scott. *The Shining Path of Peru*. New York: St. Martin's Press, 1994.

Rabe, Stephen G. *The Killing Zone: The United States Wages Cold War in Latin America*. New York: Oxford University Press, 2011.

Stern, Steve J., ed. *Shining and Other Paths: War and Society in Peru, 1980–1995*. Durham, NC: Duke University Press, 1998.

Walker, Thomas W., and Christine J. Wade. *Nicaragua: Living in the Shadow of the Eagle*. 5th ed. Boulder, CO: Westview Press 2011.

Vargas Llosa, Mario. *Death in the Andes*. New York: Farrar, Straus and Giroux, 1996.

1982–1983
General Efraín Ríos Montt conducts scorched earth campaign in Guatemala

1990
Sandinistas concede presidential elections to Violeta Barrios de Chamorro

1992
Abimael Guzmán captured, Shining Path revolt fizzles

1991
Dissolution of Soviet Union, and beginning of Cuba's Special Period

1992
Peace Accords signed for El Salvador, ending civil war

1996
Peace Accords signed for Guatemala, ending civil war

13

Neoliberalism and Its Discontents, 1980–2015

Global Connections

The early 1990s were the apex of post–Cold War Western triumphalism. The fall of the Berlin Wall in November of 1989 and the collapse and dissolution of the Soviet Union in December of 1991 seemed to many in the Western world to herald a period of peace and prosperity. Pundits and policy makers described the United States as "the world's sole superpower" and spoke of a **Washington Consensus**, which emphasized a stable system of nation-states defined by commitment to political democracy, free markets, and capitalism. China's rapid and surprising embrace of free enterprise and rapid economic growth spoke volumes about the changing world order. Some observers went so far as to declare that the victory of Western democracy over state socialism marked what some scholars called the "end of history," resolving debates about the nature and duties of the state that had begun in classical Greece.

A key component of the Washington Consensus was that national central banks remain independent of partisan interference, establishing sound economic policy immune to short-term vicissitudes. These central banks were expected to adopt the prescriptions of the **International Monetary Fund (IMF)** and the **World Bank**, dictating privatization of large state enterprises and the pursuit of foreign direct investment for domestic development. To supporters, the Washington Consensus seemed to promise untrammeled growth nurtured by economists acting above the messy realm of electoral politics.

The consensus soon showed itself to be more an illusion than reality. Within Latin America, the technocratic prescriptions of the IMF and World Bank advisers recalled the impositions of Porfírio Díaz's científicos a hundred years earlier. Critics saw the Washington Consensus as a subterfuge for a new US empire, one where wealth accrued to metropolitan bankers while the common folk struggled to stay afloat. To those on the wrong side of growing inequality, history appeared to be repeating itself, rather than ending.

The Washington Consensus lasted only a few years. The dissolution of the Soviet Union had seemed to represent the triumph of liberal Western capitalism over the state-directed economies of socialism and communism. But pell-mell Russian privatization over the course of the 1990s unleashed a frenzy of corruption and crony capitalism, as those with favorable connections amassed extensive assets and wealth at the expense of most of the population. China, by contrast, took a path of state-controlled capitalism that they called "socialist modernization". This

≡ **Pavão, a Favela in Rio de Janeiro, 1985.** This photo shows that by the mid-1980s many favelas in Rio de Janeiro had ceased to be clusters of precarious shacks and had become consolidated urban neighborhoods, characterized by multistory, cinderblock construction and electric networks. But residents built nearly everything themselves. Only in very rare cases did the state government invest in favela urbanization, as in this cable car. Two years later, the cable car fell into disrepair, and the new state administration refused to provide maintenance. The cable car ceased to operate. Residents were still on their own.

involved the privatization of certain agricultural industries and industries, a shift from heavy industrial production to consumer products, and investment in knowledge economies, all negotiated through and for the state. China's steady growth under Jiang Zenin's leadership, averaging 9.7 percent per annum in GDP between 1998 and 2000, offered a healthy alterative for foreign investors, as did the enormous supply of cheap labor that China provided. Massive development projects like the Three Gorges Dam, a monumental hydroelectric project that forced relocation for a million Chinese villagers and walled off the Yangtze River, heralded spectacular economic advances but outraged environmentalists, even within China. Similarly, the destruction of Beijing's traditional and unique *hutong* alleys and *siheyuan* courtyard houses to make way for block-style apartments and factories signaled the government's willingness to privilege economic development over China's cultural heritage.

Relatively controlled experiments in reducing tariffs and opening economies to foreign trade produced their own challenges. The European Union (EU), initially established in 1992 and then steadily expanded over the next decade, aspired to facilitate the free movement of people, goods, services, and capital across member nations. The EU created a powerful trade bloc, triggering economic growth and migration. But even the rule-bound, parliamentarian liberalism of the EU created new inequalities. Germany rose to a position of economic dominance within the EU. Less industrialized nations like Spain, Portugal, and Greece, in contrast, experienced an initial flurry of speculative growth, and then stagnated, sinking into dependence on EU subsidies. Such challenges suggested that trade liberalization could produce short-term growth, but turning short-term growth into long-term equitable and sustainable development required other institutions and protections.

The resurgence of ethnic hostilities in the aftermath of the dissolution of the Soviet Union also challenged the notion that the Washington Consensus offered a stable path to global relations. In 1991, war erupted in the Balkan Peninsula among new nations created from the ruins of the dissolved Yugoslavia, a former client-state of the Soviet Union. Unable to survive on its own, Yugoslavia was soon torn apart by issues that would come to define the early twenty-first century: sectarianism, tribalism, ethnic rivalry, and religious hatred. The breakup of Yugoslavia showed that the stable system of nation-states was easier to sketch on paper than to preserve, as the new nations of Bosnia, Croatia, Herzegovina, Montenegro, Slovenia, Macedonia, and the autonomous province of Kosovo plunged into prolonged, multilateral conflict. Ethnic "nationalisms" in the former Yugoslavia boiled over into a genocidal war that reached its nadir in the early 1990s, in the Bosnian Serbs "ethnic cleansing" campaign that took place in the town of Srebrenica,

Bosnia-Herzegovina. Bosnian Serbs executed more than 8,000 Bosniak (Bosnian Muslim) men and boys, and ordered mass expulsion of another 25,000–30,000 Bosniak civilians.

Similar conflicts exacted terrible tolls in Indonesia, Rwanda, and across the Middle East. Wherever nation-states and the presence of international bodies like the United Nations or the North Atlantic Treaty Organization were weak, local ethnic conflicts risked tilting into full-scale genocide. Rwanda was the deadliest case of all. In 1994, ethnic conflict broke out between Rwanda's two main tribal and ethnic groups, the Hutus (the majority population) and the Tutsis (the country's largest minority). The Hutus launched a genocidal campaign against the Tutsi that killed as many as 70 percent of the Tutsi population in just over three months' time. An estimated 800,000 Rwandans—nearly 20 percent of the nation—were killed during the 100-day period from April 7 to mid-July 1994. Because rape was used as a tactic of humiliation, many women survivors found themselves both as widows and pregnant with the children of their hated attackers. In the aftermath of the slaughter, more than two million Hutus were themselves displaced and became refugees. Like many other fratricidal bloodbaths that took place in this period, Rwanda's terrible conflict had no winners. Latin America, where dictatorships were being replaced by elected government, long-standing armed conflicts in Central America were winding down, and Cuba was going it alone after the fall of the Soviet Union, seemed peaceful by comparison.

Despite the failure of the Washington Consensus' claims to bring peace, its influence as a set of economic prescriptions grew stronger through the end of the twentieth century. These prescriptions constituted an ideology of their own, one commonly described as "neoliberalism." That term often seemed misplaced in the United States, where "liberal" was commonly understood to describe policies that increased federal government spending and oversight. Neoliberal policies, in contrast, required cutting government spending and employment and reducing trade barriers. To Latin Americans, however, the term made intuitive sense, as "liberal" in Latin America—particularly at the nineteenth-century apogee of Latin American Liberalism—had always referred to economic policies that emphasized private property, free trade, and political representation based on individual voting rights, rather than collective rights. The new liberals of the twentieth century—the neoliberals—prescribed this same regime, with a greater emphasis on free trade than on political rights. As in the nineteenth century, the "new liberalism" was beset by tensions. Voting rights expanded and old political oligarchies broke down, but inequality increased in the face of fiscal crisis and rapidly implemented "shock" reforms. International investors seemed to be reaping all the profits of neoliberal

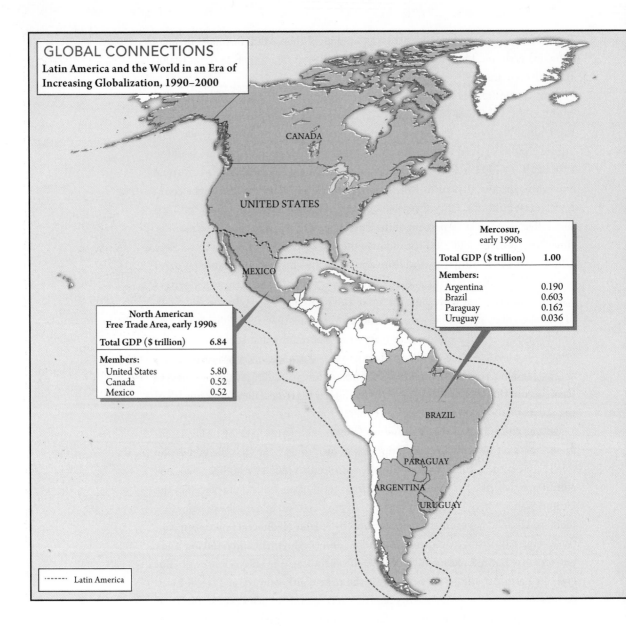

GLOBAL CONNECTIONS
Latin America and the World in an Era of Increasing Globalization, 1990–2000

Mercosur, early 1990s	
Total GDP ($ trillion)	1.00
Members:	
Argentina	0.190
Brazil	0.603
Paraguay	0.162
Uruguay	0.036

North American Free Trade Area, early 1990s	
Total GDP ($ trillion)	6.84
Members:	
United States	5.80
Canada	0.52
Mexico	0.52

CANADA

UNITED STATES

MEXICO

BRAZIL

PARAGUAY

ARGENTINA

URUGUAY

------- Latin America

reforms, while common people in Latin America—and around the world more broadly—awaited its promised benefits in vain.

Neoliberalism often marched hand in hand with globalization, the trend toward more complex and encompassing networks of trade, communications, and migration encircling the globe. If neoliberalism appeared as a set of powerful but hotly

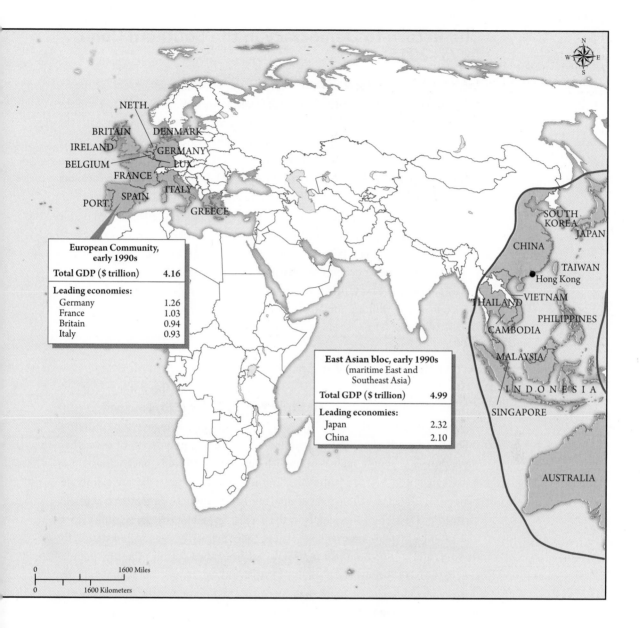

European Community, early 1990s

Total GDP ($ trillion)	4.16
Leading economies:	
Germany	1.26
France	1.03
Britain	0.94
Italy	0.93

East Asian bloc, early 1990s
(maritime East and Southeast Asia)

Total GDP ($ trillion)	4.99
Leading economies:	
Japan	2.32
China	2.10

debated policy initiatives, globalization seemed like an irresistible tide. Latin Americans had long understood that their lives were deeply affected by decisions made in Washington, London, and Madrid. By the early 2000s, they were keenly aware that their lives were also affected by decisions made in Beijing, Brussels, and Riyadh.

The Return to Democracy in the Southern Cone, 1975–2015

Latin America served as the first test case for the Washington Consensus. The region's proximity to the Washington, DC, headquarters of the World Bank and the New York headquarters of the International Monetary Fund, together with the United States' history of imposing its plans on the region, made Latin America the obvious target for early implementation. The crisis of right-wing authoritarian regimes in the Southern Cone opened the door not only to democratic reform but also to a larger reconsideration of the relationship between state and citizen. Further, a crippling debt crisis rippled across the region in the 1980s, weakening the ability of Latin American nations to resist the demands of international creditors. As a result, despite the return to democracy in the region in the 1980s, counterproductive neoliberal economic measures often hampered the emergence of a more egalitarian society. These transitions played out most clearly in the Southern Cone, where military dictatorships relinquished power to civilian regimes in Brazil, Argentina, Uruguay, and Chile in the 1980s.

Argentina's Dirty War Ends

Argentina's return to democracy was directly linked to the military regime's ill-fated gamble in the 1982 **Malvinas War**. Las Islas Malvinas, known to the English-speaking world as the Falkland Islands, lie approximately three hundred miles off Argentina's southern coast and are home to a population of fewer than three thousand people, mainly of English descent. The islands, once important as a strategic outpost for the British fleet in the South Atlantic, today are mainly dependent on sheep and the export of wool and meat products. Argentina had briefly claimed possession of the islands in the 1820s, but Great Britain seized them in 1833 and had held them ever since, using them primarily as a coaling station for its ships and a launching pad for South Atlantic naval patrols. The tiny population of the islands consisted entirely of British citizens. Argentine schoolchildren, however, had long been taught that the British domination of the Malvinas was a nefarious relic of imperial rule.

With the military regime's popularity waning as evidence of torture and economic ineptitude mounted, Argentina seized the Malvinas on April 2, 1982, hoping to trigger an outpouring of nationalist support. The regime thought that a weakened United Kingdom would give up the remote Malvinas without a fight, that the United States would recognize the Argentine claim, and that fellow Latin American nations would pledge their support. This was a costly miscalculation, proving that the dictatorship had become a violent, irrational echo chamber. Initially, Argentines greeted the April 1982 invasion of the islands with patriotic jubilation. But the regime was wrong about everything else: The British did not relinquish the islands, indeed resolving to defend their claim with full force. Prime Minister Margaret Thatcher—rapidly becoming a neoliberal icon herself—moved quickly to oust the Argentines. Ronald Reagan, Thatcher's friend and fellow neoliberal, backed her completely. Other nations cut off relations with Argentina, exacerbating its economic woes. (Chile supported the British, while Brazil remained neutral.)

On May 2, 1982, the British Navy sank the *Belgrano*, an Argentine troop ship returning from the Malvinas to the mainland, killing over 320 Argentine soldiers. The British then retook the islands themselves with relatively few casualties. By mid-June, the short-lived but hotly contested war was over, with British dominion over the Malvinas fully restored. The Argentine dictatorship unsuccessfully attempted to suppress news of the catastrophic defeat. In the wake of the humiliating Malvinas affair, the regime was forced to cede power. Over the course of 1983, it legalized political parties, restored freedom of the press, and presided over elections. Civilian President Raúl Alfonsín of the Radical Civic Union (UCR) took office in December 1983. The UCR was historically Argentina's liberal party, but Alfonsín had neither the strength nor the inclination to impose neoliberal austerity measures. Instead, he did what every other Latin American head of state was doing in the mid-1980s: He borrowed money from the IMF as fast as he could. Argentina emerged from the dark tunnel of military dictatorship to find itself on the dizzying roller coaster of hyperinflation and spiraling debt.

Brazil's Return to Democracy

General Ernesto Geisel was inaugurated president of Brazil in March of 1974, the fourth general in succession to hold the office. Geisel took the reins of a regime at the peak of its power. Its economic policies, designed to stoke the consumer power of Brazil's middle class, had proven successful in the short term. The regime's repression of the opposition had driven political opponents into hiding or exile. And its developmentalist initiatives, such as settling the Amazon and building hydroelectric dams throughout the nation, were sufficiently new that their pitfalls were not immediately obvious.

This momentum notwithstanding, evidence of the regime's reliance on torture and of corruption in military ranks posed problems. Geisel, who recognized the corrosive effects of prolonged rule on the military itself, began a gradual process of *abertura*, or opening, designed to restore civilian rule. But Geisel would not be hurried. As a beginning, he offered only mild *distensão* (decompression), without setting any schedule for a return to civilian rule.

In the meantime, Geisel accelerated state-led development, particularly in the energy sector. As a former president of Petrobras, Brazil's state oil company, Geisel knew Brazil could not overcome its dependence on foreign oil without new sources of energy. He invested heavily in ethanol production and nuclear power. The regime's support for ethanol led to the massive expansion of sugar cultivation in Brazil, now destined primarily for automotive fuel rather than food or beverages. Ethanol incentives also reshaped Brazil's growing automotive industry, subsidizing production of ethanol-fueled cars. Nuclear energy, by comparison, never fulfilled Geisel's aspirations for energy independence. Both ventures required heavy borrowing on international markets at floating interest rates, often in loans that were backed by the IMF—a recourse that would come back to haunt Brazil.

Civilian discontent soon strained the process of abertura. In October 1975, military agents in São Paulo detained journalist Vladimir Herzog for questioning. Although a member of the Brazilian Communist Party, Herzog was a moderate on the spectrum of Brazil's underground left-wing opposition. The Communist Party had opposed guerrilla resistance to the regime, favoring "popular front" activism, operating within civil society. Herzog was a news director for a São Paulo public television station who had never challenged the regime. Brazilians were shocked when military agents claimed he had hanged himself and produced a grotesquely posed photograph which showed Herzog's corpse suspended from a cord tied to the barred window of his cell with his feet on the floor, his bent knees only inches from the ground. It was obvious to all that no man could have hanged himself in such a position.

The assassination of Herzog showed that a hard line within the regime refused to countenance redemocratization. When the photograph became public, it triggered a wave of revulsion against military rule. Herzog's death gave the lie to any naive belief that the military would go quietly. Brazilians would have to achieve democracy on their own.

Civil Society Mobilization and the End of the Dictatorship

Neither of the two political parties permitted by the Brazilian military regime offered a likely venue for that mobilization. The right-wing ARENA (Alliance for National Renovation) remained supportive of the dictatorship. The centrist MDB (Democratic Movement of Brazil) had only cautiously begun a process of contestation. The military government, meanwhile, had persecuted radical underground cells nearly to extinction. Instead, opposition fermented in Brazil's civil society—indeed, it was opposition to the military regime that began to give shape and meaning to that civil society.

There were two main fronts for this mobilization. The first emerged among automotive factory workers in São Paulo's industrial suburbs. These factories had been among the direct beneficiaries of military policies. But when inflation started to climb as a result of relaxed monetary policies and rising oil prices, even well-employed factory workers felt the squeeze: government-controlled unions did little to secure wage adjustments, and workers found their real pay shrinking. In 1978, automotive workers broke with the government unions, staging an independent strike. Five hundred thousand workers walked out, making leader Luiz Inácio da Silva—known to all by his nickname, Lula—the most visible face of a growing opposition. The automotive workers soon found support among both liberation theology activists and university students and faculty, helping to build the strike into a movement.

The other prominent opposition front resulted from a national movement to create additional urban housing. After a few failed experiments with housing projects in the mid-1960s, the dictatorship had cut support for public housing. In the meantime, the regime subsidized middle-class demand through military and white-collar pension institutes. Apartment towers catering to the middle class and elites mushroomed in cities like São Paulo, Rio de Janeiro, and Recife, squeezing out previous residents. The working poor found little option other than precarious self-built homes in **favelas**, lacking property titles and legal protection. Leaders among these communities used the political thaw of the late 1970s to press for urban popular housing and to organize resistance against the eviction of residents in self-built homes. As with the automotive workers' strike, this urban

≡ **Luis Inácio Lula da Silva.** Lula and the PT (Partido dos Trabalhadores) transformed Brazilian politics in the last two decades of the twentieth century and the first decade of the twenty-first. Lula was born to an impoverished family in Brazil's northeast, then made his way into the working class as a metalworker and union leader in São Paulo during the military dictatorship. He emerged as the most visible leader in the PT during the process of redemocratization in the early 1980s. After three unsuccessful attempts, he reached the presidency in 2002. His two-term presidency coincided with a commodities boom, which helped Lula to expand redistributive government programs dramatically. The commodities bust faced by his successor provoked political crisis, revealing that Lula and the PT had made it possible for a Brazilian of humble birth to reach the presidency, but had not solved other deeply ingrained problems of Brazilian politics. This 1982 photo shows Lula early in his political career, a migrant from the poor northeast to the industrialized southeast, with many miles of rail behind him, and many more to come.

housing movement also found support among university activists and progressive Catholics, stitching together a civil society network of opposition.

The automotive workers and the popular housing activists were not alone. By the end of the 1970s, a host of identity-based movements began joining forces to call for an end to the dictatorship. Women's organizations, gay rights groups, indigenous rights associations and the Movimento Negro Unificado (Unified Black Movement) all challenged military rule, offering new previous conceptions of what it meant to be a Brazilian citizen. A pluralistic, contentious civil society began to emerge from the confines of the military dictatorship.

In 1979, a sharp spike in oil prices triggered a new round of inflation. In the short term, it forced the regime to make some concessions to the growing opposition. In 1980, the dictatorship allowed for the formation of new political parties. The industrial workers' movement of São Paulo coalesced behind the new *Partido dos Trabalhadores*, or Labor Party (PT), with Lula da Silva as its best-known politician. In Rio de Janeiro, the popular housing movement backed formerly exiled politician Leonel Brizola and his new Democratic Workers' Party (PDT). Both the PT and the PDT scrambled to establish national networks. These two parties would provide structure to the Brazilian left for the next twenty years.

In 1982, the regime allowed democratic gubernatorial elections for the first time since 1960. Opposition candidates won several states, including a victory for Leonel Brizola in Rio de Janeiro. Popular support for the regime was dwindling fast. The next two years witnessed the largest democratic mobilization in Brazilian history, as hundreds of thousands of citizens took to the streets to demand "Diretas Já," or direct elections (for the president), *now*. The *Diretas Já* campaign put the regime on notice, but not succeed in forcing the dictatorship to preside over free, democratic presidential elections. Instead, the regime allowed a carefully controlled election in a supervised electoral college. A coalition of opposition parties won, electing the political veteran Tancredo Neves as president in January of 1985. Through a series of complex backstage machinations, Neves was forced to accept José Sarney, a longtime supporter of the military regime, as his running mate.

In one of the tragic ironies of Brazilian politics, an exhausted Neves campaigned himself to his deathbed. Neves died without taking office. Instead it was Sarney, political child of the dictatorship, who took office as Brazil's first civilian president in a generation. Sarney's inauguration made clear that Brazil's transition to democracy would not be easy.

Chile after Pinochet: Democracy, Economic Growth, and Justice

Once democracy was restored in Chile in 1989, Chileans wrestled with three major policy questions. First, the new government needed to revitalize Chile's democratic tradition while maintaining harmonious relations with the military, particularly the prickly General Pinochet. Although no longer head of state, Pinochet was still commander-in-chief of the army. Second, the government had to make cautious progress remedying the human rights abuses of the Pinochet years without provoking another coup. It sought to uncover the truth about the government's atrocities, provide reparations to the families of the victims, and (at a later date) to bring to justice the perpetrators. Third, politicians agreed to continue the country's economic growth under a neoliberal, free market model, in part because the system had brought Chile economic prosperity and in part because of the constraints imposed by the Constitution of 1980, which enshrined economic liberalism and the sanctity of private property.

The leaders of the parties that led the "No" campaign against Pinochet in the 1988 plebiscite (mostly Christian Democrats and "reformed" Socialists—moderates who followed the nonviolent path of European socialism) governed under the principle that Chilean politics needed to be pragmatic and moderate, not ideological. This center-left "Coalition of Parties for Democracy," originally called the *Concertación*, agreed to slowly modify the "protected democracy" mandated by Pinochet's Constitution of 1980 to make it more democratic and easier to amend. The center-right opposition, which had formed the "Alliance for Chile" coalition, or the Alianza, accepted this principle as well. (These two coalitions have changed their names several times, but for the sake of clarity this text continues to use their original names.)

The Concertación made only incremental changes in the political system until 2005, when Pinochet's personal troubles allowed civilian politicians greater latitude. That year, Congress and socialist President Ricardo Lagos eliminated appointed senators and restored to the president the authority to dismiss members of the Joint Chiefs of Staff. Further prodemocratic reform in 2013 rewrote the law that allowed the top two vote-getters in every congressional district to take seats in the legislature (the binomial system), which automatically strengthened the influence of the second-place finisher, usually the Alianza. Further, the legislation allowed smaller parties to receive representation in both chambers. The law also required that women make up 40 percent of a party's candidates.

Chileans also had to navigate the extreme passions surrounding the Pinochet regime's abuse of human rights. Almost from the beginning of his dictatorship, international human rights organizations like Amnesty International denounced the atrocities taking place in the National Stadium and at prison facilities (chapter 11), while the regime denied these allegations of wrongdoing. The horror stories became so widespread that in 1977, the United Nations took the unusual step of passing a resolution condemning the ongoing human rights violations. Aware of the potential problems that the resolution posed, Pinochet issued a general amnesty—which opponents of the regime naturally distrusted—that welcomed opposition figures back to Chile, while simultaneously granting all members of the administration and the military immunity from any future prosecution.

When Christian Democrat Patricio Aylwin donned the presidential sash in 1989, he believed that although the Amnesty Law of 1978 limited his options, he had a moral imperative to uncover what had happened to the numerous victims of the regime. He established the first Truth and Reconciliation Commission (the Rettig Commission) to try to ascertain the truth about specific incidents of human rights violations. The Commission's findings proved disappointing to many Chileans. While it did not identify perpetrators of human rights crimes by name, nor discuss specific incidents of human rights violations, it did offer reparations to some victims. Later commissions in 2005 and 2010 found that the Pinochet dictatorship (1973–1990) had killed or disappeared 2,279 people and tortured another 30,000 citizens, primarily between 1973 and the early 1980s. Because of Pinochet's continuing roles as commander-in-chief of the army and senator for life after the return to democracy, Chile's first two democratically elected presidents treaded lightly on questions of truth, justice, and reparations in the face of the general's occasional saber-rattling threats to retake power should prosecutions for these crimes occur.

When Pinochet flew to London to undergo surgery in 1998, he inadvertently left himself open to prosecution under international law, strengthening the hand of human rights activists. A Spanish judge indicted Pinochet on charges of genocide, torture, and human rights violations, but attempts to extradite him for trial failed when the British allowed him to return to Chile because of his ill health. There, a newly elected Concertación government led by Ricardo Lagos suspended his immunity, but Pinochet's lawyers argued that the former dictator's growing mental incapacity made him incompetent to stand trial. Revelations in 2004 that Pinochet had millions of dollars squirreled away in foreign bank accounts not only played poorly in a nation where corruption was unusual, but also enabled the government to prove that the old general had sufficient mental capacity to stand trial. With this prospect hanging over his head, Pinochet died in 2006. Since then, based on the research done by members of the Truth and Reconciliation Commissions, other military men, infamous for their conduct during the Pinochet years, have been tried and sentenced to prison in the name of national reconciliation.

The two coalitions have also agreed to leave free market capitalism intact in part because it had allowed Chile to achieve some of the highest rates of growth in all of Latin America and because the Constitution of 1980 restricted the ability of politicians to alter the free market system. The Alianza agreed to modifications of pure neoliberalism to grant the state a larger role and share the country's economic prosperity more broadly. As a result, the parties have attempted to lessen the income gap between the rich and the poor while the Concertación has abjured the extreme social leveling program that Allende attempted to implement (chapter 10). Chile's strong economic growth rate has led to increasing per capita income, a rise in consumerism, and a favorable investment climate as the country gained a reputation for ease of doing business. The percentage of Chileans living in poverty has dropped dramatically, from 38 percent in 1989 to 14.4 percent in 2016. Both coalitions have embraced globalization and inked trade agreements with the United States, the Eurozone, China, Japan, and other Asian partners.

Reducing the inequities between the rich and poor has made some progress, especially since 2005. Two policies, healthcare and pensions, provide good examples of the gradualist direction of Chilean reformism. First, Pinochet had established a privatized healthcare system resembling HMOs (health management organizations) in the United States. While this system worked well for the wealthy who could afford to pay the premiums, many of Chile's poor only had access to lower quality (but nonetheless free) healthcare at government clinics, where some lifesaving procedures were not always available. Over time, especially under the reformed Socialists, the government has increased public healthcare spending to improve access to and quality of healthcare. Pinochet's controversial privatized social security system also remains largely intact, although President Michelle Bachelet—a former political prisoner of the Pinochet era who was elected in 2006 as Chile's first woman president—partially remedied this problem by establishing public funding of minimum pensions for the poorest 60 percent of Chileans in 2008.

Despite Chile's high rate of growth, income disparity remained a problem in the first decades of the twenty-first century. Both coalitions ran into difficulties with dissident student movements, which protested the lack of funding for public education. In 2006 and 2011, middle-class students led massive protests against the high costs and inequities of access to education that soon escalated to include other sectors of society. The results of the agitation proved mixed. The government in 2011, under conservative Sebastián Piñera, did grant a significant increase in the number of low-cost student loans, but other demands were shelved. The long-neglected indigenous Mapuche population benefited from an affirmative action program that granted them greater access to education. Piñera's uneven record paved the way for Michelle Bachelet's return to the presidency in 2014. During Bachelet's second term, Chile continues to move in the direction of inclusive development, reducing poverty and providing more access to education and healthcare. Against this backdrop, debates about the memory of the Pinochet years remain crucial to the understanding of human rights and democracy in Chile.

The International Debt Crisis, the IMF, and Neoliberalism, 1975–2000

The rise of neoliberal economics during the 1970s resulted from the perceived failure of state interventionist economic policies in the United States and Western Europe. The neoliberals criticized the ideas of the economist John Maynard Keynes, who, in response to the Great Depression, had called for countercyclical spending: When the economy slowed due to flagging demand, central banks and the national governments that regulated them should stimulate demand by lowering interest rates, investing in infrastructure, expanding government employment, and providing direct aid to the poor.

Into the 1970s, economists such as Milton Friedman and Friedrich Hayek argued that Keynesian policies created dependent clients of the government, stifled innovation, and slowed growth, resulting in declining productivity and employment. In Latin America, the economic independence promised by advocates of import substitution industrialization (ISI) had also proven utopian. Friedman and his colleagues argued that elected politicians could not muster the political will to curtail Keynesian measures despite creeping inflation and rising unemployment, hence the need for central banks immune to short-term political pressure. The US president Ronald Reagan and British prime minister Margaret Thatcher followed this neoliberal advice in the 1980s, cutting government spending, employment rolls, and taxes on the wealthy. The United States and British economies revived—unemployment declined, inflation slowed, and productivity increased (longer term effects of rising inequality were not yet felt). The policies implemented in the United States and Great Britain became preeminent in the IMF and the World Bank just as those institutions accrued the power to dictate terms to borrower nations. It was inevitable that Latin America would feel the effects.

The Debt Crisis and Neoliberalism in Latin America

Chile had already been Milton Friedman's test case in the 1970s (chapter 11). But Chile was hardly a typical Latin American nation: It had a small, well-educated population, with an economy heavily dependent on copper exports. As long as international demand for copper was strong, the Chilean economy would grow. Even in Chile, however, implementation of neoliberal measures—particularly cutting wages and government employment—required a violent military regime that cared nothing about public opinion. Those who cited Chile as a relative success story within Latin America often deliberately overlooked these aspects.

The Argentine military regime's halfhearted attempt to implement neoliberal measures in the late 1970s, in contrast, had been a colossal failure. The Argentine economy was larger and more complex than that of Chile, including a substantial industrial base. Haphazard curtailment of government spending and elimination of import tariffs undermined that industrial base without bringing economic growth. By the mid-1980s, the record for neoliberal policies in Latin America was decidedly mixed.

The alternative, however, appeared even worse. Nearly every Latin American government had contracted extensive loans from international lenders, including the IMF and the World Bank, in the 1970s. The 1979 spike in oil prices sent interest rates higher. Most governments responded throughout the 1980s by contracting ever-greater loans at higher interest rates in order to service existing debts without slashing spending. The largest economies, such as Brazil, Argentina, and Mexico, were the worst offenders. The new civilian leaders of Argentina and Brazil could not afford to risk their shaky popularity by imposing austerity measures. Mexico, undergoing its own process of democratic reform, was in a similar position.

By the end of the 1980s, these nations were hopelessly in debt, with inflation mounting so drastically experts referred to it as hyperinflation. Household expenses became increasingly surreal, as prices climbed from one day to the next—an attempt to keep up with rising costs that only fueled further inflation. Central banks fell behind on debt payments, and experimented with introducing new currencies in hopes of taming inflation. Private banks refused to provide further loans to debtor nations. Only the international lenders of last resort, the IMF and the World Bank, agreed to work with Latin American countries—but with strict conditions. In order to secure IMF loans or World Bank development support, Latin American governments would have to slash spending, eliminate import barriers and cut government employment. But how to implement such policies without suffering massive political rejection?

Bait-and-Switch Populists

The administration of Carlos Saúl Menem of Argentina became the prototype for a new, Latin American–style of neoliberal economic reform, leavened by populist political appeal and patronage spending. Menem was the governor of

La Rioja province in the Argentine interior when he ran for president in 1989. A member of the Peronist party (officially known as the Partido Justicialista, the Justicialist Party, or PJ), historically linked to protection of industrial labor and government patronage of the poor, he campaigned on a traditional Peronist platform, railing against the intrusion of international financial institutions and their austerity measures. Once elected, however, he became the first of several "bait-and-switch" populists of the 1990s: after campaigning with a traditional populist message, he accepted the IMF's demands and imposed austerity measures.

Carlos Saúl Menem: Argentina's Bait-and-Switch Populist. Carlo Saúl Menem was one of the prominent "bait-and-switch" populists in the 1980s–1990s in Latin America. The scion of Syrian immigrants, he first rose to national prominence as the governor of the mostly rural province of La Rioja. Menem cultivated a renegade gaucho aesthetic, with thick mutton-chop facial hair and a devil-may-care attitude, challenging the polished ways of career politicians from the capital. When he ran for president on the Peronist Party ticket in 1989, he promised a return to the salad days of Peronism, when the party protected workers with generous pension plans. Once elected, he presided over a steep decline in social spending, using short-term proceeds from the privatized public corporations to spread enough money among his loyalists to maintain temporary popularity. But he proved no better than his predecessor at resolving Argentina's deeper economic and political challenges.

What Menem came to realize was that austerity provided its own mechanisms for the distribution of patronage. The easiest way to cut government spending and employment was to privatize state-owned corporations. Privatization created massive opportunities for graft and nepotism, as foreign investment and under-the-table payoffs came rushing in. Government employment rolls shrank, but in the short term, Menem and his colleagues were awash in money. Menem could easily afford to divert funds into the same kind of social spending Evita had honed in the early 1950s—modest but symbolic rewards for political loyalists. Menem won a landslide reelection in 1995, despite ample evidence of corruption. Over the second half of the decade, Menem's administration became increasingly erratic. He turned over an economy in ruins to his successors—not a shining example for the Washington Consensus.

Alberto Fujimori of Peru—the son of Japanese immigrants to Peru—became another of Latin America's bait-and-switch populists. Like Menem, Fujimori won election based on promises to increase social spending. Once elected, Fujimori reversed positions and took the IMF's medicine, imposing harsh austerity measures. He solved the problem of "political rejection" by dissolving the Congress in 1992 and concentrating power in the executive branch. Fujimori justified these means to implement austerity measures through his success in defeating the Sendero Luminoso (chapter 12). On April 5, 1992, Fujimori set into motion an *"autogolpe,"* or "self-coup" that dissolved Congress, suspended the constitution, and put all powers into the hands of the executive branch, giving it the right to apply "drastic punishments" to terrorists. The antidemocratic nature of the Fujimori government soon began to alienate the Peruvian people. As in Menem's case, these apparent successes gradually lost their luster over the course of the 1990s, even as state-sponsored violence continued. Fujimori and his intelligence chief, Vladimiro Ilich Montesinos, presided over an extensive spy network, persecuting anyone who stood in the way of their plans. Fujimori was widely reviled by the time he was forced to flee the country in 2000, leaving evidence of high-profile corruption and bribery in his wake. In 2007, Fujimori returned to Peru, where he was tried and convicted of human rights violations, embezzlement, and other crimes. He remains in jail at the time of writing, although his daughter, Keiko, has followed in her father's footsteps, running for President in 2016.

Fernando Collor de Mello of Brazil cannot be considered a bait-and-switch populist, because he was candid about his proposed neoliberal reforms even during his 1989 presidential campaign. But his telegenic appearance gave neoliberalism a refreshing new look. Collor defeated Lula, the former labor leader, in a hard-fought campaign, Brazil's first democratic presidential election since 1960.

ECONOMICS AND COMMODITIES

The Privatization of the Rio Doce Valley Company

Back in 1942, Brazilian dictator Getúlio Vargas completed a multistage project to nationalize iron-mining interests in southeastern Brazil. Vargas used his extensive powers to seize the private holdings of foreign investors, transforming them into a state-owned conglomerate known as the Companhia Vale do Rio Doce, or Rio Doce Valley Company. Vale, as the company became known, played a key role in furnishing the raw materials for Brazil's industrialization in the 1940s and 1950s.

Fifty years later, Vale remained modestly productive, but was slow to respond to rising global demand for minerals in the 1990s. This left the state corporation vulnerable to the Washington Consensus and its trends of privatization. In 1995, President Fernando Henrique Cardoso announced plans to privatize Vale, initiating one of the greatest controversies of his tenure. Opposition to privatization emerged across the political spectrum, from unionized workers affiliated with socialist parties to oligarchic party bosses in states where Vale's operations were concentrated. But Brazil's burgeoning financial sector pressed for privatization—as did international speculators.

Cardoso eventually established a three-stage plan for privatizing the corporation in mid-1997, provoking a wave of street demonstrations in Brazil's major cities and a flurry of injunctions from opposition lawmakers. Such protestations were to no avail, as privatization went through as planned, turning Vale over to Brazilian and foreign private investors. Vale boomed in the late 1990s and early 2000s, becoming the world's largest mining firm. Within Brazil, Vale employed thousands of workers, paid ample taxes, and contributed to the growth of dozens of subsidiary companies. But Vale's growth was not without problems. The company became one of Brazil's worst polluters, as its gargantuan mining operations—some of them in the heart of the fragile Amazonian region—generated extensive toxic runoff. Vale tried to offset its environmental footprint through demarcation of forest reserves on company lands, but these reserves consisted mostly of eucalyptus groves, low in biodiversity. Vale became a symbol of the complexities of privatization and neoliberal reform, boon to some, bane to others.

- Was the privatization of Vale a net positive or a net negative for Brazil? What might have been done differently?

Collor sabotaged his own reforms by running the same kind of nepotistic operation he had derided as a candidate. He implemented economic shock policies in ways that enriched friends while impoverishing middle-class Brazilians and alienating Brazil's most powerful political figures. Brazilian media, no longer trammeled by the machinery of dictatorship, exposed Collor's schemes. Impeached in 1992, he resigned in disgrace before he could be convicted.

Vice President Itamar Franco took the reins to serve out the remainder of Collor's presidential term. Franco appointed an enterprising team of young economists to the central bank and named Fernando Henrique Cardoso as his minister of the interior. Cardoso, a distinguished sociologist and a former opponent of the military regime, had made his name with books that critiqued global capitalism for perpetuating inequality. By 1993, however, Cardoso had come to accept the apparent inevitability of neoliberal reform. As minister of the interior, he implemented the *Real* Plan, named for Brazil's new currency (the *real*), which was pegged temporarily to the US dollar. Cardoso cut government spending and implemented austerity measures to stop inflation in its tracks.

The Real Plan proved an unlikely success. Brazil tamed inflation, restoring consumer confidence and strengthening purchasing power just before the 1994 presidential election. Cardoso ran on the ticket of the Brazilian Social Democratic Party (PSDB), a party that sought to balance neoliberal economics with targeted social spending. Cardoso and the PSDB won a comfortable victory while Lula and the PT suffered another defeat. Cardoso then governed for eight years, pursuing privatization, and weathering allegations of rampant corruption. But Cardoso insulated himself from these allegations, and in the short term privatization brought foreign investment flooding into Brazil. After a 15-year period of decline, the economy finally started to grow again. Cardoso's new social spending initiatives—such as giving cash to the poor with the requirement that their children attend school—started to lift many Brazilians out of poverty. The Washington Consensus finally had a Latin American success story in the unlikely form of a former left-wing academic turned pragmatic administrator.

Contemporary Feminist Issues, 1970–2017

During the 1970s, a second wave of feminism swept the globe and energized European nations and the United States to expand women's personal liberties. In Latin America, social traditions and the powerful influence of the Catholic Church generally inhibited this trend. But because Vatican II did accept the idea of equality within the family, feminists and their supporters were able to press for reforms granting mothers equal parental authority and wives shared property rights. Other issues that keenly interested women, such as reforming divorce laws and granting reproductive freedoms, remained more controversial.

Divorce in the Southern Cone Nations

Liberals during the late nineteenth and early twentieth centuries had rewritten their legal codes to make marriage a civil ceremony. Dissolving a marriage in Latin America, however, remained exclusively within the purview of the Church and only occurred when a couple met one of the limited number of grounds for the annulment of their marriage. The Church and conservative members of society defended the sanctity of marriage as an indissoluble sacrament. Given the Church's role as society's moral compass, reformers seeking change had to proceed slowly. Because codified civil (and criminal) law governed throughout Latin America, legal change could not occur as a result of a Supreme Court decision

≡ **Feminists Marching in La Plata, Argentina.** The rise of identity politics—the creation of political groups and coalitions on the basis of race, gender, ethnicity, sexual orientation, and so forth—was one of the more striking aspects of late twentieth-century Latin American politics, and transformed traditional party structures. Identity-based groups often reacted to political crisis by advocating a politics that rejected party affiliation and sought to leverage new claims, as in the case of this feminist, antipatriarchal march in La Plata, Argentina.

(like *Roe v. Wade*, which legalized abortion in the United States), but required a statutory change to the civil code, slowing the process of reform given such widespread opposition to the measure.

As the twentieth century progressed, feminists and their supporters noted that the increasing frequency of marital breakdowns and separations provided a persuasive reason to advocate for legal change. Reformers believed that divorce, like marriage, should be a matter for the state in part because fewer people viewed marriage as a sacrament and in part because women living apart from a husband faced social stigma if they lived in an informal union with a different man. Women in such relationships also had no claim to the communal property the new, unmarried couple accumulated. Any children born from this second relationship faced the shame (and legal disadvantages) of illegitimacy. Advocates for divorce like

Brazil's senator Nelson Carneiro, who fought for change for more than two decades, argued that divorce offered the former wife more protection and freedom.

In Argentina, Brazil, and Chile, unhappy married couples resorted to tortuous legal gymnastics to circumvent the ban on divorce. In Brazil, "partners laws" extended property rights to the second family; in Argentina, couples crossed the estuary to Uruguay to get divorced. In Chile, a couple seeking an annulment went to the Civil Registry to claim that a "defect in the marriage contract" (an inaccurate detail on the marriage license, such as the wedding ceremony was not performed in the place where the couple lived) provided sufficient grounds for the annulment. None of these expedients proved wholly satisfactory.

Interestingly, the military regime in Brazil, anxious to modernize the country's legal codes, included the revision of domestic relations law in its broader reform program. To guarantee the new code would pass the legislature, President Ernesto Geisel (a Lutheran of German immigrant descent) unilaterally changed the constitutional requirement to amend any law code from a two-thirds vote to a majority vote. In Argentina, the pressure for reform mounted. Because the Church had largely remained silent about human rights abuses during the military dictatorship, the new democratic government in 1984 ignored the Church's opposition and enacted divorce legislation. In Chile, on the other hand, because the Church had spoken out against the Pinochet dictatorship, its moral authority remained intact and a divorce law was not passed until 2004, making Chile one of the last countries in the world to sanction divorce.

Reproductive Rights

Of all the issues that families faced, the question of women's reproductive rights proved the most controversial. Historically and culturally, Latin Americans had favored large families and, as a result, the Church's disapproval of birth control was not as much of an issue as it was in other parts of the world. Well into the twentieth century, particularly in rural areas, large families provided necessary laborers, and even in urban areas high infant mortality rates made larger families valuable. Even among rich elites, large families were valued as trustworthy networks for business, politics, and social connections. As a Mexican saying goes, "*a los amigos uno los escoge; los parientes son a huevo*" ("One chooses one's friends, but a family is from birth").

As Latin American urbanized and health conditions improved, however, especially after World War II, a number of factors coalesced to make small families more desirable. Foremost among these factors was Latin America's mid-twentieth century demographic boom, stemming from improvements in basic healthcare and the introduction of antibiotics around 1945. In the case of its largest cities, such as Mexico City

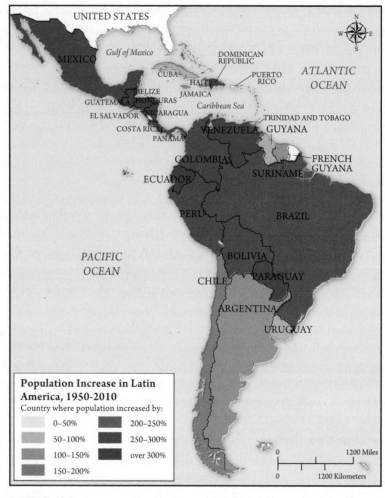

Population Increase in Latin America, 1950-2010
Country where population increased by:

- 0–50%
- 50–100%
- 100–150%
- 150–200%
- 200–250%
- 250–300%
- over 300%

≡ **MAP. 13.1**

or São Paulo, massive migration from the countryside and declining infant mortality led to exponential growth. During the 1970s, for example, Mexico City witnessed the birth of one thousand new little residents *per day.* By the start of the twenty-first century, the overall population of Latin America and the Caribbean had reached 550 million, with about four-fifths of the population residing in urban areas. In spite of all these changes, the Catholic Church, under the leadership of John Paul II (1978–2005) retained its traditional position opposing the practice of birth control.

Prior to the second half of the twentieth century, even had the Church approved and people had wanted to use them, birth control methods were unreliable and difficult to obtain, especially for unmarried couples. Beginning in the 1950s, however, scientists had begun experimenting with substances that might produce oral contraceptives. Ironically, the principal ingredient (progesterone) in the birth control pill, the most popular method of modern family planning, was derived from the *barbasco* plant, a wild yam that grew exclusively in southeastern Mexico. Eventually, barbasco picking employed some 100,000 Mexicans. For two decades, progesterone derived from barbasco remained the central ingredient in birth control pills. The discovery of a synthetic substitute in the late 1970s ended the barbasco boom. By then, however, most Latin American governments recognized women's right to acquire contraceptive devices.

Not so with abortion. The Church and conservative members of society fought tenaciously against the practice of abortion as the ultimate moral wrong. For opponents of abortion, the process involved the taking of a human life, since pro-life advocates believed that life began at conception. On the other hand, advocates of abortion reform saw the issue as one of a woman's right to choose, a question of liberty and privacy. They pointed out that numerous Latin American women secretly underwent abortions, but the lack of a legally permitted form of abortion discriminated against poorer women. While elite and middle-class women would seek treatment in a pristine new clinic, the poor resorted to back-alley practitioners who often produced disastrous results, up to and including the death of the patient.

Even before contemporary reform efforts, the Southern Cone nations (except Chile) had the most progressive legislation in Latin America regarding abortion. Traditionally, these countries recognized the legality of therapeutic abortions—those performed to save the life of the mother. Early in the twentieth century Argentina, Brazil, and Uruguay also recognized the right to compassionate abortions for victims of rape. Proof of rape, however, limited this exception as a practical matter. By way of contrast, Chile in 1989 took the opposite approach and eliminated a woman's right to abortion under any circumstance whatsoever, a measure that Nicaragua, ruled by former revolutionary and born-again conservative Catholic Daniel Ortega, also adopted in 2006. With the exception of Uruguay, where a woman's right to choose is legally accepted, these standards for limited abortion remain in place in the Southern Cone and the rest of Latin America.

Mexico: New Challenges and Protests, 1970–2000

While neoliberalism provided theoretical answers to Latin America's debt crisis, its practical applications adversely affected the poorest members of society. Curbing runaway inflation benefited everybody and satisfied foreign creditors, but the programs of privatization, deregulation and austerity each in their own way wreaked hardship on those dependent on government subsidies for economic survival. Particularly for indigenous peoples, who were often the economically least well-off members of society, neoliberalism further marginalized their existence. Indigenous peoples in Mexico forcefully protested.

The Failure of the Institutional Revolutionary Party after Tlatelolco

In the decades following the massacre of students at Tlatelolco (chapter 11), the average Mexican experienced a declining standard of living that undermined popular support for the Institutional Revolutionary Party (PRI). The PRI's industrialization program seemed to have faltered, causing higher rates of unemployment than usual. Hopes for prosperity revived in the mid-1970s, when geologists uncovered a veritable sea of petroleum in southeastern Mexico. Awash in profits because of climbing oil prices in the 1970s, the PRI increased government spending, undertook new public works projects, expanded social benefits by subsidizing many types of consumer goods and credit, and purchased privately owned businesses, converting them into state-owned enterprises. Assuming that high oil prices would continue indefinitely, Mexico borrowed from foreign banks under variable interest rate contracts. When oil prices plummeted and interest rates rose in the 1980s, the country faced economic ruin, nearly defaulting on its debt in 1982. Inflation exceeded 100 percent per year in 1986 and 1987, as the peso lost most of its value. To compound this economic tragedy, a massive earthquake devastated Mexico City in 1985, leveling countless buildings and causing many casualties.

The PRI's handpicked presidential candidate in 1988, Carlos Salinas de Gortari, appeared well prepared to resolve these problems. Trained as a technocratic economist at Harvard University, President Salinas was fluent in the economic strategies employed elsewhere in Latin America, especially in Chile, to manage fiscal crises. At the outset of his term, he privatized 85 percent of Mexico's state-owned businesses (excluding of course, Pemex, the lucrative oil company and symbol of revolutionary nationalism) and rolled back regulations hampering foreign investment and entrepreneurial growth. In the name of IMF-mandated austerity, the government eliminated many subsidies on which the poor relied and greatly reduced social spending.

Two of Salinas's measures proved particularly controversial. First, he privatized collective agriculture (the ejidos) by permitting occupants to measure, map, and register deeds for the lands that they worked that they could then rent, or even sell. The government decreed an end to any further land petitions to create ejidos, effectively ending land redistribution, a central tenet of the Revolution. In poor states like Chiapas (where 43 percent of the indigenous population still lived on ejidos), the legislation meant that young people could no longer petition for land, which threatened the indigenous communal lifestyle.

Perhaps even more controversially, Salinas signed the **North American Free Trade Agreement (NAFTA)**. Joining this agreement, he argued, meant the entrance of Mexico into the mainstream of the global economy and access to one of the world's largest markets (the United States and to a lesser degree Canada). The United States believed its businesses would benefit by cutting labor costs by building new plants in Mexico. Mexicans anticipated that NAFTA would create additional jobs for Mexican workers in the **maquiladoras**, the factories that had already emerged along the US-Mexican border. On the US side, NAFTA supporters also argued that the maquiladoras would slow undocumented immigration. In short, all three signatory parties saw NAFTA as an example of mutual comparative advantage.

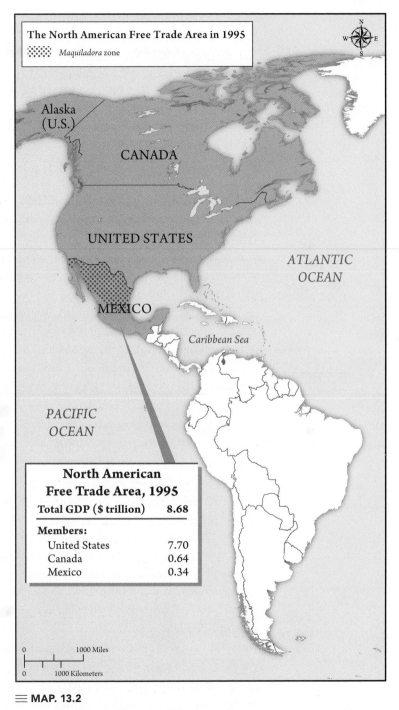

The North American Free Trade Area in 1995

:::::: *Maquiladora* zone

Alaska (U.S.)

CANADA

UNITED STATES

ATLANTIC OCEAN

MEXICO

Caribbean Sea

PACIFIC OCEAN

North American Free Trade Area, 1995	
Total GDP ($ trillion)	8.68
Members:	
United States	7.70
Canada	0.64
Mexico	0.34

0   1000 Miles

0   1000 Kilometers

≡ **MAP. 13.2**

But others heartily disagreed. Because of the likelihood of US manufacturing jobs moving south to Mexico, US labor leaders opposed the pact, as did environmentalists who feared increased pollution in the border region. Small farmers worried that US agribusiness would overtake Mexico's homegrown agriculture—a fear later borne out when US hybrid corn pushed many farmers of maize, Mexico's ancient crop and gift to the world, out of business. Many of Salinas's critics, however, argued that NAFTA would ultimately cost Mexican jobs because domestic industry would not be able to compete successfully with global giant retailers like Wal-Mart. They also worried that Mexico would be too closely tied to the US economy. Ultimately NAFTA did increase trade between the two countries and particularly benefited consumers (particularly the well-to do) in both countries. At the same time, Mexico's poor did not fare as well from NAFTA, as jobs in *maquilas* not only paid poorly but were soon undercut by even cheaper labor costs in China and elsewhere in Asia. In addition, prices for basic commodities rose dramatically, despite the supply-and-demand promises of international competition.

Although Salinas attempted to use nationalistic symbols to promote NAFTA and the privatization of rural properties, both measures contradicted two of the longest-entrenched policies of the Mexican Revolution: agrarian reform and economic nationalism. These and other neoliberal measures undermined the PRI's social base. The rural peasantry, another major leg of the PRI's populist coalition, also lost faith in the PRI. Eliminating price supports for Mexican farmers while importing subsidized grains from the United States and Canada under NAFTA ruined many subsistence farmers and ejido members.

Organized labor, too, turned against the PRI during the 1990s and deprived the party of even more economic resources once used to overwhelm the opposition in political campaigns. Even before NAFTA, the creation of the maquiladoras discouraged unionization and fundamentally altered the nature of Mexican industry. The surge in maquiladora production after the passage of NAFTA exacerbated this trend. These low-tech assembly plants hired mostly women who both possessed dexterous hand skills and the willingness to accept the low wages offered for assembly work. In addition, these employees demonstrated the docility business owners desired and tended to be transient, another highly desirable trait for employers who wanted a flexible labor force that could be laid off in times of recession. As a result of these trends, organized labor contributed less to the PRI, which tended to make the opposition more competitive in the quest for campaign funds. Because the PAN and the PRD competed so successfully for contributions, in 1996 PRI supported public funding of elections.

With the public weary of fraud (especially after what was for many a blatantly stolen election in 1988) and with PRI reformers' new commitment to democracy, public pressure forced PRI to create a Federal Election Board to oversee future contests. As opposition parties moved from their former extreme ideological stances to more moderate positions, they were able to challenge PRI in the congressional elections of 1997 and win a majority of seats.

The Zapatista Uprising of 1994

Like the Sendero Luminoso (Shining Path) in Peru, the **Zapatistas**, who took their name from Mexico's iconic agrarian reform hero, underwent a clandestine ten-year incubation period before emerging as a military force. In no other respect, however, did the Zapatistas (formally known as the Zapatista Army of National Liberation or EZLN) resemble Peru's murderous revolutionaries. As the titular leader of the Zapatistas, Subcomandante Marcos (a pseudonym adopted by Rafael Guillén, a former professor from Mexico City) explained, he and a few of his mestizo colleagues may have entered the Lacandón jungle as Marxists, but over time the Maya people residing there converted them to a different way of thinking. In other words, instead of trying to impose a foreign ideology on the campesinos as Sendero had attempted to do, the Zapatista leadership learned from the people they hoped to help. As a result, the Zapatistas' "First Declaration from the Lacandón Jungle"–perhaps the first revolutionary manifesto ever sent out over the new technology of the Internet—articulated the Mayan priority to struggle for human dignity in a just and democratic society where indigenous people could live autonomously and in liberty.

The EZLN launched their rebellion on January 1, 1994, the day of NAFTA's implementation. On the following day, their insurgent forces of about five thousand indigenous Maya took the colonial capital city of San Cristóbal de las Casas in the state of Chiapas before being driven out of town by the Mexican army. Ten days later, President Salinas declared a unilateral armistice and entered into negotiations with the rebels. During these early skirmishes, estimates of casualties ranged from one hundred to three hundred people. Although the federal army occupied much of Chiapas thereafter, the level of violence was minimal compared to guerrilla movements in Colombia and Peru. Subcomandante Marcos explained that the Zapatistas' weapons were their communications, not bullets. Because of their successful use of the Internet—at the time a new technology to most of the world—the Zapatistas engendered sympathy not just in Mexico but also beyond, as they negotiated to achieve dignity by protesting the racism and exploitation to which indigenous people had been subjected over five centuries and in particular under neoliberalism.

≡ **Subcomandante Marcos and Zapatistas in Chiapas.** The Ejército Zapatista de Liberación Nacional (Zapatista National Liberation Army) or EZLN, took its name in honor of Emiliano Zapata, the early twentieth-century campesino revolutionary. The late twentieth-century Zapatistas staged a dramatic occupation of the southern Mexican city of San Cristóbal de las Casas on New Year's Day, 1994, bringing local Maya youth together with mestizo organizers in a movement to challenge traditional political hierarchies. The Zapatistas probed at the weak points of the new North American Free Trade Agreement, demanding greater representation and resources for the rural poor, including indigenous communities.

The large number of women participating in the Zapatista movement (statistics indicated that women constituted about 30 percent of the Zapatista forces) raised the issue of gender equality and secured their fellow rebels' agreement to the Revolutionary Law for Women. Besides demanding the right to choose their own husband, deciding on the number of children they would bear, and being able to gain access to birth control, many Zapatista women demanded greater participation in community decision-making. Despite the law and these ideals of equality, at the local level and even within Zapatista ranks, women still faced paternalistic practices in their daily lives. According to the law, "uses and customs" that depended on local circumstances could restrict women's rights.

The Mexican government pursued a dual strategy to deal with the Zapatistas in the 1990s. On one hand, the occupying Mexican army conducted a "low intensity war" designed to instill fear and end resistance. Specifically, the army displaced communities suspected of being sympathetic to the Zapatistas and arrested known Zapatistas, sometimes abusing innocent victims in the process. On the other hand, the two sides negotiated. Catholic Bishop Samuel Ruiz presided over talks designed to create an indigenous bill of rights. Although Bishop Ruiz had originally been a conservative Catholic, like Archbishop Óscar Romero of El Salvador, he became a proponent of liberation theology in the 1970s and an advocate for the poor. Because both sides trusted the bishop, he was able to convince them to agree to the San Andrés Accords on Indigenous Rights and Culture in 1996. Specifically, the Accords, among other things, granted municipalities greater autonomy and redefined Mexico as a multiethnic nation.

When Vicente Fox, a member of the PAN (National Action Party) rather than the entrenched PRI party, campaigned for the presidency in 2000, he famously claimed that he would end the Zapatista uprising in fifteen minutes upon election. After President Fox made overtures to Subcomandante Marcos, the Zapatistas agreed to march peacefully to Mexico City without arms to speak to the Mexican Congress, which had not yet debated the San Andrés Accords. After a contentious discussion in congress, one of the female comandantes spoke to the legislators, pleading for them to treat indigenous people with dignity in the name of the Mexican nation.

Although Congress passed the Accords, they did so with significant amendments. Because conservative congressmen who believed in the idea of a unified nation-state could not accept the notion of semi-independent, autonomous entities within Mexico, these amendments therefore proposed to make the communities subordinate to state authorities. The Zapatistas refused to accept the revised legislation. Although the Zapatista stalemate continues today, the movement has reintroduced the question of indigenous rights into Mexico's national dialogue and has forced Mexicans to discard the discussion about assimilation.

The Drug Trade: Poisoning the Andean States, 1970–2000

Long famous for possessing desirable commodities (silver, guano, cacao, tin) that excited the greed of outsiders, the Andean nations became infamous for a new product in the 1980s and 1990s: illicit drugs. Although as valuable (if not more so)

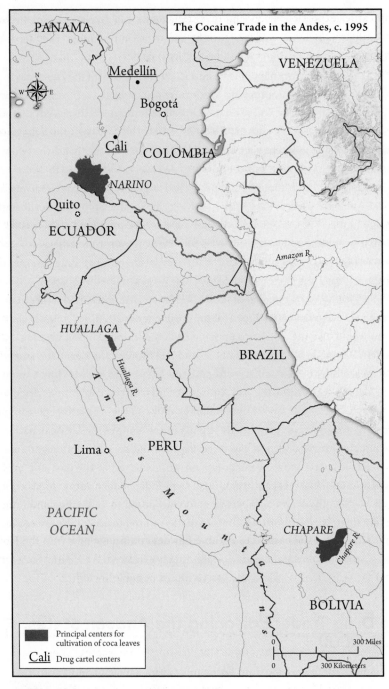

The Cocaine Trade in the Andes, c. 1995

PANAMA

VENEZUELA

Medellín

Bogotá

<u>Cali</u>

COLOMBIA

NARINO

Quito

ECUADOR

Amazon R.

HUALLAGA

Huallaga R.

A n d e s

BRAZIL

Lima

PERU

M o u n t a i n s

PACIFIC
OCEAN

CHAPARE

Chapare R.

BOLIVIA

■ Principal centers for
cultivation of coca leaves

<u>Cali</u> Drug cartel centers

0   300 Miles

0   300 Kilometers

☰ **MAP. 13.3**

than earlier export commodities, marijuana and especially cocaine had a much more deleterious effect on Andean society than did earlier goods. The drug business played out very differently in the southern Andean nations than it did in Colombia, while Ecuador generally stayed aloof from the trafficking.

Producing Coca in Bolivia and Peru

Until the 1970s coca had a limited local and international market and coca growers used only a small portion of Peru and Bolivia's farmland. That situation changed when the combination of agrarian reform measures and the abysmal economic conditions of the 1980s encouraged discharged tin miners and impoverished campesinos to move to the eastern slopes of the Andes Mountains in a desperate attempt to earn their living. Despite their hard work, fruits like bananas and papayas, as well as staples like rice, often spoiled before reaching markets, leaving these farmers impoverished until the introduction of coca.

In the United States, the fascination with marijuana had given way to a desire for harder drugs in the 1970s, including cocaine, a derivative of the coca leaf. The new demand spurred coca production in the eastern Andes and especially in the Bolivian province of Chapare, where soils proved so conducive to coca that growers could harvest four crops per year. Once planted, coca required little labor other than picking the leaves, allowing farmers plenty of time to tend the subsistence crops they also grew to feed their families. Unlike fragile fruits, coca transported easily over bumpy dirt roads. In Bolivia, the industry may have employed as many as 100,000 workers and earned some participants upwards of $150,000 per year. (For obvious reasons, the statistics are unreliable).

Converting raw leaves into cocaine involved a three-step process, requiring the use of chemicals like kerosene, sulfuric acid, and hydrochloric acid in the final stages. Bolivian processors generally completed only the first step, rendering the leaves into paste (*pasta básica*), almost all of which they sold to Colombian cartels, who then refined the paste into cocaine powder and smuggled it into the United States. As the quantity of cocaine on US streets escalated, the United States pressured the Bolivian government to use all means possible, including military force, to eradicate production. *Cocaleros* (coca farmers) led by one of their own, future president Evo Morales, strongly protested these measures in 1991, arguing that growing coca was an essential element of Bolivia's cultural heritage and should be differentiated from cocaine production designated for export. The acclaim that Morales won soon led to his emergence as a national political figure.

Peru's upper Huallaga Valley actually produced more coca than did Bolivia's Chapare, but because of the size and diversity of Peru's economy, coca production generated a smaller percentage of its gross domestic product (GDP). As in Bolivia, Peru's growers tended to be small farmers who sold leaves to processors, who then processed the leaves into more transportable paste for the Colombians. Peru's coca industry drew the attention of President Fujimori after the Huallaga Valley became the refuge for the remnants of the Sendero Luminoso following Abimael Guzmán's capture in 1992 (chapter 12). Initially, Sendero won a following in the valley by offering growers protection against eradication efforts by US and Peruvian police. Between the intensification of government military efforts in the region and a local fungus that wreaked havoc on coca plants, production levels plummeted. The Peruvian Air Force began shooting down drug-carrying planes at the same time that the Bolivian government stepped up its efforts against cocaine smugglers (but not coca growers). The diminution of production in Peru and Bolivia, however, mattered little, because by then Colombia grew more leaves than did either of the southern Andean republics.

Drug Smuggling: The Medellín and Cali Cartels in Colombia

From the outset, drug gangs in two Colombian cities, Medellín and Cali, dominated the processing of cocaine from coca paste and then the smuggling of the refined product to the United States. Beginning in the mid-1980s, however, Colombians in the southeastern region began growing their own coca in part to increase profits and in part to avoid interruption of their sources of supply from Peru and Bolivia. Drug lords like Medellín's Pablo Escobar began their careers by smuggling high-quality and much-prized "Colombian Gold" marijuana as well as cocaine into the United States. This enabled him to construct a reliable network of distributors and dealers. The market for cocaine remained small in the 1970s, allowing the cartels to rely on "drug mules," often young women visiting relatives in the United States, who smuggled small quantities of "blow" in their luggage or clothing. As law enforcement became more cognizant of these activities, smugglers became more inventive. Now mules swallowed tightly woven bags of cocaine just before they

≡ **Pablo Escobar.** At the peak of his influence, Pablo Escobar was the most powerful man in Colombia, leader of a vast organization with the power to corrupt officials at all levels of government, to wage war against rival cartels, and to ship cocaine internationally via a flexible network despite the US War on Drugs. Indeed, US policy likely helped Escobar concentrate power by eliminating smaller-scale rivals. Escobar became a prime target of the Drug Enforcement Agency and its Colombian allies, and died in a hail of bullets in 1993.

boarded planes and then voided their bowels with the intact bags (often condoms) once they passed through US customs. If a bag leaked, however, the mule died a horrible death. As time passed and profits increased, the cartels resorted to planes, cargo ships, and even submarines to smuggle their goods into the United States, usually through Florida.

Pablo Escobar and his cartel did not hesitate to murder rival gang members, people in his own organization who betrayed him, and even politicians and judges. But even as Medellín became a war zone, many of the city's poorest residents praised him (and protected him) because of his charitable spending: building public housing, constructing soccer fields, and providing other social services. In addition to being a Robin Hood–like figure in the eyes of some of the poor, Escobar hoped to further his influence and provide himself with protection by becoming politically active, even winning a seat in the national legislature as an alternate deputy representing Medellín. At the peak of his power, *Forbes Magazine* named him one of the ten richest people in the world. When Escobar and his cartel were implicated in the assassination of three Colombian politicians, public opinion turned against him. With technical support from US agents, police finally tracked him down in 1993 by tracing his cell phone, and killed him as he fled across a rooftop.

With Escobar's death and the disruption of the **Medellín cartel**, Cali's organization took over the smuggling business. The Cali cartel used different tactics and methods of operation. A decentralized organization without a kingpin, they preferred to bribe politicians and judges rather than kill them. The cartel's strategy forced them to remain aloof from the urban poor, which cost them popularity and protection. Clever at laundering money, the Cali cartel invested in a number of legitimate businesses in the city. Nevertheless, the combination of the Colombian police and US drug enforcement led to the demise of the Cali cartel in 1995.

Neither of the Colombian cartels looked favorably at the FARC or the ELN (The Revolutionary Armed Forces of Colombia and the National Liberation Army—chapter 12). Escobar had initially used the guerrillas to protect his interests, but grew tired of paying their exorbitant war taxes, which may have been as high as $110,000,000 in 1992. Escobar felt a much greater kinship with the ranchers whom guerrillas threatened with kidnapping and extortion. The ranchers in turn appreciated the firepower that Escobar's gang could bring to bear against the guerrillas. The Cali gangs in particular hated the FARC, because guerrillas had kidnapped the daughter of one of the cartel's principal leaders, holding her for ransom. Nevertheless, the FARC ultimately benefited from the cocaine trade, protecting farmers who grew large quantities of leaves and paid war taxes to the guerrillas.

Although cocaine production did generate some income for Peru, Bolivia, and Colombia, most of the wealth was untaxed and "off the books" and so had little positive effect on the national economy. Drugs certainly provided employment in all three countries, perhaps for as many as 500,000 people in Colombia. But the overall effects were overwhelmingly negative. Only a small proportion of drug profits trickled down into the communities in which the kingpins lived. High drug usage among young people had social consequences. The ecological consequences of drug trafficking were also horrendous. Approximately 10 percent of Peru's forests were cut in the 1980s to grow coca; similar deforestation occurred in Colombia. Worse, the chemicals used to process cocaine were routinely poured into nearby streams, poisoning the drinking water for humans and animals.

The Colombian government and US Presidents Bill Clinton and George W. Bush invested heavily in Plan Colombia to eradicate drug smuggling and the guerrillas (chapter 12). Colombian drug producers responded by seeking out partnerships with Mexican and Central American criminal elements to continue their unlawful activities. During the early years of the cocaine trade, the Medellín cartel flew drugs from Colombia to Florida, either dropping them at sea to waiting speedboats or landing in rural areas of the state, after which the cargo was trucked to Miami for distribution. When the crime rate in Dade County, Florida, rose dramatically in 1982, President Reagan created a task force to curtail the drug trade. Working with the Coast Guard and the Drug Enforcement Administration (DEA), the task force seized several huge shipments and cut the quantity of drugs entering Florida by approximately 50 percent. At this point an experienced Honduran drug smuggler working for the cartel, Juan Ramón Matta Ballesteros, suggested using Mexican traffickers and their preexisting marijuana smuggling routes along the mostly unprotected two-thousand-mile border with the United States. Initially, the Colombians retained most of the profits from the traffic, but by the mid-1990s the Mexican cartels, especially the Sinaloa cartel, asserted control over the enterprise. Thereafter, the presence of drug-related violence in Mexico greatly escalated (chapter 14).

Latin Americans have long protested that the drug problem is not one of controlling supply, but rather of limiting demand. In the years up to the present, such topics were taboo in the halls of the US Congress. Only when drug smuggling grew to an even more problematic degree have some US jurisdictions begun to consider the possibility of decriminalizing at least some of the activities associated with drug use as a way of addressing the problem and avoiding the singling out of poor minorities in the United States for the brunt of criminal prosecutions.

ECONOMICS AND COMMODITIES

Coca before the Narcos

In the southern Andes, the use of coca, the "sacred leaf," dated back to pre-Hispanic times. Back then, Andean priests and nobility used coca for religious ceremonial purposes. During the colonial period, the use of coca became much more widespread, as chewing or sucking the leaves helped indigenous workers endure hunger and fatigue while laboring in mines or fields. After independence the chewing of coca became one of the principal markers differentiating indigenous people from the elite. Coca became a global commodity in the 1860s, however, when the German chemist Albert Niemann discovered the chemical process that isolated coca's active ingredient, cocaine. As part of the late nineteenth-century medical revolution to locate new painkillers and curatives for disease, Peruvian cocaine, marketed by the German entrepreneur Emmanuel Merck, occupied an important niche. Although the United States also imported its share of medicinal cocaine, cocaine primarily became associated with the most iconic US product universally sold throughout Latin America.

This product, of course, is Coca-Cola. Formulated by the Atlanta pharmacist John Pemberton as a health beverage in 1886, Coke promised to stimulate the nerves and brain and cure headaches. By the turn of the century, however, the US medical community and the government had become concerned about cocaine's potentially addictive properties. As US attitudes shifted, the Coca-Cola Company in 1903 replaced the pure cocaine with a secret ingredient known as Merchandise No. 5 syrup, derived from coca leaves imported exclusively from La Libertad province in Peru. Produced by the New Jersey–based Maywood Chemical works, the process removed the cocaine from the coca leaf, leaving only the tasty syrup.

By then, Coca-Cola had expanded from a soda fountain operation to a provider of bottled beverages and in so doing had crushed all of its early competition. While Peruvian cocaine continued to be a legal medicinal commodity in Europe, the Harrison Narcotics Tax Act of 1914 outlawing cocaine importation into the United States conveniently granted

≡ **Coca Plantation in Bolivia.**

exclusion for coca leaves to Coca-Cola and the Maywood Corporation so they could continue to manufacture Merchandise No. 5 syrup. In exchange, the two corporations alerted the FBI and the Narcotics Bureau whenever they learned about illegal cocaine shipments to the United States. Coca-Cola may have removed the coca leaf additive from its formula in the 1960s, although this is not certain because the formula remains a trade secret.

Meanwhile, as US influence grew in Latin America, especially after World War II, the fight against illegal cocaine intensified. When a pro-US Peruvian dictator shut down exports from his nation in the 1950s, the production of illicit cocaine shifted to Bolivia, which up to then had produced the leaf only for its domestic market. After the Bolivian Revolution of 1952, when landless peasants received property along the eastern slope of the Andes (chapter 10) but found that they could not earn a living growing fruits and vegetables, they turned to coca production. At the same time, high-ranking Bolivian officials allegedly conspired with smugglers to supply much of the world's illicit cocaine by the mid-1960s. The real expansion of the trade would occur, however, in the 1980s.

- What questions does the history of coca use raise about contemporary drug policy?

CULTURE AND IDEAS

Narcocorridos

Narcocorridos, the tales sung about the daily lives and exploits of drug smugglers, burst onto the Mexican pop music scene in the 1980s and have grown in popularity ever since. The singers of narcocorridos reinvented the venerable northern Mexican ballad form, the *corrido*, which had reached the apogee of its popularity during the Mexican Revolution in the first half of the twentieth century, with lyrics that celebrated the heroic military victories of Emiliano Zapata and Pancho Villa against the corrupt federal army. Narcocorridos also draw inspiration from US hip hop and gangsta rap, which lionize criminals and their glamorous (if short-lived) lifestyles. Employing favorite northern Mexican instruments like the accordion, guitar, and tuba, bands played this danceable music, a version of the polka, but "pumped up on meth" as one critic stated.

Narcocorrido videos often portray the lead singer carrying an assault rifle, reflecting the artists' close relationship with drug cartels. Lyrics glorify the violence of the warring gangs, as well as their conspicuous consumption and sexual conquests. The lyrics frequently describe the grisly realities of drug gang violence: beheadings, dismemberment, and even the boiling of enemies alive. Because of their close association with gangs, the singers themselves lead precarious lives. For example, in 1992 an audience member at a concert jumped on stage and shot the most popular singer of the first generation of artists, Rosalino "Chalino" Sánchez, who returned fire. Not long thereafter, Sánchez was found murdered following another concert. Between 2006 and 2008, over a dozen Mexican musicians lost their lives due to violence.

Many influential individuals, including the former Mexican president Vicente Fox (2000–2006), have criticized narcocorridos and urged that this music be banned from the airwaves because of the unprecedented level of savage murders it seems to encourage. While most defenders of the music agree that the lyrics are purposefully offensive, they argue that the narcocorridos fit into a long tradition of music that protests social injustices. The songs relate the stories of Mexico's poor and destitute, who, if ambitious to improve themselves, have limited opportunities to gain wealth and power in such a corrupt society. Banning the music also has proven impractical, in part because powerful US radio stations with transmitters that can reach Mexico air the music. Recent immigrants to the United States enjoy the music and have made it their own, rendering narcocorridos a transborder experience. To a lesser degree, narcocorridos have also found a popular following elsewhere in Latin America, particularly in Guatemala, Honduras, Colombia, Peru, and Bolivia.

- Are the narcocorridos artistic free speech, or propaganda for traffickers? Should they be banned from the airwaves?

Urban Poverty and the Informal Sector, 1960–2000

Poverty was a dark force within Latin American cities from their inception. Colonial Spanish and Portuguese administrators accepted hunger and disease in the streets as part of the urban scenery. They expected religious institutions to ameliorate the worst aspects of this misery and took no further steps of their own. The transition to independent national governments in the nineteenth century did not change this attitude dramatically. But as national governments seized Church lands and resources, they also took up some of the burden of mitigating urban poverty, although always with reluctance.

The Resurgence of Urbanization in the 1960s

Authorities had taken few additional steps to address urban poverty in the first half of the twentieth century, and then did so in ways more often designed to drive the poor out of the cities than to improve their conditions. The effects of the Green Revolution and improvements in primary healthcare in the 1960s changed the equation of this long history of urban poverty, forcing the burgeoning population of rural poor to move to cities that could not accommodate them either.

Migrants to the city found ways to support themselves and their families, carrying cargo, cleaning streets and sewers, selling food in the streets, and countless other shifting, overlapping occupations. But few of these paid enough to enable new urban residents to rent a room, much less buy a home. Instead, recent urban residents cobbled together housing the same way they knitted together employment, taking scraps from here and there and getting by until the next crisis. Self-built housing itself became a shadow sector of the urban economy. From Buenos Aires to Mexico City, those fortunate enough to own urban property found ways to illegally subdivide it off the books (that is, without reporting either the subdivision or the resulting rental income for the purposes of taxation or other municipal requirements) and rent space to the poor, who built their own precarious dwellings. New highway networks expanded the circumference of Latin American cities, and local strongmen laid claim to the odd plots in their interstices. They then divided the plots and sold them off the books to people willing to build their own homes on lands of uncertain title.

More rarely, communities of the working poor banded together to seize and improve vacant urban space, and then to petition politicians for legal protection in return for loyalty. This pattern was common in Mexico City, where the dominance of a single party organized political patronage, helping to explain that city's remarkable territorial growth over the past century. The communities of self-built housing resulting from these varying processes went by different names throughout the region—*villas miseria* (misery villas) in Buenos Aires, colonias populares (people's colonies) in Mexico City, *callampas* (mushrooms) in Santiago, *pueblos jovenes* in Peru. Some of the terms, such as "barriadas" in Lima or "favelas" in Rio de Janeiro, have no direct translation, but were understood as the place of the urban poor, invoking images of intense crowding; precarious or nonexistent water, sewage, and electrical networks; and little access to education or health services. Urbanists recognized these as "informal" settlements, because their residents had no formal property title.

Most Populous Cities in Latin America, 1980 and 2000

● City with least 1 million inhabitants in 2000
(cities marked by blue circles are the 10 most populous)

(Population in millions)

≡ **MAP. 13.4**

As Latin America emerged from the authoritarian wave of the 1960s and 1970s, these neighborhoods grew more rapidly. This growth coincided with the rise of a new language of citizenship. Urban residents began demanding not only a right to vote but also rights to live in the city without fear that authorities would summarily evict them, destroying the homes they had built over years. Amid the hyperinflation and recession of the 1980s and early 1990s, no municipal or federal government in Latin America had the wherewithal to build housing sufficient to accommodate the urban poor. Instead, the working poor of Latin American cities demanded something simpler: guarantees that their hard-won urban foothold would be respected.

Contemporary Ideas about Informal Urbanization

Meeting this demand required both political and legal flexibility. The first part was relatively easy, as the experience of Mexico City had already shown. The second part was more difficult: no city solved the problem of granting legal rights to informal urban property.

Two schools of thought emerged to address the problems of informal urbanization. The first, elaborated by the Brazilian anthropologist and architect Carlos Nelson Ferreira dos Santos in Rio de Janeiro, can be thought of as "sites, services, and support": municipal governments can best incorporate the working poor by providing legally defined plots of land hooked to electricity, water, and sewage, with access to education and healthcare. Then, municipal governments should provide guidance to new residents of these plots as they build their own homes and neighborhoods.

The second school of thought was pioneered by the Peruvian economist Hernando de Soto, and can be characterized by his own phrase, "the mystery of capital." De Soto argued that municipal governments should immediately confer property titles on existing informal urban residences. Formal property title would enable residents to seek credit, improving not only their housing but also their employment and educational prospects, creating a virtuous cycle of improvement and rising value.

≡ **A Woman Protects Her Home in the Vidigal Favela, Rio de Janeiro.** This favela resident defends her hard-won patch of urban ground against attempted eviction in 1978. The favela residents' movement was one of the vanguards of redemocratization in Brazil, bringing new actors into Brazilian politics, forcing an expansion of the meanings of citizenship and rights. Vidigal avoided eviction but did not achieve equal protection under the law. By the late 1980s, it had fallen victim to turf battles between rival drug-trafficking syndicates.

≡ **A Man Participating in the Informal Economy in Ecuador.** This Ecuadorian street scene shows an informal (unlicensed) vendor offering to laminate documents or make a telephone connection for clients. Vendors have occupied street space in Latin American cities since the sixteenth century, so there was nothing new about informal commerce. But it became increasingly prevalent in late twentieth-century Latin America, as public employment rolls shrank and traditional firms subcontracted services rather than hiring permanent workers. Low-paid, highly flexible informal work became an ever-present feature of most sectors of the Latin American economy.

De Soto's recommendations had the theoretical appeal of simplicity and the budgetary appeal of efficiency; on paper, they required little public investment. In the neoliberal 1990s, de Soto became a star, while Ferreira dos Santos's ideas remained marginal. Latin American cities rushed to implement property-titling programs, often hiring de Soto as a consultant. However, few of these programs achieved their objectives, as property titling proved more difficult in practice than in theory. Nearly all of Latin America's urban informal neighborhoods remained only partially linked to formal property registries and their legal protections.

Urban informal property has been the most visible manifestation of a larger informal economic sector that includes any activity not legally registered but not expressly illegal either. Informal employment is as diverse as informal housing—comprising everything from selling food on the street to running an unregistered textile factory—but is even more difficult to define. The informal sector, as social scientists describe it, exists everywhere, not just as a curiosity of the developing world but as a large percentage of the overall economy wherever the rule of law is weak.

The proliferation of the informal economy undermines the formal economy by shrinking the tax base, crowding out legal employers, and weakening worker protections. Latin American cities have struggled to reduce the size of the informal sector with varying success. The neoliberal 1990s, with their focus on property and capital, brought new urgency to this challenge. At the same time, by cutting government spending, neoliberal policies often complicated efforts to regulate the informal sector. By the first decade of the twenty-first century, most Latin American politicians had recognized this as a struggle that must be faced perpetually, rather than resolved with a single magic gesture.

The Environment and Development, 1960–2000

Growing cities created environmental changes, vastly altering the landscape of the region. As the pace of urbanization accelerated in the last quarter of the twentieth century, the constraints of that process became increasingly clear. In particular, demands for electrification have taxed governments' ability to provide it. The public increasingly demands electricity and transportation, and that forests and habitat be cleared for roads or housing or to grow cattle or coffee; plastic bottles have made clean water available; and diesel trucks carry consumer goods and commercial products from one end of country to another. All these factors have placed severe stress on the environment.

Urban Environmental Issues: Electrification

To begin, twentieth-century city dwellers required electricity to power their street lights, refrigerators, air conditioners, power tools, and myriad other necessities of modern life. In Latin America, where coal deposits were scarce, planners turned to hydroelectric power to meet this demand. Dams proliferated throughout the region, particularly in nations that combined growing industrialization and plentiful rivers, like Mexico and Brazil.

In one of the region's iconic examples, São Paulo's Billings Reservoir was created by reversing the course of the Jurubatuba River so that it ran westward toward the city rather than east to the sea. When inaugurated in the 1930s, the Billings complex provided the residents of São Paulo with more hydropower than they could dream possible. Successive expansions increased that power, enabling São Paulo to grow into one of the world's largest cities. The apparent success of the Billings complex inspired construction of dams throughout the country. Brazil became a nation of hydroelectric power, and the construction of a dam was the way politicians left their mark on the landscape. By the end of the twentieth century, over five hundred major hydroelectric dams dotted the countryside—and plans were underway to build more, ever larger and farther afield.

Mexico underwent a similar process, as did Colombia and Argentina. Even relatively small Chile, with its single major city of Santiago, joined the dam-building frenzy. Less-developed nations hurried to catch up, and large percentages of World Bank funding to Latin America went into construction of hydroelectric dams to bring electricity to cities. As recently as 1980, the barriadas of Lima, the *mocambos* of Recife and the barrios of Bogotá went dark at nightfall, with only a few strands of electrical wire snaking through their interiors. By 2000, these neighborhoods were as brightly lit as middle-class neighborhoods—a transformation with ramifications not merely for convenience but also for public health, enabling refrigeration of food and medicine, among other benefits.

The massive expansion of dams has also had its costs, however. Dams displaced indigenous populations and destroyed vast tracts of forest to make way for reservoirs. Damming and the toxic industrial pollution that ensued despoiled ecosystems. And cheap electricity allowed a rate of urbanization that may itself prove unsustainable. Urban growth has tended to outstrip even the most generous hydroelectric supply, requiring ever greater investment in new dams in the next generation.

Brazil's Rolling Brownouts of 2001–2002

Hydroelectric power is proving to be especially susceptible to climate change. Two years of successive drought, coupled with the steadily rising energy demands, wreaked havoc on Brazil's hydroelectric complex in 2001–2002. Reservoir levels dropped precipitously. São Paulo experienced a series of rolling brownouts in mid-2001 as the government limited distribution in order to maintain vital services. Near the end of his second term, President Fernando Henrique Cardoso was forced to implement energy rationing, requiring residents of São Paulo to cut their consumption by 20 percent in the second half of 2001.

Cardoso had tamed inflation and restored economic productivity in the mid-1990s. International investors increasingly looked on Brazil as a Latin American success story, as its middle class grew and its largest corporations rose to global prominence. Many Brazilians, however, criticized Cardoso as a tool of international bankers. The opposition Labor Party (PT), in particular, alleged that the corporate privatization Cardoso had overseen had undermined Brazil's national patrimony and self-sufficiency.

The hydroelectric crisis seemed to bolster their argument. Whereas the military dictatorship had invested heavily in expanding hydroelectric power, Cardoso had partially privatized Eletrobras, the state electricity company, and had left expansion of new capacity to private investors. For Cardoso's detractors, forced energy rationing showed the insufficiency of neoliberal policies—investors reaped the profits of privatization, while everyday Brazilians suffered.

From another angle, the hydroelectric crisis was the inevitable outcome of Brazil's unchecked urbanization and its reliance on dam construction. São Paulo's consumption of electricity had grown exponentially since 1980. Brazil has more fresh water than any other country on earth, but even Brazil's reservoirs, it turned out, could run dry. Sooner or later, Brazil had to admit to these limits.

Energy rationing worked in the short term. Brownouts slowed São Paulo's economy, but only temporarily. The experience did little to change Brazil's reliance on hydroelectric power—the government began to invest more in natural gas generators, but also redoubled its efforts to build new dams. None of this helped Cardoso in the short term. In 2002, still suffering from the backlash against the brownouts, his party lost the presidential election, paving the way for Lula of the PT to rise to the presidency at last.

Automobile Traffic and Pollution

This cycle of hydroelectric development is part of a larger cycle of petrochemical growth. For much of the twentieth century, cheap oil enabled a pace of urbanization previously unimaginable, with immediately tangible benefits and poorly

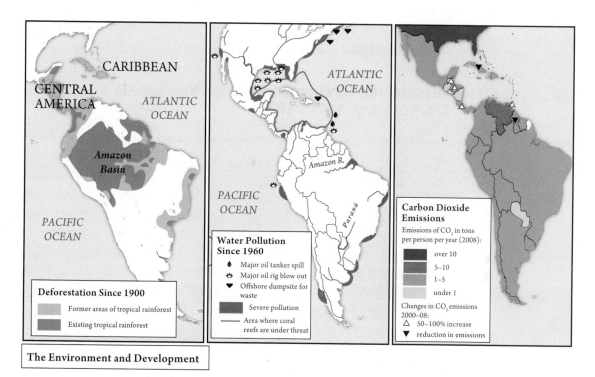

Deforestation Since 1900

- Former areas of tropical rainforest
- Existing tropical rainforest

Water Pollution Since 1960

- Major oil tanker spill
- Major oil rig blow out
- Offshore dumpsite for waste
- Severe pollution
- Area where coral reefs are under threat

Carbon Dioxide Emissions

Emissions of CO_2 in tons per person per year (2008):

- over 10
- 5–10
- 1–5
- under 1

Changes in CO_2 emissions 2000–08:
- 50–100% increase
- reduction in emissions

The Environment and Development

≡ **MAP. 13.5**

understood long-term costs. This petrochemical urbanization changed the world in dramatic ways, and those changes came particularly quickly in rapidly developing countries in the last quarter of the twentieth century—a description that fits most of Latin America.

The demand for automobiles exploded. Only a small percentage of Latin Americans owned automobiles in 1980, but car ownership is now more often the rule than the exception among city dwellers. In 1980, Mexico City had but 120 cars for every 1,000 persons; by 2015 the number had escalated to 300—more than one per family. The benefits of each of those new cars to the individual families who acquire them have been numerous, clear evidence of the expansion of the Mexican middle class and its demands for mobility. But the collective costs—in air pollution, congestion, and investment in highways and parking garages—have also been enormous, presenting a set of problems that are hardly unique to Latin America.

Describing the industrial might of São Paulo in the 1970s, the composer Caetano Veloso referred to *"a força da grana que ergue e destroi coisas belas"* ("the power of money that builds and destroys beautiful things"). Most Latin Americans, concentrating on climbing out of poverty, have had every reason to concentrate on the building of beautiful things. A growing number of Latin American communities, however, have begun to realize they must reckon also with the destruction.

Unsettling Circumstances for Venezuela's Democracy, 1970–1998

Much to the surprise of most observers of Latin America's political scene, Venezuela's once well-functioning two-party democracy faltered during the 1980s and 1990s. While so many other nations had worn themselves out in the battle against Marxist guerrillas or struggling against the excesses of authoritarian governments during the previous two decades, Venezuela's democracy proceeded comfortably, with presidents from the two parties, Acción Democrática (Democratic Action, or AD) and the Christian Democratic party (COPEI), alternating in office. But just as Mexicans increasingly questioned the viability of PRI in the last quarter of the twentieth century, by 1998 Venezuelans began to ask themselves what had gone wrong with their democracy.

From the *Caracazo* to the Breakdown of the Two Parties

By electing presidents from different political parties without resort to revolution, Venezuelans were rightly proud of the progress that they had made since the era of caudillos and military dictators. In addition to believing that votes should be counted fairly, both political parties agreed on policy fundamentals. In particular, both of these left-leaning organizations provided generous social services for the nation's poorest citizens. With Latin America's highest GDP because of the seemingly boundless supplies of oil and a growing manufacturing sector, the AD and COPEI governments could afford to be generous with state revenue to accomplish social objectives.

True, in the 1970s, President Carlos Andrés Pérez had squandered a good deal of this money by tripling the size of the federal bureaucracy and creating a large number of new state-owned manufacturing companies, but the country's inexhaustible petroleum reserves seemingly guaranteed continued growth. Generous education expenditures had significantly curtailed illiteracy, and price subsidies for household necessities kept people out of the grinding poverty so common elsewhere in Latin America. Venezuela's workers, particularly in the petroleum industry, not only received the highest wages in all of Latin America but also shared the benefits of subsidized food, healthcare, and transportation.

Just as had occurred in Mexico, plunging oil prices in the 1980s undid the two previous decades of progress and forced Venezuela's government to enact some austerity measures. In 1984, 36 percent of the population fell beneath the poverty line; by 1995, that percentage had increased to 66 percent. Both COPEI and

AD agreed on the necessity for neoliberal solutions to escape the economic crisis, beginning with slashing the salaries of government employees and privatizing a number of unprofitable state-owned companies. When these measures proved insufficient, Carlos Andrés Pérez, newly returned to the presidency in 1988, abandoned his campaign pledge to resist the neoliberal demands of the IMF. Instead, he deregulated the price of domestically consumed gasoline, provoking a series of massive demonstrations in Caracas in 1989 known as the *caracazo*.

After five·days of riots and looting, Pérez dispatched the army to restore order, an act that resulted in the death of at least 280 citizens, though an official death toll has never been established and was likely higher. In February 1992, a young colonel named Hugo Rafael Chávez Frías, influenced by the words of the Venezuelan Marxist guerrilla Douglas Bravo, led an unsuccessful barracks uprising to try and unseat Pérez and replace him with a socialist government. Soon thereafter evidence mounted of the president's corruption, leading to his impeachment. In the next election in 1994, eighty-year-old Rafael Caldera, who had served as president from 1969 to 1974, returned to that office, but the government limped along for the remainder of his term. What had gone wrong with Venezuelan democracy?

Although on paper a democratic system, Venezuela's centralized constitution in practice restricted citizens' participation. By concentrating power in each party's leadership, Venezuelan democracy excluded citizens from actual decision-making; in effect, voters merely ratified the choices that party bosses made. The party leaders selected all of the candidates for governorships and mayoralties. Voters could not split their votes, choosing some candidates from one party and some candidates from the other; they had to vote for the entire AD or COPEI ticket. Both parties controlled their own media outlets. Loyal AD operatives ran certain labor unions, while COPEI adherents directed most of the remainder. Party discipline made congress ineffective because no legislator ever crossed the aisle to vote with the opposition. In fact, roll call votes (as happens in the US Congress) never occurred. No significant ideological differences separated the parties; most battles were about questions of patronage. In short, ordinary Venezuelans felt they had little stake in the political system, especially after it stopped delivering benefits during hard times, as of course it eventually did. As a result, enthusiasm for both AD and COPEI had diminished by 1998, especially in the urban barrios, where the poorest of Venezuela's citizens lived.

The Venezuelan Election of 1998

The election of 1998 dramatically demonstrated voters' antipathy for both the AD and COPEI as the most successful presidential candidates artfully avoided association with either major party. Take, for example, the campaign of Irene Sáez, the early frontrunner who in December 1997 polled about 70 percent of the popular vote. As a former Miss Universe (1981) and mayor of a wealthy Caracas suburb, Sáez carefully wore her hair like Eva Perón and employed similar rhetoric to great effect. She promised to end corruption, to downsize the massive bureaucracy, and to refinance the public debt on more favorable terms. Her status as an outsider made her particularly appealing. But her numbers started to fall in the spring, in part because of voter concern about her lack of experience, but largely because she accepted COPEI's endorsement. By the time of the election her support had dwindled to 2 percent. The eventual runner-up in the election, a former governor, scrupulously refused the endorsement of both the national AD and the COPEI parties, although he did accept local support from the parties. Despite having both traditional parties behind him, he only won 38 percent of the tally when the election finally took place in December 1998.

After barely registering numbers in the early polls, Colonel Hugo Chávez, a Cuban-inspired socialist who was not aligned with either of the traditional political parties, emerged to win the election in a landslide with 56 percent of the popular vote. His charismatic personality, along with his flamboyant speeches peppered with rich colloquialisms that showed him to be a man of the people, pulled voters from Sáez into his camp. His three-point platform sounded like hers in some respects. He promised to end the traditional parties' monopoly over the political process and open it up to independent parties. In addition, he vowed to end corruption and poverty, an appeal that played very well with the poor and working classes. Most interestingly, he promised a complete rejection of the political past by calling for a constitutional convention to create the country's Fifth Republic, which would sweep away neoliberal policies. After his remarkable victory, Chávez kept this last promise, leading to the Constitution of 1999 and the eventual implementation of what Chávez christened the "Bolivarian Revolution."

TIMELINE

1960
New era of urbanization begins

1975
Era of neoliberal economic thought begins

1980s
Expansion of cocaine production in Colombia, Peru, and Bolivia

1980s
IMF begins lending money to debt-ridden nations

1983–1990
Democracy restored in Argentina, Brazil, and Chile

1985–2000
New wave of feminism

1989
Caracazo protest occurs in Venezuela

Conclusion

As Latin America emerged from the authoritarian period, it contended with the opportunities and challenges of neoliberalism. But this supposed economic panacea had mixed results. While foreign investors, business owners, and middle-class and elite consumers prospered (and some corrupt politicians lined their pockets), the poor experienced declining standards of living. As governments slashed social spending in the name of austerity and liberalized trade, both the urban and rural poor found their struggle to survive more challenging. Impoverished campesinos who had fled to the cities found themselves in equally dire straits because of their lack of job skills, which forced them to participate in the vagaries of the informal economy.

The benefits of the new wave of democracy that supplanted the authoritarian dictatorships of the 1970s offered the poor some glimmers of hope. Populist governments in the beginning of the twenty-first century reversed many neoliberal policies, and promised to create more egalitarian societies. Initially, these governments proved wildly popular, as they capitalized on the new ways of conceiving politics and popular culture, the subject of chapter 14.

KEY TERMS

favelas   587

International Monetary Fund (IMF)   579

Malvinas War   584

maquiladoras   603

Medellín cartel   612

North American Free Trade Agreement (NAFTA)   603

Washington Consensus 579

World Bank   579

Zapatistas   605

1989–2000
Era of bait-and-switch populists

1991
Bolivia's Evo Morales protests against coca eradication

1993
Medellín cartel kingpin Pablo Escobar killed

1994
Zapatista uprising protesting neoliberalism in Mexico

1998
Hugo Chávez elected president of Venezuela

2006
Chile elects Michelle Bachelet as president

Selected Readings

Borzutzky, Silvia, and Lois Oppenheim eds. *After Pinochet: The Chilean Road to Democracy and the Market.* Gainesville: University Press of Florida, 2006.

Clawson, Patrick L., and Lee Rensselaer III. *The Andean Cocaine Industry.* New York: St. Martin's Press, 1996.

Coppedge, Michael. *Strong Parties and Lame Ducks: Presidential Partyarchy and Factionalism in Venezuela.* Stanford, CA: Stanford University Press, 1994.

Edmonds-Poli, Emily, and David A. Shirk. *Contemporary Mexican Politics.* Lanham, MD: Rowman & Littlefield 2012.

Fischer, Bronwyn, Bryan McCann, and Javier Auyero. *Cities from Scratch: Poverty and Informality in Urban Latin America.* Durham, NC: Duke University Press, 2014.

Gootenberg, Paul. *Andean Cocaine: The Making of a Global Drug.* Chapel Hill: University of North Carolina Press, 2008.

Grandin, Greg. Empire's Workshop, *Latin America, the United States, and the Rise of the New Imperialism.* New York: Holt Paperbacks, 2007.

Holt-Giménez, Eric. *Campesino a Campesino: Voices from Latin America's Farmer to Farmer Movement for Sustainable Agriculture.* Oakland, CA: Food First Books, 2006.

Htun, Mala. *Sex and the State: Abortion, Divorce and the Family under Latin American Dictatorships and Democracies.* New York: Cambridge University Press, 2003.

Miller, Shawn W. *An Environmental History of Latin America.* New York: Cambridge University Press, 2007.

Painter, James. *Bolivia and Coca: A Study in Dependency.* Boulder, CO: Lynne Reinner, 1994.

Soto Laveaga, Gabriela. *Jungle Laboratories: Mexican Peasants, National Projects, and the Making of the Pill.* Durham, NC: Duke University Press, 2009.

14

New Identities,
New Politics,
1980–2016

Global Connections

With the end of the global Cold War in the late 1980s and early 1990s, old certainties diminished and new challenges arose. The binary division that had defined competition between the superpowers—capitalist versus communist, East versus West—seemed to crumble. It took with it an array of smaller but still substantial categories that had ordered political life for decades. For much of the twentieth century, global political trends had run toward incorporation and aggregation: granting rights of citizenship to those previously held on the margins; incorporating formerly autonomous areas into national boundaries; and creating blocs and treaty organizations. As the century closed, trends ran in the opposite direction, toward disaggregation and devolution. But this process was overshadowed by the longer history of empire and global expansion. This led to the formation of new political and cultural identities deeply shaped by histories of conflict.

Consider the case of East Timor, the eastern half of the island of Timor, north of Australia. The Portuguese colonized East Timor in the sixteenth century, bringing Catholicism, the Portuguese language, and connections to the Western world (including Brazil, for example, through Portuguese trade networks). The Portuguese also brought forcible labor exploitation, displacement, and racial hierarchy. As the Portuguese empire disintegrated in the 1970s, Marxist guerrillas struggled for autonomy, proclaiming their independence in 1975. Days later, Indonesia swept in and claimed East Timor as a province, beginning decades of abusive military rule. Over the course of the 1990s, the East Timorese negotiated a painstaking and fragile process toward sovereignty under the auspices of the United Nations, establishing full independence in 2002. This process—the disestablishment of dictatorial regimes, the splintering of states along ethnic or religious lines— was typical of the 1990s. It could not have happened without the end of the global Cold War, but its unfolding revealed the imprint of a longer history of empire. East Timor's experience with Catholic liberation theology, for example, had much in common with that of many parts of Latin America.

Processes of political change were driven by new or revived claims to group identity, often expressed in racial, ethnic, or religious terms. These group identities had no consistent ideological content or direction—they could just as easily become part of revolutionary uprisings or counterrevolutionary suppression of dissent. They required the assertion of group unity, which, in turn, tended to diminish recognition of inequalities within the group while emphasizing distinctions between

Indigenous Protest Leader. Beginning in 1990, members of CONAIE unified the different groups of indigenous people in Ecuador and began to place pressure on the national government to end neoliberal policies that damaged the poor. Initially, they began their efforts with a mass march on Quito and presented their demands to the mestizo-dominated elected government. CONAIE applied additional pressure on the state by imposing informal blockades on roads leading to Quito, rolling boulders onto the asphalt or piling trees across the roadway. Since the urban population depended on foodstuffs and other supplies brought in from the countryside, these tactics gave CONAIE considerable leverage.

629

members of the group and outsiders. As a result, they challenged understandings of citizenship and rights, both in multiparty democracies and single-party socialist states. For example, the Uyghurs, a Turkic, Muslim ethnic minority concentrated in the Xinjiang province of western China, sought greater autonomy in the 1990s and early 2000s, in keeping with global trends toward devolution and identity politics. The Chinese government responded by cracking down heavily, violently suppressing what it perceived as a separatist threat. In places like Turkey and Iraq, Kurdish minorities pressed for recognition and autonomy from their national governments. Iraq's brutal repression of the Kurds under Saddam Hussein provided one of the justifications for the US invasion of that country in 2002.

Elsewhere in the Middle East, a rapidly changing political landscape saw the rise of new types of religious-political identity. Most important was the rise of political Islam. These new Islamicists were not ethnic or religious minorities in any sense—in nearly every Middle Eastern country, Muslims constitute the vast majority of the population, and many Muslims adhere to a strict observance of their faith that was entirely apolitical—but radical Islamicists emerged from the same political power shifts and realignments that shaped the 1990s in other parts of the world.

Egypt's Islamic Brotherhood was one of the first such groups, although Egypt's heavy-handed leadership limited its widespread influence for many years. In the wake of the Soviet intervention in Afghanistan, that country—once among the most cosmopolitan and "Westernized" in the region—fractured into tribalism, which opened political space for its takeover by another radical Islamicist group, the Taliban. As a result, Afghanistan would become a haven where other militant Islamicist groups, unwelcome in their home countries could grow and flourish. Most notable among these was Al-Qaida, an organization with origins in Saudi Arabia and Yemen. Al-Qaida's attacks on Western targets in 2001 redefined the political paradigm for the early twenty-first century, just as the Cold War had for the second half of the twentieth.

By contrast, the 1990s were a decade for optimism in Latin America, characterized by redemocratization through much of the region. Military governments gave way to democratic political openings. Between the mid-1980s and mid-1990s, freely elected civilian presidents replaced the rule of the generals in Argentina, Chile, Brazil, Uruguay, Paraguay, Peru, El Salvador, Guatemala, and Honduras.

The violent conflicts between armed Marxist insurgents and military security forces that had flared across the region since the 1960s slowly came to an end, as the defeat of the guerrillas or negotiated peace accords brought an end to hostilities in nearly every country. In the 1990s, peace accords brought an end to the bloody conflicts that had savaged Guatemalan and El Salvador. The process took longer in Colombia, where the region's longest-running civil war had developed into a decades-long conflict involving militant leftists, right-wing paramilitaries, the Colombian military, narco-traffickers, and the US Drug Enforcement Administration (DEA). But this tragic era of Colombian history also slowly began to wind to a close in the 1990s. It would take two more decades until the FARC and the government finally reached a negotiated settlement in 2016.

The reopening of civil society created an opportunity for Latin Americans to reconsider many of the national myths that had undergirded the societies in which they had lived for many decades. Foremost among these were questions that had to do with representation and rights, especially for nonwhites and mestizos. Even in places such as Mexico, where the mestizo notion of "**la raza cósmica**" had served as a key trope of Mexican political identity since the 1920s, and in Brazil, where the "myth of racial democracy" had sought to unite a vast and racially diverse country since the 1930s, questions about race and ethnicity fell under new scrutiny. In countries like Guatemala and Peru, where the indigenous population had borne the brunt of political violence in recent armed conflicts, new ethnic-based political movements such as the *movimiento maya* emerged. And in Honduras, Nicaragua, Peru, and Colombia, where large Afro-descendent minorities had been left almost out entirely of the national narratives, vocal sectors emerged to demand that the national political discourse incorporate conceptualizations of race and ethnic identity in meaningful new ways.

The new opening was limited not only to people-power movements, but also to fresh ideas, such as concerns for the environment. Environmentalism emerged as a political force in the United States and Western Europe in the 1960s, but it did not take root in Latin America (nor in most regions in the Global South) until the 1990s. When environmentalism did begin to flourish in the region, it became intertwined with other aspects of identity politics, often shaped by movements to recognize indigenous rights. But indigenous people were not always the "natural environmentalists" that many people in the North romantically imagined them to be. In Paraguay, for example, indigenous people, facing poverty resulting from deforestation and government corruption, initially opposed the creation of national parks because they encroached on what little forest territory they had left to them. As with the expansion of political rights to formerly disenfranchised or unrecognized groups, protection of the environment—or at least due consideration of it—became both a source of controversy and a priority in Latin America by the 1990s.

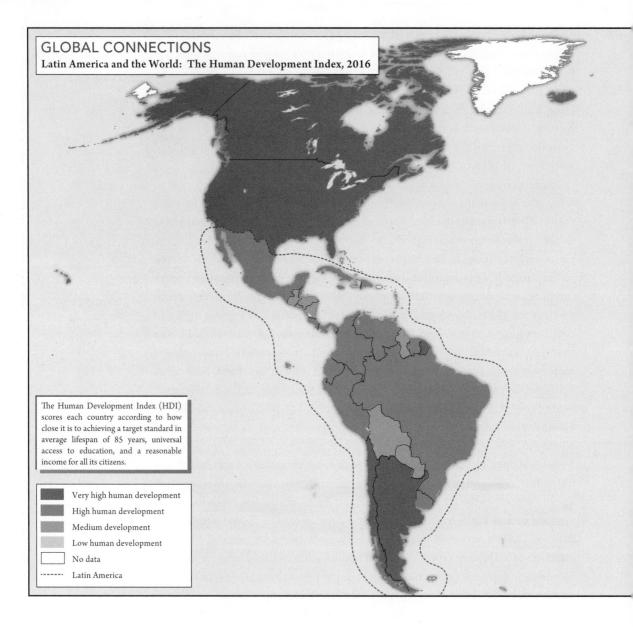

GLOBAL CONNECTIONS
Latin America and the World: The Human Development Index, 2016

The Human Development Index (HDI) scores each country according to how close it is to achieving a target standard in average lifespan of 85 years, universal access to education, and a reasonable income for all its citizens.

- Very high human development
- High human development
- Medium development
- Low human development
- No data
- ------- Latin America

The Rejection of Mestizaje and Racial Democracy, 1980–2000

The expansion of political democracy in Latin America during the 1980s and 1990s coincided with changes in the way citizens represented themselves before the state. The corporatism that structured Latin American nations in

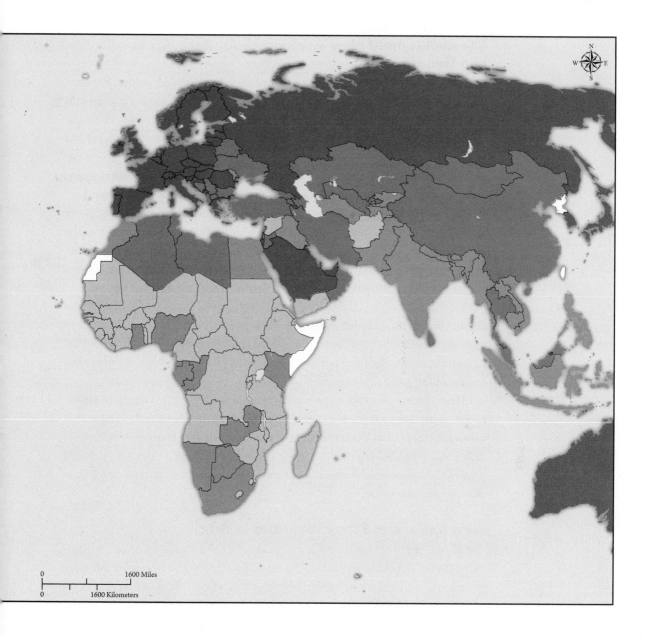

the mid-twentieth century had divided populations by occupation, with industrial workers, campesinos, soldiers, and university graduates treated as distinct classes. The authoritarian period drained corporatism of its inclusionary energy: citizenship became less a delivery of new rights and more a series of strict limitations.

The Evolution of New Thinking about Race, Class, and Gender

By the time Latin American nations returned to democracy, corporatism had atrophied. Neoliberal governments shed their bureaucratic burdens, particularly protections of particular labor categories. As Brazilian President Fernando Henrique Cardoso put it in the 1990s, "the Getúlio Vargas Era is over!" As occupation became less definitive, emphasis on racial, ethnic, religious, and gender identity grew stronger. Self-identifying as black, indigenous, evangelical Christian, or gay, for example, became more important than self-identifying as a dockworker or a lieutenant.

This rise of **identity politics** paralleled similar transitions in the United States and Western Europe. But it took on particular inflections in Latin America. The idea of harmonious racial or ethnic mixing was crucial to the foundation of a sense of modern national identity in places like Mexico, Brazil, Ecuador, Colombia, and Nicaragua. Even in countries where the idea of ethnic mixing had not been so prominent, such as Peru and Bolivia, governing elites had sought to restrict ethnic distinctions to the margins of politics. Ideas of racial harmony had always been more aspirational than real, as racism and discrimination persisted throughout the twentieth century. But the model and symbolism of racial and ethnic harmony had been a central goal to this aspiration.

In the 1980s and 1990s, a new generation of leaders criticized those aspirational ideas. Their critique was that symbols of harmonious racial and ethnic mixing, or superficially colorblind legislation that failed to recognize indigenous difference, provided cover for ongoing discrimination. This criticism gathered greater force as citizens reorganized themselves, seeking new bases for mobilization and representation.

New Racial and Ethnic Identities in Brazil

The phrase "myth of racial democracy" was itself a product of sociological analysis of the 1960s. The existence of that phrase and a supporting body of academic work describing racial disparities in Brazil shows that many Brazilians were keenly aware of ongoing racial discrimination well before the 1990s—particularly those who felt the brunt of that discrimination. But before the 1990s, suggestions that racism remained a problem in Brazil were decidedly countercultural, working against the mainstream celebration of racial mixing. In the 1990s and beyond, those suggestions began to move into the forefront. While they remained controversial, they set the terms of a new debate.

The rhetoric of racial democracy and criticisms of that rhetoric alike tended to focus on Brazilians of African ancestry. The sociological research demonstrating

Ethnic Composition in Latin America Today

- Indigenous
- Europeans
- Afro-descendant
- Mestizos

≡ **MAP. 14.1**

racial disparities, for example, focused on economic differences between *branco*, *negro*, and *pardo*—white, black, and brown, with brown (as a census category) understood to refer to citizens of mixed African and European ancestry. Brazilian Indians were largely pushed to the margins of this debate. The emergence of an indigenous movement thus came as a surprise to many Brazilians. More surprising still was the prominence of indigenous leaders from eastern and southern Brazil in that movement. Most Brazilians had wrongly assumed Indians had disappeared from these regions. Their sudden visibility largely resulted from a new self-identification as Indian by Brazilians who had previously classified themselves as *pardo*, or brown.

Several reasons explain this shift. The 1988 Constitution, which consolidated the gradual transition from military dictatorship to democracy, enshrined indigenous land rights. Communities that had no prior incentive to identify themselves as Indian now stood to recover lands they had lost during previous decades. The Catholic Church, influenced by the social gospel of liberation theology, began to recognize and emphasize indigenous identity in its ministry, in some cases helping new indigenous leaders in their appeals to government. And self-identification as "indigenous" began to offer a powerful platform for political contestation. After centuries of marginalization, Brazilians of indigenous ancestry began to seize the benefits of identifying on the basis of ethnic or racial difference.

Black mobilization was more diffuse. From the 1920s through the 1960s, localized black movements and organizations had arisen to challenge political order, without gathering national momentum. In the 1970s, self-consciously black cultural identity—often using the English term "black," rather than the Portuguese "*negro*" or "*preto*"—offered a way of proclaiming racial consciousness and questioning dominant assumptions. In the same decade, the *Movimento Negro Unificado*, or Unified Black Movement, sought to unite race-based political groups throughout the country, playing a part in the democratic mobilization that led to the dictatorship's demise.

≣ **Skateboarders in Downtown São Paulo.** Compare this photo to Figure 5.5, of the Viaduto do Chá in downtown São Paulo in the 1920s. This photo is taken nearby some seventy years later, and shows the transformation of downtown São Paulo. The privileged, well-ordered space of the elite has become the messy, democratic space of the popular classes, who develop their own uses for old promenades. This transformation of urban space was typical of the breakdown of old hierarchies and the emergence of niche consumer markets, identity groups, and challenges to elite politics.

In the 1980s, affiliation with new political parties splintered the Unified Black Movement. But as with the indigenous movement, the 1988 Constitution offered new legal tools, including land grants to communities that could prove they were founded as quilombos, or settlements of runaway slaves in the period before abolition. And black leaders mobilized to demand admission in greater numbers to Brazil's selective public universities, which remained overwhelmingly white into the twenty-first century.

Black Brazilians also challenged long-standing social codes, ostensibly colorblind but in reality deeply racist. Among the most notorious was the common practice of directing any dark-skinned visitor to an apartment building to the "service" rather than the "social" elevator. The unspoken segregation of elevators had long been a way of reinforcing assumptions about the social place and status of Brazilians of color. Changing this practice required new laws making it illegal to block anyone from using the "social" elevator. It also required a cultural change, a growing recognition that Brazilians of color deserved access to the real benefits of citizenship. The cultural transformation was more difficult to consolidate than the legal, and could only be achieved through the constant efforts of Brazilians of color claiming their rights.

Questioning Mestizaje in the Andean Nations

Inspired by Mexico's discussion of mestizaje in the 1920s (chapter 9), Andean politicians and anthropologists began debating the applicability of the idea to their own populations. Because indigenous people were stereotyped as poor, uneducated, rural, and "traditional," Andean political leaders and intellectuals hoped that the combination of indigenous migration to urban areas and a greater investment in rural education would culturally transform indigenous people into mestizos.

As the leaders of the new indigenous movements pointed out, mestizaje represented a disguised attempt to "whiten" the indigenous population—if not biologically, then at least culturally—and to assimilate them into the nation. Although the proponents of mestizaje stated that their goal was to include every citizen into the nation-state, in effect ethnic assimilation meant that indigenous people needed to relinquish all characteristics of indigeneity. Perhaps nobody stated the objectives of mestizaje more bluntly than one of Ecuador's military presidents in the 1970s. "There is no more Indian problem," he declared. "We all become white when we accept the goals of national culture." Not surprisingly, many proud indigenous groups, such as the Otavalans of northern Ecuador, resented and resisted the government's attempt to assimilate them into a melting pot dominated by the majority culture.

Despite having significant percentage of indigenous citizens, identity politics has not played a strong role in Peru's recent history. As we saw in chapter 9, Juan Velasco's military government conceptualized society in terms of class, so that all campesinos were decreed to be peasants. Then, in the 1990s, President Alberto Fujimori's government brooked no political opposition. No indigenous movement could take root in Peru as they would in Bolivia and Ecuador. Even Peru's indigenous president, Ollanta Humala (2011–2016), was reluctant to make his identity an important feature of his term in office.

Additionally, the concept of mestizaje proved intellectually unsatisfactory to the Afro-Andean population, who became increasingly outspoken in defense of their culture during the 1990s. Except in Brazil and the Caribbean, Afro-Latin Americans had remained largely invisible to the dominant culture since their emancipation from slavery. In Bolivia and Ecuador, the populations of African descent were numerically small (thirty-five thousand people in Bolivia, 4 percent of the population in Ecuador) and mostly distant from urban centers. Even in places where there was a sizable Afro-descendent population, they were often not well represented. Although more than one million Afro-Colombians lived on the remote Pacific Coast, for example, policy makers in Bogotá paid little attention to them.

Peru's once-large population of African heritage, most of which resided in Lima, underwent generations of racial mixing after emancipation in 1854, and had been incorporated statistically into the mixed-race population. Afro-Peruvians have been less involved in the kinds of multicultural movements that are commonplace elsewhere in Latin America, although there is an increased tendency to self-identify as Afro-descendent and to position their own histories within that of the African Diaspora. Peruvian singer Susana Baca, a winner of two Latin Grammy awards and the former Minister of Culture of Peru, has done much to popularize the culture and history of Afro-Peruvians and to raise their profile both nationally and internationally.

In addition to their geographical isolation, many Afro-Andeans suffered from high rates of illiteracy and unemployment, contributing to their invisibility. Increased economic activity by outsiders within their isolated and impoverished areas threatened the livelihood of the people residing there, who normally fished, farmed, and occasionally panned for gold. In western Colombia in the 1980s, large gold-mining conglomerates and logging corporations occupied lands that Afro-Colombians considered to be their own, leading Afro-Colombian activists to protest. In Ecuador, the construction of a petroleum pipeline and refinery on the Pacific coast threatened the environment of Esmeraldas province, causing Afro-Ecuadorians to raise their voices against foreign oil corporations and join forces with the new indigenous-led multicultural movement. These social movements contributed to the relative decline of the concept of mestizaje.

Susana Baca(r) on Indigenous Peoples' Day in Peru. The Peruvian singer Susana Baca grew up in the coastal region characterized by common Afro-Peruvian inheritance. African roots were rarely recognized in Peruvian national narratives in Baca's youth. Baca rose to prominence in her own community, then in cosmopolitan Lima, then more broadly. Only after achieving international fame as an icon of Black Peru did she become more celebrated nationally within Peru, as that nation gave new emphasis to African contributions to national culture.

ECONOMICS AND COMMODITIES

Otavalan Weaving and Global Entrepreneurship

The indigenous town of Otavalo in northern Ecuador was highly respected as a producer of woven goods in pre-Hispanic times. During the colonial era, Otavalan workshops supplied consumers as far away as the mines at Potosí. Although mired in depression during the nineteenth century, the town gained the reputation as the "awakening valley" after World War II because of its revival as a producer of quality handicrafts. Later, Peace Corps volunteers contributed new designs, new products like sweaters and tapestries, fresh colors, and marketing strategies. These attracted more visitors to Otavalo's Poncho Plaza. With the construction of a paved road between Quito and Otavalo in the 1970s, what had been a two-day journey was reduced to two hours, expanding the number of prospective purchasers. Soon travel companies packaged their Galápagos tours with a three-day stay in the Ecuadorian Andes, including a visit to the marketplace at Otavalo's Poncho Plaza.

Otavaleños have astutely capitalized on growing interest in their textiles and music to become prosperous international entrepreneurs. For the thousands of tourists who visit Otavalo annually, the appeal of the marketplace is in part a quest for an aesthetic ideal—the assumption that one can purchase a handmade sweater from a "real indigenous person" at a modest price in visually breathtaking surroundings. Merchants deliberately signal their indigenous heritage by dressing in traditional Otavalan attire. Women, who are the principal vendors at the Plaza, wear ruffled white embroidered blouses with two long dark skirts, a shawl, a headscarf, and gold jewelry (depending on one's wealth).

During the 1980s, Otavaleños traveled to Europe and the United States seeking new markets. The enthusiasm of international customers for Otavalan goods convinced merchants that they could expand their commercial outreach. Otavaleños and Ecuadorians in general migrated to Spain (where no visa was required) or the United States (where the large

≡ **Otavaleño Man Selling Textiles at the Market.**
The Plaza de Ponchos in Otavalo, Ecuador, hosts the largest indigenous market in South America. The Plaza derived its name from its exhaustive array of homemade textiles, a craft at which the Otavaleños have excelled since pre-Hispanic times, which attract tourists by the thousands annually. Usually, women sell at Andean markets, but in this instance an Otavaleño man is tending his wares. He is dressed in the typical clothing for Otavaleño men, with white dress pants, a dark shirt, and a single braid of hair.

Hispanic community welcomed them) to sell their wares on sidewalks and entertain passing crowds with Andean music. The resulting transnational network involved family members back in Otavalo producing goods and shipping them to sidewalk merchants abroad. Some well-known weavers sold to exclusive stores in major metropolitan areas in Europe and the United States, while young Otavalan street merchants became familiar sights in cities like New York, San Francisco, and Taos, as well as on college campuses, where they found ready interest in their colorful sweaters and CDs. Even in those difficult economic times, Otavalans found new ways to both preserve their ethnic identity and earn a decent living.

The Indigenous Movements in Ecuador, Bolivia, and Guatemala, 1980–2010

Latin America's multicultural turn in the 1980s elevated the public roles of indigenous people and Afro-Latin Americans. This contemporary **indigenismo** that stemmed from the activism of indigenous folk and Afro-Latinos themselves differed radically from the indigenista ideas of the mestizo and white intellectuals of the 1920s. Rejecting the implicit racism of the assimilationist projects that those intellectuals and national governments had long promoted, independent ethnicities now created their own organizations in an attempt to assert their rights to survive and prosper as distinct cultural nations within their countries.

The Ecuadorian Experience

The propitious moment when Ecuador returned to democracy in 1979 opened up opportunities for indigenous people. Newly empowered with the right to vote and an official commitment to promote bilingual education, the emboldened leadership of indigenous groups, assisted by nongovernmental organizations (NGOs) and both Catholic and Protestant missionaries, focused on preserving their distinctive cultures.

In 1986, Ecuador's fourteen separate indigenous ethnicities merged into a single pan-indigenous entity, the **Confederation of Indigenous Nationalities of Ecuador (CONAIE)**, a unique coalition in Latin America. As a cultural organization, CONAIE pressed the government for the recognition of the concept of **plurinationalism**—the idea that multiple autonomous indigenous nations could exist within the boundaries of the Ecuadorian nation-state. CONAIE also advocated for social and economic issues, such as the need for additional agrarian reform and the protection of the Amazonian environment from destructive petroleum drilling. Although many Ecuadorians sympathized with CONAIE's objective of environmental sustainability, politicians proved resistant to any notion of plurinationalism. Seemingly, the indigenous movement and the neoliberal state had arrived at a stalemate.

On June 4, 1990, Ecuadorians awoke to find their highways blockaded with boulders and trees, preventing commercial traffic from hauling foodstuffs from the countryside into the urban areas for an entire week. What astonished politicians was that CONAIE had managed to unify the entire indigenous population behind this nationwide blockade. Quickly the government entered into negotiations with CONAIE, but refused to accept their demand for redefining Ecuador as a plurinational state. Although Ecuador now boasted the most unified and powerful indigenous movement in the Americas, CONAIE could not sustain the blockade forever; nor could it force the government into concrete concessions. CONAIE's leadership eventually decided to form a political party, Pachakutik (Quichua for "turning point") to contest elections and hopefully assert greater influence.

Over the next few years, the party managed to elect a few representatives to Congress, increasing its numbers in every election cycle. Seven members of Pachakutik were chosen as delegates to the new assembly charged with drawing up the Constitution of 1998. Pachakutik's members, however, could only persuade their fellow delegates to employ the language of "pluricultural and multiethnic" in the Constitution to describe Ecuador's population.

As Pachakutik continued to show its political muscle, Lucio Gutierrez, newly elected president in 2002, offered four cabinet posts to the party. Although Gutierrez had campaigned as a populist whose ideas seemed to be in concert with those of

≡ **CONAIE Members Marching on Quito.** Indigenous groups challenged traditional Ecuadorian political hierarchies in the 1990s and beyond. To achieve greater political leverage, many indigenous groups united in CONAIE, the Confederation of Indigenous Nations of Ecuador. Between the early 1990s and 2005, CONAIE went from the political margins to the mainstream, becoming a key player in national politics, with the power to make or break presidencies through alliance or opposition. CONAIE mobilized against the perquisites of multinational oil companies operating in Ecuadorian territory, among other concerns about the inequalities and instability of global capital movements.

the indigenous movement, following his election he retained most of the neoliberal measures he had once denounced. Discredited by their association with the president, Pachakutik lost its political viability. In the 2006 presidential election, the Pachakutik candidate managed to win only 1 percent of the vote. The victor, Rafael Correa, who had unsuccessfully courted the party during the election, thereafter refused any overtures to Pachakutik. As a result, Ecuador's indigenous movement languished during Correa's "citizens' revolution."

Correa radically transformed Ecuador's political system. An elected constituent assembly strengthened executive authority through the Constitution of 2008, a process that Correa subsequently reinforced through control of the legislature. Correa departed sharply from neoliberal prescription by increasing government spending on social programs. He doubled welfare and housing assistance and reduced electricity rates for Ecuador's poorest citizens. (Rising oil revenues paid for these public expenditures). By 2013 federal expenditures on education and healthcare had tripled since 2005. Declining petroleum revenues, however, diminished his popularity, and he left office at the end of his third presidential term in 2017, barely able to convince the electorate to accept his chosen successor.

As CONAIE ascended into the political spotlight in the early twenty-first century, Afro-Ecuadorian organizations became more outspoken. Disparate groups created the National Afro-Ecuadorian Confederation (CNA), which successfully lobbied NGOs and the World Bank for funding for development projects. CNA sought an end to racial stereotyping. It also pressed for the passage of a statute identical to Colombia's Law 70 of 1993, which had redefined Pacific-coast Afro-Colombians as a corporate entity entitled to hold lands communally, just like indigenous people. Despite the language of Ecuador's Constitution of 1998 embracing multiculturalism, Congress refused to create legislation similar to Colombia's, on the grounds that Afro-Ecuadorians had no tradition of communal agriculture. Nevertheless, in recent years, individuals within the Afro-Ecuadorian community have played more prominent political roles. During Rafael Correa's first term, Congress passed an affirmative action statute and the president appointed a number of CNA's leaders to cabinet positions, a national first. Ironically, by promoting these individuals, critics pointed out, Correa co-opted and weakened the leadership of the CNA. By way of contrast, the trajectory for Bolivia's indigenous movement has been relatively positive.

The Indigenous Movement in Bolivia

Bolivia, the nation in South America with the largest indigenous population, also experienced the emergence of social protests in recent years. In fact, the first contemporary demonstration in the Andean region was that of a group calling itself

Túpac Katari (after the colonial-era indigenous rebel Túpac Katari) that block-aded roads in 1979 to protest the corrupt military regime. Assisted by NGOs and religious sects, various local organizations voiced opposition to the neoliberal policies of subsequent governments led by the National Revolutionary Movement (MNR). By the 1980s, the MNR had lost its interest in maintaining its linkage to the Aymara and other indigenous folk as it adopted assimilationist language. As one MNR politician said, "One will no longer be discriminated against when one stops being an Indian."

Although fragmented, indigenous groups continued to protest their situation. The neoliberal governments gradually responded by adopting a constitutional amendment that defined Bolivia as a multiethnic and pluricultural state, like Ecuador. Governments again funded bilingual education and accepted the principle of communal agriculture. Most importantly, the Law of Popular Participation of 1990 redistributed 20 percent of federal revenue to municipalities based on the premise that communities could best decide funding priorities for themselves. Although indigenous people constituted 60 percent of Bolivia's population, their priorities remained low on the neoliberal agenda, arguably because the movement's fragmentation weakened its political influence.

The relatively marginal position of the indigenous movement changed only with the growing popularity of Evo Morales, an indigenous Aymara coca farmer who originally gained national recognition for defending fellow cocaleros from US efforts to eradicate their crop. Elected to Congress in 1997, Morales tapped into popular issues beginning with a protest against the proposed privatization of the water company in Cochabamba, a measure that stood to raise rates to consumers by 400 percent. He aroused nationalist sentiment by opposing the neoliberal government's proposal to sell natural gas to foreign corporations, which then would export to Chile (the enemy that had annexed Bolivia's entire coast after the War of the Pacific) and the United States. His popularity with indigenous people coupled with his broader anti-imperialist message gave Morales a majority of votes in the presidential election of 2005, marking the first time that a self-identified indigenous person had become the president of any South American nation. Thus, even as Ecuador's indigenous movement collapsed in disarray, Bolivia's advanced as an indigenous president was inaugurated into the highest office in the land.

Evo Morales became another member of the so-called **Pink Tide**, a group of leftist presidents who rejected neoliberalism and pledged to restore government support for the nation's poor. Like Ecuador's Rafael Correa and Venezuela's late Hugo Chávez, Morales increased funding for education, healthcare and welfare assistance. As a result, he reduced Bolivia's poverty rate from 53 percent in 2005 to 29 percent in 2015. In order to pay for these programs, the government increased

≡ **Evo Morales, Hugo Chávez, and Fidel Castro.** Latin America's so-called Pink Tide was characterized by the rise to power of a new generation of leftist leaders in the late 1990s and early 2000s. The most prominent among them, Venezuela's Hugo Chávez and Bolivia's Evo Morales, sought the benediction of Cuba's Fidel Castro—a benediction Fidel Castro was happy to bestow, given Chávez's willingness to supply Cuba with subsidized Venezuelan oil. The Pink Tide terrified international investors and outraged traditional elites, but soon faced challenges of its own, as new leftist leaders sought to reconcile promised redistribution of wealth with falling revenues.

the tax rate on Bolivia's enormous exports of natural gas and other hydrocarbons. Like his fellow leftist presidents, Morales faced ongoing opposition from the middle class, who pointed out that the financial deficits caused by social programs were unsustainable. Perhaps more than any other Latin American president, Morales strongly supported affirmative action programs. At one point, women held half of his cabinet's ministerial positions.

The Maya Movement in Guatemala

Guatemala is another of the few Latin American nations with an indigenous majority (upward of 60 percent of Guatemalans are indigenous), but its native population has historically been the object of virulent racism that has left them with some of the lowest social indicators in the hemisphere. Even in the late twentieth century, power in the country remained vested in a small elite of primarily European origin and in the ladinos. Guatemala has historically been the richest nation in Central America in terms of economic and natural resources, but decades of political struggle severely hampered its economic advancement.

As we have seen (chapter 12), Guatemala suffered through an unevenly matched and bloody civil war between Marxist guerrillas (the Guatemalan National Revolutionary Unity, or URNG) and the military-controlled government from 1960 to 1996. The Maya population bore the brunt of the violence, especially during the 1980s, when the Guatemalan government came to identify the indigenous population as "internal enemies of the state." By the end of the armed conflict, Maya people accounted for more than 80 percent of the war's victims. So severe were the effects of the violence on Mayan lives and culture that some have called this period the "Mayan holocaust," while others have labeled it outright genocide.

From the ashes of the Mayan holocaust, indigenous leaders began to reinterpret the violence in terms of racism and genocide, rather than through the lens of the Cold War and anticommunism. This was the basis of *movimiento maya* (sometimes called the "Pan-Mayan" or simply the **Mayan movement**), a cultural and political movement that sought to fundamentally redefine the place of Maya people as citizens within Guatemala. The movement's leaders were largely Maya intellectuals and elites. Indigenous Mayan linguists played a major role in organizing the movement, contributing to the significance that Mayan languages played as a symbol of the movement itself.

Leaders of the Mayan movement critiqued what they described as a racist ladino (mestizo and white) nation. Their critique extended to the armed left, which they began to reexamine through the lens of racism. This reinterpretation called for a wholesale reconsideration of the Mayan experience as it related to the Guatemalan state, and they demanded a fundamental reassessment of the role Mayan people would play in postwar society and culture. In the mid-1980s, Mayan intellectuals put forth a series of mandates for the reconstruction of Mayan society based on two key principles: the conservation and resurrection of elements of Mayan culture and the promotion of governmental reform based on full equality within the framework of Guatemalan and international law.

In the early 1990s, the movement gained momentum through events surrounding the Columbian quincentenary in 1992 and the award of the Nobel Peace Prize to an indigenous female activist, Rigoberta Menchú Tum, that same year. By 1993, the Mayan movement had become a full-blown political and social crusade, built on the premise that Guatemalan nationhood had for too long perpetuated oppression and violence against the country's indigenous population. The movement's

SOCIAL UPHEAVAL

Rigoberta Menchú Tum

Rigoberta Menchú is a Ki'che' Maya woman originally from rural Guatemala who has served as an advocate for human and indigenous rights since the 1980s. For these efforts, she was awarded the Nobel Peace Prize in 1992, the first indigenous person to receive this award. While in exile in Paris in 1982, Menchú dictated her life story to an activist anthropologist. Her story, published in English as *I, Rigoberta Menchú: An Indian Woman of Guatemala*, offered both an account of her life growing up in her native village and descriptions of the mistreatment that she and other indigenous people experienced at the hands of their employers, especially on coffee plantations, where Maya people regularly migrated to perform seasonal labor. *I, Rigoberta Menchú* did much to publicize the plight of Maya people during Guatemala's period of extreme violence in the early 1980s. It also helped to persuade many who were otherwise unfamiliar with or unconvinced of the brutality of the Guatemalan government's treatment of its indigenous population.

By the end of the hostilities in 1996, Rigoberta Menchú had become an international symbol of Mayan resilience and resistance. Her work with the eponymous Rigoberta Menchú Foundation has actively championed the cause of human and political rights both in Guatemala and among indigenous peoples elsewhere in Latin America, supporting many projects involving women's rights, rural health, and peace and justice in Guatemala and across the globe. Menchú has also been active in Guatemalan politics, running for president on more than one occasion. Recognized worldwide for these efforts, she has received many international commendations beyond the Nobel Peace Prize.

In 1999, an American anthropologist published a book charging that not all of the facts that Menchú published in *I, Rigoberta Menchú* were verifiably true, an accusation eventually borne out by other investigators. The anthropologist charged that Menchú—whose father, Vicente, had been a

≡ **Rigoberta Menchú Tum at the Ancient Mexican Pyramid at Teotihuacan.**

left-wing activist killed in the Spanish Embassy fire of 1980 (chapter 12)—was not the naïve young woman she had purported to be, and that her book had been contrived as political propaganda for the URNG. Menchú's supporters countered that the book, whose title in Spanish is *Me llamo Rigoberta Menchú y asi me nació la conciencia* (*My Name Is Rigoberta Menchú, and This Is How My Consciousness was Born*, a much more evocative and transparent title than the English version), was a *testimonio* (a political genre common in Latin American literature, but not in English), and not an "autobiography" in the sense that English readers would understand it to be. Menchú herself remained largely aloof from the debates, stating only that while the book had strongly autobiographical roots, it also included elements that had not happened to her personally. She also argued that in her book she spoke collectively—in the Maya fashion—for the many people during the armed conflict who had no voice and whose story would otherwise not have been heard.

• Is this a case of clashing epistemologies (worldviews, ways of understanding)? Should we read historical documents within their own cultural contexts, or from our own?

goal was to reconfigure this power asymmetry and recover the Mayas' rightful place in the body politic. It also sought to redefine Guatemala's national culture as pluralistic. In specific terms, this called for the revitalization of more than twenty Mayan languages (several of which have many thousands of native speakers, but a few of which were largely moribund); a respect for Mayan religion and native worldviews; the creation of Mayan schools not based exclusively on European bodies of knowledge; and dramatically increased indigenous political participation.

In the short term, the Mayan movement sought recognition as an influential sector in the forging of the Peace Accords, which were being negotiated in peace talks between the guerrillas and the Guatemalan military and government in Oslo, Norway, in the early 1990s. But its long-term goal was for the nation-state to formally recognize the "multiethnic, pluricultural, and multilingual" nature of Guatemalan society. The Peace Accords, signed in December 1996, finally ended the military confrontation. For the first time in Guatemala's history, specific cultural and political rights were conceded to the Mayan peoples.

Both of these achievements were due in no small measure to the efforts of the Mayan movement. Unfortunately for the cause of Maya equality, the Guatemalan voting populace, still dominated by a ladino majority, voted down a 1999 national referendum that had promised to implement those elements of the Accords that directly addressed Maya cultural and political rights. With this stunning repudiation of their efforts and goals, the Mayan movement receded, although its impact remains in improved respect and visibility for Maya culture, language, and native people's increased political engagement.

Contemporary Mexico: Competitive Democracy, Drugs, and State Violence, 2000–Present

The presidential election of 2000 marked the evolution of Mexican democracy toward a more competitive political system. Up to that moment, the Institutional Revolutionary Party (PRI) had controlled Mexico without challenge since 1929. But scandals alleging blatant electoral fraud in 1988, corruption at the highest levels, and a declining economy had cost the party much of its popularity. The adverse effects of recent policy decisions had also disrupted the populist coalition and allowed challengers to confront the entrenched ruling party.

Vicente Fox and the Fruition of Democracy

"We're fed up with the PRI"—with its corruption, its fraudulent democratic practices, and its failed economic policies—was the message that resonated with voters in the presidential election of 2000. Vicente Fox, the nominee of the

National Action Party (PAN) and the former head of Coca-Cola for all of Latin America, offered a charismatic image that contrasted with that of his mild-mannered PRI opponent. Wearing a cowboy hat and black boots and physically towering over his PRI rival, Fox campaigned as a maverick who had renounced his membership in the PRI to serve successfully as one of the PAN's few elected state governors in the 1990s. Although PAN party leaders were reluctant to nominate him as their presidential candidate because of his relatively recent conversion, Fox's proven abilities as a fundraiser soon changed their minds.

Fox also expanded the size of PAN's constituency and won over many independents as well as some PRI voters as he moved the party toward the political center. For people seeking a candidate who embodied competitive democracy and opposition to the anemic state-led economy, Fox became the obvious choice. He promised a return to prosperity by guaranteeing a 7 percent annual growth rate as well as a transparent and efficient government, a message that appealed to disillusioned moderates. His election signaled Mexico's transition to a true competitive democracy, fulfilling the dream of the Revolution's first leader, Francisco I. Madero, who advocated that every vote should matter and be counted (chapter 7).

The arrival of competitive democracy proved to be one of the few tangible results of Fox's presidency. The PRI opposition held the majority of seats in Congress and frustrated his legislative agenda. Lacking relationships with key PRI party leaders and the patronage power to bend them to his will, Fox could accomplish little. Although his friendship with US President George W. Bush initially offered

≡ **Vicente Fox on Horseback while Campaigning for the Presidency.** Vicente Fox was the Mexican response to the Pink Tide, a believer in free trade, innovation, and entrepreneurial development. Fox challenged Mexico's long-ruling PRI (Institutional Revolutionary Party) from the right, bringing a new, probusiness coalition to power. But Fox could not resolve the challenges posed by the growing power of criminal networks in northern Mexico coupled with the volatility of migration from Mexico to the United States, and from Central America through Mexico and on to the United States.

hopes to resolve the outstanding issues between the two neighbors, the terrorist attacks on the United States on September 11, 2001, dashed those hopes, as the United States turned its attention toward the global war on terror. Finally, Fox could not deliver on his promise to restore economic prosperity. His proposed tax reforms, seeking to make the government less reliant on import/export duties for revenue, went nowhere in Congress.

In the presidential contest of 2006, pundits expected the very popular leftist mayor of Mexico City, Andrés Manuel López Obrador, to triumph. But the PAN candidate, longtime party member Felipe Calderón, countered López Obrador by pledging to work for economic reforms and improvements in education and healthcare, while retaining the neoliberal model. His campaign also strove to appeal to political moderates, as Calderón noted his opponent's resemblance to Venezuela's Hugo Chávez. Calderón's middle-class constituents (and many other Mexicans) bore little love for Chávez, who had criticized and insulted President Fox at an international meeting in 2005. Calderón won the election by a razor-thin margin, and López Obrador appealed to the Federal Electoral Court. Even after that body certified Calderón's victory, López Obrador and his adherents continued their protest, setting up a shadow government and maneuvering unsuccessfully to prevent Calderón's inauguration.

Calderón, a seasoned politician who had served in the Chamber of Deputies, had only slightly better luck with Congress than Fox. He implemented modest reforms of the judicial system, increased spending on healthcare and education, and raised the salaries of the police and army in an attempt to reduce corruption. Although President Calderón did not prevail in the battle for tax reform, he did manage other small adjustments to the economy. He capped public employee salaries and controlled the prices of some essential goods.

Calderón utterly failed to reform the state-owned oil giant Pemex, although smaller nationalized companies (like the State electric company) have been made more responsive to the open market. Most Mexicans understand that Pemex is notoriously inefficient and unable to make a profit even in the best of times; nevertheless, Calderón could not persuade Congress to reform the iconic giant. Likewise, an attempt to improve public education by introducing performance standards, bonuses for effective teachers, and tougher requirements for tenure met opposition from the powerful teachers' union. Nevertheless, Mexico's economy grew, albeit slowly, as the country expanded its trade networks to Asia and Europe, becoming less reliant on the US marketplace. To a large extent, Calderón's tenure would be remembered most for violence associated with Mexico's drug war, which escalated dramatically after Calderón attempted to undertake an unsuccessful divide-and-conquer tactic against rival cartels. By the end of Calderón's sexenio, an estimated seventy thousand Mexicans had died in violence related to the attempted crackdown. Needless to say, Mexico's descent into violence, much of which took place along the US-Mexico border, also did severe damage to the economy by staunching the normally vibrant tourist trade and by closing down the vast network of northern-border maquilas.

The presidential election of 2012 also brought a surprise, as a youthful PRI candidate, Enrique Peña Nieto, defeated the candidates from both the Party of the Democratic Revolution (PRD) and the PAN with 38 percent of the vote by making the claim that the PRI could deliver on its reform promises. Peña Nieto argued that Mexico's economy had stagnated under the PAN's leadership, registering less than 2 percent growth per year. Under his stewardship, the economy has shown greater growth, particularly as a result of the opening of several automobile manufacturing plants. His term began on a note of optimism, as he crafted a ninety-five-point "Pact for Mexico" with the leaders of the PAN and the PRD to implement reforms. While tackling educational reform and banking reform, efforts broke down when Peña Nieto touched the third rail of Mexican politics, Pemex. Instituting real reform, such as privatizing parts of Pemex, has proven impossible for all three of these post-2000 governments, as Mexico's new democracy has proven less efficient than the well-oiled PRI machine.

The Drug Trafficking Issue

As we saw in chapter 13, as the US DEA became more efficient in blocking drug trafficking across the Caribbean to Florida, Colombians began shipping cocaine through Central America and Mexico instead. During the 1980s, Mexico's drug trafficking kingpin, Félix Gallardo, invited colleagues to a meeting during which he assigned the leaders of four organizations specific geographical territories and smuggling routes to the United States. The goal was to increase operational efficiency and reduce the possibility that the police could close down the entire operation with a single raid. In PRI's final decade of dominance, drug bosses paid off the local police, but if their gangs behaved too badly, the police arrested offenders. In 1996, about four hundred individuals died because of their involvement in drug trafficking; just over a decade later, this toll would rise astronomically.

The arrival of democracy changed this situation. To clean up corruption, in 2002 President Fox ordered the police to round up cartel leaders and dismantle their organizations. Meanwhile, the Gulf Cartel had hired thirty-seven former elite commandos who had deserted from the Mexican army and called themselves the *Zetas*, effectively turning them into a private army. The four trafficking organizations eventually formed larger gangs that the US media dubbed "cartels," which occasionally fought for control of territory. Profits enabled these gangs to illegally purchase military-style hardware in the United States and even fashion their own

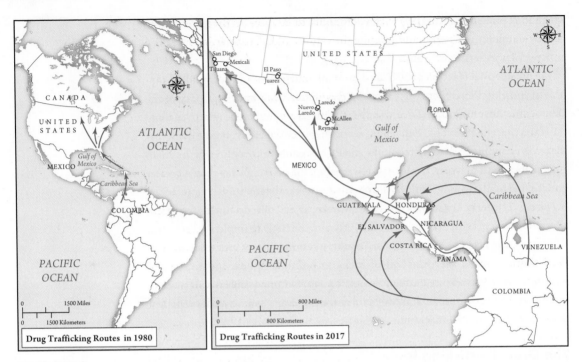

≡ **MAP. 14.2**

tanklike vehicles. Tired of payoffs to the police, the drug kingpins expanded their armies of otherwise unemployed young men and women and became virtual warlords in their respective states by 2005.

Fox's successor, Felipe Calderón, decided that he needed to end this threat to Mexico's sovereignty. Staking his presidency on eradicating the scourge of cartel violence, Calderón deployed some 45,000 soldiers to arrest the kingpins and enforce the drug laws. Unfortunately, this measure only increased the level of violence, resulting in approximately 83,000 deaths between 2007 and 2014 as a result of gang-related conflicts. In 2010 and 2011, the Zetas broke with the Gulf Cartel and launched a bloody war.

This conflict, as well as rivalries between other drug lords, left a power vacuum that encouraged the Sinaloa cartel's vicious kingpin, Joaquín "El Chapo" Guzmán, to take over new territories, provoking yet more violence. By the end of Calderón's term in 2012, drug trafficking, which now included methamphetamines and heroin, employed even more people in Mexico (allegedly 450,000) than in Colombia. Gangs expanded their operations, engaging in human trafficking, extortion, and money laundering. As the cartels grew, their influence, augmented by networks they established with cashiered former soldiers, guerrillas, and gang members, began to expand into Central America. In 2012, Peña Nieto vowed to take a softer approach, replacing the military with a new police force to lessen the violence. The cartels remained a huge problem, despite the capture of El Chapo in January 2016 and his extradition to the United States.

Violence continues to plague Mexico in the second decade of the twentieth century to a degree not seen since the Mexican Revolution of a century ago (chapter 7). One of the most shocking cases was the 2014 kidnapping and disappearance of forty-three students from Ayotzinapa Rural Teachers' College in Iguala, Guerrero. On September 26, the students commandeered several buses to travel to Mexico City to commemorate the anniversary of the 1968 Tlatelolco Massacre (chapter 11). Despite the fact that such actions are not unusual among activists in Mexico, the forty-three Ayotzinapa students were taken away in broad daylight and never seen again.

Although all the students are presumed dead and many human remains have been found in the area (some of them apparently related not to Ayotzinapa, but to other "everyday" violence), the crime remains unsolved at the time of writing. Officials and popular opinion point blame at drug gangs, public officials, and/or various branches of the Mexican security forces. The failure of authorities to fully investigate the case, account for the students, and to prosecute the guilty, despite widespread protests demanding they do so, indicates the inability or lack of will on the part of the present government to combat violence or to enforce the rule of law in early twenty-first century Mexico.

Hugo Chávez and the Bolivarian Revolution, 1998–2016

Hugo Chávez's crushing defeat of the candidates from Venezuela's two traditional parties in the 1998 elections provided him with the opportunity to undertake the dramatic reforms he had promised during the campaign. As he had correctly articulated, the Democratic Action party (AD) and Christian Democratic party (COPEI) and their neoliberal policies had no answers to the dilemmas Venezuela now faced: a moribund economy; a declining standard of living for most Venezuelans; and a corrupt political system. Chávez represented change, especially for the poorest segments of society.

The Chavista Revolutionary Program

Chávez's inaugural address reaffirmed his campaign demand that the old constitution be scrapped and a new revolutionary one be written. Because of his boundless energy campaigning and his overwhelming support among the poor, Chávez's followers constituted 95 percent of the delegates at the constitutional assembly.

Based on Chávez's draft, the final version of the Constitution of 1999 extended the presidential term from four to six years, permitted one immediate reelection, and abolished the bicameral legislature in favor of a National Assembly. In addition to strengthening the president's hand, the Constitution spoke the language of social inclusion, reserving seats in the National Assembly for indigenous people and guaranteeing their right to maintain their languages, religions, and cultures. In addition, the Constitution declared that all Venezuelans should enjoy the benefits of healthcare.

After the approval of the new constitution by 71 percent of the electorate, Chávez moved slowly to implement his reforms. Initially he deployed the army to implement Plan Bolívar 2000, a series of ad hoc actions designed to bring relief to the poorest of Venezuela's citizens. Thousands of soldiers once confined to their barracks now performed public services: repairing roads, building schools, cleaning streets, and dispensing food at discounted prices in poor neighborhoods. Like his role model Fidel Castro, the charismatic Chávez delivered lengthy speeches about his proposed reforms on television, crowding off the air a number of Venezuela's popular telenovelas. In addition to laying out a blueprint for his reforms, Chávez's speeches became increasingly critical of the nation's media, which rarely had kind things to say about their new president. Over the next four years, Chávez would face down an attempted coup, neutralize a strike by oil workers, and defeat a recall election in 2004 in which he won 59 percent of the popular vote. Each challenge seemed to strengthen his appeal, allowing him to win the presidential election of 2006 by a substantial margin.

Chávez succeeded politically because his social programs appealed to the poor and because oil revenues enabled him to spend heavily on social programs. His "missions," as he styled them, aimed to deliver social services to the country's most impoverished citizens. At the time of his election in 1998, about 80 percent of Venezuelans lived below the poverty line. At the theoretical level, each of Chávez's missions fell under the umbrella of "Twenty-First Century Socialism," a term initially coined by the German sociologist Heinz Dieterich in 1996. Arguing that both capitalism and twentieth-century socialism had failed to solve social problems such as poverty, hunger, exploitation, sexism, racism, and environmental degradation, Dieterich argued in favor of a more participatory democratic system that would allow governments to solve these problems at the grassroots level. Ultimately, though, Chávez's programs and rhetoric exploited and deepened the division between social classes.

Chávez's mission programs strongly resembled the initiatives of revolutionary leaders in Cuba and Nicaragua. *Misión Robinson*, the program designed to deliver elementary education to the illiterates of the barrio, taught over a million citizens to read. A related program, *Misión Ribas*, offered free secondary education, and

Misión Sucre provided scholarships to university. One of the most successful programs, *Barrio Adentro* ("Inside the Neighborhood") assigned 12,000 Cuban doctors to urban neighborhoods to provide healthcare in exchange for 95,000 barrels of oil per day shipped to Havana.

With much of Venezuela's population now living in urban areas, Chávez offered them deeds to the land they occupied, legalizing their homesteads and conveying other rights of citizenship. Chávez also fostered community development. He encouraged the formation of Bolivarian Circles, neighborhood organizations designed to raise citizens' consciousness and petition the government to fund their projects for housing, education, and healthcare. For the rural population, Chávez redistributed approximately nine million acres of land (mostly government owned) to 130,000 families. As of 2008, the **Bolivarian Revolution** had done much to improve the lives of many Venezuelan citizens. At that point, it was little surprise that many Venezuelan baby boys—even in a country known for the bestowing of political and even whimsical first names—were named "Hugo."

Like his proposals for domestic reform, Chávez's foreign policy brought applause from his supporters but generated growing criticism from many middle- and upper-class Venezuelans and the United States. Early on, with low oil prices hampering Venezuela's income, Chávez urged OPEC to cut production and thereby increase the price per barrel, which effectively increased oil earnings. But the growing dependence of Venezuela on oil revenues eventually created problems. In 2002, revenue from oil amounted to about half of Venezuela's income; by 2012 that figure would rise to 95 percent. Chávez initially enjoyed a growing reserve of funds for domestic social spending and his increasingly ambitious role on the international stage. Traveling to China, Chávez inked a trade deal that ultimately resulted in the loan of $50 billion in exchange for enormous shipments of oil.

More controversially, Chávez visited Iraq's Saddam Hussein (the only head of state to do so after 2000) and spent time in Iran. Increasingly he played a larger role on the Latin American diplomatic stage, loudly criticizing Yankee imperialism (and especially President George W. Bush) and the US-proposed Free Trade Area of the Americas, while offering financial assistance to members of Mercosur (the Southern Common Market, designed to promote free-market trade among the nations of the Southern Cone). Chávez antagonized moderate Latin American leaders at the Ibero-American Summit in 2007 by continually interrupted the prime minister of Spain, asserting that his predecessor was a fascist. Chávez's boorish behavior provoked King Juan Carlos of Spain to turn to Chávez and exclaim: "Why don't you shut up!"

Of all international leaders, Chávez found the aging Fidel Castro to be his true kindred spirit and role model. The Venezuelan president received a tumultuous welcome on his first official visit to Havana in 1999. The two men cemented their friendship during a pickup baseball game in which Chávez played first base and Fidel coached the Cuban squad to victory. Over the years, Castro and Chávez remained warm friends and faithful allies, much to the concern of the United States.

The Venezuelan state extended its control over much of the economy by nationalizing banks as well as steel, cement, and packaged food processors. Chávez created several new state-owned enterprises, especially in petroleum-related industries such as petrochemicals. In 2007, just before oil prices collapsed, the government bought out a number of its international partners in the petroleum business. Although this move may ultimately prove beneficial when prices increase again, for the next decade at least it proved to be a ruinous expense. The attempt to develop other state-owned industries, such as the aluminum industry in the south, floundered because of inadequate hydroelectric power.

Criticism Mounts as the Revolution Falters

The worldwide recession of 2008 led to declining oil revenues, undoing much of the social progress of the Bolivarian Revolution. Despite all of Chávez's efforts to remake Venezuelan society, many problems remained, and some have since worsened. Chávez's administration retained an ostensible framework of constitutional democracy, but in practice that democracy was increasingly distorted by authoritarian tendencies. (The same was arguably true of the long period of apparently stable constitutional rule from 1958 to 1989, suggesting more enduring conflicts in Venezuelan civil society).

Chávez's administration relied on his personal intervention by decree to solve people's problems. For political reasons, after 2008 Chávez did not want to reduce social spending despite the diminution of state income. Inflation rates that were already high (30 percent in 2010) continued to escalate. Because the state paid farmers fixed prices below the cost of production for their products, whenever possible farmers sold their products on the black market. Housewives waited in long lines to purchase necessities at the state-owned stores, only to be turned away when the shelves emptied. As a result of the food production crisis, Venezuela relied increasingly on imported staples. Although the economic situation improved briefly in 2012 when oil prices revived, the recovery was short lived. When the United States and Canada began extracting oil from shale deposits within their own borders, the price of oil plummeted to new lows and the Venezuelan state again found itself strapped for cash. Even then, most poor Venezuelans remained fiercely loyal to Chavéz, continuing to see in him the charismatic leadership and concern for ordinary Venezuelans that had eluded them for so long.

But brighter days were not on the horizon for anyone in the Bolivarian Republic. While the country's poverty rate dipped from 43 percent in 1998 to 29.5 percent in 2011, it rose steadily after that because of the Chávez administration's mismanagement of the economy. Chávez failed to curb rising crime rates (especially murders and kidnappings), alleviate high unemployment rates, or curtail enrichment among a new class of **boliburguesía**, a purported new bourgeoisie that benefited from close ties with the Bolivarian state. Chávez's electoral support subsequently began to fray after his monumental 2006 presidential victory.

By 2010, Chávez's deficit spending on domestic social policies and his insistence on price controls brought the economy to a near standstill. High rates of inflation drained savings accounts. Even though Chávez won reelection in 2012, his margin of victory had significantly narrowed. In the meantime, his doctors informed him he was suffering from cancer. Despite treatment in Cuba, Hugo Chávez died in March 2013.

Chávez's vice president, Nicolás Maduro, stepped up to replace him. A personalistic regime faces grave challenges when it loses its charismatic leader. Under Maduro, a former bus driver who served Chávez loyally, the government's policies did not change course. As a result, Venezuela's economy continued to worsen significantly, with its citizens suffering under the highest inflation rate in the world. Even more seriously, a precipitous drop in the price of oil, beginning in 2015, led to nearly unprecedented scarcity, austerity, and hardship for Venezuelans. China's loan of $20 billion in 2015 offered a brief respite, but Maduro's approval ratings plummeted. His unpopularity was confirmed by the National Assembly elections of 2015, where for the first time since 1998 the opposition won the majority of seats. Although Maduro maneuvered to delay a referendum that could unseat him, the future of Twenty-First Century Socialism without Chávez seems uncertain at best in Venezuela. By 2017, severe shortages of basic foodstuffs and consumer goods, a thriving black market only for those who can afford it, and massive cut backs in jobs, education, and healthcare have brought levels of poverty and suffering to Venezuelans that are unprecedented in a nation that was once awash with petro-dollars. These privations erode whatever positive legacy remains from Chávez's accomplishments.

The Changing Role of Women in Politics, 1990–2016

The journey toward women's political equality in Latin America has been gradual but relatively direct. Recall that, at the beginning of the twentieth century, women did not enjoy the right to vote in any Latin American country. Although Latin America is notorious for its *macho* culture, this situation was hardly unique to the region; in 1900, New Zealand was the only country in the world where women could vote without restriction, although they could be elected to office in the United States. After Ecuador granted women the franchise in 1929, other South American nations followed suit in the 1930s. Chilean women won a limited right to vote in 1931 (extended to full suffrage in 1949), followed by Brazil in 1932, while

Mexico did not grant women the vote until 1953. As women achieved the franchise, they also gained the right to stand for election, although few took advantage of this opportunity until the 1960s, when the dawn of the international women's movement opened new doors and eyes.

Although Latin America was somewhat late in granting women's political enfranchisement, the region relatively quickly elected women to political office, at least compared with the United States, which has never yet elected a woman to its highest office. While the occasional woman had been an important political figure in the region from time to time—Argentina's Eva Perón in the 1940s comes immediately to mind—the ascendance of women to political office, especially to the executive branch, did not take place until the last three decades of the twentieth century. Latin America's first woman president was Maria Estela Martínez de Perón ("Isabela"), Juan Domingo Perón's third wife, who as the elected vice president became president after Peron's death in 1974, while Lidia Gueiler Tejada served briefly as president of Bolivia after a coup in 1979. The first woman *elected* chief executive of a Latin America, however, was Violeta Chamorro, who served as president of Nicaragua from 1990 to 1997. At the time of writing, there have been eight women voted into office to serve as president of a Latin American nation.

Since the turn of the twenty-first century, the three largest countries in South America have elected female *presidentas:* Michelle Bachelet governed Chile from 2006 to 2010 and was reelected for a second term in 2014; Cristina Fernández de Kirchner was elected to the presidency of Argentina in 2007 and then reelected for a second term in 2011. Former guerrilla fighter Dilma Rousseff won the election for the presidency of Brazil in 2010 and reelected for a second term in 2014. In Central America, Laura Chinchilla served as president of Costa Rica from 2010 to 2014.

Female leadership, however, did not necessarily translate into more stable government. Brazil's Rousseff was impeached in 2016, and the same year, Argentina's Kirchner found herself facing a criminal charge for a complicated political scandal. In both cases, backlash against these leaders as women exacerbated political conflict within each country. While, generally speaking, women executives tend to be unfairly characterized in the popular imagination as "Mothers" or as "Iron Women," political scientists have demonstrated that their styles of governance, for better or worse, have proven to be very similar to that of male chief executives.

Latin America is one of the few regions of the world which boasts mandated quotas for female political representation in nearly every country, meaning that women are required by law to make up 50 percent of elected officials, cabinet members, or government ministers. Not all countries work equally hard to enforce this aspirational law. Only Venezuela, Chile, Guatemala, and Cuba do not have mandated quotas, although Cuba has nearly proportional representation anyway, and

≡ **President Michelle Bachelet of Chile and President Dilma Rousseff of Brazil.** The rise to power of women presidents in Chile, Brazil, and Argentine showed that transformation of traditional gender dynamics in Latin American politics. Sexism did not disappear, but women found ways to challenge exclusion and take center stage in national politics. The three women presidents of Latin America's Southern Cone represented three different political movements with divergent characteristics. Political crisis stymied Argentina's Cristina Kirschner (not shown here) and led to Rousseff's impeachment during her second term. Bachelet's administration from 2006 to 2010 remained stable despite economic fluctuations. After one term out of the presidency, Bachelet returned to office in a second, nonconsecutive term in 2014.

Chile has twice elected a woman president. Yet it is not, generally speaking, quotas alone that have brought women into office. Most of the women who have entered politics have followed a path to power initiated by male family members, usually husbands or fathers (Chamorro, Kirchner). Others, like Dilma Rousseff, became politically active during the military dictatorships in their respective countries.

Prior to the 1970s and 1980s, women's movements in Latin America, specifically in countries ruled by military dictatorships in the 1970s, derived political and social authority from Marianist notions of motherhood. **Marianismo** is a traditional Hispanic ideal of women that venerates them as pure, modest, and morally strong, like the Virgin Mary (who lends this view her name). It also reduces women to passive subjects of their own fates.

The crisis of the Cold War years changed this attitude when women found themselves in the vortex of violence, often left as the only ones able to speak out on behalf of "disappeared" husbands, parents, or children. These circumstances inspired women to step outside of the home to found post-Marianist movements, including groups such as the Mothers and Grandmothers of the Plaza the Mayo in Argentina (chapter 11), and CoMadres, a similar group in El Salvador. Such groups empowered their members to speak truth to power about human rights and lost loved ones, and to develop new economic and political opportunities for widows and other women displaced by conflict. These new types of organizations served as avenues for women to enter the public sphere. Moreover, direct participation in leftist movements, as was the case for both Bachelet and Rousseff, primed others for electoral political action.

But one should not underestimate the significant number of women who have served in ministerial or cabinet posts for, as studies have shown, there appear to be particular patterns to "gendered" cabinet appointments in Latin America. These reveal that even when the lengths of careers of both men and women are similar, disparities emerge between the types of government posts that men and women hold. Women most often hold lower-prestige ministerial positions that carry a "feminine" policy portfolio, such as those that address family, women's issues, the elderly, disability rights, and the like. Despite that qualification, however, women's participation in politics in Latin America has dramatically increased over the last few decades. Without a doubt, quotas and a broader understanding of the roles to be played by formerly disenfranchised sectors—measured across race, class, and gender—have created an unprecedented cultural recognition of the importance of women as actors in the public sphere.

The Evolving Ecological Debate, 1980–2000

Since the early 1960s, modern environmentalism—the idea that man-made degradation of the natural environment poses a threat to humanity itself, and that definitive action must be taken to minimize such degradation—has developed into a powerful set of beliefs and practices. While the principles of modern environmentalism may seem self-evident today, the environmentalist movement represents a radical shift in the way most humans perceive the world around them. No longer is nature seen—as it was in the recent past—as something to be conquered by civilization or to be exploited without regard for its material limits. Instead, humans increasingly recognize that the long-term survival of our species is inexorably linked to the long-time survival of our planet. This new environmental consciousness has sparked popular movements for "sustainable development" across the globe.

General Tenets of the Environmental Movement in Latin America

The environmental movement in Latin America has taken many of its cues from the United States and Europe, yet its development and overall approach have differed from these movements in significant ways. As Latin American governments tend to have fewer financial resources available to them than their Northern counterparts, they cannot spend as much money for environmental initiatives like adopting cleaner technologies, treating sewage in overcrowded cities, or even funding regulatory agencies to enforce environmental laws. Higher rates of poverty and hunger also force many people to invade protected forests and national parks in search of food, lumber, and exotic animals to sell on the black market. These regional challenges have helped to shape a distinctly Latin American environmental movement in which environmental concerns are deeply integrated into larger popular movements for social justice and equity.

Over the last generation, the antiauthoritarian political mobilizations of the 1970s and 1980s have developed into broadly based popular movements demanding a greater voice in all matters of social justice, including land, labor, health, human rights, and the environment. In recent decades, members of the most politically marginalized groups—often the indigenous populations of each country—have found that organizing around issues of environmental injustice can bring surprising access to the political arena. More so than in the United States or in Europe, environmentalism in Latin America is becoming a powerful tool in the struggle for social, political, and economic justice.

Wherever environmental initiatives have come at the perceived short-term expense of local individuals—regardless of whether those individuals are Cancún hoteliers and their well-heeled clients or poor timber-gatherers in the forests of central Mexico—they have failed. The rule of law has not proven strong enough to restrain the profit motive. And resource degradation by wealthy and politically connected actors often leads to different kinds of environmental damage by poorer actors farther out on the economic periphery. The massive expansion of agroindustrial soy cultivation in Brazil's center-west, for example, has created massive monocultural zones heavily reliant on petrochemical pesticides. Increased soy cultivation, meanwhile, also pushed settlers and small farmers farther north into the Amazon region, where they have set the rainforest ablaze and polluted waterways in order to clear land.

Even in Costa Rica, an early adapter of environmentalist policies, where more than 25 percent of the country's land has been set aside for national parks and reserves, environmental degradation in the form of deforestation for cattle ranching and road building to further develop the tourist industry have taken an enormously heavy toll.

Stopping or diverting these chain reactions has required new kinds of environmental imagination, often beginning on a local scale and then expanding. Programs for protection of sea turtles on Mexico's Pacific Coast and in Northeastern Brazil, for example, pay small fishing villages to care for the turtles, integrating this environmental stewardship into a sustainable fishery. Nearly all of these initiatives have required the painstaking construction of networks linking local knowledge and national and international leverage, a fragile but hopeful practice of environmental management.

Ecological Policy Debates in Peru

Long central to Andean peoples' perception of the sacred landscape, glaciers and glacial lakes have taken on new significance in recent times. Because of glacial lakes' ability to be both a positive force (by providing irrigation waters) and a negative one (through destructive floods), Andean people have attributed supernatural powers to these "enchanted" lakes, which can cause natural disasters if not properly propitiated with suitable offerings. Recent natural disasters involving glacial lakes have provoked scientific inquiry and environmental policy debates on how to prevent or mitigate such disasters. For example, in 1941 a glacial lake formed by glacial melt penned up behind a moraine dam of naturally accumulated rock and mud burst, sending rushing water down to the valley below. The city of Huaraz was flooded, killing five thousand people. After the disaster, the Peruvian government initiated discussions about its response, which began as a program to drain the more dangerous glacial lakes located above large population centers but gradually evolved into other potential uses for glacial lakes, principally as development projects.

A second type of disaster involving a glacier lake occurred in 1970, when a 7.7-magnitude earthquake broke off a huge portion of a glacier on Mount Huascarán, triggering an avalanche so loud it sounded like a herd of elephants, according to one witness. The avalanche of mud, debris, and water roared through the town of Yungay, killing 15,000 (55,000 others in the region died in the earthquake, making this the worst natural disaster in South American history) and burying all the city's buildings lying in its path. General Juan Velasco's authoritarian government attempted strong measures to prevent future avalanche disasters. Most notably, he mandated a zoning plan that forbade the displaced from rebuilding in these vulnerable areas. Locals resisted this plan for two reasons. First, people of middle and elite status did not want to yield their choice locations in the center of town and live among the indigenous population at higher altitudes. In addition, people were attached to their old homes and familiar surroundings, and like disaster victims all over the world, wanted to rebuild in exactly the same place. Even under the most authoritarian regime, then, local people successfully resisted attempts by national authorities to impose their rules over community and familial wishes.

Although the local urban population did want the government to manage the threats of future floods by draining lakes, policy makers in Lima recognized that glacial lakes provided opportunities for economic development. As early as the 1940s governments decided that melting glacial waters stored behind modern dams could generate massive amounts of hydroelectric power to provide energy for industrial development and electricity for coastal cities, while incidentally providing some electricity to the Andean communities. In addition, governments foresaw the possibility of increased international tourism for those interested in skiing, mountaineering, and spectacular sightseeing. To manage the lakes and promote tourism, the government needed to extend roads in the mountains, which also acted as a way to assimilate the Andean region into the nation and lessen its isolation. Thus, governments proposed a difficult balancing act. On one hand, they hoped to keep glacial lakes at their highest possible level to maximize hydroelectric projects (such as the massive Cañon del Pato hydroelectric plant, completed in 1958) while simultaneously preventing natural disasters and floods.

Neoliberalism, not surprisingly, seemed to tip the policy debate in favor of economic development. In addition to confronting the violent rebel movement Sendero Luminoso, in 1990 President Alberto Fujimori faced a nation in economic shambles. As a doctrinaire neoliberal, he privatized several of Peru's inefficient state-owned enterprises, including Electroperú, which the government sold to Duke Energy, a US corporation. Duke accomplished many of its promised goals, nearly doubling Peru's hydroelectric output during the 1990s and bringing electricity to many households once cloaked in darkness after sunset.

As critics noted, however, without the government subsidizing the cost of electricity, consumers had to pay more for electrical service, a burden which fell disproportionately on the poor. Duke Energy contemplated expanding its productivity by building additional reservoirs. But when a secondary security dam overflowed and caused some minor flooding, local residents protested, fearing a repetition of the Huaraz or Yungay disasters. When a new government replaced Fujimori in 2001, these complainants found a willing audience, and Duke's permit to build was denied. Despite concern for the effects of global warming—which exacerbates glacial melting, increasing run-off into the lakes—the policy debate over glacial lakes continues. On one hand, the Peruvian government and others in similar situations need to provide more energy to improve the lives of its citizens, especially its urban populations. On the other hand, governments have the responsibility to protect the environment and its citizens from natural disasters such as inevitable overflow floods.

Religious Pluralism: Pentecostalism in Latin America, 1960–2010

Since the 1960s, Protestantism and especially Pentecostalism experienced a dramatic expansion across Latin America, bringing widespread religious pluralism to a region of the world that had been a Catholic stronghold since the Iberian conquest. Increased religious pluralism is expressed in many forms—from Protestantism to Islam to a variety of new, esoteric religions, and even to secularism and "no religion" at all. But it is **Pentecostalism**, above all, that has come to define Latin America's new religious landscape.

The Rise of Protestantism

The conventional wisdom holds that Latin American is irreducibly "Catholic" in religion, culture, and worldview, but this perception is no longer as true as it once was. Consider the following: One metropolitan Pentecostal church in Guatemala City has more members than the number of Catholic priests in the entire country. In El Salvador ten times more people converted to Protestant churches during the 1980s than were killed during that nation's civil war. More Nicaraguans joined Protestant sects in Nicaragua during the Sandinista decade (1979–1989) than there were members of Catholic Christian Base Communities (CEBs). Or ponder this: One study found that ten thousand Brazilian Catholics abandon the Catholic Church *per day* in Latin America, mostly to become Pentecostals.

One hundred years ago, only about fifty thousand Protestants lived in all of Latin America, a figure made up nearly exclusively of foreigners—English Anglicans, German Lutherans, Swiss Mennonites—who happened to live and worship in that part of the world. By contrast, a 2006 study by the Pew Center for Religion and Public Life estimated that least 25 percent of Latin America's two billion people are "renewalists" (Pentecostals and Charismatic Catholics). While some nations claim sizable Protestant populations, such as Guatemala (around 40 percent Protestant) and Brazil (just over 20 percent of that nation's enormous population), others, such as Mexico, measure a very small Protestant population overall. But even in the case of a highly "Catholic" country like Mexico, deep pockets of Protestantism can be found in critical areas. Chiapas, for example, is nearly 40 percent Protestant, with some indigenous villages claiming nearly total Protestant homogeneity. A similar pattern is evident for a Catholic citadel like Ecuador, where, though the nation

Religious Affiliations of Latin Americans, 2017

- Catholic
- Protestant
- Unaffiliated
- Other

 MAP. 14.3

is less than 3 percent Protestant overall, nearly the entire populations of several northern Andean villages, including the prosperous town of Otavalo, Ecuador (mentioned earlier in this chapter), have converted to the Church of Jesus Christ of Latter Day Saints (the Mormon Church).

Most remarkably, virtually all of these conversions have transpired since the 1960s during a period when many social scientists were distracted by other types of social and political currents. During this tumultuous period, Marxism, authoritarianism, dependency theory, developmentalism, even radical Catholicism seemed to many outside observers to be more intellectually engaging, and perhaps, even more "authentic" to the Latin American experience than Protestantism. Yet, hidden in plain sight, Protestantism engaged many more ordinary Latin Americans than have any of these other movements, making religious conversion one of the most dynamic forces in the region during an era of extreme change and upheaval.

The Three Waves of the Protestant Movement

The Protestant presence in Latin America—the "invasion of the sects," as hostile observers often call it—began in the second half of the nineteenth century. North American and British missionaries of historical denominations such as the Methodist and Presbyterian churches came to the region bearing a message of salvation deeply embedded in the cultural norms and behaviors of Victorian society and wrapped in the flag of imperialism. While liberal and positivist leaders in the late 1800s often welcomed Protestant missionaries as harbingers of modernity and as a counterbalance to Catholic political power—as evidenced by Mexico's president Benito Juarez's snide remark that North American missionaries might "teach Indians to read rather than light candles"—it is little wonder that the population at large tended to vigorously reject both the foreigners and their alien (and for them, alienating) message. Even by 1960, the missionary movement seemed to have largely failed, as not a single country in Latin America counted more than a handful of native (that is, nonforeign) Protestants—in every case, less than 10 percent in its national census.

Scholars have classified the subsequent expansion of the movement through the region in three key waves of development. "First wave" Pentecostalism came to Latin America in the early decades of the twentieth century, brought by foreign missionaries, usually—though not exclusively—from the United States. Reviled by both Catholics and other Protestants, the first wave Pentecostals established something of a permanent presence in a few locations (especially in Brazil, where Swedish evangelists founded the *Assembleia de Deus*, now the largest non-Catholic denomination in the country). For the most part, the first wave did not penetrate the religious cultural membrane of the receiving nations.

The second wave of Pentecostals appeared in the late 1950s and early 1960s with the arrival of media-based evangelism and national "crusades." In some locations, conservative authorities viewed Pentecostalism as a spiritual alternative to communism, adding political support to the appeal of evangelism. By the mid-1960s, Protestant conversion had begun to inch up to a noticeable degree. Due to a favorable convergence of sociological, political, and even spiritual factors, the efforts of such interdenominational agencies quickly bore fruit. By the middle of the decade, locally run Protestant churches began to sprout in the urban slums and rural villages of Latin America. The context of rapid urbanization, internal migration, and the transition from agricultural to industrial economies in midcentury Latin America resulted in what one anthropologist has called "a complex bombardment of twentieth-century forces," and contributed directly to the increased number of churches. The exigencies of the Cold War in Latin America, where military governments confronted leftist insurgencies, forced many populations to struggle to persevere in a setting of violence and police states.

The third wave Pentecostalism emerged in the 1980s. Unlike the earlier two waves, which were typically—if not always—driven by foreign clergy, third wave Pentecostals developed from local leadership and domestic "consumer tastes" and preferences in religious offerings. In particular, third wave Pentecostals differ from their predecessors by their emphasis on the here-and-now, as opposed to the end-of-times concerns of other Pentecostals, who were (and are) so focused on Christ's imminent Second Coming that they have little concern for daily "worldly" matters. Third wave Pentecostals, often called neopentecostals, are fiercely focused on the present time. Like other Pentecostals, neopentecostals reify the baptism by the Holy Spirit, meaning they believe in a bodily experience of God, such as through speaking in tongues or faith healing. But their orientation is firmly grounded in the temporal world, as neopentecostals emphasize self-improvement and material advancement as signs of God's grace and favor. From this temporal orientation, neopentecostals believe in instrumentalist religious practices such as prosperity theology (the belief that God blesses the faithful with material abundance), which promises to bring about improvement in the everyday world through celestial intervention. We take a closer look at a uniquely Brazilian example of "prosperity theology" later in this chapter.

Why Pentecostalism?

Scholars have explored the Latin American affinity for Pentecostalism in a variety of ways, describing it as a "refuge of the masses" for former peasants displaced to the cities by war, economic problems, and migration, who find stability and assistance through a new life in a Pentecostal church. Others adopt a functionalist explanation, emphasizing the ways in which immigrants from the country use urban Protestant churches as voluntary organizations that enable them to save money and insulate themselves from social ills such as alcoholism and abuse. Other scholars suggest that Pentecostal attitudes help women to "domesticate machismo," or teach converts new ways to improve themselves *del suelo a cielo* (from a dirt floor to heaven). Some observers suggest that Protestant (and specifically Pentecostal) religion does not offer any particular material advantage to the poor, but does provide believers with certain new psychological strategies and attitudes that help them cope with the reality of their poverty. Finally, other analysts conclude that the real attraction of Pentecostalism is its exuberant, joyous style that appeals to Latin American sensibilities. "Pentecostalism," suggests one well-known scholar, "is its very own fiesta."

The impact of Pentecostalism (and its Catholic variation, known as "Charismatic Renewal," which is the most dynamic Catholic movement in the region) has been profound. In 2006, the Pew Forum study noted that 73 percent of Protestants in Latin America were Pentecostals. Even more significantly, the Pew study demonstrated an upsurge in what it termed "renewalist" religion within their ten-country study, meaning that people who belonged to religious groups not historically Pentecostal—mainline Protestants and, especially, Catholics—had adopted a "pentecostalized" set of beliefs and practices to enrich their own traditions. It remains to be seen if the popular papacy of the first pope from Latin America, Pope Francis (Argentina's former Cardinal Jorge Bergoglio), will alter the trajectory of religious change in the region.

Brazilian Neo-Pentecostalism

Pentecostal growth reflects Brazil's larger transformations in the past generation: Pentecostal denominations have grown as Brazil has urbanized, pushing into new frontier zones and cultivating identity politics. Since the late 1970s, neopentecostal churches have grown rapidly. Their strategies for expansion, requiring extensive contributions and recruitment by every church member and often characterized by church ownership of radio and television stations, have altered Brazil's religious and political landscape.

The Universal Church of the Kingdom of God (IURD), was the largest and most controversial of the neopentecostal churches. The church, founded in Rio de Janeiro in 1977 by Edir Macedo, is a major presence in Brazil. It owns a major media empire, as well as an airline and substantial real estate holdings. Like other neopentecostal churches, the IURD practices exorcism of "demons"; in this case, the church seeks to cast out the gods and spirits of the African diasporic religions such as Candomblé and Umbanda, denouncing them as fallen angels. The IURD is also

≡ **Pentecostal Community Baptism.** Protestant Pentecostalism emerged as a powerful religious phenomenon in the last quarter of the twentieth century throughout Latin America. Pentecostalism has been particularly strong in Central America and Brazil, attracting converts from Catholicism among the urban poor and working class, rural to urban migrants, women of all sectors, and residents of fast-growing regions. Pentecostalism offers networks of solidarity and employment prospects and an invigorating response to perceived decadence and dissolution of modern life.

an avid proponent of "prosperity theology," a doctrine that teaches that God rewards believers for their faith with material and worldly success. In practical terms, believers "plant seed money" by giving tithes and other financial offerings to the church that they believe will assure God of their faithfulness.

Because of the vast wealth the IURD and its founder have acquired, the church has frequently been accused of illegal or unethical activities such as money laundering and charlatanism. To date, both the church and Macedo have come through these scandals largely unscathed. In 2014, the IURD completed its own "answer to the Vatican," a $300 million "Temple of Solomon" in São Paulo, which the church described as a "direct replica" of the Old Testament king's residence. (This Temple of Solomon, however, also includes a helipad and a state-of-the-art multimedia system.) The dedication of the Temple, featuring a procession that included an "ark of alliance" modeled on the biblical Ark of the Covenant, was televised live

CULTURE AND IDEAS

Argentina's Naval Mechanics School Museum

During the "dirty war" of Argentina's 1976–1983 dictatorship, Buenos Aires's Escuela *Superior de Mecánica de la Armada*, or Naval Mechanics School, was perhaps the most-feared location in the country. Agents of the regime took thousands of prisoners to the Naval Mechanics School, tortured them, subjected them to forced labor, and killed them. Pregnant women among the prisoners were permitted to live only until they gave birth. Their babies were then given to military officers, and the mothers were subsequently killed. This was one of the most horrific sites of institutionalized depravity in Latin America's long history.

In 2004, Argentina began to convert the grounds and buildings of the School into a museum and archive, the *Espacio Memoria y Derechos Humanos*, or Memory and Human Rights Space. The museum opened to visitors in 2010. Its exhibition space guides visitors through the painful history of the dictatorship, displaying passports, photographs, and letters of the disappeared, paintings made by and about survivors and their experiences, and locations and instruments of torture and abuse. Tour guides, some of them survivors of torture, recount the awful history of the dirty war.

Like other museums dedicated to documenting a horrific past, the Memory and Human Rights Space urges visitors not to forget and offers a space to mourn and reflect. It also offers something that the Argentine political arena has not been able to provide: a place to hold perpetrators accountable, at least through the revelation of their acts. When the military regime ceded power in 1983, it insisted on legal amnesty from prosecution for individual officers. That amnesty was later overturned, but attempts at prosecution have generally failed, confounded by intimidation and corruption. Inside the Memory and Human Rights Space, however, the evidence stands stark and unforgettable.

- What role do sites that memorialize and interpret trauma, like the Naval Mechanics School Museum, play in the consolidation of democracy?

on Brazilian TV, and watched by millions of viewers. Given its accruing wealth, its emphasis on success, and its expansive presence, the IURD represents not only a neopentecostal religion but also a neoliberal religion.

Thousands of smaller neopentecostal sects also jostle for space in Brazil's newly diverse religious marketplace. Brazilians disillusioned with what they often took to be the apathy of the traditional Catholic Church, or alienated by liberation theology's emphasis on social gospel over personal belief, started converting to these neopentecostal churches in massive numbers. These churches preached that believers could gain control over their destiny in this life, keeping at bay the forces of social dissolution and economic disruption, a message with enormous power amid Brazil's turbulence. Neopentecostalism grew first at the margins—in poor and peripheral urban neighborhoods, and in newly settled frontier zones. But by the first decade of the twenty-first century neopentecostal conversion had grown more diverse, crossing class, racial, and geographical boundaries. Indeed, Brazilian neopentecostal churches—and not only the IURD—began expanding rapidly throughout the Americas and overseas.

Neopentecostal churches have used media ownership to attract followers but also to secure their position, in some cases earning implicit political protection in return for favorable coverage of elected leaders. Neopentecostal political pastors have supplemented that strategy by running for office themselves, forming a *bancada evangélica*, or evangelical coalition, in Brazil's congress. Although that coalition has not always voted in a unified manner, it has consistently acted to protect neopentecostal media ownership and to oppose measures of social liberalization like abortion and gay marriage.

Popular Cultural Traditions, 1970–2000

Neoliberal development, urbanization, and the emergence of newly pluralistic democratic societies are also reflected in Latin America's popular culture. Cultural expressions that had formerly been marginal came to the center, as new sites of production and distribution emerged. The market for popular culture expanded, as new generations bought televisions, compact disc players and the great novelty of the period, home computers. It would be impossible to provide a comprehensive survey of these transformations, but a few examples serve to illustrate these trends.

New Popular Music Genres

Merengue and *bachata* are two popular musical genres from the Dominican Republic. The first emerged as a genre in the 1920s, performed by ensembles featuring strings, brass, and percussion. Under the Trujillo dictatorship (chapter 8), merengue became the Dominican Republic's national music, favored by the dictator himself but also celebrated by his opponents. During the turbulent 1960s and 1970s, merengue became a vehicle for political debate. But it also became big business, as Dominican producers collaborated with partners in New York City (home to a vibrant Dominican community) to make transnational stars of its top performers. The merengue they favored was slick and upbeat, often produced as a televised spectacle with performers in lavish costumes accompanied by exuberant dancing girls. Pop-merengue's intricate dance maneuvers became staples on dance floors from New York to Guayaquil.

As merengue reached its peak as Spanish America's pop music, bachata started to emerge from its origins in working-class Santo Domingo dancehalls. In comparison with the glittery merengue of the 1980s, bachata was stripped-down, usually performed only on electric guitar, *bongo* drum and *güira*, a metal rasp. Bachata had a tinny, cutting timbre with melodramatic lyrics, nearly always about heartbreak. Like merengue, it was danced by embracing couples, but without fanfare. Commercial producers initially scoffed at bachata, dismissing it as music of the margins. But self-produced cassettes by unheralded bachata performers became all the rage in the working-class quarters of Santo Domingo. Bachata gradually overtook merengue's market share.

The shift in popularity was consolidated when Juan Luis Guerra, the Dominican Republic's biggest star and one of Latin America's most famous performers, recorded a bachata album in 1990. Scruffy bachata suddenly moved from the margins to the center. Its initial working-class practitioners and fans did not make the same transition so easily or so successfully, but bachata's newfound prominence at least signaled their rising influence.

Bachata's rise was not unique. *Cumbia*, a popular musical genre from Colombia's Afro-Caribbean coast, experienced a similar evolution in the 1990s. Popular ensembles throughout Spanish America already performed cumbia, and distinct subvarieties of the genre were already popular in the Andes, Buenos Aires, and Mexico. But like bachata, cumbia had primarily been a popular music of the urban margins. In the 1990s, as the residents of the barrios, villas miseria, and barriadas began to seek greater prominence and self-determination, cumbia became their soundtrack.

In some ways, the rise of bachata and cumbia repeated a trajectory seen earlier in the emergence of genres like samba and tango. In contrast to these earlier genres, however, bachata and cumbia were not invested with symbolic meanings of national identity. While always recognized as a Dominican genre, bachata never took over merengue's title as *the* Dominican music—and its performers and producers never sought that role. Protean cumbia was rarely even thought of as Colombian—it adapted thoroughly to whatever Latin American context in which it was being performed. These transitions reflected a new pluralism and rapid hemispheric circulation of Latin American popular culture.

Other Forms of Popular Culture

Some forms did not evolve dramatically, but nonetheless reflected the changing spirit of the times. The televised soap opera—the **telenovela** in Spanish America, or *novela* in Brazil—remained by far the most popular dramatic genre

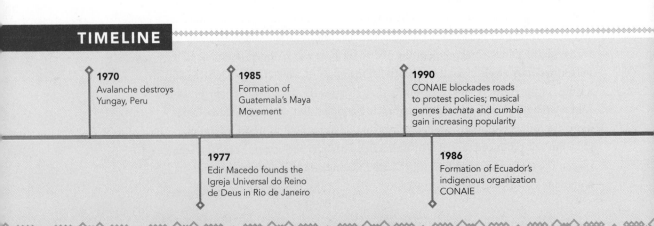

TIMELINE

1970
Avalanche destroys
Yungay, Peru

1985
Formation of
Guatemala's Maya
Movement

1990
CONAIE blockades roads
to protest policies; musical
genres *bachata* and *cumbia*
gain increasing popularity

1977
Edir Macedo founds the
Igreja Universal do Reino
de Deus in Rio de Janeiro

1986
Formation of Ecuador's
indigenous organization
CONAIE

in the region; today, its fan base extends well into the United States. In many ways the telenovelas had changed little from their origins in the *radionovelas* of the 1930s. In many cases, in fact, they *were* the old radionovelas, with the same plots updated to reflect current situations. *Marimar*, for example, produced by the Mexican station Televisa in 1994, became one of the most popular Spanish-American soap operas of the decade, broadcast throughout the continent. *Marimar* was an updated version of a *La Indomable* ("The Untamable Woman"), an old Venezuelan radionovela.

Marimar's title character is a poor orphan girl who, over the course of the series, marries a rich boy, loses him and is framed for robbery by his stepmother, goes to jail, and is subsequently released. Marimar then happens to encounter her own father—who turns out to be rich—moves to Mexico City, and adopts the identity and mannerisms of a wealthy woman to exact revenge on the evil stepmother, and winds up reunited with her sweetheart. By inviting the viewer to identify with Marimar, the telenovela offered the viewer the best of all worlds—the simple life of Marimar's youth, the luxury of her new surroundings in Mexico City, the sweet taste of revenge against the corrupt elite, and the satisfaction of being just a country girl at heart. Nothing about the storyline of this populist parable differed dramatically from the original radio version, but the updated speech, clothing, and settings gave it currency throughout the hemisphere in the 1990s.

In other ways, telenovelas did deliberately take on current issues. In Brazil, especially, novela authors prided themselves on shaping popular culture rather than simply reacting to it. The plots of Brazilian novelas of the 1990s featured elements like Internet romance, heart transplants, and the political struggles of favela residents. Even religion was not immune: during the 1990s, the Brazilian TV network Rede Record ran an unflattering soap opera called *Decadência*, based on the IURD

1990
Violeta Chamorro becomes first elected woman president in Latin America

1992
Rigoberta Menchú Tum is awarded the Nobel Peace Prize

1990
Law of Popular Participation in Bolivia

2005
Evo Morales becomes first indigenous president in South America

and Edir Macedo, although the church retaliated with a biblical costume-drama novela of its own, *Os Dez Mandamentos* (The Ten Commandments), that is still among Brazil's most popular TV shows.

Politicians feared their influence: In 1993, as impeachment loomed, President Fernando Collor de Mello used his executive power to block broadcasts of a novela that presented a thinly veiled caricature of his corrupt administration. But even Collor could not block the opening credits of the 1992–1993 telenovela *Deus Nos Acuda* (May God Help Us), which showed an elite cocktail party gradually submerged by the infiltration of a sea of mud. As the example shows, Latin America's telenovelas were designed to please a mass audience—but their political implications could be remarkably pointed.

Conclusion

The new actors and movements that emerged on the Latin American social and political landscape in the final decades of the twentieth century came from sectors that had been underrepresented or absent entirely from the national narrative in the past: women, people of indigenous and African descent, and newly minted Protestants. During the post-1980 period, ordinary people began to redefine their own lives within new identities. These new identities might be constructed around religious change and conversion, or by new understandings of self, based on ethnicity, race, or gender. As these social identities began to change, so did people's ideas of what they could and should expect from their governments. Gone were the preoccupations of the Cold War, to be replaced—however slowly—with reordered priorities and anxieties about the environment, human rights, democracy, and the construction of a civil society that reflected these vital new concerns.

KEY TERMS

Selected Readings

Becker, Marc. *Pachakutik: Indigenous Movements and Electoral Politics in Ecuador.* New York: Rowman & Littlefield Publishers, 2011.

Carey, Mark. *In the Shadow of Melting Glaciers: Climate Change and Andean Society.* New York: Oxford University Press, 2010.

Carroll, Rory. *Comandante: Hugo Chávez's Venezuela.* New York: Penguin Press, 2013.

Fischer, Edward T., and R. McKenna Brown. *Maya Cultural Activism in Guatemala.* Austin: University of Texas Press, 1996.

Garfield. Seth. *Indigenous Struggle at the Heart of Brazil: State Policy, Frontier Expansion, and the Xavante Indians, 1937–1988.* Durham, NC: Duke University Press, 2001.

Garrard-Burnett, Virginia. *Protestantism in Guatemala: Living in the New Jerusalem.* Austin: University of Texas Press, 1998.

Jalalzai, Farida. *Women Presidents of Latin America: Beyond Family Ties.* New York: Routledge, 2016.

Kampwirth, Karen, ed. *Gender and Populism in Latin America: Passionate Politics.* University Park: Pennsylvania State University Press, 2010.

Meisch, Lynn A. *Andean Entrepreneurs: Otavalo Merchants and Musicians in the Global Arena.* Austin: University of Texas Press, 2002.

Rahier, Jean Muteba, ed. *Black Social Movements in Latin America: From Monocultural Mestizaje to Multiculturalism.* New York: Palgrave MacMillan, 2012.

Stoll, David. *Is Latin America Turning Protestant? The Politics of Evangelical Growth.* University of California Press, 1990.

Stoll, David. *Rigoberta Menchú and the Story of All Poor Guatemalans.* Boulder, CO: Westview Press, 1999.

Vanden, Harry E., and Gary Prevost, eds. *Politics of Latin America: The Power Game.* 5th ed. New York: Oxford University Press, 2015.

Weyland, Kurt Gerhard, Raúl L. Madrid, and Wendy Hunter, eds. *Leftist Governments in Latin America: Successes and Shortcomings.* New York: Cambridge University, Press, 2010.

Epilogue

The Zika Epidemic

The zika virus first emerged as a threat in Brazil in 2015. Like malaria, yellow fever, and other viruses already familiar to Latin America, zika is primarily spread by mosquito, but can also be spread through sexual transmission. Zika was a newcomer to Brazil. The virus was first identified in Uganda in 1947, but did not cause a large outbreak among a human population until 2007, on the Pacific island of Yap. Zika probably arrived in Brazil in 2014, when Brazil hosted both the World Cup and an international canoe race featuring multiple teams from Pacific Island nations. Zika did not initially seem to pose a catastrophic threat, as its symptoms in most adults—body aches, fever, and rash—were similar to but milder than dengue fever, already well known in Brazil. But over the course of 2015, hundreds of Brazilian babies were born with microcephaly, or abnormally small skulls accompanied by severe brain damage; not long thereafter, it became evident that even children who did not show immediate symptoms at birth could still suffer from the most severe symptoms of the disease. Scientists soon established the connection between zika and microcephaly, and went on to establish a clear link between zika and rising incidences of Guillain-Barré syndrome, a temporary paralysis that can prove fatal to the very young, the aged, or the otherwise debilitated.

Within a matter of months, zika was transformed from a tropical disease few people had heard of into an epidemiological panic. Zika spread quickly from Brazil throughout Central and South America, and began a steady migration northward through the Caribbean and to US shores, as well as across the Atlantic. Zika is transmitted by the *Aedes aegypti* mosquito, which flourishes amid the standing water, raw sewage, and dense populations of the urban peripheries of Latin American cities. *Aedes aegypti* did not disdain the rich, but it displayed a malevolent preference for the poor, with many more opportunities to live among them.

In the 1880s, the Cuban physician Carlos Finlay identified the mosquito as the vector of the yellow fever virus. In 1900, Finlay and the US Army doctor Walter Reed used this knowledge to lead ambitious, well-coordinated efforts to eradicate yellow fever and malaria from most of Cuba through vigilant mosquito control—a strategy then reproduced in Panama and elsewhere in Latin America. In 2016, governments throughout the Americas, along with transnational epidemiology and healthcare networks, struggle to craft a response as

≡ **Child Refugees from Central America.** In the second decade of the twenty-first century, many thousands of children from Central America attempted to cross the border into the United States. Many of the children were unaccompanied minors, who had left their homes in El Salvador, Guatemala, and Honduras to escape crime, gang violence and poverty in their communities. Child immigration from Central America reached crisis proportions in the summer of 2014, when when tens of thousands of women and children crossed the border. In the United States, children were taken to shelters run by churches and other private organizations, or to Immigration and Customs Enforcement (ICE) detention centers. The children referred to the ICE centers as "*la hielera*," (the icebox).

effective as that of Finlay and Reed in the early 1900s. Although contemporary resources are much greater—Brazilian epidemiologists raced to produce genetically modified mosquitoes to reduce the spread of zika, for example—the challenges are much greater as well. Urban poverty is entrenched in Latin American cities to an extent unimaginable in 1904, while a generation of policy initiatives based on the logic of the market has left governments relatively incapable of coordinated, large-scale mosquito eradication. Zika does not lend itself to market-based solutions.

As of this writing, it is too soon to tell whether zika will be contained relatively quickly or whether it will remain a threat for years to come. But it is clear that zika flourishes at the nexus of trends that have reshaped Latin America in recent decades.

≡ **Sanitation Worker Spraying for Mosquitos in Rio de Janeiro.** Zika went from a nearly unknown disease to one of the greatest fears in the region between 2014 and 2016. This mosquito-borne virus spread rapidly in poor neighborhoods of tropical cities characterized by standing water and inadequate sanitation. Its consequences include microcephaly among newborns, a terrifying prospect for expectant parents in the zika zones. Zika spread quickly from Brazil northward, reaching the southern US by 2016. Initiatives to contain and combat zika spread equally quickly, in stark examples of the increasing interconnectedness of global life.

Migration, urbanization, inequality, and environmental degradation all play their role in the spread of zika. And it is clear that transnational networks will be necessary to contain the virus and reduce its threat. Zika is a global disease, no more Latin American in origin than the mango or the coffee bean, two other imports often associated with Latin American exchange. But it is a reminder of why and how what happens in Latin America affects the United States, for example, along with the rest of the world.

Zika presents one of many threads we can follow back through the tangles of Latin America's recent history. As scholars of Latin America based in the United States, we are enmeshed in those tangles even as we try to see beyond them, into the future and into the more distant past. Current events are too unsettled and multivarious to offer a summary. Instead, by way of an epilogue we consider the recent trajectories of several of the key themes we have been following through the book. In each section, we identify iconic cases like that of zika, which seem to exemplify and reflect broader trends.

Environmental Issues

As the twenty-first century unfolds, many Latin Americans, like people across the globe, have become increasingly aware of the importance of addressing environmental challenges. Natural disasters (earthquakes, volcanoes, tsunamis, hurricanes, and landslides) will always threaten Latin Americans because they reside in a geologically volatile part of the globe. But humans also share responsibility for some contemporary environmental problems as well as the scale of damage wrought by natural disasters.

During the nineteenth century, elites (like their colonial predecessors) viewed nature as an antagonist to be tamed and exploited. Thus, nineteenth-century Peruvians depleted the entirety of their irreplaceable guano resources; at the same time that Brazilian landowners chopped down most of the Atlantic coastal forest to clear land for sugar and coffee plantations. The result was immeasurable destruction of ecosystems and loss of biodiversity.

As Latin Americans poured into cities, especially after 1960, they exacerbated the pressure on natural resources by demanding modern conveniences, like electricity, that taxed natural resources. Worse, as automobile and bus traffic clogged colonial city streets, their diesel and gasoline emissions transformed urban jewels like Mexico City and Lima into polluted urban environments, contributing to the carbon emissions now recognized as a cause of global warming. Only in the past few decades have we understood that we must work to manage, minimize, or prevent three categories of environmental disasters: those created by natural phenomenon; those unleashed by human hands; and those like global warming that are the product of international forces. As disaster management specialists like to note, "Natural *events* turn into natural *disasters* only when human beings are affected."

The case of the 2010 earthquake in Haiti, the most devastating natural disaster ever to strike the Americas, wreaked havoc on Latin America's poorest nation. Although far from the most powerful earthquake ever to strike the Western Hemisphere, the Haitian quake caused extraordinary damage.

≡ Aftermath of Haiti Earthquake of 2010. The devastating 2010 earthquake in Haiti brought home the fatal consequences of inequality and weak governance. Shoddy construction crumbled during the quake, trapping and killing thousands of Haitians. Ineffective administration made it impossible to clear rubble and restore water and electricity. Vast sums in international aid were siphoned off by corrupt middlemen. Impoverished Haitians fled the nation, seeking opportunities elsewhere through circuitous and dangerous migrant networks. The local and international consequences of environmental catastrophe provided another example of interconnected global fortunes.

Its epicenter was located only fifteen miles from densely populated Port-au-Prince, where building codes were almost never enforced and many people lived in substandard housing in vast slums. As a result of haphazard construction, thousands of homes and public buildings collapsed in Haiti's quake; which struck just a few minutes before the end of the workday. Many of the government and health officials who would otherwise have led the nation's reconstruction were themselves killed while still sitting at their desks. In addition, centuries of deforestation caused by unsustainable agricultural practices left the mountainous Haitian landscape especially vulnerable to landslides. But like many natural disasters, the Haiti earthquake disproportionately affected the poor. An estimated 150,000 people perished and a million and a half people became homeless in a matter of minutes.

Human activity contributes directly to environmental crises. For example, the multinational Samarco Corporation built a holding dam near the Brazilian town of Bento Rodrigues to store the tailings (waste products) from its iron mines. When the dam breached on November 5, 2015, nearly sixteen billion gallons of toxic iron waste flowed into the Doce River. En route to the sea, the sludge inundated the isolated town of Bento Rodrigues, giving residents only minutes to flee to higher ground. Seventeen people died and hundreds were left homeless in the worst environmental disaster in Brazilian history. The sludge fouled riverbanks and the beaches near the river's mouth, and poisoned wildlife. Communities along the river reported levels of arsenic, lead, and mercury in their drinking water between ten and twenty times the acceptable level.

The Brazilian government's investigation revealed significant corporate negligence on the part of Samarco and its corporate partners. Besides failing to reinforce the dam, the company had recklessly increased production (and therefore the tailings) that produced more pressure on the dam. Nor had the corporation placed a warning system on the dam itself or in the town of Bento Rodrigues. As a result of this evidence of negligence, the Brazilian government fined Samarco $4.5 billion. As multinational corporations continue to extract minerals, Latin Americans worry about the possibility of future man-made environmental disasters like the Bento Rodrigues dam failure.

Finally, Latin American environmentalists see visible evidence of global warming in the melting of the glaciers that once graced numerous Andean mountains. Scientists also debate whether global warming has contributed to the intensification of **El Niño** effects, because the three largest El Niños in the past century have occurred since 1980. El Niños result from the abnormal warming of waters in the eastern Equatorial Pacific. This warming alters the flow of winds, creating heavy rains in Peru, intense hurricanes in Mexico, and persistent drought in vulnerable areas such as the "dry corridor" that runs through Guatemala, Honduras, and El Salvador. Despite the fact that it produces only 0.05 percent of global greenhouse emissions, the United Nations has identified Central America as a "hotspot" for climate change–related disasters in coming years, ranking alongside other extremely vulnerable areas, such as sub-Saharan Africa, Bangladesh, and the Maldives.

Campesinos in this region work small subsistence plots of land without the benefit of irrigation. In good times, they grow enough staples (such as corn and beans) to sell a small surplus. When a "super" El Niño arrived in 2015, corn stalks withered in the field. After farmers lost this first harvest, the drought persisted and the second crop failed as well. Without corn and beans, families lacked even the meager diet of tortillas and frijoles to sustain life. As the El Niño effect continues to linger over the dry corridor, some 3.5 million people are experiencing food insecurity despite the best efforts of relief agencies like World Food Programs to alleviate hunger. Because one in five families has experienced the effects of the drought, many people from the dry corridor have joined the flood of migrants fleeing Central America for the United States. Although the extent of the long-term consequences of global warming cannot be known, Latin Americans share the world's anxiety about their changing environment.

Commodities in the Twenty-First Century

As we have seen in previous chapters, Latin America historically has supplied Europe and the United States with primary products, mostly foodstuffs and minerals. This monocultural dependence on one or two major export crops has profoundly affected relations with the nations in the North where these products are sold. Consumers in temperate climatic zones developed a taste for the exotic commodities grown in the tropics that have now become basic staples, such as sugar, coffee, cacao, and bananas, while the Southern Cone nations exported affordable beef, mutton, and wheat to British markets. Other Latin American countries sold minerals like tin and petroleum to the United States and Western Europe. In recent years, the mineral lithium, the key element in cellphone batteries and other portable devices, has become essential for the contemporary telecommunications revolution and has promised to become the next bonanza for several South American nations. Today, commodity chains of primary products continue to link Latin America tightly to the rest of the world.

Likewise, for much of its history Latin America imported manufactured goods from Western Europe and the United States although since the 1930s the region's industrial output has dramatically increased. For the most part, however, technological innovations continue to flow from the developed world to Latin America. During the nineteenth century, inventions such as the steamship, the locomotive, and the telegraph transformed Latin America economically and contributed to the heightened sense of national identity, a process furthered by the arrival of paved highways and air transport after 1920 (the first airplane may well have been built by a Brazilian, Alberto Santos-Dumont, years before the Wright brothers' invention in 1903). Recently, the telecommunications industry has integrated nations even more tightly.

During the twenty-first century, Latin America, more than any other part of the global south, has participated in this telecommunications revolution that has proceeded through three stages. When neoliberal economics were adopted, almost all Latin American nations (beginning with Chile in 1987) privatized their telecommunications networks. As a result, governments shed thousands of state employees and their wages. At the same time, these administrations weakened the regulations controlling the industry and offered other incentives to encourage foreign investment. With the exception of Brazil, neoliberal governments replaced the former state-owned corporations with monopolistic private corporations. In Mexico, for example, the businessman Carlos Slim, famous for purchasing troubled assets at bargain-basement prices, acquired Telmex, the sole landline operator in the country. When the technology bubble burst in 2000, his international partners withdrew from their partnership, allowing him to gain majority interest in the company.

The second phase of the telecommunication revolution began after 2000, when the economy rebounded and the industry revived armed with a new business model and new international partners. Another of Slim's companies, eventually called *América Móvil*, soon dominated the Mexican market with an innovation that provided subscribers with mobile telephone service using prepaid cards. Enormously successful, América Móvil brought fame and fortune to Slim, especially after the company expanded its operations into other Latin American nations. Between 2010 and 2013, *Forbes Magazine* ranked him as the richest person in the world with assets of approximately $75 billion.

In 2012, two years after Brazil introduced the idea of national broadband network services, Slim's companies became major actors in this third phase of the telecommunications revolution. Soon Colombia created a national plan to provide 70 percent of its population with Internet access and to provide universal access to hospitals and schools, even those in remote rural areas. Over the past few years, countries have rapidly adopted 4G-LTE networks. While many sectors of Latin America's economy slumped following the recession of 2008 (especially petroleum), the telecommunications industry has prospered. Smartphone sales led by Samsung have boomed in Brazil, Mexico, Argentina, Colombia, and Venezuela. By some estimates, Latin America will have 600 million smartphones in use by 2020 with América Móvil, *Telefónica*, and AT&T among the biggest providers. Latin Americans have become eager adapters of this new technology, and statistics indicate that technology leads to job creation and higher incomes.

Cellphones, smartphones, digital cameras, laptops, and electric automobiles all require rechargeable lithium batteries. As a result, experts predict that South America's extensive deposits of lithium may become the continent's next export bonanza. A significant portion of the world's lithium supply lies beneath the great Andean salt lakes of Chile, Argentina, and Bolivia, the so-called lithium triangle of South America. Because of these new technological uses for lithium, the demand for lithium and hence the price paid for this relatively rare, lightweight mineral has rapidly increased. Experts predict that production will triple from two hundred thousand tons in the year 2000 to more than six hundred thousand tons by 2020. Because of its multiple uses as a supplier of energy, manufacturers of the new technology refer to the mineral as "white petroleum" or the "oil of the twenty-first century."

Lithium production requires technology and significant investments of capital. The remote post–Ice Age salt lakes contain a variety of salts suspended in brine beneath the surface. To get at the deposits, mining companies must first drill wells and pump the lithium-rich brine to the surface. Then, the liquefied substance is drawn into a series of holding ponds where the minerals precipitate according to weight: first table salt, then a series of other salts (like potassium) and finally solid lithium. Because rain never falls in the Atacama Desert, Chile's Salar de Atacama has proven the most profitable because the sun does all the work of evaporating moisture from the pools of brine. In the wetter Argentine salt flats in the northwestern portion of the country, removing standing water adds to the costs of production. Bolivia's remote Salar de Uyuni may hold as much as 50 percent of the world's lithium supply.

Although foreign mining corporations would like to participate in the lithium boom, their willingness to invest also depends on the favorability of the host nation's policies. Despite having a Socialist president, Chile's stable, essentially

≡ **Lithium Deposits in Salar de Uyuni.** In the sixteenth century, Andean silver became crucial to the global economy, transforming commerce and fueling the rise and fall of empires. In the twenty-first century, lithium deposits in far-flung Bolivian salt-flats such as Salar de Uyuni became vital to manufacturing cell-phones and other cutting-edge electronics. Spiking demand for lithium led to speculation, environmental damage, and resource depletion and reawakened old concerns over border infringements. Cellphone consumers rarely realized they held a little bit of Bolivia in their hands.

neoliberal economic policy has encouraged both foreign mining conglomerates and a Chilean corporation to participate. Investors have expressed a growing interest in Argentina's deposits since Mauricio Macri, who favors economic orthodoxy and foreign investment, replaced leftist Cristina Fernández de Kirchner as Argentina's president in 2015. Meanwhile, in Bolivia, President Evo Morales has gloried in his nation's promised status as the "Saudi Arabia of lithium," but his insistence that his country retain 60 percent of any profits has cooled many investors' interest. Although Comibol, German and Chinese companies have begun small-scale processing ventures, most of Bolivia's resources remain untouched. In addition, Morales faces the concerns of environmentalists who fear the accumulation of massive quantities of sludge, huge powerlines, and heavy equipment on what had been a pristine salt lake. Morales now must juggle the interests of environmentalism, enshrined in the 2008 Constitution, with the need to develop production for the benefit of citizens in South America's poorest nation.

Gender Issues: The LGBT Movement in Contemporary Latin America

The **LGBT** community has become more visible and more vocal in twenty-first century Latin America, decades after the movement began in Western Europe and the United States. Using the inclusive language of the US civil rights movement of the 1960s and 1970s, LGBT advocates in Latin America have sought the same individual liberties that other citizens enjoyed. Although there have always been gay, lesbian, bisexual, and transgendered Latin Americans, the vast majority had no socially acceptable alternative but to keep their gender preferences secret until very recent times. While the US civil rights movement in the 1960s and 1970s provided space for gay advocacy movements, Latin America's authoritarian regimes in Argentina and Brazil repressed early organizational efforts. Likewise, Fidel Castro's regime in Cuba relegated homosexuals to labor camps in the 1960s and then isolated gay men in medical camps during the AIDS crisis of the 1980s and 1990s.

Even the democracies that emerged during Latin America's third wave of democracy in the early 1990s initially did little to advance LGBT issues, for two reasons. First, the LGBT movement in many countries lacked a safe organizational structure to lobby for its causes, in part because many LGBT individuals did not feel comfortable revealing their sexual orientation to family and friends by joining such an organization and because many Latin American men who have sex with other men do not always self-identify as gay. Second, the LGBT community represented a relatively small proportion of the population in comparison with other identity-based groups, such as women, indigenous populations, or Afro-descendent groups. As Latin American LGBT organizations grew more prominent in the twenty-first century, they sought to create a nondiscriminatory safe space for nonheterosexual individuals. Cities allowed for more practical opportunities for such organizations to prosper. As a result, the quest for LGBT rights found its earliest successes in large metropolitan areas such as Rio de Janeiro, Mexico City, and Buenos Aires.

The importance of patriarchal family networks in Latin America has increased the challenges faced by LGBT individuals, who have often risked

≡ **Gay Pride Parade in Guatemala City.** Gay rights movements emerged as one of the most powerful forms of identity politics in late twentieth-century Latin America. In cities like São Paulo and Buenos Aires, Gay Pride Parades went from being relatively small gatherings in the face of mainstream opposition in the early 1990s to being part of the political mainstream in the 2000s. Gay rights emerged more slowly as a cause for political mobilization and popular celebration in relatively traditional and conservative Central America. But Guatemala had a thriving Gay Rights Parade by 2011, as this image shows, challenging traditional gender norms.

familial condemnation by identifying as nonheterosexual. The Catholic Church and Pentecostal churches have generally condemned the LGBT lifestyle as a sin and an abomination. Even leftist parties in Latin America were slow to embrace the LGBT cause, hesitant of losing broader popular support. As recently as 2014, a Pew survey indicated that in every country in Latin America except for Brazil, Mexico, Chile, Argentina and Uruguay, a majority (50 percent or more) of the population opposed same-sex marriage.

But even so, over the past twenty years, a vigorous, transnational LGBT movement has emerged to create its own network of support and advocacy. That network, in turn, has proven influential in helping to direct public attitudes toward acceptance. Old prejudices endure in many places, and violence against LGBT individuals remains distressingly common. But the cause of LGBT rights has also gone mainstream in a way few would have predicted a generation ago. In Latin America's major cities LGBT parades now attract tens of thousands of participants, including major politicians. Openly gay legislators serve in the national congresses of many Latin American countries. And the quest to legalize same-sex marriage in Latin America has made incremental headway in several nations. (It bears noting that Latin American countries tend to be conservative on marriage issues in general. Most did not even permit legal divorce until the 1970s, and Chile did not legalize the practice until 2004).

In 2007, Uruguay became the first Latin American nation to permit civil unions. Most of the countries considering this solution looked for guidance to European precedents, especially Spain's same-sex marriage statute of 2006. Civil unions were politically easier than same-sex marriage for many Latin Americans to accept because they applied to both heterosexual and homosexual couples. Because of declining marriage rates, even more conservative legislators could endorse a reform that would convey property rights on persons living in a committed relationship (defined in Uruguay as one lasting five years or more). There, a new progressive party, the *Frente Amplio* ("Broad Coalition"), came to power in 2005 on a platform that included supporting legislation permitting greater reproductive rights and broadening antidiscrimination laws. During party rallies, LGBT advocates flew rainbow flags and persuaded Frente Amplio to adopt their cause. In 2009, Uruguay's legislature modified its family law statutes to allow same-sex couples to adopt children, essentially conveying the last remaining right of traditional marriage on gay and lesbian couples. Finally, the Uruguayan government formally recognized same-sex marriage in 2013.

In Argentina, activists used the court system to bring legal challenges to the statutory definition of marriage as being between one man and one woman. The activism of several high-profile litigants brought the issue into the public spotlight, and as judges began granting exceptions to individual couples, the publicity created pressure on the federal legislature to revise the law nationally. In 2010 Argentine President Cristina Fernández de Kirchner both advocated for and then signed such legislation, making Argentina the first Latin American nation to fully legalize same-sex marriage. As of this writing, same-sex marriage laws have been approved in Brazil and Uruguay (2013), Colombia (2016) and some states in Mexico, while Chile and Ecuador allow civil unions. And in Argentina, Brazil, Uruguay, and Chile, public opinion now broadly favors same-sex marriage. The rest of Latin America is likely not far behind.

Porous Borders and Transnational Crime: Gangs

Despite the fact that the wars in Central America ended more than a quarter century ago, the region remains one of the most violent in the world, especially in what is known now as the "Northern Triangle" of El Salvador, Honduras, and Guatemala. In the second decade of the twenty-first century, Honduras had the highest homicide rate in the hemisphere and among the highest in the entire world outside a war zone. The rate of violent death per year in El Salvador was nearly as high. Guatemala's murder rates follow close behind; there, the number of women who die violently in that country is so high that Nobel Prize–winner Rigoberta Menchú called the epidemic of violence "femicidio" (femicide). In all three of these countries, much of the violence is caused by and takes place among street gangs, notably the Mara Salvatrucha (MS-13) and the 18th Street Gang (also known as Barrio or Calle 18), two notorious *maras* (the popular Spanish word for "gangs"—the proper word is *pandilla*) that have their origins in the United States. In all three countries of the Northern Triangle, gang violence is rampant, greatly feared, and, especially in the case of Honduras, largely beyond the government's control.

The gang problem is a transnational and circular one that ties Central America closely to the United States. Both MS-13 and the 18th Street gangs have their roots in Los Angeles, where many Central Americans came to live after fleeing the wars in their own countries during the 1980s. Because many of these immigrants did not have legal papers, parents bringing young children into the United States more often than not ended up working low-paying jobs with long hours, often with little choice but to leave their children with little supervision. (That said, it is important to note that the high cost of childcare produces hierarchies of care and cost for parents across all economic ranges, where immigrant women may place their own children in childcare in order to work as nannies themselves).

Some of these children drifted into Latino street gangs that emerged in the 1980s in Los Angeles. These gangs competed with already-established gangs, like the Crips and the Bloods, that controlled turf and ran criminal enterprises such as drug trafficking, prostitution, and gun sales. For young gang "wannabes," gangs seemed to offer a sense of purpose, respect, and belonging otherwise absent from their lives, though at a very heavy cost of commitment, danger, and the likelihood of early death. The lucrative crack epidemic, combined with the heavy flow of poor and traumatized immigrants in the 1980s into the United States, directly contributed to the expansion of California's Central American gangs, which quickly gained affiliates around the country over the next decade.

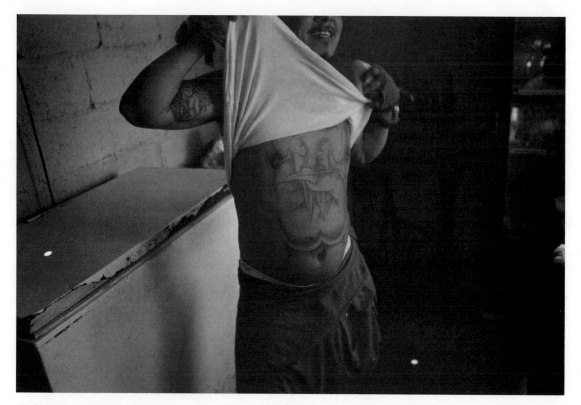

≡ **Gang Tattoos in Honduras.** Transnational criminal syndicates proved perniciously flexible, seizing opportunities for expansion and control in the economic crisis and disorder of 1990s and 2000s Central America. Following the civil wars of the 1980s, demobilized militias rarely disarmed. In many cases they turned to protection rackets, along with drug and arms trafficking. Central America was awash in guns. Meanwhile, the United States deported undocumented Central American migrants, some of whom had already established ties to gangs in cities like Los Angeles. Actors both within Central America and returning to the region from the United States strengthened growing transnational syndicates.

In the mid-1990s, US law changed to mandate the immediate deportation of non-US-born criminals if they were convicted of a felony (such as a drug possession charge). This policy resulted in the deportation of many thousands of Salvadoran and Guatemalan gang members back to prisons in home countries that many of them had left as babies or small children and to which they had no meaningful ties. With families absent or reluctant to claim them, most were likely to immediately affiliate with members of their gang, thus vastly increasing the size and power of the gangs within the home countries and creating close transnational connections between the gangs in Central America and in the United States. Violent competition among opposing gangs (sometimes directed by orders from imprisoned affiliates) contributes to the crime and insecurity that mark life in the Northern Triangle today, especially in poor areas where the rule of law and police protection are weak or nonexistent. The great migration of unaccompanied children to the United States from Honduras, El Salvador, and Guatemala in the summers of 2014 and 2015 was in large measure the response of anxious parents who were desperate to distance their vulnerable children from gang violence and away from the lures of the gangs themselves.

Because the gangs are large (MS-13, for example, is estimated to have some seventy thousand members across the United States and Central America), well-organized, firmly disciplined, and wealthy, they constitute a clear threat to the general welfare of the fragile nation-states in which they operate. This is especially true of El Salvador and Honduras, where they control physical territory and where some analysts have reported that they effectively operate as a parallel government. Both Guatemala and El Salvador adopted a *"mano dura"* (iron fist) approach to gangs in the mid-2000s, which in El Salvador went so far as to call for the arrest, imprisonment, or sometimes even the extrajudicial killing of young men with tattoos, especially body art that was clearly gang-related and or that disfigured the face. In March 2012, under an agreement brokered by negotiated by former guerrillas of the FMLN (now El Salvador's ruling political party) and a bishop from the Roman Catholic Church, MS-13 and the 18th Street Gang signed a truce, which brought an unprecedented two-year stretch of peace to the country. When the truce broke, however, in March 2015, the violence picked up where it left off. That month witnessed an average of sixteen gang-related killings per day, exceeding the daily average for the darkest days of the civil war.

The Latin Americanization of the United States

Chapter 14 demonstrated that although Brazil is often cited as the world's largest Catholic country, it can also be considered the world's largest Pentecostal country—its highly visible and hard-working Pentecostal minority continues to grow and to play an increasingly prominent role in defining the nation. In similar ways, the United States is traditionally thought of as "Anglo"—English-speaking, resting on a long history of British institutions and cultural expectations—but should also be considered Latin American, as its highly visible and hard-working Latin American minority continues to grow and to play an increasingly prominent role in defining the nation. There are over 55 million US residents of Hispanic/Latino/a origins, and another one or two million originally from Brazil. The Hispanic population of the United States is larger than the population of South Africa, South Korea, or Spain, and larger than that of any Latin American nation with the exception of Brazil and Mexico. The Hispanic population of the United States is growing far more quickly than the white/non-Hispanic population. In many US counties, Hispanics already represent a plurality of the population, larger than any other racial or ethnic group. Many Southwestern and Southern states had significant Hispanic populations. Among the top three were New Mexico (47 percent), Texas (38 percent), and California (38 percent); when adding other ethnic and racial groups, all three of these states are also "majority-minority." That presence of Hispanic/Latino/a populations will only grow over the next generation.

Some US citizens find this a worrying prospect, and fear the linguistic, cultural, and economic changes it heralds. These concerns were clearly demonstrated in the election of Donald J. Trump on a nativist and nationalistic platform to the US presidency in November 2016. Trump's political rhetoric to drastically reduce immigration, deport the 11 million undocumented Latin Americans then living in the United States, and his promise to build a wall along the nearly two-thousand-mile border between the United States and Mexico, a longtime US ally, clearly underscored these anxieties.

But in many ways, however, these changes are already upon us. And so, far from weakening the United States, Latin American Americans enrich the nation culturally while strengthening its economy. Most Americans view bilingualism positively. Many Americans lament the perceived failures of Hispanic immigrants to learn English, and accuse bilingual schools of, in practice, confining Hispanic children to the margins. Research suggests these fears are exaggerated, as the overwhelming majority of Hispanic and Brazilian immigrants, like generations of all ethnicities before them, learn to speak English and their children most certainly do.

The growing presence of Spanish—and to a lesser extent Portuguese—in the United States is a reality. But that presence is an asset, not a liability, to the United States in an increasingly global economy. Many recent academic studies have shown that the ability to speak more than one language allows the speaker not only to converse with non-English speakers of that language, but it also improves mental flexibility, superior concept formation, and metalinguistic awareness. Because English is the world's **lingua franca**

≡ **Boys Playing Soccer outside Bras Metro Station in São Paulo.** São Paulo, the largest city in South America, embodies many of the region's transformations over the past fifty years. Latin America has become heavily urbanized and industrialized. It is marked by great demographic, religious, and cultural diversity. Its economy forms a key part of global networks. Like most of the world, Latin America continues to face great challenges of inequality, violence, and environmental degradation. But it also possesses a vibrancy that continues to inspire local inhabitants and draw visitors. Like the boys playing soccer here outside the Bras Metro Station in the heart of working-class São Paulo, Latin Americans in general continue to take difficult circumstances and turn them into unlikely settings for popular creativity.

as well as the United States' official language, it is clearly advantageous for immigrants from Latin America to learn English, as have many generations of immigrants before them. And the United States is not likely to become a fully bilingual nation anytime soon. But an increasing percentage of Americans will speak both English and Spanish, and it is difficult to see this as a weakness.

Whether the presence of Latin American cultural influences like *ballet folklórico*, *quinceañeras*, and *carnitas burritos* enrich American culture or not is largely a matter of perspective. But what is clear is that these expressions represent "and also" options rather than "either/or" alternatives. Neither salsa (the music) nor salsa (the condiment) drove out rock and roll or ketchup. More seriously, fears of Latin American religious and lifestyle influence have turned out to be unfounded. Some observers have feared that Hispanic immigration would unleash a wave of Catholicism on the country, undermining the traditional Protestant denominations. Growing Catholicism, these observers have suggested, might subvert purported links between Protestantism, an ethic of hard work and economic striving, and US cultural and economic strength.

This has not happened and is not likely to happen in the future, although the US Catholic Church, where numbers had been declining with the "greying" of traditional "ethnic" populations such as Irish and Italian American Catholics, has received a significant boost with the influx of Latin American Catholic immigrants. Even so, Latin American immigrants often are not Catholic, and even when first-generation immigrants are, their children often are not. Many Hispanic and Brazilian immigrants are, in fact, Protestant—although not usually of the traditional, mainline denominations. More importantly, data suggests that—after controlling for economic background—Hispanics tend to have better educational outcomes, steadier employment, and more durable family units than the national average. Put simply, Latin Americans tend to have a beneficial influence on the United States. This positive generalization is not any truer of Latino/as than of any other population, of course, but it is far more frequently true than is the reverse proposition.

Most of the opposition to Latin American immigration to the United States focuses on the fear of job loss and depressed wages. Fears of job loss are not borne out by statistical evidence. Instead, it is clear that if undocumented Hispanic workers were suddenly removed from agricultural labor, for example, that sector of the economy would simply grind to a painful halt with catastrophic consequences, rather than adapt quickly to provide higher-paying jobs to legal residents. As for the matter of paying taxes—a common nativist complaint—even undocumented workers pay sales tax on every item they purchase, and many often pay social security and other taxes that support US social programs for which they can generally expect to receive no personal benefit. The economic effects of undocumented labor are complex and do not easily lend themselves to simple slogans and solutions.

Effects on wages are even more thorny, leading to larger concerns. Some research finds that high proportions of immigrants—in cities like Los Angeles and Miami, for example—can depress wages for low-skilled labor by as much as three percent. (This equation incorrectly assumes that immigrants from Latin America all work in the low-wage sector, which of course is patently untrue, since many are business and medical professionals, media figures, clergy, midlevel managers, and other highly skilled workers). This decrease is offset by the high productivity of immigrant labor, which tends to raise wages of skilled labor. As there are more skilled than unskilled workers, the overall effect of immigration on wages is positive. And the gains to productivity are considerable.

These overall gains, however, should not obscure the real struggles of low-wage workers, for this speaks to a larger and less salutary similarity between the United States and Latin America: the gap between the rich and the poor has widened substantially over the past generation. The role of Hispanic immigration in that rising inequality is relatively minimal, vastly outweighed by the role of the rising fortunes of the financial elite. But this rising inequality reminds us that the United States is growing more Latin American not only because of the growing presence of Spanish-speakers and of Latin American culture but also because of the increasing discrepancies of wealth separating the rich from the poor. As Latin America has become more like the United States, nurturing a diverse consumer society marked by middle-class aspirations, the United States has become more like Latin America, with protected enclaves sealed off from the presence of the poor. The Americas grow more alike.

The United States faces many of the same challenges faced by Latin America, such as high rates of gun violence and persistent patterns of racial discrimination. Our democracy is turbulent and imperfect but hopeful, our environment threatened but bountiful, our citizens contentious but patriotic. For better and for worse, we *are* Las Américas, a truth that citizens of all the Americas might embrace rather than deny. In the words of the Cuban poet José Martí, "Nor should we hide the obvious facts of a problem that can be solved, in the interests of a long and peaceful future, by means of study, good judgment, and the quiet, strong impetus of the single soul that the whole hemisphere shares."

KEY TERMS

El Niño 681	lingua franca 692	LGBT 683

Glossary

abolition In the nineteenth century, the abolition of the trans-Atlantic slave trade and then of slavery itself became controversial issues for tropical economies like those of Cuba and Brazil because production seemed to depend upon cheap labor. Under pressure from Afro-Latin Americans themselves, as well as European and national abolitionists, the "peculiar institution" was finally abolished in Cuba in 1886 and Brazil in 1888.

Alliance for Progress President John F. Kennedy's program to provide financial aid to the Latin American nations for economic development that would also improve the conditions of the poor and thereby dissuade Latin Americans from turning to communism. Despite the optimism with which Latin Americans viewed the proposal in 1961, the Alliance for Progress met with only modest success.

altiplano A highland region, most commonly the highland plateau in the southern Andes of Peru and Bolivia where people live at 12,000 feet altitude or higher. The ancestral home of the Aymara, the altiplano's inhabitants raise potatoes and herd llamas and alpacas; it also is the mining region in the Andes. The term is also used in Guatemala to describe the western highlands, home to the majority Maya population.

bancada evangélica is a neopentecostal evangelical coalition in the Brazilian congress, created in the late 1990s.

Banda Oriental was the name of the South American territories east of the Uruguay River and north of Río de la Plata. It was the easternmost territory of the Viceroyalty of the Río de la Plata. Under the terms that ended the Cisplatine War between Argentina and Brazil (1825–28) the Banda Oriental became the independent nation of Uruguay, a buffer zone between the regional powers of Argentina and Brazil.

barbudos, or guys with beards. After three years fighting in eastern Cuba, Fidel Castro, Ernesto "Che" Guevara, and the other men of the 26th of July Movement, overturned the regime of Fulgencio Batista on January 1, 1959. Their youthful bearded appearance became the style of many revolutionaries and hipsters of the 1960s and 1970s.

blanqueamiento / embranquecimento "whitening," This was the racist policy of gradually reducing the African and indigenous presence and marginalizing their cultural influence in Latin America by encouraging white immigration from Europe or intermarriage between races in Latin America. The policy was typical of Social Darwinist thought of the late nineteenth century.

blancs or "Whites." This referred to French colonials or other persons of European heritage living in Haiti prior to the Haitian Revolution in the 1790s.

boliburguesía refers to a new bourgeoisie that emerged in Hugo Chávez's Venezuela. Numerous government officials and businessmen friendly to the regime acquired huge fortunes through corruption. As Venezuela's economic situation worsened, critics have identified rampant corruption as one of the nation's greatest problems.

Bourbon reforms During the eighteenth century, the new Spanish dynasty (the Bourbons) attempted to reorganize the economic, administrative, and military structures of the colonies. It hoped to shore up Spanish America's defenses against foreign interlopers and to modernize the economic system to increase revenue from the Americas for the Crown's use in its European foreign policy objectives. Latin American colonists often resented the new taxes and other restriction of the reforms.

Business imperialism Economic domination and exploitation of poorer and weaker countries by richer and stronger states.

campesino a campesino The farmer to farmer movement, which promoted sustainable practices in Guatemala, southern Mexico, Honduras, and Nicaragua. Sustainable practices were seen as an alternative to the Green Revolution with its dependence on chemical fertilizers and genetically modified seeds. In many instances, these practices have led to "food sovereignty."

campesinos rural people, or farmers. This is the term that such people often prefer to use to refer to themselves, rather than a negative word like "peasant."

castas The Sociedad de las Castas was a hierarchical system of race classification created by Spanish elites (*españoles*) in the Americas during the eighteenth century.

The word casta, used alone, can also refer to any people of color during the colonial period: mestizos, mulattos, Afro-Latin Americans, indigenous people, and any people of racial mixture thereof—that is, all who were not classified as españoles within the system.

caudillos Regional strongmen, primarily important during the turbulent period of the early nineteenth century. Their charisma allowed them to attract followers who relied on them for benefits. Caudillos enjoyed solid support in their *patria chica* ("little country," or region) and ignored constitutional strictures to remain in power (*continuismo*) as long as possible, usually with the support of a personal army loyal to the strongman himself.

centrales large, industrialized sugar mills. These were commonly found in Cuba in particular.

charro Mexican cowboy, particularly from the north of the country, who wear distinctive outfits and like the *gauchos* of Argentina plays games of skill to display superior horsemanship. Today their outfits are frequently worn by mariachi musicians.

Charter of Punta del Este Treaty signed in August 1961 by the United States and twenty-two Latin American countries that established the Alliance for Progress to promote economic and social development in Latin America.

Christian Base Communities (CBEs) A religious movement that began in Latin America in the late 1960s in which small. autonomous groups within a parish meet regularly for Bible study, led by a priest, nun, catechist, or lay member. CBEs are often closely associated with liberation theology.

científicos Literally, "scientists." Porfirio Díaz's most influential advisors. Several occupied cabinet posts. The científicos helped Díaz create a budgetary surplus, encouraged him to build thousands of miles of railroads and modernize legal codes to encourage foreign investment. Their powerful role in government prompted outsiders to oppose Díaz's re-election in 1910.

Cisplatine War The Cisplatine War (1825–1828) was fought between the newly independent nations of Brazil and Argentina over control of the Banda Oriental, the territories east of the Uruguay River and north of Río de la Plata. The British negotiated a truce. Under its terms, the Banda Oriental became the independent nation of Uruguay, a buffer zone between Argentina and Brazil. For Uruguay, independence was neither the beginning nor the end of conflict, as the small nation would be torn by civil war for the next three decades.

Code Noir Literally the "Black Code," issued in 1685 by France's Louis XIV. It defined the conditions of slavery and established harsh controls over the conduct of enslaved people in France and the French colonies, notably Saint Domingue.

Cold War The global struggle between the West (the US, the western European nations, and Japan) and the East (the Soviet Union, Eastern Europe, and China) in the aftermath of World War II. The ideological conflict was "cold" because military conflict—"hot" wars— between the two sides rarely occurred except in Africa and Southeast Asia. The ideological struggle affected Latin America, especially after the Cuban Revolution of 1959, and lasted there through the late Cold War in the 1980s and 1990s.

colonias populares is the Mexican term for peoples' colonies or squatter settlements. These settlements emerged throughout Latin America but have different names (*villas miseria* in Argentina; *callampas* in Santiago, Chile, *barriadas* in Lima; *favelas* in Rio de Janeiro). These neighborhoods often lacked potable water, electricity, and schools, but the impoverished citizens living there hoped for a better future.

colonos sharecroppers, or resident worker on an agricultural estate (although the name may differ depending on the country). In exchange for the use of a parcel of land, the colono either provides a portion of his crop or his labor to the hacendado. "Colono" is widely used in Brazil and El Salvador.

Columbian Exchange A term coined to describe the exchange of products between Europe, the Americans, and Africa after Christopher Columbus "discovered" the Americas in 1492. For example, new food from the Americas like corn and potatoes fed many poor Europeans, while European cattle, sheep, chickens and wheat diversified the palate of indignous people. Africans contributed foodstuffs like yams and new forms of music.

Comité de Unidad Campesina (CUC) A mass popular organization made up mainly of indigenous campesinos in highland Guatemala, established in 1976 after a massive earthquake dramatically increased the nation's social, political, and economic inequalities. The organization was created to organize workers, to advance economic justice, (especially regarding land tenure), and to end state repression of campesinos.

communism In the 1840s Karl Marx conceptualized a social and conomic system based on his perceptions of the fate of the harsh labor conditions prevalent during the early stages of the industrial revolution. He believed that these conditions would lead to class warfare that would result with a victory for the workers, leading to a society where all property was publicly owned and people were paid according to their needs and abilities. In Latin America, immigrants familiar with the ideas of socialism and communism made important contributions to the early labor movement.

Confederación General de Trabajo (CGT) General Labor Confederation. A pan-union organization strengthened by Perón's campaign of factory visits and his orders to improve conditions and wages, which won him the fierce loyalty of workers.

Conquest of the Desert Military campaign directed by General Julio Argentino Roca in the 1870s that established Argentine dominance over Patagonia, and resulted in the near extermination of the native Aruacanians.

Conservatives Conservatives in the nineteenth century revered much of the Spanish tradition but proved amenable to gradual reforms as the century advanced. The preferred a strong central government, restrictions on open-ended liberties to preserve order, tariffs to generate revenue, and the preservation of Church lands and privileges as an essential part of the social order and the welfare system. In addition, they defended the Church because it preserved traditional values.

continuismo A common practice of caudillos, who often ignored or abrogated their national constitutions to remain in power indefinitely.

contras Nicaraguan troops who sought to overthrow the Sandinista regime through terror-tactics and low-intensity warfare, with US support. The word means "against," or counter-revolutionary.

cordon sanitaires sanitary barriers or quarantines designed to prevent the spread of infectious diseases, such as during the cholera epidemic of 1837 in Guatemala.

Corporatism is the idea that the political system should be organized by interest groups (like business, labor, military) that work together harmoniously to further the interests of the state. As such, political scientists often see corporatism as the foundational principle of populist regimes like that of Juan Perón in Argentina and Getúlio Vargas in Brazil.

coverture a wife's legal rights were entirely subsumed under those of her husband, who therefore outright owned all of her property, whether dowry, inheritance, earned income or real estate.

criollos people of Spanish descent born in the New World. Their diminished status during the Bourbon Reforms led many of them to fight on the patriot side during the wars of independence.

Cuba Libre A slogan that José Martí employed during the Cuban War for Independence: "Free Cuba".

Cuban Missile Crisis A thirteen-day confrontation in October 1962 between the United States and the Soviet Union over the installation of nuclear-armed Soviet missiles on Cuba It was the moment during the Cold War when the two superpowers came closest to nuclear conflict.

descamisados A term popular in 1930s-1950s to describe unskilled workers in Argentina. Eva Perón used this term to rally working class support for her husband's regime.

desparecido "disappeared one", referring to victims of extrajudicial murder by military regimes, primarily used in the 1970 to the 1980s.

Dirty Wars The Dirty Wars refer to the unequal conflicts between Latin American militaries and Marxist guerrillas beginning in the 1960s. The Dirty Wars were especially gruesome in Argentina, Chile, Guatemala, and El Salvador, where many thousands of civilians, suspected of being subversives, were tortured and disappeared. These reigns of terror generally subsided in the 1980s.

docencia libre Academic freedom, one of the results of the student strike in Argentina resulting in the University of Córdoba reforms of 1918–19.

Dollar Diplomacy An American foreign policy first articulated by President William Howard Taft. Its aim was to increase American influence by guaranteeing loans made to foreign countries, particularly in Latin America and East Asia.

Ejidos in Mexico, property in which community members individually farm designated parcels and collectively maintain communal holdings.

el corte / kout kout a literally meaning "the cut"; refers to the five-day massacre of Haitians living along the Dominican-Haitian border ordered by Rafael Trujillo on October 2, 1937.

El Niño A climate pattern result from the abnormal warming of waters in the eastern Equatorial Pacific. This warming alters the flow of winds, creating heavy rains in Peru, intense hurricanes in Mexico, and persistent drought in vulnerable areas such as the "dry corridor" that runs through Guatemala, Honduras, and El Salvador. Scientists debate whether global warming has contributed to the intensification of El Niño effects, because the three largest El Niños in the past century have occurred since 1980.

el pulpo the octopus; the nickname given to the United Fruit Company for its extensive and multi-tentacled reach in Central America.

empleados Literally, "employees". Government and commercial white-collar employees who became one of the core elements of the middle class that emerged in Latin America in the late nineteenth and early twentieth centuries.

encomienda In the era of the Spanish conquest/ encounter, leaders of expeditions and government official rewarded their followers by distributing to them groups of indigenous people. In exchange for the indigenous peoples' labor and payment of tribute, the encomendero was responsible for treating his charges humanely and providing them with religious instruction. In all too many instances, the greed for profits superseded the humanitarian motives.

Enlightenment Enlightenment ideas profoundly affected the Bourbon reformer King Charles III (1759–1788) and many of the important leaders of the Latin American wars for independence in the nineteenth century. The Enlightenment offered ideas such as the rights and liberties that free citizens enjoyed, the notion that free trade would lead to greater prosperity, and the idea that the Church ought to be stripped of its secular power (anti-clericalism). In Latin America, Enlightenment anti-clericalism led Charles III to expel the Jesuit order.

entreguistas sellouts; those accused of selling the country cheaply to foreign interests, primarily used in 1950s Brazil.

Esquipulas Accords This was the pan-Central American peace agreement brokered by Costa Rica's president Oscar Arias and signed in 1987. The insurgents agreed in general terms to commit to national reconciliation, and end to the hostilities, and to holding free, democratic elections. It also laid out a timetable for implementation.

Estado Novo the "New State". This was Getúlio Vargas's populist dictatorship with fascist leanings in Brazil from 1937 to 1945. The government sought rapid industrialization while maintaining close relationships with workers.

fascism A doctrine exalts nations and sometimes race above the individual, and stands for a strong centralized government headed by a charismatic leader. It is a form of authoritarian nationalism characterized by a totalitarian dictatorship that became influential in nations like Germany, Italy, Spain, and Portugal after World War I. Fascist parties existed in several Latin American countries in the 1930s. See corporatism and Integralistas.

favelas informal urban neighborhoods in Brazil of dwellings built mostly by the residents themselves outside of any building code, lacking property titles and legal protection. Often located on steep hillsides, they are prone to disaster during floods. See also colonias populares.

fazendeiros The owners of a plantation or large ranch in Brazil. Before 1888 these properties operated on the basis of slave labor, and thereafter with free workers. The estate included a big house (often a mill) and raised a variety of crops, particularly coffee or sugar.

Ferrocarril Central Mexicano (FCM) a railroad line that ran from Mexico City through the center of the nation, stopping at important cities like Guanajuato and Torreón before connecting with a US line in El Paso, Texas. The railroad was one of Porfirio Díaz's great achievements.

Ferrocarril Nacional Mexicano (FNM) a railroad line built in the latter part of the nineteenth century that passed through Zacatecas and Monterrey before joining a US line in Laredo, Texas. This route also had great commercial significance.

fincas farms or rural estates. In Central America especially, this is typically a large commercial enterprise, usually involved in the production of coffee.

folk Catholicism a type of Catholicism, still prevalent in parts of Latin America, in which local spirituality, legend, and shamanism are grafted onto Church dogma, creating a fusion of indigenous and Catholic beliefs.

Frente Farabundo Martí de Liberación Nacional (FMLN) A coalition of leftist guerrilla groups in El Salvador that united in 1980 to attempt to overthrow the US backed military government. After the signing of the Chapultepec Peace Accords in 1992, the FMLN became a legal political party, winning the presidency in 2009 and again in 2015.

fueros privileges, primarily referring to Church exemption from state taxation in nineteenth century Spanish America. Individual clergy (and military officers) possessed fueros, giving them the right to be tried in an ecclesiastical or military court under certain circumstances. Liberals abolished fuero throughout Latin America, arguing all citizens should be equal under the law.

gamonales a term meaning "bossism" used primarily in Peru but also in Bolivia and Ecuador to a lesser extent. The name is derived from that of a parasitic plant that squeezes the life from its host, and it refers to the exploitation of the indigenous population, mainly by highland landowners of European descent.

Gauchos Cowboys who worked on the great haciendas south and west of Buenos Aires. For the Argentine writer Domingo Faustino Sarmiento, the gauchos represented the barbarism of the provinces, a violent people who needed to be civilized. Ironically, gauchos became Argentina's national symbol in large part because of José Hernández's heroic epic poem, "Martín Fierro".

gens de couleur libres In Haiti, this term often referred to free mixed raced mulattos, frequently the children of white planters and enslaved mothers.

gente decente the elite people, also sometimes called the *gente de razón* or *gente bien*, in contrast with *los de abajo*, a phrase popularized by Mexico's famous author Mariano Azuela, who used the term as the title of his 1915 novel about the Mexican Revolution. In common use, the term has a snobbish implication, meaning "the right kind of people."

globalization Beginning in the 1990s with the Washington Consensus, opportunities existed to formalize international trade agreements (like NAFTA-The North American Free Trade Agreement between the US, Mexico, and Canada) to a degree never previously imagined. New communication links also shrank the metaphorical size of the globe.

Good Neighbor Policy was US President Franklin Roosevelt's idea to reboot US foreign policy towards Latin America by ending the era of military interventions and engaging in more equal, reciprocal relationships with Latin American nations. In practical terms, this meant the withdrawal of US troops from all parts of Latin America and the Caribbean, including Cuba, the Dominican Republic, Nicaragua, and Haiti.

Gracias por existir, mi Coronel the famous line "Thanks for existing, my Colonel" uttered by Evita Duarte, a young actress who became Perón's mouthpiece and wife, and ultimately the embodiment of the inchoate political ideology of Peronismo in Argentina.

Grandmothers (*Abuelas*) of the Plaza de Mayo Founded in 1977, the Grandmothers of the Plaza de Mayo is a human rights organization whose goal is to find the children stolen and illegally adopted during the Argentine dictatorship.

Great Depression The Great Depression of the 1930s was the most severe economic crisis that the world has ever faced. Factories closed as millions of people lost their jobs. Agricultural prices fell so low that farmers could not afford to send their crops to market. In Latin America, the Great Depression ended the export boom associated with the Age of Progress and Modernization, but opened up new opportunities for industrialization.

Green Revolution refers to the introduction of agricultural technology to Latin America in the post-World War II era. Agronomists encouraged farmers to use hybrid seeds, chemical fertilizers, herbicides and pesticides to increase productivity to meet demand as Latin American populations and foreign markets rapidly expanded. The policy had two important consequences: it favored large producers over small-scale, often indigenous, farmers and it had negative environmental effects.

gringo In Latin America, a mildly derogatory name for a person, especially an American, who is not Hispanic or Latino. Purportedly the word dates from the Mexican-American War of the 1840s.

hacendado An owner of a hacienda

hacienda A great estate. The large estate has always existed in Latin America since the time of the conquest. They have traditionally dominated the countryside, providing wealth and status to their owners. Twentieth century reformers have often prioritized agrarian reform as a means to offer hacienda employees a better life.

identity politics New political and cultural identities became prominent in the 1990s. Long held notions such as mestizaje and the myth of racial democracy in Brazil lost ground as indigenous people and Afro-Latin Americans embraced their own unique heritages. Ethnic identity, gender, sexual orientation, and evern religious affiliation superseded other ideas like class distinctions for many.

Import Substitution Industrialization (ISI) In response to the disastrous decline in exports caused by the Great Depression, many Latin American countries adopted import substitution industrialization (ISI), a trade and economic policy that advocated replacing foreign imports with domestic production. ISI would remain the dominant economic policy for most Latin American countries until the 1960s.

indigenismo The exaltation of indigenous cultures became a key component of Mexico's national identity as a means to integrate indigenous people into national life, and it quickly spread to other nations with large percentages of people of indigenous descent like Guatemala, Peru, Ecuador, and Bolivia. This cultural ideal germinated in nineteenth-century novels like Clorinda Matta de Turner's *Birds without a Nest,* and came to fruition as part of the intellectual contributions of the Mexican Revolution of 1910.

ingenios sugar cane mills.

Institutional Act Five Decree passed by the military dictatorship in Brazil in December 1968 that suspended any constitutional guarantees for Brazilian citizens, leading to the institutionalization of torture.

Integralistas A fascist movement in Brazil led by Plinio Salgado that emerged in 1932. Wearing Green Shirts, the Integralistas initially rejected anti-Semitic views in contrast to their European counterparts. Vargas cracked down on the Integralistas after he established the Estado Novo in 1937.

internados indígenas Boarding schools for indigenous children. During the 1930s the Mexican government combined an assimilationist project (teaching the children Spanish, hygiene, and practical skills) with a program designed to preserve local languages, arts, and crafts.

International Monetary Fund (IMF) International organization headquartered in Washington, DC. that fosters global monetary cooperation, facilitates international trade, and promotes high employment and economic growth around the world. The IMF is often viewed as one of the chief exponents of neoliberal policies.

jogo bonito Literally, the beautiful game. This term describes the Brazilian manner of playing soccer, characterized by a dance-like, playful offense.

juntas Provisional governments, usually composed of several individuals (often military men) who have unseated the previous government by coup or revolution. These have been prevalent throughout Latin American history.

La Cristiada The Cristero Revolt (1926–29) was a spontaneous uprising in the center-west of Mexico against President Plutarco Elías Calles who sought to diminish the hold that the Catholic Church had culturally over rural peoples. In response, the rebels attacked federal troops, burned schools, and killed teachers, viewed as the embodiment of the intrusion of the new secular state and its values into traditional rural society. With the aid of US Ambassador Dwight Morrow, a compromise was reached and the violence lessened.

ladino A person of mixed indigenous and European heritage or an indigenous person who lives as a non-Indian. In both Spanish and Portuguese America, this term was used to distinguish those of indigenous or African ancestry who adopted Spanish or Portuguese ways in contradistinction to those who remained fully *indio* or *africano*. The term is most commonly used in Central America. The word is synonymous with *mestizo*.

La Matanza literally, "the Massacre", a term used by Salvadorans to reference the killing of thousands of Salvadoran campesinos, the majority of them indigenous, in 1932 by the Hernández Martínez military government.

la raza cósmica The title of José Vasconcelos' important book which argued that the mestizo combined the best characteristics of indigenous people and Spaniards and resulted in a superior race. La raza cósmica became a key trope of Mexican political identity since the 1920s where

the "myth of racial democracy" has sought to unite a vast and racially diverse country.

latifundia A large landed estate. The word is Latin and was originally used to describe large estates in Iberia, and the term was eventually exported for use in the Americas.

La Violencia The long period of civil violence in Colombia that began with the assassination of politician Jorge Eliécer Gaitán in 1948 and ended roughly in the 1960s although violence under different guises remained an endemic problem in Colombia until 2016. The same term refers to the nadir of Guatemala's armed conflict between 1980 and 1982.

Law 900 Also called the Agrarian Reform Law, Law 900 was a Guatemalan land reform law passed on June 17, 1952. It redistributed unused lands of sizes greater than 224 acres to local peasants. Although in force for only eighteen months, the law had a major effect on the Guatemalan land reform movement.

Lerdo Law a Liberal Mexican statute, later incorporated into the Constitution of 1857, which confiscated all corporately held property, which meant the forfeiture of the Church's vast rural estates and urban properties on which the Church had collected rents for centuries. The Church was required to sell the land, hopefully to its current tenants. In most instances, however, the land ended up in the hands of large landowners.

LGBT Gay, lesbian, bisexual, or transgendered people. Using the inclusive language of the US civil rights movement of the 1960s and 1970s, LGBT advocates in Latin America have sought the same individual liberties that other citizens enjoyed. Although there have always been LGBT Latin Americans, the vast majority had no socially acceptable alternative but to keep their gender preferences secret until very recent times.

Liberals During the nineteenth century Liberals espoused many of the ideas of the Enlightenment. As modernizers seeking progress, they advocated for free trade, a federalist form of government and states' rights, considerable personal liberties for citizens, and for a variety of anti-clerical measures. They generally disdained their Spanish heritage and especially the influence of the Catholic Church.

Liberation theology a grassroots religious movement that became the focus of the Latin American Catholic Church between the 1960s and 1980s. In addition to creating a new role for the laity, the Catholic leadership at the Medellín Conference in 1968 spoke about the preferential option for the poor—the creation of Christian Base Communities that would study the Bible intensely and provide concrete ways to improve the lives of the poor.

The ideas of liberation theology inspired many on the political left to join the guerrilla movements in Central America during the late Cold War.

Ligas Campesinas Peasant leagues made up of rural cooperative and landless or small-scale farmers. During Guatemala's "Ten Years of Spring" (1944–1954), ligas campesinas provided leverage and a prominent political voice for peasants for the first time in the nation's history and were strong supporters of the reformist regimes. In the wake of the overthrow of Arbenz, campesinos leaders suffered severe repression at the hands of anti-communist paramilitary groups.

lingua franca a language that is adopted as common language between speakers whose native languages are different.

llaneros Literally, someone from the *llanos,* or plains, who often herds cattle. The name is taken from the llanos grasslands in eastern Colombia and southern Venezuela in the Orinoco Basin. Except during the wars of independence, this area has played a marginal role in both nations' history.

Malê the Bahian term for Muslim. African Muslim slaves planned and initiated the Malê Revolt, Brazil's largest slave rebellion, in 1835.

Malvinas War Also known as the Falkands War, the conflict was a ten-week war between Argentina and the United Kingdom over two British overseas territories in the South Atlantic. It began on Friday, April 2, 1982 when Argentina invaded and occupied the islands in an attempt to establish the sovereignty it had claimed over them. The conflict lasted 74 days and ended with an Argentine surrender and the return of the islands to British control. Argentina's defeat led to the demise of the military dictatorship and its return to democracy in 1983.

Mambises a term of disputed origin that came to refer to all those who volunteered for the fight against Spain in late nineteenth century Cuba—most of them free blacks and escaped slaves.

Manifest Destiny Manifest Destiny is the understanding that God had granted a covenant to the United States to spread across the North American continent "from sea to shining sea." In the nineteenth century, this involved appropriating new lands from Texas to California from Mexico, and fully absorbing the diverse populations who already lived there into the Protestant, Anglo-Saxon culture, values, religion, and political system of the United States.

maquiladoras A foreign assembly plant originally located in Mexico near the US border and now scattered throughout the hemisphere. Maquiladoras capitalize on the availability of cheaper labor costs to assemble products that are then sold in the US or elsewhere. Critics point out that the plants create pollution and take advantage of female workers.

marianismo a traditional Hispanic ideal of women that venerates them as pure, modest, and morally strong, like the Virgin Mary.

Maroon societies. Throughout the Americas, wherever African slavery existed, so-called maroon societies—colonies of runaway slaves—emerged. Most maroon societies were small and short-lived (with a few notable exceptions). In the nineteenth century, they existed at the margins of free societies, characterized by trading and raiding.

Mayan movement "Pan-Mayan" or *movimento maya.* This was a cultural and political movement that sought to fundamentally re-define the place of Maya people as citizens within Guatemala beginning in the 1980s.

Medellín cartel A Colombian drug cartel originating in the city of Medellín, Colombia. The cartel operated throughout the 1970s and 1980s and was known for the ruthlessness and violence of its tactics. At its height, it smuggled tons of cocaine each week into the United States, making hundreds of millions of dollars in profit.

mestizaje the process of assimilating indigenous people into the more inclusive hegemonic national culture. See La Raza Cósmica.

milpas A small corn field. Milpas were the basis of Mexican village agriculture from colonial times through the 1940s when the Green Revolution began. They still remain the basic agricultural unit for small-subsistence farmers across Latin America.

modernity The quest for modernity has been a goal of Latin Americans since independence. In the late nineteenth century, the elite republics made steps in this direction, but failed to create a more egalitarian society that would have had a deeper impact.

Montoneros Argentine leftist terrorist and urban guerrilla group, active during the 1960s and 1970s.

Movimiento Revolucionario 13 de Noviembre, better known as MR-13. This group of young Guatemalan idealistic cadets who led a failed coup attempt against Miguel Ydígoras Fuente in 1960 fled to the eastern portion of the country and eventually joined forces with other opposition groups. They were nearly exterminated by the military by 1968.

Mulato/a a person of mixed race black and white heritage.

NAFTA is the North American Free Trade Act entered into in 1992 by the United States, Canada, and Mexico.

By cutting tariffs between the three nations, the agreement was designed to expand trade, and from the Mexican point of view, to bring US industry to Mexico where labor costs were less expensive. Over time, NAFTA has proved controversial, as it also dislocated many Mexican farmers who could not compete with cheap, imported US grain.

nationalism Simply stated, patriotism or devotions to one's country. In the aftermath of the wars for independence, political leaders sought to imbue their citizens with a sense of national identity, not always successfully because of the prevalence of regionalism. Nationalism is often shaped by language and culture as well as geographical boundaries.

National Revolutionary Unity (URNG) A Guatemalan political party that started as a guerrilla movement 1982 but laid down its arms in 1996 and became a legal political party in 1998 after the peace process ending the Guatemalan Civil War.

National Security Doctrine Policy that emerged during the 1960s at the height of the Cold War and in response to the threat that the Cuban Revolution of 1959 might spread. The US agreed to train Latin American militaries in counter-insurgency warfare that would allow them to defeat communist insurrections within their nations. In addition, Latin American governments frequently received financial aid to assist in national development as an additional means to thwart the lure of communism.

Negritude The affirmation of the distinctive nature, quality, and validity of black culture

Neo-Liberalism Neoliberalism emerged in the 1970s in reaction to the problems associated with ISI and excessively state-dominated economies. Neo-liberals preached the need to privatize state-owned businesses, deregulate the economy, institute free trade, and impose austerity by reducing social spending. Neoliberalism disproportionately targeted the poor, and met with significant opposition.

New Imperialism At the end of the nineteenth century, Europeans embarked on the age of New Imperialism, during which they carved up Africa and large parts of Southeast Asia, and created spheres of influence for themselves in China. Europeans had fewer political effects on the independent Latin American republics, but exerted considered economic influence, especially in South America. Latin Americans were victimized by the US between 1898 and 1933. US investors came to play an enormous economic role in these smaller nations, but US interventions in the Caribbean and Central America infringed upon their sovereignty and left nationalistic scars.

noirs literally "blacks". This referred to the enslaved blacks in Saint Domingue prior to the Haitian Revolution of 1791.

obreros workers or laborers. These people worked with their hands and did physical labor, which in the twentieth century differentiated them from the middle class.

Operación Limpieza literally, "Operation Clean-up" a term used in several contexts (Guatemala, Mexico) to describe law enforcement sweeps against criminal groups or alleged political subversives.

Pact of Punto Fijo An agreement reached by the leadership of Venezuela's democratic left leaders in 1958 to establish the framework for the country's democracy and its continued support for capitalist development. The Venezuelan democratic left remained a strong ally of the United States during the Cold War. Its two major parties held sway until Hugo Chávez won the election of 1998, promising reform and an end to corruption.

pampas the fertile grasslands, mostly in Argentina and Uruguay, that stretch north for many miles from Patagonia into Uruguay and even southern Brazil. This fertile land became the hub of Argentina's wheat and cattle raising industries in the latter nineteenth century and early twentieth century which propelled the country (and to a lesser degree Uruguay and southern Brazil) to great prosperity.

Pan-Africanism The idea that peoples of African descent have common interests and should be unified politically and culturally. The leading exponent of Pan-Africanism in the early twentieth century was Marcus Garvey (1887–1940).

pardos a word used in the Spanish colonies in the Americas to refer to the tri-racial descendants of Europeans, Native Americans, and West Africans. They are defined as neither mestizo (Native American-European descent) nor mulatto (African-European descent) nor zambo (African-Native American descent). Pardos, for example, who constituted about fifty percent of the Venezuelan population, played an important role in the South American wars of independence.

patria potestad legal doctrine where the man of the house wields absolute authority over his wife and children.

Pax Porfiriana or the Porfirian Peace. Porfirio Díaz used a variety of strategies, including offering financial rewards and coercion, to bring peace to Mexico during his lengthy dictatorship from 1876 to 1911.

Paz y Trabajo The positivist political slogan for Venezuelan dictator Juan Vicente Gómez's regime (1908–1935). The profits from oil fueled considerable growth as Gómez built modern highways and completed other public works and encouraged foreign investment while terrorizing his opposition.

pelegos Members of the government-approved organized labor union created under Brazilian President Getúlio Vargas later derided by radical labor leaders for their accommodation of government and employer interests.

peninsulares First generation Spaniards born in the Iberian Peninsula who had emigrated to the New World. That the Spanish monarchy favored peninsulares for positions in government and the Church, irked criollos, many of whom would side against Spain during the wars of independence.

Pentecostalism is a variety of Christianity that emphasizes the experience of the "gifts of the Holy Spirit" manifested in physical terms, such as speaking in tongues, faith healing, or exorcism.

peones poor rural workers, often under the authority of a wealthy landowner.

Petróleos Mexicanos/Pemex is Mexico's government-owned oil company formed after Lázaro Cárdenas expropriated foreign and domestic petroleum holdings in 1938. Today it is Latin America's second most valuable economic enterprise and an important source of revenue for the Mexican government.

plurinationalism the idea that multiple autonomous indigenous nations could exist within the boundaries of a nation-state. Both Bolivia and Ecuador have adopted this language in constitutions to describe the multi-ethnic nature of their countries.

Populism an amorphous concept that became a new political strategy in the wake of the Great Depression. Populists tended to be charismatic with great rhetorical skills. Shy on ideology, populists sought to create multi-class alliances, bringing the working class into the political process for the first time. Because of conflicts within their coalitions, populist reformers generally achieved only modest success. Two of the most famous populists were Juan Perón in Argentine and Getúlio Vargas in Brazil.

positivism A philosophy advocated by Auguste Comte (1798–1857) that favors the careful empirical observation of of natural phenomena and human behavior over metaphysics. Positivism appealed to modernizers throughout Latin America, particularly in Brazil.

PRI (Institutional Revolutionary Party) A Mexican political party founded in 1929, that held power without interruption for 71 years, from 1929 to 2000.

problema indio Literally, "Indian problem." As a young intellectual in the 1920s, Guatemalan Miguel Angel Asturias attempted to characterize the problems that prevented indigenous people from being incorporated into society. Among others, these included inadequate nutrition, excessive labor demands, alcoholism, and poverty.

progress Progress became the watchword of the elite regimes of the late nineteenth and early twentieth centuries. For the elite, progress meant the imposition of political order, the encouragement or foreign investment, the importation of modern technology and immigrants, and an unhealthy interest in "whitening" their own populations. The poor and underprivileged rarely shared in the benefits of the elite vision of prosperity.

rabonas Peruvian female camp followers, who served as cooks, laundresses, nurses, lovers, mothers, and occasionally as combatants, not only in the civil wars of the nineteenth century but also in the War of the Pacific (1879–1882).

Reagan Doctrine US President Ronald Reagan (1980–1988) saw the civil wars in Central America as part of the ongoing Cold War. The Reagan Doctrine was a policy designed to weaken the Soviet Union by increasing defense spending that the Soviets could not match, and by contesting communist incursions worldwide. In Latin America, the Reagan Doctrine led the US to support the contras against the Sandinista government, and to offer large amounts of military aid to the government of El Salvador for their fight against the FMLN.

Reconquista ("reconquest") is the historical period of the Iberian Peninsula between the Islamic conquest in 711 and the fall of the last Islamic state in Iberia at Granada to the Christian kingdoms of Castile and Aragon in 1492. The Reconquista was completed just before Columbus encountered the New World, which launched Spanish and Portuguese colonial empires in the Americas.

regionalism Most Latin Americas have always identified closely with the region where they were born or came to reside as young people. This trait that was quite profound in the early days of the republics still exists today.

Rerum Novarum A papal encyclical issued by Pope Leo XIII in 1891 and considered the foundation of modern Catholic social teaching. In it, the Church stressed that the free operation of market forces must be tempered by moral obligations, condemning unrestricted capitalism, supporting the formation of trade unions and collective bargaining practices, and reaffirming the right to private property.

Revolutionary Armed Forces of Columbia (FARC) Latin America's most intractable guerrilla movement, active in Colombia from 1964 to 2016, and at its height in the 1980s and 1990s controlling large swaths of territory and responsible for tens of thousands of deaths each year. A peace agreement with the Colombian government was finally signed in 2016

Rio Treaty Shorthand title for the 1947 Inter-American Treaty for Reciprocal Assistance signed in Rio de Janeiro between the US and all the Latin American nations. The treaty guaranteed US military protection against threats of aggression against any Latin American state. In the context of the Cold War, the treaty was designed as a pact to prevent possible communist intervention in Latin America.

rurales Porfirio Díaz's infamous rural police force designed to reduce banditry and bring order to Mexico's countryside. As many of the rurales were recruited from bandit bands and occasionally reverted to their former professions, the rurales achieved only modest successes although their reputation for ferocity did have some effect.

Sandinista Insurrection The effort to overthrow the Nicaraguan dictator Anastasio Somoza that began in the 1960s and succeeded in seizing power in 1979. The Sandinistas took inspiration from the Cuban Revolution of 1959, and once in power, moved to eliminate their more moderate allies from the government.

Sandinista National Liberation Front (FSLN) A democratic socialist political party in Nicaragua. The party is named after Augusto César Sandino, who led the Nicaraguan resistance against the United States occupation of Nicaragua in the 1930s.The FSLN overthrew Anastasio Somoza in 1979, and established a revolutionary government in its place.

San Patricios A unit of 175 to several hundred immigrants (accounts vary) and expatriates of European descent who fought as part of the Mexican army against the United States in the Mexican-American War of 1846–1848.

Semana Trágica A week of an aggressive crackdowns launched by the government of middle-class reformer Hipólito Yrigoyen against protesting workers in Buenos Aires and other Argentine cities in January, 1919.

Sendero Luminoso ("Shining Path") Communist militant group in Peru founded in the late 1960s by Abimael Guzmán. At its height in the 1980s Sendero Luminoso controlled significant portions of Peruvian territory; nearly 70,000 people died in its conflict with the Peruvian government. Guzmán was captured and imprisoned in 1992.

socialism A popular European idea, especially in the nineteenth century. The objective of socialists was to force major reforms in the economic system to provide greater equality for working people. In Latin America, socialists were very active in the early labor movement. Chile's Socialist Party remains very active today, and has elected two presidents during the past forty-five years.

Social Darwinism The application of Darwin's biological theories to human societies, often to justify claims of racial superiority and rule by the strong over the weak. Social Darwinism was enthusiastically embraced by Latin American liberals in the 19th century.

soldaderas During the Mexican Revolution of 1910, the soldaderas were women who participated both as camp followers and soldiers, some becoming officers. But when the military phase of the Revolution ended in 1920, however, women found that they had won few concrete rights for themselves.

Southern Cone the region of South America comprising the countries of Uruguay, Argentina, and Chile. Its geographical area is often considered to encompass Paraguay and the southernmost regions of Brazil.

Special Period After 1989 and the collapse of the Soviet Union, Cuba had to do without the huge subsidies, largely in the form of petroleum that the USSR had been supplying since the 1960s. Although Fidel Castro tried to downplay the significance of the loss of USSR aid, the people of Cuba suffered shortages of foodstuffs. They had to revert to bicycles rather than cars and busses, and were eventually allowed to grow and market their own food raised in backyard gardens. European and Canadian tourism eventually provided some economic relief.

Sufragio efectivo y no re-elección Roughly translated as "A Fair Vote and No Boss Rule," this phrase was Francisco I. Madero's slogan when he challenged Porfirio Díaz for the presidency in 1910. Although Madero failed to bring democracy to Mexico, he did initiate the military phase of the Revolution. The phrase still appears above the signature of many government officials in Mexico even today.

telenovela televised soap opera. Largely filmed in Brazil and Mexico, these glamorous soap operas are popular throughout Latin America. They are more sophisticated than US soap operas, treating contemporary themes like corruption, drugs and violence in addition to portraying historical events.

Ten-Million-Ton Harvest Failed attempt by the Cuban government to break historic sugar production records by producing a ten million-ton sugar harvest in 1970. The campaign yielded fewer than eight million tons and deepened Cuba's economic dependency on both sugar and Soviet subsidies.

Ten Years' War (1868–1878). An inconclusive war for independence that ravaged Cuba for a decade. One of the leading intellectual figures of the independence movement was Carlos Manual de Céspedes, who was among those who issued the "Grito de Yara" in 1868.

Trans-Amazonian Highway A 2,500-mile highway in northeastern Brazil that opened in 1972 with the intention of providing a pathway for poor, landless farmers to clear the rainforest for development. Instead, the highway has brought great environmental damage to the Amazon region.

Tupameros Left-wing urban guerrilla group active in Uruguay in the 1960s and 1970s.

United Provinces of Central America (UPCA) When Mexico became a republic in 1823, Central America (Guatemala, Honduras, El Salvador, Nicaragua, and Costa Rica) broke away, declaring independence from Spain, Mexico, and all foreign powers on July 1, 1823. The region now known as Belize theoretically remained an internal province within Guatemala, though informally controlled by Great Britain, which called the territory British Honduras.

vendepatrias sellouts, those who prioritize personal profit over national loyalty, and intentionally or negligently help to facilitate foreign domination. A term used throughout Latin America to criticize those perceived to collaborate with US economic and political intervention in particular, and was widely popularized by Augusto Sandino in Nicaragua. See *entreguista* in Brazil.

villistas Followers of revolutionary leader Francisco "Pancho" Villa during the Mexiccan Revolution of 1910. Villa's followers came mainly from northern Mexico.

Vodun A Haitian belief system, otherwise known as "voodoo," that emphasizes African spirit worship and the use of supernatural protection and power. Maintaining a harmonious relationship with a good *loa* (spirit) is vital. Vodun remains a core ingredient in Haitian culture today.

War of the Triple Alliance War fought from 1864 to 1870 between Paraguay and the Triple Alliance of Argentina, the Empire of Brazil, and Uruguay. The war was the deadliest and in Latin America's history and cataclysmic for Paraguay, which suffered catastrophic losses in population and was forced to cede one third of its territory to Argentina and Brazil.

Washington Consensus was the idea that after the collapse of the Soviet Union in 1989 that the US system of political democracy, free markets, and capitalism would become the norm and would bring peace to the world. This optimistic analysis, however, quickly proved inaccurate as both democracy and neoliberalism met with resistance in many nations.

World Bank A leading neoliberal institution, the World Bank is an international financial organization that provides loans to countries for capital programs.

Zapatistas Members of the Zapatista Army of National Liberation], a left-wing revolutionary political and militant group based in Chiapas, the southernmost state of Mexico. The group takes its name from Emiliano Zapata, the agrarian reformer and commander of the Liberation Army of the South during the Mexican Revolution (1910–1920).

Sources in Latin America in the Modern World

Edited by Nicola Foote
Florida Gulf Coast University

TABLE OF CONTENTS

Credits

Chapter 1

CO1: Arturo Michelena, 1896, Wikimedia Commons; **Figure 1.1:** Columbus Memorial Library; **Figure 1.2:** Wikimedia Commons; **Figure 1.3:** Genaro García Collection, Benson Latin America Collection; **Figure 1.4:** Bulletin of the Pan American Union, 43, 1916, Benson Latin American Collection; **Figure 1.5a:** F. Loraine Petre, *Simon Bolivar*; **Figure 1.5b:** Wikimedia Commons; **Figure 1.6:** Bulletin of the Pan American Union, 48, 1918, Benson Latin American Collection; **Figure 1.7:** Columbus Memorial Library; **Figure 1.8:** Library of Congress, LC-DIG-ds-06574, Thierry

Chapter 2

CO2: John Gast, Library of Congress, LC-USZ62-737, George A. Crofutt; **Figure 2.1:** Emilia Wilson, *Maravillas*, 1910; **Figure 2.2:** Library of Congress, LC-USZ62-130816; **Figure 2.3:** Currier and Ives, Library of Congress, LC-USZ62-7555; **Figure 2.4:** Bulletin of the Pan American Union, 43, 1916, Benson Latin American Collection; **Figure 2.5:** Library of Congress, LC-USZ62-53041; **Figure 2.6:** C. B. Waite, Library of Congress, LC-USZ62-115487; **Figure 2.7:** Arturo Michelena, Bulletin of Pan American Union, 40, 1915, Benson Latin American Collection; **Figure 2.8:** Bulletin of the Pan American Union, 43, 1916, Benson Latin American Collection

Chapter 3

CO3: Arthur B. Ruhl, *The Other Americas*, 1908; **Figure 3.1:** Bryan McCann; **Figure 3.2:** James F. Fletcher, *Brazil and the Brazilians*, 1879; **Figure 3.3:** Rafael Reyes, *Two Americas*, 1917; **Figure 3.4a:** Columbus Memorial Library; **Figure 3.4b:** Library of Congress; **Figure 3.5:** Genaro García Collection, Benson Latin American Collection; **Figure 3.6:** Alan B. Chase, *Thirty Years*, 1917; **Figure 3.7:** The Miriam and Ira D. Wallach Division of Art, Prints and Photographs: Print Collection, The New York Public Library. "L'exécution de l'emperor Maxmilien." The New York Public Library Digital Collections. 1867. http://digitalcollections.nypl.org/items/510d47da-412b-a3d9-e040-e00a18064a99; **Figure 3.8a:** Biblioteca Nacional de Uruguay; **Figure 3.8b:** Instituto Moreira Salles

Chapter 4

CO4: Bulletin of the Pan American Union, 37, 1913, Benson Latin American Collection; **Figure 4.1:** Charles Pepper, *Panama to Patagonia*, 1906; **Figure 4.2a:** Marc Ferrez, Instituto Moreira Salles; **Figure 4.2b:** Instituto Moreira Salles; **Figure 4.3:** Reginold Enock, *The Andes and the Amazon*, 1907; **Figure 4.4:** René d'Harnoncourt, Benson Latin American Collection; **Figure 4.5:** Isabel V. Waldo, from Fanny Gooch, *Face to Face with the Mexicans*, 1887; **Figure 4.6:** Ernest Peixotto, *Pacific Shores from Panama*, 1916; **Figure 4.7:** René d'Harnoncourt, Benson Latin American Collection

Chapter 5

CO5: Bulletin of the Pan American Union, 45, 1917, Benson Latin American Collection; **Figure 5.1:** Genaro García Collection, Benson Latin American Collection; **Figure 5.2:** Bulletin of the Pan American Union, 38, 1914, Benson Latin American Collection; **Figure 5.3:** Bulletin of the Pan American Union, 42, 1916, Benson Latin American Collection; **Figure 5.4:** Bulletin of the Pan American Union, 42, 1916, Benson Latin American Collection;

Figure 5.5: Guilherme Gaensly, Instituto Moreira Salles; **Figure 5.6:** A. H. Keane, *Central and South America*, 1901; **Figure 5.7:** Bulletin of the Pan American Union, 39, 1914, Benson Latin American Collection; **Figure 5.8a:** Bulletin of the Pan American Union, 54, 1922, Benson Latin American Collection; **Figure 5.8b:** Bulletin of the Pan American Union, 54, 1922, Benson Latin American Collection

Chapter 6
CO6: Official Marine Corps Photo. Courtesy of the Marine Corps History Division; **Figure 6.1:** http://latinamericanstudies.org/spanwar/journal-2-17-1898/publicdomain; **Figure 6.2:** William Dinwiddie, Library of Congress, LC-USZC4-7934; **Figure 6.3:** Bulletin of the Pan American Union, 39, 1914, Benson Latin American Collection; **Figure 6.4:** Bulletin of the Pan American Union, 46, 1918, Benson Latin American Collection; **Figure 6.5:** Bulletin of the Pan American Union, 46, 1918, Benson Latin American Collection; **Figure 6.6:** Bulletin of the Pan American Union, 40, 1915, Benson Latin American Collection; **Figure 6.7:** Bulletin of the Pan American Union, 53, 1921, Benson Latin American Collection; **Figure 6.8:** Benson Latin American Collection

Chapter 7
CO7: Benson Latin American Collection; **Figure 7.1:** Bulletin of the Pan American Union, 42, 1916, Benson Latin American Collection; **Figure 7.2:** Library of Congress, LC2012593202; **Figure 7.3:** Bulletin of the Pan American Union, 51, 1921, Benson Latin American Collection; **Figure 7.4:** Bulletin of the Pan American Union, 43, 1916, Benson Latin American Collection; **Figure 7.5:** Bulletin of the Pan American Union, 40, 1915, Benson Latin American Collection; **Figure 7.6:** Modesto Brocos, Museu Nacional de Belas Artes, Brazil; **Figure 7.7:** Bulletin of the Pan American Union, 43, 1916, Benson Latin American Collection; **Figure 7.8:** Rafael Reyes, *Two Americas*, 1914

Chapter 8
CO8: Photographer unknown, public domain. www.guatemalasecular.org/blogs/2016/02/12/la-educacion-durante-la-dictadura-de-jorge-ubico/; **Figure 8.1:** Bulletin of the Pan American Union, 42, 1916, Benson Latin American Collection; **Figure 8.2:** Bulletin of the Pan American Union, 42, 1916, Benson Latin American Collection; **Figure 8.3:** Paul Fearn / Alamy Stock Photo; **Figure 8.4:** Columbus Memorial Library; **Figure 8.5:** Frans Post, Museu de Arte de São Paulo; **Figure 8.6:** Hulton Archive / Getty Images; **Figure 8.7:** Bulletin of the Pan American Union, 43, 1916, Benson Latin American Collection; **Figure 8.8:** Benson Latin American Collection

Chapter 9
CO9: Tony Frissell, Library of Congress, LC-USZC4-4321; **Figure 9.1:** Bernard Silverstein, Library of Congress, LC-DIG-ppmsca-19365; **Figure 9.2:** Bulletin of the Pan American Union, 48, 1918, Benson Latin American Collection; **Figure 9.3:** Reginald Enoch, *Peru: Its Former and Present Civilization*, 1916; **Figure 9.4:** Martín Chambí, Instituto Moreira Salles; **Figure 9.5:** Peter Henderson; **Figure 9.6:** Martín Chambí, Instituto Moreira Salles; **Figure 9.7:** Martín Chambí, Instituto Moreira Salles; **Figure 9.8:** Photo courtesy of Edward Moreiras and the Queer Tango Archive

Chapter 10
CO10: Luis Korda, Wikimedia Commons; **Figure 10.1:** Bulletin of the Pan American Union, 39, 1914, Benson Latin American Collection; **Figure 10.2:** Columbus Memorial Library; **Figure 10.3:** AP Photo / Henry Brueggemann; **Figure 10.4:** Benson Latin American Collection; **Figure 10.5:** Everett Collection Historical / Alamy Stock Photo; **Figure 10.6:** Image Source / Alamy Stock Photo; **Figure 10.7:** AP Photo / Roberto Candia; **Figure 10.8:** Guillermo Angulo (Harry Ransom Center)

Chapter 11
CO11: Benson Latin American Collection; **Figure 11.1:** Columbus Memorial Library; **Figure 11.2:** Benson Latin American Collection; **Figure 11.3:** Columbus Memorial Library; **Figure 11.4:** Keystone Pictures USA / Alamy Stock Photo; **Figure 11.5:**

Andrew Hasson / Alamy Stock Photo; **Figure 11.6:** AP Photo / Peter Bregg; **Figure 11.7:** AP Photo; **Figure 11.8:** Peter Henderson

Chapter 12

CO12: © Susan Meiselas / Magnum Photos; **Figure 12.1:** Ernesto Cardenal Papers, Benson Latin American Collection; **Figure 12.2:** Benson Latin American Collection; **Figure 12.3:** Benson Latin American Collection; **Figure 12.4:** Dennis Cox / Alamy Stock Photo; **Figure 12.5:** © Larry Towell / Magnum Photos; **Figure 12.6:** Langevan Jacques / Hulton Archive / Stringer / Getty Images; **Figure 12.7:** Carlos Bendezú, *Revista Caretas*; **Figure 12.8:** Vera Lentz / AP Photo

Chapter 13

CO13: José Roberto Serra / CPDOC-JB; **Figure 13.1:** Madalena Schwartz, Instituto Moreira Salles; **Figure 13.2:** Christopher Pillitz / Alamy Stock Photo; **Figure 13.3:** Federico Julien / Alamy Stock Photo; **Figure 13.4:** AP Photo / Gergory Bull;

Figure 13.5: Bulletin of the Pan American Union, 45, 1917, Benson Latin American Collection; **Figure 13.6:** AP Photo; **Figure 13.7:** Rogério Reis / CPDOC-JB; **Figure 13.8:** Peter Henderson

Chapter 14

CO14: Patrício Realpe; **Figure 14.1:** Juca Martins, Instituto Moreira Salles; **Figure 14.2:** AP Photo / Martin Mejia; **Figure 14.3:** Peter Henderson; **Figure 14.4:** Patricio Realpe; **Figure 14.5:** AP Photo / Javier Galeno; **Figure 14.6:** incamerastock / Alamy Stock Photo; **Figure 14.7:** AP Photo / Marco Ugarte; **Figure 14.8:** AP Photo / Estéban Félix; **Figure 14.9:** Virginia Garrard

Chapter 15

CO15: AP Photo / Eduardo Verdugo; **Figure 15.1:** Luiz Souza / Imagespi / AP Photo; **Figure 15.2:** AP Photo / Gerald Herbert; **Figure 15.3:** Jorg Schuster / picture-alliance / dpa / AP Images; **Figure 15.4:** AP Photo / Moises Castillo; **Figure 15.5:** AP Photo / Estéban Félix; **Figure 15.6:** Ed Viggiani, Insitituto Moreira Salles

Index

Page numbers in italics indicate illustrations. Page numbers in bold indicate maps.